T0189523

Communications in Computer and Information Science　1043

Commenced Publication in 2007
Founding and Former Series Editors:
Phoebe Chen, Alfredo Cuzzocrea, Xiaoyong Du, Orhun Kara, Ting Liu,
Krishna M. Sivalingam, Dominik Ślęzak, Takashi Washio, and Xiaokang Yang

More information about this series at http://www.springer.com/series/7899

Yongtian Wang · Qingmin Huang ·
Yuxin Peng (Eds.)

Image and Graphics Technologies and Applications

14th Conference on Image and Graphics
Technologies and Applications, IGTA 2019
Beijing, China, April 19–20, 2019
Revised Selected Papers

 Springer

Editors
Yongtian Wang
Beijing Institute of Technology
Beijing, China

Qingmin Huang
University of Chinese Academy of Science
Beijing, China

Yuxin Peng
Institute of Computer Science
and Technology
Peking University
Beijing, China

ISSN 1865-0929 ISSN 1865-0937 (electronic)
Communications in Computer and Information Science
ISBN 978-981-13-9916-9 ISBN 978-981-13-9917-6 (eBook)
https://doi.org/10.1007/978-981-13-9917-6

This Springer imprint is published by the registered company Springer Nature Singapore Pte Ltd.
The registered company address is: 152 Beach Road, #21-01/04 Gateway East, Singapore 189721, Singapore

Preface

It was a pleasure for us to organize the 14th Conference on Image and Graphics Technologies and Applications (IGTA 2019). The conference was organized under the auspices of the Beijing Society of Image and Graphics, and was held during April 19–20, 2019, at the University of Chinese Academy of Sciences in Beijing, China.

IGTA is a professional conference and a premier forum for image processing, computer graphics and related topics, including but not limited to image analysis and understanding, computer vision and pattern recognition, big data mining, virtual reality and augmented reality, as well as image technology applications.

IGTA 2019 collected over 152 submissions for technical presentation from different countries and regions of the world. Each of the manuscripts was assessed by at least two reviewers, with some of them being assessed by three reviewers. After careful evaluation, a total of 66 manuscripts were selected for oral and poster presentations.

The conference program included keynote presentations, oral papers, workshops, posters, demos, and exhibitions. The most recent progress in the field of images and graphics was reported. I firmly believe that the papers included in the IGTA 2019 proceedings will provide valuable reference information to scientists and engineers in the relevant fields.

On behalf of conference general chairs, I would like to heartily thank our supporters and committee members for all they have done for this conference. Thanks go to all authors for their contributions, especially to those who traveled great distances and took time from their busy schedules to attend the conference. I am also grateful to the Springer staff for their support and collaboration in publishing these proceedings. Thanks also go to the reviewers who completed the reviewing process on time. Finally, I would like to express our gratitude to our host, professors and students from the University of Chinese Academy of Sciences, who took care of the local arrangements for the conference, and to all the attendees.

April 2019   Yongtian Wang

Organization

General Conference Chairs

Yongtian Wang   Beijing Institute of Technology, China
Qingming Huang   University of Chinese Academy of Sciences, China

Executive and Coordination Committee

Guoping Wang   Peking University, China
Chaowu Chen   The First Research Institute of the Ministry of Public
     Security of P.R.C., China
Mingquan Zhou   Beijing Normal University, China
Shengjin Wang   Tsinghua University, China
Chenglin Liu   Institute of Automation, Chinese Academy of Sciences,
     China
Yao Zhao   Beijing Jiaotong University, China
Zhiguo Jiang   Beihang University, China

Program Committee Chairs

Yuxin Peng   Peking University, China
Ran He   Institute of Automation, Chinese Academy of Sciences,
     China

Organizing Chairs

Yue Liu   Beijing Institute of Technology, China
Weiqiang Liu   University of Chinese Academy of Sciences, China
Xiaoru Yuan   Peking University, China

Research Committee Chairs

Xiaohui Liang   Beihang University, China
Xiangyang Ji   Tsinghua University, China
Jian Yang   Beijing Institute of Technology, China

Publicity and Exhibition Committee Chairs

Lei Yang   Communication University of China, China
Fengjun Zhang   Software Institute of the Chinese Academy of Sciences,
     China

Program Committee

David Rempel	University of California, USA
Zhao Chaoyi	China National Institute of Standardization (CNIS), China
Stephen Bao	University of Washington, USA
Jay Kapellusch	University of Wisconsin, Milwaukee, USA
Lin Wanhong	China Astronaut Research and Training Center, China
Henry Been-Lirn Duh	La Trobe University, Australia
Takafumi Taketomi	NAIST, Japan
Jeremy M. Wolfe	Harvard Medical School, USA
Yiping Huang	Taiwan University, China
Youngho Lee	Mokpo National University, South Korea
Nobuchika Sakata	Osaka University, Japan
Seokhee Jeon	Kyunghee University, South Korea
Xiaoru Yuan	Peking University, China
Ran He	Institute of Automation, Chinese Academy of Sciences, China
Jian Yang	Beijing Institute of Technology, China
Xiangyang Ji	Tsinghua University, China
Yue Liu	Beijing Institute of Technology, China
Huimin Ma	Tsinghua University, China
Liang Wang	Institute of Automation, Chinese Academy of Sciences, China
Huijie Zhao	Beijing University of Aeronautics and Astronautics, China
Danpei Zhao	Beijing University of Aeronautics and Astronautics, China
Cheng Yang	Communication University of China, China
Jun Yan	Journal of Image and Graphics
Shihong Xia	Institute of Computing Technology, Chinese Academy of Sciences, China
Weiqun Cao	Beijing Forestry University, China
Kaichang Di	Institute of Remote Sensing and Digital Earth, Chinese Academy of Sciences, China
Xucheng Yin	University of Science and Technology Beijing, China
Fuping Gan	Ministry of Land and Resources of the People's Republic of China
Xueqiang Lv	Beijing Information Science and Technology University, China
Jianbo Liu	Communication University of China, China
HuaLin	Tsinghua University, China
Xiaozhu Lin	Beijing Institute of Petrochemical Technology, China
Hua Li	Institute of Computing Technology, Chinese Academy of Sciences, China
Jing Dong	Institute of Automation, Chinese Academy of Sciences, China
Yankui Sun	Tsinghua University, China
Li Zhuo	Beijing University of Technology, China

Qingyuan Li	Chinese Academy of Surveying and Mapping, China
JiazhengYuan	Beijing Union University, China
Yiding Wang	North China University of Technology, China
Aiwu Zhang	Capital Normal University, China
Mingzhi Cheng	Beijing Institute of Graphic Communication, China
Yahui Wang	Beijing University of Civil Engineering and Architecture, China
Siwei Ma	Peking University, China
Liang Liu	Beijing University of Posts and Telecommunications, China
Bin Liao	North China Electric Power University, China

Contents

Human Fungal Infection Image Classification Based on Convolutional Neural Network

Yuan Zhou$^{(\boxtimes)}$, Yanxia Feng, and Haiying Zhang

Faculty of Automation and Information Engineering,
Xi'an University of Technology, Xi'an 710048, China
1227482510@qq.com

Abstract. An improved algorithm for deep learning of convolutional neural network is proposed in this paper to automatically extract feature of the fungal images. Firstly, the target image of the connected area is used to detect the targets of the fungal image, and several small images of conidia in the original image are obtained. Secondly, the small image is augmented by some operations, the augmented small images are proportionally divided into training sets and validation sets, and the training accuracy and validation accuracy are obtained. Finally, the test unknown images are input into the model, and the test accuracy is obtained. Experimental results show that the measures of data augmentation and fine-tuning not only effectively avoid the over-fitting of deep learning algorithm in small samples, but also improve the accuracy. The training accuracy of the algorithm can reach 95%, the validation accuracy can reach 96%, and the test accuracy can reach 69.23%, which has good robustness and generalization.

Keywords: Fungal image classification · Data augmentation ·
Convolutional neural network (CNN) · Fine-tuning

1 Introduction

In recent years, with the aging of the population, organ transplantation, tumor radiotherapy and chemotherapy, corticosteroid application and various catheter interventions, the incidence of human fungal infections has increased year by year. From the current epidemiology, human fungal infections can be divided into primary, secondary and invasive. Their clinical manifestations are fever, pain and dyspnea, etc., because they are not specific, combined with the complexity of the fungal spore microscopic image itself and the similarity between different types of fungal morphology, so that fungal infections Accurate and timely diagnosis and treatment have great difficulties.

At present, there are mainly the following methods for manually detecting and diagnosing fungal types:

(1) Based on a combination of tissue culture and imaging. This method takes a long time.
(2) Direct microscopy. The clinical specimens (sputum, bronchoalveolar lavage fluid) were cultured and stained, then observed under a microscope [1].

© Springer Nature Singapore Pte Ltd. 2019
Y. Wang et al. (Eds.): IGTA 2019, CCIS 1043, pp. 1–12, 2019.
https://doi.org/10.1007/978-981-13-9917-6_1

(3) Antigen examination based on GM experiment and G experiment. Diagnosis of fungal infections by detecting antigenic components released by fungi into the blood [2]. This method is of great significance for early diagnosis of fungal infections, monitoring of high-risk populations and evaluation of curative effect.
(4) CT-based imaging examination. CT diagnosis is a more effective method commonly used in clinical practice. However, because CT images are mainly based on one or two morphological performance, and other performance is combined, the diagnosis is complicated and the infection category cannot be diagnosed [3].

In summary, the traditional method of artificial detection and diagnosis of fungi is not only time-consuming and laborious, but the diagnosis results are easily affected by many human factors. If computer-aided diagnosis (CAD) and artificial intelligence methods are used to automatically classify microscopic images of fungal spores, not only can the diagnostic efficiency be improved, but objective and accurate diagnosis results can be provided [4].

The content of this thesis is that the deep learning method based on convolutional neural network is adopted, and the data augmentation method and transfer learning are adopted to prevent the over-fitting problem often encountered when the deep learning algorithm is trained in small sample data sets. Thereby, the accuracy of microscopic images of fungal spores is improved to meet the high standard clinical application requirements.

2 Fungal Image Preprocessing

2.1 Fungal Conidia Target Detection

In Fig. 1, in a primitive fungal image, due to the existence of several conidums, the whole image is input for training during the detection and classification process, and the position distribution and density of each conidium in the image are obtained. Background information such as size, bubble, and the like are extracted as features of the image, and an over-fitting phenomenon occurs. Therefore, it is necessary to pretreat each conidium in the whole image [5].

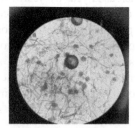 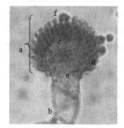

(A) Aspergillus terreus   (B) Spore-forming structure of filamentous fungi
(a. conidia head b. spore stalk c. crest sac d. bottle stem e. sylph f. conidia)

Fig. 1. Original image of filamentous fungi and its sporulation structure.

In combination with the manual marking and the target detection method, the training data is obtained by manual marking, and the test data is obtained by the target detection algorithm, thereby automatically detecting the small target area in the test image, that is, a single conidium region. The specific algorithm is:

Step 1: Convert a three-dimensional color image into a two-dimensional gray image;

Step 2: Convert the gray image into a binary image according to the empirical threshold;

Step 3: Perform expansion and corrosion on the binary image;

Step 4: Sort the size of the target connected domain;

Step 5: Calculate the coordinates and size information of the target center position to determine the specific location of the conidia;

Step 6: The single conidium position information of the original image is detected as several sub-images.

In the second step of converting the gray image into a binary image, the transformed boundary threshold can be found by the maximum inter-class variance method. The third step is mainly to reduce the amount of calculation and eliminate the influence of small gaps and small holes on the calculation of the target connected domain. In addition to considering this effect, the whole of the conidium is also considered in the process of target detection with a tangent rectangle [6].

2.2 Data Augmentation

Deep learning usually requires a large amount of data to train, at least a few hundred thousand images. A small amount of data often causes over-fitting and non-convergence. But in reality, a large number of labeled medical fungal images are expensive and difficult to obtain, so you need to "create data". In this paper, the data augmented method is adopted based on the limited labeling fungal images provided by the cooperative hospital. The specific operations include: rotate, affine transformation, scaling, mirroring in horizontal and vertical directions, contrast transformation and their combined operation. The data set has been expanded by 33 times.

When using any angle of rotation, considering the complexity of the background of the filamentous fungus image, when the data is augmented by any angle rotation, the image size changes and a blank background is generated. Therefore, the difficulty in enhancing the image data of the filamentous fungus is after the rotation. Blank background fills the problem.

As shown in Fig. 2, the original image size is $m \times n$, the angle from the horizontal plane is α, the distance from the center point to any corner point is ρ, and the position coordinate of one pixel point is (x_0, y_0), the image is rotated by θ degrees, and (x_1, y_1) is the pixel coordinates after rotate. The area of the circumscribed rectangle that is tangent to it after rotation changes, so the canvas needs to be reselected to store the rotated image matrix. In order to avoid information loss, the principle of canvas expansion is to carry all the picture information in a minimum area. The smallest canvas size selected is $M \times N$.

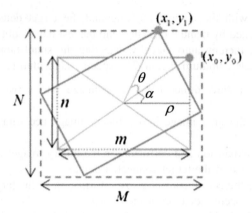

Fig. 2. Schematic diagram of pixel rotation coordinates

The horizontal and vertical coordinates after rotation are as follows:

$$x_1 = \rho \cos(\alpha + \theta) = \rho(\cos \alpha \cos \theta - \sin \alpha \sin \theta)$$
$$= x_0 \cos \theta - y_0 \sin \theta \tag{1}$$

$$y_1 = \rho \sin(\alpha + \theta) = \rho(\sin \alpha \cos \theta + \sin \theta \cos \alpha)$$
$$= x_0 \sin \theta + y_0 \cos \theta \tag{2}$$

$$M = m \cos \theta + n \sin \theta \tag{3}$$

$$N = m \sin \theta + n \cos \theta \tag{4}$$

$$x_1 = (x_0 - m/2) \cos \theta - (y_0 - m/2) \sin \theta + M/2 \tag{5}$$

$$y_1 = (x_0 - m/2) \sin \theta + (y_0 - n/2) \cos \theta + N/2 \tag{6}$$

The matrix transformation formula is obtained by the combination of Eqs. (1), (2) and (3) and (4):

$$[x_1 \, y_1 \, \mathbf{1}] = [x_0 \, y_0 \, 1] \cdot \begin{bmatrix} \cos \theta & \sin \theta & 0 \\ -\sin \theta & \cos \theta & 0 \\ 0 & 0 & 1 \end{bmatrix} \tag{7}$$

$$[x_0 \, y_0 \, \mathbf{1}] = [x_1 \, y_1 \, 1] \cdot \begin{bmatrix} \cos \theta & -\sin \theta & 0 \\ \sin \theta & \cos \theta & 0 \\ 0 & 0 & 1 \end{bmatrix} \tag{8}$$

According to the matrix transformation formula in Eq. (7), the pixel position after the image is rotated can be easily calculated. However, considering the coordinate transformation, the rotated coordinate points are not necessarily integers, and there must be some coordinate points in the new image. No corresponding pixels can be filled, or the position arrangement destroys the original neighbor relationship. The resulting rotated image will appear "empty". It can also be considered as regular noise. As shown in Fig. 3(a).

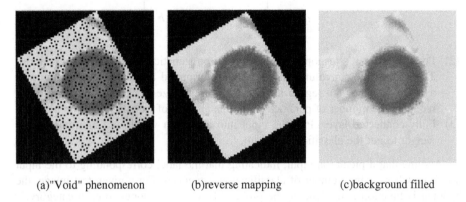

(a)"Void" phenomenon   (b)reverse mapping   (c)background filled

Fig. 3. "Void" phenomenon, reverse mapping and background fill after rotation

In order to solve this problem, a reverse mapping method, such as Eq. (8), it is adopted to take the color forward. Starting from the rotated image, find the point of the corresponding original image, and then pass the gray value in the original image, so that each pixel of the rotated image can certainly correspond to a point in the original image, Different strategies can make pixels more accurate. The effect is shown in Fig. 3(b).

Finally, for the background filling of the black background area in Fig. 3(c), considering the difference in the background color of the original image is large, it is not easy to directly assign the value, which is also the difficulty in enhancing the image data of the filamentous fungus. After many experiments, the background mean value at the width of 1/4 of the edge is selected to ensure that the filling result is close enough to the background of the adjacent edge, and the visual difference of the transition region is reduced.

3   Convolutional Neural Network

Convolutional Neural Network (CNN) is a feedforward neural network with deep learning function. Its structure includes input layer, convolution layer, pooling layer, fully connected layer and output layer. Its feature learning process including low-level to high-level feature extraction and classification. The network can recognize two-dimensional graphics of displacement, scaling and other forms of distortion invariance. During the training process, it can be implicitly learned from the training data, and can be learned in parallel [7], so in the field of image detection classification, there are a wide range of applications.

3.1   The Specific Structure and Design of Convolutional Neural Networks

(1) Convolutional layer: it's responsible for the learning of features. The calculation formula is as shown in (9).

$$q_j^{(l)} = f\left[\sum_{i \in M^{l-1}} q_i^{(l-1)} * k_{ij}^{(l)} + b_j^{(l)}\right] \tag{9}$$

(2) Pooling layer: it's responsible for aggregation statistics of adjacent area features. The map of the convolutional layer is downsampled by taking the maximum or average value of the region to reduce the input size of the next layer, thereby reducing the number of parameters and the amount of calculation of the network.
(3) Fully connected layer: Pull the input into a column vector and multiply it by a weight to get the classification result.

Assume that a picture is input, indicating that the label corresponding to the input image is, where is the number of classification categories. For a given test image, the hypothesis function is to estimate the probability value it belongs to each category.

$$h_\theta(q) = \begin{bmatrix} p(y_i = 0)|q_i; \beta \\ p(y_i = 1)|q_i; \beta \\ p(y_i = 2)|q_i; \beta \\ p(y_i = 3)|q_i; \beta \end{bmatrix} = \frac{1}{\sum_{i=0}^{k-1} e^{\theta_i^T q_i}} \begin{bmatrix} e^{\beta_0^T q_i} \\ e^{\beta_1^T q_i} \\ e^{\beta_2^T q_i} \\ e^{\beta_3^T q_i} \end{bmatrix} \tag{10}$$

In the formula, $\sum_{i=0}^{k-1} e^{\beta_i^T q_i}$ represents the normalization of the probability distribution, the sum of the corresponding probabilities is 1. β represents the parameters of the classifier, and Y represents the correct classification result. The loss function is

$$Loss(q, Y, \beta) = -\sum_{i=0}^{k-1} Y_i \bullet \log \frac{e^{\beta_i^T q_i}}{\sum_{i=0}^{k-1} e^{\beta_i^T q_i}} \tag{11}$$

Finally, the loss function is minimized according to the stochastic gradient descent method to achieve the optimal classification purpose.

Using two convolutional neural network models for comparison, in addition to the input layer and the output layer, the improved GoogLeNet network has 11 hidden layers which are 4 layers of convolution, 4 layers of pooling and 3 layers of full connections respectively [8–11]. Because of the difference in the structure of the two models, the classification performance of the two models is different. In this paper, two kinds of networks are used to detect and classify filamentous fungal images.

3.2   Fine-Tuning Training

After the data is augmented, the requirement to fully train a network is not achieved, so in order to avoid over-fitting, transfer learning is adopted. There are four main transfer methods of transfer learning: sample transfer, feature transfer, model transfer, and relationship transfer. The sample transfer is mainly applied to the problem of small target data samples effectively when the source data is very similar to the target data samples. For example, the traditional Adaboost algorithm is promoted, Dai et al. propose a boosting algorithm with transfer capability [12]. The idea of feature transfer is to find similar feature representations between source data and target data samples, such as CoCC algorithm, TPLSA algorithm and self-learning algorithm. Model transfer is to map the target data into the source data feature space, and use a unified model for learning and classification [13, 14]. For example, transfer learning from language recognition to image recognition [15].

Considering that the image similarity between the filamentous fungal image and the source data is not high, the model has little correlation as well, but it has certain similarity with the source data features. For example, the characteristics of dandelion in the ImageNet dataset are similar. Therefore, the feature transfer learning method is used to retrain the filamentous of small samples to achieve the purpose of over-fitting [16, 17]. Feature transfer first pre-trains the network on the big data set, obtaining the parameters of each layer of the network, and then copying its first n-layer parameters to the first n-layer of the target network, freezing the first n-layer parameters, and the other layers are randomly initialized. The specific operation process is:

Step 1: Use to train on the big dataset ImageNet the network and get the network parameters.

Step 2: Freeze the first n layer parameters in the network, and other layers are randomly initialized.

Step 3: Retrain the small dataset filamentous fungus image with the parameters in step 2 as the initial parameters. Get training accuracy and validation accuracy.

Step 4: Change the number of layers frozen in the network, cycle step 2 and step 3, find the optimal value of the number of transfer layers.

The purpose of transfer learning is to find the model parameters shared in the ImageNet dataset and a small number of filamentous fungal images, and to optimize the parameters of the filamentous fungal image classification model by using the source model parameters, so as to realize the characteristic transfer of data in different fields, which is beneficial to the filamentous fungal image. Classification

4   Results and Analysis

4.1   Data Augmentation and Target Detection

The collected labeled fungal image data set was used as training data and validation data. The data set contained a total of 1128 labeled fungal images, including 198 Aspergillus nidus images, 440 images of Alternaria alternata, and Aspergillus terreus 320, 170 other fungal images. Each fungus image uses four different magnifications (40X, 100X, 200X, 400X) and a fixed RGB three-channel image of 3024 × 4032 pixels. The augmented data set has been expanded 33 times with nearly 40,000 fungal images.

According to the target detection algorithm steps, three sets of target detection experiments were carried out on the Aspergillus terreus image. The experimental results were taken as the average of the multiple experimental results. The experimental precision has good stability. One set of experimental results is shown in Fig. 4.

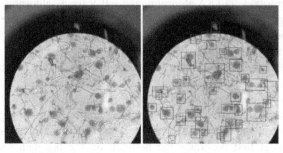

(a) Original image   (b) Target test result

Fig. 4. Target detection effect of Aspergillus terreus image

It can be seen from Fig. 5 that most fungal conidia are detectable, but some targets are still not detected, and there are leakage and misdetection phenomenon. The target detection algorithm was tested on three Aspergillus species samples, and the test results are shown in Table 1.

Table 1. Statistics on spore image detection results of Aspergillus terreus

Data set	Aspergillus terreus		
	a	b	c
Total spores	36	26	8
Number of detections	38	26	8
Number of misdetections	4	6	3
Number of missed detections	2	6	3
Accuracy (%)	94.4	76.9	62.5

As can be seen from Table 1, the accuracy of target detection is related to factors such as the total number of detections and background complexity. The more the total number of spores, the more concentrated the target distribution, and the less the background interference information, the easier the computer can detect the target.

4.2   Fine-Tune Training Results and Analysis

On the basis of data augmentation, the transfer learning strategy is used to train the network. In order to verify the effect of parameter transfer, the convolutional layer learning parameters are first frozen, the full connection layer of the source model is replaced with the 4-class Softmax classifier, and then the pre-training is performed. The model is put into the concentration training of the filamentous fungus samples, that is, the feature extraction ability and the induction ability of the pre-training model are retained. In the experiment, the number of training iterations is 100, the number of batches is 32, and the learning rate is 0.001. The results are shown in Table 2.

Table 2. Softmax classifier classification performance

Network	Training accuracy/%	Validation accuracy/%	Time/min	Parameter amount
GoogLeNet	93.1	82	53	10394614
Alexnet	74.42	71.64	32	58612952

Table 3. GoogLeNet network performance under different training parameters

Network	Training accuracy/%	Validation accuracy/%	Number of freeze layers	Trained parameter ratio/%
GoogLeNet	91	88.76	5	96.1
	92.59	90.66	4	93.98
	98.22	**96.55**	**3**	**75.4**
	94.94	94.84	2	65.66

It can be seen from Table 2 that after replacing the fully connected layer with the Softmax classifier, the training accuracy and validation accuracy of the GoogLeNet network is 10.36%–18.68%, higher than that of the Alexnet network, which is significant. The training accuracy and validation accuracy of GoogLeNet network can reach 93.1% and 82%, but the validation accuracy of Alexnet network can only reach 71.64%, which is far from meeting the clinical requirements. In order to further improve the network performance, the model parameters are fine-tuned, and different model structures use different frozen layers. Other parameters are unchanged, and the network performance changes under different trainable parameters are observed, and the number of frozen layers and training can be found. The optimal value of the parameter scale. The results are shown in Tables 3 and 4.

Table 4. Alexnet network performance under different training parameters

Network	Training accuracy/%	Validation accuracy/%	Number of freeze layers	Trained parameter ratio/%
Alexnet	80.23	79.69	4	96.9
	84.56	**83.2**	**3**	**96.17**
	84.14	82.42	2	34.25
	78.92	75.39	1	6.83

It can be seen from Tables 3 and 4 that the optimal validation accuracy of the two networks can reach 96.55% and 83.2%, and the network performance is greatly improved, indicating that the fine-tuning strategy has a significant improvement effect on the network classification. When the two networks are frozen at 3 layers, that is, the GoogLeNet network trainable parameters account for about 75%, and the Alexnet network trainable parameters account for about 96.3%, the network performance is the best. The GoogLeNet network training accuracy and validation accuracy can reach 98.22% and 96.55% respectively, which can provide reference for the clinical detection of filamentous fungi. The performance of the two network classifications gradually become better as the number of frozen layers increases, but when it increases to the optimal value, the network performance gradually deteriorates. As shown in Fig. 5.

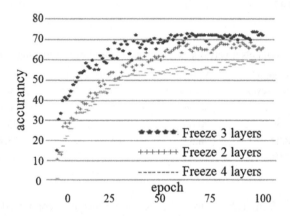

Fig. 5. Alexnet network different frozen layer accuracy changes

The performance of the Alexnet network increases first with the number of frozen layers. When the optimal value reaches reached, the performance begins to decrease. The optimal number of frozen layers is 3 layers, and the validation accuracy is up to 83.2%. After the transfer learning, the performance has improved. The main reason is the network structure is simple, and the parameters that can be migrated with a small correction range. Therefore, the accuracy is low, but the Alexnet network runs faster than the GoogLeNet network.

Figures 6, 7, 8, and 9 show the change of the accuracy and the loss value of the training process of the GoogLeNet and the Alexnet network transfer learning model. It can be seen from Figs. 6 and 7 that the GoogLeNet starts to converge 10 times in iteration, and the difference between the training precision and the verification accuracy is small, and there is no over-fitting phenomenon. The loss values of the two are close to each other in the iterative process, and finally can be reduced. By 7–10, the highest accuracy is around 95%. In Figs. 8 and 9, the Alexnet network starts to converge 20 times in iteration, but the convergence effect is not good. There is a difference between the training accuracy and the verification accuracy. There are multiple oscillations, and the final loss value is 10–15. The optimal accuracy is about 85%. This result indicates that the multi-size convolution kernel design in the GoogLeNet makes its parameter utilization higher and generalization better. The main reason for the poor performance of the Alexnet network classification is that the training dataset is too small.

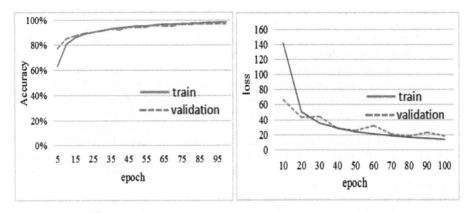

Fig. 6. GoogLeNet classification performance **Fig. 7.** GoogLeNet training process loss value

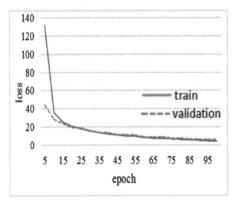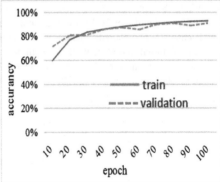

Fig. 8. Alexnet classification performance   **Fig. 9.** Alexnet training process loss value

References

1. Li, Y., Su, H., Qi, C.R., et al.: Joint embeddings of shapes and images via CNN image purification. ACM Trans. Graph. **34**(6), 1–12 (2015)
2. Gu, J., Wang, G., Cai, J., et al.: An empirical study of language CNN for image captioning. Comput. Vis. Pattern Recogn. (2017)
3. Gyvez, J.P.D., Wang, L.W.L., Sanchezsinencio, E.: Large-image CNN hardware processing using a time multiplexingscheme. In: Fourth IEEE International Workshop on Cellular Neural Networks & Their Applications. IEEE (1996)
4. Wang, W., Yang, L.J., Xie, Y.T., et al.: Edge detection of infrared image with CNN_DGA algorithm. Int. J. Light Electron Opt. **125**(1), 464–467 (2014)
5. Li, G., Yu, Y.: Visual saliency detection based on multiscale deep CNN features. IEEE Trans. Image Process. **25**(11), 5012–5024 (2016)

6. Zhang, B., Wang, L., Wang, Z., et al.: Real-time action recognition with deeply-transferred motion vector CNNs. IEEE Trans. Image Process. **27**, 2326–2339 (2018)
7. Cao, J., Pang, Y., Li, X.: Learning multilayer channel features for pedestrian detection. IEEE Trans. Image Process. **26**(7), 3210–3220 (2017)
8. Liu, P., Guo, J.M., Wu, C.Y., et al.: Fusion of deep learning and compressed domain features for content based image retrieval. IEEE Trans. Image Process. **26**, 5706–5717 (2017)
9. Kn, L., Ravindhranathreddy, B., Suryakalavathi, M.: Brain storm optimization algorithm for solving optimal reactive power dispatch problem. Chronexus.Org (2014)
10. Sun, Y.: A hybrid approach by integrating brain storm optimization algorithm with grey neural network for stock index forecasting. Abstr. Appl. Anal. **2014**, 1–10 (2014)
11. Wang, J., Hou, R., Wang, C., et al.: Improved v, -Support vector regression model based on variable selection and brain storm optimization for stock price forecasting. Appl. Soft Comput. **49**, 164–178 (2016)
12. Tajbakhsh, N., Shin, J.Y., Gurudu, S.R., et al.: Convolutional neural networks for medical image analysis: fine tuning or full training? IEEE Trans. Med. Imaging **35**(5), 1299–1312 (2017)
13. Affonso, C., Rossi, A.L.D., Vieira, F.H.A.: Deep learning for biological image classification. Expert Syst. Appl. **85**(11), 114–122 (2017)
14. Smith, R.: The 7 Levels of Change, 2nd edn. Tapeslry Press, Littleton (2002)
15. Wang, S., Liu, L., Duan, L., et al.: Accurate segmentation of Ulva prolifera regions with superpixel and CNNs. In: International Conference on Security. IEEE (2018)
16. Richter, C.D., Samala, R.K., Chan, H.P., et al.: Generalization error analysis: deep convolutional neural network in mammography. In: Computer-Aided Diagnosis (2018)
17. Jang, J., Kwon, J.Y., Kim, B., et al.: CNN-based estimation of abdominal circumference from ultrasound images (2017)

Improved RPN for Single Targets Detection Based on the Anchor Mask Net

Mingjie Li[✉], Youqian Feng, Zhonghai Yin, Cheng Zhou,
and Fanghao Dong

Foundation Department, Air Force Engineering University, Xi'an, China
13072988703@163.com

Abstract. Common target detection is usually based on single frame images, which is vulnerable to affected by the similar targets in the image and not applicable to video images. In this paper, anchor mask is proposed to add the prior knowledge for target detection and an anchor mask net is designed to improve the RPN performance for single target detection. Tested in the VOT2016, the model perform better.

Keywords: Anchor mask · RPN · Single targets detection · Timing · Time series

1 Introduction

Since the introduction of deep learning technology into the field of computer vision, all tasks for single-frame images are done well by a variety of networks. In the field of image recognition, Alexnet, VGG, Resnet [1] and more constantly refreshed the correct rate record of the Imagenet game. In the field of Target segmentation, FCN [2] and perfect application of the technology of CRF [3, 4] on it make the segmentation effect is more and more significant. AND in the field of Target Detection, the series of RCNN [5–7], the series of YOLO [8–10], R-FCN [11] and SSD [12] perform better and better by constantly improving the structure. But the target detection on the singe image frame can be affected simply if there is no prior knowledge added in the network. And with the development of target detection networks, the basic structure of RPN in also used in the all mainstream algorithm (for instance Faster-RCNN, Yolo-v3, and SSD). According to the problem and character of RPN, the concept of anchor mask is proposed in this paper, which can be used to connect to the prior knowledge to filter a lot of wrong anchors to improve the detection accuracy. An anchor mask net considering the timing characteristic is designed to join to the RPN as an auxiliary part. Passing the test in the VOT2016 data set, new RPN preforms better for single targets detection.

2 Relation Work

2.1 RPN

RPN is proposed firstly in Faster-RCNN, which generate several anchor boxes with different scales and ratios according to the anchor points on feature maps. And anchor

© Springer Nature Singapore Pte Ltd. 2019
Y. Wang et al. (Eds.): IGTA 2019, CCIS 1043, pp. 13–19, 2019.
https://doi.org/10.1007/978-981-13-9917-6_2

boxes can be adjusted to location the target and provided confidence scores by CNN. RPN is a effective structure to get proposal boxes which replace the complex procession of research boxes generation in RCNN. The structure of RPN is as showed in Fig. 1.

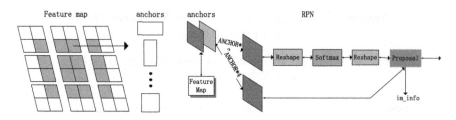

Fig. 1.

In this paper, a RPN is trained to be a target detector for video clip frames. Because RPN is the basic structure for the main steam algorithm in the targets detection field. So our anchor mask net will be useful in other networks if it is fine to RPN.

2.2   FCN

FCN is a classical structure for target segmentation. It gets the image features by the convolutional layers and pool layer firstly. After that, resize the feature maps to the same size of the original image by the fully convolutional layers and de-convolutional layers to predict the classes of each pixel.

In this paper, a similar FCN is trained to predict the valid anchor points. The structure of FCN is shown in Fig. 2.

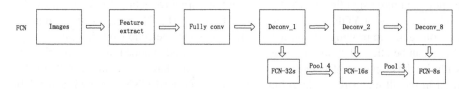

Fig. 2.

2.3   3dCNN

Three-dimensional Convolutional neural Networks (3dCNN) is firstly use for video analysis proposed in the C3D [13]. This structure integrates temporal and spatio information of video. Similar to ordinary convolution operations, 3dCNN make clip frames at different times equivalent to channels in 2dCNN. Convolutional operation is performed in each time dimension, and then an addition operation is performed on all time channels. In this paper, a 3dCNN is used to be the front end to get time information of the IOU heat maps of the first three frames. The principle of 3dCNN is shown in Fig. 3.

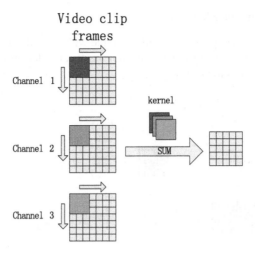

Fig. 3.

3   RPN with Anchor Mask Net

3.1   Anchor Mask and IOU Heat Map

In RPN, all the anchor points on the feature maps will be gotten operation to predict a box data and confidence scores. But there is always a few boxes marked valid, and the anchor boxes of interference target reserved. In this paper, a matrix containing only 0 and 1 is proposed to be the filter to dot multiply with feature maps before the convolution operation to get position and scores (The procession is shown in Fig. 4). The matrix which is called anchor mask is a filter to integrate prior knowledge and eliminate impossible locations. According to the highest score of all the anchor of per anchor points when we make the result boxes as ground truth, a heat map with same two-dimensional size as feature maps is made. In the heat mop, the value of each pixel is the highest IOU value of the anchors of the corresponding anchor point, and set the value less than threshold to 0. A heat map is show in Fig. 4.

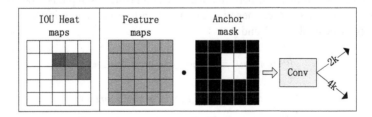

Fig. 4.

3.2 RPN with Anchor Mask Net

In order to consider the prior knowledge of the video of the previous frame and excluded interference target, a RPN with anchor mask net is designed in this paper. The structure of network is shown in Fig. 5.

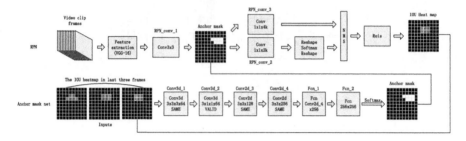

Fig. 5.

There are two stage in this network. And two network are trained in two stage. In stage 1, the IOU heat maps of last three frames was sent to the network. After two 3d Conv layers, input is compressed into one-dimensional. And after two 2d Conv layers to extract features and two Fully Convolutional layers and one Softmax layer, an anchor mask of next images which pixel is prediction of confidence scores generates.

In stage 2, the anchor mask generating in stage 1 dot multiply the feature maps before the generation of proposal boxes. According to rois of Non-maximal suppression (nms), the IOU heat map of this image generates which is used to predict anchor mask of next image. In this paper, the front end of vgg-16 is used to be the feature extractor and all the video clips are resize to (224, 224).

3.3 Losses of Network

The two networks in two stages in this be trained separately. In this paper, the video clip frames are resized to (224, 224) before put into RPN. And losses of RPN are same as Faster-RCNN. In this paper, the RPN is trained without anchor-mask to increase negative samples and the ratio between negative and positive sample is 3 (according to the SSD). The labels of others negative sample is set to −1 meaning invalid. Losses of the RPN is as Formulas 1, 2 and 3.

$$loss_{rpn\_total} = loss_{rpn\_scores} + loss_{rpn\_reg} \tag{1}$$

$$loss_{rpn\_scores} = \frac{-\sum_{i}^{n} labels_i \bullet \log(scores_i)}{n} \tag{2}$$

$$loss_{rpn\_reg} = \frac{\sum_{i}^{n}\sum_{j}^{4}R(t_j - t_{j^*})}{n} \tag{3}$$

Where $loss_{rpn\_total}$ is the total loss of RPN include the classification loss $loss_{rpn\_score}$ and regression loss $loss_{rpn\_reg}$ in Formulas 1. Where n is the number of valid anchors and $labels_i$ is the truth classification of $i - th$ anchor in Formulas 2. Where t_j is one of (t_x, t_y, t_h, t_w) which is the corresponding parameters between the ground truth and anchors and $(t_{x^*}, t_{y^*}, t_{h^*}, t_{w^*})$ is the corresponding parameters between the predict boxes and anchors. R is Robust loss function $smooth_{L1}$.

And the anchor mask net is trained with the IOU heat maps of the last threes clip frames. Losses of anchor mask net is shown in Formula 4.

$$loss_{mask} = \frac{-\sum_{i}^{M} label\_p_i \bullet \log(score\_p_i)}{M} \tag{4}$$

Where M is the number of anchor points in the feature maps. $label\_p$ is the ground truth anchor mask and $score\_p$ is the confidence scores of each pixel of anchor mask.

4 Experiment

4.1 Experimental Environment and Train Losses

Hardware Environment: AMD RYZEN 2200 and GTX1080-Ti.
Software Environment: Ubuntu16.04+tensorflow+pycharm

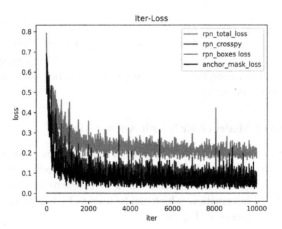

Fig. 6.

Our model get trained in the VOT2016 which is a common target tracking data set. The data set consists of short video slices of 60 different objects. In this paper, 20 images are randomly selected as a batch to train RPN. And 20 randomly selected 3 clip frames (or less) are used to train Anchor mask net as a batch. All models were trained 10,000 times, and training losses were recorded every 5 times. The relationship of Iteration and loss is shown in Fig. 6.

As the Fig. 6 shown, all losses have dropped significantly over time. And the loss of anchor mask net drops quickly. It means that the anchor mask net is useful to get temporal characteristic. The loss of RPN dropping shows RPN is useful to detect target.

4.2   Result of Anchor Mask Net

RPN and anchor mask net are trained separately and used together as Fig. 5. The model is tested on VOT2016 data set in continuous video clip frames. The part of result of test is shown in Fig. 7.

The blue boxes are ground truth boxes. The red boxes are results of RPN with anchor mask net. And the green boxes are results of RPN.

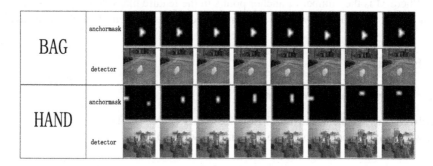

Fig. 7. (Color figure online)

As the Fig. 7 shown, the IOU of our model is higher than ordinary RPN. But it doesn't work well if the prediction of anchor mask is wrong. (For example, the result of sixth images of hand is wrong because of the wrong prediction of anchor mask).So the model is improved in the paper.

4.3   The Improved Model of RPN with Anchor Mask

For the problem of wrong prediction of anchor mask, a new generation method of anchor mask is proposed. The IOU heat map of last frame is added to the prediction to increase detection range. The new anchor mask comprehensive considerate of recent pictures and predicted information, which can be used to fix bug prediction results. The result of new RPN is shown in Fig. 8.

Fig. 8.

New anchor mask is useful as Fig. 8 shown, our model is useful for single target detection of video clip frames.

5 Conclusion

A RPN with anchor mask net is proposed in this paper, which considerate the spatio and temporal characteristic. The model is tested and improved in the VOT2016 data set, the effect of model is ideal.

References

1. He, K., Zhang, X., Ren, S., et al.: Deep residual learning for image recognition (2015)
2. Long, J., Shelhamer, E., Darrell, T.: Fully convolutional networks for semantic segmentation. IEEE Trans. Pattern Anal. Mach. Intell. (2014)
3. Krähenbühl, P., Koltun, V.: Efficient inference in fully connected CRFs with Gaussian edge potentials (2012)
4. Zheng, S., Jayasumana, S., Romera-Paredes, B., et al.: Conditional random fields as recurrent neural networks (2015)
5. Girshick, R., Donahue, J., Darrell, T., et al.: Rich feature hierarchies for accurate object detection and semantic segmentation. In: 2014 IEEE Conference on Computer Vision and Pattern Recognition (CVPR). IEEE Computer Society (2014)
6. Girshick, R.: Fast R-CNN. In: Computer Science (2015)
7. Ren, S., He, K., Girshick, R., et al.: Faster R-CNN: towards real-time object detection with region proposal networks. In: International Conference on Neural Information Processing Systems (2015)
8. Redmon, J., Divvala, S., Girshick, R., et al.: You only look once: unified, real-time object detection (2015)
9. Redmon, J., Farhadi, A.: YOLO9000: better, faster, stronger. In: IEEE Conference on Computer Vision & Pattern Recognition, Honolulu, HI, 21–26 July 2017, pp. 6517–6525. IEEE (2017)
10. Redmon, J., Farhadi, A.: YOLOv3: an incremental improvement (2018)
11. Dai, J., Li, Y., He, K., et al.: R-FCN: object detection via region-based fully convolutional networks. In: Proceedings of the 30th International Conference on Neural Information Processing Systems. Curran Associates Inc. (2016)
12. Liu, W., Anguelov, D., Erhan, D., et al.: SSD: single shot multibox detector (2015)
13. Tran, D., Bourdev, L., Fergus, R., et al.: Learning spatiotemporal features with 3D convolutional networks (2014)

Design and Analysis of Object Behavior in Media Content-User Relationship Network Model

Shan Liu[✉] and Kun Huang

Information Engineering School, Communication University of China,
Beijing 100024, China
liushan@cuc.edu.cn, hk_cuc@163.com

Abstract. The application of new media technologies and artificial intelligence technologies has promoted the prosperity of the Internet. The connection between web users and media content resources is deepening. Studying the relationship between media content and web users has become our focus. In this paper, using the theory of complex network and the Agent theory, the attribute information of media content and web users are analyzed, the objects and object clusters are classified and defined, and the behavior mechanism of related objects is designed and analyzed to realize the intelligence of the relationship network. The classification and behavior mechanisms of the objects will provide theoretical premise for realizing the visual analysis of the relationship between media content and web users, and lay the foundation for further model design.

Keywords: Complex network · Agent theory · Intelligent tag · Media content · Object behavior

1 Introduction

The development of new media technologies has promoted the prosperity of the Internet. At the same time, the popularity of technologies such as artificial intelligence has also promoted the continuous growth of media resource content and web users. On the Internet, people browse a lot of content every day and leave their own behavioral information. The relationship between web users and the content of media resources is inseparable. The dissemination of media resources content and the needs of users have become the focus of the current network services. We try to establish a relationship network for media resource content and web users, design and simulate the behavior evolution mechanism between different objects in the network, so as to realize the visual analysis of media information and the intelligent management of media resource content and web users, and to reasonably divide and accurately recommend content.

There are some studies of both media content and user. For social media corpus, Ning proposed a cluster-LDA algorithm model, which combines author structure in topic modeling to complete topic inference and author grouping [1]. Han et al. applied the concept of social networking to online shopping behavior, and proposed a new network perspective to look at the interconnection of online interests and products,

© Springer Nature Singapore Pte Ltd. 2019
Y. Wang et al. (Eds.): IGTA 2019, CCIS 1043, pp. 20–30, 2019.
https://doi.org/10.1007/978-981-13-9917-6_3

thereby to capture online product attributes that reflect the user's sociality [2]. Stephen developed a social media monitoring system to help media monitors to distill the perception of potential and actual customers of the value of media products and services, which can learn how to better meeting customer expectations [3]. Choudhury used social media with the dual characteristics of content and community to develop a content recommendation framework that combines user feedback [4]. Ma proposed a solution that combines user profiles and social network structural features to accommodate more online social networks [5]. Most of these research are based on traditional data mining algorithms and complex network frameworks. The current analysis of media and users is becoming more intelligent. Therefore, for the intelligent analysis of media resource and web users, we adopt Agent theory and intelligent tag.

The Agent-based models are in line with the behavior characteristics of the people in the real world, and can well simulate the behavior process of users in the network [6]. At present, relevant scholars have applied the theory of agents to the analysis of social public opinion [7]. It is a good model method for realizing the correlation analysis of network resource. In the previous study, we proposed a distance calculation method for measuring the relationship between media resource content and users [8]. In this paper, we design and analyze the behavior of objects and clusters in the network based on such calculation methods. Combining Agent theory with other theories, this paper studies the impact of behavioral characteristics on internal relationships of media content and web users.

In this paper, the main contributions are as follows:

- Based on Agent theory and other theories, we describe media content and web user objects in relationship network and define user clusters, media content clusters, and media content user clusters.
- Through the characteristics of media content and web users, we design the mechanism of object behaviors, conduct the behavior analysis and visual analysis in the relationship network, and provide suggestions for content recommendation, user grouping and other applications.

2 Related Theory

2.1 Complex Network and Agent Theory

A complex network is a complex relationship between object and object in the research. The object elements themselves are relatively simple, but the mechanism of action that embodies the relationships between objects shows a high degree of complexity. The structure of complex networks and other aspects show complexity.

The transformation of information technology has led to the birth of massive data, and has also promoted the current scientific research into the era of big data [9]. Quantitative analysis of data facilitates the intersection of complex science and various disciplines. Some major problems that need to be solved in the field of complex network research have been proposed [10].

Agent theory comes from the development of complex network theory. Agent has the following characteristics.

- Autonomy. The Agent can operate without the direct intervention of people or other agents, and has some control over its behavior and internal state.
- Sociability. The Agent and other Agents interact through some kind of Agent communication language.
- Reactivity. The Agent observes its environment (perhaps the physical world, the graphical world, a series of other Agents, the Internet, etc.) and responds within a certain period, and can reflect the behavior of the target by accepting certain revelation information [11].

We study the Agent theory to obtain the modeling ideas, and design the behavior of the research objects, thus helping to realize the intelligence of the network model of media content and web users.

2.2   Silhouette Coefficient

Silhouette Coefficient [12] measures the degree of similarity between clusters and clusters in a relational network, and measures whether the object enters a reasonable cluster. Silhouette Coefficient is an evaluation method for the clustering effect of clusters combining cohesion and separation.

SC (Silhouette Coefficient) has several properties: $-1 \leq SC \leq 1$; SC is closer to 1, indicating that the convergence effect of the corresponding cluster is better; $SC > 0$ means that object has entered a relatively suitable cluster.

3   Definition and Design of Object Cluster and Object Behaviors in Network Model

There are two kinds of objects in the network - media content and users, each with its own unique attributes. The attributes of an object are the key to establishing relationship between users and users, media content and media content, and media content and users. At the same time, the attributes can be translated into unique tags for users or content. Objects are an important element of a cluster.

3.1   Definition of User Cluster, Media Content Cluster and Media Content-User Cluster

In the relationship evolution network model of media resource content and web user, each cluster has its own specific theme and goals. The status between clusters and clusters is equal, when negotiating and cooperating. Most of the clusters and clusters are loosely related to each other to clarify their independence, and try to achieve no competition and contradiction between each other. In the relationship network, each cluster has several capabilities: managing itself independently, solving its own problems, and achieving its goals.

User cluster: the user cluster is a cluster of user objects.

- There is no upper limit on the number of objects in the cluster, and the convergence is based on the relevance of the user's attribute tags to cluster the user objects together.
- Certain behaviors of users entering the same cluster show holistic and consistent, such as focusing on the same type of media resource content.
- The goal of the user cluster is to form a relatively stable user community. Observing a user cluster can obtain data information of such users, such as the attributes and behavior characteristics of the group.
- For the user community, certain media resources and information can be specifically distributed, or specific needs can be provided in a centralized manner, thereby facilitating the benign development of the user cluster.

Media content cluster: the media content cluster is a cluster composed of media content objects.

- There is no upper limit on the number of objects in the cluster, and the convergence is based on the relevance of the attribute tags of the media resources to cluster the media resource content objects together.
- Certain features of the media resources entering the same cluster exhibit integrity and consistency, for example, attracting attention and browsing by the same type of users.
- The goal of the media content cluster is to form a relatively stable set of media resources. Observing a certain media content cluster can obtain data information of this type of media resources, such as the attributes and theme features of the resource set.
- For media content clusters, we can concentrate on media resources or guide users' reasonable attention, which is conducive to realizing the update and flexible calling of media resources.

User-media content cluster: the user-media content cluster is a cluster composed of user cluster and media content cluster.

- The number of objects in a cluster has a certain limit. The reason is that as the web users and media resources are continuously updated, the uncertainty of the clusters also changes. This causes the internal close relationship of the cluster to gradually fade, and the core target of the cluster is weakened. The basis of the cluster is that the tags of the web users and the media resource content objects are related to a certain extent.
- The purpose of the cluster is to make accurate recommendations and to study the hotspot evolution of related topics. Through user-media content clusters, the matching of media resources and web users and the recommended effects of related content can be seen. The information interaction between the user cluster and the media content cluster inside the cluster realizes the recommended update and the monitoring and early warning of certain topics.

3.2 Classification and Definition of Objects Behavior

The behavior of objects and clusters mainly includes joining behaviors, sharing behaviors, and leaving behaviors. The main basis is the method of measuring the distance between objects and objects [8]. Based on the previous definition of objects and object clusters, and the subsequent design of object behavior, in the relational network, we can see the autonomous action of object and visual intuitive analysis.

3.2.1 The Joining Behavior of Objects

Definition. When an object satisfies certain conditions set, or its attribute content characteristics are the same as the universal attribute characteristics of all objects in a cluster, the object will join the cluster when it plays a positive role in achieving the common goal of the cluster. The representation of the object's joining behavior is as follows:

The distance between the cluster C_i and the object x is d_{xC_i}. When the object x joins the cluster C_i, it must satisfy:

$$d_{xC_i} = \min\{d_{xC_1}, d_{xC_2}, \cdots, d_{xC_M}\}. \tag{1}$$

When the above conditions are met, the object will autonomously join the corresponding cluster. If the value of d_{xC_i} is decreasing, it will indicate that the importance of this object in the cluster is increasing. When such objects occupy the vast majority, these objects are considered to be the core objects of the cluster.

3.2.2 The Sharing Behavior of Objects

Definition. When an object enters a cluster, it persists in this cluster for a long time. The attribute content of the object is not only the same as the universal attribute of all the objects in the cluster, but also similar to the general characteristics of other clusters. It also promotes the goal of other clusters to a certain extent, thus, the object is shared by these clusters. The premise of sharing objects is that the objects are already assigned to a particular cluster, rather than independent of all clusters. The representation of the object's sharing behavior is as follows:

First, an object x needs to belong to a cluster C_i, that satisfying (1).
Then, every cluster is defined to have a shared area. That is, some other clusters can share the objects in this area with the cluster. The measure of the cluster is the object's Silhouette Coefficient. An object x in a cluster C_i, and its Silhouette Coefficient is called s_x. If the object is in the sharing area, the Silhouette Coefficient must satisfy:

$$-s_a \leq s_x \leq s_a. \tag{2}$$

In (2), s_a is set as needed. From the definition of the object's sharing behavior, the theorem of two clusters sharing same object is available.

Theorem. The distance between the cluster C_i and the object $\mathbf{x}$ is $\mathbf{d_{xC_i}}$, and if the distance between the object $\mathbf{x}$ and another cluster $\mathbf{C_j}$ is $\mathbf{d_{xC_j}}$, it satisfies:

$$d_{xC_j} \times (1 - s_a) \leq d_{xC_i} \leq d_{xC_j} \times (1 + s_a). \tag{3}$$

Thus, the object x is shared by the cluster C_i and the cluster C_j at the same time.

Proof. Considering the definition of the object's sharing behavior, when the object $\mathbf{x}$ is in the cluster $\mathbf{C_i}$, $\mathbf{d_{xC_i}} = \mathbf{min}\{\mathbf{d_{pQ_1}}, \mathbf{d_{pQ_2}}, \cdots, \mathbf{d_{pQ_n}}\}$ are satisfied. Thus, the condition $\mathbf{d_{xC_j}} > \mathbf{d_{xC_i}}$ is known. As we all know, $\mathbf{d_{xC_i}}$ is the intra-cluster dissimilarity of the object $\mathbf{x}$, and $\mathbf{d_{xC_j}}$ is the dissimilarity between the clusters of the object $\mathbf{x}$, and there is $-s_a \leq s_x = 1 - \frac{d_{xC_i}}{d_{xC_j}} \leq s_a$, $\mathbf{d_{xC_j}} \times (1 - s_a) \leq \mathbf{d_{xC_i}} \leq \mathbf{d_{xC_j}} \times (1 + s_a)$, obtained.

3.2.3   The Leaving Behavior of Objects

Definition. When an object no longer satisfies certain conditions set, or its attribute content changes, and different from the general attribute characteristics of other objects in the cluster, and no longer plays a positive role in achieving the common goal of the cluster in which it is located, the object will leave this cluster. The representation of the object's leaving behavior is as follows:

When the object x satisfies:

$$d_{xC_i} \neq \min\{d_{xC_1}, d_{xC_2}, \cdots, d_{xC_N}\}. \tag{4}$$

At the same time, the condition of the object's sharing behavior is no longer satisfied, but

$$s_x \leq -s_a. \tag{5}$$

Thus, the object leaves the cluster C_i, and enters the new object cluster according to the condition of the object's joining behavior.

4   Analysis of Object Behavior

4.1   Analysis of the Joining Behavior of Objects

With the change of time, new objects constantly appear in the relationship network, and at the same time, the behavior of objects joining the cluster occurs at the moment, as shown in Fig. 1. Several objects already exist in the initial relationship network, and a number of object clusters have been formed. These objects and cluster distribution have collected some initial objects and kept stable distribution. There are three user clusters, namely {1, 4, 8}, {2, 5, 9}, {3, 6, 7}, and four media content clusters, namely {1, 3}, {2}, {4, 5, 7, 8} and {6, 9}. These user clusters and media content clusters are related to each other and form several user-media content clusters. At this time, two new objects enter the relationship network, the user object numbered 10 and the media content object numbered 10. According to the condition of object joining behavior, compared with all clusters in the network, the user object numbered 10 is closest to the user cluster {1, 4, 8}, and the media content object numbered 10 is closest to the media content cluster {4, 5, 7, 8}. Therefore, the user object numbered 10 joins the user cluster. The media content object numbered 10 also joins the media content cluster. As a result, the cluster distribution of the relational network is updated. There are user clusters: {1, 4, 8, 10}, {2, 5, 9}, {3, 6, 7}; media content clusters: {1, 3}, {2}, {4, 5, 7, 8, 10}, {6, 9}. In addition, it is worth noting that the user-media content cluster in the network has also changed and become larger. This makes it more influential in the whole relationship network, more easily to absorb more objects, and better to achieve the goals.

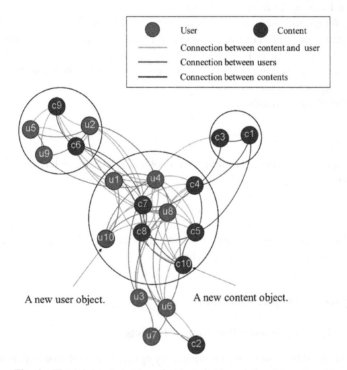

Fig. 1. The joining behavior of objects in the relationship network.

4.2 Analysis of the Sharing Behavior of Objects

In the evolution process of relationship network, the sharing behavior of objects between object clusters is very common. A specific example can be seen in Fig. 2. In the figure, there are three user clusters: {1, 4, 8, 10}, {2, 5, 9}, {3, 6, 7} and four media content clusters: {1, 3}, {2}, {4, 5, 7, 8, 10}, {6, 9}. It is worth noting that the solid circle in the figure divides the range of three independent clusters, which are a user-media content cluster (consisting of the user cluster {1, 4, 8, 10} and the media content cluster {4, 5, 7, 8, 10}), another user-media content cluster (consisting of user clusters {2, 5, 9} and media content clusters {6, 9}) and a separate media content cluster {1, 3}. There are also two dashed circles defining the range. These two areas overlap with the largest user-media content cluster. This reflects the result of object sharing behavior. The user object numbered 1 satisfies the condition of the sharing behavior of the object, and the media content object numbered 4 has the same conditions. As a result, these two objects not only belong to the cluster of objects they are in, but they also act on other clusters of objects and are used by other clusters. The sharing behavior of objects will work when recommendation or grouping.

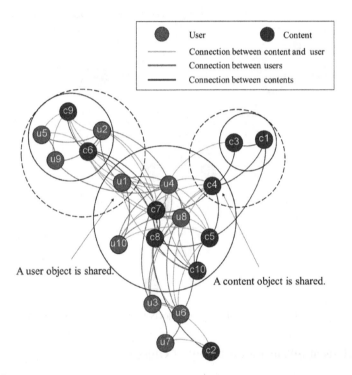

Fig. 2. The sharing behavior of objects in the relationship network.

4.3   Analysis of the Leaving Behavior of Objects

In Fig. 3, the composition of the user object cluster and the media resource content cluster in the relationship network changes as compared with the result of the object sharing behavior presented in Fig. 2. The result is a change in the user-media content cluster. The user object numbered 1 has left the user cluster where it was originally located, and the media content object numbered 4 is also not in the original media content cluster. During the evolution process, a change in the partial attribute tag of the user object numbered 1 caused a change in its distance from other user objects. A similar situation occurs for a media resource object numbered 4. As time changes, the distance between these two objects and their respective clusters increases, and the distance from other clusters shrinks, reaching the conditions for the object leaving behavior, and also satisfying the condition of the object joining behavior. As a result, the new cluster accommodates both objects. We can see that the object leaving behavior will lead to an update of the entire relationship network.

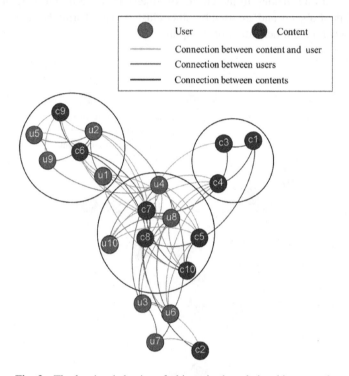

Fig. 3. The leaving behavior of objects in the relationship network.

4.4   Analysis of Silhouette Coefficient of Objects

For the behavior design of the object cluster in the relationship network, the Silhouette Coefficients of all the object nodes in our team network are calculated and counted, and the distribution of the Silhouette Coefficient of the object nodes is observed. In the Fig. 4, we can see that the Silhouette Coefficients of all objects are greater than 0. Therefore, this means that all objects enter the relevant clusters, and have sufficient rationality, which also reflects the rationality of the behavior mechanism. By distributing the Silhouette Coefficients, we can know that some objects are "shared" by different clusters. The definition of clusters and the design of behavioral mechanisms have laid the foundation for relevant analysis, accurate recommendation and information communication of media content and web users.

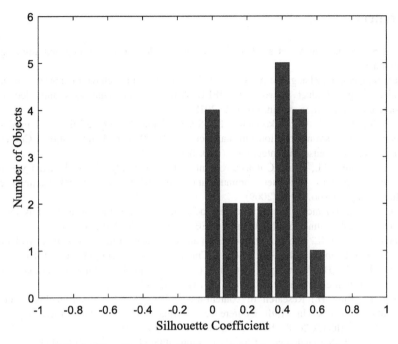

Fig. 4. The silhouette coefficients of objects in the network.

5   Conclusion

Based on the evolution of the media resource content and the web user's relationship network, this paper defines the related object clusters in the network based on the media content and web users' attribute tags, and designs the object behavior mechanism in the relationship network. The classification of object clusters and the design of object behavior will clarify the themes and targets in the relationship network. According to the internal relationship between the media contents and web users, the behavior mechanism of the object is designed to adapt to the actual evolution. Through the behavior design of objects and object clusters, the intelligence of objects in the relationship network is further advanced. Definition of object cluster and design of object behavior help to realize visual analysis of relationship network. Applications such as grouping and recommendation of the network models will also be autonomous under the design of behavior mechanism. These provide theoretical premise for realizing the visual analysis of the relationship between media content and web users, and also provide a research basis for the complete design of the entire network model, which helps to analyze the rationality of media resource and web users.

Acknowledgments. The work of this paper was supported by the Fundamental Research Funds for the Central Universities and Scientific Research Grant of Asian Media Research Center at Communication University of China.

References

1. Ning S., Qu X., Cai V., et al.: Clust-LDA: joint model for text mining and author group inference (2018)
2. Han, S., Qiao, Y., Zhang, Y.: Analyze users' online shopping behavior using interconnected online interest-product network. In: IEEE Wireless Communications and Networking Conference, Barcelona, Spain, pp. 1–6 (2018)
3. Wan, S., Paris, C., Georgakopoulos, D.: Social media data aggregation and mining for internet-scale customer relationship management. In: 2015 IEEE International Conference on Information Reuse and Integration (IRI). IEEE (2015)
4. De Choudhury, M., et al.: Connecting content to community in social media via image content, user tags and user communication. In: IEEE International Conference on Multimedia & Expo. IEEE (2009)
5. Ma, J., et al.: Balancing user profile and social network structure for anchor link inferring across multiple online social networks. IEEE Access 5, 12031–12040 (2017)
6. Guoan, Y., Ting, X., Hao, C.: The definition and classification framework of network cluster behavior. J. People's Public Secur. Univ. China (Soc. Sci. Ed.) 6, 99–104 (2010)
7. Zong, L., Gu, B.: Multi-agent modeling of network public opinion evolution in crisis communication environment. Inf. Sci. (9), 1414–1419 (2010)
8. Shan, L., Kun, H.: Research of content-user relationship based on intelligent tags in evolution network. In: 13th Conference on Image and Graphics Technologies and Applications (IGTA 2018), Beijing, China, pp. 566–577 (2018)
9. Marx, V.: The big challenges of big data. Nature 498(7453), 255–260 (2013)
10. Zhou, T., Zhang, Z., Chen, G.: The opportunities and challenges of complex networks research. J. Univ. Electron. Sci. Technol. China 43(1), 1–5 (2014)
11. Wooldridge, M., Jennings, N.R.: Intelligence agents: theory and practice. Knowl. Eng. Rev. 10(2), 115–152 (1994)
12. Rousseeuw, P.J.: Silhouettes: a graphical aid to the interpretation and validation of cluster analysis. J. Comput. Appl. Math. 20(20), 53–65 (1999)

A Method of Penicillin Bottle Defect Inspection Based on BP Neural Network

Yangbo Feng[1,3](✉), Tinglong Tang[2,3], and Shengyong Chen[1,3]

[1] Tianjin University of Technology, Tianjin 300384, People's Republic of China
13001363055@163.com
[2] China Three Gorges University, Yichang 443002, People's Republic of China
[3] Tianjin Key Laboratory of Intelligence Computing and Novel Software Technology,
Tianjin University of Technology, Tianjin 300384, China

Abstract. Penicillin bottles are widely used in freeze-drying product packaging. Under the strict GMP standard, every bottle filled with freeze-drying should be inspected before being sent to the market. Traditionally, the inspection is accomplished by grueling and time-consuming human work. To address this problem, a method based on machine learning is proposed to inspect the defects of penicillin bottles. Scale Invariant Feature Transform (SIFT) is used to features extraction and a back propagation (BP) neural network classifier is employed to detect whether the bottles are with flaws. Experiments show that the proposed method is effective for penicillin bottle defects detection with high accuracy and fast speed.

Keywords: Defect inspection · Feature extraction ·
Back propagation neural network

1 Introduction

Penicillin bottles are widely used in pharmaceutical industry to contain liquid, freeze-dried powder and other drugs [16]. However, there are inevitable kinds of flaws such as wrinkle, titling and sunken which may occur during the packing process which is shown in Fig. 1 [8].

Traditional defect inspection methods are based on manual inspection. However, the manual inspection work is laborious and time-consuming. Defect detection methods based on image processing and machine vision technology are appearing in recent years [12]. For instance, the adaptive threshold method for simple defect segmentation is often applied [21]. Texture analysis technology also plays a leading role in surface defect detection technology [6].

Though the surface detection based on image process has been successfully applied to the quality inspection, there is rare work detecting the flaws of this

The project was supported by the Opening Foundation of Tianjin Key Laboratory of Intelligence Computing and Novel Software Technology, Tianjin University of Technology, China (TJUT-KLICNST-K20180002).

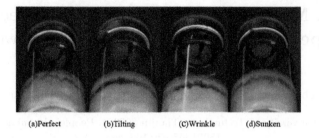

(a)Perfect   (b)Tilting   (C)Wrinkle   (d)Sunken

Fig. 1. Samples of Penicillin bottles

kind of bottle. To address this problem, the approach based on BP neural network classifier [4] and the SIFT descriptor has been proposed. Particularly, it is demonstrated that methods based on BP neural network classifier [7] are superior to the support vector machine (SVM) classifier [9]. The detection speed of this method can reach the manual detection speed. Therefore it could execute pattern classification effectively to inspect whether the vial bottles are with flaws.

The rest of this paper is organized as follows: Sect. 2 describes the related work on defect detection and correlation method. Section 3 describes the methods used in this paper; Sect. 4 describes and discusses the experimental results; Sect. 5 presents the conclusions.

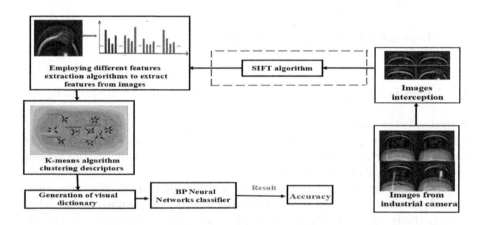

Fig. 2. Overview of the proposed method

2   Related Works

Quality of pharmaceutical products is crucial for people's health. Hence product quality testing is a significant part of the production process. Machine vision provides one cost-effective technique to accomplish these requirements. This inspection approach based on image analysis has found different applications in the product quality testing.

The objective of this paper is to achieve a high percentage of accuracy by applied to feature extraction and BP classification. Feature extraction has been applied to detect the face liveness [14] and the auto welding quality etc. Similarly, BP neural network has been applied to tackle the problem of product quality detection including defect inspection of solder bumps in the flip chip [5] and coke quality to meet requirements of a production process, etc. The research focuses on the three crucial facts: (1) The problem of bottle mouth inspection for pharmaceutical packaging bottle is effectively solved. (2) reduce the labor intensity with defect inspection more effectively; (3) selection of BP neural network achieves a high percentage of accuracy even when there are few samples.

For feature extraction, there are many descriptions and definitions of features, such as Haar, Invariant Feature Transform (SIFT) [18], Local Binary Patterns (LBP) [20], Speed Up Robust Features Scale (SURF) [3], etc. The SIFT operator is a classic method to describe the image local variance. Moreover, a small number of images can also extract a large number of features.

For classification, there are many classic classifiers, such as Support Vector Machine (SVM) [1], Multilayer Perceptron (MLP) [19], BP neural network classifiers [10], etc. BP neural network is the most widely used networks due to its simplicity and its power to nonlinear mapping.

3   Proposed Method

In this study, the LFDs method [15] and BP algorithm are used to build the inspection model. First, a model for vial defect inspection is built to analyze the performance of LFDs and BP algorithms. The model is visualized in Fig. 2. SIFT descriptor is applied to feature extraction that could generate visual dictionaries through the application of k-means clustering [13]. BP neural network classifier is used to inspect whether the vial bottles are with flaws. It is demonstrated that the proposed method is effective for defect inspection.

3.1   Images from the Industrial Camera and ROI Extraction

We have taken the images with the SR4000 3D laser ranging camera. In addition, dark-field illumination was used to obtain clear images of the surface of the object, as shown in Fig. 4. In the bottles lighting process, it could produce tilted astigmatism into the lens and obtain bright points in a dark background.

Then, the region of interest (ROI) [17] containing the vial lib is extracted based on the 3D image shown in Fig. 3. The ROI is obtained through image interception, the method deeply reduces the computational complexity and accelerates computing speed.

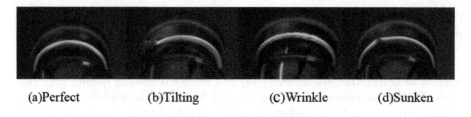

(a)Perfect   (b)Tilting   (c)Wrinkle   (d)Sunken

Fig. 3. Obtain ROI.

Fig. 4. Camera sampled images scene.   **Fig. 5.** SIFT features comparison.

3.2 SIFT Features Extraction

SIFT extracts features [11]that are invariant to scaling, rotation and partially invariant to the 3D camera view. Moreover, it is possible to reduce the possibility of noise interference because these are well oriented at spatial and frequency domain. Extracting of SIFT features is done in the following four steps:

- The scale space extreme detection
- Key point localization
- Orientation assignment
- Key point description.

By conducting a set of experiments, it is the best result that the local features are clustered into eight clusters. We averaged the results of clustering images. It is shown in Fig. 5, evidently, the defective images have a larger value than the perfect images. It demonstrates the SIFT features extraction method is very effective.

3.3 K-means Clustering in Bag Descriptors of Features

The k-means algorithm is to cluster features into K clusters which could produce the visual dictionary. The training samples are $x^{(1)}$, $x^{(2)}$, ..., $x^{(m)} \in R^n$. Firstly, random selection of K cluster centroid points which are $\mu_1, \mu_2, \ldots, \mu_k \in R^n$. Then for each sample $x^{(i)}$ to calculate which class it should belong to.

$$c^{(i)} = arg \min_{j} ||x^{(i)} - \mu_j||^2 \qquad (1)$$

For each class j that the centroid points of the class is recalculated, the result is represented by μ_j.

$$\mu_j = \frac{\sum_{i=1}^{m} 1(c^{(i)} - j)x^{(i)}}{\sum_{i=1}^{m} 1(c^{(i)} - j)} \qquad (2)$$

$c^{(i)}$ represents the closest distance between the simple i and the nearest class. Repeat the above steps until convergence. After several experiments, the best experimental results were obtained when the number of visual words K was eight. In this process, all descriptors were coded into similar visual words respectively, it is shown in Fig. 6.

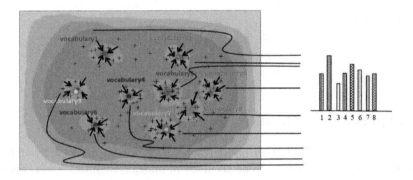

Fig. 6. Obtain a visual dictionary by clustering.

3.4   MLP-BP Neural Network Classifier

MLP-BP neural network [2] is an error back propagation neural network. In this paper, BP neural network model made up with four layers that is an ANN model with two hidden layers. This is the BP neural network structure (see Fig. 7).

The input layer input vector is $X = [x_1, \ldots, x_i, \ldots, x_n]^T$, the first hidden layer output vector is $L_1 = [l_{11}, \ldots, l_{1j}, \ldots, l_{1k}]^T$ that has k neurons, the second hidden layer output vector is $L_2 = [l_{21}, \ldots, l_{2m}, \ldots, l_{2q}]^T$ that has q neurons, the output layer output vector is $Y = [y_1, y_2]^T$. The weight matrix of between input layer and first hidden layer is denoted by $A = [a_1, \ldots, a_j, \ldots, a_k]$. The weight matrix of between first hidden layer and second hidden layer is denoted by $B = [b_1, \ldots, b_m, \ldots, b_q]$. The weight matrix of between second hidden layer and output hidden layer is denoted by $C = [c_1, c_2]$. By the forward propagation of the signal, the function f(*) is defined as neuron activation function. For the hidden layer that:

$$L_{1j} = f(net_{1j}), j = 1, 2, \ldots, k \qquad (3)$$

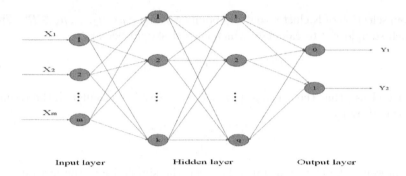

Fig. 7. BP neural network.

$$net_{1j} = \sum_{i=1}^{n} a_{ij}x_i, \ j = 1, 2, \ldots \qquad (4)$$

For the output layer:

$$y_j = f(net_j), \ j = 1, 2 \qquad (5)$$

$$net_{3j} = \sum_{i=1}^{q} c_{ij}L_{2i}, \ j = 1, 2 \qquad (6)$$

4   Experimental Results

In this section, we evaluate the robustness of the proposed method through the averaged recognition accuracy. The accuracy of image recognition was expressed as:

$$a = \frac{RightI}{AllI}100\% \qquad (7)$$

where a represents the accuracy of image recognition. $RightI$ and $AllI$ are the numbers of correctly identified test images and the numbers of all test images respectively. We selecte 2, 3, 5, and 8 cluster centers to do experiments. It is found that the experiment works best when the number of cluster centers is 8.

4.1   Comparison of Various Algorithms of Features Extraction

Randomly selecting 200 images from the remaining images for testing. Each model is tested ten times and calculate the average value. By using diverse feature extraction methods include SIFT, SURF and LBP algorithms that experiment could obtain averaged recognition accuracy in Fig. 8. In addition to, four kinds of multi-features algorithms can also achieve high precision. The averaged recognition accuracy is showed in Fig. 9.

Figure 9 shows that that SIFT algorithm obtain the highest experimental accuracy. With only ten training samples, the accuracy is higher than 95% and the accuracy is 100% when the training samples are enough. The reason is that

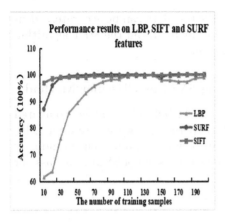

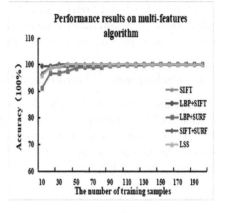

Fig. 8. Performance on LBP, SIFT and SURF algorithm

Fig. 9. Performance results on multi-features algorithms

the features extracted by the SIFT algorithm have the most obvious differences with defective and perfect images.

Then Fig. 10 shows that when LBP and SIFT methods are combined that the experimental accuracy obtained is higher than 99% even with a small number of training samples. However, methods of multi-feature integration take magnanimous time to extract features so that speed decreases. Moreover, the SIFT algorithm is faster than a various multi-feature algorithm.

Furthermore, during the experiment we randomly selecte the test samples $N \in \{40, 80, 120, 160, 200, 240, 280, 320, 360\}$ in which the positive samples and negative samples ratio of one to one when 260 training samples are given. Each set of data is randomly selected ten times and the average accuracy is showed in Fig. 10. It indicates that the SIFT and multi-features algorithms significantly

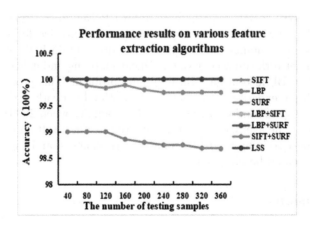

Fig. 10. Performance comparison on several algorithms

outperform LBP and SURF algorithms. All the test data can be accurately identified when SIFT and multi-features algorithms by used. But the SIFT algorithm
is faster than the various multi-feature algorithm.

4.2 Performance Comparison by Using SVM as Classifier Method

Finally, for demonstrating the proposed method is effective that we compared
it with SVM algorithm as a classifier. In the experiments, we selecte from 5, 10,
15, 20, 25, 30 images until 100 images per category for training. Then randomly
selecte 200 images to test ten times. Experimental results of SVM as a classifier
are shown in and Fig. 11.

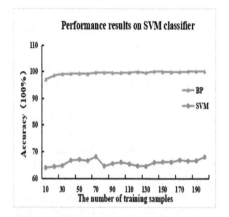

Fig. 11. Comparison of BP and SVM
experimental results on SIFT algorithms

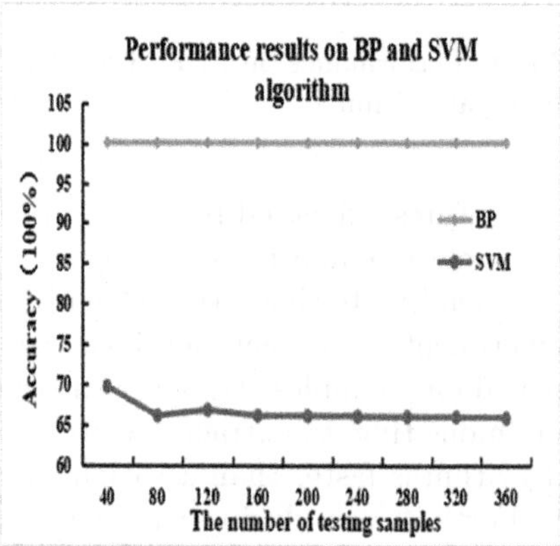

Fig. 12. Comparison of BP and SVM
experimental results on multi-features
algorithms

  Figure 11 shows that the methods base on BP Neural Network as classifier
outperform the SVM. The SVM algorithm is only effective for special small
samples. For a large number of samples it couldn't obtain high precision. But
the BP neural network could achieve non-linear mapping and it has self-learning
ability. However, BP also has a local minimum problem. This problem could be
solved by multiple experiments to obtain the optimal network.

  In addition to, we randomly selecte the test samples when 260 training samples were given. The average accuracy is showed in Fig. 12. It shows that when
selecting the best training model by multiple experiments, and the great experimental results could be obtained.

5   Conclusion

In summary, we have presented a recognition method for vials inspection using
the SIFT algorithm and BP neural network. The experimental results show that

the lowest accuracy of this method achieves 96%. Moreover, an accessible accuracy 99.6% will be obtained, even if the number of training samples is not large (10 training samples). This preliminary work demonstrates that the proposed approach is quite valid for the recognition of penicillin bottles defection.

References

1. Adankon, M.M., Cheriet, M.: Support vector machine. Comput. Sci. **1**(4), 1–28 (2009)
2. Azehoun-Pazou, G.M., Assogba, K.M., Adegbidi, H.: A novel approach of black skin lesion images segmentation based on MLP neural network. In: International Conference on Bio-engineering for Smart Technologies (2017)
3. Bay, H., Tuytelaars, T., Van Gool, L.: SURF: speeded up robust features. In: Leonardis, A., Bischof, H., Pinz, A. (eds.) ECCV 2006. LNCS, vol. 3951, pp. 404–417. Springer, Heidelberg (2006). https://doi.org/10.1007/11744023_32
4. Cun, Y.L., et al.: Handwritten digit recognition with a back-propagation network. Adv. Neural Inf. Process. Syst. **2**(2), 396–404 (1990)
5. Fan, M., Li, W., He, Z., Wei, W., Lu, X.: Defect inspection of solder bumps using the scanning acoustic microscopy and fuzzy SVM algorithm. Microelectron. Reliab. **65**, 192–197 (2016)
6. Fekriershad, S., Tajeripour, F.: Multi-resolution and noise-resistant surface defect detection approach using new version of local binary patterns. Appl. Artif. Intell. **31**(5–6), 395–410 (2017)
7. Fu, B., Guo, H., Zhao, X., Chang, Y., Li, B., He, L.: Motion-blurred sift invariants based on sampling in image deformation space and univariate search. IET Comput. Vis. **10**(7), 709–717 (2017)
8. Hanzaei, S.H., Afshar, A.: Automatic detection and classification of the ceramic tiles surface defects. Pattern Recogn. **66**, 174–189 (2016)
9. Hsu, C.W., Lin, C.J.: A comparison of methods for multiclass support vector machines. IEEE Trans. Neural Netw. **13**, 415–425 (2002)
10. Jia, J., Jia, X., Han, J., Ren, G., Department, M.V.: Diesel misfire diagnosis based on single vibration sensor and bp neural network. J. Mil. Transp. Univ. (2017)
11. Kumar, P., Henikoff, S., Ng, P.C.: Predicting the effects of coding non-synonymous variants on protein function using the sift algorithm. Nat. Protoc. **4**(7), 1073–1081 (2009)
12. Liao, S., Zhu, X., Lei, Z., Zhang, L., Li, S.Z.: Learning multi-scale block local binary patterns for face recognition. In: Lee, S.-W., Li, S.Z. (eds.) ICB 2007. LNCS, vol. 4642, pp. 828–837. Springer, Heidelberg (2007). https://doi.org/10.1007/978-3-540-74549-5_87
13. Liao, Y.N., Meng-Jun, L.I., Zhang, J.Q., Science, S.O.: Multiple target location based on k-means clustering and particle swarm optimization. Electron. Des. Eng. (2018)
14. Ning, X., Li, W., Tang, B., He, H.: BULDP: biomimetic uncorrelated locality discriminant projection for feature extraction in face recognition. IEEE Trans. Image Process. **27**(5), 1–1 (2018)
15. Sasazaki, K., Saga, S., Maeda, J., Suzuki, Y.: Vector quantization of images with variable block size. Appl. Soft Comput. **8**(1), 634–645 (2008)
16. Sindagi, V.A., Srivastava, S.: Domain adaptation for automatic OLED panel defect detection using adaptive support vector data description. Int. J. Comput. Vis. **122**(2), 1–19 (2016)

17. Solingen, R.V.: Measuring ROI of software process improvement. IEEE Softw. **21**(3), 32–38 (2004)
18. Tao, H., Yong, W., Liu, Z., Qing, G., Zhang, D.: Content based image retrieval method based on sift feature. In: International Conference on Intelligent Transportation (2018)
19. Taud, H., Mas, J.F.: Multilayer perceptron (MLP) (2018)
20. Trichet, R., Bremond, F.: LBP channels for pedestrian detection. In: IEEE Winter Conference on Applications of Computer Vision (2018)
21. Tsang, C.S.C., Ngan, H.Y.T., Pang, G.K.H.: Fabric inspection based on the Elo rating method. Pattern Recogn. **51**(4), 378–394 (2016)

An End-to-End Pyramid Convolutional Neural Network for Dehazing

Chuandong Yang[1], Zhen Liu[1], Songnan Liu[2], Jie Qin[1],
and Dong Chen[1(✉)]

[1] Ammunition Technology Office, Army Academy of Artillary and Air Defense,
Hefei 230031, Anhui, China
1092850034@qq.com
[2] Collaborative Innovation Center on Forecast and Evaluation of Meteorological
Disasters/Key Laboratory of Meteorological Disaster, Ministry of Education,
Nanjing University of Information Science and Technology,
Nanjing 210044, China

Abstract. In order to dehaze the outdoor hazy images with different fog levels faster and more accurately, a method based on convolutional neural network (CNN) is proposed, called End-to-End Pyramid Dehazing Network (EPD-Net). EPD-Net is a light-weight CNN with three modules: the T-estimation module, coarse dehazing module and pyramid pooling module. A depth estimation method based on CNN and a sky segmentation algorithm are used to estimate and modify the depth maps of outdoor image datasets, which aimed to synthesize hazy images of different fog levels. Experimental results demonstrate that on both the synthesized and the natural hazy image datasets, the proposed EPD-Net achieve superior dehazing performance than other representative dehazing algorithms in terms of objective indicators such as PSNR, SSIM, running time and the subjective visual quality.

Keywords: Dehazing · Convolutional neural network · Pyramid structrue · Sky segmentation · Outdoor images

1 Introduction

Due to bad weather such as haze and fog, outdoor images obtained by unmanned aerial vehicle, traffic monitor systems and other intelligent information processing systems are with hue shift, low contrast and low clarity. These degraded images not only affect the subjective perception of the human eyes, but also seriously affect the completion of reconnaissance, target recognition and other computer vision tasks. Therefore, it is of great significance to clear the hazy image, which is also a hot research directions in the field of computer vision. At present, the dehazing methods mainly include image enhancement method and physical model restoration method. Typical algorithms based on enhancement, such as Retinex algorithm and tone equalization algorithm [1], have strong pertinence and can effectively improve contrast brightness. However, they are not processed the image from the mechanism of image degradation, thus local distortion and loss of details often occur, which makes it difficult to adapt to hazy images

© Springer Nature Singapore Pte Ltd. 2019
Y. Wang et al. (Eds.): IGTA 2019, CCIS 1043, pp. 41–50, 2019.
https://doi.org/10.1007/978-981-13-9917-6_5

with different fog levels. Typical algorithms based on restoration, such as DCP algorithm [2] and ATM [4] can compensate image loss and improve image quality by utilizing the universal fog degradation model [3]. In recent years, deep learning has achieved good results in image dehazing by virtue of its powerful data learning ability [4–8].

However, due to the wide range of outdoor scenes and the deep depth of field, the estimation of the transmission map is inaccurate, which can lead to the lost of details and halo artifacts in output images. In response to solve the above problems, we propose the End-to-End Pyramid Dehazing Network (EPD-Net), a light-weight CNN dehazing model with three modules and a method to modify the outdoor image datasets.

- The T-estimation module is responsible for estimating the depth and relative haze level with only five skip-connected convolutional layers. The coarse dehazing module uses a re-formulated dehazing model with all parameters estimated in just one unified model.
- The pyramid pooling module is a pyramid structrue with four branches, which is designed for improving the network's ability to learn global information.
- A depth estimation method based on CNN and a sky segmentation algorithm are used to estimate and modify the depth maps of outdoor image datasets, which aimd to synthesize hazy images of different fog levels.

EPD-Net is trained end to end, which can restore the clean images directly. An overview of the proposed EPD-Net arcgutecture is shown in Fig. 1, which illustrates the three basic modules: the T-estimation module, coarse dehazing module and pyramid pooling modules.

2 Dehazing Principle Based on CNN

In the field of computer vision, the atmospheric scattering model [2] is a good explanation for the image degradation caused by the presence of haze. It is widely used in dehazing technology research and can be mathematically expressed as:

$$I(x) = J(x)t(x) + A(x)(1 - t(x)), \tag{2.1}$$

where $I(x)$ is the hazy image, $J(x)$ is the haze-free image ("scene radiance") to be recovered. There are two important parameters which affect the dehazing effect: $A(x)$ is the global atmospheric light on every x pixel coordinates which represents the intensity of ambient light, $t(x)$ is the transmission map which is a distance-relevant parameter. The transmission map $t(x)$ can be formulated as:

$$t(x) = e^{-\beta d(x)}, \tag{2.2}$$

where $d(x)$ represents the scene depth, which is the distance between the camera sensor and the object and β represents the scattering cofficient of the atmosphere.

It can be seen from Eq. (2.1), by accurately estimating the t(x) and A(x), the hazy image I(x) can be restored, namely:

$$\hat{J}(x) = \frac{I(x) - \hat{A}(1 - \hat{t}(x))}{\hat{t}(x)}. \tag{2.3}$$

Many works generally adopt a method of estimating two parameters separately which is a partial optimal solution strategy. Therefore it cannot minimize the image reconstruction errors directly but can accumulate or even amplify errors. Different from this, a unified formula T(x) in (2.4) is adopted to unify the two parameters t(x) and A (x), and directly solve the disadvantages of the two-stage strategy. This can minimize the pixel-domain reconstruction errors directly. The dehazed image can be restored by calculating:

$$J(x) = T(x)I(x) - T(x) + b, \text{ where}$$
$$T(x) = \frac{\frac{1}{t(x)}(I(x) - A(x)) + (A(x) - b)}{I(x) - 1}. \tag{2.4}$$

By this method, the global atmospheric light A(x) and the transmission map t(x) are integrated into the same variable T(x). It can be seen that T(x) is a function of the input hazy image I(x), whose value chang with the input. So it is necessary to design a input adaptive model to minimizes the recover error between the output J(x) and the input I(x) fog image and real image error.

The defogging method based CNN is divided into a training process and a dehazing process, as shown in Fig. 1. training process shows how we synthesize hazy images of different fog levels and then use the synthesized haze image datasets to train our model, whose parameters are obtained after multiple iterations of training. The whole process realizes end-to-end learning. Given a pecifiche hazy image as input of the well-trained EPD-Net, corresponding output can be obtained through three modules successively.

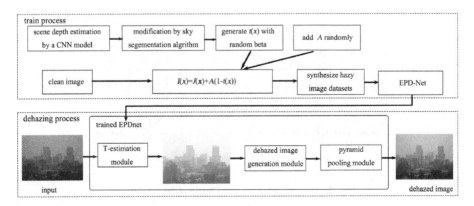

Fig. 1. Framework of dehazing method based on the proposed end-to-end pyramid dehazing network

3   End-to-End Pyramid Dehazing Network

There are three modules in EPD-Net, named as T-estimation module, coarse dehazing module and pyramid pooling module. The coarse dehazing module is a relatively simple block, which consists of several element-wise additon layers and an element-wise multiplication layer, aimed to generate coarse dehazed image via calculating Eq. (2.4).

3.1   T-Estimation Module

The T-estimation module is the essential component of EPD-Net, mainly used to estimate the haze level and the atmospheric transmission map. The output of it is the joint parameter T(x). Its structure is shown in the Fig. 2. Re-Conv indicates the basic structure which uses the convolution operator and the ReLU (Rectified linear Unit) activation function as basic operations. The numbers below indicates the convolution kernel size and the group number of convolution kernel, which is equal to the number of output feature maps. The Re-Conv operation and the ReLU operation are defined as:

$$F_s(x) = ReLU[W_s \cdot F_{s-1}(x) + B_s]$$
$$ReLU(x) = max(x, 0), \tag{3.1}$$

where W_s is the s-th layer's convolution kernel, $F_s(x)$, $F_{s-1}(x)$ are the s-th and the (s − 1)-th layer's output feature maps seperately. · represents the convolution operation, B_s is the bias of the s-th layer.

The whole structure uses only five Re-Conv structures and the number of output feature maps of each conv block is only three, which lead to light weight parameters and quick computation. The size of convolution kernels ranges from 1 to 7, which provides features at different scales. Besides, concatenating the multi-scale feature maps and the skip-connected design can compensate for the information loss caused by the convolutions. For example, concat3 combines the results of the first four layers of Re-conv operations, so the number of output feature maps is 12.

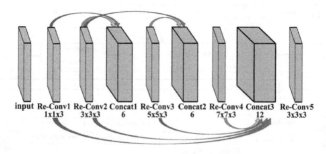

Fig. 2. A close look of the T-estimation module

3.2   Pyramid Pooling Module

Although the use of the skip-connected layer in the T-estimation module increases the connection between different layers and the multi-scale features are merged to some extent, because of the feature map from different scales do not directly affect the estimation of the final output, dehazing images obtained by the first two modules still lack global structural information, especially when the outdoor scene is wide-ranging and the target scale changes greatly. In order to solve this problem effectively, inspired by tasks such as image classification and segmentation, the pyramid pooling module is proposed to effectively solve the problem by embedding different scale features into the final result. The input of it is the concatenation of the T-estimation module and coarse dehazing module's outputs. The module structure is shown in the Fig. 3. LReLU (Leaky Rectified linear Unit) is used as the activation function before the convolution operation, which provides better gradient characteristics. Which is defined as:

$$LReLU(x_i) = \begin{cases} x_i & if\ x_i > 0 \\ a_i x_i & if\ x_i \le 0 \end{cases},\qquad(3.2)$$

where x_i is the input from the i-th channel, a_i is a fixed parameter which depends on the input data. The LRe-conv structure can be expressed as $F_s(x) = LReLU[W_s * F_{s-1}(x) + B_s]$, which is similar to Eq. (2.1). In pyramid pooling module there are three LRe-conv structrue used. Instead of using too large pooling kernel to get more global context information, we tend to capture more 'partial' information to characterize the target's overall structure. Therefore a four-branch average pooling operation with different pooling kernels is adopted. Then a LRe-conv operation is used to compress the feature maps of each size into one channel. After that, the four branch feature maps are up-sampling to the input size and then concatenated with LRe-conv2's output feature maps. Finally, tanh-conv4 is used to recover the dehazed image.

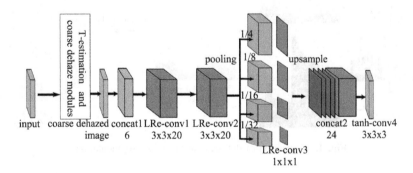

Fig. 3. A close look of the Pyramid pooling module

4   Experimental Comparison

4.1   Hazy Image Datasets Correction

Hazy datasets often don't have accurate outdoor hazy image pairs, so improvements have been made in this paper. First, we add aerial images to the RESIDES [9] dataset. Then the depth estimation model [10] is used to calculate the depth information $d(x)$ more accurately for 2200 outdoor images. After that a sky segmentation algorithm is used to identify the sky region and then increasing $d(x)$ value of the sky region because the estimation results are often lower than the real value. The sky segmentation algorithm is as follows:

Step 1: Convert to gray-scale image and perform a histogram equalization operation
Step 2: Obtain a gradient image of the gray-scale image using the Canny operator
Step 3: Use Gaussian blurring
Step 4: Transform the gradient image into a binary image
Step 5: Extract the sky region and the non-sky region by applying Morphological expansion and corrosion operations to the binary image

We select different global atmopheric lights $A \in [0.7, 1]$ and set $\beta \in \{0.6, 0.8, 1.0, 1.2, 1.4, 1.6, 1.8\}$. With different parameter combinations to generate synthetic images and each clean image corresponds to 35 different fog level synthetic images. As illustrated in Fig. 4, by using sky segmentation algorithm, the depth information of the image is modified more accurately, especially the sky area.

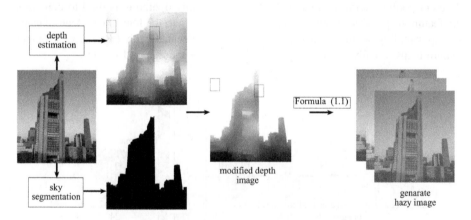

Fig. 4. Correction of datasets based on sky segmentation

In summary, the proposed algorithm for modifying the dataset is as follows:

Step 1: Use the depth estimation model to obtain outdoor image depth information;
Step 2: Use the sky segmentation algorithm to obtain the sky region;

Step 3: Correct the depth information by dividing the image into the sky area and the non-sky area;

Step 4: Use Eq. (2.1) to synthetic hazy image by setting different transmission map and atmospheric light value.

4.2 Training Details

The experimental environment is NVIDIA 1070GPU, and the program is coded by using the pytorch framework. The network input size is 512 * 512, so the training set image is randomly cropped to a fixed size. The network is iteratively trained by minimizing the mean squared loss, which can be expressed as:

$$L_{MSE} = \frac{1}{N} \sum_{x=1}^{N} \sum_{i=1}^{3} ||\hat{J}(x) - I(x)||_2, \tag{4.1}$$

where N is total number of pixel, i is the channel index.

The specific parameters are set as follows: the batch size is set to 1. We use Adam as the training optimization algorithm with learning rate of 0.02 and weight attenuation of 0.0001. After 500000 iteration of training, loss value drops to 0.002, which achieves satisfying results. 20 hazy images from the dataset were randomly selected as a synthetic test dataset, and 50 aerial images were collected from the internet as a natural hazy image test dataset.

4.3 Comparison with Other Representative Methods

To verify the algorithm's effectiveness on hazy images, we chooses the classic image enhancement-based Retinex algorithm, the restoration-based DCP algorithm, ATM algorithm and MSCNN, DehazeNet, AODNet algorithm based on deep learning as comparison algorithms respectively on the synthetic hazy image dataset and the natural hazy image dataset for comparison. Examples of the image dehazing results is shown in Figs. 5 and 6.

As can be seen from Fig. 5, Retinex algorithm needs to manually adjust the parameters for different scenes and there is a serious color shift, especially in the sky area. the DCP algorithm is too dependent on the color information, which easily causes the building's color to be supersaturated. the algorithms such as MSCNN, AODnet, DCPDN which are based on deep learning used a large number of indoor images as training set, resulting in insufficient processing intensity of the far scene, such as remaining of a small amount of fog. EPD-Net can better estimate the fog distribution and level for large depth of field and the most competitive visual dehazing results is achieved in both the sky and the ground areas. The details of the building in the distance are rich with no color shifts.

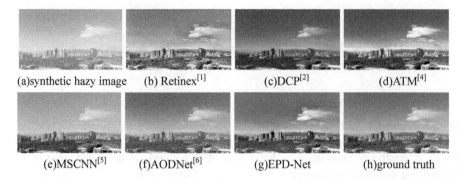

(a)synthetic hazy image   (b) Retinex[1]   (c)DCP[2]   (d)ATM[4]

(e)MSCNN[5]   (f)AODNet[6]   (g)EPD-Net   (h)ground truth

Fig. 5. Visual results on dehazing synthetic hazy image by different algorithms (Color figure online)

Figure 6 shows the dehazing effects on the actual aerial hazy image downloaded from the Internet. Retinex produces overly-enhanced visual artfacts. DCP and ATM suffer from unrealistic color tones and halation in sky area. AODNet and MSCNN blur image textural details and still remain some fog. DehazeNet darkens some regions. EPD-Net produces richer textural details and more realistic colors while suppressing artifact of over-enhancement and distorted object contours.

(a) arial hazy image   (b) Retinex[1]   (c)DCP[2]   (d)ATM[4]

(e)MSCNN[5]   (f)DehazeNet[6]   (f)AODNet[7]   (h) EPD-Net

Fig. 6. Visual results on dehazing natural hazy image by different algorithms (Color figure online)

To verify the algorithm's effectiveness from a quantitative perspective, the SSIM (structural similarity index) and PSNR (peak signal to noise ratio) are selected as full-reference evaluation indicators, and the average gradient (Ave-grad) and entropy are selected as the no-reference evaluation indicators. Indicators with larger values mean have better results. Entropy_natural and Ave-grad_natural are average Entropy value and average gradient value on natural hazy image dataset. Tests were performed on all test set images and the mean values were calculated. Besides the per-image average runnig times of all methods without GPU acceleration are shown in Table 1.

Table 1. Average objective scores on synthetic hazy image dataset and natural hazy image dataset

Index	Retinex	DCP	ATM	MSCNN	AODNet	Dehazenet	EPD-Net
PSNR	18.65	21.64	21.82	24.88	25.53	23.56	**26.21**
SSIM	0.71	0.8124	0.7947	0.8766	0.8916	0.8623	**0.9218**
Entropy	16.7265	17.528	16.9982	16.8765	17.8795	17.6564	**18.2174**
Ave-grad	11.8567	11.9213	9.9412	11.5778	12.3694	12.0178	**12.8528**
Entropy_natural	18.65	21.64	21.82	24.88	25.53	24.973	**26.21**
Ave-grad_natural	0.71	0.8124	0.7947	0.8766	0.8916	0.8831	**0.9128**
Run time(s)	**0.52**	18.49	36.70	1.78	0.67	1.94	0.89

It can be seen that the SSIM, PSNR, entrophy and average gradient results of the proposed EPD-Net are the highest among compared algorithms on synthetic hazy image dataset and entrophy and average gradient results are highest on natural hazy image dataset, indicating that the dehazing results are more closer to the clean images and global information is better preserved. Details of test images are better recovered than other methods and achieve a real-time processing speed. The results illustrate that EPD-Net can obtain high-quality, low-noise dehazing images with different fog levels effectively.

5   Conclusion

The paper proposes EPD-Net, an End-to-End pipeline that directly recover hazy images via a light-weight CNN with three modules: the T-estimation module, coarse dehaze module and pyramid pooling module. Besides, a depth estimation method based on CNN and a sky segmentation algorithm are used to estimate and modify the depth maps of outdoor image datasets, which aimed to synthesize hazy images of different fog levels. We compare EPD-Net with a variety of dehazing methods, on both natural and synthetic haze image datasets, using subjective and objective critiria. The experimental results verify the efficiency of EPD-Net, which provides a reference image dehazing solution for tasks such as automatic piloting and aerial reconnaissance.

References

1. Jobson, D.J., Woodell, G.A.: Retinex processing for automatic image enhancement. Electron. Imaging **13**(1), 100–110 (2004)
2. He, K.M., Sun, J.: Single image haze removal using dark channel prior. IEEE Trans. Pattern Anal. Intell. **33**(12), 2341–2353 (2011)
3. Tang, J., Chen, Z., Su, B., Zheng, J.: Single image defogging based on step estimation of transmissivity. In: Wang, Y., Wang, S., Liu, Y., Yang, J., Yuan, X., He, R., Duh, H.B.-L. (eds.) IGTA 2017. CCIS, vol. 757, pp. 74–84. Springer, Singapore (2018). https://doi.org/10.1007/978-981-10-7389-2_8

4. Sulami, M., Glatzer, I., Fattal, R.: Automatic recovery of the atmospheric light in hazy images. In: IEEE International Conference on Computational Photography (ICCP), pp. 1–11. IEEE (2017)
5. Ren, W., Liu, S., Zhang, H., Pan, J., Cao, X., Yang, M.-H.: Single image dehazing via multi-scale convolutional neural networks. In: Leibe, B., Matas, J., Sebe, N., Welling, M. (eds.) ECCV 2016. LNCS, vol. 9906, pp. 154–169. Springer, Cham (2016). https://doi.org/10.1007/978-3-319-46475-6_10
6. Cai, B., Xu, X., Jia, K.: Dehazenet: an end-to-end system for single image haze removal. IEEE Trans. Image Process. 25(11), 5187–5198 (2016)
7. Li, B., Peng, X., Wang, Z.: AOD-net: al-in-one dehazing network. In: IEEE International Conference on Computer Vision, Venice, Italy, 22–29 October, pp. 4770–4778 (2017)
8. Zhang, H., Patel, V.M.: Densely connected pyramid dehazing network. In: The 32th IEEE Conference on Computer Vision and Pattern Recognition, Salt Lake City, USA, 19–21 June, pp. 2261–2269 (2018)
9. Li, B., Ren, W., Fu, D., et al.: Benchmarking single-image dehazing and beyond. IEEE Trans. Image Process. 28(1), 492–505 (2019)
10. Liu, F., Shen, C., Lin, G., et al.: Learning depth from single monocular images using deep convolutional neural fields. IEEE Trans. Pattern Anal. Mach. Intell. 10, 2024–2039 (2016)

Dynamic Community Detection and Evolution Analysis

Shan Liu$^{(\boxtimes)}$ and Rui Tang

Information Engineering School, Communication University of China,
Beijing 100024, China
{liushan, rare}@cuc.edu.cn

Abstract. Social media has become an important role for the occurrence, development and evolution of public opinion events in today's network and big data era. In this context, a flocking bird-based dynamic community evolution analysis model is proposed, which takes advantage of the dynamic character- istics of the bionic algorithm itself and models the particles in the community as an agent. We also define the movement rules and evolution patterns of the particles, and visualize the evolution process of the community. In view of the proposed algorithm, we have carried out experiments on real data sets. The experimental results show that the proposed algorithm has certain advantages and practical application value.

Keywords: Community detection · Community evolution ·
Dynamic analysis · Visualization

1 Introduction

The rapid development of social network and mobile internet technology has greatly reduced the distance between users in recent years, making users more closely linked together. Users can not only easily have access to various information, but also par- ticipate in the process of information manufacturing and become the producer of information. Many existing community detection algorithms can easily identify reports belonging to the same event from a large number of reports. Therefore, how to detect the different stages of events and generate relevant abstracts from a large number of reports and make it visualizable has become a very important research focus nowadays.

Traditional dynamic network evolution algorithms usually cluster snapshots at each time, and then analyze the evolutionary relationship between neighboring communities. One disadvantage of this method is that it does not consider the temporal characteristics of dynamic networks. Clustering is based on the network structure of a single time, and it is difficult to describe and visualize the evolution characteristics of communities.

In order to solve the above problems, we propose a flocking bird based dynamic community evolution analysis model, which takes advantage of the dynamic charac- teristics of the bionic algorithm itself, models the particles in the community as an agent, and defines the movement rules and evolution patterns of the particles, so that the similar particles are close to each other and the dissimilar particles are far away from each other. Until the end of the algorithm, each agent moves in space with the

© Springer Nature Singapore Pte Ltd. 2019
Y. Wang et al. (Eds.): IGTA 2019, CCIS 1043, pp. 51–60, 2019.
https://doi.org/10.1007/978-981-13-9917-6_6

same rules, completing the evolution behavior of community formation, extinction, preservation, shrinkage, expansion, splitting, etc.

Our main contribution is that we visualize these behaviors on a two-dimensional plane, and complete the visualization of the evolution process of the dynamic community, so as to facilitate the tracking and understanding of the evolution process of the community. Furthermore, since we use agents to simulate the community behavior, we consider the temporal characteristics of dynamic networks. The agents move according to the defined rules, update their position and speed.

For the proposed algorithm, we have carried out experiments on real data sets. The experimental results verify the performance and advantages of the proposed algorithm.

2   Related Works

2.1   Community Clustering Algorithms Based on Flocking Theory

Natural bird flocking behaviors is described as follows: First, collision avoidance or separation. It means steering away from the other boids to avoid collision. Second, alignment or velocity matching. It means aiming to match the moving direction and speed to that of nearby flockmates. Third, cohesion or flock centering. It means attempting to adjust steering toward the average position of local flockmates and to stay close to the neighbors. Forth, information flocking. It means attempting to move with similar boids [11].

2.2   Dynamic Community Evolution Patterns

Leskovec et al. studied a large number of real network evolution processes and analyzed the statistical characteristics of network snapshots in each period. It was found that with the change of time, most of the networks will become denser and the average diameter will gradually decrease [1]. Asur et al. defined five key community evolution modes for the process of network evolution, i.e. community preservation, merging, splitting, formation and extinction, and defined four dynamic behaviors of nodes, i.e. node appearance, disappearance, joining and leaving. At the same time, an incremental network evolution mode detection algorithm [2] was proposed.

Palla et al. defined six models of community evolution by analyzing the evolution process of scientific research cooperative networks and user communication networks, namely, the expansion, shrinkage, merger, splitting, formation and death of communities. They found that the size of communities and the dynamic behavior within communities would affect the life cycle of communities. Small communities with stable nodes and large communities with frequent replacement of nodes could exist stably for a longer time [3, 4]. Takaffoli proposed a community evolution traceability and pattern detection method, MODEC [5]. This method traces the evolving communities by comparing the similarity of communities in temporal networks, and defines relevant rules to determine the six evolution patterns proposed by Palla. This study also analyzed the relationship between node behavior and community evolution patterns in sequential networks, and proposed that a small number of high-impact node behavior and evolution patterns are highly correlated. On the basis of Palla's evolutionary model, Bródka et al. proposed an evolutionary pattern detection method GED [6]. This method first uses the maximum group filtering algorithm CPM to find the static community structure, and then finds the continuous community by comparing the size and mutual inclusion of the community in the continuous time slice. Gliwa et al. defined a group of community evolution patterns: stability, scale change, separation, addition, splitting, merging, post-splitting merging, recession [7–10]. At the same time, a community evolution tracing method, SGCI, is proposed. Its basic idea is to find persistent communities in a fixed length of time window. The criterion is that the survival time of communities in a given length of time window exceeds the threshold.

3 Problem Formalization

Before putting forward the algorithm, we first give the definition and description of the related concepts of community evolution, and point out the main problems that need to be solved in this paper.

3.1 Dynamic Network

In order to dynamically model the network, we assume that the dynamic network DG consists of a set of time-varying network snapshots G_t, where $G_t = (V_t, E_t)$. For each time $t \in T$, V_t denotes the set of nodes in the network snapshot, and E_t denotes the set of edges between nodes in the network snapshot. Assuming that $i, j \in V_t$, each edge $(i, j) \in E_t$ has a time-varying weight $Sim_t(i, j) \in (0, 1)$, which represents the similarity between nodes i and j. In this paper, we will calculate the similarity between nodes according to a specific similarity between nodes according to a specific similarity formula. In Sect. 4, we will introduce the definition of similarity in detail.

Definition 1. Dynamic network $DG = \{G_1, G_2, \ldots, G_t\}, t \in T$, where $G_t = (V_t, E_t)$, node set $V_t, t \in T$, edge set $E_t = \{(i, j), i, j \in V_t\}, t \in T$. At time t, if $(i, j) \in E_t$, then $Sim_t(i, j) \in (0, 1)$.

3.2 Social Group

Generally speaking, a community can also be called a group, cluster or module, which is a set of nodes or edges in the network. At present, there is no clear definition of 'community'. The most widely accepted one is the definition given by Newman and Girvan in literature [11]. Assuming that the whole network is a graph composed of nodes connected to each other, the community is a subgraph, and the connection between nodes within the community is very close, while the connection between the community and the community is relatively sparse. Let us suppose that the dynamic community DC is composed of a series of community snapshots C_t that change with time. For each time $t \in T$, the set C_t contains n_t small communities, and each small community mC_t^p is also a graph composed of V_t^p as node set and E_t^p as edge set, where $p \in n_t$.

Definition 2. Dynamic cluster $DC = \{C_1, C_2, \ldots, C_t\}, t \in T$, where $C_t = \{mC_t^1, mC_t^2, \ldots, mC_t^p\}, p \in n_t$, n_t is the number of communities contained in the community set C_t. At the same time, $C_t = (V_t, E_t)$, $mC_t^p = (V_t^p, E_t^p)$, where $V_t^p \subseteq V_t, E_t^p \subseteq E_t$. That is, mC_t^p is a subgraph of C_t.

3.3   Evolution Pattern

We define seven basic ways of community evolution over successive adjacent periods.

Definition 3. Community Evolution Patterns

Continue: if the node set V_t^p in community mC_t^p and the node set V_{t+1}^q in the community mC_{t+1}^k are equal at the next moment, that is to say, only a few edges of the community have changed, while the node set remains unchanged. We call the relationship between the two communities continued.

$$\text{Evolution}(mC_t^p, mC_{t+1}^k) = \text{Continue, if } V_t^p = V_{t+1}^k \tag{1}$$

Grow: if at least half of the nodes in the community mC_t^p appear in the community mC_{t+1}^k at the next moment, we call the community mC_t^p grow and expand to the community mC_{t+1}^k at time $t + 1$.

$$\text{Evolution}(mC_t^p, mC_{t+1}^k) = \text{Grow, if } |V_t^p \cap V_{t+1}^k| > \frac{|V_t^p|}{2} \text{ and } |V_{t+1}^k| > |V_t^p| \tag{2}$$

Shrink: if at least half of the nodes in the community mC_{t+1}^k come from the previous community mC_t^p, we call the community mC_t^p shrink, and it shrinks to community mC_{t+1}^k at time $t + 1$.

$$\text{Evolution}(mC_t^p, mC_{t+1}^k) = \text{Shrink, if } |V_t^p \cap V_{t+1}^k| > \frac{|V_t^p|}{2} \text{ and } |V_{t+1}^k| < |V_t^p| \tag{3}$$

Merge: if there are two different communities mC_t^p and mC_t^q at time t, there is a community mC_{t+1}^k at the next time, so that at least s% of the nodes in the community come from the first two communities, we call the community mC_t^p and mC_t^q merge, and they merge into a community at time $t + 1$.

$$\text{Evolution}(mC_t^p, mC_t^q, mC_{t+1}^k) = \text{Merge, if } \ni mC_{t+1}^k \text{ such that}$$
$$\frac{|(V_t^p \cup V_t^q) \cap V_{t+1}^k|}{Max(|V_t^p \cup V_t^q|, |V_{t+1}^k|)} > s\% \text{ and } |V_t^p \cap V_{t+1}^k| > \frac{|V_t^p|}{2} \text{ and } |V_t^q \cap V_{t+1}^k| > \frac{|V_t^q|}{2} \tag{4}$$

Split: if there is a community mC_t^p at time t, at least s% of the elements in the community at the next moment will appear in the other two communities mC_{t+1}^k and

mC_{t+1}^l at the next moment. We call the community mC_t^p has a splitting event, and it splits into two communities mC_{t+1}^k and mC_{t+1}^l.

$$\text{Evolution}\left(mC_t^p, mC_{t+1}^k, mC_{t+1}^l\right) = \text{Split, if } \exists\, mC_{t+1}^k, mC_{t+1}^l \text{ such that}$$

$$\frac{\left|\left(V_{t+1}^k \cup V_{t+1}^l\right) \cap V_t^p\right|}{\text{Max}\left(\left|V_{t+1}^k \cup V_{t+1}^l\right|, \left|V_t^p\right|\right)} > s\% \text{ and } \left|V_{t+1}^k \cap V_t^p\right| > \frac{\left|V_{t+1}^k\right|}{2} \text{ and } \left|V_{t+1}^l \cap V_t^p\right| > \frac{\left|V_{t+1}^l\right|}{2}$$

$$(5)$$

Form: for community mC_{t+1}^k at time $t + 1$, if all nodes of the community do not belong to any community at time $t + 1$, we call that a new community mC_{t+1}^k is formed at time $t + 1$.

$$\text{Evolution}\left(mC_{t+1}^k\right) = \text{Form, if } \exists\, \text{no } mC_t^p \text{ such that } \left|V_t^p \cap V_{t+1}^k\right| > 1 \qquad (6)$$

Dissolve: for community mC_t^p at time t, if there are no nodes in the community at the next moment, then we call the community mC_t^p will disappear at time t.

$$\text{Evolution}(mC_t^p) = \text{Dissolve, if } \exists\, \text{no } mC_{t+1}^k \text{ such that } \left|V_t^p \cap V_{t+1}^k\right| > 1 \qquad (7)$$

3.4   The Problem

The main problems to be solved in this paper are as follows:

Let us suppose that $DG = \{G_1, G_2, \ldots, G_t\}, t \in T$ is a dynamic network, which divides the snapshots of the network into communities at each time. We divide G_t into communities containing n_t small communities C_t. In the dynamic community $DC = \{C_1, C_2, \ldots, C_t\}, t \in T$, evolutionary events occur in the community of the network at every two adjacent moments. EvolutionSet$(t, t+1)$ is a set of small community evolution events from t to $t + 1$. This paper is to solve a series of dynamic events   (EvolutionSet$(\text{start}, \text{start} + 1), \ldots, $EvolutionSet$(\text{end} - 1, \text{end})$),   where start $\leq t <$ end.

4   Dynamic Community Detection and Evolution Based on Flocking Theory

Traditional community clustering and evolutionary algorithms need to divide the dynamic network into a series of static network snapshots, and then cluster each static network. The problem of this kind of algorithm is that the execution speed is slow, and it is not convenient to visualize, and it is not suitable for large-scale dynamic network information flow. To solve this problem, we propose a flocking bird based community evolution model, which is mainly divided into dynamic community detection algorithm as shown in Table 1 and dynamic community evolution pattern analysis algorithm as shown in Table 2.

4.1   Dynamic Community Detection Algorithm

Each agent represents a node in the community, and all agents are placed in a two-dimensional continuous space. Each agent will have its own speed (v_x, v_y) and a position (p_x, p_y), where $v_x, v_y \in [0, 1]$ and $p_x, p_y \in [0, 1]$.

Table 1. Dynamic community detection algorithm

Input: Dataset
Output: $DC = \{C_1, C_2, \dots, C_t\}$, communities at time t

---

1 **repeat**

2   **repeat**

3   Read $data_a$

4   Create a new agent and map $data_a$ to agent a

5   Initialize the position and velocity of agent a (randomly)

6   **until** There is no new data

7   Compute the ideal distance between all agents, $d_{ideal}(i, j)$

8   **for** all agent i **do**

9   **for** all agent j $\in$ Neighbor(i) **do**

10                $v_{j\_on\_i} = v_j + \alpha \times (v_j - v_i)$

11   **end for**

12   **end for**

13   **for** all agent i **do**

14   Update i's velocity: $v_i = \sum v_{j\_on\_i}$

15   Update i's position: $p_i = p_i + \beta \times v_i$

16   **end for**

17   Extract communities according to [5]

18 **until** system is stopped

Agents can be placed arbitrarily on the plane, then read in the new community particle data and assign the particle data to the agent. Then update the ideal distance between all agents. The agents begin to move according to the defined rules, update their position and speed. This process is repeated until the end of the program.

4.2   Dynamic Community Evolution Analysis

Given the start time and end time of a dynamic network, the community identified by Table 1 is identified according to the definition of community evolution in Sect. 3.3 of this paper.

First, we set the start time and the end time. Then we use dynamic community detection algorithm to find communities at time t. From start time to end time, we calculate the evolution pattern from C_t to C_{t+1}. Finally, we will obtain the EvolutionSet from start time to end time.

Table 2. Dynamic community evolution algorithm

Input: DC={$C_1,C_2,...,C_t$}, start, end
Output: (EvolutionSet(start,start+1),...,EvolutionSet(end-1,end))
1 **for** t from start to end-1 **do**
2   **for** all mC_t^p in C_t and mC_{t+1}^k in C_{t+1} **do**
3   add Evolution(mC_t^p,mC_{t+1}^k) to EvolutionSet(t,t+1)
4   **end for**
5 **end for**

5   Experiment

In this section, we will evaluate the proposed algorithm experimentally. Firstly, we will introduce the data set used in the experiment, then introduce the evaluation criteria of the experiment and evaluate the proposed algorithm experimentally.

Table 3. July 2018 event of Changsheng vaccine

Post time	Post content
2018/7/15	Changsheng Real-name reporting Drug administration
2018/7/16	Changsheng Vaccine recall Quality problem
2018/7/17	Changsheng Discontinued Apologize Standard
2018/7/19	Changsheng Vaccine Punishment
2018/7/22	Li keqiang Instruction Account for

5.1   Datasets

The experimental data set in this paper collects 57 events lasting from January 2018 to December 2018 from the official interface API of microblog. Each event contains several microblogs, each microblog contains information such as release time, content text, etc. Table 3 shows some posts of the July 2018 Event of Changsheng Vaccine, as follows:

5.2   Experiment Results

As shown in Fig. 1, this is the result of dynamic community evolution based on flocking bird. Figure 1(a) shows that when t = 50, one community form but does not reach a steady state. Figure 1(b) shows that another community form when t = 200. Figure 1(c) shows that when t = 300, three communities are aggregated in the information space. The red community grows and with the passage of time, new nodes come in and old ones disappear. As can be seen from Fig. 1(d), the two yellow and blue communities in Fig. 1(c) merge into one community, while the red community splits into two different communities. As can be clearly seen from the four figures (a) (b) (c) (d), divisions have taken place in the red community and mergers have taken place in the yellow and blue communities. This proves that our flocking bird algorithm has the ability to dynamically detect communities and visualize evolutionary patterns.

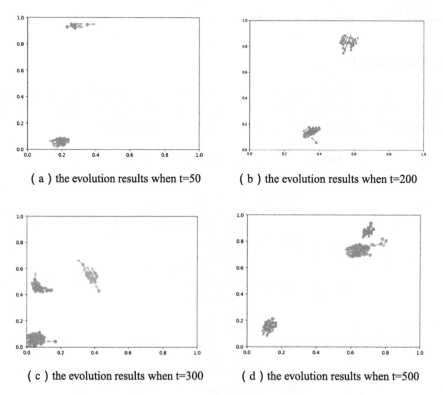

(a) the evolution results when t=50   (b) the evolution results when t=200

(c) the evolution results when t=300   (d) the evolution results when t=500

Fig. 1. The results of community evolution based on flocking theory, where $d_{th} = 0.1$, $Sim_{th} = 0.4$, N = 100 (Color figure online)

As shown in Fig. 2, our method is also applicable to event extraction and dynamic tracking throughout the life cycle. We take Changchun Changsheng Vaccine Event from July 15 to 22 as an example.

Fig. 2. The life cycle of Changchun Changsheng Vaccine Event

6 Conclusion

In this paper, a flocking bird based dynamic community evolution analysis model is proposed, which takes advantage of the dynamic characteristics of the bionic algorithm itself. The proposed method models the particles in the community as an agent, and defines the movement rules and evolution patterns of the particles, so that the similar particles are close to each other and the dissimilar particles are far away from each other. Until the end of the algorithm, each agent moves in space with the same rules, completing the evolution behavior of community formation, dissolve, continue, shrink, expansion, split, etc. At the same time, we visualize these behaviors on a two-dimensional plane, and complete the visualization of the evolution process of the dynamic community, so as to facilitate the tracking and understanding of the evolution process of the community. In view of the proposed algorithm, we have carried out experiments on real data sets. From the experimental results, the proposed algorithm has certain advantages and practical application value.

Acknowledgments. The work of this paper was supported by the Fundamental Research Funds for the Central Universities and Scientific Research Grant of Asian Media Research Center at Communication University of China.

References

1. Leskovec, J., Kleinber, J., Faloutsos, C.: Graphs over time: densification and shrinking diameters (2006)
2. Asur, S.: An Evolve-based framework for characterizing the evolution of interaction graphs. ACM Trans. Knowl. Discov. Data **3**(4), 1–36 (2009)
3. Palla, G., Barabási, A.-L., Vicsek, T.: Community dynamics in social networks. Fluctuation Noise Lett. **07**(03), L273–L287 (2007)
4. Palla, G., Barabasi, A.L., Vicsek, T.: Quantifying social group evolution. Nature **446**(7136), 664 (2007)
5. Takaffoli, M., Fagnan, J., Sangi, F., et al.: Tracking changes in dynamic information networks. In: International Conference on Computational Aspects of Social Networks. IEEE (2011)
6. Bródka, P., Saganowski, S., Kazienko, P.: GED: the method for group evolution discovery in social networks. Soc. Netw. Anal. Min. **3**(1), 1–14 (2013)
7. Gliwa, B., Zygmunt, A., Byrski, A.: Graphical analysis of social group dynamics (2012)
8. Falkowski, T., Barth, A., Spiliopoulou, M.: Studying community dynamics with an incremental graph mining algorithm. In: Learning from the Past & Charting the Future of the Discipline Americas Conference on Information Systems. DBLP (2008)
9. Yu, P.S., Aggarwal, C.C.: Online analysis of community evolution in data streams. Sdm Lars Backstrom Dan Huttenlocher Jon Kleinberg & Xiangyang (2012)
10. Saka, E.: Swarm intelligence for clustering dynamic data sets for web usage mining and personalization. Dissertations & Thesis – Gradworks (2011)
11. Newman, M.E., Girvan, M.: Finding and evaluating community structure in networks. Phys. Rev. E Stat. Nonlinear Soft Matter Phys. **69**(2), 026113 (2004)

Object Detection and Segmentation Method for Multi-category Armored Targets Based on CNN

Dong Chen, Chuandong Yang, Zhen Liu$^{(\boxtimes)}$, Xiaolong Zhang,
and Shengbin Shi

Ammunition Technology Office, Army Academy of Artillery and Air Defense,
Hefei 230000, Anhui, China
1092850034@qq.com

Abstract. A target detection method based on fisher discriminative Mask-RCNN is proposed to improve the ability of the object detection and segmentation of multi-category armored targets. The fisher discriminative layer is added to the classification branch and trained by imposing the Fisher discrimination criterion on loss function. Target segmentation is achieved by adding a mask branch network to generate binary target masks. Experimental results indicate that the proposed method can increase the mean Average Precision (mAP) by 1.3% on our dataset of four similar armored targets and achieve good segmentation results, which can better meet the need of military reconnaissance and other tasks

Keywords: Multi-category armored targets · Fisher discriminative · Mask-RCNN · Target detection · Target segmentation

1 Introduction

In military operations, there are various types of armor targets, such as tanks, self-propelled artillery, rocket launchers and anti-aircraft missiles, which have different values. If we can detect multi-category armored targets autonomously and accurately, the combat effectiveness will be maximized.

In recent years, target detection algorithms based on convolution neural network (CNN) are superior than traditional algorithms, which quickly obtained the extensive application in military field. CNN detection algorithms are mainly divided into two categories right now: single-stage algorithm [1, 2] and two-stage algorithm [3–6]. The algorithm proposed by Li et al. [5] is superior to the single-stage algorithm in speed and precision, indicating that the two-stage algorithm based on Faster-RCNN has great potential. He et al. [6] proposed Mask-RCNN, which is based on Faster-RCNN, achieved target detection and segmentation by adding mask branches. Meanwhile for multi-category target objection, it's important to distinguish the differences between them. Targets examples are shown in Fig. 1. Inspired by fine-grained image recognition tasks [7–9], fisher discriminant can maximum between class discrete degrees and

© Springer Nature Singapore Pte Ltd. 2019
Y. Wang et al. (Eds.): IGTA 2019, CCIS 1043, pp. 61–69, 2019.
https://doi.org/10.1007/978-981-13-9917-6_7

minimize within-class discrete degrees, which can improve the effectiveness of object detection tasks as well.

Fig. 1. Within-class variability and between-class similarity

Besides it is important to achieve the target segmentation for striking the certain part of the target. In order to solve the problem above, this paper proposed an improved target segmentation algorithm using fisher discriminant. There are three branches in our model: the classification branch, the regression branch and the mask segmentation branch. We add a Fisher discriminative layer after the ROI pooling layer in the classification branch to improve the detection effect for multiple types of targets.

2   Framework of Object Detection Based on CNN

As shown in Fig. 2, the target detection method consists of three stages: data acquisition, model training, and detection by trained model. In the first stage, image acquisition device was used to acquire a visible image dataset of multi-category armored targets in multiple scenarios in which contain one or more targets. In the second stage, we train the model with the training dataset. Finally, the trained model is used to test the effectiveness of our model and output the results.

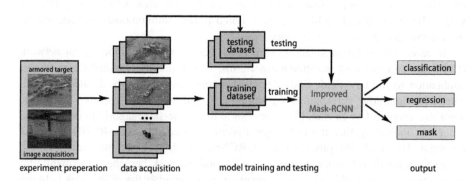

Fig. 2. Framework of object detection based on our model

2.1   Basic Structure of Mask-CNN

Mask-RCNN detection method is based on Faster-RCNN, which has two stages for detection. In the first stage, a set of object proposals are obtained by using Region Proposal Network. In the second stage, fixed-size features are extracted from proposals by using ROI (Region of interest) pooling layer and each of them have a confidence score, and the classification branch and regression branch are used after 2 fully connected layers to output the class and bounding box coordinates. Features from convolutional network are shared in the two stages, which helps to achieve faster forward inference. The backbone of Mask-RCNN we use is Resnet101 with FPN, which contributes to better feature extraction.

Mask-RCNN adopts Faster-RCNN's structure such as the classification branch and the box-regression branch to output class labels and bounding boxes' offsets. A third mask branch network is added to output binary mask for each RoI, which realize the function of target segmentation. The detection framework of Mask-RCNN is shown in Fig. 3.

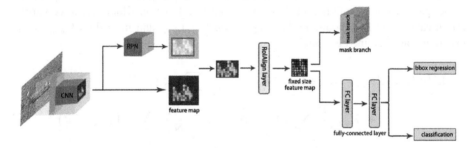

Fig. 3. Detection framework of Mask-RCNN

The mask branch network is a fully convolutional network with few parameters and more accurate spatial information, whose structure is shown in Fig. 4. The network generates a 28 * 28 mask for the blasting point target from each input RoI feature. First, four consecutive convolution operation is performed on the fixed-size feature map (14 * 14 * 256), then the deconvolution operation is used to increase the dimension of the feature map(28 * 28 * 256). And finally the 1 * 1 convolution is used and activated by sigmoid activation function. The function obtains a mask with a resolution of 28 * 28 * C, where C is 1 due to there is only one type of target. And the value of each position is a float number ranged from zero to one, which will be binarized at a threshold of 0.5.

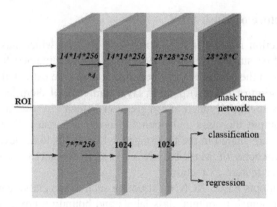

Fig. 4. The mask branch network

2.2 Loss Function of Mask-RCNN

Mask-RCNN uses back-propagation algorithm for end-to-end learning to optimize model parameters by minimizing a multi-tasking loss function which has three parts: classification loss L_{cls}, bounding box regression loss L_{box}, and mask loss L_{mask}. The loss function is defined as follows:

$$
L(\{p_i\}, \{t_i\}, \{a_i\}) = L_{cls} + L_{box} + L_{mask} = \frac{1}{N_{cls}} \sum_i L_{cls}(p_i, p_i^*)
$$
$$
+ \ \lambda_{reg} \frac{1}{N_{reg}} \sum_i p_i^* L_{reg}(t_i, t_i^*) + \lambda_{mask} \frac{1}{N_{mask}} \sum_i p_i^* L_{mask}(a_i, a_i^*)
\tag{1}
$$

where i is the index of an anchor proposed by the RPN in a mini-batch of training samples. p_i is the probability of anchor i is a target, p_i^* is the corresponding ground-truth value (0 or 1). t_i is a vector containing four predicted bounding box coordinate parameters, t_i^* is the corresponding ground-truth value of box. a_i is an array corresponding to the mask result of anchor i, and a_i^* is an array corresponding to the ground-truth value of the mask. λ_{reg}, λ_{mask} are parameters to balance each part of the loss. L_{cls} is the logistic loss of class. L_{reg} is the smooth L1 loss and L_{mask} is the average binary cross entropy loss calculated for each pixel. $p_i^* L$ indicates that only positive samples contribute to the loss. The positive samples are the anchors with Intersection-over-Union (IoU) greater than 0.5. The three branches are independent of the outputs $\{p_i\}$, $\{t_i\}$ and $\{a_i\}$.

3 Improved Mask-RCNN

3.1 Fisher Discriminative Loss Function

Fisher discriminative criterion can maximum between-class discrete degrees and minimize within-class discrete degrees [9]. We add a Fisher discriminative layer in the classification branch of Mask-RCNN. And the model is trained by inducing the value of loss function imposed on a Fisher's discriminative criterion constraint. As shown in Fig. 5, we introduces a fully-connected layer FC_c named Fisher discriminative layer in the classification branch of the Mask-RCN, which is located between the second FC layer FC_b and the softmax classification layer FC_d.

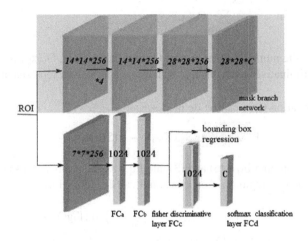

Fig. 5. Fisher discriminative layer in classification branch

The input is denoted as (X_{FD}, y_{FD}), where $X_{FD} = \{x_k\} = \{X_{FD}^1 \ X_{FD}^1, \ X_{FD}^2, \ldots X_{FD}^C\}$, x_k is a sample, X_{FD}^i is the ground-truth bounding box sample for the i-th target class, $y_{FD} = \{y_{xk} | x_k \in X_{FD}\}$ is the corresponding label vectors. Based on the loss function of the original model, the model improves the classification loss L_{cls} by adding the fisher discriminative regularization term $F(X_{FD})$ on the CNN features, which can be defined as:

$$L'_{cls} = L_{cls} + \lambda_{FD} F(X_{FD}), \qquad (2)$$

Where λ_{FD} is the balance parameter, $F(X_{FD})$ is the fisher discriminative regularization term. L_{cls} is the logarithmic loss of the category and is computed by

$$L_{cls} = -\frac{1}{|X_{FD}|} \sum_i \langle p_i, \log O_d(x_k) \rangle, \qquad (3)$$

where <m, n> is the inner product of m and n.

It can be achieved by maximizing between-class discrete degrees of X_{FD}, which is defined as $S_B(X_{FD})$ and minimizing within-class discrete degrees of X_{FD}, which is defined as $S_w(X_{FD})$:

$$S_B(X_{FD}) = \sum_{i=1}^{C} n_i(m_i - m)(m_i - m)^T$$

$$S_w(X_{FD}) = \sum_{i=1}^{C} \sum_{x_k \in X_{FD}} (O_c(x_k) - m_i)(O_c(x_k) - m_i)^T$$

$$m_i = \frac{1}{n_i} \sum_{x_k \in X_{FD}^i} O_c(x_k)$$

$$m = \frac{1}{|X_{FD}|} \sum_{x_k \in X_{FD}} O_c(x_k) \tag{4}$$

Where, n_i is the number of samples of the i-th target class, $O_c(x_k)$ is the output of the Fisher discriminative layer. m, m_i are the average feature representations of X_{FD} and X_{FD}^i.

The regularization term can be defined as:

$$F(X_{FD}) = tr(S_w(X_{FD})) - tr(S_B(X_{FD})) \tag{5}$$

Therefore, combining Eqs. (6) and (3) into Eq. (2), the improved loss function with a fisher discriminative regularization constraint can be defined as

$$L = L'_{cls} + L_{box} + L_{mask} = -\frac{1}{|X_{FD}|} \sum_i \langle p_i, logO_d(x_k) \rangle$$
$$+ \lambda_{FD}(tr(S_w(X_{FD})) - tr(S_B(X_{FD}))) + L_{box} + L_{mask} \tag{6}$$

3.2   Algorithm of the Model

The target detection algorithm consists of two parts: model training and model testing. The model is pre-trained on the COCO dataset, and then fine-tuned on the armored target dataset. After the model is trained, the test image is used for target detection. The feature is extracted by the fine-tuned model and is used to output the predicted target class positions and masks of the targets in the image.

Model training method can be described as follows. The input training samples are paired data (X_{FD}, y_{FD}) and we use the pre-training model to initialize the parameters. We trained the RPN network and the Fast-RCNN module separately. Before the stop criterion is reached, we perform the following four steps:

Step 1: Obtain the anchors through the RPN network.
Step 2: Use non-maximum suppression algorithm (NMS) to select the RoI and use the RoIAlign layer to output the feature map more accurately.
Step 3: Calculate the model loss via Eq. (4).
Step 4: Use the back propagation algorithm to update the model parameters.

The input of the testing part is an image. There are four steps before outputting the final results of target types, targets' position and the masks

Step 1: Extract the target features through the feature extraction network,
Step 2: Generate anchors through the RPN network.

Step 3: Use NMS to select the RoI and extract fixed-sized feature map by RoIAlign layer.

Step 4: Pass the feature map to the Fisher discriminative classification branch, the regression branch and the mask branch for calculation to output the predicted results.

4 Experiment Comparison

4.1 Training Details

The network is trained on a Dell precision tower 7810 workstation with an Intel Xeon E5-2683 V3 and a Nvidia Geforce 1080 GPU and is implemented by using pytorch. Image are resized to 800 pixels. The specific parameters are set as follows: the batch size is set to 2. We use Adam as the training optimization algorithm with learning rate of 0.02, momentum of 0.9 and weight decay of 0.00005. λ_{reg}, λ_{mask} are set to 1. λ_{FD} is set to 0.005. 2000 RoIs per image are used for training and 1000 RoIs per image are used for testing.

4.2 Datasets Preparation

Image acquisition is carried out in grassland, desert, mud, highway and other scenes from different height and angle range. Several different states are set for each target to increase within-class variability. Each image of different scenes contains several different targets to provide similarity between classes. 8000 images were obtained and divided into training dataset and test dataset. All images are annotated by labelme toolkit to meet the COCO data format for training and testing.

4.3 Results Analysis and Comparison

In order to verify the effectiveness of the method, we firstly compared our model with the basic model on COCO dataset, the improved model has an increase in precision including AP(average precision over all IoU thresholds), AP_{50}, AP_{75}, and AP_S, AP_M, AP_L (at different scales) as is shown in Table 1.

Table 1. AP results on COCO dataset

Model	AP	AP_{50}	AP_{75}	AP_S	AP_M	AP_L
Mask-RCNN	35.7	58.0	37.8	15.5	38.1	52.4
Improved model	36.0	58.2	38.1	15.7	38.2	52.7

Then we compare the effectiveness of different models on the multi-category armored target dataset we collected which has more obvious pertinence of within-class variability and between-class similarity. We choose the classic one-stage detection method YOLO and the two-stage method Mask-RCNN as the comparison algorithms.

The detection and segmentation results are shown in Fig. 6. The improved model have higher scores and can generate more accurate segmentation result than Mask-RCNN, such as the rocket launcher in the first column, which is of great significance for precision attack.

Fig. 6. Detection and segmentation results of different models (a) YOLOv3 (b) Mask-RCNN (c) improved model

Table 2 shows the mean average precision of different models for multi-category armored target detection in this experiment. The basic model and the improved Mask-RCNN model achieved 91.75% and 93.05% mAP respectively, which demonstrate the effectiveness of the method we use. Compared with the single-stage YOLOv3 model which achieved 91.33% mAP for the detection of armored targets, two-stage method has an advantage in precision.

Table 2. Results on military target dataset

Model	mAP				
	Tank	Self-propelled artillery	Rocket launcher	Air defense missile	mAP
YOLOv3	91.4%	90.9%	91.2%	90.7%	91.33%
Mask-RCNN	92.3%	91.7%	91.8%	91.2%	91.75%
Improved model	93.5%	92.8%	93.6%	92.3%	93.05%

5 Conclusion

Introducing deep learning into military field is a research trend. An improved object detection and segmentation method based on CNN by adding the fisher discriminative criterion is introduced, which has a demonstrable effect on military tasks such as reconnaissance and strike. The effectiveness of the improved method is verified on COCO dataset and a multi-category armored targets dataset. The accuracy of multi-category target detection is improved and the target can be segmented accurately, which can play an important role in military tasks and maximize the operational effectiveness of the ammunition.

References

1. Lin, T.Y., Goyal, P., Girshick, R.: Focal loss for dense object detection. In: IEEE International Conference on Computer Vision, pp. 2999–3007. IEEE Computer Society (2017)
2. Liu, W., et al.: SSD: single shot multibox detector. In: Leibe, B., Matas, J., Sebe, N., Welling, M. (eds.) ECCV 2016. LNCS, vol. 9905, pp. 21–37. Springer, Cham (2016). https://doi.org/10.1007/978-3-319-46448-0_2
3. Ren, S., He, K., Girshick, R.: Faster R-CNN: towards real-time object detection with region proposal networks. IEEE Trans. Pattern Anal. Mach. Intell. **39**, 1137–1149 (2015)
4. He, X.T., Peng, Y.X., Zhao, J.J.: Fine-grained discriminative localization via saliency-guided faster R-CNN. In: ACM MM (2017)
5. Li, Z., Peng, C., Yu, G.: Light-head R-CNN. In: Defense of Two-Stage Object Detector. https://arxiv.org/abs/1711.07264
6. He, K.M., Gkioxari, G., Dollár, P.: Mask R-CNN. In: Proceedings of the IEEE International Conference on Computer Vision, pp. 2961–2969 (2017)
7. He, X.T., Peng, Y.X., Zhao, J.J.: Fast fine-grained image classification via weakly supervised discriminative localization. IEEE Trans. Circ. Syst. Video Technol. **29**, 1394–1407 (2018)
8. Dai, J., Li, Y., He, K.: R-FCN: object detection via region-based fully convolutional networks. In: Advances in Neural Information Processing Systems, pp. 379–387 (2016)
9. Cheng, G., Zhou, P., Han, J.: RIFD-CNN: rotation-invariant and fisher discriminative convolutional neural networks for object detection. In: Computer Vision and Pattern Recognition, pp. 2884–2893. IEEE (2016)
10. He, K., Zhang, X., Ren, S., Sun, J.: Deep residual learning for image recognition. In: Proceedings of the IEEE Conference on Computer Vision and Pattern Recognition, pp. 770–778 (2016)

Inter-frame Relationship Graph Based Near-Duplicate Video Clip Detection Method

Xinbo Ai, Yinan He[✉], Yanzhu Hu, and Wenjia Tian

Automation School, Beijing University of Posts and Telecommunications,
Beijing, China
{axb, heyinan, tianwenjia}@bupt.edu.cn, yzhu@263.net

Abstract. The detection of Near-Duplicate Video has been studied by many scholars in recent years. This paper proposes a method for classifying and identifying infringing video by extracting video visual features, obtaining inter-frame relationship graphs, and using CNN classification network. We apply the improved weighting technique of text mining to video solution and still achieve better results. This method is robust in experiments and does not require retraining of a model in practical applications. At the same time, this method can also be applied to large-scale video retrieval. Our method has an F1 score of 95.74%.

Keywords: Near-Duplicate video · Inter-frame relationship · TF-IVF · CNN

1 Introduction

In recent years, the behavior of video infringement has spread rapidly, and many video platforms have appeared. Professional video production is difficult, long-term, and costly; the method of infringement is easy and the risk is low; the copyright awareness of the platform, authors and users is relatively weak, and the supervision and video copyright protection system is not perfect.

In response to the infringement of such videos, many scholars proposed two major types of solutions based on two different perspectives in recent years.

The first technical route is to take appropriate measures before the video is produced for later detection, such as video encryption or digital watermarking. Traditional encryption technology requires a specific decryption method to play, which increases the difficulty of video processing and limits the propagation of video, and cannot be applied on a large scale. The other is to add a special digital watermark to the video to verify the video [1]. Digital watermarking can cause the content integrity of a video to change, its validity cannot be fully guaranteed, and it is easy to be lost or destroyed.

Another way is a video near copy detection method based on video content visual features by extracting features of the video and matching the features to determine whether they are near copy videos [2]. This method needs video prepossessing, such as performing shot splitting or key frame extraction, extracting features of the genuine video and matching the matching video, and judging whether there is infringement relationship or the like according to the matching result.

© Springer Nature Singapore Pte Ltd. 2019
Y. Wang et al. (Eds.): IGTA 2019, CCIS 1043, pp. 70–79, 2019.
https://doi.org/10.1007/978-981-13-9917-6_8

In the early days of extracting video features, it was common to use a global feature descriptor to describe the content of the entire video as a whole. Global features such as HSV color space or RGB space statistics were used to express key-frames [3]. A feature proposed by Nandagopalan et al. is to use color, texture and edge histogram descriptors for retrieval [4]. However, when the image changes slightly, its characteristics vary greatly. The accuracy of the video similarity comparison based on the global feature is greatly reduced.

The other is an image description comparison method based on image local features. The local features were first proposed by Lowe in 1999. In 2004, the scale invariant feature transform feature descriptors were published, and the rotation, scale and brightness were kept invariant [5, 6]. Natsev et al. [7] used SIFT features as local features of video key-frames and combined them with color correlation graphs as video features, which achieved good detection results, but higher time complexity. Yang et al. divided each key frame, then extracted the SURF point features of each block, and compared the number of SURF points of each block according to Hilbert order, and map it to a hash value for video copy detection [8]. In addition, Qi [9] proposed the SURF and KPCA hash algorithm.

There are three categories for video similarity matching: global-based matching, segment-based matching, and frame-level based matching. The global-based video sequence matching algorithm [10] treated the video as a whole, and then searches the reference video library to determine whether there is a video similar to the query video. But this method can only detect the copy of the video as a whole. Another segment-based matching method [11] was to follow the fixed length of the video. The videos are judged according to the similarity between the reference video segment and the query video segment. A disadvantage of this type of algorithm is that it is difficult to process and detect for timing changes such as frame interpolation or frame dropping. The frame-level matching algorithm [12] was proposed to solve the defects and shortcomings of global-based matching and segment-based matching algorithms, and to deal with similar video distortions such as time series transformation. Roopalakshmi et al. [13] used a sliding window based DTW algorithm to approximate the location of a copy of a video segment. Liu et al. [14] used Relative Edit Distance Similarity (REDS) to filter out non-approximate copy video, and then proposed a dynamic programming algorithm based on detect-and-refine to generate a path matrix, and calculate the similarity between videos by using the generated path matrix. The approximate copy video segment is located. Chiu et al. [15] presented another multi-scale video approximate copy detection and localization algorithm.

In this paper, we combine the text feature structuring method to extract the local features of the video and combine them into TF-IVDF information, which can cope with more tampering conditions compared with the traditional global video features, and is faster than the local video features. The matching efficiency, the current research and strategy for text description methods has always been the hot direction of natural language processing problems. Text vectors as a method to characterize image features are rarely used in images. After extracting the video features, we will obtain the inter-frame relationship graph through the similarity calculation, and then use the deep learning method to discriminate the copy video. In our experiments, the method is proved to be efficient and robust. It can not only handle a variety of video post-processing effects, but also successfully classify three different types of infringement methods. Compared to the current method, our method proves more effective and robust of similar video detection.

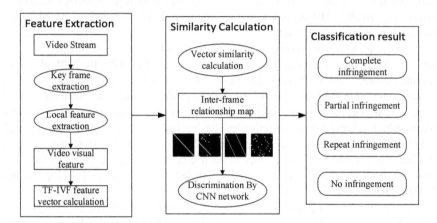

Fig. 1. The proposed approach for Near-Duplicate Video Clip Detection. Our method provides the inter-frame maps of different videos. The map is used to predict the Infringing type.

2 The Proposed Method

Figure 1 is a block diagram of the proposed method. For a genuine video clip, a total of n video key frames are extracted, and a set of key frames is formed. For the video clip to be detected, a total of m video key frames are extracted, and the key frames are composed. For the extracted video key-frames, firstly, the local features need to be extracted, and the feature structure is performed by using TF-IVF, and then the inter-frame relationship graph is obtained by performing similarity calculation on the two structured feature sets. Then, through a convolutional neural network, the obtained inter-frame relationship diagram is classified to obtain the copy video infringement type.

Video infringement is mainly divided into several major categories: one is completely infringing, and simple post-processing operations or video format conversion are performed on the original video. Post-processing has video screen brightness, contrast modification, picture cut, watermarking, cover video content, video color conversion, add end-of-slice and other completely infringing videos. The processed video length is similar to the original video, its diagram as shown in Fig. 2(a); the repeated infringement of the video is shown in Fig. 2(d). The other is partial infringement, such as editing the video, only retaining part of the original video or repeating the infringement of the video, and the infringement of the video length changes greatly, as shown in Fig. 2(b). The inter-frame relationship diagram of the video that does not constitute infringement is as shown in Fig. 2(c).

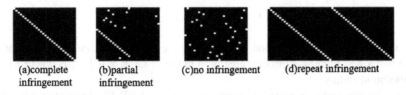

(a)complete   (b)partial   (c)no infringement   (d)repeat infringement
infringement   infringement

Fig. 2. Four type of inter-frame relationship diagrams

2.1 Video Feature Structure

(a) Local feature extraction

In local feature extraction, we use the same rotationally invariant and noise-resistant ORB algorithm, but better than the SIFT algorithms in real-time. The ORB algorithm uses FAST corner detection to extract feature points. The FAST detection algorithm [16] uses the local gray value of the image for feature point detection, which has high repeatability and noise immunity. The corner definition of the FAST algorithm is that there are enough pixels in the neighborhood around the pixel to be in a different area from the point, and the candidate feature point is defined as its original center. The formula for calculating the value of the corner point from other pixels is as shown in Eq. 1, where $I(x)$ is the gray value of the point on the circumference of the corner point, $I(p)$ is the gray value of the corner point, and ξ is the threshold value for judging whether the corner point is the feature point. If $Diff$ is greater than the threshold, we consider the point to be a feature point.

$$Diff = \sum_{x \in f_{ij}} |I(x) - I(p)| > \xi. \tag{1}$$

Since the FAST feature information does not have scale invariance and rotation invariance, the ORB algorithm uses the gray centroid method to make the feature points have directional characteristics. For any feature point P, the moments defining the neighborhood pixels of P are:

$$m_{pq} = \sum_{x,y} x^p y^q I(x, y) \tag{2}$$

where $I(x, y)$ is the gray value of the image I at the point (x, y). Then the centroid of the image is:

$$C = \left(\frac{m_{10}}{m_{00}}, \frac{m_{01}}{m_{00}}\right) \tag{3}$$

The angle between the feature point and the centroid is defined as the main direction of the FAST feature point, as follows:

$$\theta = \arctan(m_{01}, m_{10}) \tag{4}$$

In order to improve the rotation invariance of the ORB algorithm, it is necessary to ensure that x and y are in a circular area with radius r, i.e. $x, y \in [-r, r]$ where r is the neighborhood radius.

Next, the descriptor is extracted using the improved BRIEF description algorithm [17]. First, an image block p of $S \times S$ size is selected around the feature points, and a test function is defined on the image block p.

$$\eta(p; x, y) = \begin{cases} 1, & p(x) < p(y) \\ 0, & p(x) \geq p(y) \end{cases} \tag{5}$$

Where $p(x)$ and $p(y)$ are the gray values at the pixel points $x = (u_1, v_1)$ and $y = (u_2, v_2)$ in the image block respectively. Let $n_d = 256$, the template of the pixel pair compares all the pixel pairs (x, y) on the template to obtain the binary feature descriptor of the p point:

$$f_{n_d}(p) = \sum_{1 \leq i \leq n_d} 2^{i-1} \eta(p; x_i, y_i) \tag{6}$$

Since the gray value of a single pixel is easily affected by noise, when the pixel gray value is compared, the image around the feature point is preprocessed in a Gaussian smoothing manner when the video key frame is input.

(b) TF-IVF

After extracting the local features of the video, we introduce a text feature algorithm that uses the text feature as a corpus to complete the structured expression of the video. Here we call this expression TF-IVF, which consists of two parts, one is the word frequency (*TF*), and the other is the inverse video frequency (*IVF*). Where TF is defined as the frequency at which a local feature appears in the video.

$$Weight_{TF}(w) = TF(v, w) \tag{7}$$

IVF is a description of the distribution of image visual feature words in videos.

The weight of the levy in a video can be calculated according to the frequency of its appearance in the video set, because the visual features appearing in the video are different and the difference is huge. In order to balance the gap between the videos, we define the keywords in the video set. The logarithm of the square root of the ratio of the total to the number of videos containing visual feature words is IVF:

$$Weight_{IVF}(w) = IVF(w) = \lg(\sqrt{N/n + \varepsilon}) \tag{8}$$

N represents the total number of videos in the video set, n represents the number of videos in the video set containing visual feature words w, and ε is a small amount.

TF-IVF considers the word frequency and inverse video frequency together. The calculation formula is as follows:

$$TFIVF(w) = Weight_{TF} \times Weight_{IVF}$$
$$= TF(v, w) \times \lg(\sqrt{N/n + 0.1}) \tag{9}$$

In order to calculate the similarity measure in the next step, we perform normalization in this step, and the calculation formula is as follows:

$$TFIVF_i(w) = \frac{TF(v_i, w) \times \lg(\sqrt{N/n + 0.1})}{\sqrt{\sum_{i=1}^{|v|} (TF(v_i, w))^2 \times \lg(\sqrt{N/n + 0.1})}} \tag{10}$$

The TF-IVF algorithm uses the word frequency and inverse video frequency of visual feature words to measure the weight of feature words. The formula of the inverse video frequency can also be understood from the perspective of information theory: when applied to a video, the frequency of occurrence of an image local feature in the entire video is high, and when the video containing the modified image feature is rare, the weight of the feature is higher. The purpose of the *IVF* is to enhance the importance of low frequency visual feature words that appear in a small number of videos while reducing the importance of visual feature words that appear in most video.

(c) Video similarity measuring
For the two videos V_i and V_j, we represent their video frames as $\{f_1^{v_i}, f_2^{v_i}, \ldots, f_m^{v_i}\}$ and $\{f_1^{v_j}, f_2^{v_j}, \ldots, f_n^{v_j}\}$, and when calculating the similarity between the video V_i and V_j, the extracted video structured features are drawn into the vector space. After obtaining the TF-IVF structured feature matrix, each row of the matrix needs to be normalized.

The normalized matrices are defined as *TFIDFV_i* and *TFIDFV_j*. We can find the cosine of the angle by finding the product of them. The formula is given by the Eq. 11, which can be used to characterize the similarity of the contents of the two videos. This cosine value can be used to characterize the similarity of the content of the two videos. The smaller the angle, the closer the cosine value is to 1, and the more consistent their direction, the more similar the content of the video frame, the more $d_{i,j}$ will be brighter in the inter-frame relationship graph.

$$d_{i,j} = TDIVF_{Vi} \cdot TDIVF_{Vj} \tag{11}$$

2.2 Method for Judging Near-Duplicate Videos

VGGNet [18] has good portability and promotion characteristics, in order to recognize different inter-frame relationships at the same time, since our images are not very complicated, the existing deep learning neural network relies on large-scale training data and powerful computing power. The convolutional neural network VGGNet network structure is simplified, the number of network layers is large, the parameters are many, the memory required for the storage network is large, the calculation amount is large during training, and the convergence is slow, which requires a large amount of training sample data.

Since the features extracted through the bottom layer of VGGNet are better, in order to reduce the amount of calculation and reduce the dependence on a large number of training samples, it is necessary to reduce the number of fully connected layers. Change the last three layers of VGG16 to a fully connected layer. At this point, the total number of parameters required for training is reduced to 14 million. This reduces the time required for model calculations and the storage space required to save model parameters. The structure of the light-VGG network is shown in Fig. 3.

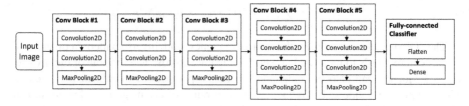

Fig. 3. Light-VGGNet structure

3 Experiments

We select the CC_WEB_VIDEO dataset [19] as the experimental dataset, which contains 12,790 videos, and the video collection of 24 popular search keywords in YouTube, Yahoo and other websites. Similar videos in the dataset, in addition to simple copy and re-release, a large part of the original video is directly edited and modified, about 27% of the repeated video, each video does not exceed 10 min.

We have modified CC_WEB_VIDEO artificially and got different post-processing infringement videos, as shown in Fig. 4.

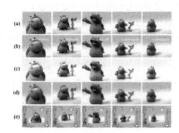

Fig. 4. Our modification

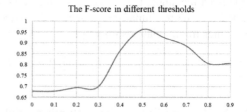

Fig. 5. F1 values for different thresholds

3.1 Complete Duplicate Detection of Post-processing Content of Video Images

Firstly, the ORB features of the key frames of a single video are extracted, the visual words of each frame are obtained, the TD-IVF video semantic feature vectors of each video are calculated, and the distance between the vectors is calculated to obtain the inter-frame relationship. For complete infringement detection, the diagonal of the matrix can be directly calculated and classified by setting different thresholds. This method can still get a more accurate result in the picture-in-picture transformation. In our experiments, the F1 values for different thresholds are shown in Fig. 5. The best results were obtained when the threshold was chosen to be 0.5, and the alignment of a single video took only 0.3 s. Comparing our method with the GLF [20], the results obtained are shown in Table 1.

Table 1. Comparison with GLC [20]

Modification method	Our method		GLC	
	Precision rate	Recall rate	Precision rate	Recall rate
Original video	100%	100%	92.7%	98.9%
Watermark	98.43%	96.87%	92%	98.6%
Video size compression	100%	100%	76.2%	98.6%
Video brightness change	96.15%	89.33%	78.3%	97.1%
Gaussian blur	85.79%	99.90%	93.6%	93.9%
Change title	89.90%	73.08%	–	–
Picture in picture	80.63%	57.88%	–	–
Change color	86.92%	86.92%	–	–

3.2 Application of CNN Network for Inter-frame Relationship Detection

In CC_WEB_VIDEO, we selected Similar video, Long version, and Major change. We also expanded the data set, including pirating modifications such as video re-sampling and video playback.

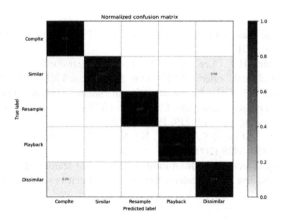

Fig. 6. Confusion matrix

After reading the key frame, we first extract the ORB feature operator for each frame of the video. In order to obtain a better operation speed, the number of feature points per frame is set to 200 at most. We can quickly get the visual words of each frame and construct a visual feature word matrix for the entire video. Then, a TD-IVF video semantic feature vector is constructed for each visual feature word, and the obtained vector is normalized to calculate the distance between the vectors. By screening the closest distance between each frame, we can draw the inter-frame relationship graph and classify the infringing video pattern through 3.2. The results obtained by the experiment are shown in Fig. 6. The average precision of our method is 94.1%, the average recall rate is 97.44%, and the F1 value is 95.74%.

4   Conclusion

In this paper, we propose a method for classifying and identifying infringing video by extracting video visual semantic features and drawing inter-frame relationship graphs, and exploring large-scale similar video retrieval. The video infringement by time transformation and cropping transformation can be embodied intuitively in the inter-frame relationship. This method can improve the effectiveness of similar video detection. The experimental evaluation results show that this method can obtain good results in a short time, and the method can effectively detect the picture-in-picture transformation, which has good robustness. Still, our program has some limitations. For example, the target detection network can directly locate the infringing video frame and the faster and better local feature operator, etc., which needs to be studied later.

Acknowledgments. This work was mainly supported by the development of digital copyright protection technology scheme based on digital image tamper identification technology, Key Project of Beijing, China (No. Z181100000618006), and also supported by data-driven security production supervision image construction technology and security management situation research (No. Z181100009018003).

References

1. Shih, F.Y.: Digital Watermarking and Steganography: Fundamentals and Techniques. CRC Press, Boca Raton (2017)
2. Chou, C.L., Chen, H.T., Lee, S.Y.: Pattern-based near-duplicate video retrieval and localization on web-scale videos. IEEE. Trans. Multimedia **17**(3), 382–395 (2015)
3. Chen, F.Q., Zhou, Y.P.: Color feature extraction of Hainan Li brocade image based on RGB and HSV. In: International Computer Conference on Wavelet Active Media Technology & Information Processing, pp. 214–219. IEEE (2016)
4. Nandagopalan, S., Adiga, B.S., Deepak, N.: A universal model for content-based image retrieval. jiP **2**, 3436–3439 (2008)
5. Lowe, D.G.: Object recognition from local scale-invariant features. In: ICCV (1999)
6. Lowe, D.G.: Distinctive image features from scale-invariant keypoints. Int. J. Comput. Vis. **60**(2), 91–110 (2004)

7. Natsev, A., Hill, M., Smith, J.R.: Design and evaluation of an effective and efficient video copy detection system. In: 2010 IEEE International Conference on Multimedia and Expo, pp. 1352–1358. IEEE (2010)
8. Yang, G., Chen, N., Jiang, Q.: A robust hashing algorithm based on SURF for video copy detection. Comput. Secur. **31**(1), 33–39 (2012)
9. Qi, Y., Qiu, Y.: SURF and KPCA based image perceptual hashing algorithm. In: SPIE (2016)
10. Song, J., Yang, Y., Huang, Z., et al.: Effective multiple feature hashing for large-scale near-duplicate video retrieval. IEEE. Trans. Multimedia **15**(8), 1997–2008 (2013)
11. Zhou, X., Zhou, X., Chen, L., et al.: An efficient near-duplicate video shot detection method using shot-based interest points. IEEE. Trans. Multimedia **11**(5), 879–891 (2009)
12. Liu, H., Lu, H., Xue, X.: A segmentation and graph-based video sequence matching method for video copy detection. IEEE. Trans. Knowl. Data Eng. **25**(8), 1706–1718 (2013)
13. Roopalakshmi, R., Reddy, G.R.M.: A novel spatio-temporal registration framework for video copy localization based on multimodal features. Sig. Process. **93**(8), 2339–2351 (2013)
14. Liu, H., Zhao, Q., Wang, H., et al.: An image-based near-duplicate video retrieval and localization using improved edit distance. Multimedia Tools Appl. **76**(22), 24435–24456 (2017)
15. Chiu, C.Y., Tsai, T.H., Liou, Y.C., et al.: Near-Duplicate Subsequence Matching Between the Continuous Stream and Large Video Dataset. IEEE. T. MULTIMEDIA. **16**(7), 1952–1962 (2014)
16. Rosten, E., Porter, R., Drummond, T.: Faster and better: a machine learning approach to corner detection. IEEE Trans. Pattern Anal. Mach. Intell. **32**(1), 105–119 (2008)
17. Calonder, M., Lepetit, V., Strecha, C., Fua, P.: BRIEF: binary robust independent elementary features. In: Daniilidis, K., Maragos, P., Paragios, N. (eds.) ECCV 2010. LNCS, vol. 6314, pp. 778–792. Springer, Heidelberg (2010). https://doi.org/10.1007/978-3-642-15561-1_56
18. Simonyan, K., Zisserman, A.: Very deep convolutional networks for large-scale image recognition. CoRR abs/1409.1556 (2014)
19. Wu, X., Hauptmann, A.G., Ngo, C.-W.: Practical elimination of near-duplicate from web video search. In: ACM International Conference on Multimedia, pp. 218–227 (2007)
20. Luan, X., Xie, Y., He, J., et al.: Near-duplicate video detection algorithm based on global GSP feature and local ScSIFT feature fusion. J. Phys. Conf. Ser. **960**(1), 012034 (2018)

The High Speed 3D Measurement Based on Interval Line Structured Light Method for Translucent Objects

Huijie Zhao[1], Xiaochun Diao[1(✉)], Hongzhi Jiang[1], and Xudong Li[2]

[1] Key Laboratory of Precision Opto-mechatronics Technology,
Ministry of Education, School of Instrument Science and Opto-electronics
Engineering, Beihang University, Xueyuan Road 37#, Haidian District,
Beijing 100191, China
1227293066@qq.com
[2] Beihang University Qingdao Research Institute, Beijing, China

Abstract. Nowadays, modern manufacturing fields may encounter plastic, nylon, porcelain and other minerals which have translucent surface that would contrast the blurring of projection. It is one of the biggest bottleneck problems in the using of new materials. There are many optical methods indicates solving this problem in the past few years where cameras are used. Among all the optical methods, epipolar line projection method is the most efficient category that could acquire dense point clouds of object surface whose accuracy is equivalent to traditional methods. This paper presents a high speed 3D profile measurement based on triangular pattern motion blur method using interval line projection which derives from epipolar line projection. The experiments indicate that the proposed method can achieve high-speed 3D measurement of translucent objects. The measurement time of translucent objects is 0.091 s.

Keywords: 3D measurement · Translucent measurement ·
High speed measurement

1 Introduction

Nowadays, modern manufacturing fields may encounter not only traditional metal materials but also like plastic, nylon, porcelain and other minerals. Components made by these new materials could achieve high mechanical strength, high temperature resistance, low weight and low cost. But these types of new materials couldn't be measured precisely with optical methods because the translucent surface would make the projected pattern blurred. It is one of the biggest bottleneck problems in the using of new materials [1–3].

There are many optical methods indicates solving this problem in the past few years where cameras are used to capture the image of objects. The main problem of measuring translucent surface is that the projected light would goes into the subsurface of objects and becomes translucent scattering. The scattering light of subsurface and direct

© Springer Nature Singapore Pte Ltd. 2019
Y. Wang et al. (Eds.): IGTA 2019, CCIS 1043, pp. 80–90, 2019.
https://doi.org/10.1007/978-981-13-9917-6_9

reflection light would be combined together on camera [4]. The measured 3D point clouds of surfaces shape are disturbed by the translucent scatter [5].

Methods aiming on this phenomenon could be classified into two categories. The first type of category is trying to give a separation of direct reflection and translucent scatter. The surface profile can be measured by analyzing the direct reflection. And also the translucent characteristic can be calculated by the information of scatter [6]. The works starts form analyzing the nature of translucent and try to separate direct reflection [7, 8]. Debevec et al. [9] builds a lamp array to give an illumination form whole angles, which can measure human faces. The method could get the elaborated information of human faces yet the device needs a large space to be implemented in manufacturing fields. O'Toole et al. [10] developed a system using primal-dual coding to separate direct reflection. Also it needs a specified optical system to fulfill this method in implementation.

The other kind of methods concentrates on separating the direct reflection lights with designed projecting patterns. Comparing with the first category, this kind of methods can be easily implemented based on existing measurement system. In other words, an existing system could achieve the measurement of translucent objects by modifying projected patterns and measuring algorithm. It makes these methods more acceptable in industrial applications. Many researchers proposed different types of patterns. Speckles projection methods [11] give the exclusive information on objects for stereo matching. Different frequency of fringes methods [12, 13] applied two frequency of patterns to calculate the subsurface scatter. Polarized fringes methods [14] also can extract the subsurface scatter and direct reflection from captured image. Laser scanning methods [15] enforces the direct reflection to increasing the signal-to-noise ratio of images. And other structural lights methods [16–18] that all devote themselves to separate the direct reflection from subsurface scatter disturbing.

Among all these methods, epipolar line projection method is the most efficient category that could acquisit dense point clouds of object surface whose accuracy is equivalent to traditional methods [3]. Since the time cost would be multiple comparing with traditional method, it still cannot be used conveniently in manufacturing situations.

This paper presents a fast measurement method using interval line projection which derives from epipolar line projection category [19]. There are many methods of high-speed measurement are proposed in recent years [20]. Among these high-speed measurement methods, the high speed measurement based on triangular pattern motion blur method is used to accelerate the measuring speed. The experiments indicate that the proposed method can achieve high-speed 3D measurement of translucent objects. The accuracy of this method is estimated by measuring a plate with translucent surface. Also the repeatability is estimated by measuring the jade plate for several times.

2   Principles

The difficulties of traditional methods for translucent measurement are firstly discussed. Then a most effective method, epipolar line projection method, is analyzed to show how the method works in translucent measurement. Thereafter, the interval line projection method and its' mathematical model is proposed. To achieve high speed measurement, the projection of triangular pattern is briefly introduced in this section. The projection of triangular pattern and interval line is also analyzed for translucent measurement.

2.1 Difficulties of Traditional Methods for Translucent Measurement

Among all the optical 3D measurement methods, sinusoidal phase shifting method is an eminent way with high accuracy and dense data. But it meets difficulties when measuring translucent surface. The brief method of sinusoidal method could be introduced as below.

A serial of phase shifting sinusoidal vertical fringe patterns is projected to the surface of object. The captured vertical fringe image of camera could be introduced as

$$I(x, y) = A + B \cos(\frac{2\pi}{\lambda}x + \frac{2\pi}{M}k), \tag{1}$$

where (x, y) is the coordinate on image, N is the period of pattern, M is the total step of phase shifting, k ranging from 0 to M is the phase shifting number of current pattern. Since the binocular system is installed horizontally, the phase is shifted horizontally as well. This phase could be used for stereo matching of left and right camera. Then the 3D point cloud can be calculated with calibration results.

However when the translucent surface is measured, one pixel of projector will not directly reflects into camera to light up a dot in image. But it will be blurred into a halo because of the subsurface scatter, as shown in Fig. 1, which would give an illuminating area on image.

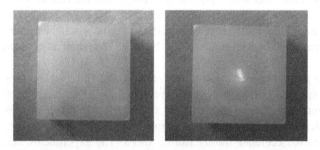

Fig. 1. Marble cube without projection and projected by one laser dot. The subsurface scatter becomes a halo on image. The direct reflection is still the most bright point in the center of the halo.

In the projection of patterns, each pixel on the pattern will be disturbed by circumjacent pixels. The weight window function of subsurface translucent scatter can be set as

$$W_T = \begin{cases} W_T(x,y) & (x,y) \in D \\ 0 & (x,y) \notin D \end{cases}, \tag{2}$$

where D is the point set composed of the neighborhood near base point (0,0). D can be expressed as

$$D = \left\{ (x,y) \middle| x \in [-\frac{d_x}{2}, \frac{d_x}{2}], \ y \in [-\frac{d_y}{2}, \frac{d_y}{2}] \right\}, \tag{3}$$

where d_x is the width of window function, and d_y is the height of window function. In addition, there is a normalization constraint of the window function $\sum_{(x,y) \in D} W_T(x,y) = 1$, which means that the energy amount of the translucent halo equals to the energy of one projection pixel if there is no translucent at all.

When the pixels on pattern are projected on translucent surface, the reflection light of each pixel will be disturbed by circumjacent pixels along with the weight window function W_T. Taking sinusoidal fringes as example, after the blurring of translucent, the fringe image captured by camera goes to

$$I_T(x,y) = \sum_{(i,j) \in D} W_T(i,j) I(x+i, y+j), \tag{4}$$

where (x,y) is the coordinate on image, (i,j) is the neighborhood pixel that would disturb the pattern on point (x,y). $I_T(x,y)$ can be written into

$$\begin{aligned} I_T(x,y) &= A \sum_{(i,j) \in D} W_T(i,j) + B \sum_{(i,j) \in D} W_T(i,j) \cos[\Phi(x+i)] \\ &= A + B \sum_{(i,j) \in D} W_T(i,j) \cos[\Phi(x) + \Phi_N(i)]. \end{aligned} \tag{5}$$

which intends that the phase will be disturbed and the modulation of pattern is decreased. The decreasing of modulation would let the phase information drowned into the noise and give a harm of calculated phase.

In proceeding, to find the direction of eliminating the disturbing of circumjacent pixels, we can concentrate on the discrete Fourier transform of $W_T(x,y)$:

$$F_w(u,v) = \sum_{(x,y) \in D} W_T(x,y) e^{-\frac{z2\pi}{N}ux} e^{-\frac{z2\pi}{N}vy}, \quad \text{where } z = \sqrt{-1}. \tag{6}$$

When $u + v = 1$, especially $(u,v) = (1,0)$, $F_w(u,v)$ becomes

$$\begin{cases} B_r = |F_w(1,0)| \\ \tan \theta_r = -\dfrac{\text{Im}_{[F_w(1,0)]}}{\text{Re}_{[F_w(1,0)]}}, \end{cases} \tag{7}$$

where B_r is the modulus of $F_w(1,0)$, θ_r is the angle of $F_w(1,0)$. It can be concluded that the disturbed modulation B_r and the disturbed phase error θ_r is essentially the modulus and angle of the first harmonic generation of the discrete Fourier transform of the weight window function of subsurface translucent scatter W_T. It gives us a general direction for the refining of projection methods. The more the weight window W_T is clustered into origin point (0, 0), the more modulus weight of first harmonic generation is allocated, and the more the real part of first harmonic generation is allocated. Obviously, this conclusion is contrary to the translucent weight window because of the nature characteristic of translucent material. So modifying the projection patterns to chop-out the disturbing part on weight window is the major works of the proposed method.

2.2   Epipolar Line Projection Method

To solve the difficulty of translucent measurement, epipolar line projection is an effective method to distract the reflections and subsurface scatter. The brief principle of this method is introduced below.

After calibration, all the epipolar lines of the system can be found. For one single epipolar line on projector, it can be used as a mask covering on the pattern data that only pixels on this line will be projected on the object. Then, on the camera image, only pixels on this epipolar line are used for 3D calculation. This method can efficiently eliminate the disturbing caused by the translucent blurring from projected patterns because of only the pixels on epipolar line of image are calculated, which all come from the reflection of projected patterns. A masked pattern to be projected is shown in Fig. 2.

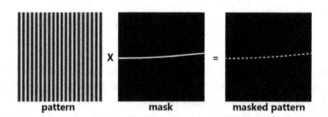

Fig. 2. Origin pattern, epipolar mask and the masked pattern. The masked pattern is the multiply of origin pattern and epipolar mask. The masked pattern is projected on translucent surface.

Based on this method, the most of translucent disturbing is cut out in this processing. A line of 3D data of object is gotten in one projection. For each epipolar line of this system, a mask could be derived and a process of projection can be illustrated. After all the epipolar line masks are 'scanned', the whole data can be fused from all the scanning results.

Obviously this method will cost multiply times of projection that would enlarge measure time epically when a frame of dense 3D data is required. And it may cost more time considering two package of camera-projector epipolar line in binocular stereo system.

This paper proposes an interval line mask method based on fast triangular pattern projection that could achieve measurement of translucent object with an acceptable speed.

2.3   Interval Line Projection Method

The first key principle of epipolar line projection method is to eliminate subsurface scatter from circumjacent pixels. Then the reflection points can be found on image also using epipolar line.

When epipolar line projection method is settled on a binocular system, both the binocular and projector are needed to be calibrated. And it needs the projection of two packages of epipolar line mask patterns, the left-camera-projector epipolar line package and the right-camera-projector epipolar line package. Interval line projection method could avoid calibration of camera-projector system. A binocular system only needs one projection serial to extract phase on both left and right camera.

However the row or column scanning is still time-costing. We can find that the weight window is spatial limited. It means when the distance between two pixels is larger than the radius of scatter function, shown in Fig. 3, the two pixels will not disturb each other.

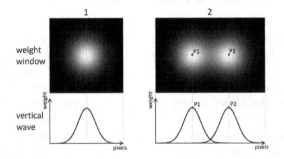

Fig. 3. Weight windows and vertical wave form of (1) single weight window and (2) two abreast weight windows that the distance equals to the radius. The two projected point P1 and P2 does not disturb each other.

Since there is no epipolar restricts on image in this method, a max modulation picking function is used on image to find the reflection line. The modulation of the whole image can be introduced as

$$B_I(x, y) = \sum_{(x,y) \in D} B(x+i, y+j) W_T(i,j), \tag{8}$$

which meets the maximum when the mask goes across current point (x, y). Based on this phenomenon, we can set a threshold function to pick the maximum modulation pixels out. Figure 4 shows how the projected pattern is masked.

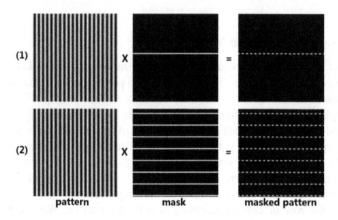

Fig. 4. Origin pattern, line mask and the masked pattern of (1) one row mask and (2) interval line mask. The masked pattern is the multiply of origin pattern and mask. The masked pattern is projected on translucent surface.

2.4   High-Speed Projection of Triangular Pattern

Since the measurement time is still longer than normal principle even using interval line projection method. A fast projection method should be used. Triangular pattern method of motion blur is suitable for the interval line projection mode. This method can give a high speed measurement with a focused projector. To provide a high-speed projection of grayscale-intensity patterns, a single binary pattern is initially projected using the DMD. The binary pattern comprises an array of basic blocks that will transform into grayscale-intensity patterns when motion is blurred.

Figure 5 shows the binary patterns, vertically blurred grayscale-intensity pattern, and horizontal wave form of triangular pattern. The wave form of patterns is determined by the intensity of 1 and 0 in the column.

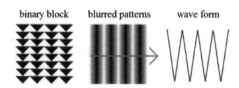

Fig. 5. Binary block, blurred patterns, and wave form of triangular wave with triangular block. The binary block is dithered into blurred pattern. One row of wave form of blurred pattern is shown.

In the conventional method, an 8-bit number is used to express the grayscale of one projection point. The micromirror on DMD is flipped in serial to give a time modulation of light. The 8-bit number expresses how the micromirror flips. The projection period is divided into 8 flip parts. The flip time of micromirror of each part is twice as much as previous flip time. In this way, any 8-bit number could be projected in 256 basic flip times. Figure 6 shows how the projected pattern is masked.

Fig. 6. Origin triangular pattern, interval line mask and the masked pattern. The masked pattern is the multiply of origin pattern and interval line mask.

3   Experiments

3.1   Interval Line Width Experiment

To find the best interval line width of translucent objects, we held an experiment that projects two lines of pattern with phase shifting. The shifted phase can be used for calculating the modulation of this projected line. In the experiment, the distance of the two lines of pattern is increasing. As shown in Fig. 7, the distances of the two lines are from 1 pixel to 18 pixels. The modulation is endurable when the interval line width is larger than 8 pixels. Because when interval line width goes larger, the measurement time expands. The best width should be around 8 pixels.

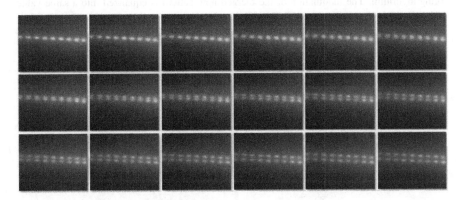

Fig. 7. 18 captured images of experiment for best interval line width finding. The distances of the two lines are from 1 pixel to 18 pixels.

3.2   Experimental Results of 3D Reconstruction

The results of the phase calculating can be used for 3D reconstruction. Figures 8 and 9 shows the reconstruction results of the jade horse statue. The experiment was conducted with a triangular pattern projection frequency of 700 Hz using VIALUX V4390 projector. As the camera capture speed is limited, the resolution of camera (BALSER acA800 camera) is reduced to reach the projecting frequency. Only two widths of patterns are projected as the resolution is reduced. The width of interval line is 8 pixels and two fringe width 4-step shape shifting patterns are used in the experiment. Totally, 64 images are captured in 0.091 s. The 3D data may easily got error on beveled surface because the phase error is enlarged.

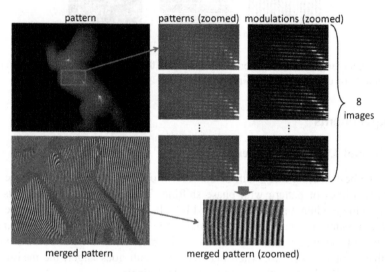

Fig. 8. One captured image and one merged pattern image of the projection serial. The same parts on 8 interval line images are zoomed and shown. Also their modulation is calculated for merging algorithm. The modulation of the merged new pattern is equalized into a same value.

Fig. 9. Reconstruction results of the jade horse statue and the picture of it. The triangular pattern projection frequency is 700 Hz. The width of interval line is 8 pixels. Two fringe width 4-step shape shifting patterns are used. 64 images are captured in 0.091 s.

The measurement accuracy of the system can be tested by measuring the jade plane. As shown in Fig. 10, the reconstructed 3D point-cloud of plane board was fitted as a standard plane. Both horizontal and vertical interval line patterns are estimated. The distances between the 3D points and the standard plane were calculated as the plane measurement errors used for evaluate the measurement accuracy. The absolute mean error of horizontal interval line is 0.061 mm, and standard deviation of errors is 0.085 mm. The absolute mean error of vertical interval line is 0.066 mm, and standard deviation of errors is 0.091 mm. The width of interval line is 10 pixels and two fringe in width of 25 and 26 pixels are used in this experiment.

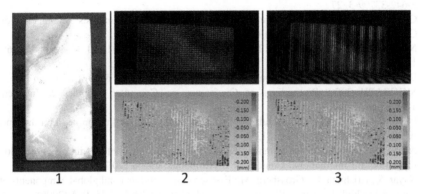

Fig. 10. Measurement deviation estimation: (1) The jade plate. (2) The absolute mean error of horizontal interval line is 0.061 mm standard deviation of errors is 0.085 mm. (3) The absolute mean error of horizontal interval line is 0.066 mm, and standard deviation of errors is 0.091 mm.

4 Conclusion

This study presents a novel high speed 3D measurement based on interval line structured light for translucent objects. The entire projection time is reduced compared with epipolar line projection method. The high speed measurement based on triangular pattern motion blur method is also used to accelerate the measuring speed. Moreover, a mathematical analyzing is used to shown how the method works on translucent measurement. The experiments indicate that the proposed method can achieve high-speed 3D measurement of translucent objects. Measurement error may be partially caused by the reduced modulation of patterns. In future works, the spectrum leakage is one of the key points for triangular patterns measurement optimization. Also enlarging the brightness of light source is one of the ways in system optimization.

References

1. Salvi, J., Fernandez, S., Pribanic, T.: A state of the art in structured light patterns for surface profilometry. Pattern Recogn. **43**(8), 2666–2680 (2010)
2. Ihrkel, I., Kutulakos, K., Lensch, H., Magnor, M., Heidrich, W.: State of the art in transparent and specular oblect reconstruction. In: European Conference on Computer Vision (2008)

3. O'Toole, M., Mather, J., Kutula, K.: 3D Shape and indirect appearance by structured light transport. In: IEEE Computer Vision & Pattern Recognition (2014)
4. Godin, G., Rioux, M., Beraldin, J.: An assessment of laser range measurement on marble surfaces. In: Proceedings of 5th Conference on Optical 3D Measurement Techniques (2001)
5. Zhang, C., Rosenberger, M.: Wavelength dependency of optical 3D measurements at translucent objects using fringe pattern projection. In: Society of Photo-optical Instrumentation Engineers Society of Photo-Optical Instrumentation Engineers (SPIE) Conference Series (2017)
6. Inoshita, C., Mukaigawa, Y., Matsushita, Y., Yagi, Y.: Shape from single scattering for translucent objects. In: Fitzgibbon, A., Lazebnik, S., Perona, P., Sato, Y., Schmid, C. (eds.) ECCV 2012. LNCS, pp. 371–384. Springer, Heidelberg (2012). https://doi.org/10.1007/978-3-642-33709-3_27
7. Curless, B.: Better optical triangulation through spacetime analysis. In: International Conference on Computer Vision (1995)
8. Nayar, S., Ikeuchi, K., Kanade, T.: Shape from interreflections. Int. J. Comput. Vis. **6**(3), 173–195 (1991)
9. Debevec, P., Hawkins, T., Tchou, C.: Acquiring the reflectance field of a human face. In: SIGGRAPH 2000: Proceedings of Conference on Computer Graphics & Interactive Techniques (2000)
10. O'Toole, M., Raskar, R., Kutulakos, K.: Primal-dual coding to probe light transport. ACM SIGGRAPH **31**, 39-1 (2012)
11. Achar, S., Nuske, S., Narasimhan, S.: Compensating for motion during direct-global separation. In: International Conference on Computer Vision (2013)
12. Nayar, S., Krishnan, G., Grossberg, M.: Fast separation of direct and global components of a scene using high frequency illumination. ACM SIGGRAPH **25**, 935–944 (2006)
13. Zhao, H., Liang, X., Jiang, H.: A dual-direction fringe projection method for the 3D measurement of translucent object. In: Society of Photo-optical Instrumentation Engineers Society of Photo-Optical Instrumentation Engineers (SPIE) Conference Series (2017)
14. Chen, T., Lensch, H., Fuchs, C., Seidel, H.: Polarization and phase-shifting for 3D scanning of translucent objects. In: IEEE Computer Vision & Pattern Recognition (2007)
15. Li, L., Ohtani, K., Baba, M.: A new measurement method of a surface shape of translucent objects by using laser rangefinder. In: IEEE Conference of the Society of Instrument & Control Engineers of Japan (2015)
16. Nie, S., Jiang, Z., Zhang, H., Wei, Q.: Image matching for space objects based on grid-based motion statistics. In: Wang, Y., Jiang, Z., Peng, Y. (eds.) IGTA 2018. CCIS, vol. 875, pp. 310–318. Springer, Singapore (2018). https://doi.org/10.1007/978-981-13-1702-6_31
17. Zhang, X., Zhang, H., Wei, Q., Jiang, Z.: Pose estimation of space objects based on hybrid feature matching of contour points. In: Tan, T., et al. (eds.) IGTA 2016. CCIS, vol. 634, pp. 184–191. Springer, Singapore (2016). https://doi.org/10.1007/978-981-10-2260-9_21
18. Ning, J., Zhihui, L., Shengdong, Y.: An independently carrier landing method using point and line features for fixed-wing UAVs. In: Tan, T., et al. (eds.) IGTA 2016. CCIS, vol. 634, pp. 176–183. Springer, Singapore (2016). https://doi.org/10.1007/978-981-10-2260-9_20
19. Zhao, H., Xu, Y., Jiang, H., Li, X.: 3D shape measurement in the presence of strong interreflections by epipolar imaging and regional fringe projection. Opt. Exp. **26**(6), 7117 (2018)
20. Zhang, S.: High-speed 3D shape measurement with structured light methods: a review. Opt. Lasers Eng. **106**, 119–131 (2018)

Pixel and Channel Attention Network for Person Re-identification

Minjie Wang[1,2], Xian Li[2,4], Jiahuan Zhang[2,3], Haoyu Zhou[2], Lei Lei[1,2], and Banghua Yang[1(✉)]

[1] School of Mechatronic Engineering and Automation, Shanghai University, Shanghai, China
wangminjie920705@163.com, yangbanghua@shu.edu.cn
[2] Institute of Materials Technology and Engineering CAS, Ningbo 315201, China
{lixian,zhangjiahuan,zhouhaoyu,leilei}@nimte.ac.cn
[3] School of Information Engineering, Yangzhou University, Yangzhou, China
[4] University of Chinese Academy of Sciences, Beijing, China

Abstract. The combination of global and partial features has been an effective method to improve the precision for Person Re-identification. However, illumination, camera angle and pedestrian pose, etc. still have adverse effects on the retrieval results. In particular, a lot of background and other redundant information is contained in the boundingbox. Meanwhile, the part-based solutions are imprecise on account of unbalanced partitioning. In order to minimize the impact of these factors on the retrieval results, we introduced the pixel, channel attention modules and middle layer supervision into the ReID system to aggregate person features. In this paper, we propose a novel architecture for Person Re-Identification, with the pixel and channel attention modules that are beneficial for feature extraction. Comprehensive experiments results on the mainstream datasets including Market-1501, DukeMTMC-ReId, CUHK03-labeled and CUHK03-detected show that our method achieves better results.

Keywords: Person re-identification · Channel attention · Pixel attention · Middle layer supervision

1 Introduction

Since 2016, pedestrian recognition has witnessed a rapid growth and the method based on deep neural network has attracted wide attention. In the meantime, the relevant datasets are expanding, and the results of various datasets have also been obviously improved. Up to now, pedestrian recognition [10,11,21] has become a hot topic in computer vision.

At present, Person Re-identification methods based on deep learning are mainly divided into the following five categories: characterization, metric, local features, video and GAN [2]. We use the method with combination of global and partial features which belongs to local features methods in the paper.

© Springer Nature Singapore Pte Ltd. 2019
Y. Wang et al. (Eds.): IGTA 2019, CCIS 1043, pp. 91–104, 2019.
https://doi.org/10.1007/978-981-13-9917-6_10

Fig. 1. Pedestrians with different illumination, camera angle, background and pose.

In early studies, global features method was the mainstream approach that used the whole image to extract feature vectors for image retrieval. Later, the global feature encountered a bottleneck, and gradually local features became popular. The commonly used methods of extracting local features include image segmentation [14], positioning of skeleton key points and pose correction [24].

The combination of global and partial features is an effective way to improve the accuracy of person re-identification. However, different illumination, camera angle, background and pose of pedestrians is an enormous challenge for pedestrian recognition (as shown in Fig. 1).

Max-pooling and mean-pooling are the most common pooling methods, which can effectively reduce the number of parameters, improve the calculation efficiency and speed up the convergence of the model in the network. However, max-pooling discards all the non-maximum activation values in the pooling domain, resulting in serious information loss. Similarly, the mean-pooling takes all the activation values in the pooling domain for averaging, then the high positive activation value and the low negative activation value may cancel each other, resulting in the loss of discriminant information. To solve above problems, we give different weights to the elements of the tensor. In Fig. 2, we assume that the upper left and lower right corner areas are redundant information and we set their weight to 0. Then, the redundant information will be removed after maxing-pooling.

In the paper, we propose a pixel and channel attention [23] network for Person Re-Identification to alleviate the above problems. The resnet50 network is used as the basic network to extract image features. Then the whole network is divided into three branches where each branch represents the global features and different local features. At the same time, the intermediate constraint is added after the first, second and third layer of resnet50. In order to reduce the negative impact of background on Person Re-identification retrieval results, we adopted the pixel attention model to enhance the person's feature information and weaken the background information. In the meanwhile, in order to reduce the information redundancy, we also adopted the channel attention model to assign different weights to each channel and enhance the ability of network feature extraction.

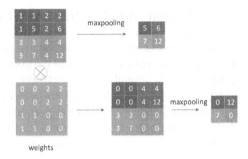

Fig. 2. max-pooling and pixel attention mechanism before max-pooling.

Due to the introduction of pixel attention and channel attention model, the network can extract effective information and reduce the loss of information during the mean-pooling and max-pooling for the feature tensor, then the defects of the both can be made up.

To summarize, the contribution of this paper is in the three aspects:

- We adopt pixel and channel attention model, which can effectively reduce redundant information, improve retrieval accuracy and accelerate model convergence.
- We use the middle layer monitoring mechanism and multiple loss functions to improve the retrieval accuracy.
- Comprehensive experiments results on the mainstream datasets including Market-1501, DukeMTMC-ReId, CUHK03-labeled and CUHK03-detected show that our method achieves better results.

2   Related Work

Deep Learning for Person Re-identification. Deep learning has been widely used in pedestrian recognition and has achieved satisfactory results [5,6,12,15, 16,20]. Compared with other deep learning projects, the dataset of pedestrian recognition is relatively small. Therefore, the method of using GAN to generate images of people and expanding datasets has been adopted by some researchers.

Li et al. [9] introduce a deep and open human regression model to alleviate the attacks caused by similar non-target people. The main idea is to use the GAN to generate an image that is very similar to the target, so as to extract the attack feature from the target person, so that the feature extractor learns to tolerate the attack through discriminative learning.

[19] proposed a new person reid model, which combines efficient embedding based on multiple convolutional network layers and is trained under deep monitoring. The model can adjust the computational resources according to the texture and other details of the image.

Part-Based Model for Person Re-identification. The local features method is one of the main methods in the field of recognition. Compared with global features, local features can better extract the feature information of each part of the person and improve the robustness of the network.

Zhang et al. [22] propose a new global feature extraction method based on local features. Global feature learning benefits a lot from local feature learning. Fu et al. [1] propose a simple and effective horizontal pyramid matching (HPM) method to make full use of various parts of a given person's information, so that even if some key parts are missing, the correct person candidates can still be identified.

[14] adopts a network called a partial convolutional baseline (PCB). Given an image input, it outputs a convolution descriptor consisting of several component level features. Through a unified partitioning strategy, PCB has achieved competitive results through state-of-the-art methods, proving that they are powerful convolutional baselines for personnel retrieval. Uniform partitioning inevitably produces outliers in each part, and these outliers are actually more similar to others. RPP reassigns these outliers to their closest component, resulting in a refinement with enhanced internal consistency of the component.

Attention Model for Person Re-identification. In order to reduce the influence of background on retrieval results. Many researchers use attentional mechanisms to weaken background tensors and redundant channel information.

Wang et al. [18] propose a new person re-identification architecture based on a new parameter-free attention layer that introduces the spatial relationship between feature map activation into the model. Li et al. [8] formulate a novel Harmonious Attention CNN model where soft pixel attention is adopted. In [13], double attention mechanism, using intra-sequence attention strategy and inter-sequence attention strategy for feature refinement and feature pair alignment is adopted.

3   Proposed Method

The section will propose a novel architecture for Re-ID that is based on Multiple Granularity Network [17]. The pixel and channel attention modules will also be described in detail.

3.1   Network Architecture

The architecture of Pixel and Channel Attention Network is shown in Figure 3. The backbone of the network is Resnet50 [3] which extracts feature information from pictures. We use the first three layers of resnet50 network to extract image features. The most obvious difference from the original version is that we divided the subsequent part after layer3 into three separate branches, sharing the same architecture as the original ResNet50. In the upper branch, We use convolution to reduce the dimension of the feature graph and get the global feature graph. Then

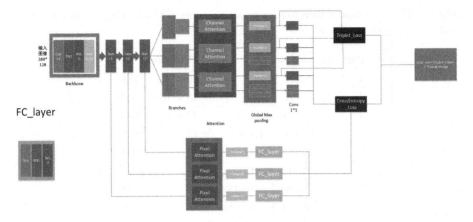

Fig. 3. Pixel and Channel Attention Network architecture. The main network is mainly divided into three branches: the first branch aggregates the global features, the second branch divides the features into two parts in the vertical direction, and the third branch divides the features into three parts in the vertical direction. Then feature map are aggregated using the channel attention module. After layer1, layer2, and layer3, an middle supervision layer was introduced, including pixel attention module.

the channel attention model is used to assign different weights to each channel to eliminate redundant information, following a global max-pooling operation. Finally, a 1×1 convolution layer with BN and ReLU is used to reduce 2048-dim features to 256-dim features. In the middle branch, the feature map is split into two stripes in horizontal orientation. In the lower branch, the feature map is split into three stripes in horizontal orientation.

During the Network, the supervisory layers are adopted in layer1, layer2 and layer3. In the supervisory layers, The pixel attention model was adopted followed by max-pooling and full connection layer.

Table 1 shows the setting information of the modules of the Network. In the table we can realize the tensor information of the modules including three branches, channel attention and pixel attention.

3.2   Channel Attention Module

In the past, the cnn-based method treated the channel features equally, which is inflexible for the actual situation. In order for the network to aggregate more useful features, we use the relation between the feature channels to form attention mechanism (see Fig. 5). The attention mechanism has been used in image super-resolution by Zhang *et al.* [23]. However, we improve the method to improve retrieval accuracy.

The key of the channel attention is how to generate different concerns for each channel. The feature map generally contains rich low frequency components and high frequency components. The low frequency components correspond to the

Table 1. Feature graph dimension information in the network. The size of the input image is set to 384×128.

Part no.	Module	Map size	Dims
1	layer1	96×32	256
2	layer2	48×16	512
3	layer3	24×8	1024
4	Branch_Global	12×4	2048
5	Branch_Part1	24×8	2048
6	Branch_Part2	24×8	2048
7	Channel Attention-1	12×4	2048
8	Channel Attention-2	24×8	2048
9	Channel Attention-3	24×8	2048
10	Pixel Attention-1	96×32	256
11	Pixel Attention-2	48×16	512
12	Pixel Attention-3	24×8	1024

Fig. 4. Channel Attention Network architecture.

flat part of the image, and the high frequency components correspond to the edge, texture and detail regions of the image.

As shown in Fig. 4, the size of the input tensor is $H \times W$ and the dimension is C. Now input features is $X = [x_1, x_2, \cdots, x_c]$. The first step is to reduce the dimension of the eigenvectors in each channel. Then the c-th element of F is determined by

$$F_c = \frac{1}{H \times W} \sum_{i=1}^{H} \sum_{j=1}^{W} x_c(i, j) \tag{1}$$

where $x_c(i, j)$ is the value at the position (i, j) in the c-th channel. By averaging the pixels in each channel, we can obtain the aggregation features. The second step then filters the resulting features to remove redundant information.

$$\{G_1, G_2, ..., G_{c_2}\} = f_1\left(\{\omega_1, \omega_2, ..., \omega_c\} \cdot \{F_1, F_2, ..., F_c\}\right) \tag{2}$$

where ω_c is the weight matrices of the each channel. The third step is to raise the dimension.

$$\{Z_1, Z_2, ..., Z_c\} = f_2\left(\{\varphi_1, \varphi_2, ..., \varphi_{c_2}\} \cdot \{G_1, G_2, ..., G_{c_2}\}\right) \tag{3}$$

where φ_{c_2} is the weight matrices of the each channel and Z_c is the output matrices which represents the weight value of each channel. Finally, the original eigenvector can be weighted by Z_c.

$$X_{result-c} = \sum_{i=1}^{H} \sum_{j=1}^{W} Z_c \cdot X_c(i,j) \tag{4}$$

3.3 Pixel Attention Module

Wang *et al.* [18] propose parameter-free spatial attention network. However, this model can only be used before the mean-pooling layer, and the parameterless model cannot use the neural network to learn to adjust the parameters. We improve the attention network (as shown in Fig. 5).

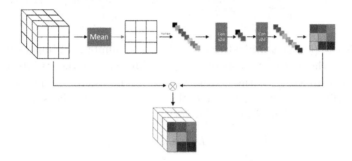

Fig. 5. Pixel Attention Network architecture.

The size of the input tensor is $H \times W$ and the dimension is C. The input features is $Y = [y_1, y_2, \cdots, y_c]$. The first step is similar with the channel attention network to reduce the dimension of the input tensor.

$$D(i,j) = \frac{1}{C} \sum_{c=1}^{C} y_c(i,j) \tag{5}$$

where $y(i,j)$ is the value at the position (i,j). The next steps are similar to the channel attention model. Then the tensor is resized a vector E.

$$E_\alpha = g_0(D), \alpha = 3 \cdot j + i \tag{6}$$

And then we convolve the vector.

$$\{I_1, I_2, ..., I_N\} = g_1(\{\eta_1, \eta_2, ..., \eta_\alpha\} \cdot \{E_1, E_2, ..., E_\alpha\})$$
$$\{J_1, J_2, ..., J_\alpha\} = g_2(\{\gamma_1, \gamma_2, ..., \gamma_N\} \cdot \{I_1, I_2, ..., I_N\}) \tag{7}$$

Then we restore the vector to a tensor.

$$K = g_4(J) \tag{8}$$

Finally, we can get the weight K of each pixel in the each channel.

$$Y_{result-c}(i,j) = K(i,j) \cdot Y(i,j) \tag{9}$$

3.4   Loss Functions

According to the recent research results, the multi-loss function is helpful to accelerate the network convergence and improve the accuracy. We employ softmax loss and triplet loss in the Network.

For i-th features f_i, the softmax loss is designed as:

$$L_{softmax} = -\sum_{i=1}^{N} \log \frac{e^{W_{y_i}^T f_i + b_{y_i}}}{\sum_{k=1}^{C} e^{W_k^T f_i + b_k}} \tag{10}$$

where N is the batchsize in the training process and C is the number of the classes. The triplet loss [4] is formulated as follows:

$$L_{triplet} = \sum_{i=1}^{P}\sum_{a=1}^{K}[m + \max_{p=1...K}\left\|f_a^i - f_p^i\right\|_2 - \min_{\substack{n=1...K \\ j=1...P \\ j \neq i}}\left\|f_a^i - f_n^i\right\|_2]_+ \tag{11}$$

where P is the pedestrian identities and K is the numbers of images from each identity. f_a^i is the feature vectors of the query image, f_p^i is the feature vectors of the positive samples, f_n^i is the feature vectors of the negative samples.

We combine the softmax loss and the triplet loss into the sum loss by the parameter λ. we set λ as 2 in the Network.

$$L_{sum} = \lambda \cdot L_{softmax} + L_{triplet} \tag{12}$$

4   Experiment

4.1   Datasets and Evaluation Protocol

Market1501 dataset [25] consists of 1501 pedestrians captured by 6 cameras and 32668 detected pedestrian rectangles. Each pedestrian is captured by at least 2 cameras and may have multiple images in one camera. The training set consisted of 751 people, containing 12,936 images, with an average of 17.2 training data per person; the test set consisted of 750 people, containing 19,732 images, with an average of 26.3 test data per person.

DukeMTMC-reID dataset [26] is a large-scale, multi-target, multi-camera pedestrian tracking dataset. It offers a new large HD video dataset recorded by 8 simultaneous cameras with more than 7,000 single camera tracks and more than 2,700 individual characters. It contains 16,522 training images (from 702 people), 2,228 query images (from another 702 people), and 17,661 gallery images.

CUHK03-NP dataset [7] contains labeled dataset and detected dataset. They divide the dataset into a training set of 767 pedestrians and a test set of 700 pedestrians.

Evaluation Protocol. In our experiment, we use Cumulative Matching Characteristic (CMC) at rank-1 and the mean average precision (mAP) to evaluate our approach on the three datasets.

4.2   Implementation Details

The input images are resized 384×128, followed by random erasing [27] and random horizontal flipping with 0.5. We also use re-ranking to improve retrieval accuracy. Batch size is set to 48 and we choose SGD as the optimizer. Ubuntu 16.04 with 1080Ti is used for the experiment.

Algorithm 1. Stochastic gradient descent, SGD

Require: learning rate ε_k
Require: initial parameter θ
while *no stop criterion* **do**
    m samples $\left\{x^1, ..., x^m\right\}$ are extracted from the training set, where x^i is corresponding to y^i.
    Compute gradient estimation: $\hat{g} \leftarrow +\frac{1}{m} \bigtriangledown_\theta L(f(x^i; \theta), y^i))$
    update: $\theta \leftarrow \theta - \epsilon \hat{g}$
end

Table 2. Comparison of results on Market1501 with Single Query. "RK" represents re-ranking operation.

Methods	Single query	
	Rank-1	mAP
SVDNet	82.3	62.1
PDC	84.1	63.4
TriNet	84.9	69.1
DuATM	91.4	76.6
DaRe	89.0	76.0
DPFL	88.9	73.1
HA-CNN	91.2	75.7
SPReID	93.7	83.4
GP-reid	92.2	81.2
SphereReID	94.4	83.6
PCB+RPP	93.8	81.6
Aligned-ReID	92.6	82.3
MGN	**95.7**	86.9
Ours	95.0	**87.5**
Ours+RK	95.8	94.4

4.3 Comparison with State-of-the-Art Methods

The results on Market1501 dataset is shown in Table 2. Our method without re-ranking in the single query achieves Rank-1/mAP = 95.0/87.5. If re-ranking operation is used, it achieves Rank-1/mAP = 95.8/94.4. Our method without re-ranking exceeds MGN by 0.6% in mAP.

Table 3. Comparison of results on DukeMTMC-reID. "RK" represents re-ranking operation.

Methods	Rank-1	mAP
DPFL	79.2	60.6
HA-CNN	80.5	63.8
DaRe	80.2	64.5
SLSR	82.9	67.8
SphereReID	83.9	68.5
CA3Net	84.6	70.2
BFE	88.7	75.8
MGN	88.7	78.4
Ours	**89.7**	**79.2**
Ours+RK	92.2	90.7

The results on DukeMTMC-reID dataset is shown in Table 3. Our method without re-ranking achieves Rank-1/mAP = 89.7/79.2. If re-ranking operation is used, it achieves Rank-1/mAP = 92.2/90.7. Compared with other existing methods, our method is slightly improved on CMC and mAP.

Table 4. Comparison of results on CUHK03-NP. "RK" represents re-ranking operation.

Methods	Labeled		Detected	
	Rank-1	mAP	Rank-1	mAP
SVDNet	40.9	37.8	41.5	37.3
DPFL	43.0	40.5	40.7	37.0
HA-CNN	44.4	41.0	41.7	38.6
Pose-transfer	45.1	42.0	41.6	38.7
MLFN	54.7	49.2	52.8	47.8
DaRe	66.1	61.6	63.3	59.0
Mancs	69.0	63.9	65.5	60.5
MGN	68.0	67.4	66.8	66.0
Ours	**80.9**	**78.7**	**78.9**	**76.4**
Ours+RK	87.5	89.0	86.2	87.5

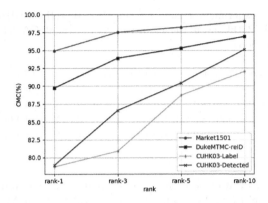

Fig. 6. CMC curves of our method on Market1501, DukeMTMC-reID, CUHK03-Labeled and CUHK03-Detected.

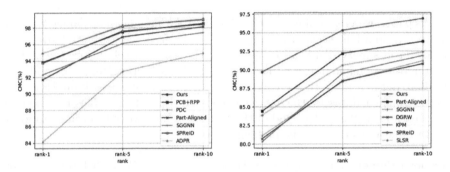

Fig. 7. CMC curves of the current methods. Left is on Market1501, right is on DukeMTMC-reID.

Table 4 shows the results on the CUHK03-Labeled and CUHK03-Detected. Our method achieves Rank-1/mAP = 80.9%/78.7% on the CUHK03-Labeled and 78.9%/76.4% on the CUHK03-Detected. They exceed respectively baseline by 12.9%/11.3% and 12.1%/10.4%. Figures 6 and 7 shows the CMC result of rank-1, rank-3, rank-5 and rank-10.

4.4 Ablation Experiment

Table 5 shows the results of the ablation experiment on DukeMTMC-reID, CUHK03-Labeled and CUHK03-Detected. For the backbone, we use the Network in Fig. 3 without channel attention and pixel attention modules. Through the Table 5, it is more effective on CUHK03-Labeled and CUHK03-Detected. On the CUHK03-Labeled dataset, the model equipped with CA and PA forms the attention-free model by 12.9% rank-1 accuracy and 11.3% mAP. On the

Table 5. Ablation experiment results on DukeMTMC-reID, CUHK03-Labeled and CUHK03-Detected. Backbone is the main Network without CA (channel attention) and PA (pixel attention).

Module	DukeMTMC-reID		CUHK03-Labeled		CUHK03-Detected	
	Rank-1	mAP	Rank-1	mAP	Rank-1	mAP
Backbone	88.7	78.4	68.0	67.4	66.8	66.0
Backbone+CA	89.6 (+0.9)	78.8 (+0.4)	80.2 (+12.2)	77.2 (+9.8)	74.9 (+8.1)	72.9 (+6.9)
Backbone+CA+PA	89.7 (+1.0)	79.2 (+0.8)	80.9 (+12.9)	78.7 (+11.3)	78.9 (+12.1)	76.4 (+10.4)

CUHK03-Detected dataset, the model equipped with CA and PA forms the attention-free model by 12.1% rank-1 accuracy and 10.4% mAP.

5   Conclusion

In this paper, we present a new network structure. Channel attention mechanism and pixel attention mechanism are added on the basic network. Moreover, the middle layer supervision is also applied, which can effectively utilize the middle layer information and improve the retrieval precision. Through experimental verification, our new network is proved effective in pedestrian recognition. However, during different datasets, the experiment results vary greatly. This may be due to differences in the background of the characters, and we will continue to work hard to find ways to solve the problem.

Acknowledgments. I would like to thank Mr. Xiao, Mr. Wang and Mrs. Yang for their guidance during the experiment. Thanks to Li for providing the experimental materials. Thanks for Zhang's help during typesetting the paper.

References

1. Fu, Y., et al.: Horizontal pyramid matching for person re-identification. arXiv preprint arXiv:1804.05275 (2018)
2. Ge, Y., et al.: FD-GAN: pose-guided feature distilling GAN for robust person re-identification. In: Advances in Neural Information Processing Systems, pp. 1230–1241 (2018)
3. He, K., Zhang, X., Ren, S., Sun, J.: Deep residual learning for image recognition. In: Proceedings of the IEEE Conference on Computer Vision and Pattern Recognition, pp. 770–778 (2016)
4. Hermans, A., Beyer, L., Leibe, B.: In defense of the triplet loss for person re-identification. arXiv preprint arXiv:1703.07737 (2017)
5. Huang, Q., Liu, W., Lin, D.: Person search in videos with one portrait through visual and temporal links. In: Ferrari, V., Hebert, M., Sminchisescu, C., Weiss, Y. (eds.) ECCV 2018. LNCS, vol. 11217, pp. 437–454. Springer, Cham (2018). https://doi.org/10.1007/978-3-030-01261-8_26

6. Le, C., Ma, H.: A method of detecting human head by eliminating redundancy in dataset. In: Wang, Y., Jiang, Z., Peng, Y. (eds.) IGTA 2018. CCIS, vol. 875, pp. 578–585. Springer, Singapore (2018). https://doi.org/10.1007/978-981-13-1702-6_57

7. Li, W., Zhao, R., Xiao, T., Wang, X.: DeepReID: deep filter pairing neural network for person re-identification. In: Proceedings of the IEEE Conference on Computer Vision and Pattern Recognition, pp. 152–159 (2014)

8. Li, W., Zhu, X., Gong, S.: Harmonious attention network for person re-identification. In: CVPR, vol. 1, p. 2 (2018)

9. Li, X., Wu, A., Zheng, W.-S.: Adversarial open-world person re-identification. In: Ferrari, V., Hebert, M., Sminchisescu, C., Weiss, Y. (eds.) ECCV 2018. LNCS, vol. 11206, pp. 287–303. Springer, Cham (2018). https://doi.org/10.1007/978-3-030-01216-8_18

10. Lv, J., Chen, W., Li, Q., Yang, C.: Unsupervised cross-dataset person re-identification by transfer learning of spatial-temporal patterns. In: Proceedings of the IEEE Conference on Computer Vision and Pattern Recognition, pp. 7948–7956 (2018)

11. Shen, Y., Li, H., Xiao, T., Yi, S., Chen, D., Wang, X.: Deep group-shuffling random walk for person re-identification. In: Proceedings of the IEEE Conference on Computer Vision and Pattern Recognition, pp. 2265–2274 (2018)

12. Shen, Y., Li, H., Yi, S., Chen, D., Wang, X.: Person re-identification with deep similarity-guided graph neural network. In: Ferrari, V., Hebert, M., Sminchisescu, C., Weiss, Y. (eds.) ECCV 2018. LNCS, vol. 11219, pp. 508–526. Springer, Cham (2018). https://doi.org/10.1007/978-3-030-01267-0_30

13. Si, J., et al.: Dual attention matching network for context-aware feature sequence based person re-identification. arXiv preprint arXiv:1803.09937 (2018)

14. Sun, Y., Zheng, L., Yang, Y., Tian, Q., Wang, S.: Beyond part models: person retrieval with refined part pooling (and a strong convolutional baseline). In: Ferrari, V., Hebert, M., Sminchisescu, C., Weiss, Y. (eds.) ECCV 2018. LNCS, vol. 11208, pp. 501–518. Springer, Cham (2018). https://doi.org/10.1007/978-3-030-01225-0_30

15. Ali, T.M.F., Chaudhuri, S.: Maximum margin metric learning over discriminative nullspace for person re-identification. In: Ferrari, V., Hebert, M., Sminchisescu, C., Weiss, Y. (eds.) ECCV 2018. LNCS, vol. 11217, pp. 123–141. Springer, Cham (2018). https://doi.org/10.1007/978-3-030-01261-8_8

16. Wang, C., Zhang, Q., Huang, C., Liu, W., Wang, X.: Mancs: a multi-task attentional network with curriculum sampling for person re-identification. In: Ferrari, V., Hebert, M., Sminchisescu, C., Weiss, Y. (eds.) ECCV 2018. LNCS, vol. 11208, pp. 384–400. Springer, Cham (2018). https://doi.org/10.1007/978-3-030-01225-0_23

17. Wang, G., Yuan, Y., Chen, X., Li, J., Zhou, X.: Learning discriminative features with multiple granularities for person re-identification. arXiv preprint arXiv:1804.01438 (2018)

18. Wang, H., Fan, Y., Wang, Z., Jiao, L., Schiele, B.: Parameter-free spatial attention network for person re-identification. arXiv preprint arXiv:1811.12150 (2018)

19. Wang, Y., et al.: Resource aware person re-identification across multiple resolutions. In: Proceedings of the IEEE Conference on Computer Vision and Pattern Recognition, pp. 8042–8051 (2018)

20. Yu, R., Dou, Z., Bai, S., Zhang, Z., Xu, Y., Bai, X.: Hard-aware point-to-set deep metric for person re-identification. In: Ferrari, V., Hebert, M., Sminchisescu, C., Weiss, Y. (eds.) ECCV 2018. LNCS, vol. 11220, pp. 196–212. Springer, Cham (2018). https://doi.org/10.1007/978-3-030-01270-0_12

21. Zhang, J., Wang, N., Zhang, L.: Multi-shot pedestrian re-identification via sequential decision making. arXiv preprint arXiv:1712.07257 (2017)

22. Zhang, X., et al.: AlignedEeID: surpassing human-level performance in person re-identification. arXiv preprint arXiv:1711.08184 (2017)

23. Zhang, Y., Li, K., Li, K., Wang, L., Zhong, B., Fu, Y.: Image super-resolution using very deep residual channel attention networks. In: Ferrari, V., Hebert, M., Sminchisescu, C., Weiss, Y. (eds.) ECCV 2018. LNCS, vol. 11211, pp. 294–310. Springer, Cham (2018). https://doi.org/10.1007/978-3-030-01234-2_18

24. Zheng, L., Huang, Y., Lu, H., Yang, Y.: Pose invariant embedding for deep person re-identification. arXiv preprint arXiv:1701.07732 (2017)

25. Zheng, L., Shen, L., Tian, L., Wang, S., Wang, J., Tian, Q.: Scalable person re-identification: a benchmark. In: Proceedings of the IEEE International Conference on Computer Vision, pp. 1116–1124 (2015)

26. Zheng, Z., Zheng, L., Yang, Y.: Unlabeled samples generated by GAN improve the person re-identification baseline in vitro. In: Proceedings of the IEEE International Conference on Computer Vision, pp. 3754–3762 (2017)

27. Zhong, Z., Zheng, L., Kang, G., Li, S., Yang, Y.: Random erasing data augmentation. arXiv preprint arXiv:1708.04896 (2017)

Infrared and Visible Image Matching Algorithm Based on SIFT and LDB

Lirui Zhang$^{(\boxtimes)}$, Min Dai, and Jinwen Tian

National Key Laboratory of Science and Technology on Multi-spectral
Information Processing Technology, School of Automation,
Huazhong University of Science and Technology, Wuhan 430074, China
hust_zlr@hust.edu.cn

Abstract. A new local feature extraction method (BSPL) is proposed and applied to heterogeneous image matching to solve the problem that the traditional SIFT features have poor matching performance in heterogeneous image matching. A number of improvements have been made to ensure that common features of heterogeneous images can be extracted efficiently. The gradient histogram-equalized image is used as the input matching image; The bilateral filtering is used to construct the scale space pyramid to replace the Gaussian filtering of the traditional SIFT, which can make the details such as the edges of the image better preserved; PCA-based LDB descriptor is used as feature expression to improve the robustness of feature expression. Experimental results show that the proposed local feature descriptor has rotation and scale invariance, and effectively improves the number of matching points, matching accuracy, matching precision and matching adaptability, which is an effective infrared and visible image matching method.

Keywords: Heterogeneous image matching ·
Gradient histogram equalization · Bilateral filtering · SIFT · PCA-LDB

1 Introduction

Heterogeneous image matching has a wide range of applications in image navigation, target recognition, and image fusion. In scene matching navigation, since the reference image adopted is visible satellite image, while the real-time image adopted is infrared image which can work all day, the matching for infrared and visible image is a key technology. The gray information of the visible image reflects the reflection intensity of the scene target, while the infrared image reflects the surface temperature distribution. Due to the difference of imaging mechanisms, it is difficult to match the infrared image with the visible image.

Generally, matching methods are based on gray information or local features [1]. Infrared and visible images are typical heterogeneous images of nonlinear grayscale. Even under the same scene, imaging effect of the two images varies greatly. There may even be cases where the image results formed by the two cameras are reversed [2]. Therefore, matching methods based on gray information for heterogeneous image are not reliable. From recent research, feature-based matching methods like SIFT [3],

© Springer Nature Singapore Pte Ltd. 2019
Y. Wang et al. (Eds.): IGTA 2019, CCIS 1043, pp. 105–115, 2019.
https://doi.org/10.1007/978-981-13-9917-6_11

SURF [4], ORB [5] have gradually become a hot spot in the field of image matching. [1] proposed an improved SIFT heterogeneous image matching algorithm based on constrained threshold for eigenvectors. However, the threshold setting needs to greatly depend on the selected sample image, which does not have good applicability. [6] proposed a heterogeneous image matching algorithm that combines SIFT and shape context. However, it only deals with the case where the two images are negatively imaged, while the actual imaging difference between the two images is more complicated. [7] proposed a visible and infrared image registration algorithm based on elliptical symmetry directional moment, but the descriptor extracted by the algorithm does not have good invariance for rotation and scale. [8] proposed to use a bilateral filtered image as the guiding image to perform multi-scale guided filtering on the scale pyramid space to achieve the edge preservation effect on multi-band SAR images. However, the multi-scale guided filtering also magnifies the image noise caused by imaging differences. [9] proposed an anisotropic scale space constructed with speckle reducing anisotropic diffusion (SRAD) to reduce the influence of noise on feature extraction, but it only applies to SAR image matching, lacking the experimental performance for infrared and visible image matching.

Although infrared and visible images have large differences in imaging effects, edge and contour information of the two images are less affected by the sensor imaging mechanism, still maintaining high similarity, which can be regarded as common features for heterogeneous images. This paper proposed an improved matching algorithm combining both bilateral filtered SIFT and PCA-LDB (BSPL). Gradient histogram equalization image is used as the matching input image to highlight the edge information as much as possible, which can also maintaining the similarity of the two images after rasterization from the gray level. Bilateral filter [10] is used instead of traditional SIFT Gaussian filtering to construct a bilateral filtering scale pyramid to better preserve image edge information. The Principal Component Analysis (PCA) method is adopted to reduce the dimension of the original LDB [11] descriptor. The PCA method can extract main features and remove those unimportant detailed features as well as image noise caused by preprocessing and bilateral filtering. Finally, the Euclidean distance is used to obtain the initial matching point pairs and the RANSAC method is used to purify these pairs. Experiment results show that the proposed method has a very significant effect on both the matching accuracy and the adaptability of the algorithm under the premise of time-consuming.

2 Algorithm Framework

In this paper, the proposed algorithm is divided into four modules: preprocessing, keypoints extraction, descriptor construction, matching and purification. The framework of the entire algorithm is as in Fig. 1. A detailed introduction for technical details of the proposed algorithm is given in Sects. 2.1–2.4.

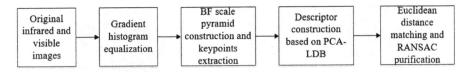

Fig. 1. Algorithm framework

2.1 Preprocessing

Due to the different imaging mechanisms of infrared and visible image, the two images are weakly correlated on grayscale. Figure 2(a) shows the onboard infrared image and visible image taken under the same scene.

In Fig. 2(a), for the mountain regions, the grayscale distribution of the two images keeps relatively consistent, but for farmland and building regions, the grayscale distribution varies greatly. However, edge and contour information of the two images are rich and similar, which can be regarded as common features of the two heterogeneous images. Since the gradient image does not consider original gray information of image, it is only related to the gradient information of a certain pixel, so the paper firstly makes Sobel gradient transform on both original images. The transformed image are shown in Fig. 2(b). Information such as edges and contours of the extracted infrared and visible images are more obvious. However, the grayscale contrast of the two images varies greatly, so histogram equalization is performed on the two images, and processed results are shown in Fig. 2(c). After Sobel transform and histogram equalization, the grayscale distribution of buildings, farmlands and mountains in Fig. 2(c) have been greatly improved compared to original images, which is more suitable for further matching.

2.2 SIFT Keypoints Extraction Based on Bilateral Filter

In SIFT algorithm, the scale space pyramid is constructed by Gaussian filter template, and the scale transform is realized by down-sampling and different scale factors. However, Gaussian filter only considers the spatial distance relationship between pixels, leaving out the similarity between the pixel values, which cannot reflect the grayscale distribution in the pixel neighborhood. [12] proposed bilateral filter, which not only considers the spatial distance relationship between pixels, but also considers the similarity between pixels values, thus greatly maintaining the overall contours and edges of the original image. $u(x)$ is the gray value of the original image at pixel x, Ω is the filter window centered on pixel x, and $u(y)$ is the pixel value of the neighborhood pixel within the template window. $u_{OUT}(x)$ is the output image, the definition of bilateral filtering is as follows:

$$u_{OUT}(x) = \frac{1}{C_{d,r}} \sum_{y \in \Omega} exp\left(-\frac{|x-y|^2}{2\sigma_d^2}\right) exp\left(-\frac{|u(x)-u(y)|^2}{2\sigma_r^2}\right) u(y) \qquad (1)$$

(a) Onboard visible reference image (left) and onboard infrared real-time image (right)

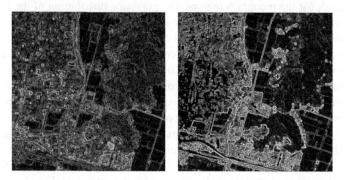

(b) Onboard visible reference image (left) and onboard infrared real-time image (right) after Sobel transform

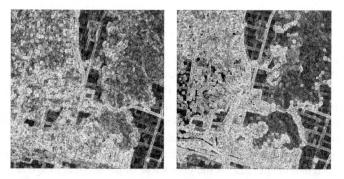

(c) Onboard visible reference image (left) and onboard infrared real-time image (right) after Sobel transform and histogram equalization

Fig. 2. Preprocessing result

$$c_{d,r} = \sum_{y \in \Omega} exp\left(-\frac{|x-y|^2}{2\sigma_d^2}\right) exp\left(-\frac{|u(x)-u(y)|^2}{2\sigma_r^2}\right) \qquad (2)$$

The first exponential function in formula (1) measures the spatial proximity between central pixel x and neighborhood pixel y. The second exponential function measures the grayscale similarity between neighborhood central pixel x and the neighborhood pixel y. $u(y)$ measures the gray value at pixel y. σ_d and σ_r are the spatial distance weight coefficient and the image gray weight coefficient. $c_{d,r}$ is the normalization coefficient, see formula (2).

In order to measure the effect of different filtering methods on edge preservation, this paper adopts an index proposed by [13] to evaluate the edge preservation effect of filtered images, namely Edge Preserve Index (EPI). Its definition is as follows:

$$EPI = \frac{\sum(|p_s(i,j) - p_s(i+1,j)| + |p_s(i,j) - p_s(i,j+1)|)}{\sum(|p_o(i,j) - p_o(i+1,j)| + |p_o(i,j) - p_o(i,j+1)|)} \tag{3}$$

$p_s(i,j)$ represents filtered image pixel and $p_o(i,j)$ represents original image pixel. The larger the value of EPI, the stronger the edge retention capability of the filter, and the maximum value is 1. The figure below shows the experimental results after Gaussian filtering and bilateral filtering under different pyramid scales:

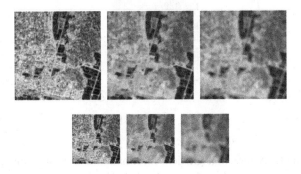

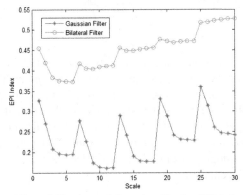

(a)   Two sets of original images, bilateral filtering images and Gaussian filtering images under different pyramid scales

(b)   Bilateral filtering and Gaussian filtering EPI index curve

Fig. 3. Results of two filtering experiments under different pyramid scales

In Fig. 3(a), bilateral filter can better preserve image edge information compared to Gaussian filter. Figure 3(b) shows the EPI exponential distribution of the two filtering methods under different pyramid scales. Each of the six points is a group, and the first image of the next group is down-sampled and filtered by the original image of the previous group. We can see that the larger the number of groups, the more blurred the image is on the scale space. Compared with Gaussian filtering, bilateral filtering can better retaining image edge information with image becoming more blurred.

2.3   Improved LDB Descriptor Based on PCA

A good descriptor should have good robustness to illumination, rotation and scaling. The LDB (Local Difference Binary, LDB) descriptor has such characteristics. Under same matching effect, the calculation speed is much faster than SIFT descriptor. Within the neighborhood of the feature point, a certain size area is selected, and the area is divided into n * n sub-blocks of the same size. Take 2 * 2 sub-blocks as an example:

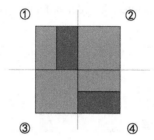

Fig. 4. 2 * 2 sub-block

The mean value, X-direction gradient information and Y-direction gradient information of each sub-block in Fig. 4 are extracted. The formula is as follows:

$$\begin{cases} I_{avg}(i) = \frac{1}{sum\_pt} \sum_{x,y \in \Omega(i)} I(x,y) \\ d_x(i) = I_{xr}(i) - I_{xl}(i) \\ d_y(i) = I_{yd}(i) - I_{yu}(i) \end{cases} \tag{4}$$

Taking area 2 in Fig. 4 as an example, the gray mean value $I_{avg}(i)$ is the sum of the pixel values in the area divided by the number of pixels sum_pt_pt; Taking area 1 as an example, the x-direction gradient information $d_x(i)$ is the sum of the pixel values of the right half area $I_{xr}(i)$ minus the sum of the pixel values of the left half area $I_{xl}(i)$; Taking area 4 as an example, the gradient information $d_y(i)$ in the y direction is the sum of the pixel values of the lower half area $I_{yd}(i)$ minus the sum of the pixel values of the upper half area $I_{yu}(i)$. LDB adopts integral image to calculate these three values, which greatly speeds up the calculation.

After each block extracts the above three values, two different sub-blocks are randomly selected from the 2 * 2 sub-blocks for comparison, which can construct a binary descriptor. The comparison function is as follows:

$$\tau(F(i), F(j)) = \begin{cases} 1, F(i) - F(j) > 0, i \neq j \\ 0, F(i) - F(j) \leq 0, i \neq j \end{cases} \tag{5}$$

Sub-block i and j form a set of correspondences. The set of correspondences represents a three-dimensional vector, and each element in the vector is 0 or 1. In order to reflect the scale invariance of the LDB descriptor, [11] proposed to divide the sub-block numbers of the feature point neighborhood into 2 * 2, 3 * 3, 4 * 4 and 5 * 5. The larger the divided sub-blocks are, the more the overall characteristics of the region can be reflected; the smaller the sub-blocks are, the more detailed the region can be reflected. According to the division, the dimension of the descriptor extracted is:

$$dimension_{sum} = 3 * \left(c_{2*2}^2 + c_{3*3}^2 + c_{4*4}^2 + c_{5*5}^2 \right) = 1386 \tag{6}$$

The factor of 3 indicates that one comparison can form a three-dimensional vector. c_{2*2}^2 indicates that the total number of comparisons in the 2 * 2 sub-block if two sub-blocks are randomly taken for comparison, and so on. Since the division of multi-scale sub-blocks makes the descriptor dimension too large, the original LDB algorithm adopts two simple methods to reduce the dimension of the descriptor: the random dimension filtering method and the entropy-based dimension filtering method. Among the two methods, the random dimension screening method has great uncertainty. The entropy-based dimension screening method only uses the entropy value of different dimensions as the dimension screening index, which does not consider the intrinsic relationship between different dimensions.

This paper proposes to apply PCA to the LDB descriptor, retaining the most important features of high-dimensional data, and removing the unimportant features to achieve the purpose of dimension reduction. It can also filter out the image noise created by preprocessing and bilateral filtering. Like PCA-SIFT, the process of calculating the covariance matrix of the descriptor and extracting the feature vector after the dimension reduction can be done offline without taking up the actual matching time. After experimental test, the descriptor dimension is set to 64 after dimension reduction.

2.4 Feature Matching and Matching Purification

In the feature matching stage, the Euclidean distance is used to describe the similarity of feature points. Then, the extracted matching points are filtered and purified by RANSAC.

3   Experimental Results and Analysis

The experimental data used in this paper is derived from two on-board visible images and infrared images under the same resolution. The infrared image size to be matched is set to 200 * 200, and the visible image size is set to 400 * 400. In order to verify the effect of the proposed algorithm BSPL, the selected test image data contains a variety of different landform information such as buildings, waters, mountains and plains. Since this paper absorbs the ideas of BFSIFT algorithm and LDB algorithm, the comparative experiment is carried out by means of control variable method. Five methods were designed for comparative experiments: The traditional SIFT method (SIFT), the proposed method without preprocessing (BSPL w/o PRE), the proposed method without bilateral filtering (BSPL w/o BF), the proposed method without PCA dimensionality reduction (BSPL w/o PCA), and the proposed method (BSPL). The following is the matching result.

In Fig. 5, SIFT and BSPL without preprocessing have good matching performance on the mountain regions, but almost fails to match for other three regions; the rest three methods have better adaptability to all these four regions. The number of feature points extracted by BSPL without bilateral filtering is less than that of BSPL and BSPL without PCA. There is not too much difference between match results for the last two methods visually. For quantitative analysis, the matching results for these four different regions are statistically analyzed. The statistical indicators include: the number of matching points after RANSAC(NUM_RANSAC), the correct matching points number(MATCH_NUM), the correct matching rate (MATCH_RATE, which equals correct matching points divides number of matching points after RANSAC), the matching time (MATCH_T) and matching center coordinate deviation(MATCH_DEV). The correct matching center point coordinate is (200, 200). The experimental results are shown in Table 1.

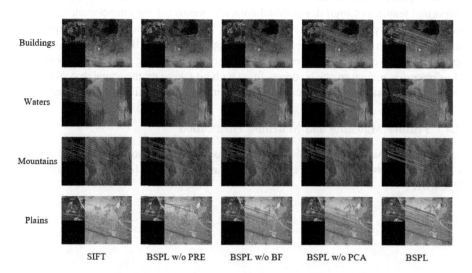

Fig. 5. Matching results of different landform areas

Table 1. Matching indicator data for different landforms

		Method 1	Method 2	Method 3	Method 4	Proposed
Buildings	NUM_RANSAC	6	5	22	54	70
	MATCH_NUM	0	0	21	49	69
	MATCH_RATE	0%	0%	95.45%	90.74%	98.57%
	MATCH_T/ms	1306	1459	1298	1990	1633
	MATCH_DEV	$(-32, 33)$	$(-61, -46)$	$(-1, 0)$	$(-1, 0)$	$(-1, 0)$
Waters	NUM_RANSAC	12	9	24	30	28
	MATCH_NUM	11	1	23	30	28
	MATCH_RATE	91.67%	11.11%	95.83%	100%	100%
	MATCH_T/ms	934	1058	908	1450	1180
	MATCH_DEV	$(1, 1)$	$(-1, 3)$	$(1, 0)$	$(1, 0)$	$(1, 0)$
Mountains	NUM_RANSAC	46	51	32	37	48
	MATCH_NUM	45	50	32	36	48
	MATCH_RATE	97.83%	98.04%	100%	97.28%	100%
	MATCH_T/ms	892	1209	1230	1607	1468
	MATCH_DEV	$(-1, 0)$	$(-1, 0)$	$(-1, 0)$	$(-1, 0)$	$(-1, 0)$
Plains	NUM_RANSAC	4	7	27	40	42
	MATCH_NUM	0	0	27	39	41
	MATCH_RATE	0%	0%	100%	97.5%	97.62%
	MATCH_T/ms	1128	1324	1181	1413	1498
	MATCH_DEV	$(-28, -12)$	$(29, -59)$	$(0, 0)$	$(0, 0)$	$(0, 0)$

From Table 1, among the five matching methods, the matching performance for SIFT and BSPL without preprocessing is poor. The matching center coordinate deviations of the rest three methods are the same with high precision. However, BSPL without bilateral filtering adopts the Gaussian filtering of the original SIFT, which does not retain the detailed information such as image contours, so the number of matching points is much smaller than BSPL and BSPL without PCA; BSPL without PCA adopts entropy value screening of the original LDB to reduce the dimension of the descriptors, while BSPL uses PCA to reduce the dimension of the descriptors. Because BSPL in this paper reduces the descriptor to 64-dimensional, which is much smaller than the original LDB 256-dimensional. Therefore, the overall cost time for BSPL is less than that of BSPL without PCA. At the same time, the amount of matching points extracted by BSPL is generally more than that of BSPL without PCA. Based on the above five indicators, the proposed method in this paper performs the best.

In order to verify the invariance of the proposed algorithm to rotation and scale, the above real-time infrared images are first rotated or scaled. And then perform the proposed matching algorithm. The selected indicators are: correct matching points number (MATCH_NUM), correct matching rate (MATCH_RATE, which equals correct matching points divides number of matching points after RANSAC) and matching center coordinate deviation (MATCH_DEV). The results are in Tables 2 and 3.

Table 2. Matching indicator data of four regions under different scaling ratios

	Scaling ratios	0.95	0.90	0.85	0.80	0.75
Buildings	MATCH_NUM	56	44	39	24	11
	MATCH_RATE	96.55%	93.62%	100%	96%	91.67%
	MATCH_DEV	(1, 1)	(1, 0)	(1, 1)	(1, 0)	(0, 0)
Waters	MATCH_NUM	14	9	9	6	4
	MATCH_RATE	100%	75%	81.81%	66.67%	66.67%
	MATCH_DEV	(−1, 0)	(−1, 0)	(1, 2)	(0, −3)	(−1, −2)
Mountains	MATCH_NUM	32	23	16	14	11
	MATCH_RATE	99.97%	95.83%	88.89%	87.5%	84.62%
	MATCH_DEV	(1, 0)	(1, 0)	(1, 1)	(2, 0)	(1, 0)
Plains	MATCH_NUM	42	29	23	9	9
	MATCH_RATE	95.45%	96.67%	95.83%	69.23%	90%
	MATCH_DEV	(0, 0)	(0, 0)	(0, 0)	(−2, 0)	(0, −2)

Table 3. Matching indicator data of four regions under different rotation angles

	Rotation angles	2	4	6	8	10
Buildings	MATCH_NUM	53	45	38	32	12
	MATCH_RATE	98.15%	100%	95%	96.97%	85.71%
	MATCH_DEV	(−1, 0)	(−1, 0)	(−1, 0)	(−1, 1)	(−1, 1)
Waters	MATCH_NUM	22	21	9	7	10
	MATCH_RATE	100%	95.45%	81.82%	77.78%	100%
	MATCH_DEV	(1, 0)	(1, 0)	(2, 0)	(−2, −3)	(0, 0)
Mountains	MATCH_NUM	34	32	23	22	18
	MATCH_RATE	97.14%	100%	92%	100%	100%
	MATCH_DEV	(−1, 0)	(−1, 0)	(−2, 0)	(−1, 0)	(−1, −1)
Plains	MATCH_NUM	49	39	29	32	23
	MATCH_RATE	100%	95.12%	100%	91.43%	100%
	MATCH_DEV	(0, 0)	(0, 0)	(0, 0)	(0, 0)	(0, 1)

In Tables 2 and 3, as the scaling ratio decreases or the rotation angle increases, the correct matching number and the correct matching rate show a downward trend. But the center point coordinate deviation can still be retained within three pixels. Therefore, the proposed algorithm can maintain good invariance for a certain range of rotation and scaling.

4 Conclusion

As the imaging mechanisms of infrared and visible images are quite different, common local feature descriptors are not effective. This paper proposes an improved image matching method (BSPL) for heterogeneous images based on traditional SIFT and

LDB. The method is designed from three aspects: image preprocessing, scale space pyramid construction and descriptor construction. Experiment results show that the proposed algorithm can extract more matching points for different geomorphological regions and ensuring the time-consuming at the same time. Matching accuracy and matching precision of the proposed method are also quite well, which is a fast, robust image matching method for infrared and visible heterogeneous image matching. In addition, this paper does not optimize too much for the final feature matching strategy. It just adopts simple Euclidean distance to match points and RANSAC method to purify. Therefore, further study can be done for the feature matching and purification part.

References

1. Ming, Z.: Registration of infrared and visible images based on improved SIFT feature. Opto-Electron. Eng. **38**(9), 130–136 (2011)
2. Wen, G., Bo, H.: Infrared and visible light images matching based on corner and edge. Inf. Technol. Netw. Secur. **37**(02), 122–126 (2018)
3. Lowe, D.G.: Distinctive image features from scale-invariant keypoints. Int. J. Comput. Vis. **60**(2), 91–110 (2004)
4. Bay, H., Tuytelaars, T., Van Gool, L.: SURF: speeded up robust features. In: Leonardis, A., Bischof, H., Pinz, A. (eds.) ECCV 2006. LNCS, vol. 3951, pp. 404–417. Springer, Heidelberg (2006). https://doi.org/10.1007/11744023_32
5. Rublee, E., Rabaud, V., Konolige, K., et al.: ORB: an efficient alternative to SIFT or SURF. In: ICCV, vol. 11, no. 1, p. 2 (2011)
6. Zhang, J., Li, J., Zhu, Y., et al.: Matching method of IR/visual images based on SIFT and shape context. Laser Infrared **42**(11), 1296–1300 (2012)
7. Chen, S., Zhang, S., Yang, X., Qi, N.: Registration of visual-infrared images based on ellipse symmetrical orientation moment. Chin. J. Eng. **39**(07), 1107–1113 (2017)
8. Wu, P., Yu, Q., Min, S.: Fast and robust SAR image matching algorithm. Comput. Sci. (7) (2017)
9. Wang, Y., Ge, Z., Su, J., Wu, W.: SAR image registration using cluster analysis and anisotropic diffusion-based SIFT. In: Wang, Y., et al. (eds.) IGTA 2017. CCIS, vol. 757, pp. 1–11. Springer, Singapore (2018). https://doi.org/10.1007/978-981-10-7389-2_1
10. Wang, S., You, H., Fu, K.: BFSIFT: a novel method to find feature matches for SAR image registration. IEEE Geosci. Remote Sens. Lett. **9**(4), 649–653 (2012)
11. Yang, X., Cheng, K.T.: LDB: an ultra-fast feature for scalable augmented reality on mobile devices. In: 2012 IEEE International Symposium on Mixed and Augmented Reality (ISMAR). IEEE Computer Society (2012)
12. Manduchi, R., Tomasi, C.: Bilateral filtering for gray and color images. In: IEEE International Conference on Computer Vision (ICCV), Bombay, India, p. 839 (1998)
13. Han, C.-M., Guo, H., Wang, C., et al.: An improved filtering method for SAR image speckle noise. J. Remote Sens. **8**(2), 121–127 (2004)

The Overview of 2D to 3D Automatic Conversion

Yunlong Cheng[1], Yun Dong[2], and Jiawei Tan[1(✉)]

[1] College of Information Science and Engineering, Northeastern University,
Shenyang 110819, China
tan_jw@foxmail.com
[2] State Grid Urumqi Power Supply Company, Urumqi 830000, China

Abstract. With the rapid development of 3D devices, the depth map extraction method of 2D to 3D conversion has become a research hot spot in the field of computer vision. In this paper, on account of collected literatures and documents, we mainly introduces two methods of automatic depth map extraction based respectively on depth clues and machine learning. The depth map extraction method based on clues of several implementation algorithms is introduced, and its respective advantages and disadvantages are summarized. While for the depth map extraction method based on machine learning, we show the process of depth map extraction as an example. Moreover the parametric method and the non-parametric method are compared, and their respective advantages and disadvantages are pointed out. Finally we summarize the improved depth map extraction algorithm in the recent years, and the technical prospect is also discussed.

Keywords: Depth map extraction · Depth clues · Machine learning · Deep learning

1 Introduction

In recent years, devices with 3D display functions, such as 3D television, smart phones, or projectors, have developed rapidly. However, the growth of 3D resources couldn't catch up with the speed of 3D devices. Therefore, it becomes very important to convert massive existing 2D resources into 3D resources.

The 2D-to-3D conversion process usually has two main steps. The first one is the depth estimation from a given monocular image, and the second one is the Depth Image-Based Rendering (DIBR) of a new image or images to form a stereo pair, or a multi-view set of images [1]. For the rendering step, there exist many algorithms with good effects on depth map generation. However, the depth estimation from a single image is still a challenging process [1].

According to the degree of artificial participation in the 2D to 3D conversion process, the depth map extraction method can be divided into three categories: manual method, semi-automatic method and automatic method. Since the automatic method without artificial participation, many scholars have been focusing on this approach,

© Springer Nature Singapore Pte Ltd. 2019
Y. Wang et al. (Eds.): IGTA 2019, CCIS 1043, pp. 116–124, 2019.
https://doi.org/10.1007/978-981-13-9917-6_12

there are a lot of advanced depth extraction techniques have appeared in the scope of automatic methods.

Based on the collection of documents, the depth map extraction automatic methods mainly divided into two categories which is based on machine learning and depth cues. Considering the chronological order of the emergence of depth map extraction technology, the algorithm divided into various stages. And the advantages and disadvantage of various methods are reviewed simultaneously. This paper is organized according to the following structure. In Sect. 2, the extraction process of depth map was introduced in detail. Then in Sect. 3, we describe the development process of depth map extraction method. Next is the summary of the improvement of depth map extraction's technology in recent years and finally the technology of depth map extraction is prospected in Sect. 5.

2   2D to 3D Processing Flow

2D to 3D conversion process is as in Fig. 1. Step 1, the depth map extraction. This is the hardest part to implement, also has many clues and methods to estimate depth maps, which will be described in detail in Sect. 3. Step 2, the generation of virtual viewpoints. One approach is an image with the original depth as a viewpoint, while the other virtual viewpoint is generated by computing the information provided by the depth map. The other one is to take the original depth maps as the intermediate image and generates images of the left eye viewpoint and the right eye viewpoint respectively through it. Step 3, Hole filling. The image obtained by virtual viewpoint generation technology contains many empty points. There are two main types of void points. The first type is the smaller void points generated by resampling or other reasons. The other one is due to the occlusion of the formation of large holes, generally appear at the edge of the object. Step 4, Synthesize the image. The images of two viewpoints are fused to generate images.

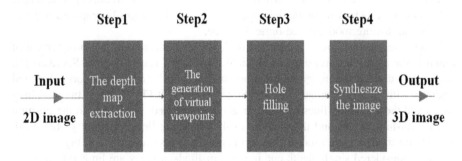

Fig. 1. 2D to 3D processing flow.

3 The Development of Depth Map Extraction Method

3.1 Depth Map Extraction Based on Depth Cues

In automatic depth map extraction, almost all algorithms use depth cues in the images. Therefore, many scholars have divided these algorithms into 3 categories: the algorithms based on monocular cues, based on binocular cues and based on mixed cues. Commonly used depth cues mainly include:

(1) Linear perspective
(2) Occlusion
(3) Shading
(4) Texture
(5) Motion Parallax
(6) Focus

Among them, (1) (2) (3) (4) (5) can be extracted from a single image, called monocular cues. (6) (7) need to be obtained from multiple images, called binocular clues. The binocular clue means using the stereo matching method to search for the corresponding pixels in the two images to calculate the disparity value. The larger the parallax is, the closer the scene is, and vice versa. The existing stereo matching methods are divided into local matching approach and global matching approach. The process of using depth cues for depth map extraction is roughly a transition from using single clue to mixed clues.

A. Depth Map Extraction Using Single Clue

- Advantages: The best effect in a particular image scene.
- Disadvantages: Just suitable for a particular image scene.

In the early days, many scholars used single depth cue to extract depths map from specific scenes. For example, Cozman and Krotkov [2] first applied atmospheric scatter to the depth extraction of outdoor images. Choe and Kashyap [3] proposed a three-dimensional texture model based on texture cue.

Linear perspective cue is often used in depth map generation, the most typical of which is the algorithm proposed by Battiato, Curti, La Cascia, Tortora, Scordato [4]. They firstly divided the image into indoors, outdoors with geometric information, and outdoors without any geometric information, as shown in Fig. 2. Then, the vanishing points and the vanishing lines of each image were detected. According to the position of the vanishing points and the gradient of the vanishing lines, different global depth distribution models were used to perform pixel depth assignment, as in Fig. 3.

Only considered single depth cue in these methods, so they are limited to a single 2D image scene with a specific depth cue or extremely demanding for the hardware equipment for image shooting. However, in practical applications, since 2D images have characteristics such as content diversity and structural complexity, extracting depth maps from complex and diverse image scenes has become the main direction of research.

     (a)   (b)   (c)

Fig. 2. Example of image categories. (a) Outdoor, (b) Outdoor with geometric appearances, (c) Indoor.

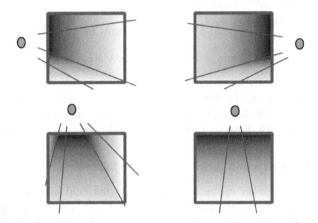

Fig. 3. Examples of the heuristic rules to generate depth gradient planes: the green circle represents the vanishing point. (Color figure online)

B. Depth Map Extraction Based on Multi-cues Hybrid

- Advantages: Suitable for a variety of scenarios.
- Disadvantages: Algorithm is complicated.

Since the depth map extraction method using single depth cue cannot be applied to different scenes, scholars tried to combine various depth cues to conduct research. For example, Han and Hong [5] used linear perspective cues to generate an initial depth map, and then used texture cues to refine the initial depth map. Ji, Wang, Li, Zhang [6] combined with linear perspective, defocus, sharpness and defocus to construct an adaptive depth model, which can construct a better depth map for different target images. Wafa, Nasiopoulos and Leung [7] combined three depth cues (haze, vertical edges, sharpness) to estimate the sparse depth map, and then obtained the complete map from the sparse depth map by an edge-aware interpolation method [8]. Representatively, Chang, Chen, Chang, and Tsai [9] proposed a 2d-3d priority depth fusion conversion system, which includes three different depth reconstruction modules. Different depth cues are used in each module to produce different depth maps, and finally a linear weighted fusion is used for the three depth maps, as in Fig. 4.

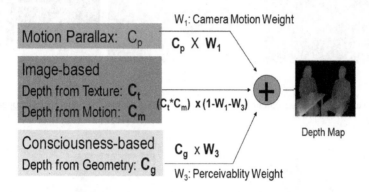

Fig. 4. The algorithm of the priority depth fusion.

The depth map extraction method based on mixed depth cues expands the scope of the scenes compared with the single clue method, and the accuracy is also improved. It is also the main research direction of the future development of depth map extraction.

3.2   Depth Map Extraction Based on Machine Learning

Due to the powerful ability of machine learning in the field of image classification, scholars have applied the machine learning to the technology of depth map extraction. Harman, Flack, Fox [10] first applied machine learning to the field of depth map extraction. The depth of other pixels is estimated by entering 5 eigenvalues of each pixel of the image (x, y, r, g, b). However, this algorithm only considered local information, didn't combine important depth clues, and ignored the global information of the image. Saxena, Chung, and Ng [11] applied Markov Random Field (MRF) to the field of depth map estimation in 2007, so as to take the global information of images into account the process of depth map extraction.

At present, the extraction methods based on machine learning depth map are mainly divided into two categories: parametric learning method and non-parametric learning method. The following will mainly introduce the extraction process of non-parametric machine learning depth map, and in the depth extraction step, the differences between the two methods and the advantages and disadvantages of each method will be explained in detail.

A. Depth Map Extraction Using a Single Clue

(1) **Parametric Learning Algorithm**

- Advantages: Considering the global information of image.

- Disadvantages: too many parameters, long training time, poor real-time performance.

Saxena, Chung, and Ng [11] used patch as the unit to extract the depth map. Firstly, local features and relative features of the image block were extracted (Local features correspond to texture, focus, gradient and other depth clues of the image block. Relative feature represents the relation of relative depth between image blocks), as in Fig. 5.

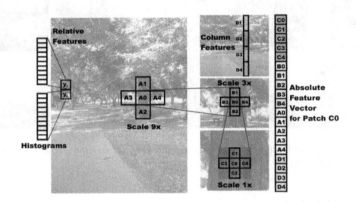

Fig. 5. The absolute depth feature vector for a patch, which includes features from its immediate neighbors and its more distant neighbors (at larger scales). The relative depth features for each patch use histograms of the filter outputs.

Having considered the relationship between the depth of each block and the depth of adjacent blocks, they proposed two models, one of which was Laplace model. The formula was as follows:

$$P(d|X; \theta, \lambda) = \frac{1}{Z} \exp \left(- \sum_{i=1}^{M} \frac{\left| d_i(1) - x_i^T \theta_r \right|}{2} - \sum_{s=1}^{3} \sum_{i=1}^{M} \sum_{j \in N_s(i)} \frac{\left| d_i(s) - d_j(s) \right|}{\lambda_{2rs}} \right)$$

(1)

Here, M is the total number of patches in the image (at the lowest scale); x_i is the absolute depth feature vector for patch I; and θ is parameters of the model. In detail, different parameter θ_r for each row is in the image. Z is the normalization constant for the model. λ_{1r} and λ_{2rs} are the Laplacian spread parameters.

(2) **Non-parametric Learning Algorithm**

- Advantages: Simple learning model.
- Disadvantages: The library image and the target image on the spatial structure have a certain similarity, but local differences.

In 2013, Konrad, Wang, and Ishwar [12] proposed a depth estimation algorithm based on non-parametric machine learning method. This algorithm calculated the

Euclidean distance between the HOG descriptor of the target image [13] and the HOG descriptor of each image in the training data set, and then found out k depth images closest to the target image in global image attributes such as color, texture and edge features in the image library, as in Fig. 6.

Fig. 6. RGB image and depth field of four 2D queries (left column), and their four nearest neighbors (columns 2-5).

B. Depth Map Fusion
Konrad, Wang, and Ishwar [12] first used the median filter method for deep fusion of the k depth maps. Then the depth values of similar regions in the image library are matched by the color, texture and other image features.

C. Depth Map Filtering
After the depth map fusion, the initial depth map needs to be filtered to ensure smooth edges. Such as adaptive filtering, cross/joint bilateral filtering and other methods.

4   Summary of New Methods

In recent years, scholars have proposed many improved algorithms to address the deficiencies of the methods that we discussed above.

In the data processing process, in order to improve the speed of image matching, Herrera et al. [14] extracted various Features of the data, including HOG, LBP, Gist, and SURF. Then k-means algorithm was used to cluster the extracted features. Finally, parameter training was carried out to improve the classification effect, and the matching model between image features and depth information was obtained.

In the process of model training, in order to classify database images more accurately, Liu, Lin, Zhang, Izquierdo [15] used the method of SVM to classify indoor images according to the rules of linear perspective clues. In order to better match database images, Yuan, Wu, and Zhu [16] proposed a monocular image depth estimation algorithm based on semantic segmentation and depth migration. Scale Invariant Feature Transform (SIFT) is utilized to represent an image in multi-scale form.

In the process of deep fusion, Xu, Jiang, Li [17] gave different weights to k similar depth maps in order to obtain more accurate initial depth map.

In the process of refining depth map, Xu, Jiang, Li [17] divided the input 2D images through the Density Based Spatial Clustering of Applications with a Noise clustering algorithm (DBSCAN), and finally improved the initial depth map according to the results of image segmentation.

5 Prospect

Currently, due to the variety of 2D images/videos content and complexity of scene structure, no matter which method for depth map extraction is used, it will have its disadvantages. Therefore, these methods are all used to find a perfect balance between accuracy and timeliness in a particular situation.

The new method for depth map extraction presents the following trends:

(1) By establishing a more complete scene classification system, different depth map extraction methods are used for images of different scenes and structures to obtain depth information.

(2) More detailed refinements are applied on existing depth map extraction methods, including increasing the diversity of feature extraction, improving the accuracy of images classification and the application of new depth cues.

(3) In the new field, the Convolutional Neural Network (CNN) is applied to the depth estimation. For example, in the aspect of unmanned driving, Yao, Sun, Fang [18] proposed a depth estimation algorithm based on Deep Convolution-Deconvolution Neural Network for depth estimation of night scenes. In the image depth estimation of foggy scenes, Cai, Xu, Jia, Qing, and Tao [19] designed an end-to-end Convolutional Neural Network model (DehazeNet) to generate depth map in the fog.

It can be foreseen that with the rapid development of depth map extraction's technology and the innovative attempts of scholars, there will be better solutions for depth map extraction.

References

1. Herrera, J.L., Del-Blanco, C.R., García, N.: Automatic depth extraction from 2D images using a cluster-based learning framework. IEEE Trans. Image Process. **319**, 3288–3299 (2018)
2. Cozman, F., Krotkov, E.: Depth from scattering. In: IEEE Computer Society Conference on Computer Vision and Pattern Recognition, pp. 801–806. IEEE Press, San Juan (1997)
3. Choe, Y., Kashyap, R.L.: Shape from textured and shaded surface. In: 10th International Conference on Pattern Recognition, pp. 294–296. IEEE Press, Atlantic City (1990)
4. Battiato, S., Curti, S., Cascia, M.L., Tortora, M., Scordato, E.: Depth map generation by image classification. In: SPIE International Society for Optical Engineering. San Jose, CA, pp. 95–104 (2004)

5. Han, K., Hong, K.: Geometric and texture cue based depth-map estimation for 2D to 3D image conversion. In: IEEE International Conference on Consumer Electronics, pp. 651–652. IEEE Press, ChiangMai (2011)
6. Ji, P., Wang, L., Li, D., Zhang, M.: An automatic 2D to 3D conversion algorithm using multi-depth cues. In: Proceedings of International Conference on Audio, Language and Image Processing, pp. 546–550. IEEE Press, Shanghai (2012)
7. Wafa, A., Nasiopoulos, P., Leung, V.C., Pourazad, M.T.: Automatic real-time 2D-to-3D conversion for scenic views. In: 7th International Workshop on Quality of Multimedia Experience, pp. 1–5. IEEE Press, Costa Navarino (2015)
8. Levin, A., Lischinski, D., Weiss, Y.: A closed-form solution to natural image matting. IEEE Trans. Pattern Anal. Mach. Intell. **350**, 228–242 (2008)
9. Chang, Y.-L., Chen, W.-Y., Chang, J.-Y., Tsai, Y.-M., Lee, C.-L., Chen, L.-G.: Priority depth fusion for the 2D to 3D conversion system. In: Proceedings of SPIE 3D Image Capture Applications, p. 680513 (2008)
10. Harman, P.V., Flack, J., Fox, S.: Rapid 2D-to-3D conversion. In: Proceeding of SPIE, pp. 78–86. Society of Photo-Optical Instrumentation Engineers Press, San Jose (2002)
11. Saxena, A., Chung, S.H., Ng, A.Y.: Learning depth from single monocular images. In: International Conference on Neural Information Processing Systems, Taiwan (2005)
12. Konrad, J., Wang, M., Ishwar, P.: 2D-to-3D image conversion by learning depth from examples. In: Proceedings of IEEE Computer Society Conference on Computer Vision and Pattern Recognition Workshops, pp. 16–22. IEEE Press, Providence (2012)
13. Dalal, N., Triggs, B.: Histograms of oriented gradients for human detection. In: Proceedings of IEEE Computer Society Conference on Computer Vision and Pattern Recognition, pp. 886–893. IEEE Press, San Diego (2005)
14. Herrera, J.L., del-Blanco, C.R., García, N.: A novel 2D to 3D video conversion system based on a machine learning approach. IEEE Trans. Consum. Electron. **736**, 429–436 (2016)
15. Liu, Y., Lin, X., Zhang, Q., Izquierdo, E.: Improved indoor scene geometry recognition from single image based on depth map. In: Proceedings of Image, Video, and Multidimensional Signal Processing, pp. 1–4. IEEE Press, Seoul (2013)
16. Yuan, H.X., Wu, S.Q., Yu, H.Q.: Semantic-level depth migration 2D to 3D algorithm. J. Comput.-Aided Des. Comput. Graph. **301**, 72–80 (2014)
17. Xu, H., Jiang, M., Li, F.: Depth estimation algorithm based on data-driven approach and depth cues for stereo conversion in three-dimensional displays. Opt. Eng. **55**, 123106 (2016)
18. Yao, G.S., Sun, S.Y., Fang, J.N.: Depth estimation of night unmanned vehicle scene based on infrared and radar. Laser Optoelectron. Progress. **312**, 158–164 (2017)
19. Cai, B., Xu, X., Jia, K., Qing, C., Tao, D.: DehazeNet: an end-to-end system for single image haze removal. IEEE Trans. Image Process. **299**, 5187–5198 (2016)

Sugarcane Node Identification Based on Structured Learning Model

Xiao Hu[1], Shuqin Li[1(✉)], Meili Wang[1,2,3], Changyou Shi[1],
Jing Shang[1], Yunhua Pei[1], Ganran Deng[4], and Deqiang Zhou[5]

[1] Department of Information and Engineering, Northwest A&F University,
Yangling 712100, China
lsq_cie@nwsuaf.edu.cn
[2] Key Laboratory of Agricultural Internet of Thing, Ministry of Agriculture
Rural Affairs, Yangling 712100, China
[3] Shaanxi Key Laboratory of Agricultural Information Perception
and Intelligent Services, Yangling 712100, China
[4] Argo-machinery Research Institute of Chinese Academy of Tropical
Agricultural Science, Zhanjiang 524091, China
[5] School of Mechanical Engineering, Jiangnan University, Wuxi 214122, China

Abstract. Sugarcane node identification is the key techniques for sugarcane cultivation mechanization. The accurate position of nodes that link two consecutive sections should be detected and transferred to microcontroller for cutting. However, current research fails to identify the sugarcane nodes for different kinds of sugarcanes and especially for those under complex background conditions. A novel approach proposed in this work is to recognize nodes of different sugarcanes under complicated background. Firstly, the sugarcane features are extracted, including the target region, target slope and sugarcane node height. Secondly, the edge probability image is generated using the structured learning model, which is trained by a dataset of labeled sugarcane images and dataset BSDS500. Thirdly, the node position is obtained using heuristic line detector. Experiments show the full recognition rate is about 90%, and the location accuracy is less than 36 pixels, which can be further applied to the automation of sugarcane cutting machines.

Keywords: Sugarcane node identification · Structured learning · Computer vision

1 Introduction

Sugarcane cultivation, in a traditional manner, is a laborious work and suffers myriad economic cost. With the achievement in computer vision, sugarcane planting has gradually shifted from manual work to mechanization. In the process of mechanical cutting, accurate sugarcane node identification is a necessity. There are several factors such as random scratches on sugarcane skin, uneven distribution of wax powder, texture chaos, and curvature of natural sugarcane, which affect the accuracy of sugarcane node identification greatly. The difference between various of sugarcanes is also a great challenge for researchers.

© Springer Nature Singapore Pte Ltd. 2019
Y. Wang et al. (Eds.): IGTA 2019, CCIS 1043, pp. 125–137, 2019.
https://doi.org/10.1007/978-981-13-9917-6_13

Recently, computer vision and machine learning have been widely applied in precision agriculture. Random forest classification has been applied to differentiate three soybean varieties from two pigweeds [1], as well as chlorophyll content prediction [2]. Cheng et al. [3] proposed an approach for pest identification using deep residual learning. Gilbertson and Niekerk [4] provided a method to determining the value of dimensionality reduction for a crop based on machine learning. A study on person reidentification, which is based on Structured learning, was carried out by Paisitkriangkrai et al. [5]. Wang et al. [6] proposed a method for wheat leaf disease segmentation using the K-means clustering. Since Moshashai et al. [7] conducted a preliminary research on sugarcane node recognition, a considerable literature has grown up around the theme of sugarcane node recognition [8–10]. Huang et al. [11] proposed a method, which is based on the Radom transform and morphological operator, to recognize sugarcane nodes. However, previous published studies are limited in a certain type of sugarcane, and only work to simple background. Furthermore, some either perform poorly when applied to another different image backgrounds or require strict sugarcane postures.

The edge detection of sugarcane is critical to the sugarcane node identification. The edge states are very different in various parts of the sugarcane. If it is close to the sugarcane node, the edges are more obvious and approximately vertical with respect to the horizontal axis, but the edge is different in other area. Recently, researches on image contour detection has been investigated [12, 13]. Dollar and Zittnick [14] take the structure present in local image patches to learn both an accurate and efficient edge detector, and it achieves state-of-the-art edge results on the BSDS500 dataset. Many scholars have conducted further research based on their edge detection result [15–17]. This study also adopted structured learning model to conduct edge detection.

The goal of this study is to identify sugarcane nodes for different kinds of sugarcanes under complicated background. The original contributions of this study include (1) proposing a method based on structured learning model to identify the nodes for different kinds of sugarcane, (2) presenting a heuristic line detector for special type line detecting, (3) proposing an approach for sugarcane target region extracting.

2 Materials

2.1 Dataset Preparation

The sugarcane samples are provided by Agro-machinery Research Institute of Chinese Academy of Tropical Agricultural Sciences (Zhanjiang, China). The raw materials were collected from different types of sugarcane and photographed using Canon-D7200 digital camera under both day and night situations. We selected several backgrounds when taking the sugarcane picture.

The data augmentation was conducted by rotated the image with degrees. Moreover, to be more general and robust, noises are added to the background. An original image dataset, containing 3,000 images, was obtained. Sample images are shown in Fig. 1: The images of (a) and (b) were rotated by $-30°$ and $+30°$, respectively. Additionally, Fig. 1(c) and (d) represent two types of sugarcane.

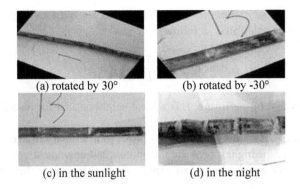

(a) rotated by 30°   (b) rotated by -30°

(c) in the sunlight   (d) in the night

Fig. 1. Sugarcane images in different states

The final dataset for structured learning model consists of BSDS500 dataset and 500 labeled sugarcane images selected randomly from the original image dataset. It was divided into three groups for training, test and validation. They contain 500 samples, 300 samples, 200 samples respectively. In addition, we labeled another 300 sugarcane images for evaluation the performance of our approach.

2.2 Node Location Accuracy Criteria

Each sugarcane node was manually marked by an area. We use the horizontal coordinate distance between the center of the marked area and all horizontal positions of one recognition node as the location accuracy criteria. The formula is following

$$\text{accuracy} = \frac{1}{N} \sum\nolimits_{i=1}^{N} |X_i - X_c|. \tag{1}$$

where X_i is a horizontal coordinate of one identified node, X_c is the horizontal coordinate of the center of the marked area, N is the number of the coordinate for one identified node. If all sugarcane nodes in one image are identified, we refer to it as full recognition.

3 Method

3.1 Extracting Sugarcane Target Region

We present an algorithm to extract the sugarcane target region from original image. The algorithm starts by executing a Canny operator [18]. Two thresholds of the Canny operator, for non-maximum suppression, are given by values greater than the default so that there are less white pixels in the background.

Then, the noise of the binary image was removed by combining a morphological operator and white pixel density filtering. A position is regarded as background if its density is less than half of the average density. This average density is calculated for values of density image except the 70% of lowest values and 10% highest values. The local density can be calculated as follow

$$\text{density}(p) = \frac{1}{|L|} \sum_{i \in L} V(i).$$

(2)

where p is a position of the image, L is a local neighbor area for position p, $V(i)$ is a pixel value.

A histogram is obtained by a horizontal project for a binary image. Two positions of histogram cut for the highest peak are the upmost and downmost vertical coordinates of target region. We use the following expression to determinate these two positions.

$$\underset{P}{\text{argmax}} \{ S^2 * K \}.$$

(3)

where P is a position of the histogram except the position of the highest peak, K is the slope of the line segment with the position P and the peak as endpoint, S is the average value from the position P to the peak.

The target region extraction is shown in Fig. 3, and the algorithm is presented as follow.

Algorithm. extracting target region

Input: An image I, a filter list F, high threshold p, low threshold q, move step s.

output: A target region image R.

BI = Canny operator (I, p, q)

  foreach f in F

      C = Close morphological operator (BI, f)

      D = Computer local density of C

      A = Average the pixel values of D, after discarding 10% of the greatest
           values and 60% of the lowest values

      D = Erase the pixels which is lower than 0.3* A

      BI = BI **and** D

  End

H = Horizontal project of BI

H = Mov sum (H, s)

Peak = Find the highest peak for H

(b, e) = Cut the peak 'Peak' using EQ (3)

R = Clip the image I from b to e rows

3.2 Estimating the Slope, Height of the Target

To calculate of the slope angle, we divide the binary image into 10 blocks along the horizontal direction. Then, we randomly sample 70% of the white pixels for each block. The sampled pixels represent approximate direction of the sugarcane target after linear fitting. The angle between the fitted straight line and horizontal axis is the slope angle.

In terms of node height estimation, we randomly select 70% of image columns. For each column, the distance between the uppermost and the nethermost white pixels is considered as the height of the column. We discard 20% of the lowest and highest height values for reducing the impact of abnormal values, and take the average of the remaining height values as the estimation of the height.

The slope and node height estimation results are shown in Fig. 2. For a given source image, (b) is target region result and the estimated slope line with star markers, (c) is node height estimation marked with circle markers, and the last row are project histogram, reshaped histogram and the highest peak cutting for histogram.

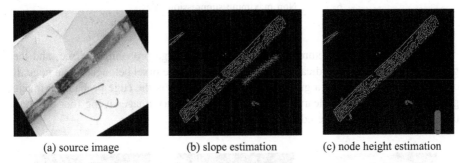

(a) source image   (b) slope estimation   (c) node height estimation

Fig. 2. Sugarcane feature extraction. (a) source image, (b) target region and the estimated slope (star markers), (c) node height estimation, the vertical axis of histograms are white pixel density (normalized).

3.3 Structured Learning Model

An edge probability image can be obtained by using structured random forest [14], which is extended from random forest [19]. The difference is the input and output for the structured random forest model are represent an image block. The structured data is often high-dimensional and complex and is difficult to compare. Hence, the structured data should be mapped to discrete data values first. Similar structures are grouped into the same discrete value, and the number of the discrete values is determined using the K-means algorithm. Additionally, the criteria for splitting a tree node is the information gain which can be calculated as follows

$$I(A) = \{\sum_{Aj=1}^{n_A}[1 - (\frac{|D_{Aj}|}{|D|})^2]\} * (-\sum_{i=1}^{n}\frac{|D_i|}{|D|}\log\frac{|D_i|}{|D|} + \sum_{Aj=1}^{n_A}\frac{|D_{Aj}|}{|D|}\log\frac{|D_{Aj}|}{|D|}). \quad (4)$$

where D represents a training dataset divided into n classes and denotes samples from the same class. A is an attribute, and the training dataset is classified into classes according to attribute A. is a class of samples whose attribute A is assigned with the same value. is the information gain of attribute A.

The BSDS500 dataset and 500 labeled sugarcane images dataset were used to train this model. The important parameter values of the model are illustrated in Table 1. Parameters used in structured random forests.

Table 1. Parameters used in structured random forests

Number	Parameter	Value
1	Trees for training	8
2	Trees for judgment	6
3	Number directions	6
4	Multi-scale flag	1
5	Layers of tree	64
6	Non maximum suppression	Yes

The output of the structured random forest is an edge probability image, and the pixel value of the image indicates the probability how the pixel belonged to an edge. It can be seen in Fig. 3. For a given sugarcane image, (b) is the edge probability image generated from structured learning model, (c–f) are binary images using four different thresholds to binarizing the edge probability image.

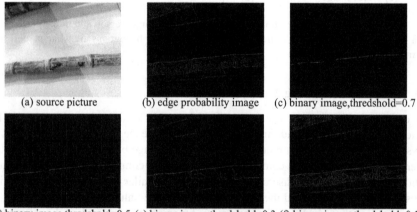

(a) source picture   (b) edge probability image   (c) binary image,thredshold=0.7

(d) binary image,thredshold=0.5 (e) binary image,thredshold=0.3 (f) binary image,thredshold=0.1

Fig. 3. Binary image of different thresholds

3.4 Sugarcane Node Identification

The edge probability image contains abundant information about sugarcane node. However, it is difficult to set a fixed threshold to adapt to various sugarcane scenarios. Our strategy is that the identification is conducted on multiple binary images which are generated from the edge probability image.

Given these parameters: the initial threshold, termination threshold and threshold delta, a series of thresholds are generated, and each threshold was used to binarize the edge probability image. Heuristic algorithm for node location was executed for these binary images.

The edges, which lie near to the sugarcane node, intersect with the horizontal axis at a high angle. This type of edge is the search target of the heuristic algorithm. Prior to the location algorithm, we eliminate the impact from the thick lines by a thinning filter process. Afterward, the heuristic algorithm is used to validate potential area according to confident index. The confident index implies how probability does his type of line appear, and is defined by the formula

$$\text{Confident}(L) = \frac{1}{H} \sum_{i=1}^{H} Q(L, i). \tag{5}$$

with

$$Q(L, i) = \begin{cases} 1, & \text{if } \left\{ \sum_{j=1}^{W} L(i,j) \right\} > 0 \\ 0, & \text{if } \left\{ \sum_{j=1}^{W} L(i,j) \right\} = 0 \end{cases}. \tag{6}$$

where L is a local area of binary image, H, W are the height and width of a local area.

The heuristic algorithm is only executed in areas of the image where the number of white pixels is large enough. In addition, the algorithm only detects the lines intersecting with the x-axis with the slope range from 70° to 110°.

Algorithm.   heuristic algorithm of node location

Input: images *IList*, widths WLlist, confident c, move step s, threshold t.

output: A node location result image *R*.

thin-filter = [1,1,1]

Foreach *I* **in** *IList*

CI = image convolve operate (*I*, thin-filter)

CI = Erase the pixel whose value is equal to sum(thin-filter)
Candidates = GetPotentialPosition (CI, s, t)
Foreach w **in** WLlist
h = tan (70) * w
Foreach p **in** Candidates
    Pat = Clip *CI* from p- w/2 to p+w/2 columns
    Confs = Computer area confident by EQ (5) for all area, with
        size of h, w under move step s in *Pat*
    $R = R$ **or** areas whose area confident is larger than c
    end
  end
end
end

To increase efficiency, we pick the potential candidate positions before the process of line segment validation. The following is the algorithm definition.

Algorithm. GetPotentialPosition

Input: An image I, threshold t, move step s.

output: Candidate positions, Candidates.

P = Vertical project (I)
P = Mov sum (P, s)
Foreach p **in** P

    If P (p) > t
        Candidates = Candidates + p if the position p is a peak
    end
end

3.5 Node Location Optimization

We refine the location results through an optimization process which is based on the line density and the distance between each two consecutive sugarcane nodes. We discard areas where the line density is low as well as these lines with extreme length. The remaining lines are assigned priorities. The more the length of a line segment is close to the estimated node height, the higher priority is assigned. An iteration procedure starts by adding an edge with the highest priority to the final result. Then, at each iteration, an edge with the highest priority among the remaining is selected and added to the final result, if the distances from this edge to each edge of the final result is greater than two times of the estimated node height. After the iteration stopping, the final result is identification.

4 Results and Discussion

4.1 Sugarcane Node Identification

Different types of sugarcane image with a resolution of 1024 by 1280, photographed under different backgrounds, were used in our experiments. Three sample images recognition are illustrated in Fig. 4. From the left to right column, each represents the original sugarcane image, the output from the structured learning model and the final result respectively. The results show that different types of sugarcane nodes can be recognized completely under different backgrounds. The further results in Table 2 show that the average full identification rate is 90% and the average computation time is 2.27 s per image.

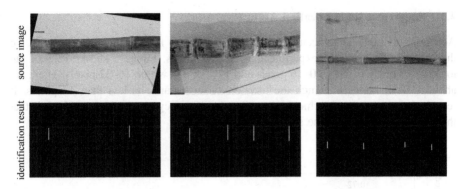

Fig. 4. Kinds of sugarcane node identifications under different backgrounds.

Table 2. Sugarcane identification experiment result.

Experiments	Experiment input		Experiment output	
	Image size	Number of images	Identification rate	Time cost
1	1024 * 1280	71	91%	166.4 s
2	1024 * 1280	71	83%	160.8 s
3	1024 * 1280	71	93%	150.6 s
4	1024 * 1280	72	93%	170.6 s
Average			90%	2.27 s

The result demonstrates that the edges of sugarcane are good feature for identification task, since the morphological characteristics of the edges in sugarcane node are different from the other region. However, if there is similar edge in sugarcane section area, it will generate pseudo identification; if the edges near node is faint enough, the node will be missed. Because of the complexity and diversity of sugarcane texture, it may miss or introduce a few sugarcane nodes during the process of selecting threshold to binarize the edge probability image. Furthermore, we attribute the less time consumption to heuristic line detector and target region extraction. The step of region of interest extraction saves execution time because much computation is executed on the target area instead of the whole image. Heuristic line detector is executed only on potential positions instead of all position of the image.

This approach works well for different types of sugarcanes under different background situations, because of using the white pixel distribution feature and the edges, which is irrelevant the color feature. Moreover, because of using the density information, our method can filter out noises such as the disturbing edges, number characters, shadows in the background.

4.2 Sugarcane Node Location Accuracy

According to the location accuracy criteria and accuracy levels defined in Sect. 2.2, we did the location accuracy experiment using 282 nodes. Figure 5 shows 72% of the location accuracy is within 0–16 pixels and 17% of it is within 16–32 pixels. There are about 93% of nodes of which the location offset distance is less than 48 pixels. It reveals that our approach achieves great location accuracy. An explanation for it is that the edges are adjacent to the sugarcane node tightly.

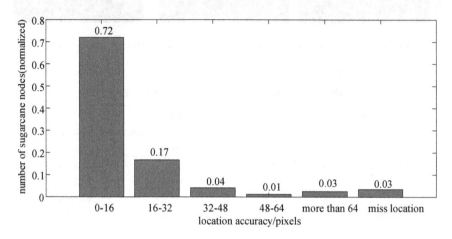

Fig. 5. Sugarcane node location accuracy in various levels, 0–16 pixels, 16–32 pixels, 32–48 pixels, 48–64 pixels, more than 64 pixels location accuracy. The most right indicates node missing (282 sugarcane images).

However, there are a few portions of location accuracies that are larger than 48 pixels. The reason is that edges near sugarcane node have a certain small distance away from center position of node in some situations.

4.3 Parameters Discussion

We conducted the experiment using 945 sugarcane edge probability images to discuss the parameters using in binarizing process. We specified the threshold range [0.9, 0.1] and the threshold delta was set to −0.02. We counted the number of white pixels of the image which was binarized from the edge probability image. Figure 6 presents the tendency of the number of white pixels. It grows slowly at the beginning but change sharply at a certain position range. The dramatic change is because the interference edges of the sugarcane section appear. The value 0.02 is chosen as threshold delta after analysis from the Table 3. However, it may cost more time execution, if we choose 0.01.

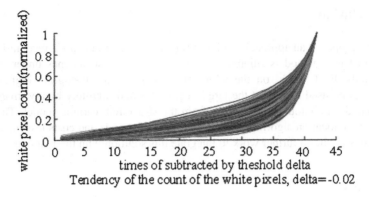

Fig. 6. Edge pixel count tendency and median position histogram

Table 3. Identification rate under different threshold deltas

Delta	0.05	0.04	0.03	0.02	0.01
Identification	86%	85%	86.2%	90%	90.56%

4.4 Sugarcane Node Contour Detection

We compared the contour generated by model trained by different datasets: the sugarcane images mixed with the BSDS500 dataset and the BSDS500 dataset. In Fig. 7, the F-score is 0.71, if the model trained by mixed dataset. But The F-score is 0.68, if the model trained by BSDS500 dataset. A possible explanation for this is that the sugarcane image dataset embodies a complement information into the structured learning model when the model is trained using sugarcane images and BSDS500.

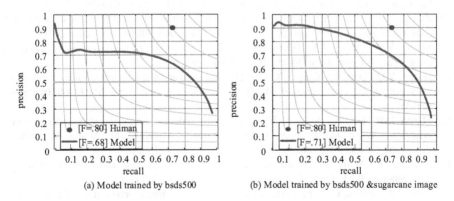

Fig. 7. F-scores of the structured learning model trained by different dataset

5 Conclusions

This study proposed an approach, aim to complete the task of the node recognition. It is verified that the method is suitable for different types of sugarcanes under different backgrounds. First, based on the white pixels density, the histogram highest peak analysis can be used to extract the target region. Second, multiply binary image were gained based on contour image output from the structured learning model. Third, the heuristic node location algorithm succeeds to locate the node and costs less time. In the next stage, we will do further work to integrate this solution with the planting machine.

References

1. Fletcher, R.S., Reddy, K.N.: Random forest and leaf multispectral reflectance data to differentiate three soybean varieties from two pigweeds. Comput. Electron. Agric. **128**, 199–206 (2016)
2. Dario, P., Maria, C., Bernardo, P., et al.: Contactless and non-destructive chlorophyll content prediction by random forest regression: a case study on fresh-cut rocket leaves. Comput. Electron. Agric. **140**, 303–310 (2017)
3. Cheng, X., Zhang, Y., Chen, Y., et al.: Pest identification via deep residual learning in complex background. Comput. Electron. Agric. **141**, 351–356 (2017)
4. Gilbertson, J.K., Niekerk, A.V.: Value of dimensionality reduction for crop differentiation with multi-temporal imagery and machine learning. Comput. Electron. Agric. **142**, 5–58 (2017)
5. Paisitkriangkrai, S., Wu, L., Shen, C., et al.: Structured learning of metric ensembles with application to person re-identification. Comput. Vis. Image Underst. **156**(C), 51–65 (2017)
6. Wang, M., Guo, S., Niu, X.: Detection of wheat leaf disease. ICIC Express Lett. Part B Appl. Int. J. Res. Surv. **6**, 1669–1675 (2015)
7. Moshashai, K., Almasi, M., Minaei, S., et al.: Identification of sugarcane nodes using image processing and machine vision technology. Int. J. Adv. Res. **3**(5), 357–364 (2008)
8. Lu, S.P., Wen, Y.X., Ge, W., et al.: Recognition and features extraction of sugarcane nodes based on machine vision. Trans. Chin. Soc. Agric. Mach. **41**(10), 190–194 (2010)
9. Zhang, W.Z., Dong, S.Y., Qi, X.X., et al.: The identification and location of sugarcane internode based on image processing. J. Agric. Mech. Res. **38**(04), 217–221 (2016)
10. Huang, Y.Q., Huang, T.S., Huang, M.Z., et al.: Recognition of sugarcane nodes based on local mean. J. Chin. Agric. Mech. **38**(2), 76–80 (2017)
11. Huang, Y.Q., Qiao, X., Tang, S.X., et al.: Localization and test of characteristics distribution for sugarcane internode based on MATLAB. Trans. Chin. Soc. Agric. Mach. **44**(10), 93–97 (2013)
12. Martin, D.R., Fowlkes, C.C., Malik, J.: Learning to detect natural image boundaries using brightness, color and textures. In: International Conference on Neural Information Processing Systems, vol. 26, pp. 1279–1286. MIT Press (2002)
13. Arbeláez, P., Maire, M., Fowlkes, C., et al.: Contour detection and hierarchical image segmentation. IEEE Trans. Pattern Anal. **33**(5), 898–916 (2011)
14. Dollar, P., Zitnick, C.L.: Fast edge detection using structured forests. IEEE Trans. Pattern Anal. **37**(8), 1558–1570 (2014)

15. Zitnick, C.L., Dollár, P.: Edge boxes: locating object proposals from edges. In: Fleet, D., Pajdla, T., Schiele, B., Tuytelaars, T. (eds.) ECCV 2014. LNCS, vol. 8693, pp. 391–405. Springer, Cham (2014). https://doi.org/10.1007/978-3-319-10602-1_26
16. Hosang, J., Benenson, R., Dollar, P., et al.: What makes for effective detection proposals? IEEE Trans. Pattern Anal. **38**(4), 814–830 (2015)
17. Xie, S., Tu, Z.: Holistically-nested edge detection. In: International Conference on Computer Vision, vol. 125, pp. 395–1403. IEEE (2016)
18. Canny, J.: A computational approach to edge detection. IEEE Trans. Pattern Anal. **8**(6), 679–698 (1986)
19. Breiman, L.: Random forests. Mach Learn. **45**(1), 5–32 (2001)

3D Human Pose Estimation
with Grouping Regression

Xuesheng He, Huabin Wang$^{(\boxtimes)}$, Yuan Qin, and Liang Tao

Key Laboratory of Intelligent Computing and Signal Processing
of Ministry of Education, Anhui University, Hefei 230031, China
wanghuabin@ahu.edu.cn

Abstract. Most of the methods for predicting the 3D human pose from single picture are to first extract the 2d joint position in the image, and then use the 2d joint coordinates to get the 3d joint position. This type of method focuses on learning the mapping from 2d to 3d, and neglects the kinematic properties of the joints. Combined with the independent characteristics of human limb joint motion, we adopt the structure of grouping regression. The limbs and trunk were divided into different joint groups, and the 3d position of the joints in each group was predicted separately. In order to make the prediction results are closer to the real human posture, we use BiLSTM to design a human joint self-constrained network to adjust prediction results and improve accuracy. Experiments show that the method of grouping regression combined with self-constrained network is superior to the current advanced method.

Keywords: 3D pose · Grouping regression · Self-constraint

1 Introduction

3D human pose estimation is a challenging subject to computer vision, which can be applied in the fields of virtual reality, motion recognition and man-machine interaction. The difficulty of this subject is that the collected images are two-dimensional signals and it is hard to extract the depth information of human body. Early methods use various invariant features such as contour [1], shape [2], SIFT [3], HOG [4] to reconstruct human body pose. Although it is easy to implement, it has the disadvantages of high algorithm complexity and low efficiency. In recent years, deep learning has been applied to 3d body posture estimation and achieved amazing results. There are two main methods involved.

(1) Learning end-to-end networking. The principle is that the 2d image is directly used as input to predict 3d joint position. For example, Li et al. [5] proposed a multi-task convolution network structure. The convolution layer is shared and the results are used for joint prediction and detection. Their method jointly controls

This work was supported in part by the National Nature Science Foundation of China under Grant 61372137 and in part by the Natural Science Foundation of Anhui Province, China, under Grant 1908085MF209.

© Springer Nature Singapore Pte Ltd. 2019
Y. Wang et al. (Eds.): IGTA 2019, CCIS 1043, pp. 138–149, 2019.
https://doi.org/10.1007/978-981-13-9917-6_14

the learning process from various aspects, improves the accuracy of the prediction results, and proves the feasibility of the 3d human pose prediction scheme combined with deep learning. However, limited by the relatively basic network structure, there is a certain distance between the predicted results and the real data. Pavlakos et al. [6] extended the method of 2d joint detection to 3d pose prediction. The 3D joint position is represented by a three-dimensional voxel, and the output of the network is a Gaussian heat map of 3d joints. This method effectively reduces the predicted 3d joint error. But it needs to store and calculate a large number of parameters, which require higher requirements on the machine and require longer training time.

The end-to-end network can obtain sufficient information in images, but it is difficult to obtain 3d pose ground-truth. Existing data sets are collected in a laboratory environment, so the trained models are not suitable for outdoor activity scenes. Chen et al. [7] proposed an automatic image synthesis method based on 3d ground-truth to alleviate the problem. However, the synthesized picture does not achieve the performance of a real picture.

(2) 3d pose estimation based on 2d joints location. The method firstly extracts 2d joints from images, and then lifts the 2d joint into three dimensions. For example, Moreno-Noguer et al. [8] transforms the 3d human pose estimation problem into a regression problem between two Euclidean distance matrices. Encode the two-way distance of the human joints, and then, network learning regression process from 2d distance matrix to 3d distance matrix. Zhou et al. [9] designed a unified model for step-by-step training. The model can be trained again to predict 3d joint position based on the trained 2d joint detection model. This method enables the 3d joint prediction to make full use of the parameters set in the 2d joint prediction network. In addition, in order to study the mapping relationship between 2d joints and 3d joints, Martinez et al. [10] has designed a good regression network by combining existing network optimization techniques. The network can obtain accurate 3D poses only with the 2D pose as input.

Since the 2d pose estimation has achieved remarkable results, a high-precision 2d pose can be obtained. Therefore, using 2d joints data to rebuild 3d poses can greatly reduce the error of prediction results. However, this kind of method focuses on exploring the mapping from 2d to 3d, neglects the kinematic properties of the joints. In actually, the movement of the human limbs is independent. For example, when the left hand is making a fixed posture, the right hand can still swing freely without being disturbed by the left hand. Combining the feature of human movement, we propose the concept of grouping regression.

As is shown in Fig. 1, the 3d joints to be predicted were grouped, and the 3d joint locations of different groups were respectively regressive by using 2d joints. Subsequently, the predicted 3d points were fused to obtain the whole body joints. Regressing different groups of joints independently can avoid internal confusion during training and can improve robustness. In addition, sufficiently utilizing the 2d joint data can deepen the influence on 3d pose estimation, effectively make up the defects of single input data and few features.

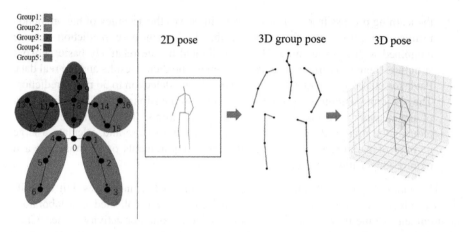

Fig. 1. A diagram of grouping regression. The limbs and trunk were divided into different joint groups, and the 3d joint positions of different groups were obtained by regressing the 2d pose. Finally, different groups of 3d joints were fused.

Although the movement of human limbs is theoretically independent of each other, it has certain coordination in daily activities. For example, humans habitually move their right hand forward as they step out of the left leg during walking. In addition, human joint movement also has its own constraints. Such as the length of limb and rotation angle of knee-joint. Fang et al. [11] designed a grammar network based on the bidirectional recurrent neural network (BRNN) to learn the constraints between human joints and adjust the prediction results of the regression network. Fang et al. verified that the BRNN has an excellent ability to learn the inherent characteristics of human joints. However, due to the low accuracy of the 3d joint obtained by the regression network in [11], the grammar network has limited ability to adjust the prediction results. In this paper, we designed the joint self-constrained network using BiLSTM, and adjusted the input method with the output of grouping regression, so that the self-constrained network structure can better learn the connection between human joints.

We have carried out detailed experiments in the public body posture dataset, for example, Human3.6M [12], MPII [13], etc. Quantitative evaluations were performed on the Human3.6M dataset with 3d joints ground-truth, including joint errors at corresponding points, and the effect of noise points on the model. For the MPII dataset, due to the lack of 3d real data for comparison, we only displayed qualitative result. The experimental results show that the proposed method is greatly improved on the basis of [10] and significantly reduces the estimation error.

Contributions: 1. The structure of grouping regression is used to solve the internal error of the joint generated by the network during training, and deeply decouple the dependence between joint points. 2. The joint self-constraint network is used to adjust the prediction results of the regression network, so that the predicted 3d joints can meet the natural constraints of human motion.

2 Related Work

3D human pose prediction methods can be roughly divided into two types, end-to-end model and two-step model. In this paper, we choose two-step model and make innovations based on our predecessors. Here is the latest related work.

2.1 2D to 3D Joints

The problem of inferring 3d joints from their 2d projections can be traced back to the classic work of Lee and Chen [14]. They showed that, given the bone lengths, the problem boils down to a binary decision tree where each split corresponds to two possible states of a joint with respect to its parent. Jiang [15] used a large database of poses to resolve ambiguities based on nearest neighbor queries. However, both of these methods only obtain rough 3D poses and cannot accurately extract position coordinates. [16, 17] regards the problem as a constrained optimization problem by minimizing the unknown 3D pose and the unknown camera 2D projection error. Such optimization-based approaches could be sensitive to initialization and local minima, and often require expensive constrained solvers. Martinez et al. [10] combined with the existing network optimization strategy to design a well-structured network, with 2d joints as input, fully learn the mapping relationship from 2d to 3d. The model is accurate and efficient, and the training time required is short, but they did not take into account the nature of human joint movement. In theory, the joints of the limbs can move independently of each other without interference. If the model processes the joints of the whole body at one time, some joints are erroneously affected by others during the training, causing deviations in the results. In order to avoid this phenomenon, we use the same structure of the network to respectively regress limbs and trunk nodes, reduce the error effect between unrelated joints, and strengthen the connection between related joints. This method can greatly improve the accuracy of prediction results.

2.2 Related Constraints

Since the image and the 2d joint data do not have depth information, 3d joints prediction is ambiguous. For example, two different 3d poses have the same 2d projection. Increasing the associated constraints can effectively limit the occurrence of similar situations and accurately recover 3d joints from 2d data. In [18], the limitation of the joint rotation angle of the human elbow and knee is used to help the reconstruction of the human joints. [9] designed the loss function to help train the network by adding the bone length constraint. [17] trained Gaussian model of human body posture in advance as a priori to avoid some low-probability and error-prone posture. These explicit coding constraints have certain effects, but they are relatively unitary and cannot greatly improve the predicted results. [11] built a grammar network which can adaptively learn human motion constraint, coordination constraint and joint symmetry constraint by using BRNN. This method shows that the BRNN is very suitable for the learning of

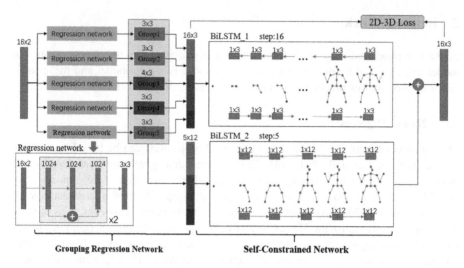

Fig. 2. Model schematic. The model is mainly composed of two parts: grouping regression network and joint self-constrained network.

joint constraints. It can not only adaptively learn the explicit constraints of human motion, but also can understand the intrinsic connection between the joints. In this paper, a similar treatment is performed for the predicted 3d joints. We use BiLSTM to design a self-constrained network combined with packet regression data. And the input mode and structure of the network were adjusted to obtain more accurate results.

3   Framework

The overall structure will be introduced from four parts, including data processing and two parts of the network structure: grouping regression network and joint self-constrained network, as well as the final network training process.

3.1   Data Processing

The model in this paper is a two-step plan. The 2d data were obtained from the stack hour-glass network proposed in [23] and fine-tuned through the human3.6m dataset. The output of the model is the 3-dimensional coordinate position of the 17 major joints of the human body. Since the error mainly comes from the distance error between the predicted 3d joints and the 3d joints ground-truth when the root joint is aligned. We used the same processing method as [10] to standardize the training data, and then predicted coordinates of the remaining 16 human main joints relative to the root joint through the network. Therefore, the root joint(coccyx) is not classified into any group in Fig. 1.

3.2   Grouping Regression Network

The regression network takes the coordinates of the 2d joint point as input. Due to the high precision of the input 2d joint points, the performance of the regression network can be effectively improved. However, the influence between human joints is not balanced. If the network ignores this imbalance and processes all the joints at the same time, it will produce wrong influence among some joints with weak relevance. In order to avoid this phenomenon, we divided the highly correlated joints into the same group, and used the regression network to train each group independently. As shown in Fig. 1, the joints are divided into 5 groups according to the order of joints provided by the dataset.

$$group\_1(r.leg) : 1 \rightarrow 2 \rightarrow 3 \tag{1}$$

$$group\_2(l.reg) : 4 \rightarrow 5 \rightarrow 6 \tag{2}$$

$$group\_3(\text{torso}) : 7 \rightarrow 8 \rightarrow 9 \rightarrow 10 \tag{3}$$

$$group\_4(l.\text{arm}) : 11 \rightarrow 12 \rightarrow 13 \tag{4}$$

$$group\_5(r.arm) : 14 \rightarrow 15 \rightarrow 16 \tag{5}$$

Subsequently, as shown in the left half of Fig. 2, the 2d joint repeatedly input into the five regression networks with the same structure to obtain different sets of 3d joints positions. Grouping regression can fully guarantee the characteristic of independence of movement of human limbs, deeply elaborate the influence of strongly related joints, and eliminate the error effects of unrelated and weakly related joints during training. Finally, the 3d position of the five sets of joints are combined into an overall joint vector as a result of the prediction of the packet regression network. The function of grouping regression is expressed as follows:

$$(g_1, g_2, g_3, g_4, g_5) = R(y_{2d}) \tag{6}$$

$$Y_{\text{reg}} = M_1(g_1, g_2, g_3, g_4, g_5) \tag{7}$$

y_{2d} expressed as a 2d joint point input. g_1, g_2, g_3, g_4, g_5 are respectively represented as 3d joints outputs of different groups.R represents the regression network. M_1 represents the process of merging each group of joints. We continue the structure of the regression network [10]. First, the input 2d joints are passed through a linear layer, and its dimension is increased to 1024. Then there are two consecutive residual connections [19] to increasing the depth of the network. Finally, a linear layer outputs the 3d joint position of the corresponding joint group. The regression network uses batch normalization [20], dropout [21], Rectified Linear Units (RELUs) [22] and other very practical network optimization strategies at present, which greatly reduces the error of the output results.

3.3   Self-constrained Network

In addition to further exploring the connection between 2d joints and 3d joints, adding the constraints of the human joints can also significantly reduce the error and super-vise the learning of the network. For example, Dabral et al. [23] added the constraint of the rotation angle of the joint point and the balance of the bone length. Although this hard-coded constraint is very effective, it is not comprehensive enough. The grammar net-work designed by Fang et al. [11] takes the predicted 3d joints as input and sets up multi-layer BRNN to fully learn the motion constraints, symmetry constraints and coordination constraints of human joints. The constraint learned through the network can better adjust the predicted 3d joint. The research of [11] shows that the BRNN has excellent ability to learn self-constraint of joints. Inspired by [11], we combine the results of grouping regression to construct two joint self-constrained network structures using BiLSTM (the transformation of the BRNN). They are joint point self-constrained network and joint group self-constrained network. The joint point self-constrained network takes single joint point as single-step input with step size of 16. And the joint group self-constrained network takes a single group of joints as single-step input with step size of 5. LSTM has the feature of selective forgetting, so BiLSTM can peel away the parts with less influence between joints and is more sensitive to the parts with strong correlations. In addition, comp-ared with Fang [11] who used repeated full-body 3d joints as the input of the BRNN, taking a single joint or a single set of joints as input ensures that the data input at each step will not be repeated, which is more consistent with the characteristics of the input mode of the RNN and can contribute to learning the connection between joints. The right half of Fig. 2 shows the structure of a self-constrained network. Since the data dimensions of the 5 groups of joints obtained by grouping regression were inconsistent, a parent joint is added to $group\_1$, $group\_2$, $group\_3$, $group\_4$ and $group\_5$ respectively before being used as the input of the joint group self-constrained network. The five groups of joints are then fused into a 5×12 vector Y_{group}. The formula is as follows:

$$Y_{group} = M_2(g_1, g_2, g_3, g_4, g_5) \tag{8}$$

$$Y_{res} = w_1 B_1(Y_{reg}) + w_2 B_2(Y_{group}) \tag{9}$$

The M_2 represents the merging process of grouped data. B_1 and B_2 represent joint point self-constrained networks and joint group self-constrained networks respect-ively. w_1 and w_2 represent the weights of the output layers of the two BiLSTMs.

3.4   Network Training Process

The input to the network is the 2d joint position $y_{2d} \in R^{16 \times 2}$. After passing the grouping regression network and the self-constrained network, the two 3d joints positions are obtained, which are Y_{res} and $Y_{group} \in R^{16 \times 3}$. The loss function is designed as the Euclidean distance between the predicted 3d joints and the 3d joints ground-truth.

$$loss = \sum_{N} ((Y_{reg} - Y_t)^2 + (Y_{res} - Y_t)^2) \tag{10}$$

During training, the loss function is minimized by gradient descent until convergence. N is the data volume of a single batch, set to 64. The learning rate was initially set at 1e−3 and gradually decreased with the progress of training. After the experiment, we found that a slight overfitting phenomenon appeared when the cycle number was too large, so we set the cycle number at 160 to obtain more accurate results.

4   Experiment and Analysis

This paper attempts to estimate the 3d pose of the human from single image. First, the 2d joint detector is used to obtain the position of the main joint of the human in the picture. Then the 3d pose of the human body is obtained by using the 2d position information of joints. The main work of this paper is to design a more refined regression model from 2d to 3d. The model is based on TensorFlow, which requires 45 ms for forward+backward pass on GTX1080. The evaluation of the model is based on two large human posture data, which are Human3.6M and MPII. Human3.6m: the largest public dataset of human 3d poses. The dataset consists of 3.6 million images covering 15 daily activities performed by actors, such as walking, eating, sitting, making phone calls and participating in discussions. It provides ground-truth of human joints in 2d and 3d. MPII: it is a standard 2d pose dataset based on thousands of youtube video clips, which contains a large number of character images and manually marked joint location information. The specific experimental results are as follows.

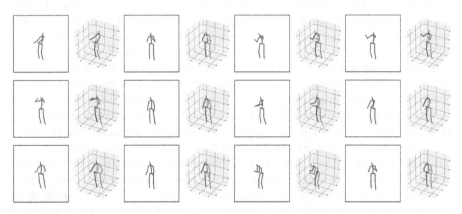

Fig. 3. Shows the predicted effect of the model under the Human3.6M dataset. On the left is the 2d joint diagram, and on the right is the prediction result.

Table 1. Detailed results on Human3.6M under Protocol #1.

	Direct.	Discuss	Eating	Greet	Phone	Photo	Pose	Purch.
Pavlakos et al. [6]	67.4	71.9	66.7	69.1	72.0	77.0	65.0	68.3
Bruce et al. [24]	91.0	88.2	85.7	95.6	103.9	92.4	90.4	117.9
Zhou et al. [9]	54.8	60.7	58.2	71.4	**62.0**	**65.5**	53.8	55.6
Martinez et al. [10]	51.8	56.2	58.1	59.0	69.5	78.4	55.2	58.1
Fang et al. [11]	50.1	**54.3**	57.0	57.1	66.6	73.3	53.4	55.7
Véges et al. [25]	50.1	54.7	56.0	56.5	67.7	76.4	53.1	54.7
Ours (single-point)	50.9	54.8	57.1	57.2	65.6	75.9	53.1	55.3
Ours (only-group)	49.8	54.7	56.4	56.4	65.2	75.2	52.7	54.6
Ours	**49.1**	54.5	**55.9**	**55.7**	64.1	73.4	**51.7**	**54.0**
	Sitting	SitingD	Smoke	Wait	WalkD	Walk	WalkT	Avg.
Pavlakos et al. [6]	83.7	96.5	71.7	65.8	74.9	59.1	63.2	71.9
Bruce et al. [24]	136.4	98.5	103.0	94.4	86.0	90.6	89.5	97.5
Zhou et al. [9]	75.2	111.6	64.1	66.0	**51.4**	63.2	55.3	64.9
Martinez et al. [10]	74.0	94.6	62.3	59.1	65.1	49.5	52.4	62.9
Fang et al. [11]	72.8	88.6	60.3	57.7	62.7	47.5	50.6	60.4
Véges et al. [25]	73.3	93.2	60.4	58.5	62.8	51.5	**48.2**	61.1
Ours (single-point)	70.2	88.3	59.3	56.9	62.0	47.7	50.6	60.6
Ours (only-group)	70.6	88.2	58.7	56.4	61.1	47.2	50.5	59.8
Ours	**69.7**	**86.5**	**58.0**	**55.5**	60.2	**46.3**	48.5	**58.9**

4.1 Standard Protocol Experiment

We train the network based on the human3.6m dataset,and achieved satisfactory results. The predicted results are shown in Fig. 3. It can be seen that the model accurately locate the specific position of the human joint point in 3d space based on the 2d joint information. To evaluate the performance of the model, we tested it in the dataset following standard protocol#1 (protocol#1: use subjects 1, 5, 6, 7, 8 for training and subjects 9, 11 for evaluation. In the case of aligning the root joints, calculating the average Euclidean distance between the predicted 3d joints and the 3d joint ground-truth, in mm). The last line of Table 1 shows our results. The experi-mental results show that our method is superior to some advanced methods in the current, and can significantly reduce the distance error between joint pairs in most active subjects. The penultimate row of Table 1 is the result of only grouping regression, and there is a certain gap compared to the final result. From the opposite side, it proves that the self-constrained network can well adjust the predicted results. In addition, we try to separate strongly related joints. We take a single joint as a group, and generate sixteen 3d joint point using the sixteen regression network. This method is called "single-point regression ". The experimental results are shown in the third row from the bottom of Table 1. Single point regression isolates the joints and breaks the dependence between them, which does not accord with the characteristics of human body movement. Therefore, the structure of single-point regression has a large error.

Table 2. Details of the effect of noise on the model. Baseline is expressed as a model of [10]. GT stands for ground-truth and TM stands for retraining model with noise data.

	Baseline	Ours	Baseline (TM)	Ours (TM)
GT	43.0	38.9	43.0	38.9
GT+N (0,2)	49.7	47.7	46.8	43.6
GT+N (0,4)	64.1	65.1	53.7	51.4
GT+N (0,6)	80.7	84.2	59.6	58.1
GT+N (0,8)	97.5	102.7	65.5	64.3

4.2 Noise Experiment

In Table 2, we examine the effect of noise points on the model. The first two columns evaluate the normal model. We add a corresponding degree of Gaussian noise to the 2d data of verification set, and calculate the error of the predicted 3d joint and the ground-truth. It can be seen that compared with the network of the Martinez et al. [10], our network can achieve amazing accuracy when the noise is small, and the error is slightly larger than [10] when the noise is large. The reason is that our network has a higher utilization of 2d input joints. At the same time, self-constrained networks learn reasonable constraints through noise-free data. When giving a high noise verification set data as input, this constraint is destroyed, and the error is increased. The network of [10] is less affected by its simple structure. In order to further prove that our network has better learning ability, in the last two columns of Table 2, we add differ-rent levels of noise to 2d training data and verification data to retrain the network. It can be seen that after retraining the two models, our model produces less error, even in the case of loud noise. Grouping regression combined with the characteristics of limb movement independence can further interpret the connection between 2d joints and 3d joints. However, the large error destroys this connection, which making the grouping regression has no advantage. In real-life situations, 2d joint data y_{2d} comes from the stack hourglass network. Although y_{2d} has a gap with the ground-truth, its distribution is regular and is not random like a noise point. Stack hourglass network does not break the connection between joints. Therefore, when using y_{2d} as the input data of the model, grouping regression also has excellent performance.

4.3 Outdoor Scene Experiment

In order to observe the predicted effect of the model in the outdoor scene, we select some images of people in the MPII dataset for testing. Since MPII does not have 3d pose ground-truth, the results cannot be qualitatively evaluated. However, it can be observed from Fig. 4 that our method accurately predicts the posture structure of the human body. Although the model in this paper is based on data from the laboratory environment, due to the full use of 2d joints and well-designed self-constrained networks, the model also accurately predicts complex and variable human poses in outdoor environments.

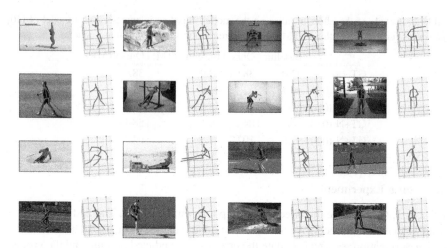

Fig. 4. 3d pose estimation based on outdoor scene character pictures in MPII dataset.

5 Conclusion

In this paper, we propose a method to predict the 3d joint position of the human body from single images based on grouping regression. This method focuses on learning the correlation between joints in the same group and avoids the influence of errors between unrelated joints, and greatly reduces the prediction error. In addition, the self-constrained network designed in combination with grouping regression can learn the inherent connection of human joints, adjust the joint position, and improve the robustness of the model.

References

1. Agarwal, A., Triggs, B.: 3D human pose from silhouettes by relevance vector regression. In: Proceedings of Computer Vision and Pattern Recognition, pp. 882–888 (2004)
2. Mori, G., Malik, J.: Recovering 3D human body configurations using shape contexts. IEEE Trans. Pattern Anal. Mach. Intell. **28**(7), 1052–1062 (2006)
3. Bo, L., Sminchisescu, C., Kanaujia, A., Metaxas, D.: Fast algorithms for large scale conditional 3D prediction. In: IEEE Conference on Computer Vision and Pattern Recognition (2008)
4. Rogez, G., Rihan, J., Ramalingam, S., Orrite, C., Torr, P.: Randomized trees for human pose detection. In: CVPR, pp. 1–8 (2008)
5. Li, S., Chan, A.B.: 3D human pose estimation from monocular images with deep convolutional neural network. In: Asian Conference on Computer Vision, pp. 332–347 (2014)
6. Pavlakos, G., Zhou, X., Derpanis, K. G.: Coarse-to-fine volumetric prediction for single-image 3D human pose. In: IEEE Conference on Computer Vision and Pattern Recognition, pp. 1263–1272 (2017)

7. Chen, W., Wang, H., Li, Y.: Synthesizing training images for boosting human 3D pose estimation. In: Fourth International Conference on 3D Vision (3DV) (2016)
8. Moreno-Noguer, F.: 3D human pose estimation from a single image via distance matrix regression. In: IEEE Conference on Computer Vision and Pattern Recognition (2017)
9. Zhou, X., Huang, Q., Xiao, S.: Towards 3D human pose estimation in the wild: a weakly-supervised approach. In: IEEE International Conference on Computer Vision, pp. 398–407 (2017)
10. Martinez, J., Hossain, R., Romero, J.: A simple yet effective baseline for 3D human pose estimation. In: IEEE International Conference on Computer Vision (2017)
11. Fang, H., Xu, Y., Wang, W., Liu, X., Zhu, S.C.: Learning knowledge-guided pose grammar machine for 3D human pose estimation. In: Proceedings of the AAAI Conference on Artificial Intelligence (2018)
12. Ionescu, C., Papava, D., Olaru, V., Sminchisescu, C.: Human 3.6M: Large scale datasets and predictive methods for 3D human sensing in natural environments. IEEE Trans. Pattern Anal. Mach. Intell. **36**(7), 1325–1339 (2014)
13. Andriluka, M., Pishchulin, L., Gehler, P., Schiele, B.: 2D human pose estimation: new benchmark and state of the art analysis. In: IEEE Conference on Computer Vision and Pattern Recognition, pp. 3686–3693 (2014)
14. Lee, H.J., Chen, Z.: Determination of 3D human body postures from a single view. Comput. Vis. Graph. Image Process. **30**(2), 148–168 (1985)
15. Jiang, H.: 3D human pose reconstruction using millions of exemplars. In: 20th International Conference on Pattern Recognition, pp. 1674–1677 (2010)
16. Wang, C., Wang, Y., Lin, Z., Yuille, A.L., Gao, W.: Robust estimation of 3D human poses from a single image. In: IEEE Conference on Computer Vision and Pattern Recognition, pp. 2369–2376 (2014)
17. Bogo, F., Kanazawa, A., Lassner, C., Gehler, P., Romero, J., Black, M.J.: Keep it SMPL: automatic estimation of 3D human pose and shape from a single image. In: European Conference on Computer Vision (2016)
18. Akhter, I., Black, M.J.: Pose-conditioned joint angle limits for 3D human pose reconstruction. In: IEEE Conference on Computer Vision and Pattern Recognition (CVPR), pp. 1446–1455 (2015)
19. He, K., Zhang, X., Ren, S.: Deep residual learning for image recognition. In: IEEE Conference on Computer Vision and Pattern Recognition (CVPR), pp. 770–778 (2016)
20. Ioffe, S., Szegedy, C.: Batch normalization: accelerating deep network training by reducing internal covariate shift. ArXiv e-prints (2015)
21. Srivastava, N., Hinton, G., Krizhevsky, A.: Dropout: a simple way to prevent neural networks from overfitting. J. Mach. Learn. Res. **15**(1), 1929–1958 (2014)
22. Hinton, G.E.: Rectified linear units improve restricted boltzmann machines Vinod Nair. In: 27th International Conference on International Conference on Machine Learning, pp. 807–814 (2010)
23. Dabral, R., Mundhada, A., Kusupati, U., Afaque, S., Sharma, A., Jain, A.: Learning 3D human pose from structure and motion. In: European Conference on Computer Vision (2017)
24. Xiaohan, N.B., Chun, Z.S., Ping, W.: Monocular 3D human pose estimation by predicting depth on joints. In: IEEE International Conference on Computer Vision (ICCV), pp. 3467–3475 (2017)
25. Véges, M., Varga, V., Lőrincz, A.: 3D human pose estimation with siamese equivariant embedding. arXiv e-print arXiv:1809.07217 (2018)

Vascular Model Editing for 3D Printing Based on Implicit Functions

Beizhan Wang, Qichao Ge, Qingqi Hong$^{(\boxtimes)}$, Yangjing Li,
Kunhong Liu, and Ziyou Jiang

Software School, Xiamen University, Xiamen 361005, China
hongqq@xmu.edu.cn

Abstract. 3D printing can quickly identify prototype to form the geometric model of the blood vessel, and then we use the printed model to do surgery simulation, so as to help the doctor to evaluate the success rate of the operation. However, current modeling technologies of 3D printing are based on explicit modeling method. These explicitly represented models need an extremely complicated geometric transformation before printing, which leads to damage of models. In this paper, we adopt implicit modeling technique to reconstruct the vascular model, and then propose a vascular model editing method for 3D printing, which includes extending the blood vessel inlets and outlets, designing the open section, and constructing the wall. Experimental results show that the extension of the vascular port makes model completely retain the information of the blood vessel inlets and outlets, which facilitate subsequent operation.

Keywords: 3D printing · Implicit modeling · Model editing

1 Introduction

Computer-aided diagnosis technology is based on medical imaging and the assistance of computer technology, such as computer graphics, virtual reality, which have commonly been considered as an effective way for providing high-quality visualization [1]. With the help of these methods, doctors could do preoperative planning, postoperative evaluation, and virtual surgery simulation, thus to improve the success rate of operation. However, if doctors only use image processing, virtual reality and other technologies to analyze the three-dimensional model of blood vessel, the final result may not be very ideal. During preoperative planning, doctors can not accurately evaluate risk and unexpected situations. For example, doctors may also overlook some detailed vessel structure which may lead to serious consequences. It is urgent need to develop more suitable and more accurate vascular models for clinical application and research.

The 3D printing technology has been in existence for over two decades and has been used for engineering and industrial applications [2]. However, the application of such techniques in the area of biomedical devices has been slow due to the stringent

This work was supported in part by the National Natural Science Foundation of China under Grant No. 61502402, 61772023, and 61802322, and the Fundamental Research Funds for the Central Universities under Grant No. 20720180073.

© Springer Nature Singapore Pte Ltd. 2019
Y. Wang et al. (Eds.): IGTA 2019, CCIS 1043, pp. 150–160, 2019.
https://doi.org/10.1007/978-981-13-9917-6_15

performance criteria and concerns related to reproducibility and quality [3]. Traditional 3D printing is utilized for the rapid prototyping of 3D models originally generated by CAD, SolidWorks [4], which cannot represent the objects with very detailed internal structure. When converted into STL files, models are prone to grid disorder, breakage and so on. Those kind of models is not good enough for medical application. Thus, we use implicit modeling to overcome the disadvantages in traditional methods. Implicit representations allow for efficient constructive solid geometry (CSG) operations, which is especially suitable for the 3D modeling of complex organic shapes [5]. Recently, various implicit modeling methods have been developed for reconstructing vascular structures [6].

In this paper, we propose a geometric model editing method based on implicit functions, and perform function operations on the vascular model to meet the requirement of 3D printing, including extension of vessel outlets and inlets, construction of the open section, and thickening of the vessel wall. In order to facilitate the operation of the printed model and retain important information at the beginning and end of vascular model, we propose to extend outlets and inlets without bending. And we also cut the last part of the central lines to make the open vessel orifice, which could easily inject fluid to simulate blood flow. We thicken the vessel wall to facilitate a 3D printer software recognition. After finishing those operations, the model can be printed.

2 Related Work

The combination of 3D printing technology and medical imaging technology brings new opportunities for medical development. The clinical application of this emerging technology is robustly studied in many medical fields.

Martelli et al. conducted a systematic review of articles on 3D printing applications in surgery [7]. A total of 158 studies met the inclusion criteria, 71.5% of which were used for anatomical models and 25.3% for surgical guidance and protocol. Most of the previous model editing was based on explicit modeling. There are many ways to reconstruct the 3D model from 2D images, such as data imaging and communication imaging (DICOM) [8], magnetic resonance angiography (MRA) [9], computed tomography angiography and rotational digital subtraction angiography (DSA) [11]. In order to reduce the number of outlets, Ryan et al. proposed [10] to join up to five vessels into a single flow outlet. Ionita et al. [11] reduced the number of outlets by merging the small vessels in closed loops. Thickening the vessel wall can also use various methods, such as Boolean operators to connect surface [10], thickening the surface of each triangle [11]. Boolean operations are also good way to connect the support structure to the blood vessels [10].

Song et al. [12] proposed the function representation based on 3D printing, f-rep model representation. Compared with the traditional slicing method, this method has obvious advantages in terms of computing time and memory consumption. Li et al. [13] showed how implicit representation can easily solve problems encountered in additive manufacturing. He used some very simple implicit shape blending functions to combine different shapes that are individually modeled.

3   Method

3.1   Extension of Inlets and Outlets

An implicitly modeled blood vessel is selected to extend its inlets and outlets. The prolongation of blood vessel inlets and outlets is the basic step, and also is the first step of blood vessel editing. We traverse the central lines of each blood vessel which are a set of points. First, we extend the central lines of the blood vessel. The extension methods of this paper are as follows: We find the last two points or the beginning two points of each central lines, A (x1, y1, z1), B (x2, y2, z2), connect them into lines, and calculate the expression of their straight lines. It is best to extract several points on the line according to the extension direction of the blood vessel center line, about 5–7 points, and add them to the end or beginning of the data of the central axis. The central line of the blood vessel is extended at the entrance and exit now. When dealing with the entrance, we will encounter a problem that many central lines are at the same starting point. At this time, we need to judge whether the entrance is the same. If so, we only need to extend it once. We set up a value, which points to the starting point of the branch of the vessel that we did that last time. If this value is the same as the point we are dealing with at present, it means the same entrance, then we will not deal with it this time. By doing this, the extension of the center line is over. See algorithm 1 for details.

Then we can employ the implicit modeling method [14] to model the new vessels, which consists of three steps, fitting the control points of blood vessel cross section, combining the cross section contour to form a branch of blood vessel, and merging the branches to form a complete blood vessel.

Program 1 Extension of inlets and outlets

```
{CenterLines is the center axis of blood vessel, Frenet is the space
of Frenet frame, inter_point is the length of vessel segment per
modeling, branchLCLPS is vessel data};
  First_point=branchCLPS(1,:,:)
  for i← 0:num_brances do
      first_point=branchCLPS(1,:,:)
      if First_point==first_point then
          Calculate the linear expression through first_point and
          second_point of the blood vessel, add the first 6 point on the
          expression to the centerLines
      First_point=first_point
      end if
  Calculate    the    linear    expression    through    last_point
      andsecondlast_point of the blood vessel add the first 6 point on
      the line on the expression to the centerLines.
  Recalculate the Frent space of the blood vessel
      for j←0:num_point-1 to inter+point do
          Implictmodel(CenterLines,Frent, j+inter_point)
      end for
  end for
```

3.2 Design of Open Section for Inlets and Outlets

On the basis of extended, we need to deal with the open vascular. According to the extended central lines, we extract part of the central line from start T to end T. If it is an outlet, start T must be on the extended part of the central line and close to the last point; if it is an inlet, end T must be on the extended part of the central lines and close to the first point. Then we calculate the space size of the segment, and set all the values in the segment space to null. As shown in Fig. 1, the gray plane intercepts the vascular area A, A is the part that is discarded to construct an open vascular orifice, B is the cross section of the intercepted blood vessel, C is the extravascular area. We can only set area A as empty, so that there is no value gradient between it and area B and area C. In the later extraction of isosurface, since there is no value here, the open vascular orifice can be made.

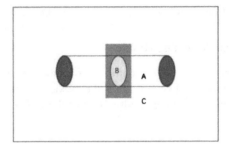

Fig. 1. Partial vascular instance

3.3 Construction of Vessel Wall Structure

On the premise that an open cross section has been constructed, we need to construct a thick vessel wall. As shown in Fig. 2. Firstly, two isosurfaces are determined. Assuming that the two isosurfaces are value1 and value2 (value1 > value2), the surface with value 1 is closer to the center of the blood vessel, and the surface with value 2 is closer to the outer wall. We cannot use these two isosurfaces as thick vessel walls directly, because the two isosurfaces are not connected together. Area B is the part whose value is greater than value1, area C is less than value2, area A (x) is greater than Value2 and less than value1. Area E is the empty area in the design of opening section for entrance and exit in the previous step.

Now the value of region B is set to value 4 (value 4 < 0), so there must be an equivalent surface with value 0 when the value changes from value 1 to value 4. Similarly, the values of region C, which is less than value 2, and region E are set to value 3 (value 3 < 0). Thus, between the equivalence surface of value 2 and region C and region E, the value changes from value 2 to value 3, and there must be an equivalence surface of value 0. Now we extract the equivalent surface of value 0, and it will appear in the closed, thick vessel wall of area D, so that the structure of the vessel wall is completed.

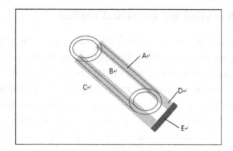

Fig. 2. Construct a diagram of the vessel wall

4 Result

The method proposed in this paper has been tested on multiple sets of real vascular data. The experimental results of two typical data sets are shown below.

4.1 Implicit Vascular Modeling Results

We select the appropriate data of the central lines of the blood vessel and adopt the implicit modeling method [14] to construct the blood vessel model. As shown in Figs. 3 and 4, satisfactory modeling results can be achieved, even for complex blood vessel data.

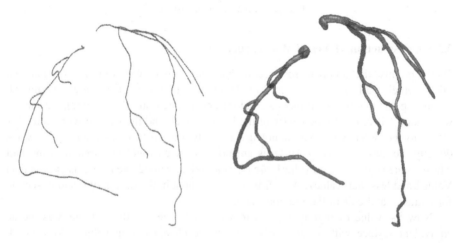

a. central line data of dataset 1   b. vascular model of dataset 1

Fig. 3. Vascular modeling result of dataset 1

a . central line data of dataset 2   b. vascular model of dataset 2

Fig. 4. Vascular modeling result of dataset 2

4.2 Editing Results of Vascular Model

4.2.1 Extension of Inlets and Outlets of Blood Vessels

After getting the data of the central lines, we can extend it according to the method presented in Subsect. 3.1. By comparing with the figure below, the extension of the central lines can be clearly seen. We use implicit functions modeling on the basis of extending the center line (Figs. 5, 6, 7 and 8).

a. central lines of extended inlets and outlets   b. vascular model

Fig. 5. (a) The result of extending the inlets and outlets for the dataset 1; (b) The dataset 1 vascular model was constructed by implicit modeling after prolongation.

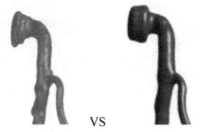

VS

Fig. 6. The left figure is the dataset 1 before extended, and the right one is after the extension; the difference between the two can be clearly seen.

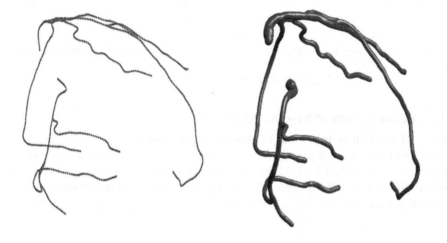

a.   Central lines of extended inlets and outlets   b.   Vascular model

Fig. 7. (a) The result of extending the entrance and exit for the central lines of dataset 2; (b) The dataset 2 vascular model was constructed by implicit modeling after prolongation.

VS

Fig. 8. Contrast figure dataset 2 before and after lengthening

4.2.2 Design of Open Section

After prolonging the outlet and inlet of the blood vessel, we can see that each port of the blood vessel model is closed. Next, an open section is constructed near the orifice of the blood vessel by using the tangent plane. We design open sections for both dataset1 and dataset2. As shown in the following Figs. 9, 10 and 11:

Fig. 9. Dataset 1 vascular model with open orifice;

Fig. 10. Dataset 2 vascular model with open orifice

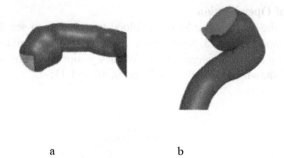

a   b

Fig. 11. (a) Details of dataset 1 open vascular orifice; (b) Details of dataset 2 open vascular orifice

4.2.3   Vessel Wall Structure

We set a thick vascular wall outside the vascular model with open vascular orifice. As shown in the following Figs. 12 and 13:

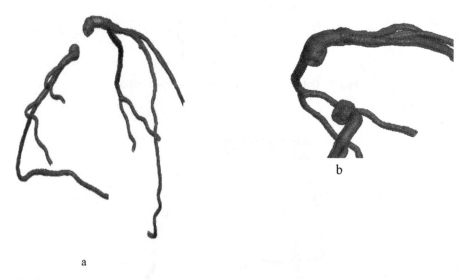

Fig. 12. (a) Model of dataset 1 vascular wall thickening; (b) Enlargement of dataset 1 specific details

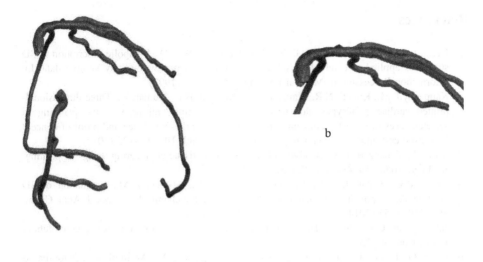

Fig. 13. (a) Model of dataset 2 vascular wall thickening; (b) Enlargement of dataset 2 specific details

4.2.4   Running Time of Experiment

The examples shown in this paper are all tested on a PC with Inter Core i7-7700 CPU @ 3.60 GHz and 8.0 GB of memory. The experimental running environment is in MATLAB software. The following table shows the running time of each method tested with dataset 1 and dataset 2. It can be seen that the more branches of blood vessels, the more time each method takes (Table 1).

Table 1. Running time each methods

	Extension of outlets and inlets	Open section	Vascular wall
Dataset 1	66.665088 s	2.923378 s	0.403513 s
Dataset 2	37.915735 s	2.662431 s	0.211394 s

5   Conclusions

This paper focuses on the design of vascular models suitable for 3D printing. We use implicit modeling technology, with the following advantages the extension of the entrance and exit of blood vessels, thickening of blood vessel wall, and the design of open cross-section of blood vessels. For vascular extension, we adopt straight line elongation based on the end or the front two points, meanwhile, we can also extend the tangent line based on the last point, maybe there is a better method of elongation, which will need further study and investigation. We will continue to optimize the method in the future work.

References

1. Gerig, G., Koller, T., Székely, G., Brechbühler, C., Kübler, O.: Symbolic description of 3D structures applied to cerebral vessel tree obtained from mr angiography volume data. In: Information Processing in Medical Imaging, pp. 94–111 (1993)
2. Kappanayil, M., Koneti, N.R., Kannan, R.R., Kottayil, B.P., Kumar, K.: Three-dimensional-printed cardiac prototypes aid surgical decision-making and preoperative planning in selected cases of complex congenital heart diseases: Early experience and proof of concept in a resource-limited environment. Ann. Pediatr. Cardiol. **10**, 117–125 (2017)
3. Bose, S., Vahabzadeh, S., Bandyopadhyay, A.: Bone tissue engineering using 3D printing. J. Mater. Today **16**, 496–504 (2013)
4. Gross, B.C., Erkal, J.L., Lockwood, S.Y., Chen, C., Spence, D.M.: Evaluation of 3D printing and its potential impacton biotechnology and the chemical sciences. J. Anal. Chem. **86**, 3240–3253 (2014)
5. Jin, X., Tai, C.L., Zhang, H.: Implicit modeling from polygon soup using convolution. J. Vis. Comput. **25**, 279–288 (2009)
6. Hong, Q., Li, Y., Li, Q., Wang, B., Yao, J., Wu, Q., She, Y.: An implicit skeleton-based method for the geometry reconstruction of vasculatures. J. Vis. Comput. **32**(10), 1251–1262 (2016)
7. Martelli, N., Serrano, C., Brink, H., Pineau, J., Prognon, P., Borget, I., Batti, S.: Advantages and disadvantages of 3-dimensional printing in surgery: a systematic review. J. Surg. **159**(6), 1485–1500 (2016)
8. Marro, A., Bandukwala, T., Mak, W.: Three-dimensional printing and medical imaging: a review of the methods and applications. J. Curr. Probl. Diagn. Radiol. **45**, 2–9 (2016)
9. Hernández-Hoyos, M., Anwander, A., Orkisz, M., Roux, J., Douk, P., Magnin, E.: A deformable vessel model with single point initialization for segmentation, quantification and visualization of blood vessels in 3D MRA. In: Medical Image Computing and Computer-Assisted Intervention, pp. 735–745 (2000)
10. O'Hara, R., Chand, A., Vidiyala, S., Arechavala, S.: Advanced 3D mesh manipulation in stereolithographic files and post-print processing for the manufacturing of patient-specific vascular flow phantoms. In: International Society for Optics Engineering, SPIE (2016)
11. Ionita, C.N., et al.: Challenges and limitations of patient-specific vascular phantom fabrication using 3D Polyjet printing. In: International Society for Optics and Photonics, SPIE (2014)
12. Song, Y., Yang, Z., Liu, Y., Deng, J.: Function representation based slicer for 3D printing. J. Comput. Aided Geom. Des. **62**, 276–293 (2018)
13. Li, Q., Hong, Q., Qi, Q., Ma, X., Han, X., Tian, J.: Towards additive manufacturing oriented geometric modeling using implicit functions. J. Vis. Comput. Ind. Biomed. Art **1**(1), 9 (2018)
14. Hong, Q., et al.: Accurate geometry modeling of vasculatures using implicit fitting with 2D radial basis functions. J. Comput. Aided Geom. Des. **62**, 206–216 (2018)

Design and Implementation of Hardware Accelerator for Gaussian Filter Based on HLS

Zonghao Tian, Zhen Liu[✉], Shuguang Wang, and Dong Chen

Army Academy of Artillary and Air Defense, Hefei 230031, Anhui, China
tzh1109180769@163.com

Abstract. Gaussian noise often appears in images, and in order to enhance the image quality, it is necessary to use a gaussian filter to preprocess the acquired image. The gaussian filter hardware accelerator module is designed through algorithm pipeline design and HLS instruction optimization by the HLS developed by Xilinx. At last, we analyze the image processing speed and resource occupancy on different hardware platforms. Experimental results show that the gaussian filter based on FPGAs is much faster than that on CPUs, and reduces the difficulty of porting the algorithm on different hardware platforms, which greatly shortens the development cycle of the project.

Keywords: Hardware accelerator · Field programmable gate arrays (FPGA) · High level synthesis (HLS) · Gaussian filter

1 Introduction

In recent years, real-time image recognition and tracking have been continuously developed with the rise of AI (Artificial Intelligence). In engineering problems, fast and efficient image processing capabilities is the key indicator for embedded platforms. At present, the image processing is generally performed on a PC or ARM platform, and the execution efficiency is lower, which cannot meet the real-time requirements. Therefore, many experts gradually turn to FPGA for image processing to make the algorithm accelerated on the hardware platform. Although the traditional hardware platforms such as DSP, ARM and GPU have the advantages of low price and easy programming in image processing, they have a big gap with FPGA in terms of performance, efficiency and cost [1].

The circuit on FPGA is designed by the hardware description language VHDL or Verilog [2], and realizes complex digital logic functions through a large number of logic gate circuits. For software engineers, it is difficult to porting image processing algorithms on hardware platform, and the development cycle is long. In 2012, Xilinx developed the tool HLS for software engineers, which can reduce the difficulty of FPGA design and shorten the engineering development cycle.

Gaussian noise is ubiquitous in images, and in order to improve the capability and accuracy of target feature extraction, recognition and tracking, it is necessary to carry out gaussian filter denoising on the images. Gaussian filter is not difficult to implement at the algorithm level, but the real-time performance of calculations on the CPU is poor.

© Springer Nature Singapore Pte Ltd. 2019
Y. Wang et al. (Eds.): IGTA 2019, CCIS 1043, pp. 161–171, 2019.
https://doi.org/10.1007/978-981-13-9917-6_16

For this reason, this paper uses HLS design the hardware accelerator of the gaussian filter, and optimizes the module for image denoising.

2 High Level Synthesis (HLS)

In the long-term engineering practice, it is found that hardware and software engineers often perform their own duties and have no understanding of each other's professions. In other word, hardware engineers do not understand algorithms and software engineers do not understand hardware circuit design, which brings great inconvenience to porting algorithms to hardware platforms. The development and design of FPGA relies on the hardware description language (HDL), and the algorithm should be converted into RTL code according to the hardware logic process in the engineering development, which is difficult and inefficient. When the hardware platform changes, the RTL code need be rewritten, and have a long development cycle.

HLS [3] is a compiler that can convert functions written in high-level languages such as C, C++ or SystemC into RTL code, simplifying the development and design of FPGA and shortening the cycle. System engineers can fully understand the design concepts of software serial and hardware parallel by HLS, and coordinate the design of hardware and software from a system-level perspective, reducing the threshold and cycle of FPGA development and improving development efficiency. Figure 1 briefly describes the FPGA development design process using HLS:

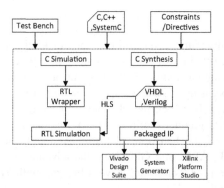

Fig. 1. The design flow chart of HLS

As can be seen from Fig. 1, system engineers can write algorithm code and Test Bench test files through high-level languages such as C and C++, and debug the performance by algorithm optimization or tool instruction optimization to achieve the optimal resource consumption and timing. Then, source code function simulation is conducted to ensure the correctness of design functions. After the function verification is passed, the HLS can be used for code synthesis, and the high-level language can be converted into RTL code which is used for RTL simulation. When the design timing and function requirements are met, it is packaged as an IP core which can be used in the whole project.

The design process of FPGA based on HLS separates the functions of software implementation from the hardware and does not need to care about the details of the underlying RTL, which reduces the difficulty of development and increases the flexibility of design. It can verify the function by C/RTL co-simulation, and obtain the small-area, high-throughput RTL circuits through continuous algorithm and instruction optimization. In addition, the development process uses high-level programming language to facilitate the maintenance and modification of functions. When replacing the hardware platform, only the algorithm code needs to be re-synthesized and simulated without considering the change of RTL code, and it increases the robustness of functional modules.

3 Gaussian Filter Algorithm

Gaussian filter is a linear filter [4], which is suitable for eliminating gaussian noise and used for image denoising. Cameras often generate a large amount of random noise which generally follows the normal distribution during imaging and image transmission. Equation (1) gives one-dimensional probability distribution of gaussian noise:

$$p(x) = \frac{1}{\sqrt{2\pi}\sigma}\exp(-\frac{(x-\mu)^2}{2\sigma^2})$$ (1)

Where μ is expected value, and σ is standard deviation.

Fig. 2. The picture with gaussian noise

As can be seen from Fig. 2 that gaussian noise appears randomly in the image, which reduces the image quality and affects the feature extraction and target recognition in the later stage. Therefore, combined with the nature of gaussian noise, the image is preprocessed by gaussian filter.

The process of gaussian filter is the pixels are weighted and averaged by itself and other pixels in the surrounding area with the gaussian kernels, where the gaussian kernels, also known as gaussian templates, is of vital importance. Equation (2) gives a two-dimensional gaussian function with $\mu = 0$:

$$\varphi(x,y) = \frac{1}{2\pi\sigma^2} \exp(-\frac{x^2+y^2}{2\sigma^2}) \tag{2}$$

The continuous two-dimensional gaussian function is discretized by gaussian kernel. Assuming that the gaussian kernel size can be expressed as $(2k+1) \times (2k+1)$, and the element value at any position (i, j) in the gaussian kernel can be expressed as $M(i, j)$:

$$M(i,j) = \frac{1}{2\pi\sigma^2} \exp(-\frac{(i-k-1)^2+(i-k-1)^2}{2\sigma^2}) \tag{3}$$

Where, σ affects the performance of gaussian filter, and it can be determined by the size of gaussian kernel:

$$\sigma = ((kenerl-1) \times 0.5 - 1) \times 0.3 + 0.8 \tag{4}$$

Gaussian filter can be described as the process of convolution between gaussian kernel and image, and it can be divided into direct convolution method and row-column separation calculation method according to the way of implementation.

Where, the direct convolution calculation method is that the two-dimensional gaussian kernel slides on the image, and replace the pixel value of the point with the weighted sum of the gaussian kernel M and the pixels. Each convolution operation requires $(2k+1) \times (2k+1)$ multiplication and $(2k+1) \times (2k+1)-1$ addition, and the calculation process is shown in Fig. 3:

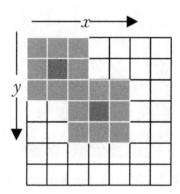

Fig. 3. The direct convolution calculation method

The row-column separation convolution calculation convert the two-dimensional gaussian kernel into two one-dimensional gaussian kernels according to the linear separability property of the gaussian filter. In other words, the one-dimensional convolution operation of the row (column) direction is carried out first, and then the other.

The certain point convolution operation requires $2 \times (2k+1)$ multiplication and $4k$ addition, which greatly reduces the complexity of the algorithm.

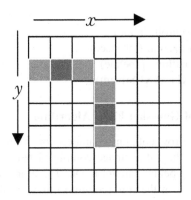

Fig. 4. The row-column separation convolution calculation method

4 Design and Implementation of Gaussian Filter Based on HLS

In the third part of the paper, two methods of gaussian filter are analyzed, in which the row-column separation convolution is less complex and better than the traditional gaussian filter algorithm. To this end, the row-column separation convolution calculation is used in image preprocessing. However, in the process of convolution calculation, there is a cross-row operation problem in the column direction (as shown in Fig. 4), and it need to wait for data in the parallel computing process of FPGA. Therefore, line buffer and window buffer are used in the design of gaussian filter to realize the traversal of a frame and pipeline design of filter process [5, 6].

Line Buffer: Row cache when the image matrix operation is performed, the line buffer size is set by the size of image width. When the data is all out, our data is all aligned, and the design is correct. In fact, the line buffer is implemented in BRAM of FPGA, and the data moves in order.

Window Buffer: Usually a set of registers, used in conjunction with line buffer, the data flows from line buffer to window buffer, as shown in Fig. 5.

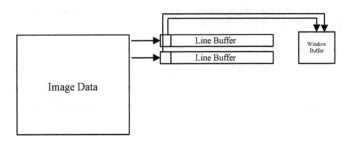

Fig. 5. The flow diagram of cache

In HLS, the row-column separation convolution algorithm is completed by C/C++, and then the algorithm is further optimized by the optimization instruction of HLS in order to achieve high throughput and low latency. The optimization process can generally be as follows:

(1) Rough optimization (unroll, inline)
(2) Memory access optimization (interface)
(3) Fine optimization (dataflow, pipeline)
(4) Bus optimization (AXI4, AXI-Stream)

4.1   Parallel Analysis of Gaussian Filter Algorithm

Pipeline parallelism: In the row-column separation convolution calculation process, it does not need to wait for the entire image completed before proceeding to the next operation, thus forming a pipeline parallel mode. Therefore, when part of the convolution calculation completes in the row (column) direction, the other can be directly performed, and the throughput rate is increased;

Data parallelism: In the row-column separation convolution calculation process, the multiplication and addition operations between data and convolution kernel can be carried out simultaneously;

Task parallel: The image processed in this paper is rgb three-channel format, and the gaussian filter of each channel is independent of each other without correlation, which constitutes the parallel processing of tasks.

4.2   Design of Gaussian Filter Based on HLS

According to the design process of HLS (Fig. 1), the hardware design [7] of gaussian filter can be simplified as shown in Fig. 6:

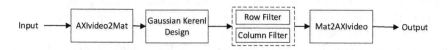

Fig. 6. Gaussian filter process based on HLS

In the process of image filter, the image data is transmitted in AXI-Stream format, and the data stream is converted into HLS::Mat format by AXIvideo2Mat, which is convenient for image pixel calculation and storage.

(1) Gaussian Kernel Design

Assuming that the size of gaussian kernel which is symmetric about the center is $2k-1$. A $1 \times k$ window buffer whose type is HLS::window is created to store gaussian parameters and reduce the resources occupied on the hardware platform.

(2) Row Filter

Assuming the size of the image is $H \times W$, the convolution can be calculated according to the sequence of image pixel data in row direction. Therefore, create a $1 \times (2k - 1)$ window buffer, and the image pixels flow into the window buffer one by one. At the same time, a1 $\times W$ line buffer is used to store the convolution calculation result. The image pixels are sequentially transferred to the window buffer, and the whole buffered data is moved to the left until the gaussian filter is completed in the row direction.

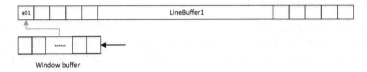

Fig. 7. The data stream of row direction gaussian filter

Where, the black arrow represents the inflow direction of image pixels, and the blue arrow represents the storage location of the calculation results in line buffer. After completing a convolution calculation, the data cached in the window buffer moves to the left.

(3) Column Filter

As can be seen from Fig. 7, in the process of column gaussian filter, the window buffer and line buffer need to be designed due to the problem of cross-row calculation. Create $2k - 2$ line buffer which size is $1 \times W$ and a window buffer which size is $(2k - 1) \times 1$. When the $2k - 2$ line buffer is full of data, the first pixel of each line buffer is stored in front of the $2k - 2$ position of the window buffer. When the new data flows to the line buffer again, the convolution calculation can be performed, and then the window buffer moves one column to the right for the next convolution operation.

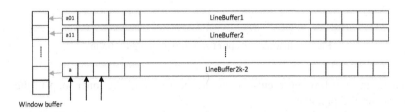

Fig. 8. The data stream of column direction gaussian filter

Figure 8 describes the data stream movement rule of gaussian filter in the column direction, where the black arrow indicates the direction in which the image pixels flow into line buffer, and the blue arrow indicates the direction in which the pixels in each line buffer move to the window buffer.

(4) The Pipeline Design of Row-Column Convolution

Through the analysis of the method proposed in this paper, it can be seen that the convolution calculation in the row direction is consistent with image data stream. Therefore, use "#HLS PIPELINE II=1" instruction to design the pipeline, and directly store the result of the row convolution into the line buffer. When the $(2k - 2) \times W + 1$ cycle begin, the convolution starts in the column direction, and it is not necessary to wait for the whole image processing completed and then turn to the other direction convolution computation, which reduce the delay of the whole of the gaussian filter module.

(5) Instruction Optimization Based on HLS

The optimization instructions provided by HLS are used to optimize the gaussian filter algorithm, such as inline, dataflow and unroll, to realize the coordinated configuration of resource and processing speed. The detailed instruction is shown in Fig. 9:

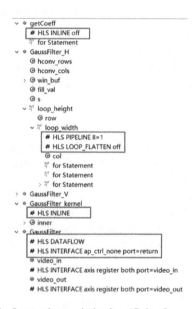

Fig. 9. Instruction optimization (Color figure online)

Where, the red box represents the command to unroll the inner loop in the algorithm and set the pipeline.

At last, the data is converted into AXI-Stream format through Mat2AXIvideo, and the hardware acceleration module of gaussian filter is completed. The whole project is shown in Fig. 10:

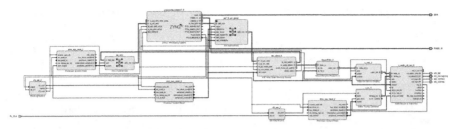

Fig. 10. The hardware acceleration project of gaussian filter

In the process, the image is stored in DDR [8] which is accessed through the VDMA module, and the image data is transmitted to the Gaussfliter Pcore, and the process of image denoising is completed.

5   Experimental Environment and Performance Evaluation

In this paper, the UltraScale+ ZCU102 Evaluation Platform, Xilinx TE0720 Platform and PC are used to implement the algorithm, and the experimental results and resource occupancy of gaussian filter on different platforms are compared and analyzed. The PS parts of the UltraScale+ ZCU102 Evaluation Platform and the Xilinx TE0720 Platform are dual-core ARM Cortex-A9 processors. The core processors are: XCZU9EG-FFVB1156-2-I and Z-7020CLG484; the CPU of the PC platform is Inter. (R) Core (TM) i7-7700HQ, and the frequency is 2.81 GHz.

Gaussian kernel setting: The size of the gaussian kernel is 25, and the standard deviation σ and the parameter values of each position of the gaussian kernel can be calculated from Eqs. (3) and (4).

First, the gaussian filter is implement on the UltraScale+ ZCU102 Evaluation Platform, Xilinx TE0720 Platform and PC. Table 1 shows the time-consuming of Fig. 2 on different platforms:

Table 1. Time-consuming for different platforms

Platform	ZCU102	TE0720	PC
Time-consuming	0.0057 s	0.0054 s	0.066 s

It can be seen that hardware acceleration of gaussian filter based on FPGA is about 12 times faster than CPU's, and the acceleration effect is obvious.

In addition, porting the Gaussfilter Pcore from the Xilinx TE0720 Platform to the UltraScale+ ZCU102 Evaluation Platform. The program code does not need to be modified, and it only changes the core processor in the HLS in order to generate the IP corresponding to different platforms, which greatly improved the porting efficiency and robustness of the module in different platforms. Figure 11 shows the resource consumption of the Gaussfilter Pcore on these two platforms:

Name	BRAM_18K	DSP48E	FF	LUT
DSP	-	-	-	-
Expression	-	-	-	-
FIFO	0	-	55	280
Instance	72	16	2618	4048
Memory	-	-	-	-
Multiplexer	-	-	-	-
Register	-	-	-	-
Total	72	16	2673	4328
Available	280	220	106400	53200
Utilization (%)	25	7	2	8

(a) TE0720

Name	BRAM_18K	DSP48E	FF	LUT
DSP	-	-	-	-
Expression	-	-	-	-
FIFO	0	-	55	280
Instance	72	16	1789	2954
Memory	-	-	-	-
Multiplexer	-	-	-	-
Register	-	-	-	-
Total	72	16	1844	3234
Available	1824	2520	548160	274080
Utilization (%)	3	~0	~0	1

(b) AX0720

Fig. 11. Resource consumption comparison of the two computing platforms

It can be seen that the arithmetic unit of the gaussian filter algorithm and the pipeline design of the data stream will not change when the platform changes, so the resource consumption of BRAM_18 k and DSP48E is the same in the two platforms. However, due to the performance and manufacturing of each processor, the layout and wiring of RTL is different in the process of algorithm synthesis and implementation, which results the consumption of FF and LUT are different.

The gaussian filter hardware acceleration based on HLS is to use C++ high-level language, through the HLS tool to complete the synthesis and implementation of the source code, and generate the corresponding Verilog, VHDL and SystemC code, as shown in Fig. 12:

Fig. 12. The report of synthesis and implementation based on HLS

Through analysis, it is found that the hardware code generated by the HLS is thousands of lines, and the control of the data stream needs to be defined in detail. The whole project is difficult for developers who are not familiar with the hardware, which extends the development cycle and make the efficiency lower.

6   Conclusion

In this paper, C++ is used to complete the gaussian filter hardware acceleration module based on the Vivado HLS. Compared with the HDL, the difficulty and complexity of porting the software algorithm to the hardware platform are reduced, and shortened the development cycle. Experiments show that gaussian filter hardware acceleration based on FPGA is more effective than the traditional method realizing on PC, and the algorithm can be transplanted to different hardware platforms, which provides a better solution for image real-time processing on embedded platforms.

References

1. Xilinx, Xilinx Vivado design suite [EB/OL] 20 Dec 2017. https://www.xilinx.com/support/do cumentation/sw_manuals/xilinx2017_4/ug940-vivado-tutorial-embedded-design.pdf
2. Dang, H.S., Wang, L., Wang, X.Q.: Development and application of FPGA based on Vivado HLS. J. Shanxi Univ. Sci. Technol. **02**, 155–159 (2015)
3. Xilinx, Xilinx Vivado design suite tutorial: High-Level-Synthesis [EB/OL] 02 Feb 2018. https://www.xilinx.com/support/documentation/sw_manuals/xilinx2017_4/ug902-vivado-high-level-synthesis.pdf
4. Zhang, Z.: Digital Image Processing and Machine Vision. Posts and Telecom Press, Beijing (2016)
5. Peng, X.W., Zhang, T.: Edge detection hardware acceleration based on Vivado HLS. Embed. Technol. **43**(5), 70–74 (2017)
6. Ding, S.S., Chai, Z.L.: Design and implementation of hardware accelerator for SURF detection based on HLS. Microelectron. Comput. **32**(9), 133–137 (2015)
7. Guo, F.S.: OpenCV application with Xilinx FPGA/Zynq using HLS design flow. Electron. Eng. Prod. World **14**(2), 50–52 (2014)
8. Ruan, Y.Z., Yuan, Z., Yu, J.H., Ding, S.S., Chai, Z.L.: Realization of video image processing system based on the zynq-7000. Softw. Guid. **17**(9), 148–152 (2018)

Fusion of Global and Local Gaussian-Hermite Moments for Face Recognition

Guojie Song[(⊠)], Dan He, Puchun Chen, Jidong Tian, Bin Zhou,
and Li Luo

School of Science, Southwest Petroleum University, Chengdu, China
cylsgj@126.com

Abstract. In automatically recognizing human faces, it is an important problem how to extract the effective features from the corrupted face. This paper propose a new face recognition algorithm based on fusion of global and local Gaussian-Hermite moments (GHMs). Firstly, in order to solve the interference of noise on features, we use the GHMs of face image as facial feature. Second, we construct the face image spatial pyramid to extract the global and local features of the face, and then we compute scatter-ratio to seclect highly discriminative feature. Lastly we use sparse representation classifier to improve the robust of algorithm. Experiments on ORL, FERET and Yale A face databases reveal that the accuracy of proposed algorithm is better than traditional algorithm, especially when the face images are corrupted by salt&pepper noise.

Keywords: Face recognition · Gaussian-Hermite moments · Spatial pyramid · Scatter-ratio · Sparse representation classifier

1 Introduction

In the past two decades, biometric models which include face recognition, iris recognition, DNA recognition and so on have been widely researched [1]. Face recognition has many advantages such as non-intrusive, non-compulsion and concealment, so it becomes one of the most important research in computer vision. Face feature extraction is the key step in face recognition. It is a crucial issue to obtaining the effective features from face images disturbed by uneven illumination, random noise, occlusion, and so on [2, 3].

In general, face feature extraction methods can be divided into two categories: global feature-based algorithm and local feature-based algorithm. Many methods are proposed to capture global-based feature from the whole human face image. In 1991, Turk [4] proposed eigenface method which project face images onto a feature space by extracting the feature vector of face images. Faruqe [5] used Principle Component Analysis (PCA) and Support Vector Machine (SVM) [6, 7] to tackle face recognition problem (PCA + SVM). Belhumeur [8] used Linear Discriminant Analysis (LDA) [9] to project face sample onto a set of projection subspaces made up of discriminant vectors, and then used Fisher discriminant criterion function [10, 11] to identify the face. There are other global-based face feature extraction methods such as Canonical

© Springer Nature Singapore Pte Ltd. 2019
Y. Wang et al. (Eds.): IGTA 2019, CCIS 1043, pp. 172–183, 2019.
https://doi.org/10.1007/978-981-13-9917-6_17

Correlation Analysis (CCA) [12, 13], Independent Component Analysis (ICA) [14] and so on.

The global-based face recognition algorithm performance can be affected greatly when the captured face images are disturbed by illumination variations. In such case, the local-based face recognition algorithms which are designed by focusing on certain number of distinct face areas (nose, chin, eyes, chin, and mouth) can perform better. Local Binary Patterns (LBPs) [15] divide the face image into several sub-images from which the LBP feature distributions are extracted and concatenated into face feature. Gabor transform [16] can effectively extract the local spatial and frequency domain information of the image, so it has been widely used to capture local feature [17, 18]. However, the face features obtained by Gabor transform are extremely sensitive to noise. Besides, the effectiveness of a local feature-based face recognition algorithm is highly dependent on the face localization and the registration model.

In order to overcome the problem caused by misalignment and improve the accuracy of face recognition, the global and local features of face image often are combined to design face recognition algorithm based hybrid-feature. The 2D Krawtchouk moments (KCMs) based hybrid-feature method captures the KCMs of the full, left, right, upper and lower parts of the face images. The KCMs is shown to perform well in the presence of noise, tilt, and expression changed [19]. Because the selection of KCMs is heuristic without any mathematical justification, Rahman computed the scatter-ratio of moments to select the highly discriminative KCMs [20]. Because the distribution of zero-crossings of Gaussian-Hermite polynomial is smooth and even, Gaussian-Hermite moments (GHMs) have excellent robustness to noise comparing with other moments [21–23]. Imran [24] selected highly discriminative GHMs as a set of feature for recognizing facial expression. The experimental results of Imran show that the information of facial expression is effectively captured by using GHMs method.

With the advent of compressive sensing and further research on the optimization of 1-norm [25–27], Wright proposed the Sparse Representation Classifier (SRC) [28]. The main idea of the SRC algorithm is to cast the face recognition problem as one of classifying among multiple linear regression models and solved the model by computing ℓ_1-minimization. The SRC algorithm can't tolerate big pose variation or misalignment, so scholars proposed feature-based sparse classification such as Gabor + SRC [29], LDA + SRC [30] and so on.

In this paper, we design a new face recognition algorithm which use GHMs to extract face feature and then use SRC to classify feature. The structure of the paper is organized as follows. Section 2 introduces the principle of GHMs + SRC algorithm. Section 3 shows the experimental result. Section 4 summarizes the whole article and gives the conclusion.

2   GHMs + SRC

In this section, we give a new face recognition algorithm called GHMs + SRC. This algorithm constructs the face image space pyramid to compute GHMs. Then, it computes the scatter-ratio of GHMs for selecting the highly discriminative GHMs. Lastly, for the reason of occlusion and corruption can be handled uniformly and robustly in face images by SRC, it selects SRC as classifier.

2.1 Human Face Description Based on Gaussian-Hermite Moments

This section gives the method of obtaining GHMs of the image and shows the relation between compression factor and face image reconstructed.

Let $I(u, v)$ be a square integrable 2D image intensity signal, whose size is $U \times V$. The Gaussian-Hermite moment of order (p, q) for face image is defined as

$$G_{pq} = \frac{4}{(U-1)(V-1)} \sum_{u=0}^{U-1} \sum_{v=0}^{V-1} I(u, v) \hat{H}_p(u, U; \sigma) \hat{H}_q(v, V; \sigma) \tag{1}$$

Where $p \in N^1$, $q \in N^1$, $\hat{H}_p(u, U; \sigma)$ is the discrete orthogonal Gaussian-Herimte polynomial.

$$\hat{H}_p(u, U; \sigma) = (2^p p! \sqrt{\pi} \sigma)^{-1/2} \exp\left\{-[(2u - U + 1)/(U-1)]^2/2\sigma^2\right\} \atop H_p((2u - U + 1)/((U-1)\sigma)) \tag{2}$$

Where σ is polynomial scale factor. $H_p((2u - U + 1)/((U-1)\sigma))$ is given by

$$H_p((2u - U + 1)/((U-1)\sigma)) = \sum_{m=0}^{p/2} \frac{(-1)^m p!}{k!(p-2k)!} \{2(2u - U + 1)/[(U-1)\sigma]\}^{p-2m} \tag{3}$$

The image $I(u, v)$ can be restored [21] from its GHMs of orders $(0, 0)$ up to (n, n) by

$$\hat{I}(u, v) = \sum_{p=0}^{n} \sum_{q=0}^{n} G_{pq} \hat{H}_p(u, U; \sigma) \hat{H}_q(v, V; \sigma) \tag{4}$$

Let $\alpha(0 < \alpha < 1)$ be the compression factor. The value of n is obtained using $n = \lfloor \sqrt{\alpha UV} \rfloor - 1$, where $\lfloor \sqrt{\alpha UV} \rfloor$ denotes the largest integer contained in $\sqrt{\alpha UV}$. Scale factor σ is given by

$$\sigma = \begin{cases} 0.9n^{-0.52} & n \geq 1 \\ 1 & n = 0 \end{cases} \tag{5}$$

We can select compression factor α to control GHMs. The resolution of the reconstructed image is improved with the increase of compression factor α.

In Fig. 1. When we select $\alpha = 0.05$ to reconstruct face image, the reconstructed image contain facial contour and facial organs relative position. As the increase of α, the quality of reconstructed face image is better. Especially, we can capture the full information of nose, eyes, mouth from the reconstructed image with $\alpha = 0.4$.

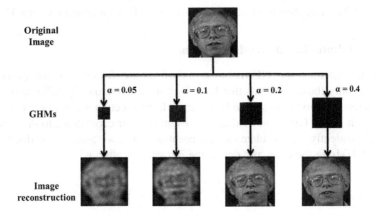

Fig. 1. Human face GHMs and its reconstruction

Human fuse global and local face information to dentify face [31], which let them have extremely strong facial-recognition skills. Therefore, we design a face hybrid-type GHMs face features recognition algorithm.

2.2 GHMs Extraction Based on Spatial Pyramid

This section uses the face image space pyramid model to extract the global and local GHMs. The high-layer of the image space pyramid can be used to calculate local GHMs, while the original image which is locate in the bottom of pyramid model can be used to calculate global GHMs.

Let K be the total number of layers in the pyramid. In k-th layer, the face image is divided into k^2 regions which are equal in size and do not overlap with each other [32]. Figure 2 is an example of the division of the space pyramid, it shows 1-th layer, 2-th layer and 3-th layer. In face image spatial pyramid, the higher pyramid we select, the stronger image locality we can observe. We select different compression factor to compute the GHMs for each layer of pyramid.

Fig. 2. Face image segmentation diagram

Let f_{ij} be the j-th image of i-th category in the face data set, where $i \in (1, 2, \ldots, C), j \in (1, 2, \ldots, \lambda^i)$. C is the total number of face categories. The i-th category has λ^i samples. We create a K-layers space pyramid for image f_{ij} to calculate GHMs, and then the GHMs of f_{ij} is merged into a column vector M_{ij}.

2.3   Scatter-Ratio Based GHMs Screening

In order to construct the GHMs-based hybrid image feature for the purpose of recognition, only those moments that have high discrimination capability and contain less interference information should be selected. In this section we compute the scatter-ratio for each of the GHMs individually to estimate their capabilities to describe face image independently. To calculate the scatter-ratio, firstly, we quantify the discriminant ability of GHMs in the class and define the intraclass scatter as

$$SW^\ell = \sum_{i=1}^{C} \sum_{j=1}^{n_i} \left(M_{ij}^\ell - \mu_i^\ell \right)^2 \tag{6}$$

Where M_{ij} is GHM vector which is calculated from the j-th face image of i-th category. The length of M_{ij} is D. M_{ij}^ℓ is the ℓ-th GHM of M_{ij}. n_i is the total number of training samples in class i. μ_i^ℓ is given by

$$\mu_i^\ell = \frac{1}{n_i} \sum_{j=1}^{n_i} M_{ij}^\ell \tag{7}$$

Then, we quantify the ability of GHMs to discriminate between classes, and define the interclass scatter as

$$SB^\ell = \sum_{i=1}^{C} n_i \left(\mu_i^\ell - \mu^\ell \right)^2 \tag{8}$$

Where μ^ℓ is the mean of the ℓ-th GHM which is given by

$$\mu^\ell = \frac{1}{\sum_{i=1}^{C} n_i} \sum_{i=1}^{C} \sum_{j=1}^{n_i} M_{ij}^\ell \tag{9}$$

Last, the scatter-ratio of the ℓ-th GHM can be defined as

$$\varpi^\ell = \frac{SB^\ell}{SW^\ell} \tag{10}$$

Since the SW^ℓ describes how strongly GHMs in same classes contrast each other, the moments of the training face images that have low SW^ℓ values are useful for distinguishing among the available classes. The SB^ℓ describes how strongly GHMs in different class contrast each other and thus high SB^ℓ values indicate big class variability [20]. The set of moments having high values of ϖ^ℓ are capable of discriminating between the classes. The ϖ^ℓ is arranged in descending order of their magnitudes as

$$\Phi_{ij}^{sort} = \left[\psi_{ij}^1; \psi_{ij}^2; \ldots \psi_{ij}^D\right] \tag{11}$$

Where $\psi_{ij}^t (t \in 1, 2 \ldots D)$ is GHM. We choose the first $J(J < D)$ GHMs as the hybrid face image feature and use PCA to reduce the dimension of feature to S.

The above contents describe how to get the effective features of face. When constructing a complete face recognition algorithm, the choice of classifier will seriously affect the performance of face recognition algorithm. In the following, we use the SRC classifier to make the algorithm strongly robust for corrupted face image.

2.4   Sparse Representation Classifier (SRC)

Sparse representation theory [33] considers that the feature of a test face can be linearly represented by the face feature database. Theoretically, the linearly represented coefficient vector whose entries are zero except those associated with the same class. The essence of sparse representation is to find a set of extremely sparse coefficients corresponding to the face feature database to represent the face features linearly. Thus the problem of sparse representation can approximately be summarized as the following l1-minimization problem

$$\hat{x} = \arg\min_{x} \|y - \Gamma x\|_2 + \lambda \|x\|_1 \tag{12}$$

Where y is the eigenvector of the test face. Γ is a dictionary of features for entire training set. The regularization factor is λ, which is used to balance reconstruction error and sparse. Solved the problem, we can obtain $\hat{x}$ which is a set of extremely sparse coefficients. In $\hat{x}$ the coefficients corresponding to class $i \in (1, 2, \ldots C)$ are reserved and other coefficients are set to 0. Let $\delta_i(\hat{x})$ be the reconstructed coefficients. So the test sample residual is given as

$$r_i(y) = \|\Gamma \delta_i(\hat{x}) - y\|_2 \tag{13}$$

The sample classification result is $class(y) = \arg\min_i r_i(y)$. $class(y)$ indicates the category of y. In the real face recognition scene, there are exiting external disturbances which can cause errors in classification result. We use I with the same size as training image to represent the error term. We add feature B calculated from I to feature dictionary Γ. Equation (13) is transformed as

$$\begin{bmatrix} \hat{x} \\ \hat{b} \end{bmatrix} = \arg\min_{x,b} \left\| y - [\Gamma, B] \begin{bmatrix} x \\ b \end{bmatrix} \right\|_2 + \lambda \left\| \begin{bmatrix} x \\ b \end{bmatrix} \right\|_1 \tag{14}$$

Classification result is given by

$$class(\mathbf{y}) = \arg\min_i \|\boldsymbol{\Gamma}\boldsymbol{\delta}_i(\hat{\mathbf{x}}) + b\boldsymbol{B} - \mathbf{y}\|_2 \tag{15}$$

3 Numerical Experimental Results and Discussions

In this paper, the ORL, FERET, Yale A face datasets are used to verify the correctness of the proposed GHMs + SRC algorithm. The Gabor + SRC, LDA + SRC, PCA + SVM face recognition algorithms are used to verify the effectiveness of the proposed GHMs + SRC algorithm.

The ORL face dataset which is made by the University of Cambridge includes 400 face images gathered from 40 people. The captured face images of ORL dataset have different types of distortions and a little illumination variations. The ORL face image's size is 92×112. The FERET face dataset which is established by the U.S. Department of Defense includes 1199 people. In such a case, the FERET dataset used in the experiments includes 420 face images obtained from 60 people. Comparing with the face image of ORL, the images of FERET have visible variation on illumination and expression. The FERET face image's size is 80×80. The Yale A face dataset which is created by Yale Center for Computer Vision and Control includes 165 images obtained from 15 volunteers. It contains the variation of illumination, expressions and posture as well as the human eye occlusion caused by glasses. The Yale A face image's size is 137×147. Figure 3 shows partial images of the ORL, FERET, Yale A face dataset.

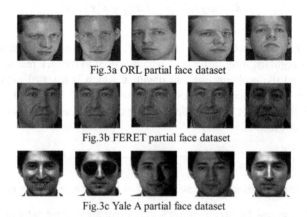

Fig.3a ORL partial face dataset

Fig.3b FERET partial face dataset

Fig.3c Yale A partial face dataset

Fig. 3. Partial face dataset

In this paper, we scale the size of all the face images to 120×120. In the k-th layer of the pyramid we select the compression factor as $\alpha = 2^{k-1}/20$, and the total number of pyramid layers is not more than 6.

3.1   Standard Face Data Set Experimental

3.1.1   ORL Dataset

In ORL face dataset, we use the first 5 images of each person as training images and the remaining images are test images. The recognition rate results are given in Table 1.

Table 1. ORL face dataset recognition rate/%

Algorithm	The number of features				
	20	40	60	80	100
GHMs + SRC	91.00	95.50	96.50	97.50	98.00
Gabor + SRC	64.50	92.00	96.50	95.50	97.50
LDA + SRC	89.00	95.50	95.50	95.50	95.50
PCA + SVM	92.50	95.00	94.00	94.50	95.00

From Table 1, it can be seen that four algorithms can gain the excellent recognition accuracy, especially when more features is used. When the number of features is selected as 20, the recognition rate of GHMs + SRC algorithm is lower than PCA + SVM algorithm and higher than Gabor + SRC, LDA + SRC. The recognition rate of GHMs + SRC algorithm is better than the other three algorithms when the number of features is more than 40, and the peak of the recognition is 98%. In ORL face dataset, the performance of GHMs + SRC algorithm is generally better than that of the other three algorithms.

3.1.2   FERET Dataset

FERET dataset contains variation in posture, expression and huge illumination variation. Comparing with the ORL dataset, the face image recognition of FERET dataset is more complex. We select the first four faces of each person as the training image and the remained images are the test images. Table 2 shows the recognition rate.

Table 2. FERET face dataset recognition rate/%

Algorithm	The number of features				
	20	40	60	80	100
GHMs + SRC	67.78	78.33	80.56	82.78	85.00
Gabor + SRC	37.22	52.22	63.89	72.22	78.33
LDA + SRC	48.89	66.11	71.67	79.44	83.33
PCA + SVM	58.33	58.89	60.00	58.89	58.33

As can be seen from Table 2, four algorithms not gain good recognition accuracy. The recognition rate of PCA + SVM algorithm can maintain about 60%, while the recognition rate of the remaining three algorithms can get about 80% accuracy when more feature is selected. On the whole, the recognition rate of GHMs + SRC algorithm is obviously higher than the other methods.

3.1.3 Yale A Dataset

The Yale A dataset is difficult to recognize because the images of Yale A data have difference illumination, posture and occluded. The first 5 images of each person in Yale A face dataset are selected as the training images and the remaining images are test images. The recognition rate results are shown in Table 3.

Table 3. Yale A face dataset recognition rate/%

Algorithm	The number of features				
	20	30	40	50	60
GHMs + SRC	83.33	86.67	88.89	87.78	90.00
Gabor + SRC	82.22	88.89	90.00	91.11	92.22
LDA + SRC	81.11	82.22	82.22	81.11	83.33
PCA + SVM	84.40	85.56	86.67	86.67	86.67

In Table 3, it is obvious that the LDA + SRC show worst performance. It can also be seen that the PCA + SVM acquire the highest recognition accuracy compared with the other three algorithms when the number of feature is 20. From last line of Table 3, we can find that the PCA + SVM algorithm accuracy is insensitive to the number of features, which is around 86.67%. From the mean recognition rate of observation of Table 3, Gabor + SRC and GHMs + SRC algorithms performance is better than that of PCA + SVM.

Experiment on the ORL and FERET face dataset show that the recognition performance of GHMs + SRC algorithm is superior to the other three algorithms. For the Yale A face dataset, the recognition accuracy of GHMs + SRC is only slightly less than Gabor + SRC. In conclusion, comparing with the LDA + SRC and PCA + SVM using global features and the Gabor + SRC using local features, the GHM + SRC algorithm fusing global and local features is generally better.

3.2 Noise Occlusion Experiment Results and Analysis

How to recognize face image corrupted by noise is an important problem in automatically face recognition. To further verify the performance of the proposed GHMs + SRC algorithm, we add 5%, 10%, 15%, 20%, 25%, 30% salt&pepper noise to the three face dataset. In noisy dataset, the way of experiment is same as Sect. 3.1. The recognition rate is follow as

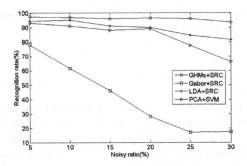

Fig. 4. Noisy ORL face dataset recognition rate

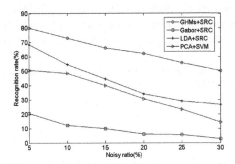

Fig. 5. Noisy FERET face dataset recognition rate

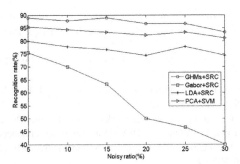

Fig. 6. Noisy Yale A face dataset recognition rate

Figures 4, 5 and 6 show the recognition rate under different noise ratio. The recognition accuracy of GHMs + SRC algorithm keep a stable trend in Figs. 4 and 6, but in Fig. 5 its recognition rate decrease by 20% with the increase of noise ratio. It also can be seen that the recognition rate of proposed GHMs + SRC algorithm is obviously higher than the other three algorithms for each noise ratio. At the same time, comparing with Gabor + SRC, LDA + SRC and PCA + SVM algorithms, the recognition rate of GHMs + SRC algorithm decreases slowly. To sum up, the GHMs + SRC algorithm proposed by this paper is extremely insensitive to recognize face image corrupted by salt and pepper noise.

4   Conclusion

In this paper, we proposed a new face recognition algorithm named GHMs +SRC. Firstly, the algorithm extracts the hybrid-feature by computing the GHMs in the each layer of the face image space pyramid. Then, it screens the features of highly discriminative power by computing scatter-ratio. Finally, it uses SRC to classify the feature.

The experiment results on ORL, FERET and Yale A standard face datasets show that the GHMs + SRC algorithm fusing global and local image information perform better than the Gabor + SRC, LDA + SRC and PCA + SVM algorithm. At the same time, GHMs is robust for noise, so numerical results also show that the GHMs + SRC algorithm can capture the effective features from face image disturbed by salt&pepper noise. All in all, the GHMs + SRC algorithm have a good performance for face recognition.

Acknowledgements. This work was supported by the National Natural Science Foundation of China under Grant No. 41674141 and No. 41204074.

References

1. Otti, C.: Comparison of biometric identification methods. In: International Symposium on Applied Computational Intelligence and Informatics (2016)
2. Buciu, I.: Overview of face recognition techniques. J. Electr. Electron. Eng. 1(1), 173–176 (2008)
3. Singh, R., Om, H.: An overview of face recognition in an unconstrained environment. In: IEEE Second International Conference on Image Information Processing, pp. 672–677 (2010)
4. Turk, M., Pentlad, A.: Eigenfaces for recognition. J. Congnitive Neurosci. 3(1), 71–86 (1991)
5. Hasan, M., Faruqe, M.: Face recognition using PCA and SVM. In: International Conference on Anti-Counterfeiting, pp. 97–101 (2009)
6. Vapnik, V., Cortes, C.: Support-vector networks. Mach. Learn. 20(3), 273–297 (1995)
7. Ma, L., Song, D., Liao, L., Wang, J.: PSVM: a preference-enhanced SVM model using preference data for classification. Sci. China Inf. Sci. 60, 1869–1919 (2017). https://doi.org/10.1007/s11432-016-9020-4
8. Belhumeur, P.N., Kriegman, D.J.: Eigenfaces vs. Fisherfaces: recognition using class specific linear projection. IEEE Trans. Pattern Anal. Mach. Intell. 19(7), 711–720 (2002)
9. Zhao, H., Yuen, P.C.: Incremental linear discriminant analysis for face recognition. Trans. Syst. Man Cybern. Part B. 38(1), 210–221 (2008)
10. Wu, X., Mao, X., Chen, L., Xue, Y., Rovetta, A.: Kernel optimization using nonparametric Fisher criterion in the subspace. Pattern Recognit. Lett. 54, 43–49 (2015)
11. Yang, M., Zhang, L., Feng, X., Zhang, D.: Sparse representation based fisher discrimination dictionary learning for image classification. Int. J. Comput. Vis. 109(3), 209–232 (2014)
12. Lei, G., Zhou, J., Li, X., Gong, X.: Improved canonical correlation analysis and its applications in image recognition. J. Comput. Inf. Syst. 6(11), 3677–3685 (2010)

13. Givens, G.H., Beveridge, J.R., Lui, Y.M., Bolme, D.S., Draper, B.A., Phillips, P.J.: Biometric face recognition: from classical statistics to future challenges. Wiley Interdiscip. Rev.: Comput. Stat. **5**(4), 288–308 (2013)
14. Kim, J., Choi, J., Yi, J., Turk, M.: Effective representation using ICA for face recognition robust to local distortion and partial occlusion. IEEE Trans. Pattern Anal. Mach. Intell. **27** (12), 1977–1981 (2005)
15. Ahonen, T., Hadid, A., Pietikainen, M.: Face description with local binary patterns: application to face recognition. IEEE Trans. Pattern Anal. Mach. Intell. **28**(12), 2037–2041 (2006)
16. Lee, T.S.: Image representation using 2D gabor wavelets. IEEE Trans. Pattern Anal. Mach. Intell. **18**(10), 959–971 (1996)
17. Shen, L., Bai, L.: A review on Gabor wavelets for face recognition. Pattern Anal. Appl. **9**(3), 273–292 (2006)
18. Kamaruzaman, F., Shafie, A.: Recognizing faces with normalized local Gabor features and spiking neuron patterns. Pattern Recognit. **53**, 102–115 (2016)
19. Rani, J.S., Devaraj, D.: Face recognition using Krawtchouk moment. Shadhana **37**(4), 441–460 (2012)
20. Rahman, S.M.M., Howlader, T., Hatzinakos, D.: On the selection of 2D Krawtchouk moments for face recognition. Pattern Recognit. **54**, 83–93 (2016)
21. Yang, B., Dai, M.: Image analysis by Gaussian-Hermite moments. Sig. Process. **91**(10), 2290–2303 (2011)
22. Yang, B., Kostková, J., Flusser, J., Suk, T.: Scale invariants from Gaussian-Hermite moments. Signal Process. **132**, 77–84 (2016)
23. Yang, B., Li, G., Zhang, H., Dai, M.: Rotation and translation invariants of Gaussian-Hermite moments. Pattern Recognit. Lett. **32**(9), 1283–1298 (2011)
24. Imran, S.M., Rahman, S.M.M., Hatzinakos, D.: Differential components of discriminative 2D Gaussian-Hermite moments for recognition of facial expressions. Pattern Recognit. **56**, 100–115 (2016)
25. Candes, E.J., Wakin, M.B.: An introduction to compressive sampling. IEEE Sig. Process. Mag. **25**(2), 21–30 (2008)
26. Rezagah, F.E., Jalali, S., Erkip, E., Poor, H.V.: Compression-based compressed sensing. IEEE Trans. Inf. Theory **63**, 6735–6752 (2016)
27. Yang, A.Y., Sastry, S.S, Ganesh, A., Yi, M.: Fast ℓ 1-minimization algorithms and an application in robust face recognition: a review. IEEE International Conference on Image Processing. IEEE (2010)
28. Wright, J., Yang, A.Y., Ganesh, A., Sastry, S.S., Yi, M.: Robust face recognition via sparse representation. IEEE Trans. Anal. Mach. Intell. **31**(2), 210–227 (2009)
29. Yang, M., Zhang, L.: Gabor feature based sparse representation for face recognition with Gabor occlusion dictionary. In: European Conference on Computer Vision, pp. 448–461 (2010)
30. Adamo, A., Grossi, G., Lanzarotti, R., Lin, J.: Robust face recognition using sparse representation in LDA space. Mach. Vis. Appl. **26**, 837–847 (2005)
31. Meaux, E., Vuilleumier, P.: Facing mixed emotions: analytic and holistic perception of facial emotion expressions engages separate brain networks. Neuroimage **141**, 154–173 (2016)
32. Xie, Z.: Infrared face recognition based on adaptive dominant pattern of local binary pattern. In: Tan, T., Ruan, Q., Wang, S., Ma, H., Di, K. (eds.) IGTA 2015. CCIS, vol. 525, pp. 28–36. Springer, Heidelberg (2015). https://doi.org/10.1007/978-3-662-47791-5_4
33. Cheng, H., Liu, Z., Yang, L., Chen, X.: Sparse representation and learning in visual recognition: theory and applications. Sig. Process. **93**(6), 1408–1425 (2013)

A Visual-Inertial Information Fusion Method for SLAM Front-End Odometry

Xinguo Yu, Tai Li[✉], and Zhizhong Zeng

National Engineering Research Center for E-Learning,
Central China Normal University, Wuhan 430079,
People's Republic of China
litai@mails.ccnu.edu.cn

Abstract. In a pure visual odometry, a pose transformation matrix between adjacent two frames is estimated by an algorithm based on pixel variation between images. However, pure monocular visual odometers cannot obtain absolute scales; in addition, relying solely on recursive calculations will inevitably lead to cumulative errors. For pure inertial solution calculations, the low-precision IMU will diverge very quickly in a short time. We derive the IMU prediction form based on Lie group and Lie algebra, and apply it to VIO. Based on the idea of graph optimization in pure visual SLAM, the IMU relative measurement information between frame and frame is converted into constraint node. The side of the pose is involved in the optimization framework. Using the IMU preintegration theory, these IMU's are processed relative to the measurement so that it is decoupled from the absolute pose (or only requires linear operations to correct), which greatly increases the speed of optimization. In addition, this optimized architecture also makes the unacceptable gravity of the accelerometer measurement an advantageous condition - the presence of gravity will make the entire system observable to the absolute attitude.

Keywords: Visual-inertial odometry · SLAM

1 Introduction

In the slam framework, a good front end can provide a good initial value for the back end for optimization. It can be said that the efficiency and robustness of the front end (mile meter) will directly affect the performance of the entire system. In pure visual odometers, the transformation matrix between the two frames is typically estimated based on pixel variations between two images or keyframes, minimizing reprojection errors or minimizing photometric errors (feature point methods or direct methods) [1, 2]. However, pure monocular visual odometers have problems in that they cannot estimate metric scales; in addition, simply relying on recursive operations inevitably leads to cumulative errors. For pure inertial solution calculation, due to the existence of random noise, the low-precision IMU will diverge very quickly in a short time.

On the other hand, a single moving camera is an external sensing sensor that allows us to measure the appearance and geometry of a 3D scene with unknown metrics; the Inertial Measurement Unit (IMU) is a proprioceptor that allows monocular vision and

© Springer Nature Singapore Pte Ltd. 2019
Y. Wang et al. (Eds.): IGTA 2019, CCIS 1043, pp. 184–192, 2019.
https://doi.org/10.1007/978-981-13-9917-6_18

gravity The metric scale is observable and provides robust and accurate motion estimation between frames [3–6]. VIO applications range from GPS autonomous navigation environments to 3D reconstruction and augmented reality.

There are already many VIO information integration solutions, such as MSCKF, VINS-MONO, ICE-BA, etc. MSCKF maintains a pose FIFO, arranged in chronological order, which can be called a sliding window. If a feature point is observed in several poses of the sliding window, a constraint is established between these poses to update the pose of key frames. VINS-Mono uses a tightly coupled, nonlinearly optimized approach to achieve high-precision visual inertial ranging by merging preintegrated IMU measurements and feature observations. In addition, VINS-Mono also performed four degrees of freedom pose map optimization to achieve global consistency. ICE_BA has renovated the VI-SLAM numerical solver. Compared to traditional solvers, ICE-BA offers an accurate solution with significantly higher computational efficiency. The ICE-BA solver allows for the use of very large measurements to achieve higher accuracy and robustness. ICE-BA solves the unresolved global consistency problem of many of the most advanced SLAM systems: the binary constraint function that minimizes the projection function during loop closure. In this paper, we proposed a visual inertial information integration method to fusion camera and IMU information.

To achieve this goal, we will do the following:

(1) Using the IMU preintegration theory, deriving the IMU preintegration formula, and combine with the SLAM graph optimization method, the IMU relative measurement information between frame and frame is converted into the constraint node (carrier pose) to participate in the optimization framework;
(2) Construct a visual odometer, select key frames, and construct a pose constraint between the two key frames;
(3) Realize the fusion of IMU and vision sensor, and complete the pose optimization between two frames based on the framework of graph optimization.

2 IMU Preintegration for VIO (Visual-Inertial Odometry)

An IMU commonly includes a 3-axis accelerometer and a 3-axis gyroscope and allows measuring the rotation rate and the acceleration of the sensor with respect to an inertial frame. The measurements of an IMU come from a 3-axis accelerometer and a 3-axis gyroscope, are namely $\omega_{wb}^b(t)$ and $\alpha^w(t)$, which in behalf of rotation vector and acceleration of the body (IMU) w.r.t to an inertial frame.

2.1 IMU Sensor Model and Kinetic Model

The gyroscope measurement model can be written as:

$$\widetilde{\omega}_{wb}^b(t) = \omega_{wb}^b(t) + \mathbf{b}_g(t) + \mathbf{\eta}_g(t). \tag{1}$$

The accelerometer measurement model can be written as:

$$\tilde{\alpha}^b(t) = \mathbf{R}_b^{wT}(_w\alpha(t) - _w\mathbf{g}) + \mathbf{b}_a(t) + \mathbf{\eta}_a(t). \tag{2}$$

In our notation, $\omega_{wb}^b(t)$ is the instantaneous angular velocity of B relative to W expressed in coordinate frame B, while $_w\alpha(t)$ is the acceleration of the sensor; $_w\mathbf{g}$ is the gravity vector in world coordinates. We neglect effects due to earth's rotation, which amounts to assuming that W is an inertial frame.

The IMU kinetic model can be written as:

$$\dot{\mathbf{R}}_b^w = \mathbf{R}_b^w(\omega_{wb}^b)^\wedge, \dot{\mathbf{v}} = \alpha^w, \dot{\mathbf{p}}^w = \mathbf{v}^w. \tag{3}$$

which describes the evolution of the pose and the velocity of Body (IMU).

2.2 Position, Velocity and Rotation

We can get the state at time $t + \Delta t$ by integrating the Eq. (3):

$$\mathbf{R}_{b(t+\Delta t)}^w = \mathbf{R}_{b(t)}^w \text{Exp}(\omega_{wb}^b(t) \cdot \Delta t), \tag{4}$$

$$\mathbf{v}^w(t + \Delta t) = \mathbf{v}^w(t) + \alpha^w(t) \cdot \Delta t, \tag{5}$$

$$\mathbf{p}^w(t + \Delta t) = \mathbf{p}^w(t) + \mathbf{v}^w(t) \cdot \Delta t + \frac{1}{2}\alpha^w(t) \cdot \Delta t^2. \tag{6}$$

In these three equations, $\omega_{wb}^t(t)$ represents the coordinate of the "angular velocity vector" at time t in the body system, $\omega_{wb}^w(t) \cdot \Delta t$ represents the coordinate of the "rotation vector" at time t in the body system. For the sake of conciseness, some upper and lower tag numbers are omitted below:

$$\mathbf{R}(t) \doteq \mathbf{R}_{b(t)}^w; \ \omega(t) \doteq \omega_{wb}^b(t); \ \alpha(t) \doteq \alpha^b(t); \ \mathbf{v}(t) \doteq \mathbf{v}^w(t); \ \mathbf{p}(t) \doteq \mathbf{p}^w(t); \ \mathbf{g} \doteq \mathbf{g}^w,$$

Bring the measurement model into the discrete equation of motion:

$$\begin{aligned} \mathbf{R}(t + \Delta t) &= \mathbf{R}(t) \cdot \text{Exp}(\omega(t) \cdot \Delta t) \\ &= \mathbf{R}(t) \cdot \text{Exp}((\tilde{\omega}(t) - \mathbf{b}^g(t) - \mathbf{\eta}^{gd}(t) \cdot \Delta t)). \end{aligned} \tag{7}$$

$$\begin{aligned} \mathbf{v}(t + \Delta t) &= \mathbf{v}(t) \cdot {}_w\alpha(t) \cdot \Delta t \\ &= \mathbf{v}(t) + \mathbf{R}(t) \cdot (\tilde{\alpha}(t) - \mathbf{b}^a(t) - \mathbf{\eta}^{ad}(t)) \cdot \Delta t + \mathbf{g} \cdot \Delta t, \end{aligned} \tag{8}$$

$$\begin{aligned} \mathbf{p}(t + \Delta t) &= \mathbf{p}(t) + \mathbf{v}(t) \cdot \Delta t + \frac{1}{2}\left[\mathbf{R}(t) \cdot (\tilde{\mathbf{a}}(t) - \mathbf{b}^a(t) - \mathbf{\eta}^{ad}(t) + \mathbf{g})\right] \cdot \Delta t^2 \\ &= \mathbf{p}(t) + \mathbf{v}(t) \cdot \Delta t + \frac{1}{2}\mathbf{g} \cdot \Delta t^2 + \frac{1}{2}\mathbf{R}(t) \cdot (\tilde{\mathbf{a}}(t) - \mathbf{b}^a(t) - \mathbf{\eta}^{ad}(t)) \cdot \Delta t^2 \end{aligned} \tag{9}$$

In the above formula, the noise term uses $\mathbf{\eta}_{gd}$ and $\mathbf{\eta}_{ad}$ which are different from the continuous noise terms $\mathbf{\eta}_g$ and $\mathbf{\eta}_a$. The covariance relationship between discrete noise and continuous noise is as follows:

$$\text{Cov}(\mathbf{\eta}^{gd}(t)) = \frac{1}{\Delta t}\text{Cov}(\mathbf{\eta}^g(t)), \tag{10}$$

$$\text{Cov}(\mathbf{\eta}^{ad}(t)) = \frac{1}{\Delta t}\text{Cov}(\mathbf{\eta}^a(t)). \tag{11}$$

Further assuming that Δt is constant (ie, the sampling frequency is constant), each discrete moment is represented by $k = 0, 1, 2, \ldots$, and the aforementioned three discrete motion equations can be further simplified (symbol simplification) as:

$$\mathbf{R}_{k+1} = \mathbf{R}_k \cdot \text{Exp}((\widetilde{\mathbf{\omega}}_k - \mathbf{b}_k^g(t) - \mathbf{\eta}_k^{gd} \cdot \Delta t)), \tag{12}$$

$$\mathbf{v}_{k+1} = \mathbf{v}_k + \mathbf{R}_k \cdot (\widetilde{\mathbf{\alpha}}_k - \mathbf{b}_k^a - \mathbf{\eta}_k^{ad}) \cdot \Delta t + \mathbf{g} \cdot \Delta t, \tag{13}$$

$$\mathbf{P}_{(k+1)} = \mathbf{p}_k + \mathbf{v}_k \cdot \Delta t + \frac{1}{2}\mathbf{g} \cdot \Delta t^2 + \frac{1}{2}\mathbf{R}_k \cdot (\widetilde{\mathbf{a}}_k - \mathbf{b}_k^a(t) - \mathbf{\eta}_k^{ad}(t)) \cdot \Delta t^2. \tag{14}$$

2.3 IMU Preintegration for Rotation, Velocity, and Position

The motion between two consecutive keyframes can be defined in terms of $\Delta \mathbf{R}$, $\Delta \mathbf{v}$ and $\Delta \mathbf{p}$ from all measurements in-between [7]. We use IMU preintegration described in [8]:

$$\Delta \widetilde{\mathbf{R}}_{ij} \approx \Delta \mathbf{R}_{ij} \cdot \text{Exp}(\vec{\delta}\varphi_{ij}) = R_i^T R_j \text{Exp}(\vec{\delta}\varphi_{ij}), \tag{15}$$

$$\Delta \widetilde{\mathbf{v}}_{ij} \approx \Delta \mathbf{v}_{ij} + \varphi \mathbf{v}_{ij} = \mathbf{R}_i^T (\mathbf{v}_j - \mathbf{v}_i - \mathbf{g} \cdot \Delta t_{ij}) + \delta \mathbf{v}_{ij}, \tag{16}$$

$$\Delta \widetilde{\mathbf{p}}_{ij} \approx \Delta \mathbf{p}_{ij} + \delta \mathbf{p}_{ij} = \mathbf{R}_i^T (\mathbf{p}_j - \mathbf{p}_i - \mathbf{v}_i \cdot \Delta t_{ij} - \frac{1}{2}\mathbf{g} \cdot \Delta t_{ij}^2) + \delta \mathbf{p}_{ij}. \tag{17}$$

3   Visual-Inertial Odometry

3.1   ORB Feature Extraction and Matching

In visual part, we use ORB (Oriented FAST and Rotated BRIEF) feature in processing pictures.

Fig. 1. An example of the ORB feature extraction. The center of the color circle is the extracted ORB feature point.

Fig. 2. An example of the ORB feature matching. The figure above shows all the matches, and the figure below shows the initial screening matches.

The biggest advantage of the ORB feature algorithm is its fast calculation speed [2]. This is first of all thanks to the use of FAST to detect feature points, and FAST's detection speed is as famous as its name. Again, the descriptor is calculated using the BRIEF algorithm.

The extracted features can be made rotationally invariant by using improved fast corner points. The representation of the unique binary string of the descriptor not only saves storage space, but also greatly shortens the matching time. The short line inside the circle indicates the direction in which the feature point rotates in Fig. 1.

After we matching the ORB features in-between two consecutive keyframes, we can estimate pose between these two keyframes based on the EPnP method [9].

The Fig. 1 is an example of the ORB feature extraction. And Fig. 2 is an example of ORB feature matching between two frames.

3.2   Visual-Inertial Sensor Information Fusion

Our visual inertial ranging system is responsible for tracking sensor pose, velocity and IMU deviation at frame rate. Once the camera pose is estimated, the map points in the local map are projected and matched to the key points on the keyframes. We then optimize the current frame by minimizing the reprojection errors for all matching feature points and IMU error terms.

The status to be estimated is as follows:

$$\theta = \left\{ \mathbf{R}_{wb}^j, {}_w\mathbf{p}_b^j, {}_w\mathbf{v}_b^j, \mathbf{b}_g^j, \mathbf{b}_a^j \right\}, \tag{18}$$

$$\theta^* = \underset{\theta}{\arg\min} \left(\sum_k \mathbf{E}_{proj}(k,j) + \mathbf{E}_{IMU}(i,j) \right). \tag{19}$$

The feature reprojection error is defined as follows:

$$\mathbf{E}_{proj}(k,j) = \rho\left((\mathbf{x}^k - \pi(\mathbf{X}_C^k))\sum_k((\mathbf{x}^k - \pi(\mathbf{X}_C^k))\right), \tag{20}$$

$$\mathbf{X}_C^k = \mathbf{R}_{cb}\mathbf{R}_{bw}(\mathbf{X}_w^k - {}_w\mathbf{p}_b^j) + {}_c\mathbf{p}_b. \tag{21}$$

where $\mathbf{x}_k$ is the keypoint location in the image, $\mathbf{X}_w^k$ the map point in world coordinates, and $\sum_k$ the information matrix associated to the keypoints scale, and ρ is the Huber robust cost function.

The IMU term $\mathbf{E}_{IMU}$ is :

$$\mathbf{E}_{IMU}(i,j) = \rho\left(\left[\mathbf{e}_R^T \mathbf{e}_v^T \mathbf{e}_p^T\right]\sum_I \left[\mathbf{e}_R^T \mathbf{e}_v^T \mathbf{e}_p^T\right]^T\right) + \rho\left(\mathbf{e}_b^T \sum_R \mathbf{e}_b^T\right) \tag{22}$$

$$\mathbf{e}_R = \mathrm{Log}\left(\left(\Delta R_{ij}\mathrm{Exp}\left(\mathbf{J}_{\Delta R}^g \mathbf{b}_g^j\right)\right)^T \mathbf{R}_{bw}^i \mathbf{R}_{wb}^j\right) \tag{23}$$

$$\mathbf{e}_v = \mathbf{R}_{bw}^i\left({}_w\mathbf{v}_b^j - {}_w\mathbf{v}_b^i - \mathbf{g}_w \cdot \Delta t_j^i\right) - \left(\Delta\mathbf{v}_j^i + \mathbf{J}_{\Delta v}^a \mathbf{b}_a^j\right) \tag{24}$$

$$\mathbf{e}_p = \mathbf{R}_{bw}^i\left({}_w\mathbf{p}_b^j - {}_w\mathbf{p}_b^i - {}_w\mathbf{v}_b^i\Delta t_{ij} - \frac{1}{2}\mathbf{g}_w\Delta t_{ij}^2\right) - \left(\Delta\mathbf{p}_{ij} + \mathbf{J}_{\Delta p}^g \mathbf{b}_g^i + \mathbf{J}_{\Delta p}^a \mathbf{b}_a^j\right) \tag{25}$$

$$\mathbf{e}_b = \mathbf{b}^j - \mathbf{b}^i. \tag{26}$$

where $\sum_I$ is the information matrix of the preintegration and $\sum_R$ is the bias random walk and ρ is the Huber robust cost function. We use bundle adjustment as the optimize method for the pose estimated [10]. We use g2o as our optimizing tool [11].

4   Experimental Results and Analysis

The monocular visual-inertial online initialization and camera-IMU extrinsic calibration method can be found in [12]. We experimented on the EuRoC Dataset [13–15].

Fig. 3. The map and the trajectory on MH_02_easy bag.

Fig. 4. The current frame that the system is processing.

The Figs. 3 and 4 are the results of the system running on the MH_02_easy.bag dataset.

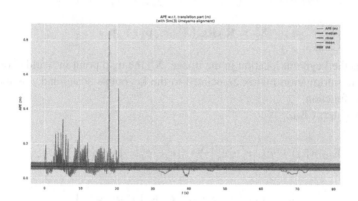

Fig. 5. The APE w.r.t. translation part (m) on V1_02_MEDIUM bag.

The Fig. 5 is the APE w.r.t. translation part(m) on V1_02_medium bag.

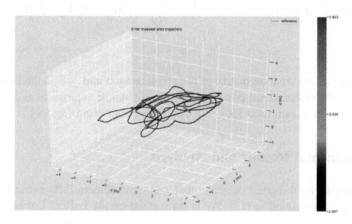

Fig. 6. The error mapped onto the trajectory (APE w.r.t. translation part (m) on V1_02_MED-IUM.bag).

The Fig. 6 shows that the APE w.r.t. translation part (m) on V1_02_MEDIUM bag mapped ontp the trajectory. We can see that most APE of the trajectory in the Figs. 5 and 6 is between 0.007 and 0.430 (m).

Table 1. Scale and RMSE (translation part) on sequences.

Sequence	Scale	RMSE
MH_02_easy	1.004957	0.035109
MH_03_medium	1.002120	0.038132
V1_01_easy	1.021709	0.089590
V1_02_medium	1.062517	0.082057
V2_01_easy	0.974105	0.073224
V2_02_medium	0.993937	0.066430
V2_03_difficult	1.014616	————

The Table 1 shows that Scale and RMSE (translation part) on sequences. From the Table 1, we can see that we basically estimated the metric scale of the map, and the error is about 0.06. On the MH easy and medium-level datasets, our system performed better with a margin of error of around 0.035. On easy and medium sequences of the V1 and V2, the trajectory RMSE is between 0.066 and 0.089. On the difficult level of the sequence, the trajectory error increases sharply. During the experiment, it was found that in the V2_03_difficult sequence, due to the fast running speed of the aircraft and the strong sloshing, at this time, the odometer part will track the loss.

The results of experiments shows that our method can integrate the image information from camera and inertial information from IMU measurements. The cameras provide rich information of the environment for building 3D models, localizing the camera and recognizing already visited places. And IMU sensors provide self-motion information, allowing to recover metric scale for monocular vision, and to estimate gravity direction, rendering absolute pitch and roll observable.

5 Conclusion

In this paper, we derive the IMU pre-integration equations and apply it to visual inertial information integration. We use a method of visual inertial information integration to apply the method of graph optimization to the process of visual inertial information integration. We have experimented with this method and analyzed the experimental results. The analysis results show that we can effectively integrate the camera and IMU data, estimate the measurement scale of the map more accurately and estimate the carrier pose and its motion trajectory, and achieve the expected goal.

Acknowledgement. This work is supported by National Natural Science Foundation of China (Grant No. 61877026).

References

1. Engel, J., Koltun, V., Cremers, D.: Direct sparse odometry. IEEE Trans. Pattern Anal. Mach. Intell. **PP**(99), 1 (2016)
2. Mur-Artal, R., Tardós, J.D.: ORB-SLAM2: an open-source SLAM system for monocular, stereo, and RGB-D cameras. IEEE Trans. Robot. **33**(5), 1255–1262 (2017)
3. Shen, S., Michael, N., Kumar, V.: Tightly-coupled monocular visual-inertial fusion for autonomous flight of rotorcraft MAVs. In: 2015 IEEE International Conference on Robotics and Automation (ICRA). IEEE (2015)
4. Tong, Q., Li, P., Shen, S.: VINS-mono: a robust and versatile monocular visual-inertial state estimator. IEEE Trans. Robot. **PP**(99), 1–17 (2017)
5. Hartley, R., Zisserman, A.: Multiple View Geometry in Computer Vision. Cambridge University Press, Cambridge (2003)
6. Indelman, V., Williams, S., Kaess, M., et al.: Information fusion in navigation systems via factor graph based incremental smoothing. Robot. Auton. Syst. **61**(8), 721–738 (2013)
7. Lupton, T., Sukkarieh, S.: Visual-inertial-aided navigation for high-dynamic motion in built environments without initial conditions. IEEE Trans. Robot. **28**(1), 61–76 (2012)
8. Forster, C., Carlone, L., Dellaert, F., Scaramuzza, D.: On-manifold preintegration for real-time visual-inertial odometry. In: IEEE Trans. Robot. (2016). https://doi.org/10.1109/TRO. 2016.2597321
9. Moreno-Noguer, F., Lepetit, V., Fua, P.: Accurate non-iterative O(n) solution to the PnP problem. In: IEEE International Conference on Computer Vision (2007)
10. Triggs, B., Mclauchlan, P.F., Hartley, R.I., et al. Bundle adjustment—a modern synthesis. In: International Workshop on Vision Algorithms: Theory & Practice (1999)
11. Kuemmerle, R., Grisetti, G., Strasdat, H., Konolige, K., Burgard, W.: g2o: a general framework for graph optimization. In: IEEE International Conference on Robotics and Automation (ICRA) (2011)
12. Yang, Z., Shen, S.: Monocular visual-inertial state estimation with online initialization and camera-IMU extrinsic calibration. IEEE Trans. Autom. Sci. Eng. **14**, 39–51 (2016). https:// doi.org/10.1109/tase.2016.2550621
13. Mur-Artal, R., Tardós, J.D.: Visual-inertial monocular SLAM with map reuse. IEEE Robot. Autom. Lett. **2**(2), 796–803 (2016)
14. Leutenegger, S., Lynen, S., Bosse, M., et al.: Keyframe-based visual-inertial odometry using nonlinear optimization. Int. J. Robot. Res. **34**(3), 314–334 (2014)
15. Burri, M., et al.: The EuRoC micro aerial vehicle datasets. Int. J. Robot. Res. **35**(10), 1157–1163 (2016)

A Multiscale Image Denoising Algorithm Based on Dilated Residual Convolution Network

Chang Liu$^{(\boxtimes)}$, Zhaowei Shang, and Anyong Qin

College of Computer Science, Chongqing University, Chongqing 400044, China
{changliu37,szw,ayqin}@cqu.edu.cn

Abstract. Image denoising is a classical problem in low-level computer vision. Model-based optimization methods and deep learning approaches are the two main strategies for solving the problem. Model-based optimization methods are flexible for handling different inverse problems but are usually time-consuming. In contrast, deep learning methods have fast speed but the performance of these convolutional neural networks (CNNs) is still inferior. To address this issue, here we propose a novel deep learning model that combines the dilated residual convolution and multi-scale convolution groups. Due to the complex patterns and structures inside an image, the design of hybrid dilated convolution is utilized to learn those patterns. Specifically, the skipped connection is utilized to speed up the training process while maintaining the denoising performance. In order to show the capacity of the proposed work, we do an ablation study to validate the effect of dilated convolution and multi-scale convolution group. Experimental results have demonstrated that our enhanced denoiser can not only achieve promising denoising results, but also become a strong competitor in practical application.

Keywords: Image denoising · Dilated convolution · Multiscale · Residual learning

1 Introduction

Image denoising is a classical yet still active topic in computer vision. It has become an essential and indispensable step in many image processing applications. In recent years, various algorithms have been proposed, which include nonlocal self-similarity (NSS) models [1], sparse representation models [2], and deep learning approaches [3–6]. Among them, BM3D [7], WNNM [8] and CSF [9] are considered as the state-of-the-art methods in non-depth learning approaches. NSS models like BM3D provide high image quality and are very effective in Gaussian denoising with known noise level. Recently, many state-of-the-art CNN algorithms like IRCNN [10] outperform the non-local and collaboration filtering approaches.

Since the deep learning methods have achieved massive success in classification [11] as well as other computer vision problems [12, 13]. A lot of CNNs have been proposed in image denoising. Aiming at image restoration task, it is important to use the prior information properly. Many prior-based approaches like WNNM involve a

© Springer Nature Singapore Pte Ltd. 2019
Y. Wang et al. (Eds.): IGTA 2019, CCIS 1043, pp. 193–203, 2019.
https://doi.org/10.1007/978-981-13-9917-6_19

complex optimization problem in the inference stage, which leads to achieve high performance hardly without sacrificing computation efficiency. To overcome the limitation of prior-based methods, several discriminative learning methods have been developed to learn the models in the inference procedure. This kind of models can get rid of the iterative optimization procedure in the test phase. According to the work of [3, 10], image denoising can be seen as a Maximum A Posteriori (MAP) problem from the Bayesiaonvolution, which can enlarge the receptive field and keep the amount of calculn perspective. The deep CNNs can be used to learn the prior as a denoiser. The motivation of this work is whether we can increase the prior from the view of convolution itself. The work of [14] shows the design of multi-scale convolutions which can help to extract more features from the previous layer. Reference [15] introduced the work of dilated cation. Subsequently, the work of [13] shows that dilated residual network can perform better than the residual network in the image classification. In the image denoising task, due to the little difference between adjacent pixels, the dilated convolution can bring more discrepancy information from the front layer to the back layer. In addition, it could increase the generalization ability of the model and require no extra computation cost.

This paper proposes an enhanced denoiser based on the residual dilated convolutional neural network. Inspired by the residual learning insight [3], this paper modifies the dilated residual network based on residual learning. We treat image denoising as a plain discriminative learning problem. Contrary to the existing various residual networks, we use multi-scale convolution to extract more information from the original image and hybrid dilated convolution module to avoid the gridding effect. The paper compares several state-of-the-art methods, such as BM3D, IRCNN, DnCNN [3] and FFDnet [17]. For gray image denoising, the experimental result shows that the proposed enhanced denoiser can make the processed image better with only half parameters of other CNN methods. And we can handle the color image denoising task by using the same network. In addition, the proposed model has a competitive run time performance.

In summary, this paper has the following two main contributions:

Firstly, we propose a lightweight and effective image denoiser based on multi-scale convolution group. The experiments shows that our proposed model can achieve better performance and speed over the current state-of-the-art methods.

Secondly, we show the proposed network can handle both gray and color image denosing robustly without the increment of parameters.

2 Related Work

Here, we provide a brief review of deep learning methods in image denoising. Harmeling et al. [18] was firstly to apply multi-layer perception (MLP) for image denoising task, which image patches and large image databases are utilized to achieve excellent results. In [6], a trainable nonlinear reaction diffusion (TNRD) model was proposed and all the parameters can be simultaneously learned from training data through a loss based approach. It can be expressed as a feed-forward deep network by unfolding a fixed number of gradient inference steps. DeepAM [4] was consisted of proximal mapping and end continuation. It is the regularization-based approach for image restoration, which enables the CNN to operate as a prior or regularizer in the alternating minimization (AM) algorithm. IRCNN [10] uses the HQS framework to show that CNN denoiser can bring strong image prior into model-based optimization methods. All the above methods have shown that the decoupling of the fidelity term and regularization term can enable a wide variety of existing denoising models to solve image denoising problem.

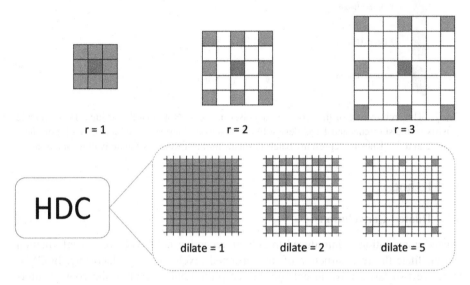

Fig. 1. Illustration of the dilate convolution and Hybrid Dilated Convolution (HDC) architecture. The pixels (marked in lavender) contributes to the calculation of the center pixels (marked in yellow) through three different dilation rate.

Residual learning has multiple realizations. The first approach is using a skipped connection from a certain layer to another layer during forward and backward propagations. This was firstly introduced by [19] to solve the gradient vanishing when the researchers need training very deep architecture in image classification. In low-level computer vision problems, Bae et al. [5] implemented a residual module within three convolution block by a skipped connection. Another residual implementation in image denoising is transforming the label into the difference between the input data and the clean data. The residual learning has been proven to be effective in many visual tasks.

The main idea of dilated convolution is to increase the image resolution by inserting "holes" between pixels. The dilated convolutions enable dense feature extraction in deep CNNs and enlarge the receptive field of convolutional kernel. Chen et al. [20] designed an atrous spatial pyramid pooling (ASPP) scheme to capture multi-scale objects and context information by using multiple dilated convolution. In image denoising, Wang et al. [21] proposed an approach to calculate receptive field size when dilated convolution is included.

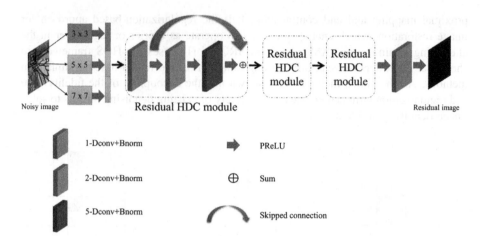

Fig. 2. The architecture of the proposed denoiser network. Note that the residual HDC module consists of the shortcuts and HDC design block. "s-Dconv" represents dilated convolution, here s = 1, 2 and 5; "Bnorm" represents batch normalization; "PRelu" is the activation function.

3 Method

3.1 Dilated Convolution

Dilated convolution is introduced to enlarge receptive field. The context information can facilitate the reconstruction of the corrupted pixels in image denoising. In CNN, there are two basic ways to enlarge the receptive field to capture the context information. We can either increase the filter size or the depth. According to the existing network design [19], using the 3×3 filter with a large depth is a popular way. In this paper, we use the dilated filter and keep the merits of traditional 3×3 convolution. In Fig. 1, the image filtered by different dilate rate shows the different receptive field. A dilated filter with dilation factor α can be simply interpreted as a sparse filter of size $(2\alpha + 1) \times (2\alpha + 1)$. For kernel size K = 3 and dilate rate r = 2, only 9 entries of fixed positions can be non-zeros. But the use of dilated convolutions may cause gridding artifacts [15]. It occurs when a feature map has higher-frequency content than the sampling rate of the dilated convolution. And we notice that the hybrid dilated convolution (HDC) proposed by [13] addressed this issue theoretically. The HDC module can naturally integrated with the original layers of network, without adding extra modules. It can make better use of receptive field information. 1 dilate convolution and 5 dilate convolution will extract features at different level. In other word, the dilated convolution can extract information at different scale.

3.2 Multiscale Convolution Group

Multiscale feature extraction is a common technique in solving computer vision problems. It can make use of feature maps in different levels. In deep CNNs, the 3×3 kernel and 5×5 kernel can extract different scale of features. The addition of the multiscale structure will not only increase the width of network, but also improves the generalization of network. Inspired by the Inception module, we proposed the multi-scale convolution group. For image denoising task, due to the unchanged size of output image, we remove the pooling layer and apply three scale filters with different numbers. The number of each kind of filters is 12, 20, 32. The reason is that the sum of the feature map is 64 and this combination achieves the balance between feature extraction and parameters. Differing from the Inception module, we concatenate the feature maps directly. It can significantly reduce the parameters. Considering of the computation cost, we only use the multiscale module in the first layer.

3.3 Architecture

Our proposed network structure illustrated in Fig. 2 is inspired by [10] and [13]. It consists of eleven layers. The first layer is the multiscale convolution group. The residual connection starts from the second layer. Each dilated convolution will be followed by the batch normalization (BN) [22] layer and parametric rectifield linear unit (PRelu) [16]. Such network design techniques have been widely used in recent CNN architecture. In particular, it has been pointed out that this kind of combination can not only enables fast and stable training but also tends to better result in Gaussian denoising task [10]. The PReLU and BN layer can accurate the convergence of net-work. The task of image denoising is going to recover a clean image from a noisy observation. We consider the noisy image y can be expressed as y = x + G, where x stands for the clean image, and G is the unknown Gaussian noise distribution. Owing to residual learning strategy applied, the labels are obtained by calculating the difference between the input image and the clean image. So the output of our network is the residual image, which is the prediction of the noise distribution.

4   Experiments

4.1   Training Details

Due to the characteristic of Gaussian convolution, the output image may produce boundary artifacts. So we apply zero padding strategy and use small patches to tackle with this problem. The number of feature maps in each layer is 64. And the depth of network is set to eleven which is kind of lightweight framework. The patch size of input images is 45×45. The Adam [25] solver is applied to optimize the network parameters. The learning rate starts from 10^{-3} and then is fixed to 10^{-4}. The learning rate is decreased 10 times after 60 epoches. The network parameters are initialized using the Xavier initialization [16]. And we trained 100 epoches to get the result, it almost takes half a day to train a denoising model with the specific noise level. 400 images of publicly available Berkeley segmentation (BSD500) [6] and Urban 100 datasets [26] are utilized to train the Gaussian denoising model. In addition, we generated 3200 images via image rotation, cropping and flipping. For the test data set, BSD68 and color version of BSD68 (CBSD68) are used. Note that all those image are widely used for the evaluation of denoising models and they are not included in the training datasets.

4.2   Ablation Study

In order to show the capacity of the proposed network, we remove some "feature" of the model, and seeing how that affects performance. Table 1 shows the results of ablation study. We keep the number of layers and the number of channels per layer unchanged. The result of removing dilated convolutions proves that the dilated convolution can extract more context information in image denoising. And the result of removing multi-scale convolution group demonstrates that multi-scale feature extraction can improve the performance of the proposed model with only a few parameters increased.

Table 1. The ablation study about performance comparison in terms of average PSNR (db) results for BSD68 dataset, the best results are highlighted.

Methods	$\sigma = 15$	$\sigma = 25$	$\sigma = 50$	$\sigma = 75$
No dilated convolution	31.678	29.172	26.205	24.612
No multi-scale convolution group	31.737	29.247	26.314	24.778
Proposed	**31.751**	**29.258**	**26.323**	**24.793**

For color image denoising, the compared deep learning methods will increase the number of layers or the number of channels to handle the color image problem. We do an ablation study to show that the reason we keep the number of layers and channels unchanged. Table 2 shows that increasing the number of layers or channels does not lead to the improvement of performance. In other word, the more complex model does not improve the generalization capabilities of the model.

Table 2. The ablation study about performance comparison in terms of average PSNR (db) results on the color version of BSD68 dataset, the best results are highlighted

Methods	$\sigma = 15$	$\sigma = 25$	$\sigma = 50$
14 layers, 64 channels	34.05	31.40	28.02
11 layers, 96 channels	34.02	31.38	28.00
Proposed	**34.10**	**31.43**	**28.09**

4.3   Denoising Results

We compared the proposed denoiser with several state-of-the-art denoising methods, including two model-based optimization methods BM3D and WNNM, one discriminative learning method TNRD, and four deep learning methods included IRCNN, DnCNN, FFDnet and DDRN [21]. Figure 3 shows the visual results with details of different methods. It can be seen that both BM3D and WNNM tend to produce over-smooth textures. TRND can preserve fine details and sharp edges, but it seems that artifacts in the smooth region are generated. The deep learning methods and the proposed method can have a pleasure result in the smooth region. It is clearly that the proposed method can preserve better texture than the other methods, such as the region above the balcony fence.

Table 3. Performance comparison in terms of average PSNR (db) results for BSD68 dataset, the best results are highlighted.

Methods	$\sigma = 15$	$\sigma = 25$	$\sigma = 50$	$\sigma = 75$
BM3D	31.075	28.568	25.616	24.212
WNNM	31.371	28.834	25.874	24.401
TNRD	31.422	28.923	25.971	–
IRCNN	31.629	29.145	26.185	24.591
DDRN	31.682	29.181	29.213	24.617
DnCNN	31.718	29.228	26.231	24.641
FFDnet	31.631	29.189	26.289	24.788
Proposed	**31.751**	**29.258**	**26.323**	**24.793**

(a) Noisy/20.175dB (b) BM3D/29.534dB (c) WNNM/28.961dB (d) TNRD/29.765dB

(e) IRCNN/30.068dB (f) DnCNN/30.161dB (g) FFDnet/30.041dB (h) proposed/30.201dB

Fig. 3. Denoising results of one image from BSD68 with noise level 25

In order to show the capacity of the proposed model, we do the quantitative and qualitative evaluation on widely used testing datasets. The average PSNR results of different methods on the BSD68 are shown in Table 3. BSD68 consists of 68 gray images, which has diverse images. We can have the following observation. Firstly, the proposed method can achieve the best average PSNR result than those competing methods on BSD68 data sets. Compared to the benchmark method BM3D on BSD68, the WNNM and TNRD have a notable gain of between 0.3 dB and 0.35 dB. The method IRCNN can have a PSNR gain of nearly 0.55 dB. In contrast, our proposed model can outperform BM3D nearly 0.7 dB on all the four noise levels. Secondly, the proposed method is better than DnCNN and FFDnet when the noise level is below 75. This result shows that the proposed method has the better trade-off between receptive field size and modeling capacity.

(a) CBM3D / 24.31dB   (b) CDnCNN / 24.98dB   (c) CFFDnet / 24.88dB   (d) proposed / 25.05dB

Fig. 4. Color denoising results of one image from the CBSD68 dataset with noise level 50 (Color figure online)

For color image denoising, we use the same network parameters. The only difference is the input tensor becomes $45 \times 45 \times 3$. The visual comparisons are shown in Fig. 4. It is obviously that CBM3D generates false color artifacts in some region while the proposed model can recover the image with more natural color and texture structure, like more sharp edges. In addition, Table 4 shows that the proposed model can outperform the benchmark method CBM3D among three noise level. In the meantime, the proposed method is more effective than three deep CNN methods in the color BSD68 dataset.

Table 4. Performance comparison in terms of average PSNR (db) results on the color version of BSD68 dataset, the best results are highlighted.

Methods	$\sigma = 15$	$\sigma = 25$	$\sigma = 50$
CBM3D	33.52	30.71	27.38
CDDRN	33.93	31.24	27.93
CDnCNN	33.89	31.23	27.92
CFFDnet	33.87	31.21	27.96
Proposed	**34.10**	**31.43**	**28.09**

We give a brief calculation about the amount of parameters in Table 5. Note that the values are different for gray and color image denoising due to the different network depth. For instance, DnCNN uses 17 convolution layers for gray image denosing and

20 for color image denoising, whereas FFDnet takes 15 for gray and 12 for color. In addition, FFDnet set 64 channels for gray image and 96 channels for color image. However, the proposed method can outperform the other method without the increment of the parameters. It indicates that our model is more robust without sacrificing the computing resource.

Table 5. The amount of parameters for three different methods. The color denoiser contains more parameters due to the deeper architecture.

Methods	DnCNN	FFDnet	Proposed
Gray/param	5.6×10^5	5.5×10^5	3.3×10^5
Color/param	6.7×10^5	8.3×10^5	3.4×10^5

We also compare the computation time to check the applicability of the proposed method. BM3D and TNRD are utilized to be the comparison due to their potential value in practical applications. We use the Nvidia cuDNN-v6 deep learning library to accelerate the GPU computation and we do not consider the memory transfer time between CPU and GPU. Since both the proposed denoiser and TNRD support parallel computation on GPU, we also provide the GPU runtime. Table 6 lists run time comparison of different methods for denoising images of size 256×256, 512×512 and 1024×1024. For each test, we run several times to get the average runtime. We can see that the proposed method is very competitive in both CPU and GPU computation. Such a good performance over the BM3D is properly attributed to the following reasons. First, the 3×3 convolution and PRelu activation function are simple effective and efficient. Second, batch normalization is adopted, which is beneficial to Gaussian denoising. Third, residual architecture can not only have a larger model capacity, but also accelerate the inference time of deep network.

Table 6. Runtime of different methods on gray images of different size with noise level 25

Size	Device	256×256	512×512	1024×1024
BM3D	CPU	0.69	2.85	11.89
	GPU	–	–	–
TNRD	CPU	0.47	1.33	4.61
	GPU	0.010	0.032	0.116
DnCNN	CPU	0.74	3.41	12.1
	GPU	0.014	0.051	0.200
FFDnet	CPU	0.44	1.81	7.24
	GPU	0.006	0.012	0.038
Proposed	CPU	0.41	1.62	4.68
	GPU	0.004	0.009	0.032

5 Conclusion

In this paper, we have designed an effective CNN denoiser for image denoising. Specifically, with the aid of skipped connections, we can easily train a deep and complex convolutional network. A lot of deep learning skills are integrated to speed up the training process and boost the denoising performance. The model-based and prior-based approaches are the popular way to tackle with denoising problem. Followed by the instruction of prior-based model, we show the possibility of increasing the features by using multiscale module and residual HDC module. Extensive experimental results have demonstrated that the proposed method can not only produce favorable image denoising performance quantitatively and qualitatively, but also have a promising run time by GPU. There are still some work for further study. First, it would be a promising direction to train a lightweight denoiser for practical applications. Second, how to extend the proposed method to other image restoration problems like image deblurring would be interesting. Third, it would be a challenging work to investigate how to denoise the non-Gaussian noisy according to some properties of gaussian denoising models.

References

1. Mairal, J., Bach, F., Ponce, J., Sapiro, G.: Nonlocal sparse models for image restoration. In: IEEE International Conference on Computer Vision, pp. 2272–2279 (2010)
2. Dong, W., Zhang, L., Shi, G.: Nonlocally centralized sparse representation for image restoration. IEEE Trans. Image Process. Publ. IEEE Sig. Process. Soc. **22**(4), 1620 (2013)
3. Zhang, K., Zuo, W., Chen, Y., Meng, D., Zhang, L.: Beyond a gaussian denoiser: residual learning of deep cnn for image denoising. IEEE Trans. Image Process. **26**(7), 3142–3155 (2017)
4. Kim, Y., Jung, H., Min, D., Sohn, K.: Deeply aggregated alternating minimization for image restoration. In: IEEE Conference on Computer Vision and Pattern Recognition, pp. 284–292 (2017)
5. Bae, W., Yoo, J., Chul Ye, J.: Beyond deep residual learning for image restoration: persistent homology-guided manifold simplification. In: Computer Vision and Pattern Recognition Workshops, pp. 1141–1149 (2017)
6. Chen, Y., Pock, T.: Trainable nonlinear reaction diffusion: a flexible framework for fast and effective image restoration. IEEE Trans. Pattern Anal. Mach. Intell. **39**(6), 1256–1272 (2017)
7. Dabov, K., Foi, A., Katkovnik, V., Egiazarian, K.: Image denoising by sparse 3-D transform-domain collaborative filtering. IEEE Trans. Image Process. Publ. IEEE Sig. Process. Soc. **16**(8), 2080 (2007)
8. Gu, S., Zhang, L., Zuo, W., Feng, X.: Weighted nuclear norm minimization with application to image denoising. In: Computer Vision and Pattern Recognition, pp. 2862–2869 (2014)
9. Schmidt, U., Roth, S.: Shrinkage fields for effective image restoration. In: IEEE Conference on Computer Vision and Pattern Recognition, pp. 2774–2781 (2014)
10. Zhang, K., Zuo, W., Gu, S., Zhang, L.: Learning deep CNN denoiser prior for image restoration. In: IEEE Conference on Computer Vision and Pattern Recognition, pp. 2808–2817 (2017)

11. Krizhevsky, A., Sutskever, I., Hinton, G.E.: ImageNet classification with deep convolutional neural networks. In: International Conference on Neural Information Processing Systems, pp. 1097–1105 (2012)
12. Ronneberger, O., Fischer, P., Brox, T.: U-net: convolutional networks for biomedical image segmentation. In: International Conference on Medical Image Computing and Computer-Assisted Intervention, pp. 234–241 (2015)
13. Wang, P., Chen, P., Yuan, Y., Liu, D., Huang, Z.: Understanding convolution for semantic segmentation. In: IEEE Winter Conference on Applications of Computer Vision (2017)
14. Szegedy, C., Liu, W., Jia, Y., Sermanet, P., Reed, S., et al.: Going deeper with convolutions. In: IEEE Conference on Computer Vision and Pattern Recognition, pp. 1–9 (2015)
15. Yu, F., Koltun, V., Funkhouser, T.: Dilated residual networks. In: IEEE Conference on Computer Vision and Pattern Recognition, pp. 636–644 (2017)
16. He, K., Zhang, X., Ren, S., Sun, J.: Delving deep into rectifiers: surpassing human-level performance on imagenet classification. In: IEEE International Conference on Computer Vision, pp. 1026–1034 (2015)
17. Zhang, K., Zuo, W., Zhang, L.: FFdnet: toward a fast and flexible solution for cnn based image denoising. IEEE Trans. Image Process. 27(9), 4608–4622 (2017)
18. Harmeling, S., Schuler, C.J., Burger, H.C.: Image denoising: can plain neural networks compete with BM3D. In: Computer Vision and Pattern Recognition, pp. 2392–2399 (2012)
19. He, K., Zhang, X., Ren, S., Sun, J.: Deep residual learning for image recognition. In: IEEE Conference on Computer Vision and Pattern Recognition, pp. 770–778 (2016)
20. Chen, L.C., Papandreou, G., Kokkinos, I., Murphy, K.: Deeplab: Semantic image segmentation with deep convolutional nets, atrous convolution, and fully connected crfs. IEEE Trans. Pattern Anal. Mach. Intell. 40(4), 834–848 (2018)
21. Wang, T., Sun, M.: Dilated deep residual network for image denoising. In: IEEE 29th International Conference on Tools with Artificial Intelligence (ICTAI), pp. 1272–1279 (2017)
22. Ioffe, S., Szegedy, C.: Batch normalization: accelerating deep network training by reducing internal covariate shift. In: International Conference on Machine Learning, pp. 448–456 (2015)
23. He, K., Zhang, X., Ren, S., Sun, J.: Identity mappings in deep residual networks. In: European Conference on Computer Vision, pp. 630–645 (2016)
24. Deng, J., Dong, W., Socher, R., Li, L.J., Li, K., Li, F.F.: ImageNet: a large-scale hierarchical image database. In: IEEE Conference on Computer Vision and Pattern Recognition, pp. 248–255 (2009)
25. Kingma, D., Ba, J.: Adam: a method for stochastic optimization. In: Proceedings of the 3rd International Conference on Learning Representations (2015)
26. Huang, J.B., Singh, A., Ahuja, N.: Single image super-resolution from transformed self-exemplars. In: IEEE Conference on Computer Vision and Pattern Recognition, pp. 5197–5206 (2015)

Model-Driven Dynamic Visualization
of Spatiotemporal Data in GIS

Weiyi Kong[1,2], Li Yang[3(✉)], Jianlong Ren[1,2], Chun Zuo[1,2],
and Fengjun Zhang[1,2]

[1] Institute of Software, Chinese Academy of Sciences, Beijing, China
kawaiiq@foxmail.com, renjianlong16@otcaix.iscas.ac.cn,
zuochun@sinosoft.com.cn, fengjun@iscas.ac.cn
[2] University of Chinese Academy of Sciences, Beijing, China
[3] State Key Laboratory of Computer Science, Institute of Software,
Chinese Academy of Sciences, Beijing, China
yangli2017@iscas.ac.cn

Abstract. Compared with static spatial data, spatiotemporal data can better represent dynamic real-world phenomena. Many models and temporal GIS applications have been proposed to process, manage and analyze spatiotemporal data. However, most of these works mainly focus on static representation and storage in database and lack enough support for dynamic visualization. Furthermore, most spatiotemporal data models are usually specially designed for specific problems, making it difficult for interdisciplinary data integration. In this paper, we propose a model-driven approach for dynamically visualizing spatiotemporal data in animation, with a property-pluggable model and a modular web-based GIS. Demonstration on 2 real-world datasets shows that our method can integrate multi-source heterogeneous data, while keeping simple, pluggable structure for future customization and extension.

Keywords: Model-driven · Dynamic visualization ·
Spatiotemporal data model · GIS

1 Introduction

Geographic information system (GIS) is an important tool for managing and analyzing geospatial information, which has been widely applied in various fields [1–5]. However, traditional GIS only supports static spatial data [6], which limits its performance on handling time-related information. The world is dynamic, and information changes with time. Therefore, started from 1980s [7], many temporal GIS and spatiotemporal data models were proposed to process, manage, and analyze spatiotemporal data [8] on various fields [9–12]. However, most of proposed models and applications mainly focus on representation and storage of data in databases but pay less attention on how to visualize it.

Most of current GIS visualize geographic data based on static visualization. They map data to visual elements, like scatters [13, 14], lines [15], polygons [14, 16], heatmaps [14], or charts [17, 18] and then display them on maps or other interfaces. For

© Springer Nature Singapore Pte Ltd. 2019
Y. Wang et al. (Eds.): IGTA 2019, CCIS 1043, pp. 204–215, 2019.
https://doi.org/10.1007/978-981-13-9917-6_20

spatiotemporal data, static visualization method integrates all information at different times together and displays static images. This is simple, compatible with most GIS, and suitable for analyzing relations between data collected at different timepoints. But it has limitations for visualizing complex spatiotemporal data, such as those whose dynamic process cannot be simply represented by just setting different styles and symbols for different objects and timepoints, for example, changes of European countries and their territories in history.

Dynamic visualization, instead, animated the dynamic process in a more vivid way, attracting attention on places where changes occurred. Animation is formed by switching frames, which represent information of a timepoint. With interferences of other timepoints excluded, dynamic visualization can contain more information on each timepoint, making it possible to handle more complex spatiotemporal data. Many GIS capable of handling spatiotemporal data support dynamic visualization using animations [9, 19, 20]. However, there are still some limitations of them.

A possible way for dynamic visualization is to let static GIS cover server-side rendered animation formatted images, like GIF, or videos, on the map. This is adopted by some GIS application [19]. It is simple but lacks flexibility in some cases, for example, setting conditions to only display interested elements, or changing style to distinguish the content from others. This requires the backend to re-render the data, which increases backend burden.

Another problem is that many of these works [9, 20] focus on specific problems and disciplines, making it hard to be applied to other problems or integrate interdisciplinary data. Furthermore, highly customized model structure also makes it hard for using well-developed tools which avoids "reinventing the wheel", like OpenLayers, Leaflet, ArcGIS, GeoServer, etc., causing extra works to transform data into common format which can be truly used by these tools for visualization.

In this paper, we propose a model-driven approach for dynamic visualization in animation of spatiotemporal data, using web-based GIS. Our goal is to find a pattern for dynamic visualization. The main contributions of this paper are as follows:

Formal Data Model for Dynamic Visualization. We propose a formal data model which can integrate multi-source, heterogeneous data and a property-pluggable structure for customization. The structure is simple for customization, and compatible with open standard data formats.

Architecture of Modular Web-Based GIS. We propose an architecture of web-based GIS using the data model, which is demonstrated to be module-pluggable and extensible.

2   Data Model

Here, we propose a model for dynamic visualization in the form of animation. This model can integrate heterogeneous data and is property-pluggable for customization. Our Model is mainly based on snapshot model [8].

2.1   Model Structure

As shown as Fig. 1, model is divided into three properties: layer, timeline and style, which is defined as follows:

$$model = [layer, timeline, style] \tag{1}$$

where *layer* contains all snapshots that can be used to show on maps, representing each spatiotemporal object, *timeline* orders each snapshot on a timeline, and *style* tells what each spatial object looks like, indicating GIS how to render them.

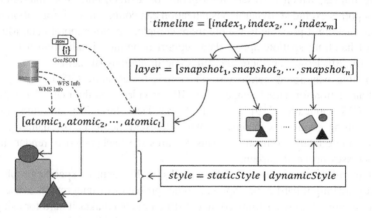

Fig. 1. Structure of data model for dynamic visualization.

Dynamic process is represented by snapshots in *layer*, indexed by *timeline*, and styled by *style*.

layer is an array. Each snapshot object represents the status of the data at some timepoint. The array is defined as follows:

$$layer = [snapshot_1, snapshot_2, \ldots, snapshot_n] \tag{2}$$

$$snapshot = [atomic_1, atomic_2, \ldots, atomic_l] \tag{3}$$

n is the number of *snapshot* objects in *layer* array. Each snapshot in *layer* array is made of several *atomic* objects, as described in (3), which describes some spatial objects. l indicates the number of *atomic* objects that make the snapshot, which can be different in each *snapshot*. Types of *atomic* object can be various without restriction.

snapshot elements in *layer* array don't have to be sorted according to time. Its order is decided by objects in *timeline* in (1), which is also an array describing the order of snapshots. It is defined as follows:

$$timeline = [index_1, index_2, \ldots, index_m] \tag{4}$$

$$index = [i, info] \tag{5}$$

m is the number of timepoints in *timeline*. Each *index* element in (4) is an object defined as (5), where *i* is a number representing the real index of snapshot object in *layer*, and *info* describes what happened at the corresponding timepoint, which can be a string or a json encoded object. A *snapshot* object in *layer* can be reused by various *index* objects, which reduces redundant data.

style in (1) indicates how the object is rendered by the system, including colors, opacity, width of edges, etc. Basically, there are two types of style: static style and dynamic style. Static style gives a fixed style configuration for all spatial objects, while dynamic style uses visual mapping to map spatial objects with different values to different style, just like what static visualization does. The data structure of style object depends on frontend implementation solution. For example, the frontend of our system is mainly built with OpenLayers, so its structure in our system implementation corresponds to related OpenLayers API [21].

2.2   Property-Pluggable Structure for Customization

All properties in the model are optional and new properties can also be appended. Types of data and their visualization method will be decided according to their provided properties. For example, if timeline is not provided (by setting it to undefined or null) in (1), it means that this is a static geospatial data, so GIS would display a static layer instead of an animation.

Another possible case is that some new properties with specific display forms are required to be added into the model. For example, to add a line-chart-based statistical indicator as a new display object, we need just concatenate the new property into corresponding unit of the model array. So the definition of *model* is extended as follows:

$$Model = [layer, timeline, style, chart] \tag{6}$$

where *chart* is the feature description of charts, which can be chart object like Echarts option. Similarly, for data defined by (6), if both *layer*, *timeline* and *style* are not provided, it means that the data describes and would be rendered as charts and displayed on some statistical interfaces.

This pattern requires support of GIS frontend for visualization, because the frontend is responsible for deciding how to render data. Related method will be introduced in Sect. 3.2.

2.3   Integrating Multi-source Heterogenous Data

To avoid dependency on specific data type, structure of *atomic* object in (3) has no restriction. Both client-side and server-side rendered data are supported. Data to be rendered by client-side is encoded in general format, such as GeoJSON, KML, etc. Large-scale data is imported as server-side rendered data, which is published to backend GIS server, like GeoServer. Its connection parameters are saved with *atomic* object to avoid performance problems in frontend caused by the huge amount of calculation. When loading server-side rendered data, GIS frontend automatically requires actual data according to the parameters saved in *atomic* object.

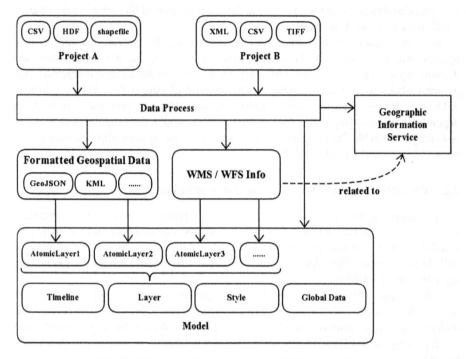

Fig. 2. Data flow of importing data of different projects.

The process of importing data is shown as Fig. 2. Different projects may have various types of data and files. An ETL system [22] is used to transform them into the required form of data model for visualization.

3 Model-Driven Web-Based GIS Design

The model can well represent heterogenous data, but it still needs a GIS interface for visualization. Here, an architecture of web-based GIS is proposed. Unlike traditional GIS applications often needs some prerequisite software such as ArcGIS, Web-based GIS can be simply visited through a browser. And with the help of responsive web design [23], it is easy for web-based GIS to support both PC and mobile devices.

3.1 System Architecture

The architecture of our web-based GIS is divided into several layers, shown as Fig. 3. The frontend is separated from the backend, which contains an HTTP server providing API for frontend to require model data, a server supporting WMS and WFS, and databases to store model data. At the bottom it is the data process layer which handles original data.

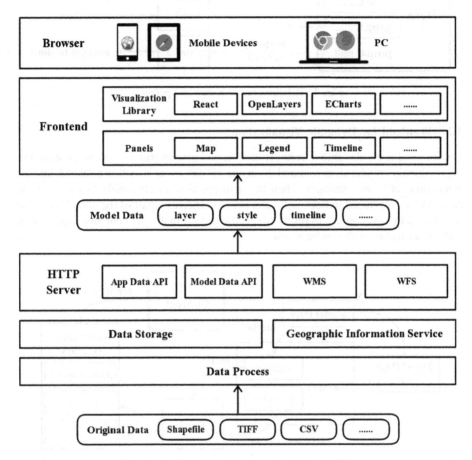

Fig. 3. Architecture of proposed web-based GIS.

Original data is processed and transformed into the form of our model and then exported to data storage. Some large-scale data is not suitable for browser-side rendering, so it is published to a GIS server for server-side rendering.

Frontend is made of a few panels. Each panel is designed to visualize a part of the data and provide some related operations. To achieve this goal, as shown as Fig. 4, each panel is related to some properties of the model. If the required properties exist, the panel will visualize the corresponding contents. Otherwise, the data will be ignored.

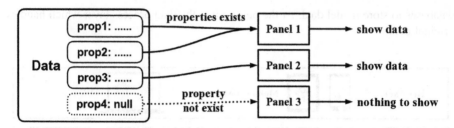

Fig. 4. Relations between data and panels.

3.2   Frontend for Dynamic Visualization

The frontend is divided into a manager module and several panel modules, as shown in Fig. 5. Firstly, model data required from the HTTP server's API are loaded into an annotation set in the manager. Then the manager notifies all panels to visualize the data. As we introduced in Sect. 3.1, each panel visualizes a part of the data. It can also be invoked by other panels to fulfill its specific tasks. Finally, all contents displayed on each panel make up the entire result.

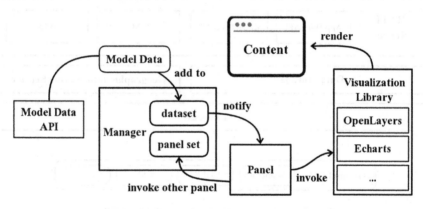

Fig. 5. Module division of frontend.

The frontend consisted of four main panels: map, details, timeline, and legend. Map panel displays the base map (base map is also considered as model data, containing layers that make the background), layers, and other elements to display on the base map. Details panel displays details of selected area on map. Time panel provides time control for spatiotemporal data. And Legend panel, as its name, display legends of spatial objects displayed on map.

Figure 6 shows an example of how the panels work when playing an animation. The manager module notifies all panels to visualize data, as we discussed before. Initially no area is selected, so nothing is displayed on detail panel. When play command is sent to time panel, it regularly invokes map panel to switch currently displayed snapshot, by which an animation is formed.

With proposed pluggable structure, the system is open for extension. New features can be included by reediting related panels or adding new panels to the frontend, without modifying other existing modules. By presenting and processing data separately, Changing or extension of displayed content does not require any modification of the backend and the data model structure, and vice versa. Therefore, the iteration of the frontend and backend, or the system and model, can be done separately.

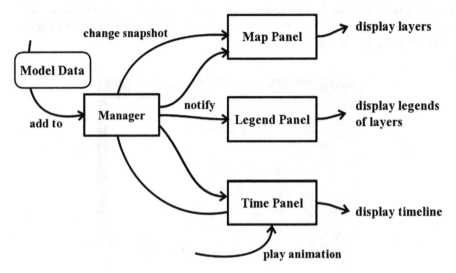

Fig. 6. An example of playing an animation of spatiotemporal data.

4 Demonstration

We implement a GIS based on proposed data model and system design. The system interface is shown as Fig. 7. Map panel is the background of the entire interface, displaying base maps and layers on it. Details and style panels are on the right side. At the bottom it is the timeline panel providing time control and displaying information at current timepoint.

As discussed in Sect. 2.3, layers are made of atomic layers that can be parameterized to get server-side rendered data through WMS or WFS, or client-side rendered vector data encoded in common format. The flexible design enhances the system ability to integrate and visualize heterogeneous data. We have implemented WMS-based visualization and GeoJSON-based visualization methods and conducted several experiments for illustration.

Two interdisciplinary datasets are collected for the system demonstration. Firstly, we animate the process of countries participating in the Belt and Road Initiative. The result is shown as the top part of Fig. 8. As timepoint switching through time, more and more countries joined the initiative and are shown on the map. On each timepoint, details, including participating countries and signed documents, will be shown on the right part of time panel. Geometries in the layer are encoded in GeoJSON format. In this way, the data is rendered in the browser, which is more flexible to customize its style, and has better user experience with no lag time of requiring additional data from a server. Compared with static visualization, the animation can express the evolution process of a time-varying event more efficiently, such as the order of countries participating in the Belt and Road Initiative. Also, more information (documents signed by each participating country) is contained on each timepoint, which is hard to achieve using statically visualizing methods.

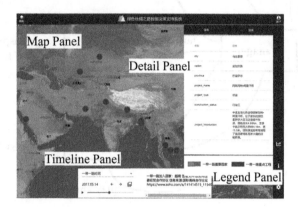

Fig. 7. Interface of our system.

For WMS-based visualization, data about the key research area of the Belt and Road Initiative is collected and published to GeoServer with connection parameters saved in data models. The result is shown at the left part of bottom of Fig. 8. In this way, when current snapshot changes, e.g. map is moved or zoomed, the frontend will automatically get related images rendered by the server.

The last dataset used for system demonstration is collected online from USGS Earthquake Hazards Program [24]. We visualized locations of all significant earthquakes in past 30 days on another base map which use services of Open Street Map [25]. Data is downloaded in the format of GeoJSON and imported to the system without complex transformation because it can be directly used as an atomic layer. Visual map parameters are set in the style attribute of the data model. Therefore, earthquakes with different magnitude is mapped to points with different colors and radii. The result is shown as the right part of the bottom right part of Fig. 8.

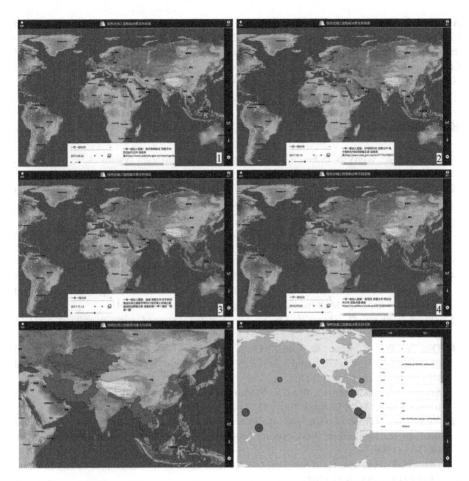

Fig. 8. Demonstration of the system. Top: animation of countries participating in the belt and road initiative. Bottom left: WMS-based visualization. Bottom right: data of earthquake.

5   Conclusion

In this paper, we propose a model-driven approach for dynamic visualization in GIS for interdisciplinary spatiotemporal data, including: (1) a formal data model to integrate multi-source heterogeneous data and (2) an architecture of modular web-based GIS to visualize model data. The model and the system are modular designed for customization and extension, and compatible with open geospatial data formats. The approach was implemented and demonstrated with data collected from different projects. The result shows that our approach has better support for dynamic animation and is suitable for more application scenarios.

Acknowledgments. This work was supported by the Strategy Priority Research Program of Chinese Academy of Sciences (No. XDA20080200), the National Key Research and Development Program of China (No. 2018YFB1005002), the National Natural Science Foundation of China (No. 61572479), the National Natural Science Foundation of China together with the National Research Foundation of Singapore (No. 61661146002).

References

1. Li, X., et al.: WebVRGIS based traffic analysis and visualization system. Adv. Eng. Softw. **93**, 1–8 (2016)
2. Ali, T.A.T., Saeed, R.A., Fageeri, S.O.: Web-based GIS business hotels tourism sites in Khartoum, Sudan. In: 2017 International Conference on Communication, Control, Computing and Electronics Engineering (ICCCCEE), pp. 1–5 (2017)
3. Lyu, H.-M., Sun, W.-J., Shen, S.-L., Arulrajah, A.: Flood risk assessment in metro systems of mega-cities using a GIS-based modeling approach. Sci. Total Environ. **626**, 1012–1025 (2018)
4. Varatharajan, R., Manogaran, G., Priyan, M.K., Balaş, V.E., Barna, C.: Visual analysis of geospatial habitat suitability model based on inverse distance weighting with paired comparison analysis. Multimedia Tools Appl. **77**, 17573–17593 (2018)
5. Zheng, J., Zhang, D., Zhang, Z., Lu, X.: An integrated system of video surveillance and GIS (2018)
6. Que, X., Wu, C., Chen, R., Liu, J., Lu, C.: Spatiotemporal data model for geographical process analysis with case study. In: 2016 15th International Symposium on Parallel and Distributed Computing (ISPDC), pp. 390–394 (2016)
7. Siabato, W., Claramunt, C., Ilarri, S., Manso-Callejo, M.A.: A survey of modelling trends in temporal GIS. ACM Comput. Surv. **51**, 1–41 (2018)
8. Yuan, M.: Temporal GIS and spatio-temporal modeling. In: Proceedings of Third International Conference Workshop on Integrating GIS and Environment Modeling, Santa Fe, NM (1996)
9. Gebbert, S., Pebesma, E.: A temporal GIS for field based environmental modeling. Environ. Model Softw. **53**, 1–12 (2014)
10. Wood, G., Whyatt, D., Hackett, D., Stevens, C.: Spatio-temporal challenges in representing wildlife disturbance within a GIS. Environ. Technol. Innov. **7**, 44–53 (2017)
11. Liu, C., Qian, J., Guo, D., Liu, Y.: A spatio-temporal scenario model for emergency decision. GeoInformatica **22**, 411–433 (2018)
12. Yang, Z., Chen, M., Bchen, D.: A study on representation and application of temporal coordinate reference systems in GIS. In: 2018 26th International Conference on Geoinformatics, pp. 1–5 (2018)
13. Barrile, V., Postorino, M.N.: GPS and GIS methods to reproduce vehicle trajectories in urban areas. Procedia – Soc. Behav. Sci. **223**, 890–895 (2016)
14. Li, M., Choudhury, F., Bao, Z., Samet, H., Sellis, T.: ConcaveCubes: supporting cluster-based geographical visualization in large data scale. Comput. Graph. Forum **37**, 217–228 (2018)
15. Langat, P.K., Kumar, L., Koech, R.: Monitoring river channel dynamics using remote sensing and GIS techniques. Geomorphology **325**, 92–102 (2019)
16. Jeppesen, J.H., Ebeid, E., Jacobsen, R.H., Toftegaard, T.S.: Open geospatial infrastructure for data management and analytics in interdisciplinary research. Comput. Electron. Agric. **145**, 130–141 (2018)

17. Mollalo, A., Alimohammadi, A., Shirzadi, M.R., Malek, M.R.: Geographic information system-based analysis of the spatial and spatio-temporal distribution of Zoonotic Cutaneous Leishmaniasis in Golestan Province, North-East of Iran. Zoonoses Public Health **62**, 18–28 (2015)
18. Qiu, X., Zhang, F., Zhou, H., Du, L., Wang, X., Liang, G.: Multimodal visual analysis of vector-borne infectious diseases. In: Wang, Y., Jiang, Z., Peng, Y. (eds.) IGTA 2018. CCIS, vol. 875, pp. 135–145. Springer, Singapore (2018). https://doi.org/10.1007/978-981-13-1702-6_14
19. Zavala-Romero, O., Chassignet, E.P., Zavala-Hidalgo, J., Velissariou, P., Pandav, H., Meyer-Baese, A.: OWGIS 2.0: open source Java application that builds web GIS interfaces for desktop and mobile devices. In: Proceedings of the 22nd ACM SIGSPATIAL International Conference on Advances in Geographic Information Systems, pp. 311–320. ACM, Dallas (2014)
20. Zhang, J., et al.: Visual analysis of public utility service problems in a metropolis. IEEE Trans. Vis. Comput. Graph. **20**, 1843–1852 (2014)
21. OpenLayers. https://openlayers.org/
22. Kimball, R., Caserta, J.: The Data Warehouse ETL Toolkit: Practical Techniques for Extracting, Cleaning, Conforming and Delivering Data (2004)
23. Sarabadani Tafreshi, A.E., Marbach, K., Norrie, M.C.: Proximity-based adaptation of web content on public displays. In: Cabot, J., De Virgilio, R., Torlone, R. (eds.) ICWE 2017. LNCS, vol. 10360, pp. 282–301. Springer, Cham (2017). https://doi.org/10.1007/978-3-319-60131-1_16
24. USGS Earthquake Hazards Program. https://earthquake.usgs.gov/
25. OpenStreetMap. https://www.openstreetmap.org/

DCNN Transfer Learning
and Multi-model Integration for Disease
and Weed Identification

Jingxian Wang[1,2], Miao Li[1,2(✉)], Jian Zhang[1,2], WeiHui Zeng[1,2],
and XuanJiang Yang[1,2]

[1] Institute of Intelligent Machines, Chinese Academy of Sciences, Hefei 230031, China
{mli,jzhang,whzeng}@iim.ac.cn
[2] University of Science and Technology of China, Hefei 230026, China
{wjx2016,xjyang}@mail.ustc.edu.cn

Abstract. For the complex image segmentation problem and high complexity of model caused by digital processing technology, we first use data enhancement technology to expand dataset size, and then use deep convolutional neural networks (CNNs) multi-model integration method combined transfer learning to identify crop disease and weed. On the one hand, we make full use of the prior knowledge learned from big dataset of four single deep CNNs (VGG, Inception-v3, ResNet and DenseNet). By parameter fine-tuning, the CNNs are reused in the agricultural field to alleviate the over-fitting problem caused by insufficient data sources. On the other hand, two or more CNNs are combined by the direct average method to complete multi-model integration. We directly average the category confidence generated by different models to obtain the final prediction result. The experimental results show that the combination of deep CNNs and transfer learning is effective and the CNNs multi-model integration method can further improve the identification accuracy compared to the single CNN model. The validation accuracy of crop disease and weed dataset can reach 97.14% and 99.22% respectively by using multi-model integration and transfer learning.

Keywords: Deep CNN · Multi-model integration · Transfer learning ·
Crop disease and weed · Image-based identification

1 Introduction

Disease and grass damage are two major factors threatening crop yield and quality. With the rapid development of computer vision technology, many researchers have used image processing technology to identify crop disease and weed. At present, crop disease identification based on image processing technology have achieved a lot of research results. Li et al. [1] extracted five types of shape parameters in wheat mildew images, and identified three common wheat mildew diseases through principal component analysis and discriminant analysis, with

© Springer Nature Singapore Pte Ltd. 2019
Y. Wang et al. (Eds.): IGTA 2019, CCIS 1043, pp. 216–227, 2019.
https://doi.org/10.1007/978-981-13-9917-6_21

an accuracy higher than 86.7%. In the research of weed identification, researchers identify weed by using differences in color, location, shape, multi-spectral and texture features. For example, Meyer et al. [2] extracted the ultra-green and ultra-red features of color features, and integrated the fuzzy classification algorithm to identify wheat and weeds.

There are still some problems using image processing technology for disease and weed identification, such as powdery disease and leaf folding of weeds. In recent years, CNN as a deep learning model, has been used in the field of crop disease and weed identification. In terms of crop disease identification, Lucas et al. [3] used AlexNet model to identify 6 known diseases of apples from 2539 images and compared them with the results of expert identification. Kawasaki et al. [4] used three layers of CNN to train dataset containing two diseases and healthy leaves of cucumber. Similar studies are also available [5,6]. In crop weed identification, Potena et al. [7] used unmanned ground vehicles equipped with multi-spectral cameras to perform real-time and automatic crop and weed classification task. Lightweight CNN was used for fast binary image segmentation, and then deep CNN was used for classification of crop and weed based on feature extraction. Guillermo et al. [8] used deep CNN to identify plants based on vein patterns. There are also some plant identifications that combine CNNs with traditional machine learning methods [9,10].

The crop disease and weed identification method based on CNN can solve the semantic gap problem and reduce the computational complexity. However, it is difficult to obtain and lable a large, domain-specific dataset to train deep CNNs. Transfer learning can solve the over-fitting problem caused by small dataset for deep learning training. At present, it has been a trend to combine CNN with transfer learning to solve the crop disease problem. Amanda et al. [11] applied transfer learning to train a deep CNN to identify three cassava diseases and two pests. Guan et al. [12] used CNN to evaluate the severity of four apple black rot diseases. They built shallow CNNs training from scratch and used deep CNNs combined with transfer learning. The result proved that the combination of VGG and transfer learning achieved the highest accuracy 90.4%. There are few researches on the application of deep transfer learning techniques for weed identification. Mostafa et al. [13] used GoogLeNet, AlexNet and VGGNet, three powerful and popular deep CNNs to identify plant types in images and evaluate different factors affecting network performance.

The use of single DCNN model combined with transfer learning can effectively extract high-level abstract features of images and reduce over-fitting phenomenon. All deep network models have their own structural improvements, and the fusion of multiple networks' results may achieve better identification effect. The CNN model is integrated by training multiple network models and synthesizing their prediction results. Model integration can significantly improve the generalization ability of the learning model. In this paper, two or more of the four CNN models (VGG, Inception-v3, ResNet and DenseNet) are integrated for crop disease and weed identification through permutation and combination. Finally, the direct average method is used to integrate the final image identification results. In other words, multiple different single CNN models are trained first, and then the category confidence generated by different models is directly averaged to obtain the final prediction result, which is used as the final classification of the corresponding input image.

2   Proposed Method

2.1   The Overall Idea of the Algorithm

The flow of this algorithm is shown in Fig. 1. This paper firstly performs data enhancement operations on the collected original datasets to expand the number of images, which can increase generalization ability of the model. Then we use ImageNet large-scale dataset to obtain pre-trained model of deep CNNs. With the help of these pre-trained models, we used disease and weed dataset to conduct transfer learning opration on the four single network frameworks of

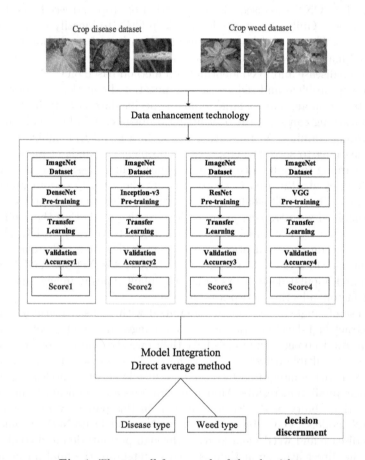

Fig. 1. The overall framework of the algorithm

VGG16, Inception-v3, ResNet and DenseNet to adjust parameters, and the network weight parameters are adapted to our dataset. Finally, two or more models of these four networks are integrated, and the direct average method is adopted for model integration. The integrated model is used for decision recognition.

2.2 CNN Identification Model Framework for Crop Disease and Weed

In this paper, we use 4 different deep CNNs to identify disease and weed, which have different characteristics. VGG [14] proposed that the depth of CNNs and the small convolutional kernels play a great role in result. By repeatedly stacking $3*3$ small convolutional kernels and $2*2$ maximum pooling layers, VGG network successfully constructed 16–19 layers of CNN. Tabel 1 lists the architecture of VGG. The $1*1$ convolution kernel can reduce dimension and increase non-linearity. The $3*3$ convolution kernel is the superposition of multiple convolution kernels, which can increase the spatial receptive field and reduce network parameters.

Table 1. The architecture of VGG network

Name	Description
Input image size	$224*224$
Pretreatment	Subtract the mean
Convolution kernels	$3*3, 1*1$
Padding	1 for $3*3$
Max-pooling	$2*2$
The activation function	Relu

Inception-v3 [15] is based on the Inception architecture. On the one hand, it splits a large two-dimensional convolution into two smaller one-dimensional convolutions, which saves lots of parameters and accelerates the operation. In particular, it increases the expression capacity of a layer of nonlinear extension model. On the other hand, Inception-v3 optimizes the structure of Inception Module. Inception-v3 used branch in the branch.

ResNet [16] has deep network hierarchy and residual connection. Compared with traditional DCNN structure, ResNet used residual connection to solve the degradation problem caused by excessively deep network. Deep residual network consists of a series of residual blocks, the form of a residual block is:

$$x_{l+1} = Relu(x_l + f(x_l, w_l)) \tag{1}$$

x_l and x_{l+1} respectively represent the input and output of the lth residual block. Relu() is the corrected linear unit function, f() is the residual mapping function, and w_l is the parameter of the residual block. The convolutional layer consists of a series of neurons, each containing a set of learnable weights and a bias. The jth feature map of the ith layer can be calculated as:

$$y_j^i = \sigma(\sum_{m=1}^{M} w_{jm}^i * y_m^{i-1} + b_j^i) \tag{2}$$

where w_{jm}^i is weight of the mth feature map, y_m^{i-1}(m = 1, ..., M) is the mth feature map in the (i − 1)th layer, b_j^i is the jth bias in the ith layer, and $\sigma()$ is the non-linear activation function.

DenseNet [17] is CNN with dense connections. In this network, there is a direct connection between any two layers. We illustrate the relationship between DenseNet and ResNet through two formulas. The first formula is for ResNet. Here, x_l represents the output of layer l, and H_l represents the nonlinear transformation. For ResNet, the output of layer l is the output of layer l − 1 plus the nonlinear transformation to output of layer l − 1.

$$x_l = H_l(x_{l-1}) + x_{l-1} \tag{3}$$

For DenseNet, $[x_0, x_1, \ldots, x_{l-1}]$ indicates that the output feature map from layer 0 to l-1 will be used for channel concatenation.

$$x_l = H_l([x_0, x_1, \ldots, x_{l-1}]) \tag{4}$$

The dense connection structure can alleviate gradient disappearance problem, enhance feature propagation, and greatly reduce the amount of parameters.

2.3 Training Mechanism

There is a positive correlation between the amount of training data and the size of deep learning model. In order to solve the over-fitting problem, we introduce transfer learning strategy. Using transfer learning can bring three benefits. (1) The initial accuracy of the model is much higher than without transfer learning. (2) The rate of performance improvement of the model is faster during the training process. (3) The model using transfer learning has better convergence. In this paper, We use the ImageNet dataset [18] to obtain the pre-trained model. That is, first we train models with prior knowledge through a large-scale dataset, and then we continue training the pre-trained model using our dataset to adjust the weight parameters. Finally, the parameters of the identification model will adapt to our dataset. The process is shown in Fig. 2.

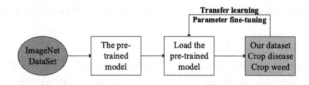

Fig. 2. The process of transfer learning

2.4   Multi-model Integration Method

The four deep network frameworks of VGG, Inception-v3, ResNet, and DenseNet all have their structural improvements. Therefore, the fusion of multi-model identification results is helpful to improve identification accuracy. There are three most common model integration algorithms in the model integration approach. In this paper, we use the direct average method to integrate two or more of the model results. Suppose there are a total of N models to be integrated. For a test sample x, the prediction result is N C-dimensional vectors (C is mark space size of the data). The Direct average method directly average the category confidence generated by different models to obtain the final prediction results.

$$Final\_score = \frac{\sum_{i=1}^{N} s_i}{N} \tag{5}$$

where s_i is the score of single model. The combinations of model integration include single model, double model integrations, three model integrations, and four model integrations.

3   Material and Experiment

3.1   Material Preparation

Figure 3 shows the samples of each crop disease and weed. The crop disease dataset includes 2,430 images from cucumber and rice diseases that have been assigned to 8 categories of labels. The weed dataset includes 1964 images of corn and 7 kinds of various weeds. These original images are all from complex natural environment. Their shooting is unrestricted, and they vary in image size, light intensity, plant posture, and camera Angle. Table 2 lists the number of images for training and validation in the experiment. The number of images in the training set and validation sets is approximately 4:1. As can be seen from Table 2, the scale of our dataset is small. The distribution of each disease is uneven, while the number of samples in each weed category is relatively uniform.

Table 2. The number of samples in each crop disease and crop weed

Class	1	2	3	4	5	6	7	8
Disease images for training	160	161	116	555	38	161	40	714
Disease images for validation	39	40	29	139	9	40	10	179
Weed images for training	164	152	210	300	224	183	187	154
Weed images for validation	40	38	52	75	56	45	46	38

(1) Cucumber downy mildew (2) Cucumber powdery mildew (3) Cucumber target spot (4) Rice blast

(5) Rice false smut (6) Rice flax spot (7) Rice bacterial blight (8) Rice sheath blight

(a) Corn (b) Amaranthus retroflexus (c) Goosegrass (d) Green bristlegrass

(e) Lamb's-quarters (f) Portulaca oleracea (g) Shepherd's purse (h) Solanum nigrum

Fig. 3. Example each from every crop disease and crop weed

3.2　Data Enhancement Technology

With the increase of network depth, over-fitting problem is caused when the dataset is small. Therefore, data enhancement technology is necessary for this situation. The premise of data enhancement is that CNN can robustness classify an object in different places. That is, it has invariant properties. In practical applications, we need to identify images with different scenes and perspectives. This article uses five data transformation techniques. (1) horizontal flip: boolean value, random horizontal flip. (2) shear range: floating point number, shear strength. (3) zoom range: floating point number, the magnitude of the random scaling. (4) width shift range: floating point number, a certain ratio of the width of the picture, the amplitude of the horizontal offset of image. (5) height shift range: floating point number, a certain ratio of the height of the picture, the amplitude of the vertical offset of image (6) rotation range: integer, the angle that the image rotates randomly. Figure 4 shows examples of cucumber disease and weed image after data enhancement.

3.3　Implementation of Experiments

Before the experiment, we standardize the hyperparameters of all experiments. The gradient descent method is mainly used to perform weight update in the network model to minimize the loss function. The momentum-based SGD optimization algorithm is adopted in this paper. The technique accelerates SGD training by accelerating training in the main direction and attenuating oscillation in the unrelated directions. The parameter is updated by:

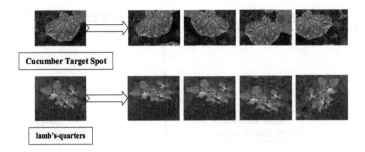

Fig. 4. Examples of cucumber disease and weed image after data enhancement

$$\nu_t = \gamma \nu_{t-1} + \eta \nabla_\theta J(\theta) \tag{6}$$

$$\theta = \theta - \nu_t \tag{7}$$

The momentum term γ is set to 0.9 in this paper. The SGD algorithm with momentum can make the network converge faster and reduce the oscillation process. The learning rate is set to 0.001. It is the rate of decline toward the minimum of the cost function. In all experiments, the program runs 200 epochs. In an epoch, all data in the training set complete training. Batch size represents a set of samples selected in the training set to update the weights. Use a large batch size when the network is small and a small batch size when the network is large. Since the deep network of this paper is large, we set the batch size to 32.

4   Results and Discussion

Figure 5 shows the training process of crop disease dataset under different depth CNNs and transfer learning strategies. Among them, the red line and green line respectively represent the accuracy trend of training process and validation process. It can be seen that the starting point of training and validation of VGG network is higher than other networks. This shows that in this network, the parameters learned from the big dataset can be better transfered to our disease dataset. And the training time of all deep network frameworks have been greatly reduced with the help of transfer learning, and the curve has converged around 20 Epochs. This proves that the method based on deep network frameworks and transfer learning can effectively solve the over-fitting problem caused by small-scale dataset.

Figure 6 shows the training process of crop weed dataset under different depth CNNs and transfer learning strategies. It can be seen that the initial training accuracy and validation accuracy of VGG model are higher than the other three networks. Among them, Inception-v3 network has the lowest training starting point and validation starting point, but the accuracy of the final stable convergence is relatively high. Among the four networks, the accuracy curve process

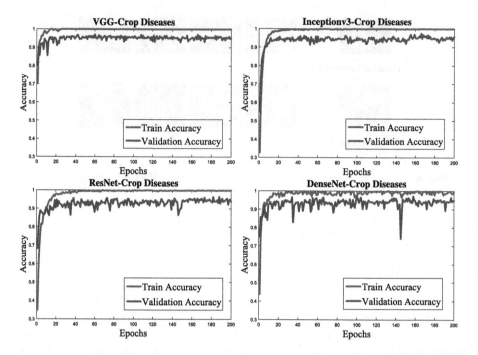

Fig. 5. The training process of crop disease images under different CNNs and tansfer learning

of the three networks Inception-v3, ResNet, and DenseNet fluctuated more than the VGG framework. With the increase of training time, the accuracy curve of all networks tend to be stable. Compared with Fig. 5, it can be seen that the network convergence time in the training process of crop weed dataset is longer than that of crop disease dataset.

Table 3 shows the experimental results of the single model and multi-model integration on the crop disease dataset. Among them, 0 represents DenseNet model, 1 represents Inception-v3 model, 2 represents ResNet, and 3 represents VGG model. [0,1] represents the integration accuracy of DenseNet and Inception-v3 model. It can be seen from the validation results of single model that the VGG model is most suitable for identifying our crop disease dataset, with an accuracy of 96.35%. In the multi-model integrated network, the integration of DenseNet and VGG model has the best effect on the crop disease identification, and the validation accuracy can reach 97.14%. The results exceeds the identification accuracy of single model, indicating that the method based on CNN model integration is effective for crop disease identification.

Table 4 shows the experimental results on the weed dataset. Overall, whether it is single model or multi-model integration, the identification accuracy of crop weed dataset is higher than crop disease dataset. This is related to the difficulty and distribution of the data in the dataset. It can be seen from Table 4 that

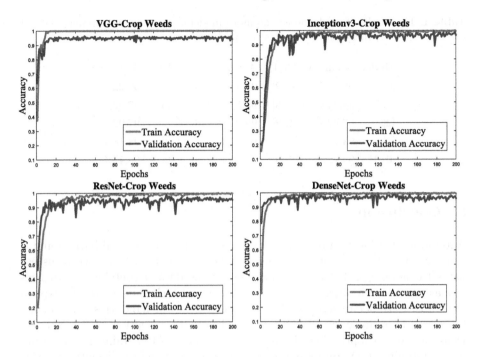

Fig. 6. The training process of crop weed images under different CNN and tansfer learning

Table 3. The results of single model and multi-model integration on crop disease dataset ([0]-DenseNet, [1]-Inception-v3, [2]-ResNet, [3]-VGG)

Model	Accuracy	Model	Accuracy	Model	Accuracy
[0]	95.83%	[0, 2]	95.42%	[0, 1, 2]	95.83%
[1]	95.83%	[0, 3]	97.14%	[0, 1, 3]	96.61%
[2]	95.21%	[1, 2]	95.63%	[0, 2, 3]	96.35%
[3]	96.35%	[1, 3]	96.09%	[1, 2, 3]	96.00%
[0,1]	96.67%	[2, 3]	95.21%	[0, 1, 2, 3]	96.10%

Inception-v3 network in the single model has the highest accuracy 98.44% for crop weed identification. In the multi-model integration experiment, the integration model of DenseNet and Inception- v3, the integration model of Inception -v3 and ResNet, the three models integration of DenseNet, Inception-v3 and ResNet, all achieved the highest validation accuracy of 99.22%. The result exceeds the accuracy of all single model identification, indicating that the method based on model integration is also effective for crop weed identification.

Table 4. The results of single model and multi-model integration on crop weed dataset ([0]-DenseNet, [1]-Inception-v3, [2]-ResNet, [3]-VGG)

Model	Accuracy	Model	Accuracy	Model	Accuracy
[0]	98.18%	[0, 2]	98.44%	[0, 1, 2]	99.22%
[1]	98.44%	[0, 3]	94.53%	[0, 1, 3]	97.92%
[2]	97.92%	[1, 2]	99.22%	[0, 2, 3]	97.92%
[3]	93.75%	[1, 3]	96.61%	[1, 2, 3]	98.18%
[0, 1]	99.22%	[2, 3]	96.88%	[0, 1, 2, 3]	98.44%

5   Conclusion

Automatic identification of crop disease and weed under natural background is beneficial to improve crop yield and quality. This paper takes a crop disease dataset containing 2,430 samples and a crop weed dataset containing 1966 samples as the research object. The data enhancement technique is used to expand the dataset size before entering the network. On the one hand, this paper makes full use of four single deep CNN frameworks (VGG, Inception-v3, ResNet and DenseNet) to learn prior knowledge from big dataset. After training and parameter fine-tuning, they are reused in crop disease and weed to alleviate the overfitting problem caused by insufficient data sources. On the other hand, we train multiple network models and synthesize their predicted results. Through permutation and combination, two or more of the four CNN models are used for model integration to identify crop disease and weed. Finally, the integrated algorithm of direct average method is adopted for the final image identification. The experimental results show that: (1) The combination of deep CNN frameworks and transfer learning strategy is effective, which can significantly improve the initial training accuracy of deep CNNs and shorten the training time. (2) The CNN multi-model integration method can further improve the identification accuracy compared to the single CNN model. The DenseNet and VGG model integration has the best effect on crop disease identification, and the validation accuracy is 97.14%. For crop weed dataset, the validation accuracy using model integration is 99.22%. In the future, we will develop the crop disease and weed identification system under the natural environment based on this method.

Acknowledgments. We thank the reviewers for their thoughtful comments and suggestions. This work is supported by Anhui Science and Technology Research Project: Key Technologies and Integrated Applications of Intelligent Monitoring of Energy-saving Ecological Agriculture and Forestry Planting in Jinzhai County (1604a0702017).

References

1. Li, J., Gao, L., Shen, Z.: Extraction and analysis of digital images feature of three kinds of wheat diseases. In: International Congress on Image and Signal Processing (2010)
2. Meyer, G.E., Neto, J.C., Jones, D.D., Hindman, T.W.: Intensified fuzzy clusters for classifying plant, soil, and residue regions of interest from color images. Comput. Electron. Agric. **42**(3), 161–180 (2004)
3. Nachtigall, L.G., Araujo, R.M., Nachtigall, G.R.: Classification of apple tree disorders using convolutional neural networks. In: IEEE International Conference on Tools with Artificial Intelligence (2017)
4. Kawasaki, Y., Uga, H., Kagiwada, S., Iyatomi, H.: Basic study of automated diagnosis of viral plant diseases using convolutional neural networks. In: Bebis, G., et al. (eds.) ISVC 2015. LNCS, vol. 9475, pp. 638–645. Springer, Cham (2015). https://doi.org/10.1007/978-3-319-27863-6_59
5. Jiang, L., Jie, H., Zhao, G., Mei, F., Zhang, C.: An in-field automatic wheat disease diagnosis system. Comput. Electron. Agric. **142**, 369–379 (2017)
6. Durmu, H., Güne, E.O., Kirci, M.: Disease detection on the leaves of the tomato plants by using deep learning. In: International Conference on Agro-Geoinformatics (2017)
7. Potena, C., Nardi, D., Pretto, A.: Fast and accurate crop and weed identification with summarized train sets for precision agriculture (2016)
8. Grinblat, G.L., Uzal, L.C., Larese, M.G., Granitto, P.M.: Deep learning for plant identification using vein morphological patterns. Comput. Electron. Agric. **127**, 418–424 (2016)
9. Cugu, I.; Sener, E.E.C.B.B.A.E.O.I.O.A.A.: Treelogy: A novel tree classifier utilizing deep and hand-crafted representations (2017)
10. Tang, J.L., Dong, W., Zhang, Z.G., He, L.J., Jing, X., Yang, X.: Weed identification based on k-means feature learning combined with convolutional neural network. Comput. Electron. Agric. **135**, 63–70 (2017)
11. Ramcharan, A., Baranowski, K., Mcclowsky, P., Ahmed, B., Hughes, D.P.: Using transfer learning for image-based cassava disease detection. Front. Plant Sci. **8** (2017)
12. Wang, G., Sun, Y., Wang, J.: Automatic image-based plant disease severity estimation using deep learning. Comput. Intell. Neurosci. **2017**, 2917536 (2017)
13. Ghazi, M.M., Yanikoglu, B., Aptoula, E.: Plant identification using deep neural networks via optimization of transfer learning parameters. Neurocomputing **235**, 228–235 (2017)
14. Simonyan, K., Zisserman, A.: Very deep convolutional networks for large-scale image recognition (2014)
15. Szegedy, C., Vanhoucke, V., Ioffe, S., Shlens, J., Wojna, Z.: Rethinking the inception architecture for computer vision. In: Computer Vision and Pattern Recognition (2016)
16. He, K., Zhang, X., Ren, S., Sun, J.: Deep residual learning for image recognition. In: Computer Vision and Pattern Recognition (2016)
17. Gao, H., Zhuang, L., Weinberger, K.Q.: Densely connected convolutional networks (2016)
18. Deng, J., Dong, W., Socher, R., Li, L.J., Li, K., Li, F.F.: ImageNet: a large-scale hierarchical image database. In: IEEE Conference on Computer Vision and Pattern Recognition (2009)

3D Human Pose Lifting: From Joint Position to Joint Rotation

Zeye Wu[1,2] and Wujun Che[1,3(✉)]

[1] Institute of Automation, Chinese Academy of Sciences, Beijing 100190, China
{wuzeye2016,wujun.che}@ia.ac.cn
[2] School of Computer Science and Technology, University of Chinese Academy of Sciences, Beijing 100049, China
[3] AICFVE of Beijing Film Academy, Beijing 100088, China

Abstract. 3D human pose estimation is a fundamental task in computer vision. However, most of the related works focus on recovering human joint positions, which provides sparse and insufficient pose information for many applications like 3D avatar animation. Therefore, this paper presents a deep network for recovering joint angles from 3D joint positions, which learns the prior dependence between them. We test the validity and robustness of our method. We also discuss some details in designing and training the network. Our method is simple, effective and extensive. It can be combined with work of 3D human pose estimation that predict 3D joint positions from image or depth data to produce more detailed and natural poses. It builds a map between two joint sets with different numbers of joints, which provides a framework to unify multiple datasets for human pose estimation with different annotation formats.

Keywords: 3D human pose · Deep Neuron Network · Residual connection

1 Introduction

Human pose estimation is a key technique for many applications such as human-computer interaction, video retrieval, digital entertainment and virtual reality. It is also a fundamental task in computer vision and has been drawing great interest among researchers during the past decades. Conventional methods capture human poses through wearable hardware devices and sensors, which take expensive cost and have tedious procedures. In recent years, more researchers turn their eyes on marker-less 3D human pose estimation based on RGB images or depth data. These methods can be categorized into generative methods and discriminative methods.

Generative methods build a human body model first, then project the model into image/depth space and align the projection to image features or fit the 3D body model to the range data [1, 2]. A human body model could be a skeleton with geometric bones [1–3], deformable triangulated meshes model [4, 5]. The more complex the human body model is, the slower the pose estimation process runs. Therefore, generative methods should consider a trade-off between efficiency and model details. Besides, these methods can easily converge to a local minimum because the fitting error functions are usually non-convex.

© Springer Nature Singapore Pte Ltd. 2019
Y. Wang et al. (Eds.): IGTA 2019, CCIS 1043, pp. 228–237, 2019.
https://doi.org/10.1007/978-981-13-9917-6_22

Discriminative methods focus on the relation between image features and human poses, and do not model the physical projection process. Some researchers consider human pose estimation as a classification task that aims to classify the image pixels to correct body parts and recognize the pixels of joints. They use Gaussian process [6], Markov random field [7], random decision trees [3, 9] and Markov chain Monto Carlo [8] to solve the problem. Discriminative methods are usually faster than generative methods, but they need large training datasets to learn the corresponding map from original data to final poses and their performances strongly depend on the datasets.

Some researchers combine the two types of methods by initializing the human pose using discriminative models [10] and then optimizing the pose within the neighborhood of initial inference [11–13]. More recently, researchers have been using deep learning methods to solve the 3D human pose estimation problem [14–22]. However, most of them recover a set of human joint positions, which is sparse and provides insufficient information for many applications like 3D avatar animation. This paper therefore aims to lift joint positions to joint angles. In addition, some other "lifting" methods have been explored. For example, [23] provide a method of recovering human shape and pose from sparse MoCap markers; [24, 25] focus on lifting 2D joints locations to 3D space.

In this paper, we design a neuron network that recover 3D joint angles from given 3D joint positions. We use residual connections to predict the joint rotation iteratively, which makes the results converge more easily. We use synthetic human model data based on [22, 23] for supervised training and three MoCap datasets are used [24, 26, 27]. Experiment results show the validity of our model to recover natural poses represented by 3D joint angles, which can be combined with other work that predicts 3D human joint positions and produce human poses that contain more details. We also compare the performances of different network architectures and different training losses. The remainder of this paper is organized as follows. Section 2 describes our model. Section 3 provides the experimental results and evaluations. The conclusion and future work are given in Sect. 4.

2 Proposed Method

2.1 Network Architecture

The proposed neuron network recovers natural joint rotation from 3D joint positions. Specifically, a set of given joints is denoted by $\{J_{i_k}, k = 1, \ldots, m\}$ and their positions by $\{P_{i_k} \in \mathbb{R}^3, k = 1, \ldots, m\}$. The output joints, of which the rotations will be predicted, is denoted by $\{J_{o_k}, k = 1, \ldots, n\}$, with their positions denoted by $\{P_{o_k} \in \mathbb{R}^3, k = 1, \ldots, n\}$ and their rotation angles by $\{\theta_{o_k} \in \mathbb{R}^3, k = 1, \ldots, n\}$ in axis-angle representation. We establish a map $f^* : \mathbb{R}^{3m} \to \mathbb{R}^{3n}$ to recover proper joint angles θ_o from given P_i. We obtain the map f^* such that $f^* = \min_f \frac{1}{|D|} \sum_{x \in D} S(f(P^x)_\theta, \theta^x)$, where D represents a human pose dataset, x is an instance in D, $S(\cdot, \cdot)$ measures the distance between two poses and $f(P^x)_\theta$ means the θ component of the output $f(P^x)$.

The two sets of joints, the input and the output, do not need to be exactly the same. In practice, we adopt 19 input joints and 24 output joints in our model. The input and the output have similar limb joints but are different in head and torso parts. The details of our pose representations are following.

We use Skinned Multi-Person Linear (SMPL) model [28] to encode the output human body. It is a popular parametric mesh model for human body, whose deformation is controlled by the shape parameter β and the pose parameter θ. The pose is modelled by the relative rotation of 23 joints and global rotation of the root joint. Our network take both rotations and shape parameters as output, but we don't use shape parameters to directly supervise the training of our network since the shape is not our focus. We combine it with rotation parameters to compute 3D joint positions' losses, which indirectly supervise the training procedure.

Figure 1 illustrates the human pose representations we used for the input and the output. The output representation, SMPL model, has 6 joints on its breast and torso since it needs those joints to control the mesh deformation. Actually, we can infer these joints' information when the limbs and head are known using the symmetrical structure prior of the human body. This prior knowledge can be learned through a neuron network. Therefore, we do not use all the 24 joint of SMPL as input. Instead, we use 14 input joints for limb and head rotation, and for face direction, we have extra 5 facial keypoints.

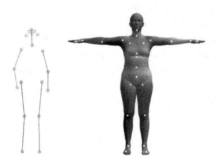

Fig. 1. The human pose representations. Left: input skeleton joint positions. Right: human mesh model controlled by SMPL parameters (including rotation and shape), the white points are the control joints [28].

The neuron network is designed based on identity mappings [29]. Figure 2 shows the architecture of our model. The dotted box represent the basic residual block consisted of two units with the same structure. The unit is a linear layer with 512 neurons, followed by a batch normalization layer, a ReLU activation layer and a dropout layer. The residual block takes (θ, β, P) as input and $(\Delta\theta, \Delta\beta) + (\theta, \beta)$ as output, where $(\theta, \beta) \in \mathbb{R}^{72+10}$ is an initial guess of human pose or the result pose of the last residual block, $(\Delta\theta, \Delta\beta) \in \mathbb{R}^{72+10}$ is the estimation of poses' changes and $P \in \mathbb{R}^{57}$ is the given joint positions. We use a regressor to obtain the correspondent 19 joints from a parameterized SMPL mesh model.

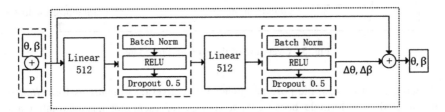

Fig. 2. A diagram of our model based on residual connections.

The residual block structure is repeated three times to build the pose-lifting network and to gradually approach the true poses. Additionally, inspired by [22], we explore another way of constructing the network: reusing a residual block for three times, which equally means using three residual blocks with the same weights. There are more parameters in the former network and therefore it has more powerful representation ability. But the latter network is smaller and also makes full use of residual blocks. It's hard to determine the better one from the two structure by theoretical analysis only. By experiment, we find that the former one has a better performance comprehensively. We will discuss the two network structures in details in Sect. 3.

2.2 Training

Dataset. We obtain a set of SMPL parameters $\{(\theta, \beta)\}$ based on the work of [22, 23]. We retain 1000 samples as our test set denoted by MT. Then, to increase the amount of training data, we split $\{(\theta, \beta)\}$ into two parts, $\{\theta\}$ and $\{\beta\}$, and randomly recombine the samples from the two subsets. Finally, we use a joint regressor $Reg(\cdot)$ to obtain correspondent ground truth joint positions $\{P\}$. Here, human shape recovery is not our focus. Therefore, our training data contains an extensive variety of human poses but the amount of different shapes is not so large as the amount of poses. We do not use shape parameter β to supervise the network training. Instead, we combine it with pose parameter θ to compute joint positions as supervision terms. We also take θ as a direct supervision term.

Loss Functions. The training loss L consists of two parts, the joint position loss L_{pos} and the joint rotation loss L_{rot}. The training procedure is illustrated in Fig. 3. A set of joint positions is input into our network. It passes through three residual blocks in the network and finally the network outputs the required joints' rotations and shape parameters. The rotations are supervised directly by the ground truth (L_{rot}). A renderer receives the rotations and shape parameters to produce a mesh model and then the mesh model regresses to a set of joint positions, which is self-supervised by the input (L_{pos}).

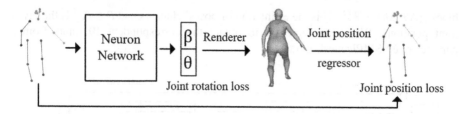

Fig. 3. Overview of the training procedure.

When computing L_{rot}, the pose parameter θ is converted to matrices form $Rod(\theta)$ using the Rodrigues formula, because the axis-angle representation has the rotation axis and the rotation angle be coupled together and therefore it is not suitable for optimization. For computing L_{pos}, we use the same regressor Reg as mentioned before to obtain joint positions from predicted meshes. The formulas of losses are as follows:

$$L_{pos} = \|Reg(f(P)) - P\|_2^2 \tag{1}$$

$$L_{rot} = \|Rod(f(P)_\theta) - Rod(\theta)\|_2^2 \tag{2}$$

where $f(P)$ is the output of the network, $f(P)_\theta$ is the rotation component of the output vector and $Rod(\cdot)$ means using Rodrigues formula to compute the rotation matrix of an "axis-angle" triple. Finally, the loss is the weighted sum of L_{pos} and L_{rot}.

$$L = w_{pos}L_{pos} + w_{rot}L_{rot} \tag{3}$$

Training Details. Our network is trained for 500,000 iterations and the mini-batch is of size 20. The input positions is of 19 joints and the output pose is of 24 joints. The training procedure takes Adam [30] as the optimizer with a learning rate of 0.00001 and a decay rate of 0.0001. We save model weights in the middle process of training and eventually choose a best model. Our code is implemented using PyTorch and the training of 500,000 iterations is performed on a Tesla K20 m GPU in less than 3 days.

3   Experiments and Evaluations

3.1   Quantitative Results

Pose Recovery Under Noises. Our method is based on the result of 3D joint positions. On one hand, it can lift the pose data in terms of information quantity, but on the other hand, it also relies on the quality of the given 3D joint positions. Therefore, we also test our model under different levels of Gaussian noises. We generate datasets with Gaussian noises in a similar way of generating training data. We report the mean per joint angle error (MPJAE) since our model is aim to recover joint angles given 3D joint positions. We also report several common used metrics for evaluating 3D joint position error as an additional assessment of our model, including the mean per joint position error (MPJPE), MPJPE after rigid alignment of the prediction with ground truth (denoted as MPJPE ARA).

The results are shown in Fig. 4. We can see that the joint position error and joint rotation error increase linearly as the noise level grows linearly. Figure 5 shows the visualization results under noises. We find that although the predicted mesh models are very different from the ground truth model, they fit the input skeleton well and their rotation pose are natural. It proves that our model has learned the dependency between joint rotations and joint positions and is able to recover valid joint rotations from joint positions. Our model takes 0.066 ms to process each frame of data averagely (15143.75 fps) in GPU and 0.223 ms (4485.87 fps) in CPU. As a post-process, our model satisfies the requirements of real-time applications.

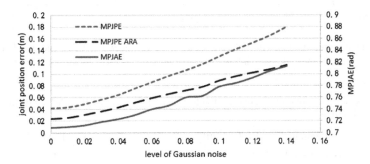

Fig. 4. The joint position errors (MPJPE, MPJPE ARA) and the joint rotation error (MPJAE) under different levels of Gaussian noises.

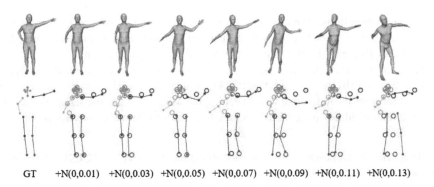

GT   +N(0,0.01)   +N(0,0.03)   +N(0,0.05)   +N(0,0.07)   +N(0,0.09)   +N(0,0.11)   +N(0,0.13)

Fig. 5. The visualizations of the output pose under different levels of Gaussian noises. Top: the recovered mesh models. Bottom: the input skeletons with noises, where the circle centers indicate the point positions of ground truth.

Repeat or Reuse. We explore three variant architectures of our network as shown in Fig. 6. Network (a) is the baseline model that contains one residual block. There are three residual blocks in network (b) and in network (c), one residual block is reused three times. We report MPJPE, MPJPE ARA, MPJAE and the percentage of correct keypoints (PCK) within a distance threshold of 150 mm of three networks in Table 1.

From Table 1, we can see that network (b) has a much better performance than network (c) does in 3D joint position errors and their MPJAEs are nearly the same. And network (c) has a higher MPJPE and lower PCK than baseline (a). Therefore, reusing residual block is not a good way to improve network performance.

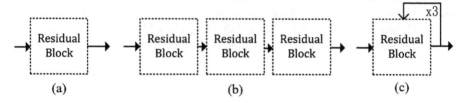

Fig. 6. Three configurations of network structures: (a) network with one residual block, (b) network with 3 repeated residual blocks, (c) network with one residual block iterated 3 times.

Table 1. Results of different network structures. MPJPE and MPJPE ARA are in mm and MPJAE is in radian.

Configuration	MPJPE	MPJPE ARA	PCK@150 mm	MPJAE
Network (a)	64.6	39.8	90.3%	0.070
Network (b)	41.5	23.8	97.5%	0.071
Network (c)	87.9	37.2	80.3%	0.070

Residual Connections. We also test the improvement made by residual connections by compare the network (a), (b) with their no-residual-connection variants denoted by (a-nres) and (b-nres). Table 2 shows the results of the comparisons. If the network predict joint rotations directly instead of regressing residuals of poses, the PCKs of network (a) and (b) decline and MPJPE ARAs increase, i.e. the residual connections help reduce joint position error while keeping the MPJAE nearly the same. The results illustrate that residual connections are greatly helpful to network convergence.

Table 2. The residual connections' influence on the results. MPJPE and MPJPE ARA are in mm and MPJAE is in radian.

Configuration	MPJPE	MPJPE ARA	PCK@150 mm	MPJAE
Network (a)	64.6	39.8	90.3%	0.070
Network (a-nres)	71.2	39.5	87.6%	0.069
Network (b)	41.5	23.8	97.5%	0.071
Network (b-nres)	59.2	39.5	92.3%	0.069

3.2 Qualitative Analysis

In this section, we show some qualitative results and evaluation of our model.

Figure 7 displays the visualization of our model of best configuration (network with 3 repeated residual blocks, trained using both position loss and rotation loss). The joint rotations recovered by our model are natural and similar to the ground truth data.

Fig. 7. Results of our network of the best configuration. Column 1, 4 & 7: 3D positions of the input 19 joints. Column 2, 5 & 8: the mesh models of ground truth. Column 3, 6 & 9: the SMPL mesh models whose parameters are predicted by our network.

Figure 8 shows the visualizations of using only 3D joint position losses when training the network of best model structure. When the training process is only supervised by joint position loss, the human mesh models have twisted surfaces although their joints are at right places. Their joint rotation parameters are very wrong so that the poses are invalid, which also proves that the joint rotation information is of great significance for human pose recovery.

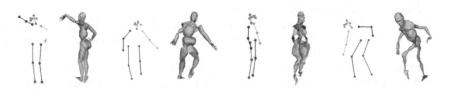

Fig. 8. Results of our network trained with 3D joint position loss only. The mesh models are twisted since the predicted joint rotation parameters are unnatural and invalid.

4 Conclusion and Future Work

This paper has proposed a deep network that recovers 3D joint rotations from 3D joint positions. In other words, we design an effective model to learn the prior dependence of joint rotations on joint positions. It can be combined with most work of 3D human pose estimation that predict 3D joint positions from image or depth data so that we can obtain more details of the poses and more useful pose data for applications. Besides, our model builds a map between two joint sets with different numbers of joints, which provides a framework to unify multiple datasets for human pose estimation with different annotation formats. Future work will consider building a benchmark dataset and evaluation procedure for detailed human pose estimation based on the proposed method.

Acknowledgements. This work is supported by the National Key R&D Plan of China (No. 2017YFB1002804) and the National Natural Science Foundation of China (No. 61471359).

References

1. Wei, X., Zhang, P., Chai, J.: Accurate realtime full-body motion capture using a single depth camera. ACM Trans. Graph. (TOG) **31**, 188 (2012)
2. Knoop, S., Vacek, S., Dillmann, R.: Sensor fusion for 3D human body tracking with an articulated 3D body model. In: International Conference on Robotics and Automation, pp. 1686–1691 (2006)
3. Shuai, L., Li, C., Guo, X., Prabhakaran, B., Chai, J.: Motion capture with ellipsoidal skeleton using multiple depth cameras. IEEE Trans. Vis. Comput. Graph. **23**, 1085–1098 (2017)
4. De Aguiar, E., Stoll, C., Theobalt, C., Ahmed, N., Seidel, H., Thrun, S.: Performance capture from sparse multi-view video. In: International Conference on Computer Graphics and Interactive Techniques, vol. 27, p. 98 (2008)
5. Wu, C., Stoll, C., Valgaerts, L., Theobalt, C.: On-set performance capture of multiple actors with a stereo camera. In: International Conference on Computer Graphics and Interactive Techniques, vol. 32, pp. 1–11 (2013)
6. Urtasun, R., Darrell, T.: Sparse probabilistic regression for activity-independent human pose inference. In: Computer Vision and Pattern Recognition, pp. 1–8 (2008)
7. Anguelov, D., et al.: Discriminative learning of Markov random fields for segmentation of 3D scan data. In: Computer Vision and Pattern Recognition, pp. 169–176 (2005)
8. Siddiqui, M., Medioni, G.: Human pose estimation from a single view point, real-time range sensor. In: 2010 IEEE Computer Society Conference on Computer Vision and Pattern Recognition - Workshops, pp. 1–8 (2010)
9. Girshick, R., Shotton, J., Kohli, P., Criminisi, A., Fitzgibbon, A.: Efficient regression of general-activity human poses from depth images. In: 2011 International Conference on Computer Vision, pp. 415–422 (2011)
10. Kanaujia, A.: Coupling top-down and bottom-up methods for 3D human pose and shape estimation from monocular image sequences. In: Computer Vision and Pattern Recognition (2014)
11. Orriteurunuela, C., Rincon, J.M.D., Herrerojaraba, J.E., Rogez, G.: 2D silhouette and 3D skeletal models for human detection and tracking. In: International Conference on Pattern Recognition, pp. 244–247 (2004)

12. Sigal, L., Balan, A.O., Black, M.J.: Combined discriminative and generative articulated pose and non-rigid shape estimation. In: Neural Information Processing Systems, pp. 1337–1344 (2007)
13. Agarwal, A., Triggs, B.: Monocular human motion capture with a mixture of regressors. In: Computer Vision and Pattern Recognition, p. 72 (2005)
14. Ouyang, W., Chu, X., Wang, X.: Multi-source deep learning for human pose estimation. In: 2014 IEEE Conference on Computer Vision and Pattern Recognition, pp. 2337–2344 (2014)
15. Haque, A., Peng, B., Luo, Z., Alahi, A., Yeung, S., Fei-Fei, L.: Towards viewpoint invariant 3D human pose estimation. In: Leibe, B., Matas, J., Sebe, N., Welling, M. (eds.) ECCV 2016. LNCS, vol. 9905, pp. 160–177. Springer, Cham (2016). https://doi.org/10.1007/978-3-319-46448-0_10
16. Pavlakos, G., Zhou, X., Derpanis, K.G., Daniilidis, K.: Coarse-to-fine volumetric prediction for single-image 3D human pose. In: Computer Vision and Pattern Recognition (2016)
17. Shafaei, A., Little, J.J.: Real-time human motion capture with multiple depth cameras. In: 2016 13th Conference on Computer and Robot Vision (CRV), pp. 24–31. IEEE (2016)
18. Tekin, B., Katircioglu, I., Salzmann, M., Lepetit, V., Fua, P.: Structured prediction of 3D human pose with deep neural networks. arXiv preprint arXiv:1605.05180 (2016)
19. Zhou, X., Sun, X., Zhang, W., Liang, S., Wei, Y.: Deep kinematic pose regression. In: European Conference on Computer Vision, pp. 186–201 (2016)
20. Mehta, D., et al.: VNect: real-time 3D human pose estimation with a single RGB Camera. ACM Trans. Graph. **36**, 1–14 (2017)
21. Mehta, D., Rhodin, H., Casas, D., et al.: Monocular 3D human pose estimation in the wild using improved CNN supervision. In: 2017 Fifth International Conference on 3D Vision (3DV) (2017)
22. Kanazawa, A., Black, M.J., Jacobs, D.W., Malik, J.: End-to-end recovery of human shape and pose. In: Computer Vision and Pattern Regognition (CVPR) (2018)
23. Loper, M., Mahmood, N., Black, M.J.: MoSh: motion and shape capture from sparse markers. In: International Conference on Computer Graphics and Interactive Techniques, vol. 33, p. 220 (2014)
24. Akhter, I., Black, M.J.: Pose-conditioned joint angle limits for 3D human pose reconstruction. In: Computer Vision and Pattern Recognition, pp. 1446–1455 (2015)
25. Martinez, J., Hossain, R., Romero, J., Little, J.J.: A simple yet effective baseline for 3D human pose estimation. In: International Conference on Computer Vision, pp. 2659–2668 (2017)
26. Ionescu, C., Papava, D., Olaru, V., Sminchisescu, C.: Human 3.6 m: large scale datasets and predictive methods for 3D human sensing in natural environments. IEEE Trans. Pattern Anal. Mach. Intell. **36**, 1325–1339 (2014)
27. EIA-0196217, F.b.N.: CMU graphics lab motion capture library (2000). http://mocap.cs.cmu.edu
28. Loper, M., Mahmood, N., Romero, J., Ponsmoll, G., Black, M.J.: SMPL: a skinned multi-person linear model. In: International Conference on Computer Graphics and Interactive Techniques, vol. 34, p. 248 (2015)
29. He, K., Zhang, X., Ren, S., Sun, J.: Identity mappings in deep residual networks. In: Leibe, B., Matas, J., Sebe, N., Welling, M. (eds.) ECCV 2016. LNCS, vol. 9908, pp. 630–645. Springer, Cham (2016). https://doi.org/10.1007/978-3-319-46493-0_38
30. Kingma, D.P., Ba, J.: Adam: a method for stochastic optimization. In: International Conference on Learning Representations (2015)

Estimation of 6Dof Pose Using Image Mask and Bounding Box

Yibo Cui, Pengyuan Liu[✉], and Junning Zhang

Department of Missile Engineering in Army Engineering University,
Shijiazhuang, Hebei, China
1164322995@qq.com

Abstract. One of the basic problems of computer vision is to calculate the 6Dof pose of objects. At present, many object recognition methods can give masks and bounding boxes of objects, but in military and industrial fields, 6 Dof pose information is also needed. In this paper, a pose estimation method based on mask, bounding box and object CAD model information is proposed, which can quickly calculate object pose. We use the prior information of object CAD model to generate template data related to the sampling value of object contour and the pose. Then, the input contour is sampled and matched to the corresponding pose template by using the input mask and bounding box, and the pose of the object is obtained. By using the method proposed in this paper, the pose of the object can be obtained quickly, and the accuracy of naked eye recognition can be basically achieved. It has strong compatibility and anti-occlusion ability. As a conclusion, in this paper, a new method of pose estimation is proposed, which can use masks and bounding boxes to quickly estimate the 6Dof pose of objects with known CAD models.

Keywords: Algorithm · Mask · Bounding box · CAD · Pose

1 Introduction

At present, with the continuous development of neural network, the accuracy of computer vision in object recognition is getting higher and faster, but in many military and industrial scenarios, the accurate recognition often requires the 6Dof pose information of the object. Considering that the current representative methods (such as MASK-RCNN [1]) can give masks and bounding boxes of objects, and the information of CAD model of industrial objects is often known, this paper designs a method that can use the above information to calculate the pose of objects.

In industrial production, the CAD model information of an object is often obtained earlier than that of the product itself. Using the prior information provided by the CAD model and software rendering, the Mask image of an object in different pose can be obtained. The Mask image mainly contains the contour information of the object projected to the camera plane in this pose. Different pose can be obtained by sampling algorithm (detailed introduction in 2.1). Sampling information of contour is saved as template data.

© Springer Nature Singapore Pte Ltd. 2019
Y. Wang et al. (Eds.): IGTA 2019, CCIS 1043, pp. 238–245, 2019.
https://doi.org/10.1007/978-981-13-9917-6_23

In practice, the information of object masks and bounding boxes can be obtained by camera data and object recognition methods. Now, the object recognition methods are quite mature. The most representative methods are real-time object recognition using neural networks, such as Mask-RCNN [1], YOLO [2], SSD [3]. These methods can output the masks and classifications of objects, which overcome the shortcomings of object masking and classification performance in pattern recognition. The methods above are not introduced too much in this paper, we mainly use the masks output by the above methods as an input-data for pose estimation.

In the aspect of pose estimation, although there are some methods such as Posenet [4], SSD-6D [5], BB8 [6], which use neural network to estimate pose, the training time is long and the adaptability of industrial deployment is poor. Once the object changes, it needs to be retrained, which takes a long time and is a black box system. In contrast, our algorithm, which uses contour sampling to match position and pose, is more convenient to deploy in practical industrial applications.

The matching algorithm uses the template data generated in the first step and the masks and bounding box information output from the object recognition method to find the pose of the object that meets the corresponding conditions. The overall process is shown in Fig. 1.

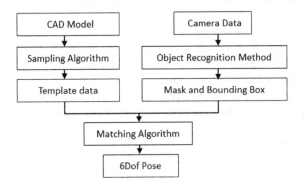

Fig. 1. The overall process

2 Sampling and Matching Algorithms

2.1 Contour Sampling Algorithm

This algorithm is inspired by papers [7–10]. The core algorithm of template data generation using object CAD model is the sampling algorithm based on object contour. Firstly, the object's mask can be rendered by the object's CAD model under the specified pose. Then, the object's bounding box can be obtained by the object's mask. And, according to different needs, the contour of the object is sampled at a certain distance on the bounding box (Fig. 2). Of course, the same equidistant sampling method can also be used in the boundary box from other angles, but the simplest and most efficient method is the direct use of the boundary sampling method mentioned below.

(a) Rendered image   (b)Mask image   (c) Sampling image

Fig. 2. An example of contour sampling, on the left is an rendered CAD model image by OpenGL the middle is the mask and the right is the contour of the CAD model which is sampling by the same distance

Based on the length L of the left bounding (similar to other boundaries) box border, we divide it into N equal parts, and each interval L/n is a sampling abscissa point. We traverse every point on the contour to calculate the distance from the point to the left border when its abscissa is equal to the sampling abscissa point. Since each sampling abscissa point may correspond to multiple contour sampling distances, the maximum and minimum values of the multiple distances are taken as the sampling values on the sampling abscissa. In this way, we transform the contour information into a set of sampling values.

Because the contour may vary in size, it is necessary to normalize the sampling value, that is, the length of the left bounding box should be in the same length. In the experiment, the left bounding box is 128px in length, which can ensure both the sampling accuracy and the sampling speed.

The advantage of the above sampling method is to obtain a set of features of the contour, so the sampling value, which is invariant to the contour scaling, but sensitive to the rotation of the object.

In the designated distance, taking the center of the object CAD model as the center, the contour of the object is sampled at different rotation angles, then the contour sampling values and the rotation angles are saved as the template data.

2.2   Pose Matching Algorithm

The pose of rigid body consists of rotation (R) and displacement (T). The matching process of the rotating part is as follows:

Because the object masking resolution of different frames is different, if the object resolution is too low, it will affect the quality of the data collected by the sampling algorithm. If the object resolution is too high, the sampling speed will decrease. So, the same as the sampling algorithm, the output contour information is first normalized and compared in the same scale.

If the sampling data of the actual mask of the object is S^{in}, group i of template data is S^i, each group has n sampling values, then the L_1 distance between the actual mask sampling data and each group of data in the template is calculated. The L_1 distance of group L_i is:

$$L_i = \sum_{j=1}^{n} |S_j^{in} - S_j^i| \tag{1}$$

Ideally, to a rigid body, the sampling values should be the same when the R and T are the same. That is to say, the rotation angle that makes the distance to be zero in the template data is the rotation angle corresponding to the contour. In practice, because the length of the pixel is a discrete integer value and there is rounding error, the value of the proposed distance can not be zero, so the rotation angle corresponding to the minimum value satisfying the threshold in all the results is taken as the right one. Therefore, the rotation angle corresponding to the minimum value satisfying the threshold in all the results is taken as the rotation angle obtained by the current matching, and the matching failure is considered when the threshold is not satisfied.

Then the angle information can be transformed into rotation matrix R, means the rotation information of the object can be obtained.

The translation algorithm is as follows:

When generating template data, because the object is sampled at a specified distance and the size of the CAD model is known, the size of the bounding box corresponding to the object is inversely proportional to its distance, that is, the smaller the bounding box is, the farther the object is, which is consistent with the naked eye recognition, then the distance between the center of the model and the plane of the camera can be obtained by (2):

$$D = (w_{in}/w_i) \cdot D_i \tag{2}$$

Among them, w_{in} is the width of bounding box (it can also be the border height), w_i is the boundary width of template data matching its rotation, and D_i is the distance specified when template data acquisition, D is the distance between the center of the model and the center of the camera. According to the ratio between the center position of the object and the distance (pixels) to the upper left corner of the boundary box, the coordinates of the object center point can be obtained.

Similarly, because the prior information of the size of the CAD model is known, the actual physical distance represented by each pixel in the template can be calculated, (t_x, t_y) can be inferred from the proportion of formula (2), so we can get the displacement vector of object:

$$T = \begin{pmatrix} t_x \\ t_y \\ t_z \end{pmatrix} \tag{3}$$

$$t_z = \sqrt{t_x^2 + t_y^2 + D^2} \tag{4}$$

In practical experiments, because the sub-pixel level information can not be obtained, there will be errors when only using the pixel to calculate, but when the object moves near the depth axis, i.e. near the camera center, it can be approximated as follows:

$$T \approx \begin{pmatrix} 0 \\ 0 \\ D \end{pmatrix} \tag{5}$$

At this time, the pose of the object is more accurate. In practical, it is easy to align the camera's optical center to the center of the object's boundary frame, so this method can be used to eliminate errors.

After obtaining the rotation R and displacement T of the object, the world coordinates of the object can be obtained by combining the internal and external parameters of the camera.

This matching method has three main advantages:

1. High accuracy. In theory, as long as the number of templates is large enough, the accuracy of pose matching can reach a high level, but the speed will decrease. In view of this situation, parallel search, tree structure and more efficient database can be used to make up for the shortcomings of speed.
2. Strong anti-interference ability. In fact, there may be occlusion and other factors that could interference the result. Considering that each border of the bounding box can be sampled, it can be re-matched by other borders when the sampling matching fails.
3. Good compatibility. The size of the input data is unlimited, and the higher the resolution of the input data, the better the effect. This method can be fused with almost any framework which output is mask.

The main drawbacks of this matching method are:

1. Because the algorithm is based on masks and bounding boxes, it is impossible to judge the accurate pose of a symmetrical object at a special angle (such as a sphere).
2. Because this algorithm does not use any acceleration strategy, its real-time performance is not good.

3   Experimental Data

3.1   Template Data Generation Time

The experimental environment is Y7000 notebook, the CPU is Core i7, the system is Ubuntu 16.04, the program is written in Python and the software for rendering model is OpenGL. The time for generating template data is as follows:

The three rotating axes (pitch, yaw and roll) are divided into 30, 40 and 50 parts respectively. Divide the border into 20 and 30 pieces on average as sampling coordinates, and the image is 256*256px. Under these conditions, the time-consuming for template data generation is shown in Table 1.

Table 1. Template data generation time

Rotating axis equal fraction	Sampling axis flat fraction	Time (min)
30	20	5
30	30	7
40	20	16
40	30	20
50	20	50
50	30	75

3.2 Actual Performance and Performance Under Occlusion

The test was divided into three scenarios:

(1) When the object is close to the depth axis (i.e. when the camera's optical center is close to the center of the object's bounding box), this method has the best performance. As shown in Fig. 3 (a), on the left is the input mask, and the right is the rendered image of the object in the 6dof pose we calculated. In the right side, two red dots represent the upper left corner and the lower right corner of the object bounding box.

Fig. 3. When the object is closed to the depth axis, on the left is the input mask and the right is the rendered image of CAD model in the pose we matched

Without any optimization, the template data is saved in. TXT format, and the recognition time of each image is about 3–4 s.

(2) When the object is far from the depth axis. As shown in Fig. 4, the depth of the object is basically correct, but the position of the other two axes is slightly deviated, but most of them are still in the bounding box.

(3) When the object is occluded. Because the input data will inevitably be partially occluded or undetected in practical application, we can only rely on the detected contour to calculate the pose. The effect is shown in Fig. 5.

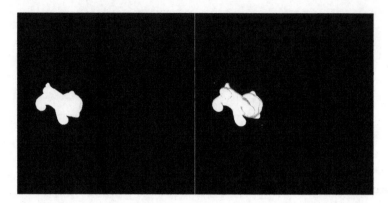

Fig. 4. When the object is far to the depth axis, on the left is the input mask and the right is the rendered image of CAD model in the pose we matched

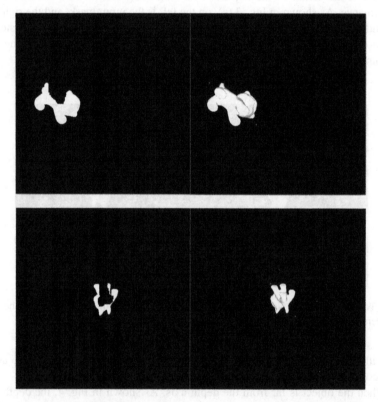

Fig. 5. Effect of pose estimation under occlusion: when occlusion occurs in the middle of an object shows on the top; when the outline of an object has a large error

4   Conclusion

Using the masks and bounding boxes obtained from image detection and the known information of the object CAD model, we design a method that can quickly and effectively calculate the pose of the object, and this method can be used to calculate the pose of the object well in the case of occlusion and contour missing.

References

1. He, K., Gkioxari, G., Dollar, P., et al.: Mask R-CNN. IEEE Trans. Pattern Anal. Mach. Intell. **99**(1), 2961–2969 (2017)
2. Redmon, J., Divvala, S., Girshick, R., et al.: You only look once: unified, real-time object detection (2015)
3. Liu, W., et al.: SSD: single shot multibox detector. In: Leibe, B., Matas, J., Sebe, N., Welling, M. (eds.) ECCV 2016. LNCS, vol. 9905, pp. 21–37. Springer, Cham (2016). https://doi.org/10.1007/978-3-319-46448-0_2
4. Kendall, A., Grimes, M., Cipolla, R.: PoseNet: a convolutional network for real-time 6-DOF camera relocalization. In: IEEE International Conference on Computer Vision (2015)
5. Kehl, W., Manhardt, F., Tombari, F., et al.: SSD-6D: making RGB-based 3D detection and 6D pose estimation great again (2017)
6. Rad, M., Lepetit, V.: BB8: a scalable, accurate, robust to partial occlusion method for predicting the 3D poses of challenging objects without using depth (2017)
7. Qi-ai, W., Ming-wu, R.: A tank shooting method simulation based on image analysis. In: Tan, T., Ruan, Q., Chen, X., Ma, H., Wang, L. (eds.) Advances in Image and Graphics Technologies, IGTA 2013. CCIS, vol. 363, pp. 136–144. Springer, Heidelberg (2013). https://doi.org/10.1007/978-3-642-37149-3_17
8. Shi, Y., Guo, F., Su, X., Xu, J.: Edge detection in presence of impulse noise. In: Tan, T., Ruan, Q., Wang, S., Ma, H., Huang, K. (eds.) Advances in Image and Graphics Technologies IGTA 2014. CCIS, vol. 437, pp. 8–18. Springer, Heidelberg (2014). https://doi.org/10.1007/978-3-662-45498-5_2
9. Xiao, Y., Ma, Y., Zhou, M., Zhang, J.: Deep multi-scale learning on point sets for 3D object recognition. In: Wang, Y., Jiang, Z., Peng, Y. (eds.) IGTA 2018. CCIS, vol. 875, pp. 341–348. Springer, Singapore (2018). https://doi.org/10.1007/978-981-13-1702-6_34
10. Wu, Z., Wang, P., Che, W.: A method of registering virtual objects in monocular augmented reality system. In: Wang, Y., Jiang, Z., Peng, Y. (eds.) IGTA 2018. CCIS, vol. 875, pp. 483–493. Springer, Singapore (2018). https://doi.org/10.1007/978-981-13-1702-6_48

Multi-Attention Network for 2D Face Alignment in the Wild

Xin Liu, Huabin Wang[✉], Rui Cheng, Xiang Yan, and Liang Tao

Key Laboratory of Intelligent Computing and Signal Processing
of Ministry of Education, Anhui University, Hefei 230031, China
wanghuabin@ahu.edu.cn

Abstract. Most existing algorithms based on Convolutional Neural Networks (CNNs) for face alignment ignore the significance of attention mechanism. In this paper, we propose a Multi-Attention Network (MANet) for robust face alignment. Our attention mechanism includes multi-level feature attention and multi-scale attention. Multi-level feature attention is introduced for the purpose of paying attention to features of different levels, specifically, high-level feature attentions are essential for correlations among neighboring regions whereas low-level feature attentions focus on detailed description for local parts. While multi-scale attention is designed to obtain better representation the features of different scales. The attentions mentioned above are utilized for better feature presentation and information flow, thus our network is guided to emphasize the key information and suppress the less significant information. The experimental results on 300 W and WFLW datasets demonstrate the superiority of the proposed method over the state-of-the-art approaches.

Keywords: Face alignment · Multi-attention · CNNs

1 Introduction

The task of face alignment or facial landmark detection [1, 2] has attracted substantial attention in the computer vision community. Facial landmarks are useful for emotion recognition [3] and expression analysis [4].

Recently, CNNs [1, 2, 5] have significantly boosted the performance of face alignment. Diverse network architectures have been extensively studied. Hourglass [6] network has been proved very effective in the task of human pose estimation. The architecture of hourglass enables the network to capture features from different scales. Naturally, the hourglass network has been applied to face alignment and has inspired a volume of research works [1, 2, 7, 8]. Although great progress has been made by HG (hourglass), there still exist a lot of challenging cases, such as large view variations, different expressions, and partial occlusions, even state-of-the-art algorithms may fail to locate the landmarks correctly.

This work was supported in part by the National Nature Science Foundation of China under Grant 61372137 and in part by the Natural Science Foundation of Anhui Province, China, under Grant 1908085MF209.

© Springer Nature Singapore Pte Ltd. 2019
Y. Wang et al. (Eds.): IGTA 2019, CCIS 1043, pp. 246–255, 2019.
https://doi.org/10.1007/978-981-13-9917-6_24

To alleviate above problems, one crucial aspect of deep learning methods is to leverage the visual attention mechanism. Visual attention is an essential mechanism of the human brain for understanding scenes effectively [6]. Following this strategy, we propose a multi-attention network which combines the attention mechanism with the stacked hourglass network. More specifically, our attentions in this paper include multi-level feature attention and multi-scale attention. For instance, high level feature attentions learn a better representation of correlations among neighboring regions in the attention map, which is indispensable for inference of the occluded parts. Low level attentions explicitly focus on detailed description for local parts. It is proved beneficial to distinguishes the ambiguous background based on features attention of different level. We show the effectiveness of the proposed framework on broadly used 300 W and WFLW datasets.

In summary, our contributions are as follows:

- We propose a Multi-Attention Network with different attention mechanism to automatically learn the contextual representations, driving the model to focus on region of interest.
- We propose a multi-scale attention module to improve the feature representation ability for different scales.
- Our algorithm achieves state-of-art results in 300 W benchmark, that is, 3.81% Normalized Mean Error (NME) in common dataset and 7.50% NME in challenge dataset.

2 Relate Work

2.1 Face Alignment

Recently, work based on Convolutional Neural Networks (CNNs) has revolutionized face alignment. Trigeorgis et al. [5] apply the recurrent neural networks to face alignment. Lv et al. [9] present a deep regression architecture with two-stage reinitialization to explicitly deal with the initialization problem by face detection. Newell et al. [6] first propose an stacked hourglass network and stack up several hourglass modules to generate prediction for human pose estimation. A similar strategy is adopted in [1, 2, 8]. Bulat et al. [8] also employ stacked hourglass network with a novel residual block to solve the 2D and 3D face alignment problem. Wu et al. [2] propose an algorithm which the boundary information is introduced into key point regression. Feng et al. [1] present a new loss function and achieved superiority performance. Valle et al. [10] present a real-time facial landmark regression method based on a coarse-to-fine Ensemble of Regression Trees (ERT).

2.2 Visual Attention Mechanism

Attention is a behavioral and cognitive process of selectively concentrating on a discrete aspect of information [11]. However, common algorithms usually ignore the influence of attention mechanism, resulting in that the key information is not highlighted and the uncorrelated information is not suppressed [12]. Various features carry information with different impacts on prediction, thus it should be treated appropriately. Attention mechanism helps the network improve the representation ability of importance degrees. Very recently, since the visual attention model is computationally efficient and is effective in understanding images, it has achieved great success in various tasks such as semantic segmentation [13] and human pose estimation [14]. Inspired by these works, we propose a method with attention mechanism to help the network improve the ability of feature representation. Specifically, we aim at guiding the network focus on important features and suppressing unnecessary ones.

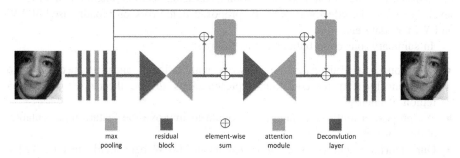

Fig. 1. Overview of our proposed network. The basic structure is a 2-stacked hourglass network. Each hourglass is an multi-scale attention module. We also apply multi-level attention at the end of each hourglass.

3   The Proposed Method

In this section, we display the architecture of the proposed multi-attention convolutional neural network (MANet) for face alignment. Firstly, we discuss about the architecture of the network, which is based on the stacked hourglass network. Then, we focus on the implement of the multi-attention mechanism.

3.1   Network Overview

Figure 1 is an overview of our proposed network. Specifically, the input of model is a face image with spatial resolution 128×128. The full network starts with a 3×3 convolution layer with stride 1, followed by residual blocks to increase feature channels and a max pooling to bring the resolution down from 128 to 64. Operating at the full input resolution of 128×128 requires a significant amount of GPU memory, so the 64×64 is the highest resolution in the hourglass module. It is proved efficient in costs and not affect the network's ability to produce precise predictions. Across the entire hourglass all residual modules output 256 features. At the end of each hourglass module, we feed the features into the attention module (As shown in Fig. 2). Then, we employ a deconvolution layer to increase the spatial resolution to 128×128, followed by a residual block and a convolution layer with 1×1 kernels to produce heatmaps. Expect the first layer, all convolution layers are equipped with batch normalization. ReLU is the activation function.

3.2 Multi-level Attention

Huang et al. [15] propose a new architecture, DenseNet. It iteratively concatenates the input features with the output features, enabling each convolution block to receive raw information from all the previous blocks. The DenseNet has shown superior performance in pose estimation [16] and parameter efficiency. Our work is similar to these methods. Since features from different levels focus on different representations: low level pay more attention to fine details while high level encode global representations. To make information flow more efficiently across different level. An illustration is shown in Fig. 1, later layers receive information from the early layers. The skip connectivity improves the feature reuse in the network forward and gradient propagation during the backward process. Then, we feed the combined feature into our attention module for the purpose of paying attention to features of different levels. In this way, our model is guided to capture and combine features across levels effectively.

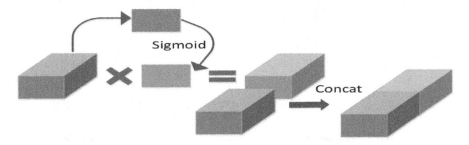

Fig. 2. Architecture of our attention module. The features are adaptively refined through our attention module.

3.3 Multi-scale Attention

The design of the hourglass is motivated by the need to capture information at each scale. The network effectively process and consolidate features across scales. Convolution operations are applied at each scale to obtain various features and bring them together for output predictions. Features from each scale carry information with different impacts on prediction, thus should be treated unequal. To this end, multi-scale attention module is designed to obtain better representation the features of different scales, shown as Fig. 3.

Concretely, existing works based on the hourglass network for face alignment follow the strategy in [6]. Hourglasses in these works which just down-sampled and up-sampled modules. Therefore, we propose a multi-scale attention module to maintain the key information for each scale. To achieve this, we concat features with same scale and feed the processed features into the attention module (Fig. 3). The features are adaptively refined through our attention module. Hence, our model has the ability to focus on features of different scales. In a nutshell, the multi-scale attention module is introduced to emphasize the meaningful features for scales.

More importantly, We employ ESP (Efficient Spatial Pyramid) module proposed by Mehta et al. [17] rather than the common residual module in the hourglass. ESP module learns multi-scale representations by using dilated convolutions with different receptive field in parallel. Dilated convolutions are a special form of standard convolutions in which the effective receptive field of kernels is increased by inserting zeros (or holes) between each pixel in the convolutional kernel. It is clear that different receptive field of kernels can boost the data representation ability of the deep neural network. Specifically, convolution layers with small kernel size focus on details while local evidence is essential for identifying features like eyes and lips. Meanwhile, the deep network can learn the global information about landmarks relationship with larger receptive field.

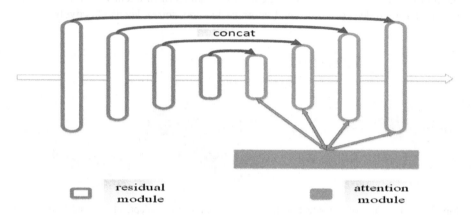

Fig. 3. Multiscale attention module. Concretely, we concat features with same resolution and feed the processed features into the attention module.

4   Experiment Results

In this section, we evaluate our method on 300 W dataset [18] and Wider Facial Landmarks in the Wild (WFLW) dataset [2]. We first introduce our implementation details and experimental settings. Then we compare our algorithm with state-of-the-art approaches on 300 W and WFLW.

4.1   Datasets

300 W is the most widely-used in-the-wild dataset for 2D face alignment. It covers a large variation of identity, expression, illumination conditions, and occlusions. The training set consists of 3148 face images in total. We present the results on common subset and challenge subset. All face images in 300 W are labeled by 68 landmarks.

Wider Facial Landmarks in the-wild (WFLW) is introduced by [2] for the sake of facilitating future research of face alignment. WFLW contains 10000 faces (7500 for training and 2500 for testing) with 98 fully manual annotated landmarks. Compare with previous dataset, faces in the proposed dataset covers large variations in occlusion, pose, make-up, illumination, blur and expression.

4.2   Performance Evaluation Metric

For WFLW dataset, we utilize the inter-ocular (outer-eye-corner distance). For 300 W dataset, we compare with the results that reported to be normalized by inter-pupil (eye-centre-distance) on 300 w dataset. The NME for inter-pupil (or inter-ocular) is computed as follows:

$$Error_i = \frac{\frac{1}{N}\sum_j^N |P_{ij} - G_{ij}|_2}{|L - R|_2},$$

where N is the number of total landmarks, P_{ij} and G_{ij} is the location of prediction and ground truth respectively. L and R are the locations of left eye center (left outer-eye-corner) and right eye center (right outer-eye-corner) in i^{th} face image.

4.3   Training Details

For training, we perform image flipping, scaling (between 0.7 and 1.3), rotation (between −30 and 30°) and adding color jittering to augment the data. The inputs are RGB images with resolution of 128×128. The network is optimized by ADAM with an initial learning rate of 2.5e-4 which is decayed by two after every 40000 iterations. The experiments are conducted on Ubuntu 16.04 with a Nvidia 1080 GPU card with a mini-batch size of 10 for 100000 iterations using PyTorch. We train our model with L2 loss:

$$Loss = \frac{1}{2}\sum_{i=1}^{N}\sum_{k=1}^{K} \|H_P - H_G\|^2,$$

where N is the number of training samples and K is the number of landmarks, H_P and H_G are the predicted heatmaps and the ground-truth heatmaps of each hourglass. Intermediate supervision is introduced for better information flow through the network. During inference, the predicted landmark locations L_k is decoded from the predicted heatmap $H_k(x)$ by taking the locations with the maximum value as follows:

$$L_k = \arg\max H_k(x)$$

4.4   Evaluation on 300 W and WFLW Datasets

We compare the performance of our model with state-of-the-art networks for 2D face alignment on 300 W and WFLW datasets. Firstly, we report NME on the Testset and 6 typical subsets of WFLW on Table 1. Our method achieves 5.41% NME on WFLW testset. Our performance on WFLW is slightly worse than the LAB [2] proposed by Wu et al.. It is worth noting that we just employ a 2-stacked hourglass network as basic structure. However, the LAB employs 8-stacked hourglass as backbone, so it is time consuming and inefficient in cost for the LAB to achieve the performance. Our proposed model is simple yet effective. Then, experimental results on 300 W are shown in Table 2. Our method significantly outperforms previous methods by a large margin. Note that, our method achieves 7.50% NME on the Challenging (IBUG) subset which reflects the effectiveness of handling large view variations and exaggerated expressions. Apart from 300 W challenge set, results on 300 W common testsets are shown in Table 2. Relying on multi-attention mechanism, our method achieves 3.81% NME on 300 W common set. This indicates that our proposed MANet is robust against extreme head pose and exaggerated expressions. The experimental results on both 300 W and WFLW demonstrate the effectiveness of multi-attention mechanism. Example of qualitative outputs on WFLW dataset are shown in Fig. 4.

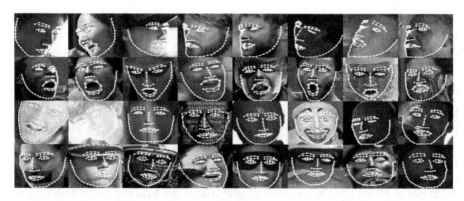

Fig. 4. Examples of face landmarks obtained using our method on WFLW testing data set. Observe that our method copes well with large view variations, different expressions, and partial occlusions.

Table 1. Evaluation of MANnet on Testset and 6 typical subsets of WFLW (98 landmarks) in terms of NME. Note that error is normalized by outer eye corner distance.

Algorithm	Testset	Pose	Expression	Illumination	Make-up	Occlusion	Blur
ESR (IJCV14) [19]	11.13	25.88	11.47	10.49	11.05	13.75	12.20
SDM (CVPR13) [20]	10.29	24.10	11.45	9.32	9.38	13.03	11.28
CFSS (CVPR15) [21]	9.07	21.36	10.09	8.30	8.74	11.76	9.96
DVLN (CVPRW17) [22]	6.08	11.54	6.78	5.73	5.98	7.33	6.88
LAB (CVPR18) [2]	**5.27**	10.24	**5.51**	**5.23**	**5.15**	**6.79**	6.32
MANet	5.41	**10.03**	5.56	5.54	6.03	7.00	**6.25**

Table 2. Results on 300 W dataset in terms of the NME. Note that error is normalized by the inter-pupil distance.

Algorithm	Common	Challenge	Full
PCPR (ICCV13) [23]	6.18	17.26	8.35
SDM (CVPR13) [20]	5.57	15.40	7.5
CFAN (ECCV14) [24]	5.50	17.00	7.58
ESR (IJCV14) [19]	5.28	17.00	7.58
LBF (CVPR14) [25]	4.95	11.98	6.32
TCDCN (CVPR14) [26]	4.73	9.98	5.76
MDM (CVPR2016) [5]	4.83	10.14	5.88
RAR (ECCV2016) [27]	4.12	8.35	4.94
TRDRN (CVPR17) [9]	4.36	7.56	4.99
DCFE (ECCV2018) [10]	3.93	7.54	4.55
MANet	**3.81**	**7.50**	**4.54**

4.5 Ablation Experiments

we conduct several experiments to evaluate the effectiveness of multi-level attention and multi-scale attention on the 300 W common Set. We use HG, ML and MS to denote the hourglass, multi-level attention and multi-scale attention respectively. We compare these model (HG+MS, HG+ML, HG+ML+MS) with the baseline of a 2-stackd hourglass network (HG) on the Common subset of 300 W dataset. The experimental results are shown in Table 3. It is clear that all the combinations have better results compared with the baseline model. The network in conjunction with the multi-level attention or the multi-scale attention has yielded improvement respectively. Note that the multi-level attention really make a difference for the final predictions, the NME is dropped about 7.6% compared with the baseline. The proposed multi-scale attention is sample yet powerful, the NME is dropped about 6.6%. Finally, we employ both multi-level attention and the multi-scale attention in our model, the NME is decreased to 3.81%. The experimental results demonstrate that our proposed multi-level attention and multi-scale attention are efficient.

Table 3. Analysis performance to evaluate the effectiveness of multi-level attention and multi-scale attention on 300 W Common Set in terms of the NME (inter-pupil).

Algorithm	HG	HG+MS	HG+ML	HG+ML+MS
NME	4.18	3.90	3.86	**3.81**

5 Conclusion

In this paper, we propose a Multi-Attention Network (MANet) for 2D face alignment, which adaptively boosts the data representation ability of the deep neural network by using the attention mechanism. Specifically, multi-attention mechanism includes multi-level attention and multi-scale attention. Multi-attention is introduced to enhance the key information and drop the less significant information. The experiments show that multi-attention mechanism can guide the network to capture important information effectively and give more precise location results. Our attention network achieves outstanding performance on 300 W and WFLW datasets.

References

1. Feng, Z., Kittler, J., Awais, M., et al.: Wing loss for robust facial landmark localisation with convolutional neural networks. In: Computer Vision and Pattern Recognition, pp. 2235–2245 (2018)
2. Wu, W., Qian, C., Yang, S., et al.: Look at boundary: a boundary-aware face alignment algorithm. In: Computer Vision and Pattern Recognition, pp. 2129–2138 (2018)
3. Li, S., Deng, W., Du, J., et al.: Reliable crowdsourcing and deep locality-preserving learning for expression recognition in the wild. In: Computer Vision and Pattern Recognition, pp. 2584–2593 (2017)
4. Pantic, M., Rothkrantz, L.J.: Automatic analysis of facial expressions: the state of the art. IEEE Trans. Pattern Anal. Mach. Intell. **22**(12), 1424–1445 (2000)
5. Trigeorgis, G., Snape, P., Nicolaou, M.A., et al.: Mnemonic descent method: a recurrent process applied for end-to-end face alignment. In: Computer Vision and Pattern Recognition, pp. 4177–4187 (2016)
6. Newell, A., Yang, K., Deng, J., et al.: Stacked hourglass networks for human pose estimation. In: European Conference on Computer Vision, pp. 483–499 (2016)
7. Yang, J., Liu, Q., Zhang, K., et al.: Stacked hourglass network for robust facial landmark localisation. In: Computer Vision and Pattern Recognition, pp. 2025–2033 (2017)
8. Bulat, A., Tzimiropoulos, G.: How far are we from solving the 2D & 3D face alignment problem? (and a dataset of 230,000 3D facial landmarks). In: International Conference on Computer Vision, pp. 1021–1030 (2017)
9. Lv, J., Shao, X., Xing, J., et al.: A deep regression architecture with two-stage re-initialization for high performance facial landmark detection. In: Computer Vision and Pattern Recognition, pp. 3691–3700 (2017)
10. Valle, R, Buenaposada, J.M., Valdes, A., et al.: A deeply-initialized coarse-to-fine ensemble of regression trees for face alignment. In: European Conference on Computer Vision, pp. 609–624 (2018)
11. Salisbury, D.F.: Cognitive psychology and its implications for designing drill and practice programs for computers. J. Comput. Based Instr. **17**(1), 23–30 (1990)
12. He, X., Peng, Y.: Multi-attention guided activation propagation in CNNs. In: Lai, J.-H., et al. (eds.) PRCV 2018. LNCS, vol. 11257, pp. 16–27. Springer, Cham (2018). https://doi.org/10.1007/978-3-030-03335-4_2
13. Fu, J., Liu, J., Tian, H., et al.: Dual attention network for scene segmentation. arXiv preprint arXiv:1809.02983 (2018)
14. Chu, X., Yang, W., Ouyang, W., et al.: Multi-context attention for human pose estimation. In: Computer Vision and Pattern Recognition, pp. 5669–5678 (2017)
15. Huang, G., Liu, Z., Van Der Maaten, L., et al.: Densely connected convolutional networks. In: Proceedings of the IEEE Conference on Computer Vision and Pattern Recognition, pp. 4700–4708 (2017)
16. Tang, Z., Peng, X., Geng, S., et al.: CU-net: coupled U-nets. arXiv preprint arXiv:1808.06521 (2018)

17. Mehta, S., Rastegari, M., Caspi, A., et al.: ESPNet: efficient spatial pyramid of dilated convolutions for semantic segmentation. In: European Conference on Computer Vision, pp. 561–580 (2018)
18. Sagonas, C., Tzimiropoulos, G., Zafeiriou, S., et al.: 300 faces in-the-wild challenge: the first facial landmark localization challenge. In: International Conference on Computer Vision, pp. 397–403 (2013)
19. Cao, X., Wei, Y., Wen, F., et al.: Face alignment by explicit shape regression. Int. J. Comput. Vis. **107**(2), 177–190 (2014)
20. Xiong, X., La Torre, F.D.: Supervised descent method and its applications to face alignment. In: Computer Vision and Pattern Recognition, pp. 532–539 (2013)
21. Zhu, S., Li, C., Loy, C.C., et al.: Face alignment by coarse-to-fine shape searching. In: Computer Vision and Pattern Recognition, pp. 4998–5006 (2015)
22. Wu, W., Yang, S.: Leveraging intra and inter-dataset variations for robust face alignment. In: Computer Vision and Pattern Recognition, pp. 2096–2105 (2017)
23. Burgosartizzu, X.P., Perona, P., Dollar, P., et al.: Robust face landmark estimation under occlusion. In: International Conference on Computer Vision, pp. 1513–1520 (2013)
24. Zhang, J., Shan, S., Kan, M., et al.: Coarse-to-fine auto-encoder networks (CFAN) for real-time face alignment. In: European Conference on Computer Vision, pp. 1–16 (2014)
25. Ren, S., Cao, X., Wei, Y., et al.: Face alignment at 3000 FPS via regressing local binary features. In: Computer Vision and Pattern Recognition, pp. 1685–1692 (2014)
26. Zhang, Z., Luo, P., Loy, C.C., Tang, X.: Facial landmark detection by deep multi-task learning. In: Fleet, D., Pajdla, T., Schiele, B., Tuytelaars, T. (eds.) ECCV 2014. LNCS, vol. 8694, pp. 94–108. Springer, Cham (2014). https://doi.org/10.1007/978-3-319-10599-4_7
27. Xiao, S., Feng, J., Xing, J., Lai, H., Yan, S., Kassim, A.: Robust facial landmark detection via recurrent attentive-refinement networks. In: Leibe, B., Matas, J., Sebe, N., Welling, M. (eds.) ECCV 2016. LNCS, vol. 9905, pp. 57–72. Springer, Cham (2016). https://doi.org/10.1007/978-3-319-46448-0_4

Virtual-Real Fusion Processing Based on Parallel Distribution

Hongyu Zhai, Tongtong Zhang$^{(\boxtimes)}$, and Richeng Xu

School of Computer Science and Technology,
Changchun University of Science and Technology,
Changchun 130022, Jilin, China
1205295658@qq.com

Abstract. For the demand of domestic digital film industry to improve the quality and efficiency of special effects film and television works, This paper studies the transmission quality of virtual and real fusion and the fusion efficiency, and proposes a better video transmission method combined with virtual and real fusion technology, which made the digital video industry more complete. Firstly, the Hadoop platform is built as the basis of distributed transmission, and then the parallel distributed transmission method and the virtual and real fusion technology proposed in this paper are combined to complete the experiment. In this paper, the efficiency of this method is compared with other existing advanced transmission methods. The experimental results show that the efficiency and transmission quality are improved compared with other methods.

Keywords: Virtual-real fusion · Hadoop platform · Distributed transmission · Virtual-real material stitching

1 Introduction

The research on the problems related to the virtual and real occlusion processing plays a decisive role in the improvement and practical application of the AR system, which can also be used to solve the important problems in practical applications. Due to the limitations of key technologies such as image foreground segmentation and 3D depth extraction, there is no complete universal solution at home and abroad. At the same time, the distributed virtual and real integration process is more icing on the digital TV industry. Whitaker et al. [1] and Du et al. [2] proposed an algorithmic structure for dealing with the problem of virtual and real fusion in augmented reality from two directions. Whitaker et al. used a multi-angle field of view and three-dimensional reconstruction to build a stereo model of the real scene, thereby the plane was restored to achieve occlusion. Wloka et al. [3] used a two-view approach to solve the virtual and real occlusion problems of the solid model in real scenes. The method proposed by Tian et al. [4] achieves the construction of stereo model using the semi-automatic method of key frame pixels, which completes the virtual and real occlusion and obtains a better result. Haouchine et al. [5] proposed an improved scheme to extract the contour part that obscured virtual object in the real scene and calculate the feature to restore the

Y. Wang et al. (Eds.): IGTA 2019, CCIS 1043, pp. 256–269, 2019.
https://doi.org/10.1007/978-981-13-9917-6_25

occlusion plane, which make it possible to complete the stereo reconstruction only using the single view.

Video data transmission [6] is an important part of data transmission and plays an important role in many fields. However, the development of video is becoming more and more networked. At this time, the video transmission method is not limited to the rapid development of video data. Video transmission data are currently divided into the following two categories at home and abroad: distributed storage transmission and centralized storage transmission in video transmission [7], In fact, in the real application, these two types of transmission are not mutually exclusive. Actually, In terms of distributed transmission [8], it is very difficult for video data to achieve an ideal distributed processing result. The combination of video analysis transmission technology and augmented reality is almost non-existent. Therefore, it can be said that a better video transmission method combined with virtual and real fusion technology [9] will make the digital video industry more complete.

2   Virtual and Real Fusion Method Based on Parallel Distributed Transmission

Through the design of the MapReduce program [10] and the design of the key-value pairs in parallelization, the Hadoop platform [11] is constructed, and then the virtual-real fusion transmission method based on distribution is obtained by combining parallel distributed transmission with virtual-real fusion technology (Fig. 1).

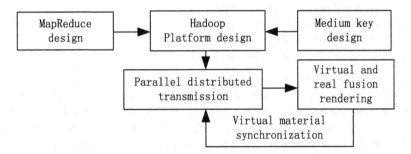

Fig. 1. The framework of virtual and real fusion processing method

2.1   Parallel Distributed Processing of Video

This paper improves and applies the distributed transmission strategy, which directly segments the video data stored on the corresponding node (the size of the segmentation is consistent) of the HDFS and then transmits the segmented video to the HDFS [12]. And then the frame extraction and identification of license plates, recognition of face and other video analysis and transmission tasks are completed in the stage of map and reduce stages respectively. The specific process is shown in Fig. 2.

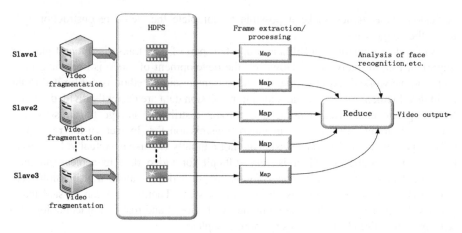

Fig. 2. Flowchart of MapReduce processing for distributed transmission

In order to achieve the balance of the load on the video system as much as possible in the video transmission, this paper improves a set of video allocation algorithm which makes full use of the equalization method. The algorithm is as follows: a video list called video_list.txt will be obtained during the operation of the algorithm. The system defines a class named VideodlistrInputFormat, which is used to complete the cutting of the video_list.txt document. The document is read in row-major order, each row consists of two columns, where the save path is stored in the first column and the file size (unit: MB) in the second column. The internal distribution of the file is as follows:

hdfs://master:9000/user/hadoop/1.mp4 462
hdfs://master:9000/user/hadoop/2.mp4 172
hdfs://master:9000/user/hadoop/3.mp4 748
hdfs://master:9000/user/hadoop/4.mp4 807

According to the above stored data, the size of the video to be transmitted and analyzed can be quickly obtained by the MapReduce processing flow x MB (x needs to be larger than the blocksize value), and the HDFS block size value defaults to: blocksize, and the number of slave nodes of the Hadoop system is N. So that the data of a node is about: (x/N) MB, when the size of the above distribution data is obtained, the VideoDistribution task is completed, and the processing flow is as shown in Fig. 3:

It can be seen that this improved algorithm is a relatively highly applicable algorithm. This algorithm makes full use of the distributed method to transmit visual and audio materials and achieves good results. In this scheme, we encapsulate the format conversion, transmission and other functions of MP4Box and FFepeg, and combine the corresponding video parsing methods to pave the way for subsequent video fusion transmission.

This section builds the Hadoop platform to lay the foundation for distributed transport and completes the configuration of the processing environment. There are several video package formats including MP4, AVI, MOV, etc. The MP4 format is more stable in encoding and decoding of compressed video, And the transmission of parallel

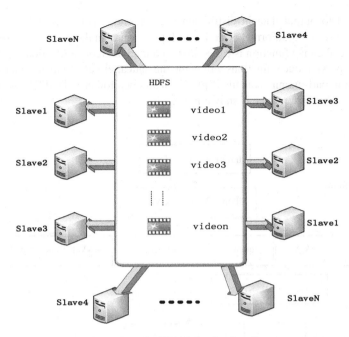

Fig. 3. Video distributed distribution diagram

distributed video for Hadoop platform will also cause difficult processing and transmission efficiency problems due to format, so this experiment unified format for MP4.

2.1.1 MapReduce Programming

The completion of this experiment builds a distributed program [13]. The program we build here is mainly through the improvement and optimization of existing templates. Since MapReduce programs process different tasks by distinct ways, we must design a medium-key pair based on video parallelization distributed processing. Here we mainly design key-value pairs: video segmentation, images, and so on. Hadoop-based on that platforms cannot provide complex data types, the design here is done strictly according to the data flow. The design of this program mainly includes the following three aspects:

(1) The task execution part, the program starts to execute the task, and then the initialization of the task processing configuration is achieved.
(2) Construct a map function to facilitate manipulation of key-value pairs.
(3) Construct the reduce function and complete the statistical data.

2.1.2 Design of Key-Value Pairs in Video Parallelization

In Hadoop we need to define an input class for video data, we can't simply use the default class TextInputFormat of its input. The input format is too simple to analyze and process the data and can not complete the experiment, so the SequenceFileInputFormat is used to input more efficient input classes. Hadoop's basic output class, TextOutputFormat, is mainly used to output data in distributed trans-mission. This class inherits the OutputFormat class. OutputFormat is similar to InputFormat. In the distributed operation of MapReduce, the map function is called first. and then the reduce function is called after running map. All reduce functions will name the data after parallel distributed operation and store it in part-nnnnn. This file is placed in an open folder in HDFS. Hadoop's data class relationship inheritance is shown in Fig. 4.

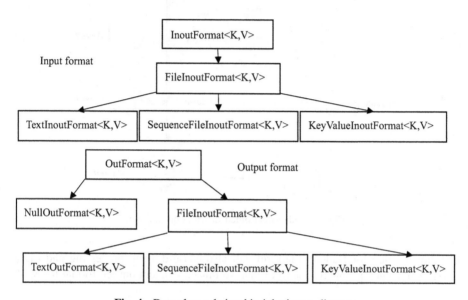

Fig. 4. Data class relationship inheritance diagram

All input classes of the program are derived from FileInputFormat <k, v> in Fig. 4. All output classes are derived from FileOutputFormat <k, v> in Fig. 4. FileInputFormat is a subclass of InputFormat, which includes the MultiPathFilter based on the PathFilter with the prefix '-' or '.' and some of its own PathFilters. The listStatus () function calls MultiPathFilter and will complete the input process in the getSplits() function. The capacity of the previously mentioned fragment is calculated by the getSplits() function. The result of the calculation will first get the minSize and maxSize of the input fragment, and then calculate the size by minSize and maxSize. Here we first debug the "mapred.min.split.size" and "mapred.max.split.size". Here the shards are placed in the splits, and the files are placed in the input data table obtained by listStauts(). The next step is to complete the traversal of the segmentation judgment of all the files, and finally the fragmentation value (splitSize) is calculated. The splitSize is calculated by the following steps:

"Math.max(minSize, Math.min(maxSize, blockSize))" is necessary to ensure that between minSize and maxSize, if "minSize <=blockSize <=maxSize" is satisfied, it is set to blockSize. When all the video's inputSplist is drawn, it is integrated into the splits. The video limit is given here. FileOutputFormat inherits from OutputFormat, where OutputFormat completes RecordWriter. This part mainly completes the serialization operation of video files. RecordWriter mainly processes all key-value pairs one by one, and puts the result into a specific position in OutputFormat after processing. The class processed by row here is a RecordWriter.

The VideoInputFormat class proposed in this paper is derived from the FileInputFormat <Text, VideoObject> class owned by the platform. The VideoInputFormat class is designed to take the form of a complete video clip without cutting and the value can only be smaller than the size of the HDFS block. The VideoRecordReader class is derived from the RecordReader <Text, VideoObject> class. The purpose of this class is to turn a good slice into a convenient key/value pair, where the key is the slice name and the value is the slice content. This is also an instance of VideoObject. Here is the encoding for the VideoInputFormat class:

```
public class VideoInputFormat extends FileInputFormat<Text,
VideoObject> {

public RecordReader<Text, VideoObject> createRecordReader(InputSplit
inputSplit,

    TaskAttemptContext taskAttemptContext) throws IOException {

      VideoRecordReader myVideoRecordReader = new VideoRecordReader();

        return myVideoRecordReader;

    }}
```

The shards are encoded by the VideoRecordReader class to get the data, and then the data stream is converted into the value of the VideoObject we need. The core code of the initialization is as follows:

```
public void initialize (InputSplit split, TaskAttemptContext context)
throws IOException {

    FileSplit myFileSplit = (FileSplit)split;

    Context myContext = context;

    Configuration myConfiguration = myContext.getConfiguration();

    start = 0; end = 5;

filename=split.getPath().getName().substring(0,split.getPath().getN
ame().indexOf('.'));

    myContext .getNumReduceTasks());

    videoReader = new VideoReader(fileIn, myConfiguration);

    videoDivider = new VideoDivider(end, videoReader.readVideoFile());
```

2.2 Virtual and Real Fusion Material Stitching

The experiment was completed simultaneously by four desktops, each of which controlled different video images and each machine was a separate node. It is also the key of this experiment that all the nodes images are fused into one image [14] and the sense of "enhancement" can be generated correctly. These details need to be dealt with in two parts: synchronous output virtual material and synchronization of virtual material [15].

(1) Synchronous output virtual material

First of all, in order to solve the problem of inconsistent output pictures, the problem is transformed into a specific problem that how to control the synchronization buffer exchange of each node frame. If the problem is not solved, the output picture slice caused by the frame buffer exchange being out of synchronization may occur, as shown in Fig. 5.

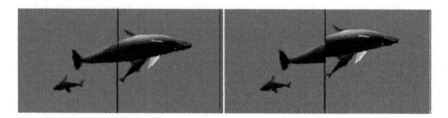

Fig. 5. Inconsistent output caused by unsynchronized buffer exchange

The synchronization control in all nodes of the experiment is as shown in Fig. 6, and all the splicing parts and the service parts are synchronously controlled by the master node. The master node will notify all nodes on standby when all the pictures start to be merged, and block the early completion when all the nodes are fused and ready for next splicing image. Open the channel when all the nodes are ready to splice the image, and then draw according to the divided display position. At this time, the operation completed in advance will also wait for the unfinished, and all the completed operation will reach a final point. All the nodes at this time receive the SwapBuffers command and then complete the video frame synchronization operation. When all the node video frames are completed, the master node will release a new screen operation command, and then repeat the operation until all the frames are completed.

(2) Synchronization of virtual material

The synchronous display of material relies mainly depends on the ability of all service nodes to process scene information synchronously. This paper mainly completes the operation of distributed virtual and real fusion material transfer through LAN. All virtual material will be stored in each node when the initialization command is issued by the master node. For all video frames that have not been manipulated, it is necessary to monitor whether the material changes in real time, so as to maintain the synergy of all images to display the virtual scene. In order to satisfy the simultaneous processing of all node data, the data update judgment of the processing node is continuously performed. If the data is not consistent, the master node performs the blocking command.

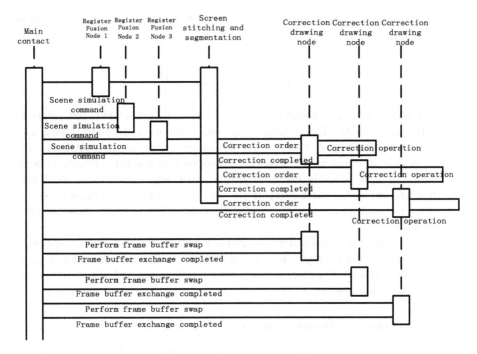

Fig. 6. Synchronization process

3 Depth-Based Hierarchical Clustering Virtual Fusion Method

3.1 Depth Data Hierarchical Clustering Method

The so-called data clustering is the process of dividing an abstract or tangible sample object into a number of sets with the same or similar characteristics according to its intrinsic properties. Cluster analysis is widely used in many fields, such as fuzzy control, market analysis, performance evaluation, etc. The core purpose is to construct the group with the greatest difference, and then configure all individuals to the most appropriate group one by one. The first step for depth data to complete hierarchical clustering is to randomly screen out K materials and set them into meta-cluster centers in turn; and then calculate the distance between the remaining samples and them according to formula (1).

$$D_{HK} = \sqrt{\frac{1}{n_H n_k} \sum_{\substack{i \in H \\ j \in K}} d_{ij}^2}. \qquad (1)$$

d_{ij}^2 :The Euclidean distance squared between any of the X samples of class H and any Xj sample of class K.

If the K class is generated by the combination of class I and class J, the recursion formula (2) is:

$$D_{HK} = \sqrt{\frac{n_I}{n_I + n_J} D_{HI}^2 + \frac{n_J}{n_I + n_J} D_{HJ}^2}.$$ (2)

After finding the cluster center which is the closest to the material sample, you can configure it to the cluster class corresponding to the center of cluster class; if there is an incorrect classification, you must correct the sample, after all the samples of the material have been corrected, the cluster center will be screened again. Finally, in order to ensure that it is correctly classified into the matching cluster class, the Udine objective function is required to check. If the value is called a stable value, or the center has been at lowest value, then the hierarchical clustering of depth data has been completed.

In the case that the virtual and real occlusion is not too complicated, the position of the virtual scene is always higher than the real scene, which means that the real scene can never be blocked. However, in most videos, real scenes and virtual scenes are occluded from each other.

3.2 Virtual and Real Object Occlusion Consistent Rendering

The viewpoint state can be completely represented by a polynomial curve fitting vector, which accurately plots the information about its rotation and displacement changes of the viewpoint. In a three-dimensional virtual scene, the texture rendering plane will have a related reaction due to the change of the viewpoint motion when rendering the texture image. That is to say, there is a certain guiding relationship between viewpoint and plane.

If the depth value of the real object corresponding to the pixel point is greater than the depth value of the virtual object, the pixel needs to be redrawn to achieve occlusion consistency; conversely, no process is performed. The previous occlusion rendering methods can be divided into three types: culling the pixels of the occluded area on the virtual object, redrawing the real object pixels on the virtual object, and rendering by special methods. For example, drawing a virtual mask in front of a virtual object renders an occlusion plane through OpenGL, and some scholars convert the depth value z of the real scene into an OpenGL depth buffer z' value, which is between 0–1. The conversion can find the conversion relationship between z and z' by performing polynomial curve fitting on the z and z' of the center of the identification card several times. It is also possible to obtain the depth value of the near-far clipping surface according to the formula as shown in formula (3).

$$z' = ((1/z\_near - 1/z))/((1/z\_near - 1/z\_far)).$$ (3)

In the algorithm, the real object pixel that has an occlusion relationship with the virtual object is redrawn, and the RGB information of the real object which is the pixel in the color image when the virtual object is not registered is copied to the image which is registered. In this way, the effect that the real object occludes the virtual object can be achieved, and then a virtual-real fusion image with occlusion consistency is obtained.

4 Experimental Results and Mathematical Analysis

The experiment of this chapter is divided into two parts: The first part is the performance comparison of three distributed transmission methods, which is used to judge whether the proposed method is more suitable for the transmission of virtual and real fusion; the second part combines the optimal transmission method and the deep consistency-based fusion method to realize the virtual-real fusion effect based on parallel distributed transmission.

In the first part of the experiment, we used Canon Red to produce of four-segment video with 2.13 GB. The experiment compares the three methods according to the parameters of the four-segment video. The video data is summarized as Table 1:

Table 1. Video data overview table

Experimental data name	Material size (MB)	Processing time (s)
a.mp4	456	22:57
b.mp4	184	09:28
c.mp4	784	38:22
d.mp4	842	40:48

The experiment compares the three transmission methods by the time cost that the following tasks needed: Frame extraction, Hdfsupload, Hdfs download, Video split. Here we apply the time instructions in the Linux system to get the time required to complete various tasks in the experiment.

The test steps are as follows:

(1) In the frame transmission process, we directly use the instruction "ffmpeg" to extract frame on each node of the four- segments of video. The four files are directly extract frames on a single node by using the instruction "time ffmpeg -i 1. Mp4 image%d.jpg". All videos have 164,856 frames, and once a file is saved on HDFS, the extra 64B space is unnecessarily occupied. Therefore, when all the frames are stored, there will be about 10M in fsimage. The second refresh will consume this much occupied space. It can be said that it is the key problem of frame distributed transmission. So this method can only handle a small amount of video.

(2) Hadoop is video segments by physical segmentation, txt. Files and distributed data processing are both suitable for this type of method, but the files of MP4 format are quite unsuitable, which is closely related to its storage method, many information of this file is not evenly distributed. Video frame will be destroyed if it is segmented by the physical segmentation. Only those previously mentioned software, such as Ffmpeg, MP4Box, which can logically segment the MP4 format

data, can meet the processing requirements of this experiment. This experiment not only tests the distributed operation time of single-point transmission, but also compares the determination of slice size. Experiments are carried out on 1 GB, 2 GB, and 3 GB videos. These sets of experimental data are all tested according to the same processing. The analysis progress time is shown in Fig. 7:

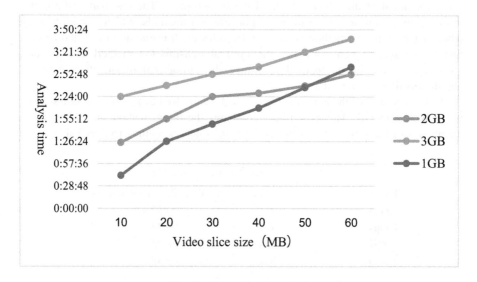

Fig. 7. Video slice test chart

According to the experiment, it can be seen that when the slice is in the 10 MB size, the processing effect is the best, so the slice is set to 10 MB in the whole system.

(3) In the distributed transmission strategy, the data is uniformly distributed to each data node on the cluster and cut at the same time, and then uploaded to the HDFS. The time of each phase is shown in Table 2:

Table 2. Distributed transmission policy processing

Experimental group naming	Video name	Allocation time	Fragmentation duration	Transmission time	Storage point
Frame extraction	a.mp4 and b.mp4	52.137 s	24.762 s	1 m 12.011 s	Slave a
Single node cutting	c.mp4	1 m 8.132 s	23.894 s	1 m 26.293 s	Slave b
Distributed cutting	d.mp4	1 m 34.324 s	22.784 s	1 m 28.869 s	Slave c

The comparison of the test results of the three video distributed processing strategies is shown in Fig. 8:

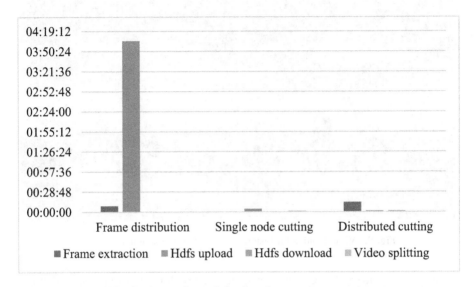

Fig. 8. Comparison of distributed processing strategies

Obviously, this test can reflect the excellent completion of HDFS-based video transmission in the Hadoop platform of this article. However, the three types of distributed solutions have obvious differences. The distributed transmission method of the whole experimental application has very high efficiency compared with the former two methods. Therefore, the experiment in this paper applies a distributed video transmission strategy. The method can solve the problem that is affected by the size and quantity of the material, and it is also the reason for its outstanding effect. According to the fusion part of the experiment, it can be clearly seen that the distribution mechanism of the Hadoop platform solves the efficiency problem. In addition, the stability of the Hadoop platform in this experiment is also reflected by its long-term work.

Combining the method of virtual and real fusion consistency, the virtual and real fusion processing is completed through the distributed transmission strategy, and Fig. 9 is obtained.

As is shown in the experimental diagram, the four pictures from left to right are represented by video screenshots respectively: the first picture shows that the panda and the person have not merged with each other; the second picture shows that the panda and the person are fused with each other and the they are in the same plane without occlusion relationship; the third picture shows that when the panda moves to the person, the person blocks the panda; the fourth picture shows that the panda is in front of the person, and the panda blocks the person. It can be seen that the virtual and real fusion experiment based on distributed transmission is ideal. The virtual object panda can achieve correct occlusion relationship with people during the movement process. The transmission process is also smooth, and the virtual and real fusion occlusion edges are smooth,

Fig. 9. Virtual and solid fusion effect diagram in different frames

which is conform to human perception, and there is no deformation of people and virtual objects, changes in pixel definition, etc., affected by the transmission mechanism.

5   Conclusion

In order to meet the demands of multi-collaboration digital film and television to complete the film and television, the parallel distributed transmission method is combined with the virtual and real fusion. As is shown in experiments, we combine the virtual and real materials by the parallel distributed method and achieve the distributed transmission of the merged video, which make the efficiency greatly improve either in fusion or in transmission.

Specifically, first, this paper analyzes Hadoop's main systems and models that include HDFS processing system and MapReduce computing framework, and fully analyses the distributed processing mode on HDFS file system and MapReduce's distributed computing process and principle. Then, the distributed transmission method proposed in this paper is analyzed. At the same time, the practicability of parallel distributed transmission is obtained by comparing the other two existing methods. Combining with virtual-real fusion technology, the efficiency of the two-way task mentioned above is improved, and the fusion effect of virtual-real fusion is not affected.

Acknowledgments. This work is supported by the Youth Science Funds of National Natural Science Foundation of China (61602058); Key Science and Technology Program of Jilin Province, China (20170203003GX,20170203004GX, 20180201069GX); Technology development plan of Jilin Province, China (20190103031JH, 20190201255JC). Thanks to the reviewers for their comments and suggestions.

References

1. De Gaspari, T., Sementille, A.C., Vielmas, D.Z.: A virtual studio system with augmented reality features. In: Proceedings of the 13th ACM SIGGRAPH International Conference on Virtual-Reality Continuum and Its Applications in Industry, pp. 17–25. ACM, Shenzhen (2014)
2. Whitaker, R.T., Chris, C., Breen, D.E.: Object calibration for augmented reality. J. Comput. Graph. Forum **14**(3), 15–27 (2010)
3. Du, C., Chen, Y.L., Ye, M.: Edge snapping-based depth enhancement for dynamic occlusion handling in augmented reality. In: 2016 IEEE International Symposium on Mixed and Augmented Reality (ISMAR), Merida, Mexico, pp. 54–62. IEEE(2016)
4. Tian, Y., Long, Y., Xia, D.: Handling occlusions in augmented reality based on 3D reconstruction method. J. Neurocomput. **156**, 96–104 (2015)
5. Zhang, C., Xu, R.C., Han, C.: An occlusion consistency processing method based on virtual-real fusion. In: Proceedings of the 11th International Symposium on Photonics and Optoelectronics. CRC Press (2018)
6. Qinying, L., Xiaolin, G., Deqin, S.: Research on secure storage strategy for cloud storage. J. Comput. Res. Dev. **48**, 240–243 (2011)
7. Burrows, M.: The Chubby lock service for loosely coupled distributed systems. In: 7th Symposium on Operating Systems Design and Implementation, pp. 335–350. USENIX, Washington (2006)
8. Yingzhuang, L., Wei, L., Xianyi, L.: Design of massive video conversion platform based on cloud computing. J. Exp. Technol. Manag. **29**, 98–100 (2012)
9. Xing, C., Junfeng, L.: Working together to enhance the reality to create the future. J. Electron. World **02**, 5 (2019)
10. Weiwei, Z.: Research and improvement of load balancing optimization under Hadoop platform. Hebei University of Economics and Business, Shijiazhuang (2017)
11. Fengrong, Z.: Research on Hadoop scheduling algorithm based on ant colony algorithm. J. Comput. Inf. Technol. **24**, 24–26 (2016)
12. Yanlong, Y., Zhuang, L., Kai, Y.: Research on high performance massive data processing platform based on Hadoop. J. Comput. Sci. **40**, 100–103 (2013)
13. Thusoo, A., Sarma, J.S., Jain, N.: Hive - a petabyte scale data warehouse using Hadoop. In: 26th IEEE International Conference on Data Engineering. IEEE Press, Long Beach (2010)
14. Zhao, Y., Zhou, Y., Xu, D.: A novel multi-focus image capture and fusion system for macro photography. In: Tan, T., Ruan, Q., Wang, S., Ma, H., Huang, K. (eds.) IGTA 2014. CCIS, vol. 437, pp. 19–28. Springer, Heidelberg (2014). https://doi.org/10.1007/978-3-662-45498-5_3
15. Wu, Y., Liu, C., Lan, S.: Real-time 3D road scene based on virtual-real fusion method. J. Sens. J. IEEE **15**, 750–756 (2015)

Exploring a Facial Defect Skin Detection Algorithm with Probability Distribution Model

Xingyuan Ren[1(✉)], Xiangyuan Qi[2], and Zhen Wang[2]

[1] National Marine Data and Information Service, Tianjin 300171, China
renxingyuan@163.com
[2] Institute of Science and Technology,
Tianjin University of Finance and Economics, Tianjin 300222, China
qxy@stu.tjufe.edu.cn, wangzhen@tjufe.edu.cn

Abstract. The defects detection of facial skin plays a key role for the evaluation of skin health and cosmetic effect. Two typical defects, color spots and wrinkle, are detected by using their probability distribution from facial digital picture. The color spots have dominant characteristics relative to the normal skin in the corresponding color space. A new Cr-Angle A-H color space is constructed, and histogram segmentation of spots region in this space is applied by using its Poisson distribution characteristics in the facial region. Wrinkles have unique orientation and texture morphological features in facial region. The maximum filter response image and texture direction field are calculated by using Gabor filters, then Gaussian Mixture Model is used to calculate the probability value of each data vector to segment wrinkle area according to the different probability distribution. The experimental results verify the validity and accuracy of the proposed algorithm for skin defect detection.

Keywords: Skin defect detection · Color space · Poisson distribution · Gabor filter · Texture direction field

1 Introduction

Nowadays people pay more and more attention to own facial skin healthy, and use cosmetics to make themselves look more attractive. How to evalue the efficacy of these products requires an objective quantitative evaluation of the skin. With the development of image processing technology in recent years, the accuracy of defect detection of facial skin image has a significant improvement, and there is no need to use magnifying glasses, dermatoscope, spectrometers or macroscopic photography, which are obviously of high cost and location limitations. The most common defects of facial skin are color spots, another crucial indicator for facial skin healthy is wrinkle. Since these features are different from normal skin in facial picture, it is possible to detect these defects of facial skin in the evaluation of skin health and the efficacy of cosmetic.

This work presented in the paper is partially supported by the Natural Science Foundation of Tianjin (Grant No. 16JCYBJC42000).

Y. Wang et al. (Eds.): IGTA 2019, CCIS 1043, pp. 270–283, 2019.
https://doi.org/10.1007/978-981-13-9917-6_26

Cuxia et al. [1] proposed a color spots detection algorithm, which used wavelet homomorphism filtering correction method and morphological image processing algorithm. Matsui et al. [2, 3] designed a facial beautification system, which used ε-filter bank [4] to remove the bad facial components, such as color spots and wrinkles, but there was no independent detection and extraction of color spots and wrinkles. Ng [5] and Batool et al. [6] carried out wrinkle detection but didn't take into account the effect of color spots. Mukaida et al. [7, 8] extracted and analyzed color spots and wrinkles according to their respective characteristics, such as size, shape and pixel distribution, but their color and texture attributes are not used.

In this paper, a facial skin defect detection algorithm is proposed by using their probability distribution from facial digital picture. We noticed that Cr in YCrCb color space and Angle A calculated in RGB color space have good visual feedback for color spots, and H in HSV color space is independent of illumination intensity, so the three color channels are combined and transformed into a new distance space. When the histogram of the distance space is segmented, the threshold can be calculated appropriately based on the Poisson distribution of the color spots region, finally the color spots region can be detected and extracted accurately. Wrinkles have unique orientation and texture morphological features in facial region. The Gabor filters in different directions are designed to extract features, the maximum filter response image and texture direction field are obtained from those Gabor filters. Gaussian Mixture Model is used to calculate the probability value of each data vector, then wrinkle area could be segmented on the maximum filtered response image according to a different probability distribution.

2 Color Spots Detection

In order to extract color spots accurately from ROI face region, the skin region of the human face is divided. Because the face is an uneven surface, the skin color of the same face varies from place to place. Thus the ROI image is divided into non-overlapping sub-images with width and height setting as 100 pixels.

2.1 Color Space Selection

The selection of color space plays a key role in pattern recognition. Angelopoulou [9] indicates that the skin color of different ethnic groups is the same in tone, and the saturation information of skin also has stability. In the YCrCb color space, Cr and Cb represent tone and saturation respectively, which can be effectively used to detect skin. Through the cluster analysis of pixels, the range of pixel values of color spots and normal skin is different both in Cr channel of YCbCr and in Angle A channel of RGB color space. There are two peaks on the two channels histogram statistics, the larger one represents the number of normal skin pixel value, and the smaller one represents the number of defect skin pixel value. We believe that Cr channel and Angle A channel have good visual feedback on color spots [10, 11]. In addition, in order to eliminate the influence of different illumination brightness during defect detection, we select the H channel in HSV color space [12]. As a result, the Cr-AngleA-H color space is constructed to detect skin defects. Angle A transform function is defined as formula (1)

$$\text{AngleA} = \cos^{-1}\left(B/\sqrt{R^2 + G^2 + B^2}\right), \tag{1}$$

where R, G and B are red, green and blue channel. The range of channel value is set as Cr for [0, 255], Angle A for [0, 90], and H for [0, 360].

Skin color distribution center (C_x, C_y, C_z) is composed of the three values of transverse coordinates corresponding to the maximum wave peaks in the Cr, Angle A, H histograms, which is defined as

$$(C_x, C_y, C_z) = \left(\arg \max_k H_k(V_{Cr}), \arg \max_k H_k(V_{AngleA}), \arg \max_k H_k(V_H)\right). \tag{2}$$

The V is the pixel observation value of each channel, H_k is the pixel statistics of each color channel in the histogram and k is the histogram transverse coordinate value. To synthetically calculate the three channels, the distance transformation between the pixel observations and the skin color distribution center is defined as

$$D(x, y) = \sqrt{[V_{Cr}(x, y) - C_x]^2 + [V_{AngleA}(x, y) - C_y]^2 + [V_H(x, y) - C_z]^2}. \tag{3}$$

2.2   Threshold Determination

After calculating the distance transform value, we need to determine a threshold value to distinguish the defective skin from the normal skin. By observing the histogram of distance transform value, we noticed that the pixel value in the sub-image approximately obeys Poisson distribution in statistics. As a discrete probability distribution, Poisson distribution is suitable to describe the number of random factors occurring in unit space. In the sub-image, the skin pixel of defect can be regarded as a discrete random factor, and through histogram statistics, Poisson distribution curve can be used to fit the distance value.

The distance value D(x, y) is divided into L levels $[1, 2, \cdots, L]$, where the statistical value of the distance is used n_k, the total of the distance values is indicated by $N = n_1 + n_2 + \cdots + n_L$. Probability distribution of distance value D (x, y) is defined as $p_k = \frac{n_k}{N}, \forall p_k \geq 0$, and Poisson curve fitting function of the distribution is defined as

$$f_k(\lambda) = \frac{\lambda^{|k-m|+\lambda}}{(|k-m|+\lambda)!} e^{-\lambda}, m = \arg \max_k(p_k), \tag{4}$$

In order to make $f_k(\lambda)$ and p_k in the same size, it convert formula (4) to formula (5):

$$f_k'(\lambda) = f_k(\lambda) \times \frac{\max(p_k)}{\max(f_k(\lambda))}, \tag{5}$$

where $\lambda = 0, 1, \cdots, L$, optimal curve p_k^* is a value which guarantee the least difference between p_k and $f_k'(\lambda)$. The λ^* is defined as $\lambda^* = \arg\min_\lambda \left(\sum_{k=0}^{L} |f_k'(\lambda) - p_k| \right)$, so

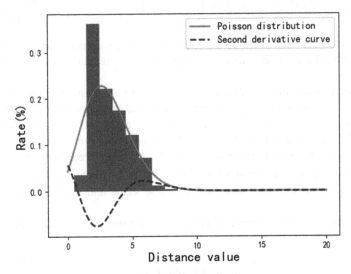

Fig. 1. Histogram of distance transform value. The solid line is the optimal Poisson distribution curve, and the dashed line is the second derivative curve.

$p_k^* = f_k'(\lambda^*)$. The threshold t is set to the dependent variable value of the inflection point of p_k^*, $t = \arg\max_k (\nabla(p_k^*))$, where ∇ represents the second derivative. Therefore, if $D(x, y) > t$, the corresponding pixel belongs to a skin defect, otherwise, it belongs to normal skin. The optimal curve and its second derivative curve are shown in Fig. 1, where the solid line represents the optimal Poisson distribution curve and the dashed line represents its second derivative curve.

3   Wrinkle Detection Method

After the face image is preprocessed and divided into sub-images, in this section, we introduce wrinkle detection method into 2 subsections: Gabor feature extraction and wrinkle area segmentation.

3.1   Gabor Feature Extraction

Gabor filter is a linear filter, which can extract spatial local frequency features as an effective texture detection tool. Due to wrinkles have unique orientation and texture morphological features in the facial region, it is appropriate to use Gabor filter to screen out wrinkles on sub-images as first step. In two-dimensional space, a Gabor filter is obtained by superposition of a Gaussian function and a trigonometric function. The two-dimensional Gabor kernel function is defined as

$$g(x, y) = \exp\left(\frac{x'^2 + \gamma^2 y'^2}{-2\sigma^2}\right) \cos\left(\frac{2\pi x'}{\lambda} + \psi\right), \begin{bmatrix} x' \\ y' \end{bmatrix} = \begin{bmatrix} \cos\theta \; \sin\theta \\ -\sin\theta \; \cos\theta \end{bmatrix} \begin{bmatrix} x \\ y \end{bmatrix}, \quad (6)$$

where (x, y) is the coordinate of the filter core, other parameters are defined as: the wavelength λ, the direction angle θ, the phase ψ, the standard deviation σ, and the aspect ratio γ.

In order to make full use of the characteristics of Gabor filter and take into account the feature of wrinkle direction, different directions of Gabor filters are designed to extract features [6]. $\{g_k(x, y), k = 0, 1, \cdots, K - 1\}$ represents the set of Gabor filters with angles $\alpha_k = -\pi/2 + \pi k/K$, where K is the total number of filters, and the directional angle range of the filter set is $[-\pi/2, \pi/2]$. $I(x, y)$ represents the input image of gray value, and $I_k^f(x, y)$ denotes the images filtered by the filter set $g_k(x, y)$ with two Gabor features, (a) the maximum filter response value and (b) the texture direction value.

The maximum filter response value is the maximum value at the pixel position in the filter set, and calculated as

$$I'(x, y) = \max_k I_k^f(x, y), \quad (7)$$

where $I'(x, y)$ is the maximum filter response image, which will be used to detect wrinkle region.

The texture direction value is the k value of the direction angle corresponding to the maximum filter response value, which is calculated as follow:

$$\theta_I(x, y) = \arg\max_k I_k^f(x, y). \quad (8)$$

The rendering method of the binary image of texture orientation field is composed two steps: first, we select a pixel with horizontal texture direction; second, we connect the pixel with two adjacent pixels with horizontal lines, so the length of each horizontal line is 3 pixels. The set of maximum filter response and the texture direction filed at each pixel, $\{I'(x, y)\theta_I(x, y)\}$, constitutes Gabor features for wrinkle regions detection.

In high resolution face images, normal skin has irregular granular texture and its orientation angle is random, while wrinkles have regular line skin texture, and its direction angle has certain regularity. This is represented by the majority of pixels appearing in groups with horizontal orientations. As a result, a set of horizontal lines could be used to describe the wrinkle area of the face because of two significant properties, (a) a dominant angle of zero degrees and (b) pixel with zero orientation angle appear in cluster.

3.2   Wrinkle Area Segmentation

We combine Gaussian Mixture Model (GMM) algorithm with Markov Random Field (MRF) to segment the wrinkle area from ROI image. GMM can be used to calculate the probability value of each sample data vector according to its distribution probability for any given data sample set, and then classify data according to the calculated results. Gaussian Mixture Model is defined as

$$p(x) = \sum_{k=1}^{K} \pi_k N(x|\mu_k, \sigma_k), \sum_{k=1}^{K} \pi_k = 1, 0 \leq \pi_k \leq 1, \tag{9}$$

where μ_k and σ_k represent mean and variance respectively, π_k is the weight of each component. Under GMM, the density function of the pixel (x, y) observation is as

$$f(I'(x,y)|\Pi, \Theta) = \sum_{k=1}^{K} \pi_k(x,y)N(I'(x,y)|\mu_k, \sigma_k), \tag{10}$$

where $N(I'(x,y)|\mu_k, \sigma_k)$ represents the standard normal distribution, $\Theta = \{(\mu_k, \sigma_k); k = 1, \cdots, K\}$ is the parameter set of GMM distribution, $\Pi = \{\pi_k(x,y); x = 1, \cdots, N_1; y = 1, \cdots, N_2; k = 1, \cdots, K\}$ is the mixed proportional set of GMM distribution.

Assuming that the statistics of a single pixel are independent of each other, the joint conditional density function of the whole image can be written as

$$p(L'|\Pi, \Theta) = \prod_{x=1}^{N_1} \prod_{y=1}^{N_2} \sum_{k=1}^{K} \pi_k(x,y)N(I'(x,y)|\mu_k, \sigma_k), \tag{11}$$

Let L' denote the ensemble of random variables $I'(x,y)$ as follows:

$$L' = \{I'(x,y); x = 1, \cdots, N_1; y = 1, \cdots, N_2\}, \tag{12}$$

As we know, MRF could take account of spatial correlation among adjacent pixels, and impose spatial smoothness constraint. Therefore, for MRF model, the prior distribution of the mixed proportion of pixels (x, y) depends on its adjacent pixels. According to Bayesian theorem, the posterior probability can be written as

$$p(\Pi, \Theta|L', \Omega) \propto p(L'|\Pi, \Theta, \Omega) \times p(\Pi|\Omega), \tag{10}$$

Let $\Omega = \{\theta_I(x,y); x = 1, \cdots N_1; y = 1, \cdots N_2\}$ denote the set of orientation angles of all pixels. As a result, we use both of two Gabor features, the maximum filter response and the texture direction filed, as prior distribution to segment the wrinkle area.

The prior joint distribution of all pixels is defined by the Gibbs distribution as follow

$$p(\Pi) = \frac{1}{Z} \exp\left(-\frac{U(\Pi)}{T}\right), \tag{14}$$

where Z is the normalized constant, $U(\Pi)$ is the Gibbs energy function, and T is a constant of temperature.

The Expectation Maximization (EM) algorithm is selected to estimate the parameters of GMM. On the basis of the maximum likelihood, the EM algorithm finds the optimal parameter set through multiple iterations as follows:

(1) Assigning the initial values to the parameters. The k-means clustering algorithm is used to cluster the samples, the initial mean value and variance are set to μ_k and σ_k. π_k is set to the proportion of all types of samples to the total number of samples.

(2) Estimation step (E-step). Take the optimal lower bound of likelihood function, the probability density value of each sample point under each component of GMM model is calculated, and the posterior probability of π_k is obtained.

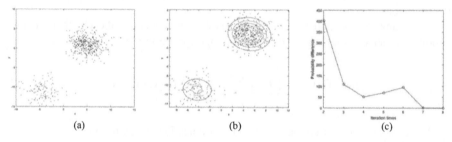

(a)   (b)   (c)

Fig. 2. Classification results. (a) Experimental sample sets generated by two sets of single Gaussian distributions. (b) The classification result after iterations of the GMM-MRF algorithm, the curve represents the probability distribution function. (c) Iterative curve of the EM algorithm.

(3) Maximization step (M-step). Update each parameter value according to the posterior probability estimated in the previous step.

(4) Iteration. Iterate over the E and M steps and update the three parameter values repeatedly until they converge. The convergence condition is the slight change of parameters.

Figure 2 shows the classification result after many iterations of the GMM-MRF algorithm for an experimental sample set, where the curve in Fig. 2(b) represents the probability distribution function.

In the M-step of the EM algorithm, we cannot directly apply the prior distribution to estimate the model parameters form the observations. Various approximations have been introduced to tackle this problem. Recently, Nguyen [13] introduced a novel way of incorporating spatial correlations in MRF model which allows a close form solution at the M-step. A factor $G_{x,y}^j$ was introduced, which is proportional to the produce of both posterior probabilities and prior distribution of the neighboring pixels. Then, they also proposed a Gibbs energy function update an EM iteration t based on $G_{x,y}^j$. Batool [6] improved Nguyen's GMM-MRF model by incorporating texture direction filed to the factor $G_{x,y}^j(\Omega)$, which is given as follows:

$$G_{x,y}^j(\Omega) = \exp\left\{ \sum_{i \in \{\eta_{x,y}\}} h(j, \theta_i)(z_i^j + \pi_i^j) \right\}, \tag{15}$$

where $\eta_{x,y}$ is the neighborhood of the pixel (x, y) and z_i^j is the posterior probability. The factor $h(j, \theta_i)$ controls the mixing proportions of a pixel based on the orientation field angles in its neighborhood only with the binary case of background and wrinkled skin.

We believe that the more prior information is used, the more accuracy iteration result could be obtained. The detected defect area such as color spots is incorporated in EM iteration. Therefore, the factor $h(j, \theta_i)$ is redefined for triple case as follow:

$$h(j, \theta_i) = \left\{ \begin{array}{c} 1 \ for j = 0 \\ \beta \ \cos(\theta_i) for j = 1 \\ 0 \ for j = 2 \end{array} \right\}, \tag{16}$$

where $j = 0$ denotes the distribution representing background skin, $j = 1$ denotes the distribution of wrinkled skin, and $j = 2$ denotes the distribution of detected defect area. This increase the mixing proportion π_i^j and probability of pixel being include in the wrinkled area than binary case. The parameter β has a value greater than 1, which guarantees the value of the factor $h(j, \theta_i)$ increase even that a pixel and its surrounding neighbors have orientation angles closer to zero.

The EM algorithm is used to find mixing proportions and to maximize the posterior distribution. During direction clustering, image segmentation composes image clustering and label classification, and the pixels with the same properties are classified into one class. The result of the EM is a labeled image where every pixel is assigned the label j with the larger posterior probability value $z_{x,y}^j$.

3.3   Algorithm Flow

The wrinkle detection algorithm of this paper is as follows:

Input: facial skin image with wrinkle I ,
Output: image segmented out of wrinkle region I_w .

1: Gobor filter $I_k^f(x,y) = I * g_k(x,y)$.

2: The maximum filter response image $I'(x,y) = \max_k I_k^f(x,y)$.

3: The texture direction field $\theta_I(x,y) = \arg\max_k I_k^f(x,y)$.

4: Segmenting the image $I'(x,y)$ using GMM-MRF Model, and the result is the binary image I_B.

5: merging the binary image I_B and the texture direction field $\theta_I(x,y)$, and the result is the binary image $B = I_B * \theta_I(x,y)$.

6: The wrinkle image is $I_w = I * B$.

---

4   Experiments and Results Analysis

The algorithm is implemented with Python programming language and computer vision library Opencv. Among them, Opencv is used to implement the transformation of special color space, Gabor filter, and python realizes the fitting of Poisson distribution curve and the selection of threshold value and GMM-MRF image segmentation algorithm. The experiment uses Bosphorus Database [14], which contains images of different skin qualities. We start this section from preprocessing of ROI extraction from original facial image, then show the results of color spots and wrikle detection respectively.

4.1   Face Region Extraction

Before facial defect detection, it is necessary to extract the region of interest (ROI) face area for the subsequent processing. The process steps are face region detection, face contour detection, internal face area detection and the ROI extraction. Figure 3 shows the image processing result at each step, which includes face region detection, face contour detection and face ROI extraction.

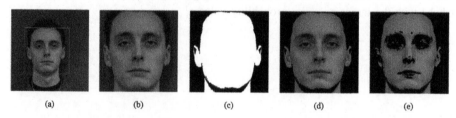

(a)   (b)   (c)   (d)   (e)

Fig. 3. Preprocessing of ROI extraction. (a) Original image, (b) Face region, (c) Face contour, (d) Internal face area, (e) Region of interest (ROI).

Face region detection algorithm uses Haar+Adaboost face detection principle [15, 16]. This method is based on the integral graph, Adaboost algorithm and cascade detector as follows:

(1) Extracting face features. The Haar-like feature is used to represent the face and the integral graph is used to realize the fast calculation of the feature value.
(2) Training classifiers. The Adaboost algorithm is used to select some rectangular face features as the weak classifiers, then the weak classifiers are constructed into a strong classifier by using the weighted voting method.
(3) Constructing cascade classifier. Several trained classifiers compose a cascade classifier in series connection, which can effectively improve the detection speed of the classifier.

Before extracting the region of interest, we need to determine the contour of the face and find the skin region according to the contour of the face. First, the connected region of face region is extracted, in which the largest connected region is the face contour. Then the binary face contour image and the face region image are multiplied to obtain the face skin region.

The Haar+Adaboost algorithm is further applied to extract the facial feature points, that is, the non-skin region of the face, including the eyes, eyebrows, mouth and nostrils. The corresponding sub-regions are segmented from the whole human face, and then face features are extracted from these sub-regions. The eyes, eyebrows, mouth and nostrils were extracted by using the Sobel edge, the HSV color space, the YCbCr color space, and Gauss difference respectively. The ROI is obtained by removing these facial features from the face, that is, the skin color region to be detected.

4.2 Color Spots Detection Results

In order to verify proposed algorithm with a stable distinction between normal skin and color spots, the process includes the following steps: excluding the pixels of normal skin, extracting the pixels of defective skin, and then detecting the spots defects of sub-images in turn. The pixel values of the defective skin region were detected in the sub-images with color spots, so this algorithm has a stable distinction between the normal skin and the defective skin. In order to verify the robustness of the proposed algorithm under different illumination conditions, the contrast experiments under different luminance conditions were designed. In the experiment, four luminance levels were added to the original image, and the proposed algorithm was applied to detect the image. According to the results of the experiment, under different illumination conditions, the proposed algorithm can effectively detect color spots regions. This is thanked to the color space used in this paper, which adds the H channel and excludes the influence of Illumination on color spots detection, so the algorithm is robust under different illumination conditions. The experimental results are shown in Fig. 4.

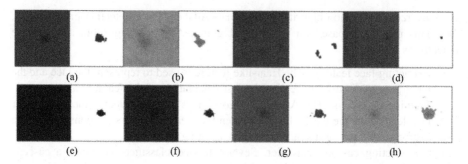

Fig. 4. Color spots detection results. (a) – (d) are four different skin images with color spots and the detection results under our proposed algorithm. (e) – (h) are four luminance levels and the detection results under our proposed algorithm. (Color figure online)

For the sake of verifying the dominant characteristics of color spots relative to normal skin in Cr-AngleA-H color space, a comparative experiment was designed in different color spaces. RGB, HSV, YCrCb and CrCb are common skin detection color spaces [17, 18]. Therefore, the four kinds of color space were selected and compared with the color space used in this algorithm. In the experiment, the original images were transformed into different color spaces. The experimental results in Figs. 4(a)–(b) and 5 (a)–(d) show that the color space used in this algorithm can effectively detect color spots regions.

In the experiment, the algorithm in this paper was compared with several common image segmentation algorithms which are dynamic threshold algorithm, Sobel, Canny and Otsu algorithm. The dynamic threshold algorithm calculates the mean of pixel value of sub-image, and take the mean value as the center to determine a fluctuation range. If the observed pixel value is outside of the range, it is considered to be a color spots region. Compared with other common image segmentation algorithms, the detection results of this algorithm keep the actual size and shape of the skin defect region, and have fewer false detection areas. The experimental results are shown in Fig. 5(e)–(h).

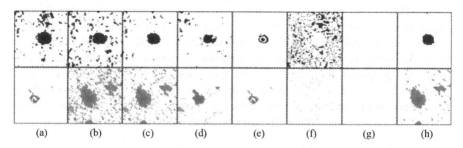

Fig. 5. The comparison experiment results of color spots detection, and the original images is from Fig. 4(a) and (b). (a) RGB color space, (b) HSV color space, (c) YCrCb color space, (d) CrCb color space, (e) The dynamic threshold algorithm, (f) Sobel image segmentation algorithm, (g) Canny image segmentation algorithm, (h) Otsu segmentation algorithm. (Color figure online)

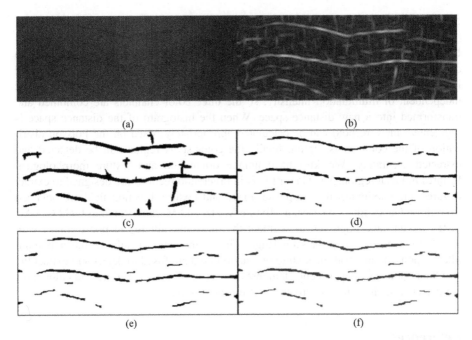

Fig. 6. The wrinkle detection experiment results. (a) The original image, (b) The maximum filtered response image, (c) The image segmentation result, (d) The texture direction field with horizontal angle, (e) The binary wrinkled image, (f) The wrinkle region extracted from the original image.

4.3 Wrinkle Detection Results

Experiments were conducted on sample image from Bosphorus Database as shown in Fig. 6(a), a wrinkled sub-image is derived from the pre-processed face image. The original image was filtered by Gabor in different directions, and the color spots defect was also detected and saved for later usage. According to the filtered image group, the maximum filtered response image is obtained as shown in Fig. 6(b). Then the EM algorithm was implemented to segment maximum filtered response image by using improved GMM-MRF model algorithm. The number of iterations was selected to be in the range 5–10 where a smaller number was sufficient enough for smaller cropped facial region. The image segmentation result is shown in Fig. 6(c). Based on the segmented result, the texture direction field with angle closed to zero can be obtained, as shown in Fig. 6(d). The segmented binary image was fused with the texture direction field image and the binary wrinkled image was obtained as shown in Fig. 6(e). Finally, the wrinkled region was extracted by multiplying the original image, and the experimental result is shown in Fig. 6(f).

5 Conclusion

In this paper, a facial skin defect detection algorithm for face image was proposed to detect color spots and wrinkle area. Due to Cr in YCrCb space and Angle A calculated in RGB space have good visual feedback for color spots, and H in HSV space is independent of illumination intensity, so the three color channels are combined and transformed into a new distance space. When the histogram of the distance space is segmented, the threshold can be calculated appropriately based on the Poisson distribution of the color spots region, finally the color spots region can be detected and extracted accurately. Wrinkles have unique orientation and texture morphological features in facial region. The Gabor filters in different directions are designed to extract features, the maximum filter response image and texture direction field are obtained from those Gabor filters. Gaussian Mixture Model and Markov Random Field (GMM-MRF) model have improved to segment the maximum filtered response image with detected defect area as prior knowledge. The segmentation results of the maximum filter response image and the texture orientation field are fused to detect and extract the wrinkle region. The experiments demonstrate that most of the wrinkles and color spots are detected to show the effectiveness of our algorithms.

References

1. Chu, X., Wu, X., Huang, Y.: A color spots detection algorithm based on facial skin image. Microcomput. Inf. **25**(21), 249–251 (2009)
2. Matsui, T., Arakawa, K., Nomoto, K.: A nonlinear filter system for beautifying face images with enhancement using interactive evolutionary computing. In: International Symposium on Intelligent Signal Processing and Communications, pp. 534–537. IEEE (2006)
3. Arakawa, K., Nomoto, K.: A nonlinear image processing system for beautifying face image using interactive evolutionary computing and its subjective test. IEEJ Trans. Electron. Inf. Syst. **131**(3), 576–583 (2011)
4. Harashima, H., Odajima, K., Shishikui, Y., Miyakawa, H.: ϵ-separating nonlinear digital filter and its applications. Electron. Commun. Japan **65**(4), 11–19 (1982)
5. Ng, C.C., Yap, M.H., Costen, N., et al.: Wrinkle detection using hessian line tracking. IEEE Access **3**, 1079–1088 (2015)
6. Batool, N., Chellappa, R.: Detection and inpainting of facial wrinkles using texture orientation fields and Markov random field modeling. IEEE Trans. Image Process. **23**(9), 3773–3788 (2014). A Publication of the IEEE Signal Processing Society
7. Mukaida, S., Ando, H.: Extraction and manipulation of wrinkles and spots for facial image synthesis. In: IEEE International Conference on Automatic Face and Gesture Recognition, pp. 749–754. IEEE Computer Society (2004)
8. Mukaida, S., Ando, H.: Age manipulation of facial images focused on spots and wrinkles. J. Inst. Image Inf. Telev. Eng. **59**, 761–768 (2005)
9. Angelopoulou, E.: Understanding the color of human skin. In: Proceedings of SPIE, vol. 4299, pp. 243–251. The International Society for Optical Engineering (2001)
10. Chang, C.Y., Li, S.C., Chung, P.C., et al.: Automatic facial skin defect detection system. In: International Conference on Broadband. IEEE (2010)
11. Chang, C.-Y., Liao, H.-Y.: Automatic facial spots and acnes detection system. J. Cosmet. Dermatol. Sci. Appl. **03**(1), 28–35 (2013)

12. Tao, L., Peng, Z., Xu, G.: Skin color characteristics of human body. J. Softw. **12**(7), 1032–1041 (2001)
13. Thanh, N., Jonathan, W.: Fast and robust spatially constrained Gaussian mixture model for image segmentation. IEEE Trans. Circuits Syst. Video Technol. **23**(4), 621–635 (2013)
14. Savran, A., et al.: Bosphorus database for 3D face analysis. In: Schouten, B., Juul, N.C., Drygajlo, A., Tistarelli, M. (eds.) BioID 2008. LNCS, vol. 5372, pp. 47–56. Springer, Heidelberg (2008). https://doi.org/10.1007/978-3-540-89991-4_6
15. Wang, M., Lin, X.: The ART2 neural network based on the adaboost rough classification. In: Tan, T., Ruan, Q., Chen, X., Ma, H., Wang, L. (eds.) IGTA 2013. CCIS, vol. 363, pp. 44–53. Springer, Heidelberg (2013). https://doi.org/10.1007/978-3-642-37149-3_6
16. Xu, P., Long, Y., Zheng, D., Liu, R.: The face-tracking of Sichuan golden monkeys via S-TLD. In: Tan, T., et al. (eds.) IGTA 2016. CCIS, vol. 634, pp. 85–91. Springer, Singapore (2016). https://doi.org/10.1007/978-981-10-2260-9_11
17. Xu, Z., Zhu, M.: A review of color-based skin detection. Chin. J. Image Graph. **12**(3), 377–388 (2007)
18. Chen, D., Liu, Z.: Overview of skin color detection technology. J. Comput. Sci. **29**(2), 20–194 (2006)

Universal Framework of Seals Erasing with Generative Adversarial Network

ZiQiang Chen(✉), ZhenYu Ding, and ShiQing Wang

School of Software Engineering, University of Science and Technology of China,
Hefei 230026, China
{sa517034,sa517059,sa517363}@mail.ustc.edu.cn

Abstract. In last decades, methods based on deep learning has dominated many application fields, such as image inpainting, image super high-resolution and image denoising. In the Optical Character Recognition (OCR), we need to erase all seals due to some special reason like improving the performance of invoices and receipts recognition. However, owing to the diversity of the shape, color and position of the seals, it is very difficult to erase all seals without affecting the original information of the invoices and receipts. At present, there are two common methods to erase seals, one is from the perspective of computer graphics, the other is from the perspective of computer software, like PhotoShop. Nevertheless, the common weakness is the poor robustness and inefficient. So, In this paper, We propose an end-to-end network for erasing seals, and we have four contributions. (1) We first propose a universal framework to do the seals erasing by using Generative Adversarial Network (GAN). (2) Training the seals erasing network by the images synthesised by scripts and seals crawled on the website, instead of spending high cost to collect images by ourselves. (3) In terms of speed, due to using end-to-end predict script, using our method to erase all seals on the 512 * 512 RGB image with padding is only 800 ms, much faster than the traditional methods. (4) There is also improvement on the invoices and receipts with the same parameter on the Convolution Recurrent Neural Network (CRNN), the average accuracy of the sequences by using our method is 91.3% higher than the original images is 89.7% on the 800 quota invoice test images.

Keywords: Deep learning · Generative adversarial network · Optical Character Recognition · Seals erasing

1 Introduction

Recently, with the development of deep learning, the OCR becomes more and more mature. Shi et al. [1] had proposed Convolution Neural Network (CNN) and Recurrent Neural Network (RNN) to deal with this task at first. The CRNN uses CNN to extract the features of the image, and then, uses the Long Short-Term Memory (LSTM) unit to predict the sequences. The LSTM can deal these

© Springer Nature Singapore Pte Ltd. 2019
Y. Wang et al. (Eds.): IGTA 2019, CCIS 1043, pp. 284–292, 2019.
https://doi.org/10.1007/978-981-13-9917-6_27

Fig. 1. The real images with seals

variational length of the inputs, at different time steps, the LSTM uses the softmax function to get the output sequences. Any other algorithms, such as with detection at first like Connectionist Text Proposal Network (CTPN) [2] or with attention [3] is similar with the CRNN by using the CNN and RNN.

Rapid and accurate text recognition is essential in these days, however, due to the exists of seals, the recognition and detection become more difficult, like the Fig. 1 shows the complicated scenes. In order to improve the performance of recognition and detection, we need to eliminate the effect by the dirty noise, so we need to erase these seals. The traditional method used to erase the seals is using PhotoShop or other simple images by converting the images to the binary images and erasing the seals by set the thresh value. These methods need to spend time to adjust the thresh value or learn how to use these software, the accuracy and the speed is not good. So we propose this universal seals erasing network by using Generative Adversarial Network [4].

As a new framework of generative model, GAN proposed by Ian GoodFellow, is able to do the various tasks, and since then it has become one of the most popular research areas. A Generative Adversarial Net have two neural networks, a generator and a discriminator, where the generator tries to produce realistic samples that cheat the discriminator, while the discriminator tries to distinguish real samples from generated ones. The most original generative model G parameterized by θ takes a random noise z as input and output is a sample $G(z; \theta)$, so the output can be regarded as a sample drawn from a distribution: $G(z; \theta) \sim p_g$. Meanwhile, we have a lot of training images x drawn from p_{data}, and the training objective for the generative model G is to approximate p_{data} using p_g, and the conditional GAN [5] is the extention of the GAN, just the architecture add the additional information to help the GAN to have better performance. Inspired by the GANs, many algorithms come up to transfers a image from domain A to domain B, such as pix2pix conditional GAN [6] or CycleGAN [7]. So our method is inspired by the pix2pix conditional GAN, to do the image to image translation.

2   Proposed Method

2.1   Architecture of the Seals Erase Universal Framework

2.1.1   The Seals Detection Network

In this section, we introduce the pipeline of our algorithm, in order to do the end-to-end seals erase network, so the seals detection network is needed essentially, such as like Single Shot MultiBox Detector (SSD) [8], You Only Look Once [9], Towards Real-Time Object Detection with Region Proposal Networks [10], due to considering the balance of speed and accuracy, we choose SSD as our base detector network. The SSD use the multi-scale feature map for detection, the every feature map can get multi bounding boxes, at last using the Non-Maximum Suppression to remove the repeated bounding boxes, to get the last results. We get a good seals detection network at last, because the seals is not the small object and we can feed the network many synthesised seals images, so it's very easy to train a good seals detection network.

2.1.2   The Seals Erasing Network

The Second step is training a seals erasing network, the main structure of network we used is aforementioned, inspired by the pix2pix conditional GAN and CycleGAN, these papers compare these different methods with transforming one image to another image. The pix2pix conditional GAN use two images, these two images are stored by pair, but the CycleGAN is the unsupervised image-to-image translation, it can transform the image A to image B, these images are unpair. Finally, according to the experiments results, the pix2pix conditional GAN with the Wasserstein GAN's (WGAN) [11] loss can have a better appearance, so we choose this architecture. The generator network of our network is the "U-Net" [12], the "U-Net" architecture are often used to do the semantic segmentation, but it can get the good performance on the image generator also, The U-Net is an encoder-decoder with skip connections between mirrored layers in the encoder and decoder stacks, so every feature map layer in U-Net can stack with the before layer. At first we do the down sample to extract the features, and then we do the up sample to reconstruct the images. Compared with the original GAN using the binary cross-entropy loss, we use the WGAN's loss to get the more better reconstructed images. The original binary cross-entropy loss can meet many problems, such as gradient vanishing, just like when the discriminator can identity the images are true or false easily, the gradient number of the discriminator is zero, so the discriminator can not train well. In order to get a better result, We reference the WGAN's structure, the last layer of discriminator does not use the sigmoid function, meanwhile the losses of generator and discriminator don't use the log function. In order to make the training process more stable

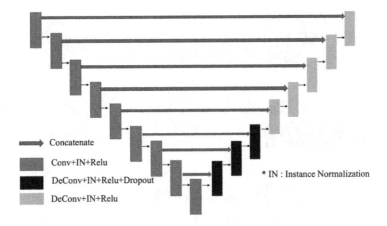

Fig. 2. The generator using 'U-Net' network

and the result is good, the generator uses modules of the form Convolution-Instance Normalization-ReLu, and the discriminator uses modules of the form Convolution-Instance Normalization-Leaky ReLu. The Instance Normalization [13] is just do the normalization on the one image, is improved can produce more high quality images on image transfer. The discriminator uses the "Patch-GAN" which only penalized which only penalizes structure at the scale of image patches. A similar PatchGAN architecture was previously proposed in [14], for the purpose of capturing local style statistics, so we use the PatchGAN to get the more better performance.

2.1.3   The Predict Phase

The predict phase uses the seals detection network and the seals erasing network, we use the detection network to detect all seals, and get all coordinates corresponding with every seals, then we crop all seals by these coordinates and send to the seals erasing network. At last, we paste the result images of seals erasing network on the original images by these coordinates.

2.1.4   The Recognition Network

We use the text recognition network, CRNN, to prove our method can improve the precision rate of the sequences. At first, we do the line detection, and then send the detection area to CRNN network. The CRNN extracts the feature at first, then uses the RNN modules to identity the output, at last, use the Connectionist Temporal Classification (CTC) [15] loss to train the whole network.

2.2   Training Mechanism

According to the above research, we construct these seals erasing framework, the settings of the generator is shown in Fig. 2, the other network parameters is setting in the discriminator is also a neural network, at first we not only use

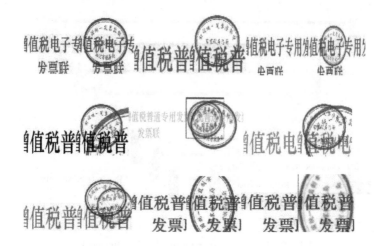

Fig. 3. The sample of seals erasing network training data

the L1 or L2 loss to control the low-frequency is similar, but also we use the "PatchGAN" [6] to distinguish the image is real or fake, The L1 or L2 loss can control the images is similar, but the image will blur, the discriminator loss can control the image more clear, so, we decide to use this two losses. This discriminator tries to classify if each $N \times N$ patch in an image is real or fake. We run this discriminator across the image, averaging all responses to provide the ultimate output of D, and we set the N is 70.

3   Material and Experiments

3.1   Material Preparation

We all know the deep learning neural network need a large amount data, so we need to feed lots of data to network, but the cost of collecting images with seals is very high, so we need to use many other computer graphics knowledge to produce these data. There are many experiments show synthesis images is useful to computer vision job, such as vehicle license plate recognition [16], the authors uses the computer graphic scripts to generate data. In order to make our model more robust, We synthesis about 20k images by using complicated backgrounds images and different types of seals cropped from other real images and crawler from the website by Poisson Image Editing [17] to train the detection network, meanwhile use the same method to synthesis about 200k images with different seals but small background images stored with their correspond clean images, just shown on Fig. 3, there are all 256 * 256 RGB images.

3.2   Implementation of Experiments

To optimize our networks, we follow the standard approach form: we alternate between one gradient descent step on D, then one step on G. So the loss of the GAN is:

Quota ID

Quota Number

Quota Value

Fig. 4. The main sequences we take focus on

$$L_{cWGAN}(G, D) = \mathbb{E}_{x \sim P_r}\left[D(x)\right] - \mathbb{E}_{x \sim P_g}\left[D(G(x))\right] \tag{1}$$

Previous approaches to conditional GANs have found it is useful to mix the GAN objective with a more traditional loss, such as L2 distance. The discriminator's job remains unchanged is to distinguish the image is real or fake, but the generator is tasked to not only fool the discriminator but also to be near the ground truth output in an L2 sense. We also explore this option, using L1 distance rather than L2 as L1 encourages less blurring:

$$\mathcal{L}_{L1}(G) = \mathbb{E}_{x,y \sim p_{\text{data}}(x,y), z \sim p_z(z)}\left[\|y - G(x,z)\|_1\right] \tag{2}$$

So, our final object is :

$$G^* = \arg \min_G \max_D \mathcal{L}_{cWGAN}(G, D) + \lambda \mathcal{L}_{L1}(G) \tag{3}$$

In addition, we divide the objective by 2 while optimizing D, which slows down the rate at which D learns relative to G. We use minibatch SGD and apply the RMSProp [18] solver, with a learning rate of 0.0002, and the λ is 100. By set the minibatch size equal 1, the batch normalization termed "instance normalization". Meanwhile, In order to reduce overfit, we use the dropout [19]. When we do the deconvolution, the first three layers, we use the dropout, can help us to reduce overfit a lot. When we use the dropout, we set the number is 0.5 to avoid overfitting.

4   Results and Discussion

In this study, we pay more attention on the seals erasing network, so we need to take focus on the result images of the seals erasing network, the Fig. 5 shows the good cases, can erase a large areas of all seals, but we also have the bad cases, the Fig. 6 show the bad cases. The reason of the bad cases is these types of seals are less, so the model can not learn the clean images corresponding with these types of seals. The right side of these images are the original images with seals,

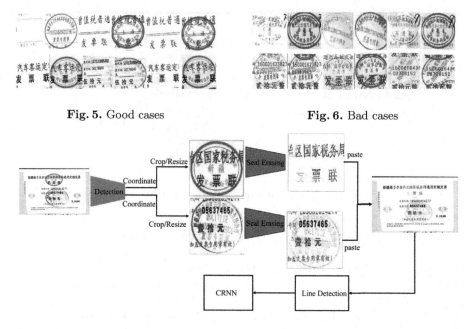

Fig. 5. Good cases   **Fig. 6.** Bad cases

Fig. 7. The total phase of seals erasing and recognition

the left side are the result without seals, we can see the result of these images, our method can erase different type seals, so this is a universal seal erasing network. In order to prove our method can help to do the recognition, we use the output images of the seals erasing network to train and test the CRNN. For example, we use the quota invoice to test our method, the Fig. 7 shows the total phases, at first, we use the detection network to get the coordinate to crop and resize these seals by 256 * 256 from the 512 * 512 RGB images with padding. Then we use the seals erasing network to erase these seals, at last, we use the output images of seals erasing to paste on the original images and use the recognition network. Because we only take focus on the three main sequences (QI represents the Quota ID, QN represents the Quota Number, QV represents the Quota Value, the dataset "Before" represents the data before seals erasing, the dataset "After" represents the data after seals erasing), just shown by the Fig. 4, so we calculate the average sequence precision, at last the output images of seals erasing network can get the better performance from on the Table 1, the QI can get the more higher architecture, because the QI sequences can be affected by these seals like the "5" can be transfer to "6" when the outline of the seals across the "5". Meanwhile, we compare our method with other traditional method, such as images inpainting, the images inpating need the mask, so we use the seals coordinate from the seals detection network to make the masks. Then we use the images inpating method to do the seals erasing, the Fig. 8 shows the result of the same image, we can see our method can get the better result.

Table 1. Comparison of different dataset

Dataset	QI	QN	QV	Average
Before	84.5%	90.0%	94.5%	89.7%
After	87.5%	91.3%	95.0%	91.3%

Fig. 8. The result of image inpating

5 Conclusion

In this paper, we first introduce the universal framework to do the seals erasing by the generator and adversarial network, compare with the traditional methods, to convert images to binary images or use the photo shop, our method is very easy, and can be used widely, like to erase watermarks also. This method is not the end-to-end training network architecture, in the next time, we will search a proper method combined seals detection and seals erasing. Our method can be used not only in the seals but also others jobs like watermarks erasing, images denoising etc. In summary, this is an innovative method to do the seals erasing and can transfer to other jobs.

Acknowledgements. The work is partially supported by School of Software, University of Science and Technology of China. We also acknowledge to the authors of the real image examples but we do not own the copyrights of them to verify the performance of our method.

References

1. Shi, B., Bai, X., Yao, C.: An end-to-end trainable neural network for image-based sequence recognition and its application to scene text recognition. IEEE Trans. Pattern Anal. Mach. Intell. **39**(11), 2298–2304 (2015)
2. Tian, Z., Huang, W., He, T., He, P., Qiao, Y.: Detecting text in natural image with connectionist text proposal network. In: Leibe, B., Matas, J., Sebe, N., Welling, M. (eds.) ECCV 2016. LNCS, vol. 9912, pp. 56–72. Springer, Cham (2016). https://doi.org/10.1007/978-3-319-46484-8_4
3. Wojna, Z., Gorban, A.N., Lee, D.S., et al.: Attention-based extraction of structured information from street view imagery. In: IEEE 2017 14th IAPR International Conference on Document Analysis and Recognition (ICDAR) - Kyoto, 9–15 November 2017, pp. 844–850 (2017)
4. Goodfellow, I.: NIPS 2016 tutorial: generative adversarial networks (2016)
5. Mirza, M., Osindero, S.: Conditional generative adversarial nets. Comput. Sci. 2672–2680 (2014)
6. Isola, P., Zhu, J.Y., Zhou, T., et al.: Image-to-image translation with conditional adversarial networks (2016)
7. Zhu, J.Y., Park, T., Isola, P., et al.: Unpaired image-to-image translation using cycle-consistent adversarial networks (2017)
8. Liu, W., et al.: SSD: single shot multibox detector. In: Leibe, B., Matas, J., Sebe, N., Welling, M. (eds.) ECCV 2016. LNCS, vol. 9905, pp. 21–37. Springer, Cham (2016). https://doi.org/10.1007/978-3-319-46448-0_2
9. Redmon, J., Divvala, S., Girshick, R., et al.: You only look once: unified, real-time object detection (2015)
10. Ren, S., He, K., Girshick, R., et al.: Faster R-CNN: towards real-time object detection with region proposal networks. In: International Conference on Neural Information Processing Systems (2015)
11. Arjovsky, M., Chintala, S., Bottou, L.: Wasserstein GAN (2017)
12. Ronneberger, O., Fischer, P., Brox, T.: U-Net: convolutional networks for biomedical image segmentation. In: Navab, N., Hornegger, J., Wells, W.M., Frangi, A.F. (eds.) MICCAI 2015. LNCS, vol. 9351, pp. 234–241. Springer, Cham (2015). https://doi.org/10.1007/978-3-319-24574-4_28
13. Ulyanov, D., Vedaldi, A., Lempitsky, V.: Instance normalization: the missing ingredient for fast stylization (2016)
14. Li, C., Wand, M.: Precomputed real-time texture synthesis with markovian generative adversarial networks. In: Leibe, B., Matas, J., Sebe, N., Welling, M. (eds.) ECCV 2016. LNCS, vol. 9907, pp. 702–716. Springer, Cham (2016). https://doi.org/10.1007/978-3-319-46487-9_43
15. Graves, A.: Connectionist temporal classification. In: Graves, A. (ed.) Supervised Sequence Labelling with Recurrent Neural Networks. SCI, vol. 385, pp. 61–93. Springer, Heidelberg (2012)
16. Wang, X., Man, Z., You, M., et al.: Adversarial generation of training examples: applications to moving vehicle license plate recognition (2017)
17. Rez, P., Gangnet, M., Blake, A.: Poisson image editing. ACM Trans. Graph. **22**(3), 313–318 (2003)
18. Hinton, G., Srivastava, N., Swersky, K.: Lecture 6D - a separate, adaptive learning rate for each connection. Slides Lect. Neural Netw. Mach. Learn. (2012)
19. Hinton, G.E., Srivastava, N., Krizhevsky, A., Sutskever, I., Salakhutdinov, R.R.: Improving neural networks by preventing co-adaptation of feature detectors. Comput. Sci. **3**(4), 212–223 (2012)

Pupil Segmentation Method Based on Treasure Theory and Region Growing

Kang Yao[1,2] and Weiwei Fu[1,2(✉)]

[1] University of Science and Technology of China, Hefei 230000, China
Xkk9866@yeah.net
[2] Suzhou Institute of Biomedical Engineering Technology,
Chinese Academy of Sciences, Suzhou 215000, China
Fuww@Sibect.ac.in

Abstract. Aiming at the problems of blurred pupil edge and occlusion of upper and lower eyelids in low resolution images, a heuristic pupil region segmentation method is proposed, which mainly uses the gray level features of pupil region to locate. Firstly, N points are randomly initialized on the whole graph. Each point is iterated in a random step and direction to find the location of the pixel whose gray value is less than the global minimum gray value. When all points in the graph are not moving, all points are selected as seed stores to grow the region. The region after growing is the pupil region. Finally, isolated points are removed by morphological changes. And fill the hole. The results show that the algorithm can overcome the pupil pose change, eyelid, eyelash occlusion and other problems, and show good robustness and accuracy compared with other algorithms.

Keywords: Treasure theory · Pupil segmentation · Region growing

1 Introduction

Pupil location plays an important role in line of sight tracking, iris recognition and medical diagnosis. In line-of-sight tracking, we can judge the direction of sight or the location of the pupil according to the movement of the pupil, and then we can know people's psychological activities; in iris recognition, we can extract the iris region by pupil location, and then we can extract features; in medical treatment, we can judge a person's mental state by monitoring the pupil condition [2]. In a word, pupil localization has great research value. At present, the most practical pupil location algorithms are Hough transform, Bayesian classification and threshold segmentation. (1) Hough transform is a commonly used pupil location method, which consumes a lot of time and space, and can not meet the real-time requirement. (2) Bayesian classification method is fast, suitable for low resolution images, easy to be disturbed by facula, blurred eyelashes, and low robustness of location. (3) Threshold segmentation method is fast, but has poor anti-interference and general positioning accuracy. Dai [6] uses Adaboost algorithm and Camshire algorithm to track and determine the face dynamically. Secondly, the integral projection and Hough transform ellipse detection are used to locate the human eye, and the opening and closing state of the human eye is judged according

© Springer Nature Singapore Pte Ltd. 2019
Y. Wang et al. (Eds.): IGTA 2019, CCIS 1043, pp. 293–299, 2019.
https://doi.org/10.1007/978-981-13-9917-6_28

to the area of the ellipse. Yang [7] proposed a novel method to locate eyes accurately. The method consists of two parts: the first part is to segment the face region by skin color clustering segmentation algorithm, to filter the segmentation map geometrically, and to find possible eye pairs by calculating the center of mass of the holes in the candidate face region; the second part is to combine the two methods based on monitoring the face region and the approximate position of the eyes. The proposed eye model uses a new Hough transform ellipse monitoring algorithm to accurately locate the position of the human eye. Hough transform is used to fit the pupil. It is better for the pupil to be completely exposed, but the detection accuracy is lower when the pupil is occluded. Guo [8] explored a new method of automatic image segmentation. A new method of automatic image segmentation was proposed. The data of image feature space were clustered by Gauss finite mixture model and expectation maximization algorithm. The number of image regions to be segmented was determined by information theory criterion (ITC), and the image was segmented by Bayesian probability. The appropriate number of regions can be determined. However, Bayesian method needs to determine more parameters and has a narrow application area. Song [9] proposed a simple and effective iris inner edge location algorithm. Based on the gray histogram of iris image, the gray threshold of separating pupils was determined by searching the gray distribution range of pupil area, and the inner edge of iris was located by gray projection method. Zhang [10] used Hough transform circle detection method to detect the pupil radius. The algorithm used threshold segmentation and image 2. The measurement of pupil radius is realized by the steps of value, edge detection and Hough transform circle detection. Liu [11] proposed an eye detection method based on deep convolution neural network. The network optimization and loss optimization are carried out. Eye detection is solved as a regression problem. The whole process is end-to-end, i.e. from the input of the original picture to the output of the final eye category and location. The accuracy of this method is 98.39% for all images in ORL face database and 95.15% for eyes without sunglasses in AR face database. The experimental results verify the effectiveness, high accuracy and strong generalization ability of the proposed method. But neural network needs a large sample size, and different people have different pupil characteristics. In the absence of a large number of training sets, traditional image processing is still the best choice.

In this paper, a new pupil location method based on pupil feature points is proposed. This method is based on the theory of digging treasures to search random points by jumping. It uses the gray-level semantic features of pupils to segment pixels, and combines morphological operations to complete pupils and remove interference electricity. The accuracy of location is high. This method can effectively overcome the influence of upper and lower eyelids and eyelashes on the segmentation of pupil boundary, and can locate the pupil region under various postures.

2   Data Acquisition

2.1   Camera Image Acquisition

In this system, the infrared camera is used to capture the eye image of eye tracker users in real time, and the center of pupil is obtained by digging treasure theory. Firstly, the image is preprocessed, including image gray processing, noise removal processing and so on. They are mainly to reduce the impact of the environment on the image and ensure the quality of the image, which is the premise of human eye segmentation.

Eye images collected by the device are shown in Fig. 1 below. Due to different eyelash length, eyelid thickness and pupil exposure, traditional threshold segmentation is difficult to accurately locate and has low robustness.

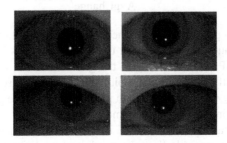

Fig. 1. Camera acquisition display

3 Pupil Location Method Based on Treasure Theory

3.1 Pupil Segmentation Based on Treasure Theory

Through the analysis of the images acquired by the camera, we propose a pupil segmentation algorithm based on treasure theory (TTPS). The steps are as follows:

Step 1: Randomly initializing N points in the image, called engineers. As shown in the following Fig. 2, the small blue circle represents the position of the initialized engineers.

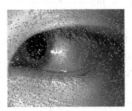

Fig. 2. Initialization of Random Point Diagram (Color figure online)

Step 2: Setting the random step size X_step and Y_step in the horizontal and vertical directions of each engineer, and to select the random direction through the different random step size in two directions. If the gray value of the destination is higher than the current global minimum gray value Global_G, the engineer returns to the original position [x0, y0]. As shown in the following formula (1). I Represents Image Matrix.

$$I\,(x_0 + X\_step, y_0 + Y\_step) > Global\_G \tag{1}$$

$$P = (1 - \frac{Changi}{AvgChange}) \times 100\% \tag{2}$$

Step 3: In order to prevent some engineers from falling into the local optimum, a probabilistic activation algorithm is set up. When $Chang_i$ is less than AvgChange, the probability of P moves directly to the global centroid, and the probability of $1 - P$ moves directly to the random point according to the second step, regardless of whether the gray value of the random point is less than the global minimum gray value. P is shown in the following formula (2).

Step 4: Set the maximum number of iterations K for all engineers. When the number of iterations exceeds K or the number of engineers in the target area has reached a certain level, the iteration stops. The location found at this time is the pupil position. As shown in the following Fig. 3.

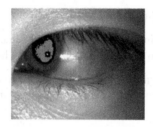

Fig. 3. Iterative K-times display

Step 5: Regional growth. In the third step, the pupil area location has achieved high accuracy, but because the number of random initial points is not enough, the pupil area coverage is incomplete, so the technology of regional growth is used to cover the pupil area adequately. Firstly, all the engineer points in the third step are selected as seed pixels, i.e. the starting point of the region growth. Then, the neighborhood around the seed pixels and the pixels satisfying certain conditions are merged into the region where the seed pixels are located, i.e. less than a certain gray threshold. At this time, the threshold is the global minimum gray value plus 10, because the nearer the edge, the higher the gray value of the pupil, but 10 is the pupil and iris. The boundary between them can better separate the iris. The new pixels continue to grow around as seeds until no more pixels satisfy the conditions can be included. The formed area is the complete area of the pupil, as shown in the following Fig. 4.

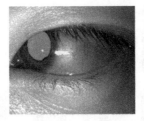

Fig. 4. Regional growth display

Step 6: Morphological transformation. The scatter plot formed by engineers can be filled with small voids and connected with adjacent objects and smooth boundaries by morphological closed operation, that is, expansion before corrosion. After that, the morphological opening operation is performed. First corrosion and then expansion can eliminate the small objects, separating the objects at the fine points and smoothing the boundary of the larger objects. For image X and structural element S, symbols $X \circ S$ are used to represent S to open image X and symbols $X \cdot S$ are used to express S to close image X. They are defined as (3) and (4):

$$X \circ S = (X \ominus S) \oplus S \tag{3}$$

$$X \cdot S = (X \oplus S) \ominus S \tag{4}$$

The image after morphological operation is shown as follows:

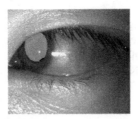

Fig. 5. Image after morphological operation

The area obtained from the above steps is the pupil area. By testing various illumination conditions and pupil posture, the results are shown in Fig. 6 below. From the results of region segmentation, the algorithm has the advantages of translation rotation, scale invariance, high robustness, strong anti-noise ability and anti-illumination imbalance. After morphological closing and opening operations, corneal reflection highlights can be filled and isolated noise points can be removed, which increases the integrity of pupil segmentation.

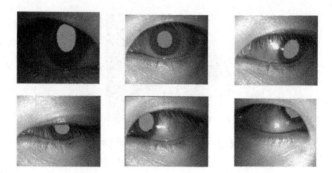

Fig. 6. Segmentation effect in various situations

4   Experimental Results and Analysis

4.1   Environmental Preparation

The pupil size detection algorithm is simulated and validated on a Python 336-based computer with i5 2.8 GHz main frequency and 8 GB memory. The image resolution is 256 * 208. The designed program realizes the functions of image stream preprocessing, image graying and pupil area location based on treasure theory.

4.2   Algorithm Comparison

Three different segmentation methods are used to segment the image. Through the results of pupil segmentation, the following conclusions are drawn:

1. The segmentation algorithm based on threshold is difficult to segment completely in dark light because of the color of eyelashes and pupils is similar, and the effect is shown in the Fig. 7(a).
2. The pupil segmentation algorithm based on Hough circle transform has lower detection accuracy when the pupil is oblique and occluded. Hough transform needs different parameters for different pupil shapes and attitudes, and its robustness is low. The processed result is shown in the Fig. 7(b).

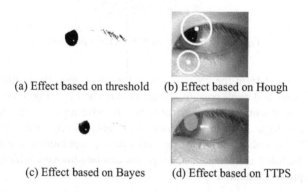

(a) Effect based on threshold   (b) Effect based on Hough

(c) Effect based on Bayes   (d) Effect based on TTPS

Fig. 7. Comparison of segmentation effects of various algorithms

3. Based on Bayes segmentation algorithm, when eyelashes are dense and pupils are covered, Eyelashes are easy to be misclassified and pupil segmentation is incomplete., and the effect is shown in the Fig. 7(c).
4. Our algorithm has high segmentation accuracy for pupils, as shown in the following Fig. 7(d).

5 Summary

In this paper, infrared light is used to collect human eyes. The difference of gray scale and shape between pupil and peripheral iris, eyelashes and eyelids is the key factor for pupil location and size calculation. Whether stable and accurate pupil shape can be extracted directly affects the accuracy of calculation. The proposed pupil segmentation algorithm based on the treasure theory can effectively extract the gray-scale semantic features of pupils. By calculating the average gray-scale in a certain window, the interference between eyelashes and iris can be effectively reduced and the segmentation effect can be more accurate. However, due to a large number of search steps based on the treasure theory and the strategy of region growth, this algorithm has a large amount of calculation and is difficult to achieve. Insufficiency of time detection. The next step is to set up the initial random points effectively and reasonably, so as to improve the detection efficiency.

References

1. Jinhuan, Y.P., Zhou, Z., et al.: One-time calibration method based on iris recognition in line-of-sight tracking. J. Comput. Aided Des. Graph. **25**(7) (2013)
2. Li, Q., Cai, X.: Significance of pupil observation in monitoring the condition of patients with craniocerebral injury. Chin. J. Nurs. **17**(6), 51 (2000)
3. Zhang, H., Wang, S., Li, X., et al.: Research and implementation of pupil recognition method based on Hough transform. LCD Disp. **31**(6) (2016)
4. He, Z.: Research on Iris Recognition Algorithms. Changsha University of Technology (2013)
5. Mu, K., Shi, Y.: Application of several threshold segmentation methods in pupil detection. Beijing Biomed. Eng. **24**(6), 443–445 (2005)
6. Dai, M., Luo, L., Chen, Y.: Detection of driver fatigue. Technol. Mark. **17**(8), 17–19 (2010)
7. Yang, Q., Gui, W., Hu, H., et al.: Innovative eye location algorithms in driver fatigue driving. Comput. Eng. Appl. **44**(6) (2008)
8. Guo, P., Lu, H.: Research on Bayesian probabilistic image segmentation. J. Opt. **22**(12) (2002)
9. Song, H., Chen, H., Zhang, L.: Pupil segmentation based on gray histogram minimum span threshold method. Chin. Printing Packag. Res. **03**(2) (2011)
10. Zhang, Z., Meng, K., Chao, L.: Research on pupil radius measurement algorithm based on threshold segmentation and Hough transform. J. Inner Mongolia Agric. Univ.: Nat. Sci. Edn. **4**, 145–148 (2013)
11. Liu, J., Chen, Z., Fan, X., et al.: Eye detection based on deep convolution neural network. Mod. Electron. Technol. (18) (2018)

Object Recognition and Localization Base on Binocular Vision

Rongjie Duan$^{(\boxtimes)}$, Shizhong Li, Zehui Yuan, and Ya Zhang

College of Mechatronics Engineering, North University of China,
No. 3, Xueyuan Road, Taiyuan, People's Republic of China
751465825@qq.com, lishizhong@nuc.edu.cn,
yuanzehui1985@126.com, deronjet@sohu.com

Abstract. Autonomous grasping of manipulator is a challenging problem, due to the difficulties and accuracy of object recognition and localization. This paper presents a binocular vision-based approach, which enables to recognize and locate object accurately with a binocular. This approach, which is based on the limitation of the application of the traditional manipulator, aims to achieve autonomous grasp of manipulator. The main contribution of this paper is to construct the recognition and localization system. Firstly, the left camera of the binocular is used to collect the image information, and the TensorFlow is used to imply the ResNet to build the recognition system; Then the principle of the ranging of the binocular is used for locating the target object; Finally, tests have been performed in three different indoor environments to achieve autonomous grasping of manipulator. The proposed object recognition and localization approach is testified by successfully autonomous grasping of manipulator, and experimental results show that the accuracy reaches 89.83% averagely.

Keywords: Binocular vision · Object recognition and localization · ResNet · Manipulator

1 Introduction

With the development of science and technology, a large number of mechanical arms have been applied to people's lives. The traditional manipulator can only carry out the movement according to the prescribed path, and not exchange the information with the outside world, which limits the scope of the application. Therefore, the manipulator has a lot of research space in the autonomous grasping, and the recognition and localization of the object is a challenge problem in autonomous grasping of manipulator. In this paper, a vision based approach is presented, which enables to recognize and locate object with a binocular, to achieve autonomous grasping of manipulator.

Nowadays, lots of methods for recognition and localization have been explored. The binocular vision is used for imitating humanity. Human being observe an object from two angles with two eyes, and the distance of object is obtained according to the fell parallax [1]. The method of stereo machine vision is accurately based on this principle. In [2], an approach of the object recognition and localization based in binocular stereo vision is introduced. Through dealing with two images what are

© Springer Nature Singapore Pte Ltd. 2019
Y. Wang et al. (Eds.): IGTA 2019, CCIS 1043, pp. 300–309, 2019.
https://doi.org/10.1007/978-981-13-9917-6_29

capture from difference points in the ca, the object in the images is analyzed and the localization is computed with the real-time and accuracy requirements by the system.

In [3–5], there are many methods of object recognition because the objects have different characteristics from the other that are seen in shape, material, size and so on. Quickly recognizing the object applies to the shape decomposition in [3]. However, the precision of the method is low. In [4], the template matching method shows high accuracy, but the whole image space should to be traversed to get the features, so it will cost much time and the object will be missed if images distort seriously. And in [5], contour recognition is used to obtain the information of target, but it has high requirements to target scaling and rotation, except the real-time should to be improved.

The binocular vision is widely used in object recognition and location. In [6–9], there are difference method to achieve object location: in [6], the paper use least-squares fitting method to accurately determine coordinates of one matching point and four boundary points. The dense stereo disparity information is used to 3D reconstruction of the scene and the triangulated information is used to build the Digital Elevation Map (DEM) for detecting obstacles in [7]. [8] proposes a new multi-object detection system based on binocular stereo vision, finally the number and position of objects can be determined. In [9], this paper proposes a method to use MATLAB to calibrate camera and use OpenCV to rectify and match images, distance between camera and object can be get via the disparity value, and the experiments show that this distance measurement method can be effective within a certain range. However, both of them only use the binocular vision to achieve object location, we can't determine the categories of object. In [10], they use SURF algorithm for object recognition and get the localization of the object according to 3d reconstruction principle, however the complexity of the 3d reconstruction principle is much larger than that of binocular localization.

In the field of autonomous grasping of manipulator, visual sensors are generally used to recognize and locate objects in the environment. In [11], the paper provide information for robot accurate grasping through the technology of binocular stereo vision calibration and 3-D reconstruction principle. The robot target recognition and positioning crawling platform based on binocular vision is researched and developed in [12], and it can effectively solve the problem of sorting of loose parts. An autonomous grasp method for the embedded mobile manipulator with an eye-in-hand CMOS camera is proposed in [13], image information and inverse kinematics are used to achieve autonomous grasping. In [14], a novel model-based scooping grasp for the picking of thin objects lying on a flat surface is proposed, and the results shows the overall grasp success rate of 84%. However, the relative works of autonomous grasping with binocular vision can't simultaneously achieve object recognition and location.

This research is aimed to construct a object recognition and localization system with a binocular for achieving manipulator grasping autonomously. The remainder of the paper is organized as follows: in Sect. 2, the recognition system is described. While the principle of binocular ranging what is used for object localization is described in Sect. 3. And in Sect. 4 the performance of the proposed method is tested and the experiment results are reported. The conclusions and future works are contained in Sect. 5.

2 Object Recognition

2.1 Object Recognition Frame

Creating accurate machine learning models capable of localizing and identifying multiple objects in a single image remains a core challenge in computer vision. In November 2015, Google released TensorFlow, which can define, train and deploy machine learning models, is an open source deep learning software library [15, 16]. The recognition system designed in this paper is programmed with TensorFlow and OpenCV to achieve the object recognition.

Neural networks have been proven to be good classifiers for those linear inseparable problems and many developments were achieved on the structure of networks to enhance the performance of classification or clustering [17]. Deep residual networks can make the training process faster and attain more accuracy compared to their equivalent neural networks. ResNet achieve this improvement by adding a simple skip connection parallel to the layers of convolutional neural networks. In Fig. 1, this is a ResNet residual learning unit, which is equivalent to changing the learning goal, no longer learning a complete output H(x), but only learning the difference between the output and the input H(x) − x [18]. The result of image recognition shows that the ResNet have significant contribution of convolution neural network.

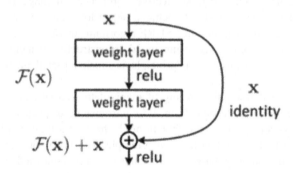

Fig. 1. ResNet residual learning unit

2.2 Object Recognition

In order to achieve the object recognition, the TFRecord datasets which can be read by TensorFlow should be made and TensorFlow is used to imply the ResNet. TFRecords is a simple binary file format. It lets you put one or more strings of bytes into a file [6]. The TensorFlow is used for achieve ResNet V2, and contrib.slim library is also used to help build the ResNet. The recognition system is constructed by training the TFRecord model into the ResNet, using the camera to record the image information, the result of object recognition is shown in Fig. 2.

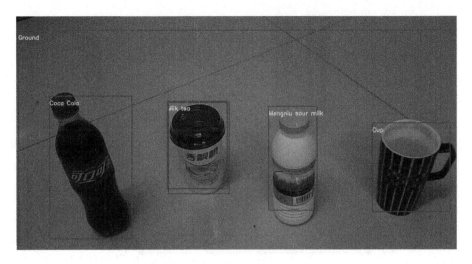

Fig. 2. The result of object recognition

3 Object Localization

After object recognition, the binocular vision can get the distance of object. There are two kinds of object localization algorithm: global-based stereo matching and local-based stereo matching [19]. The former can apparently improve the performance of the disparity image, and it can solve the problems that arise form accurately matching the pixels of weak texture regions and occluded regions, but it's high computation complexity with low matching efficiency. The local-based stereo matching algorithms obtain the accurate parallax in rich texture regions easily, but in weak texture regions, the accuracy of the stereo matching is uncomfortable. Since the real-time of the object localization algorithm [20] that uses improved Sobel kernel is performed in the proposed range finding system, and it's widely used for robot in real environments.

The principle of binocular ranging is used to obtain the distance between the camera to the target object. Figure 3 depicts an imaging configuration with two projective system, C_l and C_r represent the optical centre of the left and right camera, the line which connecting the C_l and C_r is called the base line L, and parameter f is the focal length of the left and the right camera. The difference between coordinates dx_l and dx_r is called a horizontal disparity on the life image and the right image, respectively. dX_l and dX_r are the distances from the target to the left camera optical axis and the right camera optical axis. h_l and h_r are the horizontal centre coordinate of the left image and the right image, respectively [21, 22].

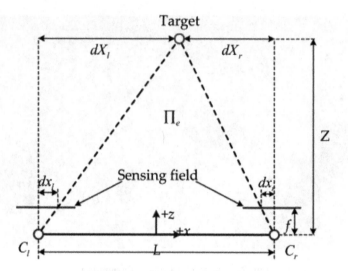

Fig. 3. Standard binocular stereo vision system configuration

Considering the similar triangles in Fig. 3, we can obtain:

$$\frac{dX_l}{dx_l} = \frac{Z}{f}, \tag{1}$$

$$\frac{dX_r}{dx_r} = \frac{Z}{f}, \tag{2}$$

$$L = dX_l + dX_R \tag{3}$$

Where

$$dx_l = (x_l - h_l) \times \text{the actual light sensing pixel distance,}$$

$$dx_l = (x_l - h_l) \times \text{the actual light sensing pixel distance}$$

Combine the Eqs. (1)–(3), we can get:

$$Z = \frac{L \times f}{(dx_l + dx_r)} \tag{4}$$

Where Z expresses the distance from the target to the baseline L.

4 Experiments

In this part, the experimental results with our object recognition and localization are reported. As is shown in Fig. 4, the manipulator is used for to testify the accuracy of object recognition and localization with accomplishing the automatic grasping.

A mobile platform equipped with manipulator is used to grasp, and the binocular which is equipped on the end-effector of the manipulator is used to recognize and locate object.

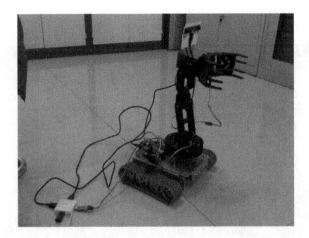

Fig. 4. The hardware system

When searching the object, the position of the manipulator is shown in Fig. 5, other joints remain fixed except rotating the joint 6.

Fig. 5. The initial pose of manipulator

In the process of recognition, when the object is not found, as Fig. 6 shows, the upper left corner of the image displays the name of the target which is looked for, the distance between camera and the target is 7999.95 cm, which means infinity. When the target is recognized, the system automatically rings the target object with a red rectangle and displays the distance between the camera and the object in real time, it can be seen in Fig. 7.

Fig. 6. Object not detected

Fig. 7. Object detected (Color figure online)

After accomplish to recognize and locate the target, the position of the end-effector of the manipulator to the object is known, the inverse kinematic of the manipulator is used for achieving the object grasping [23]. The autonomous grasping process is shown in Fig. 8.

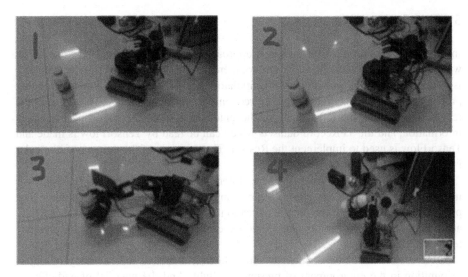

Fig. 8. The process of autonomous grasping

The experimental results of 30 times with autonomous grasping are reported as Table 1, the test are performed in three different environments, which is day, day with light, and night with light, respectively.

Table 1. The 30 experimental results with autonomous grasping

Experience environment	Target object	The number of successfully grasp	The rate of successfully grasp
Day	Mengniu	27	90%
	U-Loveit	30	100%
Day with light	Mengniu	26	86%
	U-Loveit	28	93%
Night with light	Mengniu	24	80%
	U-Loveit	27	90%

According to the data of the Table 1, we can draw some conclusions:

a. Light affects the result. The surface of the object would reflect light with the light is turned on, so the accuracy of object recognition is lower.
b. The roughness of the surface of the object affects the result. The rougher the surface, the easier it will be grasped.
c. The results show that the accuracy of autonomous grasping reaches 89.83% averagely, it's higher than the rate of 84% in [14].

5 Conclusions

In this work we present a vision-based approach for recognizing and locating object with a binocular in different indoor environments. A mobile platform with manipulator is used. Autonomous grasping of manipulator is a different and more challenging problem, due to the accuracy of object recognition and localization. To construct the recognition system, the left camera of the binocular is used for collecting the image information, and the TFRecord datasets which can be read by TensorFlow is made and TensorFlow is used to implement the ResNet. The principle of the ranging of binocular is used for locating the object.

Tests have been performed in three different indoor environments by using the inverse kinematic of manipulator to achieve autonomous grasping of manipulator. The proposed object recognition and localization approach is testified by successfully autonomous grasping of manipulator, and experimental results show that the accuracy reaches 89.83% averagely.

Future works will be devoted to study how to improve the accuracy of object recognition in the environment of presence of light. And the material of end-effector would be studied to achieve better grasping of object.

References

1. Maravall, D., Fernandez, E.: Contribution to the matching problem in stereo vision. In: LAPR International Conference on Pattern Recognition, 1992, Conference A: Computer Vision and Applications, Proceedings, vol. 1, pp. 411–414. IEEE (1992)
2. Liu, W., Wang, Z., Ning, X., et al.: An object recognition and location based on binocular stereo vision. In: International Forum on Computer Science-Technology and Applications, pp. 97–99. IEEE (2010)
3. Jia, Y.U., Fang, J.: DCT face recognition algorithm based on weighted wavelet. Comput. Eng. Appl. **48** (2012)
4. Ding, X.F., Wu, H., Zhang, H.J.: Review on shape matching. Acta Automatic Sinica **27**(5), 678–694 (2001)
5. Liu, H., Qin, S.: Recognition and servo tracking of moving target based on image features. Chin. J. Sci. Instrum. **29**(3), 644–648 (2008)
6. Wang, J., Mei, T., Kong, B., et al.: Research on object recognition of intelligent robot base on binocular vision. Appl. Mech. Mater. **127**, 300–304 (2011)
7. Neethu, S., Vinuchackravarthy, S.: Object detection using binocular vision. In: International Conference on Advances in Computing. IEEE (2016)
8. He, Z., Ren, Q., Yang, T., Li, J., Zhang, Y.: Multi-object detection based on binocular stereo vision. In: Zhang, Z., Huang, K. (eds.) IVS 2016. CCIS, vol. 664, pp. 114–121. Springer, Singapore (2016). https://doi.org/10.1007/978-981-10-3476-3_14
9. Tong, S., Wenbo, L., Jing, W.: Distance measurement system based on binocular stereo vision. Electron. Meas. Technol. **4**, 013 (2015)
10. Dehai, W., Wei, H., Qunzhe, C.: Object recognition and localization based on binocular stereo vision. J. Jilin Univ. (Inf. Sci. Edn.) (2016)
11. Hui, J., Yang, Y., Hui, Y., et al.: Research on identify matching of object and location algorithm based on binocular vision. J. Comput. Theoret. Nanosci. **13**(3), 2006–2013 (2016)

12. Xu, W., Lei, Z., Yuan, Z., et al.: Research and development of target recognition and location crawling platform based on binocular vision. In: Materials Science & Engineering Conference Series (2018)
13. Jiao, J., Cao, Z., Zhao, P., et al.: Autonomous grasp of the embedded mobile manipulator with an eye-in-hand camera. In: IEEE International Conference on Networking. IEEE (2014)
14. Lévesque, F., Sauvet, B., Cardou, P., et al.: A model-based scooping grasp for the autonomous picking of unknown objects with a two-fingered gripper. Robot. Autonom. Syst. **106**, 14–25 (2018). S0921889017308898
15. Goldsborough, P.: A tour of TensorFlow (2016). https://arxiv.org/pdf/1610.01178.pdf
16. Abadi, M., Barham, P., Chen, J., et al.: TensorFlow: a system for large-scale machine learning (2016). https://arxiv.org/pdf/1605.08695v2.pdf
17. Krizhevsky, A., Sutskever, I., Hinton, G.E.: ImageNet classification with deep convolutional neural networks. In: International Conference on Neural Information Processing Systems, pp. 1097–1105. Curran Associates Inc. (2012)
18. He, K., Zhang, X., Ren, S., et al.: Deep residual learning for image recognition. In: IEEE Conference on Computer Vision and Pattern Recognition, pp. 770–778. IEEE Computer Society (2016)
19. Hong, G.S., Kim, B.G.: A local stereo matching algorithm based on weighted guided image filtering for improving the generation of depth range images. Displays **49**, 80–87 (2017)
20. Ding, X.L., Zhao, Q., Li, Y.B., et al.: A real-time and effective object recognition and localization method. Appl. Mech. Mat. **615**, 107–112 (2014)
21. Lai, X.B., Wang, H.S., Xu, Y.H.: A real-time range finding system with binocular stereo vision. Int. J. Adv. Robot. Syst. **9**, 1 (2012)
22. Huang, G.S., Zhang, W.L.: Recognizing and locating of objects using binocular vision system. In: International Conference on Advanced Robotics and Intelligent Systems, pp. 135–140. IEEE (2013)
23. Craig, J.J.: Introduction to Robotics: Mechanics and Control, pp. 78–99. Pearson Education, Inc. (2005)

Effects of Dynamic Disparity on Visual Fatigue Caused by Watching 2D Videos in HMDs

Ruiying Shen[1(✉)], Dongdong Weng[1,2], Jie Guo[1], Hui Fang[1], and Haiyan Jiang[1]

[1] Beijing Engineering Research Center of Mixed Reality and Advanced Display, School of Optics and Photonics, Beijing Institute of Technology, Beijing, China
crgj@bit.edu.cn
[2] AICFVE of Beijing Film Academy, 4, Xitucheng Rd, Haidian, Beijing, China

Abstract. As working at a video display terminal (VDT) for a long time can induce visual fatigue, this paper proposed a method to use dynamic disparity on the situation of video watching in head-mounted displays (HMD), based on the accommodative training. And an experiment was designed to evaluate whether it can alleviate visual fatigue. Subjective and objective methods were combined in the experiment under different disparity conditions to evaluate the visual fatigue of the subjects. The objective assessment was the blink frequency of the subjects, achieved by the eye tracker. The subjective assessment was questionnaire. However, we came to the conclusion that dynamic disparity caused by the movement of left and right eye images in the HMD can't effectively alleviate visual fatigue. According to the change of the average eye blink frequency ratio of the subjects during the experiment, the change of the visual fatigue over time was analyzed.

Keywords: Dynamic disparity · Visual fatigue · Accommodative training · HMD · Eye tracking · Blink

1 Introduction

Visual fatigue in the VDT, manifested as (1) painful irritation (burning) accompanied by lachrymation, reddening of the eyes and conjunctivitis; (2) double vision; (3) headaches; (4) reduced power of accommodation and convergence; and (5) reduced visual activity, sensitivity to contrast, and speed of perception [1]. It brings a lot of trouble to work and life [2]. Close-up visual tasks for a prolonged time straining the ciliary muscles may cause abnormalities in the accommodative function of the lens, which is known as pseudo myopia and is considered to be a part of refractive myopia. It's an important cause of VDT visual fatigue [3]. Studies using objective test methods found that although the response to stimuli in patients with visual fatigue was normal, there was a significant minor fluctuation of accommodation [4]. Tosha et al.'s findings showed that patients with visual fatigue tended to have an accommodation delay after gazing at a close-range target for a period of time (90 s or longer), and the accommodation lag that occurred when patients with mild visual fatigue symptoms continued closely gazing remained stable. In patients with severe symptoms, the amount of

© Springer Nature Singapore Pte Ltd. 2019
Y. Wang et al. (Eds.): IGTA 2019, CCIS 1043, pp. 310–321, 2019.
https://doi.org/10.1007/978-981-13-9917-6_30

accommodation lag increased with time [5]. The performance of accommodative dysfunction is poor accommodative facility, and insufficient eye accommodation etc. Accommodative dysfunction can be alleviated by accommodative training, which is derived from a common knowledge that by relaxing the contracted focus-adjustment muscles around the eyeball, known as the ciliary and extraocular muscles, the degree of pseudo myopia can be reduced.

Takada et al. used stereoscopic video clips to train subjects with visual fatigue [3]. The results showed that the visual acuity of the subjects was significantly improved by continuous accommodation training [2]. Sterner et al. studied the effect of flip lens-training on accommodative function, and their results showed that accommodative training significantly increased the accommodative facility and accommodative function of the subjects, and the subjects did not regain any subjective symptoms in the next two years [6]. Our research aims to apply the accommodative training to the head-mounted display virtual reality environment, and explore whether the visual fatigue can be reduced when subjects watching 2D video in the virtual environment.

Human 3D perception is due to the existence of distance between the two eyes, which makes the imaging of object in the retina have a slight difference. This difference is processed through the human visual system to produce depth perception. For the HMD, a pair of optical systems are usually used to create depth perception, which include two small screens to guide the users to receive the left and right eye images with disparity [7]. But the stereoscopic display is somewhat different from human vision. The binocular vision is achieved through the combination of convergence and adjustment mechanisms. In the human visual system, the two mechanisms are tightly coupled because the stimuli that drive them are consistent [8]. But for the head-mounted displays, the virtual image is focused at a fixed depth away from the eyes, while the depth of the virtual objects, and hence the binocular disparity, varies with the content [9–11]. When viewing a video, the eyes accommodate to a fixed screen distance while they converge to the simulated distance of the object of interest. For the design of experiment, we change the relative disparity of the human eye fusion by changing the distance between the left and right eye images of the helmet, and generate the depth change of the screen to simulate the adjustment mechanism of the human eye when viewing the near and far objects in the real environment. Since the focal plane of the helmet is fixed, our experiment is essentially to explore whether the physical adjustment and physiological adjustment of the human eye will work under the influence of cognitive adjustment, thereby achieving the expectation of alleviating the dysfunction of accommodation and reducing visual fatigue. We compared the visual fatigue of dynamic disparity groups with the static disparity group.

Takeda et al. studied the characteristics of accommodation evoked by perceived depth sensation. The subjects looked at three different two-dimensional stimuli and two different three-dimensional stimuli. For the two-dimensional stimuli, a manifest accommodation without any accompanying vergence was found because of an apparent depth sensation even though the target distance was kept constant. For the three-dimensional stimuli, larger accommodation and clear vergence were evoked because of binocular disparity and a stronger depth sensation. These results revealed that brain depth perception had an effect on accommodation [12].

Therefore, in order to achieve the effect of relieving visual fatigue of VDT in the virtual reality environment, it is worthwhile to study the influence of creating different depth perceptions through dynamic disparity. We designed and performed an experiment using a combination of subjective and objective assessment to explore the effects of different disparity conditions on visual fatigue. According to the changes of the blinking data, visual fatigue within one hour of the experiment were discussed.

2   Materials

2.1   Hardware System

In order to test whether dynamic disparity can alleviate visual fatigue, the evaluation experiment was carried out. Subjects wore HTC VIVE head-mounted display to view different videos in virtual scenes (Fig. 1). The display has a viewing angle of 110° and a combined resolution of 1200×2160 pixels or 1200×1080 pixels per eye. The HTC VIVE system also includes a tracking and positioning system with two base stations and an interactive control handle. In order to monitor the eye condition of the subject in real time, the aSee Pro VR eye tracker combined with the HMD was used to obtain the blink data. The computers running the virtual scene and the eye tracker are all above the NVIDIA GeForce GTX 960. The experimental room was managed, with proper illumination conditions, no glare scattered light source and noise isolation. The subjects sat in a comfortable chair to avoid physical fatigue.

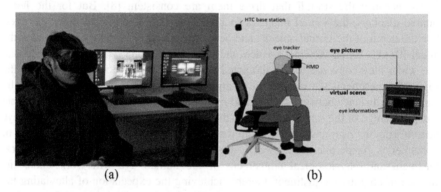

Fig. 1. The experimental scene. (a) Illustration of a user watching video through HMD. (b) The schematic of our system.

2.2   Software System

Subjects used HMD to view the documentary in a virtual scene created by Unity3d. The scale of the virtual environment and the real environment is consistent. The scene is a simple room of 6 m * 8.5 m * 4 m with a screen in it, as shown in Fig. 2. This is a within-subject experiment. According to the three conditions, it consisted of three groups: a control group with a static disparity in which the images of the left and right eyes overlapped (static group), a group of disparity changing at a constant speed with a screen motion of 0.01 m/s (constant speed group), and a group of disparity changing at a variable speed with jumping 0.05 m per 5 s (non-constant speed group). These two speed settings also ensure that the total motion distances of the screen are the same throughout the experiment.

The disparity change of the screen in the human eyes is generated by the horizontal movement of the left and right eye cameras presenting the screen. As shown in Fig. 3 (a), the size of the two screens are both 2.76 m * 1.55 m, and the vertical distance of the plane where the screen is located is 3 m from the camera. The field angle is 45°. When the left eye camera is on the right side of the center and the right eye camera is on the left side, it corresponds to the cross disparity, and conversely, the corresponding non-cross disparity. The subjects will have a relatively low visual fatigue when the binocular disparity is around −0.2° to 0.2° [13]. The conventional recommendation for the stable disparity size is generally within 1° [14]. In this case, this experiment ensured that the disparity is within 1°, and the specific range and moving speed were finally determined by a preliminary experiment. For the dynamic disparity groups in the adjustment plane, the center of the left eye image moves from 0.6 cm of the left of the point O to −2 cm of the right of the O (The right eye image moves symmetrically with respect to the left eye image), at this time the screen at the converging surface will move far from near, and the angle of view will remain 45°, as shown in Fig. 3(b).

Fig. 2. The virtual scene, as seen through the HMD.

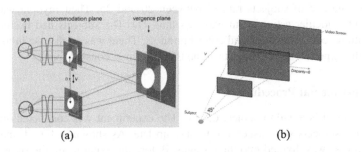

(a)   (b)

Fig. 3. (a) Disparity adjustment schematic diagram. (b) The changes of the screen in vergence plane.

2.3 Stimuli

The documentaries used in experiment were from the first three episodes of National Treasures, each duration is 1 h. These three videos' brightness and content are similar. A group watched an episode of video. To rule out the possibility of content affecting visual fatigue, this paper quantitatively evaluated the impact of the selected three videos' content complexity on blinking [15]. Among the 14 features for texture analysis on the gray level co-occurrence matrix (GLCM), only 4 features are irrelevant [16, 17]. Among these four features, the entropy value is a measure of the amount of information in the image, which indicates the complexity of the texture in the image. Therefore, a Pearson correlation analysis was carried out between the mean entropy value of every 30 s of the videos and the average value of the blink numbers in every 30 s [18].

In the calculation, a 1/12 down sampling of the image is performed. Then it was compressed into 16 gray levels. The results showed that for the static group, the correlation coefficient between the entropy and the blinks is -0.208, which is significant at the level of confidence of 0.95 ($p = 0.03 < 0.05$). It can be found that the correlation between entropy and blinks is very weak, indicating that the change of entropy of experimental video is not enough as a factor to affect visual fatigue. For the non-constant speed group, the Pearson correlation coefficient is 0.021, and is not significant ($p = 0.831 > 0.05$). For the constant speed group, the Pearson correlation coefficient is -0.075, and is not significant ($p = 0.434 > 0.05$). Therefore, in the experimental group, the entropy value change of the video used in the experiment is not a factor that can affect the blink. It could be concluded that the content of the videos we chose didn't affect the blink results which suggested the visual fatigue state.

3 Methods

3.1 Subjects

17 subjects (10 males and 7 females), most of whom were recruited from Beijing Institute of Technology, participated in the entire experimental process. Before the experiment, they were asked to fill in the basic information and eye disease questionnaire. The age of subjects ranged between 20 and 25. Their myopia was below $-2.0D$ and binocular astigmatism was less than 1D. The subjects had normal stereo vision with no color weakness and color blindness. There was no disease in their eyes. Prior to the experiment, all subjects signed an informed consent form.

3.2 Experimental Procedure

This experiment is a within-subject design. The experiment was conducted during the day and the subjects were asked not to stay up late. As shown in Fig. 4, the experimental process was divided into three stages. Before the experiment, the subjects were first familiar with the experimental instrument and rested for 20 min. They could not watch any electronic screen during the break. Then they filled out the basic information scale and the VFS and SSQ. In the experiment, the subject wore an HMD combined with an eye tracker and sat in a soft chair to watch video for an hour. After the experiment, the subjects filled in the VFS and SSQ again. The above experiment was carried out at the same time for three consecutive days. The first day was the control condition, the second day was the non-constant speed condition, and the third day was the constant speed condition.

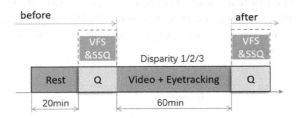

Fig. 4. Procedure of experiment. Q: questionnaire, Disparity 1: static group, Disparity 2: constant speed group, Disparity 3: non-constant group.

3.3 Measurements

For the assessment of visual fatigue, we adopt a combination of subjective and objective evaluation. The subjective questionnaires were visual fatigue scale (VFS) and simulator sickness questionnaire (SSQ), as it can cause motion sickness in the virtual reality environment [14, 19, 20]. SSQ has 16 items that can test symptoms of nausea, oculomotor and disorientation. VFS consists of 24 items, and the five symptoms that can be tested for visual fatigue are: eye strain, general discomfort, nausea, focusing difficulty, and headache.

The objective measurement was blink characteristics, Blinking is a basic function of the eye and helps to remove corneal and conjunctival irritation. The increased visual load is associated with an increasingly uncomfortable dryness sensation, so the increased blinking frequency is considered evidence of visual fatigue [21–24]. Eye blinking data has recently been widely used as a feature of visual fatigue [15, 25].

In this experiment, blink information was obtained by eye tracker. The eye images of the subjects were obtained in real time through the aSee Pro VR eye tracker and the blink data in the experiment were processed through the eye tracker supporting software. As shown in Fig. 1(b), the eye tracker was embedded in the HTC VIVE helmet, which illuminated the eye through an infrared LED ring, recorded eye movements in real time through small camera and sent the data back to the computer for processing. It was determined to be blinking when one eye is closed. In order to eliminate the error caused by different states of the same subject under three experimental conditions and difference between different subjects, the method of calculating the blink rate growth radio was adopted. We took the average blink frequency of the first five minutes as a reference, then calculated the growth rate of the nth five-minute's average blink frequency relative to it.

4 Results

4.1 Results of Subjective Measurements

In order to assess whether the experimental conditions would cause motion sickness and obtain the subjects' assessment of the visual discomfort, we had the subjects to fill in the SSQ and VFS before and after the experiment. The average changes of the scores before and after the experiment are presented in Fig. 5. The higher the score, the more serious the symptoms. The three factors of the SSQ scale and the total are multiplied by the corresponding weights.

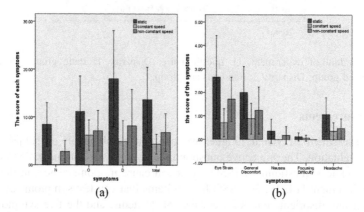

Fig. 5. The mean changes in factor scores. (a) The score of each symptom in SSQ. (N: nausea, O: oculomotor, D: disorientation) (b) The score of each symptom in VFS.

As displayed in the figure, the scores of these two scales are both the highest in the static group. Except the focusing difficulty symptom, scores in the constant speed group are lower compared to the non-constant speed group. The differences of the scores between the groups were analyzed by the Friedman method. For SSQ, the differences between the three groups in nausea score ($\chi^2 = 13.632$, P = 0.001 (<0.05)), and total score ($\chi^2 = 8.291$, P = 0.016 (<0.05)) are significant. The differences of oculomotor and disorientation between the three groups are not significant. For the results of VFS, the difference in eye strain score ($\chi^2 = 10.773$, P = 0.005 (<0.05)) is significant, and other differences in general discomfort, nausea, focusing difficulty, and headache are not significant between the three groups.

This result shows that dynamic disparity groups had lighter simulator sickness and visual fatigue symptoms than the static group. The result that eye strain score of VFS is lower in the dynamic disparity groups is significant. The nausea and total scores of SSQ are lower in the dynamic disparity groups and are significant, indicating that instead of causing more motion sickness the dynamic disparity conditions can alleviate it to a certain extent. This may be due to its reduction of visual discomfort. In the dynamic disparity groups, the scores of the above symptoms are the lowest in the condition of constant speed group, indicating that the constant change of disparity can better alleviate motion sickness and visual discomfort. As for the same item—nausea in the two scales, the results' significance is different. That because their sub-items are different, and in the significant SSQ questionnaire, there are more sub-items.

4.2 Results of Objective Measurements

The growth ratio of average blink frequency per five minutes are presented in Fig. 6. It can be seen that in the first 15 min, the blink frequency ratio of the three groups decreased slightly; In the last ten minutes, the highest value was reached at 50 min, and decreased at 55 min; The blink frequency ratio was in a stable fluctuation in the static group and same in the constant speed group at 20–45 min. According to this, it can be divided into three stages: 10–15, 20–40, 45–55 min.

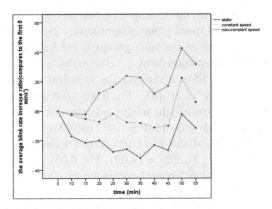

Fig. 6. The growth ratio of average blink frequency per five minutes to the initial five minutes.

The trend of the constant speed group and the static group is similar. While the variable speed group goes up in the middle stage. Its blink frequency ratio increased at 15–35 min and decreased at 40 min, after which it increased in 45 min. A two-factor repeated measures analysis of variance was used to analyze the effects of different disparity condition over time on the blink frequency ratio of the subjects. It aimed to determine whether there was a significant difference in the blink frequency ratio between the three different disparity condition groups in the significance level $\alpha = 0.05$. The statistics are performed using SPSS 22.0. The data contains two dependent variables: different disparity conditions (v) and time periods (*time*).

In the 10–15 min, for the interaction term $v * time$ ($\chi^2 = 3.056$, P = 0.217 (>0.05)) and v ($\chi^2 = 3.200$, P = 0.202 (>0.05)), the dependent variable satisfies the spherical hypothesis. The effect test in the subject indicates that the interaction term is not statistically significant ($F(2, 32) = 0.167$, P = 0.847 (>0.05)); v has no statistically significant effect on blinking ($F(2, 32) = 2.962$, P = 0.066 (>0.05)); *time* has no statistically significant effect on blinking ($F(1, 16) = 0.232$, P = 0.636 (>0.05)). Thus, the blink frequency ratio at this stage is not significantly different between the three groups.

In the 20–40 min, for the interaction term $v * time$ ($\chi^2 = 67.686$, P = 0.001 (<0.05)), the dependent variable does not satisfy the spherical hypothesis, and is corrected using Greenhouse-Geisser correction; v satisfies the spherical hypothesis ($\chi^2 = 3.194$, P = 0.203 (>0.05)); $time$ ($\chi^2 = 19.187$, P = 0.024 (<0.05)) is corrected using Greenhouse-Geisser. The effect test within the subject indicates that the interaction term is not statistically significant (F(4.203, 67.246) = 0.923, P = 0.460 (>0.05)); v has statistically significant effect on blink (F(2, 32) = 9.452, P = 0.001 (<0.05)); $time$ has no statistically significant effect on blinking (F(2.673, 42.776) = 0.214, P = 0.866 (>0.05)). Regarding the results of the pairwise comparison, the difference between the static group and the non-constant speed group is significant (P = 0.03 < 0.05), and the average difference of the blink frequency ratio is −0.430 ± 0.108; There is no significant difference between the static group and the constant speed group (P = 0.074 > 0.05). There is no significant difference between the non-constant speed group and the constant speed group (P = 0.129 > 0.05). That is, the blink ratio of the non-constant speed group is significantly higher than that of the static group, and the difference between the other groups is not statistically significant.

In the 45–55 min, the interaction term $v * time$ satisfies the spherical hypothesis ($\chi^2 = 13.184$, P = 0.157 (>0.05)); v satisfies the spherical hypothesis ($\chi^2 = 2.462$, P = 0.292 (>0.05)); $time$ ($\chi^2 = 10.463$, P = 0.005 (<0.05)) is corrected using Greenhouse-Geisser. The effect test in the subject indicates that the interaction term is not statistically significant (F(4, 64) = 0.115, P = 0.977 (>0.05)); v has statistically significant effect on blink (F(2, 32) = 4.555, P = 0.018 (<0.05)); $time$ has statistically significant effect on blink (F (1.331, 21.302) = 14.081, P < 0.05). Regarding the results of comparing v with each other, the difference between the static group and the non-constant speed group is significant (P = 0.004 < 0.05), and the average difference in the blink frequency ratio is −0.438 ± 1.32. There is no significant difference between the static group and the constant speed group (P = 0.148 > 0.05). There is no significant difference between the non-constant speed group and the constant speed group (P = 0.176 > 0.05). Regarding the results of comparing time with each other, the 45 min' blink frequency ratio with 50 min' blink frequency ratio and it with 55 min' blink frequency ratio are significantly different. The average difference is −0.274 ± 0.061 and −0.152 ± 0.028, respectively. There is no significant difference in the blink frequency ratio between 50 min and 55 min (P = 0.175). That is, at the last stage, the blink frequency ratio of the non-constant speed group is significantly higher than that of the static group, and the difference between the other groups is not statistically significant. And at the 50 min, the blink frequency ratio increases to the top in all groups.

This result shows that the growth trend of the blink frequency ratio in order of high-to-low is non-constant speed group, constant speed group and static group. In 20–40 min and 45–55 min, the difference between the static group and the on-constant speed group is significant. There is no significant difference between the constant speed group with the other two groups. This indicates that the objective visual fatigue of the subjects is the lowest in the static group and higher in the dynamic disparity groups. Among the dynamic disparity groups, the constant speed group had lower visual fatigue than the non-constant speed group. The blinks of the three groups reached their peak in 45–50 min.

5 Discussion

There is a distinction between the subjective and objective measurements. For the objectively measured results, it showed a decrease in performance of the human vision system, which refers to visual fatigue. Whereas the visual discomfort is its subjective counterpart [26]. This experiment's results show that the subjects' visual discomfort reduced in the dynamic disparity condition, especially in the constant speed condition. While the visual fatigue is higher in the dynamic disparity groups, especially in the variable speed condition. Koulieris et al. as well as other work by Konrad et al showed that manipulating disparity alone could not cause a significant change of eye accommodation [27, 28]. That could be the reason that the visual fatigue can't be reduced by dynamic disparity. As for the visual discomfort, maybe there was a delay in the feeling of the subjects, or the mechanism of the two is different.

According to the blink data, the ratio of blinking frequency in the static group and the constant speed group can be divided into three stages: declining (0–15 min), smooth fluctuation (15–45 min) and rising (45–50 min). While the non-constant speed group can be divided into four stages: declining (0–15 min), rising (15–30 min), declining (30–45 min) and rising (45–50 min). And they all started to grow rapidly in 45–50 min until the peak, which dropped in 50–55 min. These phenomena may be due to the fact that the subject had an adaptation process to the scene at the beginning. Since the variable-speed disparity can cause visual fatigue more quickly, the blink frequency started to increase first. As the fatigue of the subject increased, the duration of the blink increased, so the blink frequency decreased a little, but it was still higher than the base value [29]. So, at 40 min of the variable speed group, and 55 min of all three groups, there is a drop. The most notable is that at 50 min, the blink frequency ratio of each group reaches the highest value. The video content was not the end there, and had no difference from the content at other time periods. This shows that there is a significant increase of fatigue in 45–50 min when watching 2D video. The study of Guo also indicated that during the 60 min' task in the VR, the visual fatigue increased severe quickly in the last 20 min [30].

6 Conclusion

This study aimed to explore whether dynamic disparity can alleviate the visual fatigue caused by watching video for long period in head-mounted displays. We designed three sets of controlled trials, in which disparity was used as a control variable. The trials were composed of static group, constant speed group and non-constant speed group. Subjective and objective data were combined to evaluate the visual fatigue.

For the results of the subjective questionnaire, it indicated that the subjects felt lower visual discomfort and motion sickness under dynamic disparity conditions. In the dynamic disparity groups, the constant speed condition made the subjects feel the lowest degree of visual discomfort and motion sickness. For the results of objective measurement, the blink data showed the fatigue changes of subjects who watched 2D video for 55 min on an HMD. It can be seen that the variation tendency of the blink ratio in the static group and the constant speed group is similar, and the blink radio in the constant speed group is higher, but there is no significant difference. There is a significant difference between the non-constant speed group and the static group in the 20–40 min and 45–55 min, and the non-constant speed group has a higher blink ratio. The conclusions reached are inconsistent with the subjective conclusions, it seems that the dynamic disparity condition did not reduce the objective fatigue of the subjects, and in the variable speed group, the visual fatigue increased. According to the analysis of the results, we came to the conclusion that dynamic disparity achieved by the movement of left and right eye images in the HMD can't effectively alleviate visual fatigue.

There are some limitations in the experiment should be pointed out. In the design of the experiment, the order of the three groups was fixed, although the effect of video content on blinking was excluded. The experiment was carried out according to the static group, the non-constant speed group, and the constant speed disparity group. In the measurement of objective data, only the blink frequency was tested. It can be combined with other characteristics such as blink duration to measure the visual fatigue of the subject for the future work. Based on the results, in order to achieve the goal of relieving the visual fatigue of viewing 2D screens for a long time in a virtual reality environment by accommodative training, improvements in helmet hardware are required.

Acknowledgement. The authors would like to thank all the volunteers, and all publications support and staff. This work was supported by the National Key Research and Development Program of China (No. 2018YFB1005002) and the National Natural Science Foundation of China (No. U1605254).

References

1. Kroemer, K.H.E., Grandjean, E.: Fitting the Task to the Human: A Textbook of Occupational Ergonomics, 4th edn. Taylor & Francis/Hemisphere (1989)
2. Yamazaki, T., Kamijyo, K., Fukuzumi, S.: Quantitative evaluation of visual fatigue encountered in viewing stereoscopic 3D display. Proc. Soc. Intell. Des. **31**(1), 245–247 (1990)
3. Takada, M., Miyao, M., Matsuura, Y., Takada, H.: Accommodation training in foreign workers (2013)
4. Simmers, A.J., Gray, L.S., Wilkins, A.J.: The influence of tinted lenses upon ocular accommodation. Vis. Res. **41**(9), 1229–1238 (2001)
5. Tosha, C., Borsting, E., Ridder, W.H., Chase, C.: Accommodation response and visual discomfort. Ophthalmic Physiol. Opt. **29**(6), 625–633 (2010)
6. Sterner, B., Abrahamsson, M., Sjöström, A.: Accommodative facility training with a long term follow up in a sample of school aged children showing accommodative dysfunction. Doc. Ophthalmol. Adv. Ophthalmol. **99**(1), 93–101 (1999)
7. Arsalan Naqvi, S.A., Badruddin, N., Malik, A.S.: Effects of stereoscopic screen disparity on pupil diamete (2013)
8. Schor, C.M.: A dynamic model of cross-coupling between accommodation and convergence: simulations of step and frequency responses. Optom. Vis. Sci. **69**(4), 258–269 (1992)
9. Kramida, G.: Resolving the vergence-accommodation conflict in head-mounted displays. IEEE Trans. Vis. Comput. Graph. **22**(7), 1912–1931 (2016)

10. Sherstyuk, A., State, A.: Dynamic eye convergence for head-mounted displays. In: ACM Symposium on Virtual Reality Software & Technology DBLP, pp. 43–46 (2010)
11. Oskam, T., Hornung, A., Bowles, H., et al.: OSCAM - optimized stereoscopic camera control for interactive 3D. ACM Trans. Graph. **30**(6), 1 (2011)
12. Takeda, T.: Characteristics of accommodation toward apparent depth. Vis. Res. **39**(12), 2087–2097 (1999)
13. Ujike, H., Watanabe, H.: Visual fatigue of viewing stereoscopic display with different ranges of binocular disparity. I-Perception **5**(4), 381 (2014)
14. Kuze, J., Ukai, K.: Subjective evaluation of visual fatigue caused by motion images. Displays **29**(2), 159–166 (2008)
15. Iatsun, I., Larabi, M.C., Fernandezmaloigne, C.: Study of visual fatigue/discomfort generated by S3D video using eye-tracking data. In: IS&T/SPIE International Symposium on Electronic Imaging (2013)
16. Haraclick, R.M.: Texture features for image classification. IEEE Trans. SMC **3**(6), 610–621 (1973)
17. Ulaby, F.T., et al.: Textural infornation in SAR images. IEEE Trans. Geosci. Remote Sens. **24**(2), 235–245 (1986)
18. Fisher, R.A.S., Bennett, J.H.: Statistical Methods, Experimental Design and Scientific Inference. Oxford University Press, Oxford (1990)
19. Munafo, J., Diedrick, M., Stoffregen, T.A.: The virtual reality head-mounted display Oculus Rift induces motion sickness and is sexist in its effects. Exp. Brain Res. **235**(3), 889–901 (2017)
20. Kennedy, R.S., Lane, N.E., Berbaum, K.S., et al.: Simulator sickness questionnaire: an enhanced method for quantifying simulator sickness. Int. J. Aviat. Psychol. **3**(3), 203–220 (1993)
21. Yang, F., Yu, X., Huang, J., et al.: Robust eyelid tracking for fatigue detection. In: IEEE International Conference on Image Processing (2013)
22. Ya-yuan, T.: A fatigue testing method based on machine vision. In: Tan, T., Ruan, Q., Chen, X., Ma, H., Wang, L. (eds.) IGTA 2013. CCIS, vol. 363, pp. 72–77. Springer, Heidelberg (2013). https://doi.org/10.1007/978-3-642-37149-3_9
23. Luckiesh, M., Moss, F.K.: The eyelid reflex as a criterion of ocular fatigue. J. Exp. Psychol. **20**(6), 589–596 (1937)
24. Yamada, F.: Frontal midline theta rhythm and eye blinking activity during a VDT task and a video game: useful tools for psychophysiology in ergonomics. Ergonomics **41**(5), 678–688 (1998)
25. Kim, D., Choi, S., Park, S., et al.: Stereoscopic visual fatigue measurement based on fusional response curve and eye-blinks. In: International Conference on Digital Signal Processing (2011)
26. Lambooij, M., Ijsselsteijn, W., Fortuin, M., et al.: Visual discomfort and visual fatigue of stereoscopic displays: a review. J. Imaging Sci. Technol. **53**(3) (2009)
27. George, D., et al.: Accommodation and comfort in head-mounted displays. ACM Trans. Graph. **36**(4), 87 (2017)
28. Konrad, R., Padmanaban, N., Molner, K., et al.: Accommodation-invariant computational near-eye displays. ACM Trans. Graph. **36**(4), 1–12 (2017)
29. Ji, Q., Yang, X.: Real-time eye, gaze, and face pose tracking for monitoring driver vigilance. Real-Time Imaging **8**(5), 357–377 (2002)
30. Jie, G., Dongdong, W., et al.: Subjective and objective evaluation of visual fatigue caused by continuous and discontinuous use of HMDs. J. Soc. Inf. Display **27**, 108–119 (2018)

Detection of Small Moving Targets in Videos Using Skew Normal Mixture Model

Yuhui Shao and Fang Dai[✉]

School of Science, Xi'an University of Technology, Xi'an 710054, China
daifang@xaut.edu.cn

Abstract. Background modeling method is one of the most commonly methods for target detection. Gaussian mixture model (GMM) is a widely used background modeling method which can get good performance in video of surveillance scenes. However, when the GMM is directly applied to the detection of small moving targets, it may cause problems such as incomplete and missing detection of the target contour. Therefore, we propose a new background modeling method by using skew normal mixture model (SNMM). A skew normal mixture model is established at each pixel position in frames of video. After updating the frames of video, the parameters of the background model SNMM are updated, and the detection of small moving target is performed. Experimental results show that the SNMM can obtain better contour of the small moving targets in videos than the GMM.

Keywords: Small moving target detection · Gaussian mixture model · Skew normal mixture model

1 Introduction

Moving target detection, a hot topic in computer vision, is widely applied in traffic monitoring, vehicle navigation, industrial detection and intelligent security etc. In terms of moving target detection, three methods are commonly used, they are optical flow method, frame difference method and background modeling method. The optical flow method [1] is capable of detecting the target of independent motion and estimating its motion speed, but its calculation is complex and sensitive to changes in illumination conditions. The frame difference method [2] is simple and easy to implement, which has good robustness to dynamic scenes. However, when the moving target moves slowly, it will appear 'empty holes' in detection result. The background modeling method is simple and robustness to the background variations, which is commonly employed to detect the moving target.

The detection of small moving target in videos is very difficult, and the state-of-the-art algorithms of small moving target detection are mostly aimed at small moving targets in aerial video and weak targets in infrared images. In [3], the improved Oriented FAST and Rotated BRIEF (ORB) feature matching algorithm is proposed to obtain a precise background motion model, and then the continuous four-frame image differential multiplication and morphological processing are used to accurately segment the small moving targets in the aerial video. The method has good real-time

© Springer Nature Singapore Pte Ltd. 2019
Y. Wang et al. (Eds.): IGTA 2019, CCIS 1043, pp. 322–330, 2019.
https://doi.org/10.1007/978-981-13-9917-6_31

performance, but the detection results depend on the accuracy of the results of ORB feature matching. In [4], after the motion compensated image is obtained by image motion background modeling, the adaptive segmentation threshold is used to binarize the difference image to detect the slow dim target. The algorithm avoids the noise and compensation error to be segmented into moving targets through adaptive threshold correction, but the detection result depends on the accuracy of the motion compensation image. In [5], by extracting the sparse features of the infrared image, the original image is restored to the background image and the target image using the adaptive weighted parameter inexact augmented Lagrangian multiplier method, and then the target image is segmented by a threshold to obtain the infrared weak target. The algorithm has a high false alarm rate for complex background situations. In [6], a global saliency model is constructed to extract the visual salient regions which contain dim and small targets and then detected dim and small targets by their temporal relativity in multi-frames. When the background is too complicated, the algorithm can't get a good detection result.

Small moving targets make up a small portion of the total area of the image and contain a small number of pixels. It is difficult to extract the edge, color feature and other features of small moving targets accurately. So we use pixel-based background modeling method to detect the small moving targets under surveillance videos. The detection results of the GMM [7] for small moving targets is not ideal, such as the contour of the small target is not complete enough and sometimes it may be lost. Therefore, we propose a new background model using a skew normal mixture distribution (SNMM). Our proposed method has better adaptability to the external dynamic environment, has certain robustness to the shadow, the detected target contour is more complete and has higher performance for detection of small moving targets.

The rest of the paper is organized as follows. In Sect. 2, we introduce the skew normal mixture model and give a parameter update method using the ECME algorithm. In Sect. 3, we present two matching rules and give a new parameter update method. In Sect. 4, the videos of different scenes are selected to test the effectiveness of SNMM. In Sect. 5, the conclusions are presented.

2 Skew Normal Mixture Model and Its Parameter Estimation

2.1 Skew Normal Mixture Model

Azzalini first proposed a skew normal distribution [8] in 1985. A random variable Y follows a skew normal distribution with location parameter ξ, scale parameter σ^2 and skewness parameter λ, if its density function is given by

$$\psi(y|\xi, \sigma^2, \lambda) = \frac{2}{\sigma} \phi(\frac{y - \xi}{\sigma}) \Phi(\lambda \frac{y - \xi}{\sigma}), \tag{1}$$

where $\phi(\cdot)$ is the density function of the standard normal distribution and $\Phi(\cdot)$ is the cumulative distribution function of the standard normal distribution. We called that $Y \sim SN(\xi, \sigma^2, \lambda)$.

At any time t, the historical gray values about a pixel at position (x, y) is

$$\{X_1, X_2 \ldots X_t\} = \{I(x, y, i) : 1 \le i \le t\}, \tag{2}$$

where I denotes the image sequence. The historical gray value of each pixel is modeled by some weighted skew normal distribution [9], that is

$$P(X_t) = \sum_{k=1}^{g} \omega_{k,t} \, \psi(X_t | \xi_{k,t}, \sigma_{k,t}^2, \lambda_{k,t}), \tag{3}$$

where g is the number of skew normal distributions, $\omega_{k,t}$, $\xi_{k,t}$, $\sigma_{k,t}^2$, and $\lambda_{k,t}$ are the weights, location parameters, scale parameters, and skewness parameters of the kth skew normal distribution of the pixel at time t. $\psi(X_t | \xi_{k,t}, \sigma_{k,t}^2, \lambda_{k,t})$ is the probability density function of the kth skew normal distribution of the pixel at time t. Equation (3) is called the skew normal mixture model (SNMM).

2.2   Parameter Estimation for SNMM via ECME Algorithm

Assuming that the first t frames are used as the observation sequence, that is, the historical gray value at each pixel at time t is known which is $\{X_1, X_2 \ldots X_t\}$. We obtain the location parameters, scale parameters, and skewness parameters by implementing an ECME algorithm [10] at each pixel at time t.

Given an initial value $\theta = (\omega_{k,t}, \xi_{k,t}, \sigma_{k,t}^2, \lambda_{k,t}), k = 1, \ldots g$, and some calculation formulas which are as follows.

$$\delta_k = \lambda_{k,t} / \sqrt{1 + \lambda_{k,t}^2}, \quad \Gamma_k = (1 - \delta_k^2) \sigma_{k,t}^2, \quad \Delta_k = \sigma_{k,t} \delta_k,$$

$$z_{ik} = \frac{\omega_{k,t} \psi(X_i | \xi_{k,t}, \sigma_{k,t}^2, \lambda_{k,t})}{\sum_{k=1}^{g} \omega_{k,t} \psi(X_i | \xi_{k,t}, \sigma_{k,t}^2, \lambda_{k,t})},$$

$$s_{1ik} = z_{ik} (\xi_{T_{ik}} + \mathrm{M}_{T_k} \tau_{1ik}), \quad s_{2ik} = z_{ik} (\xi_{T_{ik}}^2 + \mathrm{M}_{T_k}^2 + \mathrm{M}_{T_k} \xi_{T_{ik}} \tau_{1ik}), \tag{4}$$

$$\mathrm{M}_{T_k} = \sqrt{\frac{\Gamma_k}{\Gamma_k + \Delta_k^2}}, \quad \tau_{1ik} = \frac{\phi\left(\dfrac{\xi_{T_{ik}}}{\mathrm{M}_{T_k}}\right)}{\Phi\left(\dfrac{\xi_{T_{ik}}}{\mathrm{M}_{T_k}}\right)}, \quad \xi_{T_{ik}} = \frac{\Delta_k}{\Gamma_k + \Delta_k^2} (X_i - \xi_{k,t}).$$

The ECME algorithm is as follows.

E-step: compute z_{ik}, s_{1ik}, s_{2ik}, for $i = 1, \ldots t$ and $k = 1, \ldots g$.

CM-step:

$$\omega_{k,t} = t^{-1} \sum_{i=1}^{t} z_{ik}, \tag{5}$$

$$\xi_{k,t} = \sum_{i=1}^{t} (z_{ik}X_i - \Delta_k s_{1ik}) / \sum_{i=1}^{t} z_{ik}, \tag{6}$$

$$\Delta_k = \sum_{i=1}^{t} (X_i - \xi_{k,t}) s_{1ik} / \sum_{i=1}^{t} s_{2ik}, \tag{7}$$

$$\Gamma_k = \sum_{i=1}^{t} \left(z_{ik}(X_i - \xi_{k,t})^2 - 2(X_i - \xi_{k,t})\Delta_k s_{1ik} + \Delta_k^2 s_{2ik} \right) / \sum_{i=1}^{t} z_{ik}, \tag{8}$$

$$\sigma_{k,t}^2 = \Delta_k^2 + \Gamma_k, \tag{9}$$

$$\lambda_{k,t} = \Delta_k / \sqrt{\Gamma_k}, \tag{10}$$

repeat this process until a suitable convergence rule is satisfied.

3 SNMM for Detecting Small Moving Targets

3.1 Background Model Estimation

It is considered that not every skew normal distribution can be properly represented as a part of background, so it is necessary to exclude the skew normal distribution that may belongs to the foreground target. Perform a sort on the values of $\omega_{k,t}/\sigma_{k,t}$ for skew normal distributions at each pixel at time t, and we select the first B skew normal distributions to represent the background,

$$B = \arg\min_b (\sum_{k=1}^{b} \omega_{k,t} > T), \tag{11}$$

where T is a threshold which is set to 0.7.

3.2 Small Moving Target Detection

The pixel value of the image at time $t+1$ is represented by X_{t+1}, and the pixel value X_{t+1} is matched with the B background distributions at the corresponding pixel positions. The pixel is regarded as the background when the matching is successful, otherwise it is regarded as the foreground. We have given two matching rules.

Matching rule 1: Let

$$F(u_\alpha) = \int_{-\infty}^{u_\alpha} \frac{2}{\sigma} \phi\left(\frac{X_{t+1} - \xi}{\sigma}\right) \Phi\left(\lambda \frac{X_{t+1} - \xi}{\sigma}\right) dX_{t+1} = \alpha, \tag{12}$$

if

$$u_{0.003} < X_{t+1} < u_{0.997},\tag{13}$$

then the match is considered successful, otherwise the match is considered to have failed.

Matching rule 2: According to the property of the skew normal distribution: ① As $\lambda=0$, the $SN(\xi,\sigma^2,\lambda)$ density reduces to the density of $N(\xi,\sigma^2)$. ② As $\lambda \to \infty$, the $SN(\xi,\sigma^2,\lambda)$ density tends to the half-normal density. We have rule 2

$$\left|X_{t+1} - \xi_{k,t}\right| < D \cdot \sigma_{k,t},\tag{14}$$

where D is set to 3.

Selecting the 'viptraffic' video to compare the detection results of the two matching rules. The detection results are shown in Fig. 1 and the single frame detection time are shown in Table 1. Considering that the detection results of the two matching rules in Fig. 1 are close and the average single frame processing time is high when the matching rule 1 is used, we keep the matching rule 2 as the matching rule of SNMM in this paper.

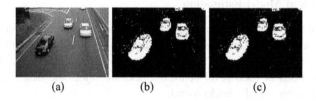

| (a) | (b) | (c) |

Fig. 1. Detection results of video 'viptraffic' (a) the video frame; (b) the detection result when the matching rule 1 is used; (c) the detection result when the matching rule 2 is used.

Table 1. Single frame detection time.

Matching rule	Matching rule 1	Matching rule 2
Single frame detection time	70s	2s

3.3   Background Model Update

It will cost too much time to implement an exact ECME algorithm for every pixel of a new frame. We propose a new parameter update method to reduce the calculation time. If the formula (14) is satisfied, the current pixel X_{t+1} is matched with one of the g skew normal distribution, then $M_{k,t}$ is set to 1 for matched distribution, otherwise, it's set to 0. The weights $\omega_{k,t+1}$ of skew normal distributions at time $t+1$ are updated by the following formula

$$\omega_{k,t+1} = (1 - \alpha)\omega_{k,t} + \alpha M_{k,t}, \tag{15}$$

where α is the learning rate which is set 0.01.

The location parameters ξ, scale parameters σ, and skewness parameters λ remain same for unmatched skew normal distributions. The location parameters ξ, scale parameters σ, and skewness parameters λ for matched skew normal distribution are updated according to the recursive parameter estimation method [11]. Let $\tilde{\theta} = \{\xi, \sigma^2, \lambda\}$, the parameter update formula is as follows.

$$\tilde{\theta}_{t+1} = \tilde{\theta}_t + \{(t+1)I_c(\tilde{\theta}_t)\}^{-1}s(X_{t+1}, \tilde{\theta}_t), t = 0, 1, \ldots, \tag{16}$$

where

$$I_c(\tilde{\theta}_t) = \begin{pmatrix} (1 + \lambda^2 a_0)/\sigma^2 & \left(E(Z)\frac{1+2\lambda^2}{1+\lambda^2} + \lambda^2 a_1\right)/\sigma^2 & \left(\frac{b}{(1+\lambda^2)^{\frac{3}{2}}}\right)/\sigma \\ \left(E(Z)\frac{1+2\lambda^2}{1+\lambda^2} + \lambda^2 a_1\right)/\sigma^2 & (2 + \lambda^2 a_2)/\sigma^2 & -\lambda a_2/\sigma^2 \\ \left(\frac{b}{(1+\lambda^2)^{\frac{3}{2}}}\right)/\sigma^2 & -\lambda a_2/\sigma^2 & a_2 \end{pmatrix},$$

$$Z = (X_{t+1} - \xi)/\sigma, \ b = \sqrt{2/\pi}, \ \delta = \lambda/\sqrt{1+\lambda^2}, \ E(Z) = b\delta,$$

$$\text{var}(Z) = 1 - (b\delta)^2, \ a_k = a_k(\lambda) = E\left\{Z^k\left(\frac{\varphi(\lambda Z)}{\Phi(\lambda Z)}\right)^2\right\} \quad (k = 0, 1, 2),$$

$$s(X_{t+1}, \tilde{\theta}_t) = (s_\xi, s_\sigma, s_\lambda)^T, \ T = \varphi(\lambda Z)/\Phi(\lambda Z),$$

$$s_\xi = \frac{Z}{\sigma} - \frac{\lambda}{\sigma}T, \ s_\sigma = -\frac{1}{\sigma} + \frac{Z^2}{\sigma} - \frac{\lambda Z}{\sigma}T, \ s_\lambda = \frac{Z}{\sigma}T,$$

the a_k is evaluated numerically.

If the number of matched skew normal distributions is zero, a new skew normal distribution is established to replace the least weight skew normal distribution. For the new skew normal distribution, the location parameter is the current pixel value, the scale parameter is an initial high value, the skewness parameter is a constant close to zero and the weight is a low value.

4 Experimental Results

The experimental environment of this paper is: windows 7 operating system, eight core Inter Core i7-4790 CPU @ 3.60 GHz and 8 GB of RAM, and MATLAB R2014a. During the execution of the algorithm, the value of $t+1$ in Eq. (16) is set to a constant of 200, and the value of a_k is approximated by $Z^k(\phi(\lambda Z)/\Phi(\lambda Z))^2$.

We use the indoor video 'camouflage', the outdoor video 'fountain' and the traffic scene video 'bank' to test the effectiveness of SNMM. The first two videos both contain the change background, but the initial frame does not contain the moving target. The

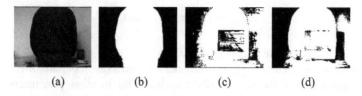

(a)   (b)   (c)   (d)

Fig. 2. Detection results of 'camouflage'. (a) the video frame; (b) the Ground truth; (c) the target detection result of GMM; (d) the target detection result of SNMM.

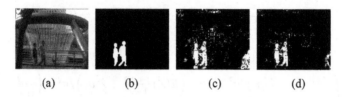

(a)   (b)   (c)   (d)

Fig. 3. Detection results of 'fountain'. (a) the video frame; (b) the Ground truth; (c) the target detection result of GMM; (d) the target detection result of SNMM.

Table 2. Quantitative evaluation results of 'camouflage'

Algorithm	Prec	Rec	F_1	Sim	MCC	PCC
GMM	0.901	0.729	0.806	0.675	0.520	76.030
SNMM	0.830	0.974	0.896	0.812	0.756	87.508

Table 3. Quantitative evaluation results of 'fountain'

Algorithm	Prec	Rec	F_1	Sim	MCC	PCC
GMM	0.869	0.456	0.599	0.427	0.614	96.168
SNMM	0.814	0.704	0.755	0.607	0.749	98.453

third video's background stays the same, but it include moving target in the initial frame. The first two videos are used to show the performance of the SNMM against background noise. The third video is used to show the performance for detecting small moving targets.

We compare SNMM with GMM, and the precision, recall, F1 parameter, similarity (Sim), Matthew correlation coefficient (MCC), correct classification percentage (PCC) are used as metrics [12] to evaluation algorithm performance.

For the 'camouflage' and 'fountain' videos, the detection results are shown in Figs. 2 and 3, and the quality evaluation results are shown in Tables 2 and 3. By comparing the detection results in Figs. 2 and 3, we find that the SNMM is less affected by noise. The recall, F1, similarity, MCC, and PCC values of SNMM are higher than GMM and the precision value of GMM is higher.

For the traffic scene video 'bank', the detection results are shown in Fig. 4, and the quality evaluation results are shown in Table 4. In Fig. 4, for the 75th frame, by comparing the results of the columns (c) and (d), it can be seen that the overall contour of the pedestrian detected in the column (d) is more complete (as indicated by the red box marks). For the 500th frame and the 1100th frame, some stationary vehicles in the "bank" video start to move, and the small target detection results in columns (c) basically do not see the actual vehicle shape (such as the red frame marks), in contrast, the results in column (d) are more in line with the real vehicle shape. In the 1100th frame, the vehicle detection results are less affected by shadows (as indicated by the green box marks). The precision, recall, F1, similarity, MCC, and PCC value of SNMM are all better than GMM.

In the traditional GMM, it is assumed that the historical gray value of the pixel at a specific pixel position in the image sequence obeys the Gaussian distribution. However, in the actual monitoring video, the pixel value sequence is not always obey Gaussian distribution, and there is a certain deviation. Therefore, using a skew distribution can better describe the variation of the pixel and obtain better target detection results.

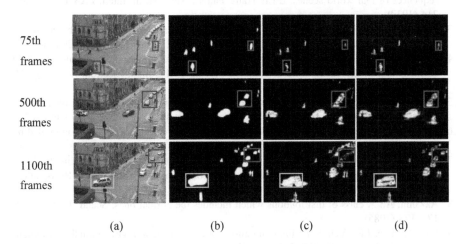

75th frames

500th frames

1100th frames

(a)   (b)   (c)   (d)

Fig. 4. Detection results of 'bank'. (a) the video frames; (b) the Ground truths; (c) the detection results of GMM; (d) the detection results of SNMM. (Color figure online)

Table 4. Quantitative evaluation results of 'bank'

Algorithm	Prec	Rec	F_1	Sim	MCC	PCC
GMM	0.792	0.635	0.680	0.528	0.690	98.781
SNMM	0.821	0.657	0.729	0.575	0.729	99.102

5   Conclusion

A new background modeling method is proposed for small moving target detection in videos. For each pixel, a skew normal mixture model is established to detect small moving targets in the video. The proposed method overcomes the problems of incomplete and missing target contour in detection results of GMM. Compared with the GMM, the proposed method is robust to background dynamics, and the detection results are more complete and accurate for small moving targets in video.

Acknowledgments. This paper has been partly supported by Xi'an science and technology planning project (No. 201805037YD15CG21(7)), China.

References

1. Barron, J.L., Fleet, D.J., Beauchemin, S.S.: Performance of optical flow techniques. Int. J. Comput. Vis. **12**, 43–77 (1994)
2. Jain, R., Nagel, H.H.: On the analysis of accumulative difference pictures from image sequences of real world scenes. IEEE Trans. Pattern Anal. Mach. Intell. **PAMI-1**(2), 206–214 (1979)
3. Liu, W., Zhao, W., Li, C., Xu, Z., Tian, K.: Detecting small moving target based on the improved ORB feature matching. Opto-Electron. Eng. **42**, 13–20 (2015). (in Chinese)
4. Yan, J., Duan, H., Xu, Q., Yang, Y.: Slow dim target detection based on adaptive threshold segmentation in the background of complex moving background. Electron. Des. Eng. **24**, 77–80 (2016). (in Chinese)
5. Xiong, B., Huang, X., Wang, M.: Infrared dim small target detection based on adaptive target image recovery. J. Huazhong Univ. Sci. Technol. **45**, 25–30 (2017). (in Chinese)
6. Yi, X., Wang, B., Zhou, H., Qin, H.: Dim and small infrared target fast detection guided by visual saliency. Infrared Phys. Technol. **97**, 6–14 (2019)
7. Stauffer, C., Grimson, W.E.L.: Adaptive background mixture models for real-time tracking. In: 1999 IEEE Computer Society Conference on Computer Vision and Pattern Recognition, Fort Collins, USA, pp. 246–252 (1999)
8. Azzalini, A.: A class of distributions which includes the normal ones. Scand. J. Statist. **12**, 171–178 (1985)
9. Lin, T.I., Lee, J.C., Yen, S.Y.: Finite mixture modelling using the skew normal distribution. Statistica Sinica **17**, 909–927 (2007)
10. Basso, R.M., Lachos, V.H., Cabral, C.R.B., Ghosh, P.: Robust mixture modeling based on scale mixtures of skew normal distributions. J. Comput. Statist. Data Anal. **54**, 2926–2941 (2010)
11. Titterington, D.M.: Recursive parameter estimation using incomplete data. J. Roy. Statist. Soc. **46**, 257–267 (1984)
12. Panda, D.K., Meher, S.: Adaptive spatio-temporal background subtraction using improved wronskian change detection scheme in gaussian mixture model framework. J. IET Image Process. **12**, 1832–1843 (2018)

Spectral Pooling Based CNN Model Compression for Light Field Depth-Estimation

Xuanyu Zhang[1], Guosheng Yang[2], and Jing Jiang[3(✉)]

[1] Beijing University of Posts and Telecommunications, Beijing, China
Xuanyu_Zhang@bupt.edu.cn
[2] Beijing Aeronautical Technology Research Centre, Beijing, China
[3] Beijing Union University, Beijing, China
xxtjiangjing@buu.edu.cn

Abstract. In the design of the traditional CNN model, there is always a balance between the spatial dimension and the number of channels. The high-dimensional spatial resolution is to preserve more detailed local information, while the large number of channels ensures more complex feature representation. For the current Light-field depth estimation algorithm, the designers usually choose to maintain a high spatial dimension in the network to improve the accuracy of the depth estimation, which results in a situation where the model has a large size and will take up huge amount of computing resources in the depth estimation process. In this paper, we introduce an effective pooling method: spectral pooling, to improve the problems of the original Light-field depth estimation network mentioned above. We transfer the light field feature map to the frequency domain through Fourier transform and reasonably reduce the size of the feature map in the frequency domain to an arbitrary size. The method can be used to reduce the complexity of the network and speed up training with similar performance to the original algorithm. More importantly, the new model with less memory demand can be better applied to light mobile device.

Keywords: Spectral pooling · Light-field · Depth-estimation · Network scale · Memory demand

1 Introduction

The light field camera realizes the function of digital focusing through the structure of the lens, the microlens array and the image sensor. Images with different depth positions can be calculated with one exposure [9], thereby completing various purposes such as three-dimensional depth estimation and panoramic deep image synthesis. There have been many methods proposed to estimate the three-dimensional depth information. We find a similarity of most neural networks for light field depth estimation:

This work is partially supported by the Fundamental Research Funds for the Central Universities (2018RC54), and partially by the Fundamental Research Funds for the New Start Plan Project of Beijing Union University (Zk10201604).

© Springer Nature Singapore Pte Ltd. 2019
Y. Wang et al. (Eds.): IGTA 2019, CCIS 1043, pp. 331–342, 2019.
https://doi.org/10.1007/978-981-13-9917-6_32

a large number of convolution layers are stacked in the network to extract effective image features, which always comes along with the heavy complexity of the network calculation, slow convergence rate and a large memory demand during depth estimation, etc. therefore, it is considered to use pooling layer in appropriate position of the network, which can reduce the calculation cost and increase the acceptance domain of the intermediate node and the output node. By using appropriate pooling methods, we can streamline the model's size and reduce its computational complexity at runtime, so that it can be better applied to mobile devices.

At present, the conventional pooling methods include maximum pooling, averaging pooling, etc., but the above methods use the maximum value or average value of each window as the result of the pooling mapping which can only reflect very local and unrepresentative information. In addition, the above-mentioned pooling reduction factor is usually fixed. This kind of uncontrollable reduction factor often leads to a problem that the image dimension is cut too fast, resulting in serious loss of effective information. In order to avoid the above problems, we adopt the method of spectral pooling, which utilizes the uneven distribution of information in the frequency domain to retain more representative information and reduce the approximation loss. In addition, the spectral pooling allows us to specify any size as the dimension of output dimension, which makes it possible to reduce the size of feature map in a slow and controllable way depending on the actual situation of the network, and reduce the loss of valid information.

The spectral pooling transforms the output feature map of the upper layer into the frequency domain by Fast Fourier transform (FFT), and determines the upper and lower limits of the truncation frequency in the frequency domain by manually setting the required reduction coefficient gamma (0 to 1). The frequency domain matrix performs the truncation of the high frequency part, thereby achieving the purpose of pooling dimensionality reduction. It exploits the non-uniformity of the spectral density of the data with respect to frequency. That is, the power spectra of inputs with spatial structure, such as natural images, carry most of their mass on lower frequencies. Therefore, filter higher frequencies in the spectral pool will not only cause great damage to the input information, but can even be regarded as a kind of denoising. Through experimental detection, the convolutional neural network using spectral pooling is significantly better than the Max-pooling convolutional neural network in terms of information preservation.

With the result of our experiments, we can draw a conclusion that we can make good use of the spectral pooling for dimensionality reduction due to light-field images' characteristics of uneven distribution in the frequency domain. Therefore, in this paper, we introduce some spectral pooling layers to the original neural network of depth estimation, use FFT transform and the truncation in frequency domain to reduce the network complexity and maintain the accuracy of the depth estimation based on the retained useful information of light field.

2   Related Work

The spectral pooling was first proposed by Rippel et al. [1], which has obvious advantages in speeding up network convergence and reducing the loss of useful information. In practice, the DFTs are the computational bottlenecks of spectral pooling. However, we note that in convolutional neural networks that employ FFTs for convolution computation, spectral pooling can be implemented at a negligible additional computational cost, since the DFT is performed regardless. So, it's suitable to apply spectral pooling in CNN. In fact, many scholars have tried to simplify their CNN models by applying the spectral pooling method to achieve the purpose of speeding up the convergence rate and improving network performance. For example, Khan et al. proposed to use "Spectral Dropout" [2] to accelerate the convergence rate of deep convolutional neural networks; Wang proposed using "CS unit" [3] to speed up network convergence and reduce complexity.

On the other hand, in terms of traditional algorithm of obtaining 3D depth information, the most representative method is to use epipolar plane images (EPIs), which are angled and spatially oriented by two-dimensional slices. Composition [4, 5]. EPI consists of straight lines with different slopes, so its inherent dimension is much lower than the original dimension, which makes image processing and optimization of depth estimation easier. For example, Wang et al. [10] explained each epipolar plane image patch with a dictionary composed of a small number of atoms with known disparity values. Wanner and Goldluecke [6] use structured tensors to calculate the slope in EPIs, and use the fast total variation denoising filter to refine the initial. Parallax map. Zhang et al. [7] also used EPIs to find matching lines and proposed a rotating parallelogram operator to eliminate the influence of occlusion on depth estimation. Heber et al. [11] presents a novel deep regression u-shaped network to extract geometric information from Light Field (LF) data with an encoding and a decoding part.

These traditional optimization methods have inevitable trade-offs between computation time and performance. In order to balance speed and performance on the basis of traditional methods, Shin et al. [8] adopted a continuous convolutional CNN, which achieved good results in terms of speed and performance. Anisimov et al. [12] utilized result of Semi-Global Matching (SGM), which achieved a reduction of computations when finding the best depth match. There is a large number of convolution layers are stacked in these neural networks to extract more effective image features. However, though some authors use the correlation of the light field features between different perspectives to reduce the number of images required for the calculation, the overall calculation is still very heavy and it takes long for the network to reach convergence when training. The memory requirements of the machine are also high during depth-estimation, which is a certain challenge for lightweight mobile device. Based on the above principles, this paper combines the relevant principles of spectral pooling, optimizes at the level of network structure, reduces the amount of computation and memory demand when model is running.

3 Specific Method

3.1 Discrete Fast Fourier Transform

Since the Fourier transform has an interesting property,

$$f(M) \otimes f(N) = F(M) \times F(N) \tag{1}$$

it is often used as an advantageous way to simplify convolution operations. When we are going to filter an M by N image with an M by N frequency response, the complexity is $O((MN)^2)$ in the spatial domain but $O(MN)$ in the frequency domain once the Fourier transform is performed. In order to reduce the time spent in the Fourier transform and inverse transform, the classical FFT algorithm has been widely used in the decades since it was proposed [13]. Through the FFT algorithm, we can further reduce the above complexity to $O(MN \log MN)$.

The formula of the discrete fast Fourier transform can be expressed as Eq. 2.

$$F\{f(x)\} = \frac{1}{N} \sum_{x=0}^{N-1} f(x) W_N^{ux} \tag{2}$$

$$F^{-1}\{F(u)\} = \sum_{u=0}^{N-1} F(u) W_N^{-ux}$$

where N means the number of samples in f(x) and W_N is $e^{-j\frac{2\pi}{N}}$.

For the two-dimensional discrete fast Fourier transform algorithm which is wildly used in CNN, we can express it as Eq. 3,

$$F(u, v) = \frac{1}{MN} \sum_{x=0}^{N-1} \sum_{y=0}^{N-1} f(x, y) e^{-j2\pi(ux + vy)} \tag{3}$$

where M, N mean the number of samples in 2 dimensions of $f(x, y)$.

3.2 Spectral-Pooling

The idea of spectral pooling is based on the law of uneven distribution of images in the frequency domain. The unimportant components of the image are truncated in the frequency domain. The specific implementation principle is as follows: We assume that the input of the spectral pooling layer in the network is which should be pooled to the size $H \times W$. First, we transform the input X into the frequency domain $F(X)$ by FFT, and determine the distribution of the main information according to the frequency domain distribution characteristics of the image. Then we set the upper f_{up} and lower f_{down} limits of the cutoff size in the frequency domain, the truncation frequency f_{mask} can be randomly selected from the range (f_{down}, f_{up}). After that, a masking matrix is created, which has the same szie as the output $H \times W$. All the values over f_{mask} will be set zero, and the others will be set 1. On the other hand, we will construct and splice the original image matrix in the frequency domain to satisfy the need of size. And the main information to be retained will be extracted from the original matrix Orignal($0 \sim$ f) by multiplying the mask matrix and the original matrix in frequency domain. This can ensure that the dimension of the middle layer feature map is reduced after *iFFT* under the premise of satisfying the main information retain. The algorithm is summarized in Fig. 1.

Through spectral pooling, we can artificially control pooling size and avoid the loss of information caused by excessively fast dimension reduction. In addition, the spectral pooling can effectively filter out the information redundancy among adjacent pixels before pooling and extract the most useful information in the image, which can ensure that the extracted information is more representative.

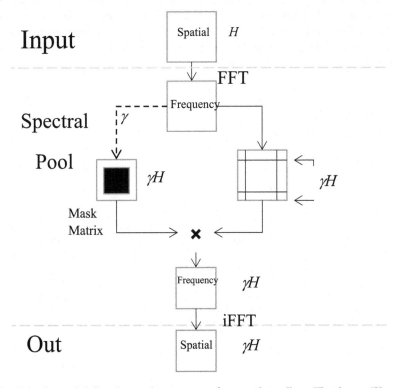

Fig. 1. This figure briefly shows the process of spectral pooling. The input ($H \times H$) is transformed from the spatial domain to the frequency domain by Fourier transform. In the frequency domain, we will create a masking matrix ($\gamma H \times \gamma H$) based on the masking frequency, where γ represents the size reduction rate we want to achieve, the black portion represents the reserved frequency range ($0 \sim$ masking frequency) and will be set 1, while the white part will be set 0 and be discarded. Then the masking matri will multiply with the adjusted input martix to achieve size reduction. We can change the parameter (gamma) arbitrarily to achieve different reduction purposes. At the end, the inverse Fourier transform is used to return spatial domain.

3.3 Network Design

The network structure is shown in Fig. 2. Based on Shin's EPI-net [8], the light field dataset is sliced in four directions: horizontal, vertical, left and right diagonals, and the multi-stream network is constructed for four viewpoints with a consistent baseline. Similar to the traditional optical flow estimation and stereo matching methods [15], we encode each image stack at the beginning of the network. Then carry out the multi-stream part which consists of three blocks. After the multi-stream part, we use the stacked layer to connect all the features of different streams. The relationship between the features passed through the multi-stream network is then gathered through the merged network which consists of eight blocks. The types of blocks in the network mainly include CON and CON_SP. The only difference between them is that CON_SP has a spectral pooling layer after the first convolution operation. The convolutional layers in the network all use a small 2×2 kernel with stride 1 to measure small disparity values (± 4) pixels. At the same time, in order to ensure the accuracy of the depth estimation, we also use the data augmentation method before training, we rotate the original light-field data set and other operations, and use the patch-wise method to further expand the data set (Figs. 3 and 4).

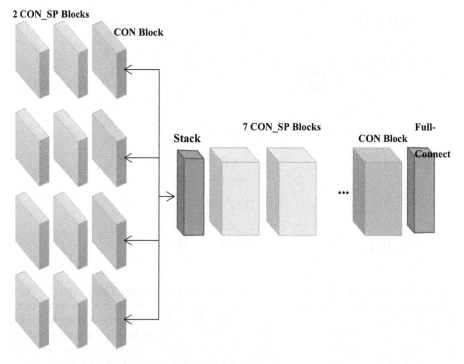

Fig. 2. Network structure

Fig. 3. CON Block's Structure, where CON_2D represents a 2-dimensional convolution layer, BN represents batch normalazation layer, RELu is used for delinearization.

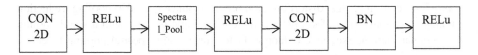

Fig. 4. CON_SP Block's Structure. The only difference from CON block is the spectral pooling layer with RELu added after the first convolution operation.

4   Simulation Results

4.1   Spectral Pooling in Information Preservation Aspects

In order to better illustrate the advantages of spectral pooling in terms of information preservation, we designed the following experiments to compare the information loss of the light-field image after pooling process. In the first experiment, the max-pooling was used as a comparison on the basis of the same number of parameters. And the results are showed in Fig. 5. It can be seen from the comparison that, after spectral pooling, the information retained by the image is more representative. We can draw a important conclusion that spectral-pooling has an advantage for information preservation under the same pooling reduction rate.

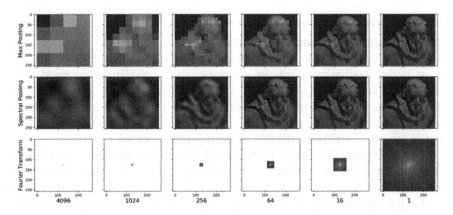

Fig. 5. Experiment one: comparison between spectral-pooling and max-pooling

In Experiment 2, compared with the fixed reduction rate of other pooling methods, we manually set a series of spectral pooling coefficients to resize the feature map to any arbitrary size that we want. The experimental results are shown in Fig. 6.

From Experiment 2, we can demonstrate the advantages of spectral pooling in avoiding excessive dimensionality reduction. these advantages can be well applied to complex deep neural networks, such as light field depth estimation networks. We can determine the appropriate pooling coefficient by analyzing the specific situation at different network. For example, we can reduce the pooling factor or don't use the pooling layer to avoid information loss where the feature extraction is important, and increase the pool size appropriately in other places to reduce more dimension. There is a problem that the edge distortion is more pronounced as the pooling reduction parameters increase. Therefore, we recommend multiple pooling with a small pooling factor rather than an excessive reduction factor for a single spectral pooling layer.

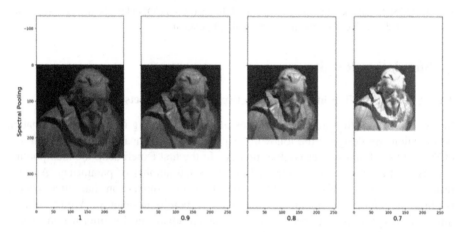

Fig. 6. Experiment two: arbitrary size of output map after one spectral pooling process

4.2 Comparison Between Two Networks

4.2.1 Complexity and Convergence Rate

As we discussed before, one spectral pooling process only needs a Fourier transform and an inverse Fourier transform, its complexity can be negligible compared to the convolutional layers. On the other hand, the computational complexity of the convolutional layer in the original network can be expressed as $n^2 k^2 hw$, where h, w represents the height and width of the input image, n represents the number of channels of the input image, and k represents the size of the convolution kernel.

The feature map of the original network only has a slight change in size due to the different padding selection of the convolution layer (input: 512, output: 492). When estimating the network complexity, for the sake of convenience, the approximate size is not changed, then the original The complexity of the CON block of the network is roughly $n^2 \times k^2 \times 512^2$.

Moreover, in the new neural network containing the spectral pooling layer, the size of feature map will change accordingly due to spectral pooling. So, in order to compare the computational complexity more intuitively, we use the calculation formula mentioned above to calculate and sum the number of floating-point operations required for every convolution operation in different networks. The results are shown in Table 1. By comparing the result, it can be seen that the spectral pooling layer reduces the computational complexity of the convolution layer by reducing feature map's size in the network, which will directly lead to a significant reduction in the computational complexity of the whole network.

Table 1. Comparison of computational complexity (original model complexity is 1)

Output size/Input size	Complexity (Floating point calculation times)	Ratio
Original	1.346162×10^{12}	1
40%	3.945668×10^{11}	0.2931
25%	2.513492×10^{11}	0.1867

We chose one of our new network models (50%) and trained it on the graphics card, its convergence curve is shown in Fig. 7. From the result, we can know that when the output size of the model is 50% of the input, the light-field depth estimation network can converge to an acceptable loss value after approximately 150 epoch of training.

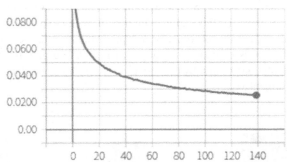

Fig. 7. Loss Rate of new model when training

4.2.2 Memory Occupancy in Depth-Estimation

In Sect. 4.2.1, we have known that the spectral pooling can effectively reduce the size of the feature map. This feature will directly reflect on the machine memory requirements when the model is running. In order to prove this, we directly observe the memory occupancy of the model in the process of depth-estimation. To more clearly compare the application of the two models on the mobile device, we choose CPU (Intel Core i5) as the hardware. Model 1 is a model whose output's size is half as the input, and Model 2 is a quarter. The result we obtained is shown in Table 2. By analyzing the results of the above experiment, we can intuitively get that the introduction of spectral pooling can effectively reduce the memory requirements, which provides great convenience for depth estimation on lightweight CPU mobile devices.

Table 2. Memory Occupancy of Models in Depth-estimation on CPU (Intel Core i5, 8 GB, Virtual Memory 2 GB, Total available memory is 10 GB). Percentage represents the ratio of Memory Occupancy to Total available memory 10 GB).

Model	Memory occupancy	Percentage
Original	8.97–9.15 GB	90.50%
Our model 1(50%)	6.63 GB	66.30%
Our model 2(25%)	5.25 GB	52.50%

4.2.3 Comparison of Depth Estimation Accuracy

Compared with the operation of convolution, pooling can reduce the computational complexity by reducing the dimension of tensor flowing in the network, but it will also bring the loss of information. By analyzing the information distribution of light field images and comparing the features of different pooling methods, we choose spectral pooling as our pooling layer in the network. The purpose is to maintain the accuracy of depth estimation while achieving pooling. We try different pooling methods in our depth-estimation network, and compare their effects when the pooling size is the same. The results are shown in Fig. 8. Through the analysis of the results we chose spectral pooling as our method. To this end, we did the following experiment, using the trained model and the original model to perform depth estimation in the same scene, and the obtained depth map is compared as shown in Fig. 9. We perform a bilinear interpolation on the depth map output by our model to satisfy the consistency with the original in the spatial dimension.

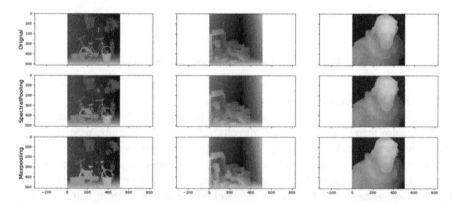

Fig. 8. Different pool methods with the same pool size (50%). All output results are restored to the same size (512, 512) by bilinear interpolation algorithm.

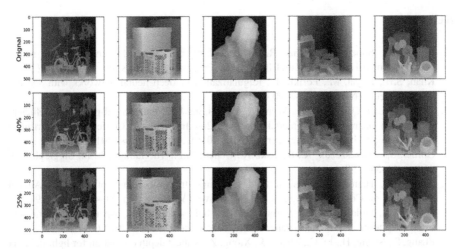

Fig. 9. Depth results predicted by different models in 5 scenarios above. The first row represents the original model's output, the model in the middle row cuts the output to 40% of the input, and output size of model in the third row reduces to 25% of the input. All output results are restored to the same size (512, 512) by bilinear interpolation algorithm.

We also compare and quantify ours with other algorithms under the same hardware conditions. The results are presented in Table 3.

Table 3. Quantitative comparison between accuracy and time under the same machine conditions

Method	MSE	Runtime(log10)
Ours (50%)	6.43	0.02
Epi1	1.22	2.0
Epi2	2.07	1.1

5 Conclusion

In this paper, a new method is proposed in the field of depth estimation using light field image. We achieved pooling the feature map in the frequency domain, slowly reducing the size of feature maps in a controllable way. Experiments show that our method can reduce the computational complexity of the network and accelerate network convergence. In addition, spectral pooling ensures a smaller size of the model, thereby reducing the model's need for machine memory when running. In the future, we will adjust the reduction factor of each pooling layer according to the situation of different positions in the network to achieve more optimal preservation of effective information. And parameter adjustment will be one of the efficient ways to improve performance. We will also take advantage of other depth estimation algorithms to further improve our performance.

References

1. Rippel, O., Snoek, J., Adams, R.P.: Spectral representations for convolutional neural networks. In: Advances in Neural Information Processing Systems, pp. 2449–2457 (2015)
2. Khan, S.H., Hayat, M., Porikli, F.: Regularization of deep neural networks with spectral dropout. Neural Netw. **110**, 82–90 (2019)
3. Wang, Z., Lan, Q., Huang, D., Wen, M.: Combining FFT and spectral-pooling for efficient convolution neural network model. In: 2016 2nd International Conference on Artificial Intelligence and Industrial Engineering (AIIE 2016). Atlantis Press (2016)
4. Gortler, S.J., Grzeszczuk, R., Szeliski, R., Cohen, M.F.: The lumigraph. In: Siggraph, vol. 96, pp. 43–54 (1996)
5. Levoy, M., Hanrahan, P.: Light field rendering. In: Proceedings of the 23rd Annual Conference on Computer Graphics and Interactive Techniques, pp. 31–42. ACM (1996)
6. Wanner, S., Goldluecke, B.: Variational light field analysis for disparity estimation and super-resolution. IEEE Trans. Pattern Anal. Mach. Intell. **36**, 606–619 (2014)
7. Zhang, S., Sheng, H., Li, C., Zhang, J., Xiong, Z.: Robust depth estimation for light field via spinning parallelogram operator. Comput. Vis. Image Underst. **145**, 148–159 (2016)
8. Shin, C., Jeon, H.-G., Yoon, Y., So Kweon, I., Joo Kim, S.: Epinet: a fully-convolutional neural network using epipolar geometry for depth from light field images. In: Proceedings of the IEEE Conference on Computer Vision and Pattern Recognition, pp. 4748–4757 (2018)
9. Ng, R., Levoy, M., Brédif, M., Duval, G., Horowitz, M., Hanrahan, P., et al.: Light field photography with a hand-held plenoptic camera. Comput. Sci. Tech. Rep. CSTR **2**, 1–11 (2005)
10. Wang, T.-C., Efros, A.A., Ramamoorthi, R.: Occlusion-aware depth estimation using light-field cameras. In: Proceedings of the IEEE International Conference on Computer Vision, pp. 3487–3495 (2015)
11. Heber, S., Yu, W., Pock, T.: Neural EPI-volume networks for shape from light field. In: Proceedings of the IEEE International Conference on Computer Vision, pp. 2252–2260 (2017)
12. Anisimov, Y., Didier, S.: Fast and efficient depth map estimation from light fields. In: 2017 International Conference on 3D Vision (3DV), pp. 337–346. IEEE (2017)
13. Cooley, J.W., Tukey, J.W.: An algorithm for the machine calculation of complex Fourier series. Math. Comput. **19**, 297–301 (1965)
14. Dansereau, D.G., Pizarro, O., Williams, S.B.: Linear volumetric focus for light field cameras. ACM Trans. Graph. **34**, 15-1 (2015)
15. Dosovitskiy, A., et al.: Flownet: learning optical flow with convolutional networks. In: Proceedings of the IEEE International Conference on Computer Vision, pp. 2758–2766 (2015)

3D Surface Splicing Based on Principal Component Feature Extraction

Kaiyue Li[1,2,3]($\boxtimes$), Qingyu Meng[1,2,3], Mingquan Zhou[1,2,3],
and Pengbo Zhou[1,2,3]

[1] College of Information Science and Technology,
Beijing Normal University, Beijing 100875, People's Republic of China
kaiyueli@mail.bnu.edu.cn
[2] Engineering Research Center of Virtual Reality and Applications,
Ministry of Education (MOE), Beijing 100875, People's Republic of China
[3] Beijing Key Laboratory of Digital Preservation and Virtual Reality
for Cultural Heritage, Beijing 100875, People's Republic of China

Abstract. In order to achieve automatic splicing for complex 3D surfaces, the parametric surface representation method for fractured surfaces of fragmented objects with thickness was analyzed and then a surface splicing method based on eigenvector of mixed subscript was proposed in this paper. In this method, geometric features of a surface were extracted based on principal components and directed subscripts and undirected subscripts were adopted to form mixed eigenvectors, and then the matching relationship between two surfaces was determined based on two similarity judgments. This method effectively lowered surface splicing error. Surface splicing experiments of broken cultural relic fragments verified the feasibility and effectiveness of this method.

Keywords: 3D splicing · Surface shape · Principal component analysis · Mixed subscript

1 Introduction

Automatic restoration of complex 3D fragmented objects is an important research topic in computer graphics, which includes surface shape feature representation of fragmented objects, calculation of complementary shape matching based on such representation as well as 3D splicing and shape restoration of matching objects. Related researches can provide reliable technical support for industrial Computer - Aided Design (CAD), cultural relic restoration, surgical plastic surgery, spinal correction and so on. Many scholars at home and abroad have done a lot of related researches. In 1980, Faugeras and his team members became the first to apply free surface matching based on 3D data to the study of Renault's component monitoring. This study was also intended for the understanding of the free surface matching represented by 3D data based on least square method in computer vision [1]. In the surface matching algorithm [2, 3], the iterative closet point algorithm is commonly adopted as basic algorithm. However, many surface matching algorithms have been studied out with efforts of researchers. Barequet et al. [4–6] adopted directed subscript for partial surface

© Springer Nature Singapore Pte Ltd. 2019
Y. Wang et al. (Eds.): IGTA 2019, CCIS 1043, pp. 343–352, 2019.
https://doi.org/10.1007/978-981-13-9917-6_33

matching. Funkhouse et al. [7] used spherical harmonics to represent the shape matching algorithm; Osada et al. [8] applied a shape distribution method to identify 3D targets; Zhang et al. [9] applied harmonic map to match 3D surfaces. Brunnstrom et al. [10] adopted genetic algorithms to overcome surface matching difficulty of 3D free-form bodies.

Surfaces of fragmented objects are extremely complicated for their randomness when in fragmentation. Although some progress has been made in the research on shape representation, matching calculation and automatic splicing technology for surfaces, the result is still unsatisfactory. The reason is that in practical applications, most of surfaces are difficult to describe with an equation, which brings certain difficulties to surface similarity calculation. However, any surface has its own inherent features. In calculation of surface matching, as long as eigenvectors reflecting local properties of surfaces can be obtained, it can be ensured that the error between matching surfaces is the smallest in similarity calculation, which provides reliable support for automatic surface splicing and restoration of fragmented objects.

Surface matching methods are mainly divided into two categories: matching between a surface and a standard surface, and matching between least time criterion and standard surface [11]. Automatic 3D surface matching can be realized by comparing the similarity of descriptive shape features between two surfaces, and the key is to find an appropriate shape description method and a feature selection scheme. Restoration technology for fragmented objects based on surface shape feature extraction includes the following processes: (1) data acquisition; (2) 3D object modeling and feature extraction; (3) complementary shape matching; and (4) object splicing; (5) model repair, as shown in Fig. 1.

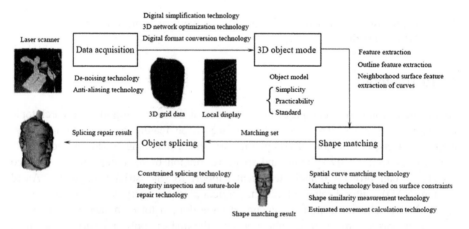

Fig. 1. Framework of 3D fragmented object restoration technology

In this paper, the representation and splicing of surface shape of 3D fragmented objects were studied. Firstly, mixed subscript eigenvectors of two surfaces were extracted based on Principal Component Analysis (PCA), and the adjacency relationship between them was judged based on shape features of fragment surfaces, and then the matching relationship between them was judged based on the similarity calculation result of the eigenvectors to achieve automatic splicing of 3D surfaces.

2 Surface Feature Extraction Based on PCA

A suitable method for describing surface shape is the key to whether two 3D surfaces corresponding to a fragment of a fragmented object can be matched and spliced. Therefore, the first thing to address is to analyze surface representation and features. In practical applications, most surfaces are difficult to describe with an equation, which brings some difficulties to surface similarity matching and splicing. However, each surface has its own certain features distinguishable from other surfaces. Therefore in order to effectively identify a surface, surface processing is required to extract surface features. This feature may reflect local features of the surface and be easy to calculate.

Assume that an object to be restored has n fractured surfaces and the eigenvector of each surface has p components, which are respectively represented as $X_1, X_2, \ldots X_p$, and they constitute the original data matrix of surface features of the fragmented object $X = \left(x_{ij}\right)_{n \times p}$, $i = 1, 2, \ldots n; j = 1, 2, \ldots p$. Due to differences in performance parameters of laser scanners, the acquired 3D surface data of objects is often affected by the dimension and magnitude of indexes. In order to eliminate such effect, it is necessary to normalize original data or preprocess the data with other methods to obtain a matrix $X = \left(x'_{ij}\right)_{n \times p}$ and improve the comparability of surface feature data

$$x'_{ij} = \frac{x_{ij} - \overline{x_j}}{S_j}. \tag{1}$$

Where $\overline{x_j} = \frac{1}{n} \sum_{i=1}^{n} x_{ij}$, $S_j = \frac{1}{n-1} \sum_{i=1}^{n} \left(x_{ij} - \overline{x_j}\right)^2$ $i = 1, 2, \ldots n; j = 1, 2, \ldots p$.

Step one: establish correlation coefficient matrix R of P feature components after surface data X is normalized.

$$R = \left(r_{ij}\right)_{p \times p}, r_{ij} = \frac{S_{ij}}{\sqrt{S_{ii}} \sqrt{S_{jj}}}. \tag{2}$$

Where $S_{ij} = \frac{1}{n-1} \sum_{k=1}^{n} \left(x_{ki} - \overline{x_i}\right)\left(x_{kl} - \overline{x_j}\right)$. The correlation coefficient matrix R indicates the degree to which P feature components are related to each other.

Step two: calculate the eigenvalue λ_i of correlation coefficient matrix R and corresponding unit eigenvectors $u_1, u_2, \cdots u_p$.

$$\lambda_1 \geq \lambda_2 \geq \cdots \geq \lambda_p > 0; \quad u_i = \left(u_{i1}, u_{i2}, \cdots, u_{ip}\right). \tag{3}$$

Step three: calculate the variance contribution rate α_k and cumulative variance contribution rate $\alpha(k)$ of each principal component of surface eigenvector.

$$\alpha_k = \frac{\lambda_k}{\sum_{i=1}^{p} \lambda_i}, \alpha(k) = \frac{\sum_{i=1}^{k} \lambda_k}{\sum_{i=1}^{p} \lambda_i}. \tag{4}$$

Where the variance contribution rate α_k indicates the amount of information of P original feature components extracted based on the k-th principal component, which reflects the percentage of the k-th principal component's integrated original feature information. Cumulative variance contribution rate $\alpha(k)$ represents the amount of information of original features retained by the first k principal components, reflecting the percentage of integrated original variable of first k principal components.

Step four: determine the number of principal components. The principle is to obtain enough original information with fewer principal components. On the one hand, we should make k as small as possible; on the other hand, we should make $\alpha(k)$ as big as possible. In practical applications, $\alpha(k) \geq 80\%$ is generally adopted. Large cumulative contribution rate $\alpha(k)$ of first k ($1 \leq k < P$) principal components indicates that the first k principal components already contain most of the information of the original variables. In this case, the first k principal components can be adopted to form an integrated evaluation function.

Step five: extract principal components of eigenvectors and provide the score evaluation function Y_i of each principal component.

$$Y_i = u_{i1}x_1 + u_{i2}x_2 + \ldots + u_{ip}x_p, i = 1, 2, \ldots k. \tag{5}$$

Step six: Since the principal components of eigenvectors are not related to each other, they are generally integrated based on weighted arithmetic mean, and the variance contribution rate of each principal component is weighted:

$$F = \alpha_1 Y_1 + \alpha_2 Y_2 + \ldots + \alpha_k Y_k. \tag{6}$$

3 Surface Eigenvector Based on Subscript

Curvature is an important geometric feature of a surface and is an important part of differential integral research. Not only curvature but also direction should be considered in judging the similarity of corresponding points on two matching surfaces. According to the Euler's theorem, the curvature of a point on a surface can be uniquely determined by the principal curvature and direction angle, and Gaussian curvature is only related to intrinsic properties of the surface. In addition, the properties of a point can be judged according to the sign of Gaussian curvature. Gaussian curvature and average curvature can be calculated and obtained based on the principal curvature. Therefore, Gaussian curvature and mean curvature on a surface can be adopted as eigenvectors of a surface, and the direction of each point on the surface should be taken into consideration in the matching process. However, if the initial matching point pair is calculated based on the curvature, there may be many matching point pairs and thus a large number of false matching point pairs with similar curvatures, which will affect the efficiency of surface matching calculation. Therefore, it is necessary to classify the types of feature points. In general, the eigenvector of a point on a surface is composed of feature quantities such as normal vector, main direction, Gaussian curvature, mean curvature and neighborhood type of points on the surface.

Subscript is a geometric quantity for surface features, which can be divided into undirected subscript and directed subscript. The former is a scalar with rotation and translation invariance and the latter is a vector that describes the direction of a point on a surface. Therefore, in order to perform principal component analysis to curvature feature data based on analysis of surface representation and feature extraction of fragmented objects, this paper proposed using the directed subscript and undirected subscript of points on surfaces to form directed eigenvectors and undirected eigenvectors of their surface shapes and using rough matching technology and refined matching technology to calculate surface matching of objects, so as to accomplish the splicing of fractured surfaces of fragmented objects.

In this paper, a total of 30 groups with broken cultural relic fragments of different shapes were used as sample data, and PCA was adopted to analyze the feature data of fractured surfaces. According to relevant archaeological literatures, surface features of an archaeological fragment can be divided into 13 feature components, which are respectively represented by $x_1, x_2, x_3, x_4, x_5, x_6, x_7, x_8, x_9, x_{10}, x_{11}, x_{12}, x_{13}$. If x_{ij} represents the data about the i-th cultural relic fragment surface in the j-th feature component, $X = (x_{ij})_{30 \times 13}$, and then a 30 × 13 original data matrix is obtained. The original data was normalized into a normalized matrix table according to Eq. (1), and the correlation coefficient matrix of the normalized matrix was obtained according to Eq. (2), and then the eigenvalues of the correlation matrix were solved according to Eq. (3) to obtain the number of principal components of the surface eigenvectors. See Table 1.

Table 1. Principal component extraction table about variance decomposition of surface feature data

Component	Initial eigenvalues			Extraction sums of squared loading		
	Total	% of variance	Cumulative %	Total	% of variance	Cumulative %
1	5.4069	41.591	41.591	5.4069	41.591	41.591
2	1.5153	11.656	53.248	1.5153	11.656	53.248
3	1.3518	10.398	63.646	1.3518	10.398	63.646
4	1.1448	8.806	72.452	1.1448	8.806	72.452
5	0.8611	6.623	79.076	0.8611	6.623	79.076
6	0.7499	5.768	84.845			
7	0.5287	4.067	88.912			
8	0.4551	3.500	92.413			
9	0.3328	2.560	94.973			
10	0.253	1.946	96.919			
11	0.1817	1.397	98.316			
12	0.1459	1.122	99.439			
13	0.0729	0.560	100.000			

Table 1 shows that the cumulative contribution rate of the first five common factors reaches 79.076%, which can reflect 79.076% of information amount of 13 indexes in original eigenvectors. P feature component data of sample fragments was normalized and substituted into Eq. (5) to calculate the principal component value, and then the comprehensive principal component evaluation value of each sample fragment was obtained according to Eq. (6). In practice, the number of principal components of the comprehensive evaluation model for surface feature data may be determined by calculating the load factor according to the automatic registration parameter requirements of surfaces to be matched in different application fields.

4 Automatic Surface Splicing Based on Mixed Subscript

Assume that the point cloud data for objects to be matched and spliced was obtained by scanning them with a 3D scanner and a triangular mesh model was obtained by triangulation based on the same subdivision criterion. After the triangular mesh was obtained, eigenvectors such as normal vector, main direction, curvature and type of points on surfaces to be matched were calculated. Moreover, an eigenvector table was constructed for each surface to store eigenvectors of points on surfaces. If a fractured surface of two pieces of an object can be spliced (i.e., the corresponding points P_i and Q_j on two surfaces are a matching pair), their undirected eigenvectors are equal or similar, and their directed eigenvectors will show opposite normal vector direction and same or similar main direction after being translated and rotated. In practical applications, an allowable error value can be set for the results of two similarity judgments where necessary and the two eigenvectors are considered equal or similar as long as the result is within the allowable error range.

In this paper, the normal vector, main direction, Gaussian curvature and mean curvature of the surface and types of points on a surface were adopted to form directed eigenvectors and undirected eigenvectors of the surface respectively. The surfaces were matched by the quadratic matching technology. First, the matching point sets with possible matching relationships were screened out by comparing undirected features of triangular mesh vertices. Then the matching point sets on the two surfaces were obtained by comparing the similarities of directed features and conducting two similarity calculations to achieve surface matching.

There are two kinds of termination conditions for the splicing algorithm. The first kind is that the calculated registration error of two adjacent registration results in the iterative registration process is smaller than the predetermined registration error parameter. This parameter is set in a human-computer interaction manner based on factors such as specifications, instrument type, material, and damage of the registration object before the splicing algorithm is executed, so as to avoid excessive iteration of the algorithm. The second one is a condition in which the number of iterations is larger than the upper limit parameter setting of the number of iterations. This parameter is set according to empirical values from experts in corresponding field before the surface splicing algorithm is executed. The purpose is to control possible divergence in the algorithm.

5   Simulation Experiment and Analysis

5.1   Experimental Platform

Hardware platform for algorithm verification was: Intel Core i7 3.33 GHz CPU, 16 GB memory, 2 GB graphics memory. Software platform was: Visual Studio 2010 and Open GL of image programming interface. The algorithm performance evaluation index was Mean Average Precision (MAP). The MAP was defined as the average of the area under multiple recall rate_precision curves, and the larger the MAP, the better the retrieval performance.

5.2   Experimental Data

The object under experiment was taken from 3D model data about some fragments of terracotta warriors and horses in the third archaeological excavation in Pit One of Terracotta Warriors and Horses of The First Emperor of Qin. The 3D point cloud model for fragments of terracotta warriors and horses was obtained using a hand-held scanner with a resolution of 3.91 mm. The scanned 3D relics point cloud model was not processed, so actual noise data was included.

5.3   Result Analysis

The first experiment was conducted to verify the feasibility of the algorithm.

The experiment shows that the method proposed in this paper can be adopted for accurate spatial transformation of the 3D model for warrior template part corresponding to internal structure of the 3D model for cultural relic fragments of terracotta warriors and horses, as shown in Fig. 2.

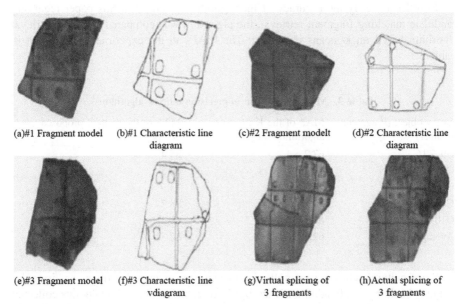

(a)#1 Fragment model   (b)#1 Characteristic line diagram   (c)#2 Fragment modelt   (d)#2 Characteristic line diagram

(e)#3 Fragment model   (f)#3 Characteristic line vdiagram   (g)Virtual splicing of 3 fragments   (h)Actual splicing of 3 fragments

Fig. 2. Splicing result of 3D model for G10-13 terracotta warrior fragments

In order verify the effectiveness of the algorithm proposed in this paper, a total of 40 sets of terracotta warrior fragments with different degrees of damage were randomly selected. Table 2 shows the representative data of 9 groups. The performance index of the algorithm for the experimental group data: the initial matching time was 1.416 s; the final matching time was 1.555 s; the average number of iterations was 13 times; the average splicing error was 1.7233 mm and the standard deviation was 1.0265 mm. The experimental data shows that the proposed algorithm with good convergence can effectively avoid divergence that is easy to occur in the existing splicing algorithm.

Table 2. Experimental data about splicing of terracotta warrior fragments

Experiment group (No.)	Initial splicing time (S)	Optimized splicing time (S)	Number of iterations (times)	Splicing error (mm)	Standard deviation (mm)
1	1.235	1.291	6	1.9398	1.1806
2	1.297	1.536	7	3.3640	1.8964
3	1.357	1.162	9	1.8148	1.2685
4	1.544	2.078	15	1.2137	0.8876
5	1.278	1.236	15	0.8902	0.6468
6	1.940	1.885	3	2.0588	0.0012
7	1.569	2.164	17	1.2549	0.9435
8	1.235	1.405	18	1.6741	1.5766
9	1.198	1.242	24	1.2992	0.8372

The second experiment was conducted to verify the effectiveness of the algorithm.

In order to verify the accuracy of the algorithm proposed in this paper regarding candidate matching fragment retrieval, the algorithm was compared with the retrieval algorithm based on k-means clustering. The MAPs in the experiment are shown in Table 3.

Table 3. MAP comparison in precision ratio of algorithms

Query object (Fragment number)	MAP of the K-means algorithm (%)	MAP of the method proposed in this paper (%)
G9-6-16	67.2	85.4
G9-6-23	58.3	76.5
G10-4-6	54.2	73.6
G10-6-5	71.5	88.7
G10-36-1	61.2	87.4
Average	62.48	82.32

Since cultural relics are naturally fragmented, the fractured surfaces are irregular and may be defective. In addition, after digitization, the number of data points collected in fragmented object fragments is also very large. Therefore, due to the discrete processing of fragments of fragmented objects and error in similarity calculation, a large error will occur when the surface of the fractured object is spliced, which affects the automatic surface splicing of the fractured object.

6 Conclusion

The comprehensive evaluation model for surface feature data obtained based on principal component factor analysis can be substituted for several related feature data using several unrelated comprehensive evaluation indexes such as directed subscripts and undirected subscripts. It can avoid mutual overlap and interference of feature data and can reflect surface geometric structure information in original feature components of original surfaces. In this paper, the parametric surface representation method for fragmented objects with thickness and their feature calculation method have been analyzed. Directed eigenvectors and undirected eigenvectors are considered as constituting directed subscripts and undirected subscript, respectively. The matching relationship between surfaces has been determined based on two similarity judgments. This model has effectively lowered 3D matching and splicing error of fractured surfaces of fragmented objects and can be applied to applications such as cultural relic restoration and medical plastic surgery.

Acknowledgement. The authors would like to thank the anonymous reviewers for their constructive comments. This project is supported by the Qingdao Municipality's Independent Innovation Major Project (2017-4-3-2-xcl).

References

1. Wang, Y., Peterson, B.S., Staiba, L.H.: 3D brain surface matching based geodesics and local geometry. Comput. Vis. Image Underst. **89**, 252–271 (2003)
2. Li, Q., Zhou, M., Geng, G.: Fractured surfaces matching for reassembling broken objects. J. Chin. Mini-Micro Comput. Syst. **34**(7), 1675–1679 (2013)
3. Papaioannou, G., Karabassi, E.A., Theoharis, T.: Virtual archaeologist: assembling the past. **21**(2), 53–59 (2001)
4. Barequet, G., Sharir, M.: Partial surface matching by using directed footprints. Comput. Geom.: Theor. Appl. **12**(1–2), 45–62 (1999)
5. Barequet, G., Sharir, M.: Partial surface and volume matching in three dimensions. Trans. Pattern Anal. Mach. Intell. **19**(9), 929–948 (1997)
6. Pan, X., Zhang, L., Jie, Y., et al.: Algorithm for three-dimensional partial surface matching. J. Nanjing Univ. Aeronaut. Astronaut. **36**(5), 544–549 (2004)
7. Funkhouser, T., Min, P., Kazhdan, M., et al.: A search engine for 3D models. ACM Trans. Graph. **21**, 83–105 (2003)
8. Osada, R., Funkhouser, T., Chazelle, B., et al.: Matching 3D models with shape distributions. ACM Trans. Graph. **21**(4), 807–832 (2002)
9. Winkelbach, S., Wahl, F.M.: Pairwise matching of 3D fragments using cluster trees. Int. J. Comput. Vis. **78**(1), 1–13 (2008)

10. Dyshkant, N.: Comparison of point clouds acquired by 3D scanner. In: Gonzalez-Diaz, R., Jimenez, M.-J., Medrano, B. (eds.) DGCI 2013. LNCS, vol. 7749, pp. 47–58. Springer, Heidelberg (2013). https://doi.org/10.1007/978-3-642-37067-0_5

11. Wu, D., Hong, J., Ding, Y., Zhao, W.: Surfaces matching algorithm based on the least time criterion. J. Xian Jiaotong Univ. **05**, 500–503 (2002)

12. Shucheng, Z., Mingquan, Z., Guohua, G.: 3D image segmentation based on wavelet transform adaptive threshold. Comput. Appl. Soft. **23**(10), 20–22 (2006)

An Automatic White Balance Algorithm Based on Pixel Luminance and Chromaticity

Heding Xu[✉], Hong Zhang, Bo Rao, Yifan Yang, and Zeyu Zhang

Image Processing Center, Beihang University,
No. 37 Xueyuan Road, Haidian District, Beijing 100083, China
xuheding@buaa.edu.cn

Abstract. Automatic white balance (AWB) is a crucially important part of digital still camera. It keeps constant color of an image by eliminating the color cast caused by non-canonical illuminant. A dynamic threshold is used to remove outliers in C_b and C_r components and detect the near-white region in an image. And we also describe a technique using both the internal illumination and all pixels in the near-white region to estimate the illuminant. The results show that the proposed technique is superior or comparable to the existing AWB algorithms. The algorithm is attractive for practical applications because of the low complexity.

Keywords: Automatic white balance · Near-white region ·
YC_bC_r color space · Illuminant estimation

1 Introduction

Illumination affects the color distribution of a certain object in a digital camera [1]. It can result in color instability such that when illuminated by different light sources, the same object appears to have different colors. A white object will appear reddish under a low color temperature. Conversely, it will appear bluish under a high color temperature. And maintaining color constancy is critical in plenty of image processing applications, such as object detection [2], color enhancement [3], etc. Therefore, we can process the image with AWB method to eliminate the color cast [4]. They usually consist of two steps: illuminant estimation and color compensation [5].

In the step of illuminant estimation, AWB algorithms try to find achromatic color (the neutral color). Since the neutral color is achromatic, we can consider that any color component of the neutral color comes from the light source [6]. Therefore, most AWB algorithms try to find the neutral color and then to estimate the illuminant.

Early AWB algorithms always make certain assumptions about low-level features, including gray world method (GWM) [7], perfect reflector method (PRM) [8], fuzzy rule method (FRM) [9], etc. And in the recent years, some new methods using high-level features have emerged, including correlation of color [10] and neural network method based on color constancy [11]. While high-level-feature-based methods typically have better performance than low-level-feature-based methods, they spend more time on computation. Starting from reality, in the digital cameras, low-level-feature-

© Springer Nature Singapore Pte Ltd. 2019
Y. Wang et al. (Eds.): IGTA 2019, CCIS 1043, pp. 353–359, 2019.
https://doi.org/10.1007/978-981-13-9917-6_34

based methods can perform reasonably in a short time with limited computing capability [12].

We propose a technique using image statistics to get the near-white region in the YC_bC_r color space. The proposed method takes pixels' weighted average in the near-white region to estimate the illuminant. Experimental results show that the proposed method performs better than other AWB methods in subjective and objective evaluation.

2   Related Work

We denote the image value with $f(x)$. It relates to the power distribution of illuminant spectrum $i(\lambda)$, the surface reflectance of spectrum $r(x, \lambda)$ where x is the pixel location and the camera spectral response function $c(\lambda)$ for a Lambertian surface corresponding to a light with wavelength λ by

$$f(x) = \int_w i(\lambda)r(x, \lambda)c(\lambda)d\lambda. \tag{1}$$

Where w is the visible spectrum.

Assuming only one light source illuminates the scene, then the observed illumination of the light source depends on the power distribution of illuminant spectrum and the camera spectral response function [10]. The illuminant I is defined by:

$$I = \int_w i(\lambda)c(\lambda)d\lambda. \tag{2}$$

Because only the image value f is known, estimating illuminant is an inappropriate problem without other assumptions.

GWM works under the assumption that, we can get an achromatic image by the average of reflectance of a scene if the original image has sufficient color variations [7].

PRM assumes that the brightest pixel in an image conveys many information about the illumination of the scene [8]. And the brightest pixel is defined as the reference white point [7].

In the FRM, the image is processed in the YC_bC_r color space. They proposed the idea of near-white region and considered the C_r to C_b ratio of white objects was between -1.5 to -0.5 [9]. The method obtains the gains of C_b and C_r to adjust images through several fuzzy rules [7].

Based on FRM, Weng et al. proposed the mean absolute deviation (MAD) method to remove outliers that have large C_b and C_r values. The method depends on mean absolute deviation in C_b and C_r component. Then the method computed the average reflectance by remaining pixels that have small C_b and C_r values, not the entire image [13].

3 The Proposed Method

A dynamic threshold is used to detect the near-white region in an image, which is different to predefined threshold in previous methods. Similar to previous methods, our method consists of white point detection and image adjustment. First, we can convert the image values from RGB to YC_bC_r color space to obtain the chromatic components easily.

As discussed in [6], for a neutral color, the chromaticity C_b and C_r are considered to come from the light source. Conversely, for a chromatic color, its values contain illumination from the scene and illumination from the light source. In order to represent the level of illumination from the light source contained in a color, Thai et al. proposed an illumination factor $h(x)$ where x is the pixel location [12]. The illuminant is given by:

$$I = \frac{\int f(x)h(x)dx}{\int h(x)dx}. \tag{3}$$

The role of $h(x)$ is to lower the influence of chromatic color pixels to the illuminant estimation. Liu et al. [9] observed that the smaller C_b and C_r values pixels have, the more neutral pixels are. We define $h(x)$ as following:

$$h(x) \propto \exp\left(-\frac{|C_b(x) + C_r(x)|}{\delta^2}\right). \tag{4}$$

$C_b(x)$, $C_r(x)$ denote chromaticity C_b and C_r of a pixel, where x is the pixel location. And δ is the parameter that controls the influence of a pixel in the illuminant estimation process. Setting a smaller value for δ, a pixel has less influence.

Based on the color characteristics observed by Liu et al. [9], we define a near-white region composed of pixels that satisfy the following relationships:

$$|C_b(i,j)| < \frac{Y(i,j)}{\sigma}. \tag{5}$$

$$|C_r(i,j)| < \frac{Y(i,j)}{\sigma}. \tag{6}$$

Where $C_b(i,j)$, $C_r(i,j)$, $Y(i,j)$ denote chromaticity C_b, C_r and luminance Y of pixel (i,j), and $\sigma \geq 1$ is the parameter which controls the range of the near-white region. Setting a larger value for σ, less pixels are selected as the near-white region.

Let $T_k(i,j)$ denote corresponding values of the pixel (i,j), where $k = \{1, 2, 3\}$ represent R, G and B channels. From Eqs. (3) to (6), the illuminant in the image defined as $\bar{T}_k$ is computed by:

$$\bar{T}_k = \sum_N \rho(i,j)T_k(i,j). \tag{7}$$

Where N is the number of image pixels in the near-white region. The averaging coefficient $\rho(i,j)$ is defined as:

$$\rho(i,j) = \frac{1}{\bar{\rho}} \exp\left(-\frac{|C_b(i,j) + C_r(i,j)|}{\delta^2}\right). \tag{8}$$

Where $\bar{\rho}$ is the normalized factor such that $\sum_N \rho(i,j) = 1$.

The following step is adjusting the image color to the estimated illuminant. The Von Kries model is used to adjust the image color [14]. Each channel gain ∂_k is computed by counting the luminance $\bar{Y}$ in the near-white region:

$$\partial_k = \frac{\bar{Y}}{\bar{T}_k}. \tag{9}$$

Where $\bar{Y} = \sum_N \rho(i,j)Y(i,j)$.

The value of each image pixel is adjusted by:

$$T_k^*(i,j) = \partial_k T_k(i,j). \tag{10}$$

Where $T_k^*(i,j)$ is the adjusted image value of channel k at pixel (i,j).

4 Experimental Results

In order to demonstrate the performance of our method, we present many experimental results to test our algorithm against other low-level-feature-based AWB algorithms including GWM [7], PRM [8], FRM [9] and MAD [13].

The experiments were conducted on datasets supplied by Gehler et al. [15] and Cheng et al. [16]. Every image in the datasets contains a Macbeth ColorChecker chart.

We used the average chromaticity of the achromatic patches of Macbeth Color-Checker as objective evaluative values to compare different methods [17]. The average chromaticity is defined by:

$$d = \sqrt{C_b^2 + C_r^2}. \tag{11}$$

If the value of d is smaller, the method has better performance.

We first studied the parameters σ, δ by setting them to different values and observing the values of average chromaticity. Experiments show that for most images we can obtain the best results when $\sigma = 4$, $\delta = 1$. Therefore, we used these values for all the experiments presented in this paper. Performance of AWB methods are demonstrated in Fig. 1. As can be seen, our method can eliminate color cast.

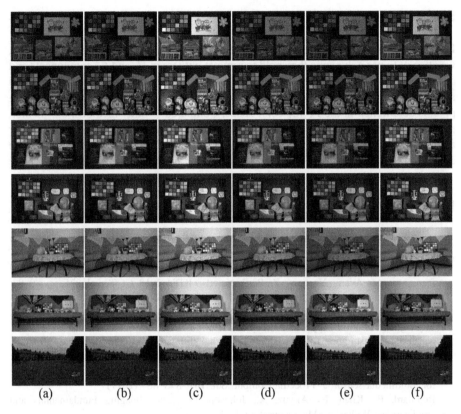

Fig. 1. Results of AWB methods on image datasets. From *top* to *bottom*: pictures, toys, books, snacks, table, sofa and outdoors image. From *left* to *right*: original images, GWM, PRM, FRM, MAD and our method. (a) The original image. (b) GWM. (c) PRM. (d) FRM. (e) MAD. (f) Our method.

We use Eq. (11) to evaluate the AWB algorithms objectively. The results are shown in Table 1, which demonstrate that our algorithm performs better than other algorithms in the test. The subjective evaluation shows that our algorithm can improve the image quality significantly.

Table 1. Average chromaticity values obtained from the Macbeth ColorChecker in images.

Test image	Original	GWM	PRM	FRM	MAD	Ours
Pictures	27.99	2.85	19.88	13.59	11.30	**1.72**
Toys	5.05	2.71	3.93	4.60	4.44	**1.82**
Books	43.50	7.51	13.62	9.87	5.47	**4.15**
Snacks	23.44	5.86	14.95	6.91	8.41	**3.38**
Table	23.96	10.90	12.28	12.67	6.15	**3.97**
Sofa	24.58	9.30	12.40	13.20	2.91	**2.86**
Outdoors	9.48	7.39	8.10	7.51	9.24	**2.08**

5 Conclusion

In this paper, we have proposed an automatic white balance algorithm. In our method, we attempt to use a dynamic threshold to remove outliers in C_b and C_r components and detect the near-white region in an image. The proposed method takes pixels' weighted average in the near-white region to estimate the illuminant. And the weight of each pixel is determined in the YC_bC_r color space. Compared to other methods, our method performs better in the objective evaluation. The subjective results also show that our algorithm is superior or comparable to other algorithms. Therefore, our method can be applied in digital cameras as a robust technique for automatic white balancing.

References

1. Jung, J., Ho, Y.: Color correction algorithm based on camera characteristics for multi-view video coding. Signal Image Video Process. **8**(5), 955–966 (2012)
2. Luo, Z., Zhang, H., Zhang, Z., Yang, Y., Li, J.: Object detection based on multiscale merged feature map. In: Wang, Y., Jiang, Z., Peng, Y. (eds.) IGTA 2018. CCIS, vol. 875, pp. 80–87. Springer, Singapore (2018). https://doi.org/10.1007/978-981-13-1702-6_8
3. Ghani, A.S.A.: Underwater image quality enhancement through integrated color model with Rayleigh distribution. Appl. Soft Comput. **27**, 219–230 (2014)
4. Nakano, N., Nishimura, R., Sai, H., et al.: Digital still camera system for megapixel CCD. IEEE Trans. Consum. Electron. **44**(3), 581–586 (1998)
5. Zhang, Y.Y., Gao, Y.F., He, Y.S., et al.: Research on the color temperature & white balance for multimedia sensor. J. Procedia Comput. Sci. **107**, 878–884 (2017)
6. Reinhard, E., Khan, E., Akyuz, A., Johnson, G.: Color Imaging Fundamentals and Applications. Wellesley, Massachusetts (2008)
7. Lin, J.: An automatic white balance method based on edge detection. In: IEEE International Symposium on Consumer Electronics. IEEE (2006)
8. Barnard, K., Martin, L., Coath, A., et al.: A comparison of computational color constancy algorithms–part: II experiments with image data. J. IEEE Trans. Image Process. **11**(9), 985 (2002)
9. Liu, Y.C., Chan, W.H., Chen, Y.Q.: Automatic white balance for digital still camera. J. IEEE Trans. Consum. Electron. **41**(3), 460–466 (2004)
10. Finayson, G.D., Hordley, S.D., Hube, P.M.: Color by correlation: a simple, unifying framework for color constancy. J. IEEE Trans. Pattern Anal. Mach. Intell. **23**(11), 1209–1221 (2001)
11. Cardei, V.C., Funt, B., Barnard, K.: Estimating the scene illumination chromaticity by using a neural network. J. Opt. Soc. Am. A **19**(12), 2374–2386 (2002)
12. Thai, B., Deng, G., Ross, R.: A fast white balance algorithm based on pixel greyness. J. Signal Image Video Process. **11**(3), 525–532 (2017)
13. Weng, C.-C., Chen, H., Fuh, C.-S.: A novel automatic white balance method for digital still cameras. In: IEEE Conference on Circuits and Systems, pp. 3801–3804 (2005)
14. West, G., Brill, M.H.: Necessary and sufficient conditions for von Kries chromatic adaptation to give color constancy. J. Math. Biol. **15**(2), 249–258 (1982)
15. Gehler, P.V., Rother, C., Blake, A., et al.: Bayesian color constancy revisited. In: IEEE Computer Society Conference on Computer Vision and Pattern Recognition (CVPR) (2008)

16. Cheng, D., Price, B., Cohen, S., et al.: Beyond white: ground truth colors for color constancy correction. In: IEEE International Conference on Computer Vision (ICCV). IEEE Computer Society (2015)
17. Li, X.-J., Fang, S., Yang, X., et al.: An algorithm of automatic white balance based on dynamic threshold. In: International Conference Information Computing & Automation (2007)

Attention-Based GAN for Single Image Super-Resolution

Dongqi Huo, Rong Wang[(⊠)], and Jianwei Ding

People's Public Security University of China, Beijing 102623, China
251955875@qq.com, dbdxwangrong@163.com

Abstract. Single Image Super-Resolution task based on GANs has shown a great improvement in all methods, but still has the optimization problems of texture details and distortion of local regions in super-resolved images. In this paper, we proposed an attention-based GAN architecture to solve preceding problems. Specifically, we first implemented attention mechanism in both Generator and Discriminator. Secondly, we adopted a three-step training for all architecture models and adjusted the adoption frequency of attention implement to make pre-trained model perform better. Extensive experiments on **Set5, Set14** and **BSD100** showed that the better pre-trained model of ours not only remedied the distortion of local regions, but also achieved the better perceptual quality than the original architecture.

Keywords: Super-resolution · Generative Adversarial Network · Attention mechanism

1 Introduction

The technique of generating high-resolution (HR) images from low-resolution (LR) images is called images super-resolution (SR), which is one of the most important parts in Computer Vision (CV). Single image super-resolution (SISR) based on Deep Learning begins with SRCNN proposed by Dong et al. [1], which used deep convolution neural networks (CNN) to find the correlation between the image pixels in both LR images and HR images. It not only brought a prosperous development of SISR in Deep learning, but also provided the idea of the following various network architecture and training strategies. Since Generative Adversarial Networks (GAN) proposed by Goodfellow [2], it have achieved great success in generation tasks in CV. From the perspective of the evolution, [2, 14–18] have made the foundation of the basic models, from the perspective of unstable training process, [11, 26, 27] etc. were proposed to stabilize the training process of GANs and improve the diversity of generated samples. From the perspective of tasks, it has achieved the better performance in image-to-image translation [19–22], image super-resolution [3, 4, 23] and text-to-image synthesis [24–26]. Among those, the method of SR based on GANs have been the state-of-the-art, like SRGAN [3]. It adopted special loss function and model architecture to solve the lack of high-frequency in SR images greatly, the achievements were shown in Fig. 1.

The technique of SISR were developed, but it also had some problems of texture details in super-resolved images, and it also had distortion of content in local region of

Y. Wang et al. (Eds.): IGTA 2019, CCIS 1043, pp. 360–369, 2019.
https://doi.org/10.1007/978-981-13-9917-6_35

images came out in some cases. Attention mechanism has been widely used in Natural Language Processing (NLP), Image Recognition, Voice Recognition and any other types of Deep Learning tasks. In CV, attention mechanism had ability to complement distal features with local features rather than just features in local regions [26, 31–33]. Self-attention (intra-attention) can calculate the response of a position in the sequence by focusing on all positions in the same sequence. [30, 34, 35] have improved the advantage of the attention mechanism in architectures or tasks and it had good performance in SAGAN in GANs recently. We used Self-attention (SA) in SISR task to handle the preceding problems and enhanced the quality of super-resolved images.

| 4×Downsampled | SRResnet | SRGAN | Ours | Original |

Fig. 1. The comparison of $4 \times$ downsampled, SRResnet, SRGAN, our model and original image.

In this paper, we improved the property of our new architecture through distinguishing the HR images super-resolved by ours and the original to get better visual perception for SISR. The subsequent of this paper is organized as follows: We introduce our model in Sect. 2 and show the results of experiment in Sect. 3. Finally, we draw the conclusions and discuss future research in Sect. 4.

2   Method

2.1   Basic Architecture

The architecture we used is shown in Fig. 2. Following Goodfellow et al. [2]. Discriminator D_{θ_D} and Generator G_{θ_G} optimize the following max-minimum problems in alternating manner:

$$\min_{\theta_G} \max_{\theta_D} E_{I^{HR} \sim p_{train}(I^{HR})}[\log D_{\theta_D}(I^{HR})] + E_{I^{LR} \sim p_G(I^{LR})}[\log(1 - D_{\theta_D}(G_{\theta_G}(I^{LR})))] \quad (1)$$

We referred to SRGAN to make our architecture. The Generator contains residual blocks with the number as a hyperparameter, and three convolutional layers with batch-normalization layers [13]. We used ParametricReLU [4] as the activation function in the latter two layers followed the residual blocks. The discriminator contains eight filter kernels, two dense layers and sigmoid activation function. We adopted perceptual loss function unlike current well-used loss function such as Wasserstein losses [16, 17]. The loss function contains content loss and adversarial loss, content loss can be divided into MSE loss and VGG loss in different step in whole process.

The pixel-wise MSE loss is calculated as:

$$l_{MSE}^{SR} = \frac{1}{r^2WH}\sum_{x=1}^{rW}\sum_{y=1}^{rH}(I_{x,y}^{HR} - G_{\theta_G}(I^{LR})_{x,y})^2 \tag{2}$$

The VGG loss is calculated as:

$$l_{VGG/i,j}^{SR} = \frac{1}{W_{i,j}H_{i,j}}\sum_{x=1}^{W_{i,j}}\sum_{y=1}^{H_{i,j}}(\sigma_{i,j}(I^{HR})_{x,y} - \sigma_{i,j}(G_{\theta_G}(I^{LR}))_{x,y})^2 \tag{3}$$

We adopted pre-trained 19 layers VGG network with ReLU activation for VGG loss, $\sigma_{i,j}$ indicates the feature map obtained by the j-th convolution before the i-th maxpooling layer in VGG19 network. [3] have adopted VGG22 and VGG54 for the experiment, VGG54 showed the better property and it also be adopted in our experiment.

The Adversarial losses is calculated by internal architecture, it's also same like what was used in [19, 20]. We used generated images as the input of Discriminator to balance performance of both Generator and Discriminator in training process. We usually multiply Adversarial losses by a scale parameter and added it to content loss as our loss function, the Adversarial losses calculated as:

$$l_{Gen}^{SR} = \sum_{n=1}^{N} -\log D_{\theta_D}(G_{\theta_G}(I^{LR})) \tag{4}$$

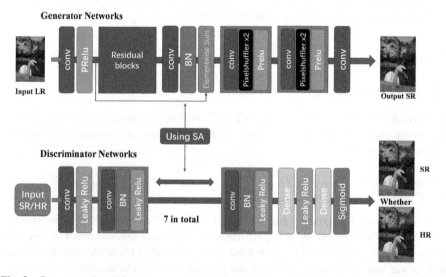

Fig. 2. Our network architecture, we adopted SA implement in both Generator and Discriminator, all have been used only once.

2.2   Self-Attention in Architecture

In order to make model capturing global dependencies efficiently, and make generated images less distortion in visual effects, we used Self-Attention model in architecture as shown in Fig. 3. The image features are first transformed into three feature space by 1×1 conv f, g, h, where $f(x) = W_f x$, $g(x) = W_g x$ is to calculate the attention. We can calculate attention map β by

$$\beta_{j,i} = \frac{\exp(r_{ij})}{\sum_{i=1}^{N} \exp(r_{ij})}, \text{ where } r_{ij} = f(x_i)^T g(x_j), \tag{5}$$

$\beta_{j,i}$ indicates the extent to which the model attends to the ith location when synthesizing the jth region. It should be noted that $\beta_{j,i}$ calculated by softmax function is performed on each row. Then the output of the attention layer is $o \in \mathbb{R}^{C \times N}$, where

$$o_j = \sum_{i=1}^{N} \beta_{j,i} h(x_i), \text{ where } h(x_i) = W_h x_i \text{ is the preceding third } 1 \times 1 \text{ conv } h, \tag{6}$$

W_f, W_g and W_h are learned weight matrices. We use $M = c/8$ to be the output kernels in f and g in our experiments, by the way, M is a variable parameter if you want to change. In final, we multiplied the output of the attention layer by a scale parameter and added back the input feature map, where output y_i is $y_i = \gamma o_i + x_i$ and γ is initialized as 0 at first.

In our architecture, we proposed Self-Attention (SA) in both discriminator and generator for once. The frequency and location of implement in architecture is adjustable.

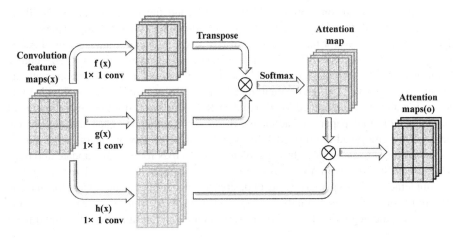

Fig. 3. Self-Attention implement in our architecture, where $\otimes$ refers to matrix multiplication.

2.3 Two Time-Scale Update Rule

[11, 30] have used divided leaning rates for generator and discriminator to accelerate and stabilize training process. Considering different sensitivity of discriminator and generator for learning rate in training GANs, to make sure using fewer generator steps per discriminator steps, the learning rate we used in discriminator is four times which used in generator in any training process in our experiments. We compared different training process model to test whether this training skill would improve results or not. The results were shown in Fig. 5 and Sect. 3.4.

3 Experiment and Analysis

3.1 Data

For training, the large dataset can improve the generator to super-resolve more natural images because of those richer textures. We used DIV2K dataset [6] and Flickr2K dataset [7], both of them are 2K-resolution dataset. The DIV2K usually to be used in images super-resolved tasks and Flickr2K was used to enrich our dataset in our experiments.

For testing, we used three widely used benchmark datasets **Set5** [8] (contains 5 images), **Set14** [9] (contains 14 images except 3 single channel images), **BSD100** [10] (contains 100 images) and the Test and Validation section of PIRM dataset [5] (contains 200 images in all). All lower resolution images were obtained by $4 \times$ down-sampling from High resolution images using bicubic kernel function in experiments.

3.2 Training Details

The training step run on NVIDIA Titan V GPU and the test step run on NVIDIA GTX1050Ti GPU. Generator has 16 identical residual blocks and set mini-batch size to 16. We used 96×96 for the spatial size of HR patch, and all optimization used Adam [12] with $\beta_1 = 0.9$. The SRResNet [3] network was trained with 5×10^5 update iterations with the learning rate of 10^{-4} and another 5×10^5 update iterations with the learning rate of 10^{-5}. For the original model, the results of training SRGAN with VGG losses initialized by the trained MSE-based SRResNet network for the generator are not as well as original paper, we adopt the-three-step training for each model. For the original, we employed the trained MSE-based SRResNet network as initialization for the generator of training MSE-based content loss SRGAN for 3×10^5 update iterations and trained SRGAN with VGG losses for 2×10^5 update iterations. The reason why we implement this step is to avoid undesired local optima for the generator and the discriminator can receive relatively good super-resolved images instead of extreme fake ones at the beginning [3, 4]. For ours, we employed the same first step and trained

MSE-based content loss SRGAN for 1×10^5, 2×10^5 and 3×10^5 iterations with SA implement, and the following is same as the original. VGG feature maps were rescaled by a factor of 1/12.75 to obtain VGG losses to correspond to MSE loss. All SRGAN model were trained with half of update iterations with the learning rate of 10^{-4} and another a half of update iterations with the learning rate of 10^{-5} (except for MSE-SEGAN for 1×10^5 iterations, it kept learning rate of 10^{-4} for all iterations). We also adopted TTUR [11] in SRGAN with VGG losses initialized by MSE-based SRGAN for 2×10^5 as the comparison to verify the performance of this implement in SISR.

3.3 Perceptual Quality

The peak signal-to-noise ratio (PSNR) [3, 28, 29] can be maximized by minimizing mean square error (MSE) to evaluate and compare qualities of SR images. But the results of PSNR-oriented approaches too smoothed to lose high-frequency, and PSNR metric doesn't match subjective evaluation of human perception. The author of [36] claimed that it has much difference between distortion and perceptual quality, and the pictures performed better in distortion always lost more texture judged by our visual perceptual. We can observe the comparison in Fig. 4, the image on the left in a couple lost more texture than which on the right and the right achieved perceptual score lower than the left. Perceptual index we used calculated by ((10−Ma) + NIQE)/2, where Ma's score and NIQE get from [37, 38], and lower perceptual index represents better quality.

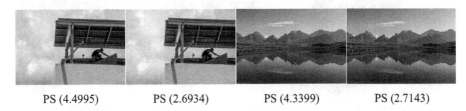

PS (4.4995)   PS (2.6934)   PS (4.3399)   PS (2.7143)

Fig. 4. Correlation of Perceptual score (PS) and visual perceptual, the images on the left generated by MSE-based SRResnet, the images on the right image generated by our model.

3.4 Results and Analysis

We used four preceding datasets to test our architecture, we extracted a few images to calculate single images perceptual score in Fig. 5, calculated whole parts of dataset mean perceptual score in Table 1. We used four pre-trained model to text three datasets respective in we implemented in Sect. 3.2, it also showed TTUR's effect to SR in our architecture in Fig. 6.

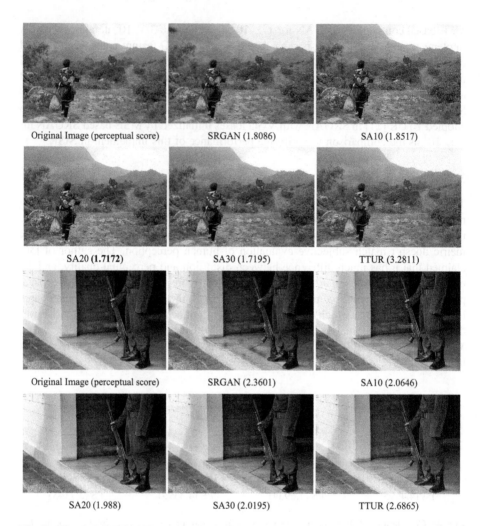

Fig. 5. We used "SRGAN" to represent original architecture, "SA10" to represent MSE-based GAN with SA for 1×10^5 iterations, "SA20" to which with SA for 2×10^5 and "SA30" to which with SA for 3×10^5 iterations, we also used "TTUR" to represent MSE-based GAN with SA for 2×10^5 iterations and adopted TTUR in following VGG losses GAN's training.

We can observe the difference between original images and images super-resolved by different models and training steps from Fig. 5 and Table 1. From the comparison of perceptual scores from single images and average perceptual scores from three testing datasets, the better pre-trained model of ours is "SA20" which based in MSE-GAN with SA for 2×10^5 iterations. The "SA30" has the same property with the original, and the performance of "SA10" is worse than the original with little difference. It should be noted that applicable step of training with SA can obtain the better result, not as much as better, too much steps of training with SA can cause severe distortion of texture. We can also observe that the model with SA can also remedy the situations that the images super-resolved by SRGAN have severe distortion of local regions in single image.

Table 1. Average Perceptual score of three dataset. The results of different datasets performed obvious difference, but different model performed almost similarly in the same datasets.

Model	Set	BSD100	PIRM
SRGAN	2.789	2.3117	2.3554
VGG10w	2.8654	2.4021	2.4253
VGG20w	**2.7114**	**2.2174**	**2.3391**
VGG30w	2.8053	2.3466	2.4643
VGG20w (TTUR)	×	3.6681	×

Fig. 6. Comparison of which if use TTUR [11] or not, the image which on the left is SRGANSA20, the right is TTUR. We can see the TTUR's images have unnatural texture.

TTUR [11] used to stabilize the training process, especially make both Generator and Discriminator in the last phase of training. We adopted this training skill to make the model perform better at first, but the result showed using TTUR has unsatisfactory effect on SISR tasks in Fig. 6. The detail texture features lost severely, it was replaced by square and unnatural texture features.

4 Conclusion

We proposed our architecture with attention mechanism (Self-Attention) in both Generator and Discriminator. Comparing performance of each different step experiment, the MSE-based SRGAN training with SA showed the better result and results of training for 2×10^5 iterations are the better in our model. Our architecture not only achieved the better perceptual scores, but also handled the distortion of local regions in results of original architecture. It showed the attention mechanism (Self-Attention) can be used to improve the property of SISR tasks based on GANs model. In final, we adopted TTUR in the better model of ours and the results of this implement generated unnatural texture features, it demonstrated the TTUR may not be applicable to this series of architecture. In the future, we will continue improving the architecture to make model more robust to adjust to diverse images, the problems of current architecture couldn't handle the super-resolved problems of different distance of scenes in images will be our next research.

Acknowledgments. This work is supported by National Key Research and Development Plan under Grant No. 2016YFC0801005. This work is supported by Grant No. 2018JKF617.

References

1. Dong, C., Loy, C.C., He, K., Tang, X.: Learning a deep convolutional network for image super-resolution. In: Fleet, D., Pajdla, T., Schiele, B., Tuytelaars, T. (eds.) ECCV 2014. LNCS, vol. 8692, pp. 184–199. Springer, Cham (2014). https://doi.org/10.1007/978-3-319-10593-2_13

2. Goodfellow, I.J., Pouget-Abadie, J., Mirza, M., et al.: Generative adversarial nets. In: International Conference on Neural Information Processing Systems (2014)

3. Ledig, C., Theis, L., Huszar, F., et al.: Photo-realistic single image super-resolution using a generative adversarial network (2016)

4. He, K., Zhang, X., Ren, S., et al.: Delving deep into rectifiers: surpassing human-level performance on ImageNet classification (2015)

5. Blau, Y., Mechrez, R., Timofte, R., Michaeli, T., Zelnik-Manor, L.: The PIRM challenge on perceptual super resolution (2018). https://www.pirm2018.org/PIRM-SR.html

6. Agustsson, E., Timofte, R.: NTIRE 2017 challenge on single image super-resolution: dataset and study. In: CVPRW (2017)

7. Timofte, R., et al.: NTIRE 2017 challenge on single image super-resolution: methods and results. In: CVPRW (2017)

8. Bevilacqua, M., Roumy, A., Guillemot, C., Alberi-Morel, M.L.: Low-complexity single-image super-resolution based on nonnegative neighbor embedding. In: BMVC (2012)

9. Zeyde, R., Elad, M., Protter, M.: On single image scale-up using sparse-representations. In: Boissonnat, J.-D., et al. (eds.) Curves and Surfaces 2010. LNCS, vol. 6920, pp. 711–730. Springer, Heidelberg (2012). https://doi.org/10.1007/978-3-642-27413-8_47

10. Martin, D., Fowlkes, C., Tal, D., Malik, J.: A database of human segmented natural images and its application to evaluating segmentation algorithms and measuring ecological statistics. In: IEEE International Conference on Computer Vision (ICCV), vol. 2, pp. 416–423 (2001)

11. Heusel, M., Ramsauer, H., Unterthiner, T., Nessler, B., Hochreiter, S.: GANs trained by a two time-scale update rule converge to a local nash equilibrium. In: NIPS, pp. 6629–6640 (2017)

12. Kingma, D., Ba, J.: Adam: a method for stochastic optimization. In: International Conference on Learning Representations (2015)

13. Ioffe, S., Szegedy, C.: Batch normalization: accelerating deep network training by reducing internal covariate shift. In: International Conference on Machine Learning. JMLR.org (2015)

14. Mirza, M., Osindero, S.: Conditional generative adversarial nets. Computer Science, pp. 2672–2680 (2014)

15. Mao, X., Li, Q., Xie, H., et al.: Least squares generative adversarial networks (2016)

16. Arjovsky, M., Chintala, S., Bottou, L.: Wasserstein GAN (2017)

17. Gulrajani, I., Ahmed, F., Arjovsky, M., et al.: Improved training of Wasserstein GANs (2017)
18. Radford, A., Metz, L., Chintala, S.: Unsupervised representation learning with deep convolutional generative adversarial networks. CoRR, abs/1511.06434 (2015)
19. Isola, P., Zhu, J.-Y., Zhou, T., Efros, A.A.: Image-to-image translation with conditional adversarial networks. In: CVPR (2017)
20. Zhu, J.-Y., Park, T., Isola, P., Efros, A.A.: Unpaired image-to-image translation using cycle-consistent adversarial networks. In: ICCV (2017)
21. Taigman, Y., Polyak, A., Wolf, L.: Unsupervised cross-domain image generation. In: ICLR (2017)
22. Liu, M., Tuzel, O.: Coupled generative adversarial networks. In: NIPS (2016)
23. Sønderby, C.K., Caballero, J., Theis, L., Shi, W., Huszár, F.: Amortised map inference for image super-resolution. In: ICLR (2017)
24. Reed, S., Akata, Z., Mohan, S., Tenka, S., Schiele, B., Lee, H.: Learning what and where to draw. In: NIPS (2016)
25. Reed, S., Akata, Z., Yan, X., Logeswaran, L., Schiele, B., Lee, H.: Generative adversarial text-to-image synthesis. In: ICML (2016)
26. Zhang, H., et al.: StackGAN: text to photo-realistic image synthesis with stacked generative adversarial networks. In: ICCV (2017)
27. Karras, T., Aila, T., Laine, S., Lehtinen, J.: Progressive growing of GANs for improved quality, stability, and variation. In: ICLR (2018)
28. Kim, J., Kwon Lee, J., Mu Lee, K.: Accurate image super-resolution using very deep convolutional networks. In: CVPR (2016)
29. Lai, W.S., Huang, J.B., Ahuja, N., Yang, M.H.: Deep Laplacian pyramid networks for fast and accurate super-resolution. In: CVPR (2017)
30. Zhang, H., Goodfellow, I., Metaxas, D., et al.: Self-attention generative adversarial networks (2018)
31. Bahdanau, D., Cho, K., Bengio, Y.: Neural machine translation by jointly learning to align and translate (2014). arXiv:1409.0473
32. Gregor, K., Danihelka, I., Graves, A., Rezende, D.J., Wierstra, D.: DRAW: a recurrent neural network for image generation. In: ICML (2015)
33. Yang, Z., He, X., Gao, J., Deng, L., Smola, A.J.: Stacked attention networks for image question answering. In CVPR (2016)
34. Vaswani, A., et al.: Attention is all you need. arXiv:1706.03762 (2017)
35. Xu, T., et al.: AttnGAN: fine-grained text to image generation with attentional generative adversarial networks. In: CVPR (2018)
36. Blau, Y., Michaeli, T.: The perception-distortion tradeoff. In: CVPR (2017)
37. Ma, C., Yang, C.Y., Yang, X., Yang, M.H.: Learning a no-reference quality metric for single-image super-resolution. CVIU 158, 1–16 (2017)
38. Mittal, A., Soundararajan, R., Bovik, A.C.: Making a completely blind image quality analyzer. IEEE Signal Process. Lett. 20(3), 209–212 (2013)

Tiny Vehicle Detection from UAV Imagery

Jinze Li, Rong Wang$^{(\boxtimes)}$, and Jianwei Ding

People's Public Security University of China, Beijing 102623, China
lijinzewudi@126.com, dbdxwangrong@163.com

Abstract. In the past decade, great progress has been made in general object detection based on deep convolutional neural networks. However, object detection from Unmanned Aerial Vehicles (UAV) imagery received not so much concern. In this paper, a densely connected feature mining network is proposed for high accuracy detection. Specifically, multi-scale predictions are used to enhance the feature representation of the tiny vehicles. Furthermore, a stream-lined one-stage detection network is used to achieve satisfactory trade-off between speed and accuracy. Finally, a improved distance metric function is integrated into the priors clustering process, which can lead to a better prelim-inary location before training. The proposed architecture is evaluated on the highly competitive UAV benchmark (UAVDT). The experimental results show that the proposed dense-darknet network has achieved a competitive perfor-mance of 42.03% mAP (mean Average Precision) and good generalization ability on the other UAV benchmarks.

Keywords: Tiny vehicle detection · Convolutional neural networks · Unmanned Aerial Vehicles

1 Introduction

In recent years, with the continuous development of artificial intelligence methods represented by deep learning in the field of image processing [26–28], a large number of object detection methods use deep convolutional neural networks. These detection models based on deep convolutional neural networks fall into two categories. One is the region proposal based framework, which adopts a two-step method with two-stage classification, further regression, two-stage features and feature alignment, so its advantage is high precision, such as Faster R-CNN [2], SPP-net [5] and R-FCN [6]. The other is the regression based framework. This one-stage framework locates objects based on global regression and classification, directly establishing the mapping of image pixel points to bounding box coordinates [1]. There is no doubt that their pioneers are YOLO [3] and SSD [4], and it is the one-stage streamlined network structure design that makes them faster.

At the same time, with the advantage of high mobility, Unmanned Aerial Vehicles (UAV) are used in agriculture, construction, public safety and other fields. However, the UAV images are diverse in terms of angle of view, background, texture, color, etc.

© Springer Nature Singapore Pte Ltd. 2019
Y. Wang et al. (Eds.): IGTA 2019, CCIS 1043, pp. 370–381, 2019.
https://doi.org/10.1007/978-981-13-9917-6_36

The existing deep learning network does not exhibit sufficient excellent effects in the object detection task of the aerial photography from the drone. The rapid development of urban transport infrastructure has led to a sharp increase in the demand for intelligent systems capable of monitoring the safety of traffic and pedestrians on the streets. Fundamental to these applications are a large number of benchmarks for object detection at the angle of unmanned aerial vehicles. To this end, a large number of UAV object detection and tracking datasets have been recently proposed,such as UAV123 [9], VisDrone 2018 [15], UA-DETRAC [8] and UAVDT [7]. UAVDT, one of these UAV datasets, has re-evaluated the current top deep based object detection frameworks [2, 4, 6, 10] in the field of general object detection [11–13]. Extensive experiment results show that the current state-of-the-art methods perform relative worse on some of these datasets. Due to the new challenges (e.g., cluttered urban environments, data imbalance, frequent occlusion, high density, small object, and camera motion) appeared in UAV based unconstrained real scenes, many innovative algorithms or improved fusions of classical algorithms are constantly being proposed. Yolov3 [21] uses the same techniques as the feature pyramid network to predict boxes from multiple scales. CornerNet [25] abandons the traditional anchor box mechanism and gets a pair of coordinate points to locate the object through corner pooling. Unfortunately, this kind of network is still difficult to train. A recent research [18] indicates that convolutional neural networks can be easier to train if they have much short connections between the early and later layers. In order to explore the performance of dense blocks combine with one-stage multi-scale training in UAV detection tasks, we used the dense-darknet as the core architecture to extract the vehicle features. We test our model on UAVDT benchmark and it obtains 42.03% mean average precision. To further evaluate the generalization capabilities of the model, we randomly extracted several images containing a large number of high-speed moving tiny vehicles from the UA-DETRAC dataset. The experimental result shows that our proposed learner has good performance in all categories.

The subsequent of this paper is organized as follows: We introduce our network architecture in Sect. 2. In Sect. 3, we perform experiment, present results, analysis and compare our method with others. Finally, we draw the conclusions and discuss future research in Sect. 4.

2   Method

Inspired by multi-scale training, densely connected feature extraction, and single-stage real-time network inspiration, we combine the idea of feature pyramids, darknet53 and DenseNet, refer to Fig. 1.

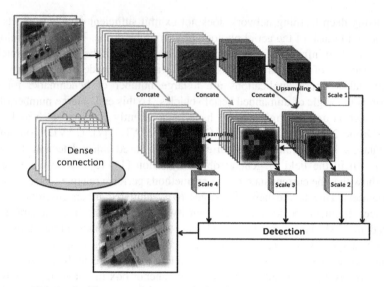

Fig. 1. Architecture of our convolutional neural network is shown.

2.1 Muti-scale Training Architecture

Multi-scale training in object detection can help identify extremely large or small objects. A larger convolution window can see larger objects after convolution, and vice versa can only see smaller section. In extreme cases, if we use the minimum convolution window of 1 multiplied by 1, the final convolved image granularity is exactly the same as the input image granularity. Conversely, if the convolution window of the image length multiplied by width is used, only a coarse-grained feature output can be encoded.

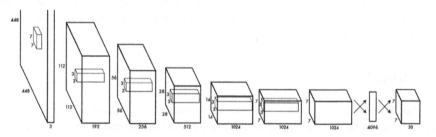

Fig. 2. YOLO architecture diagram.

For the yolov1 [3] network model shown in Fig. 2, each layer uses the same size convolution window, and it becomes powerless to identify very large objects or ultrasmall objects.

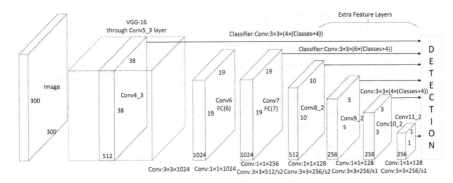

Fig. 3. SSD is synthesized using feature maps of different convolutional layers, connecting six convolutional layers to the final detection layer for classification and regression.

As shown in Fig. 3, the SSD [4] network architecture goes further. The feature map of the last detection layer is jointly generated by the feature maps of the previous multiple scales. This improves the detection of multi-scale objects with the computational complexity allowed. However, SSD also has obvious defects. For very small objects with only a few tens of pixels, the high-level feature map of SSD can no longer capture such small objects.

In order to solve the above problem, the FPN [16] network is proposed. This feature pyramid network does not blindly sample and extract semantic features to identify objects, but performs upsampling from each layer of the top layer (top-down) to obtain more accurate pixel location information. Upsampling to restore the feature map is a good way to alleviate the problem of pixel misalignment. The dense-darknet model we used is basically consistent with the yolov3 structure. It also absorbs a multi-scale prediction method similar to FPN (as shown in Fig. 4).

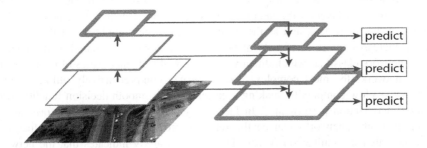

Fig. 4. A feature pyramid network with three scales.

2.2 Dense Connection

ResNet [14] was a masterpiece of image classification, which brought the detection of deep learning to a higher level. Later, many famous state-of-art networks [17, 19, 21] were also improved on the basis of ResNet. Huang et al. [20] proposes a stochastic depth network method similar to dropout[alexnet] to improve ResNet. Each step in the training process randomly "drops" some layers, which can significantly improve the generalization performance of ResNet. It shows that the neural network does not have to be a progressive hierarchy. That is to say, a layer in the network can depend not only on the features of the immediately preceding layer but also on the features of the previous layer. Meanwhile, randomly throwing away many layers during the training process will not break the convergence of the algorithm, indicating that ResNet has obvious redundancy, and each layer in the network extracts only a few features (so-called residuals). Based on the above two observations, Gao et al. [18] proposed the Dense Block structural unit, each layer is directly connected to all the layers in front of it to achieve the reuse of features (as shown in Fig. 5).

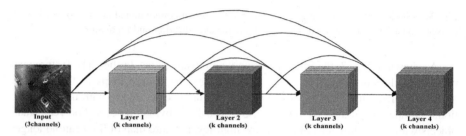

Fig. 5. Schematic diagram of a dense block, which reuses image shallow bottom features by concating them to deep semantic features.

DenseNet, consisting of dense blocks and transitional convolution and pooling layers, requires only a few features to be learned at each level, resulting in a significant reduction in parameter quantities and computational complexity. What's more, the dense connection network has good resistance to over-fitting, especially for applications where training data is relatively scarce [18]. There is a relatively straightforward explanation for the reasons why dense-shortcut can resist overfitting: the features extracted by each layer of the neural network are equivalent to a nonlinear transformation of the input data, and as the depth increases, the complexity of the transformation increases (more composite of nonlinear functions). Compared to the general neural network classifier, which directly depends on the characteristics of the last layer of the network (the most complex), DenseNet can comprehensively utilize features with low shallow complexity, making it easier to get a smooth decision function with better generalization performance. In fact, DenseNet's generalization performance is better than other networks can be theoretically proved: a conclusion [22] that was published almost simultaneously with DenseNet on arXiv indicates that the network structure similar to DenseNet has a smaller generalization error bound.

2.3   Darknet-53 Backbone

The real-time positioning and classification of objects from the images obtained by UAVs is a basic requirement for vehicle detection tasks. Although the two-stage network has the advantage of high precision, it is difficult to meet the needs of real-time detection. One-stage networks tend to have good trade-offs in speed and accuracy.

In the pictures taken by the Unmanned Aerial Vehicles (UAVs), the pixel of most objects usually does not exceed 0.5% of the image size. The bottleneck of the CornerNet [25] algorithm is the correct matching of a pair of corner points. Once a corner matching error occurs, at least two or more objects will be affected, which has a great influence on the IoU calculation. However, each cell in YOLOv3 [21] is only responsible for predicting the object whose center is in it. Even if there is an error, it is only related to the confidence of a single object, and will not affect other objects. Therefore, YOLOv3 does not have such a problem.

We replace residual connections in darknet53 [21] with a dense connection and slightly adjust the number of convolutional layers of the densely connected module(the growing rate of each dense block is 64, 128, 256, 512 and 1024 respectively), and

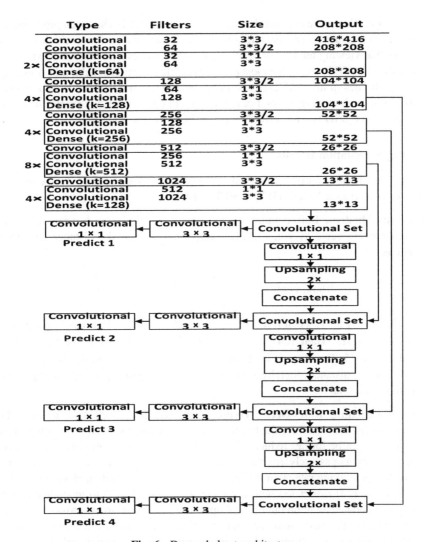

Fig. 6. Dense-darknet architecture.

finally output on four scales (operations similar to yolov3, but one more scale). The first scale adds some convolution layers after the base network and outputs the box information. The second scale is upsampled from the convolutional layer of the second to last layer in scale-1 and then added to the feature map of the previous densely connected block, and the box information is output again after passing through multiple convolutions. It is twice as large as the first scale. The third scale and the fourth scale are operated in the same way. We still retain 1×1 convolution and 3×3 convolution for controlling the number of channels in the middle of dense connections. Our dense-darknet network model is shown in Fig. 6.

3   Experiment and Analysis

In this section, We use the existing darknet53.conv.74 model that has been pre-trained on the ImageNet to exact the precise bird's-eye-view feature and perform vehicle detection from a mobile viewing angle. For verifying the effectiveness, the model is extensively evaluated on UAVDT, one of the most popular vehicle detection benchmarks nowadays. About 80k frames in the UAVDT benchmark dataset are annotated over 2.7k vehicles with 0.84 million bounding boxes. For the purpose of comparison, we employ 4 state-of-the-art detectors, SSD [4], FasterRCNN [2], R-FCN [6] and RON [10].

3.1   Implementation Details

We train our dense yolo-based methods on a machine with CPU i7 7700x and 24G memory, as well as a Nvidia GTX 1080 Ti GPU.

Dimension Clusters. Before training, We almost use the same k-means clustering method on every scale as yolov2 [24], except that we use the distance calculation formula as:

$$d(\text{box, centroid}) = \sqrt{1 - \text{IOU}^2(\text{box, centroid})} \tag{1}$$

As shown in Fig. 7, when $\text{IOU} = 0.9$, $d^2 = 0.19$, which is 19 times larger than the original $d^2 = 0.01$. When $\text{IOU} = 0.5$, $d^2 = 0.75$, which is 3 times larger than the original $d^2 = 0.25$. Therefore, this distance metric can directly amplify the influence of the IOU on the distance, thereby guiding the more accurate prior clustering, which seems more reasonable.

Adaptive Learning Rate Decay Hyperparameter. It is well known that when training a model, it is usual for the training loss to oscillate back and forth between two values and cannot be further reduced due to excessive learning rate. Instead of relying on metaphysics to passively try the lr (learning rate) hyperparameter, it is better to actively design learning rate attenuation. In the experiment, we adopted adaptive cosine decay function [23] associated with normalized loss (see Eq. 2) to guarantee that the learning rate update can jump out of local optimum and the binarized cross entropy loss function may continuously reduced, and then there are dense connections so that the network can reduce over-fitting, which greatly improves the training efficiency.

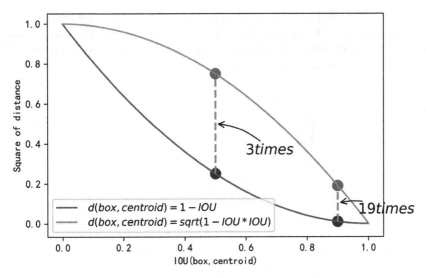

Fig. 7. Our distance metric function (red) vs the original function (blue) (Color figure online)

Here we denote that the loss values as l, the expectation of l as μ and the standard deviation as σ. We set hyperparameters α and β to control the minimum learning rate. The updated learning rate is as follows:

$$lr^* = lr \times [(1 - \alpha)c_d + \alpha] \times [|1 - \mu|/\sigma + \beta] \tag{2}$$

Where c_d refers to cosine attenuation function value, it could be defined as:

$$c_d = 0.5 \times [1 + \cos(g_s\pi/d_s)] \tag{3}$$

Where d_s indicates the number of decay steps (i.e. the number of iterations required to decay from the initial learning rate to the minimum learning rate) and g_s indicates the current training epoch. g_s takes the form:

$$g_s = \min(g_s, d_s) \tag{4}$$

In practice, in order to prevent the model from falling into local optimum, we update the g_s value to 20000, 5000 and 5000 respectively when iterating to 20000, 40,000 and 45000 times.

3.2 Experiment on UAVDT

As one of the latest UAV vehicle detection datasets, the UAVDT benchmark consists of 100 video sequences, which are captured by DJI Inspire 2 drone platform. There are three categories of vehicles in the UAVDT data set, labeled as cars, trucks, and buses. Consistent with the real situation, more than 90% of the tag categories in the picture are cars, which leads to a huge imbalance in training data. Although the ROC curve and the

PR (Precision-Recall) curve are commonly used in the classification imbalance problem, in the context of the category imbalance, the number of negative examples causes the growth of FPR to be inconspicuous, thence would result in ROC curves tend to present an overly optimistic estimate compared to PR curves.

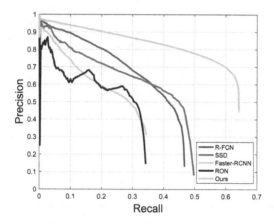

Fig. 8. Comparison of PR curves of our method and other methods.

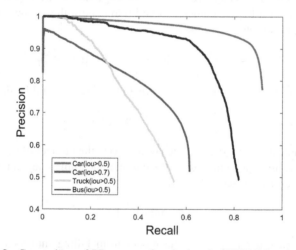

Fig. 9. Comparison of PR curves of each class in UAVDT benchmark.

Figure 8 shows that our model is more remarkable on UAVDT than other methods and has excellent coverage for positive samples. Figure 9 shows the PR curves for each class. To further evaluate and analyze our method, we calculate the average precision for each category separately in Table 1. The results show that our method can fully extract the semantic features of car through huge amount of labels, especially after adding improved distance metric clustering and adaptive learning rate techniques. But for the buses and trucks with very similar appearance and size to cars, the model's discriminating ability is still very limited. The examples in Fig. 10 illustrates this point.

Table 1. Comparison of each class average precision on UAVDT of our method (%)

Method	Car			Truck			Bus		
	AP50	AP60	AP70	AP50	AP60	AP70	AP50	AP60	AP70
Dense_darknet	73.3	66.2	49.3	29.9	27.7	21.2	42.1	40.7	37.8
Dense_darknet + tip 1	73.7	67.3	51.5	30.0	28.1	22.1	42.1	40.9	37.9
Dense_darknet + tip 1 + tip 2	**74.0**	68.2	53.8	**30.1**	28.6	22.9	**42.2**	41.3	38.4

Remarks: tip 1 means learning rate attenuation optimization, tip 2 means cluster optimization.

We randomly extracted some images from the UA-DETRAC dataset to test the generalization ability of our model. The results in Fig. 11 show that our model has good generalization capabilities for other drone vehicle datasets.

Fig. 10. Left column: Examples of correctly detected images from a bird's-eye view. The middle column: examples of images detected from a side view, there exists undetected problem when cars gather together and occlude each other. Right column: A large number of truck tags are incorrectly judged as car.

Fig. 11. The results on the UADETRAC dataset suggest that our network has successfully learned some kind of "pattern" from the perspective of drones, rather than simple violent memories.

4 Conclusion

In this paper, we proposed a densely-connected vehicle detection model which was based on yolov3 network and trained with a adaptive learning rate decline followed cosine learning-rate schedule. Our architecture makes predictions on multiple scales and implements dense connections between convolutional layers of the same size in each scale. We used a more reasonable k-means cluster distance metric which was proved to improve the detection effect. Our architecture made a mean average precision of 42.03% on UAVDT benchmark, which far surpassed SSD (33.62%) and R-FCN (34.35%).

With deep-learning-based computer vision tasks fueling these drones, we can predict that drones will be used more widely than ever before in previously unimaginable applications, delivering more efficiency and convenience than surveillance cameras with fixed camera angle, scale and view. In the class imbalance data benchmark, how to accurately mine the characteristics of the labelled data with less quantity, or in other words, how to use more powerful methods for weakly supervised drone image detection will be our future research direction.

Acknowledgments. This work is supported by National Key Research and Development Plan under Grant No. 2016YFC0801005. This work is supported by Grant No. 2018JXYJ49.

References

1. Zhao, Z.Q., Zheng, P., Xu, S.T., Wu, X.: Object detection with deep learning: a review (2018)
2. Ren, S., He, K., Girshick, R., Sun, J.: Faster R-CNN: towards real-time object detection with region proposal networks. In: International Conference on Neural Information Processing Systems (2015)
3. Redmon, J., Divvala, S., Girshick, R., Farhadi, A.: You only look once: unified, real-time object detection (2015)
4. Liu, W., et al.: SSD: single shot multibox detector. In: Leibe, B., Matas, J., Sebe, N., Welling, M. (eds.) ECCV 2016. LNCS, vol. 9905, pp. 21–37. Springer, Cham (2016). https://doi.org/10.1007/978-3-319-46448-0_2
5. He, K., Zhang, X., Ren, S., Sun, J.: Spatial pyramid pooling in deep convolutional networks for visual recognition. IEEE Trans. Pattern Anal. Mach. Intell. **37**(9), 1904–1916 (2014)
6. Dai, J., Li, Y., He, K., Sun, J.: R-FCN: object detection via region-based fully convolutional networks (2016)
7. Du, D., Qi, Y., Yu, H., Yang, Y., Duan, K.: The unmanned aerial vehicle benchmark: object detection and tracking (2018)
8. Wen, L., Du, D., Cai, Z., Lei, Z., Chang, M.C., Qi, H., et al.: UA-DETRAC: a new benchmark and protocol for multi-object detection and tracking. In: Computer Science (2015)
9. Mueller, M., Smith, N., Ghanem, B.: A benchmark and simulator for UAV tracking. Far East J. Math. Sci. **2**(2), 445–461 (2016)
10. Kong, T., Sun, F., Yao, A., Liu, H., Lu, M., Chen, Y.: RON: reverse connection with objectness prior networks for object detection. In: CVPR (2017)

11. Everingham, M., et al.: The 2005 PASCAL visual object classes challenge. In: Quiñonero-Candela, J., Dagan, I., Magnini, B., d'Alché-Buc, F. (eds.) MLCW 2005. LNCS (LNAI), vol. 3944, pp. 117–176. Springer, Heidelberg (2006). https://doi.org/10.1007/11736790_8

12. Lin, T.-Y., et al.: Microsoft COCO: common objects in context. In: Fleet, D., Pajdla, T., Schiele, B., Tuytelaars, T. (eds.) ECCV 2014. LNCS, vol. 8693, pp. 740–755. Springer, Cham (2014). https://doi.org/10.1007/978-3-319-10602-1_48

13. Russakovsky, O., Deng, J., Su, H., Krause, J., Satheesh, S., Ma, S., et al.: ImageNet large scale visual recognition challenge. Int. J. Comput. Vis. **115**(3), 211–252 (2015)

14. He, K., Zhang, X., Ren, S., Sun, J.: Deep residual learning for image recognition (2015)

15. Zhu, P., Wen, L., Dawei, D., Xiao, B., Ling, H., Hu, Q., et al.: VisDrone-DET2018: the vision meets drone object detection in image challenge results (2018)

16. Lin, T.Y., Dollár, P., Girshick, R., He, K., Hariharan, B., Belongie, S.: Feature pyramid networks for object detection (2016)

17. Xie, S., Girshick, R., Dollár, P., Tu, Z., He, K.: Aggregated residual transformations for deep neural networks (2016)

18. Gao, H., Zhuang, L., van der Maaten, L., Weinberger, K.Q.: Densely connected convolutional networks. In: IEEE Conference on Computer Vision & Pattern Recognition (2017)

19. Chen, Y., Li, J., Xiao, H., Jin, X., Yan, S., Feng, J.: Dual path networks (2017)

20. Huang, G., Sun, Y., Liu, Z., Sedra, D., Weinberger, K.Q.: Deep networks with stochastic depth. In: Leibe, B., Matas, J., Sebe, N., Welling, M. (eds.) ECCV 2016. LNCS, vol. 9908, pp. 646–661. Springer, Cham (2016). https://doi.org/10.1007/978-3-319-46493-0_39

21. Redmon, J., Farhadi, A.: YOLOv3: an incremental improvement (2018)

22. Cortes, C., Gonzalvo, X., Kuznetsov, V., Mohri, M., Yang, S.: AdaNet: adaptive structural learning of artificial neural networks (2016)

23. Pleiss, G., Chen, D., Huang, G., Li, T., van der Maaten, L., Weinberger, K.Q.: Memory-efficient implementation of DenseNets (2017)

24. Redmon, J., Farhadi, A.: YOLO9000: better, faster, stronger (2017)

25. Law, H., Deng, J.: CornerNet: detecting objects as paired keypoints (2018)

26. Zhang, T., Wang, R., Ding, J.: A discriminative feature learning based on deep residual network for face verification. In: Wang, Y., Jiang, Z., Peng, Y. (eds.) IGTA 2018. CCIS, vol. 875, pp. 411–420. Springer, Singapore (2018). https://doi.org/10.1007/978-981-13-1702-6_41

27. Zhang, X., Wang, R., Ding, J.: Abnormal event detection by learning spatiotemporal features in videos. In: Wang, Y., Jiang, Z., Peng, Y. (eds.) IGTA 2018. CCIS, vol. 875, pp. 421–431. Springer, Singapore (2018). https://doi.org/10.1007/978-981-13-1702-6_42

28. Zhou, J., Wang, R., Ding, J.: Deep convolutional features for correlation filter based tracking with parallel network. In: Wang, Y., Jiang, Z., Peng, Y. (eds.) IGTA 2018. CCIS, vol. 875, pp. 461–470. Springer, Singapore (2018). https://doi.org/10.1007/978-981-13-1702-6_46

SGM-Based Disparity Estimation Under Radiometric Variations

WeiMin Yuan[1(✉)], XiaoYan Tong[1], and Bin Xiao[2]

[1] School of Astronautics, BeiHang University, Beijing 100191, China
yuanweimin@buaa.edu.cn
[2] Civil Aviation Flight University of China, Guanghan 618307, Sichuan, China

Abstract. The semi-global matching (SGM) performances excellent in stereo correspondence field, it reaches a good trade-off between correspondence accuracy and computational complexity. However, the performance of SGM is limited under radiometric variations, such as varying lighting and exposure conditions. In this paper, an improved SGM method is presented to remedy this problem. To eliminate the discrepancy of illumination between the stereo images, both histogram equalization and binary singleton expansion are adopted in pre-processing stage. The weighted median filter is adopted after conventional LRC in the disparity refinement stage to remove the outlier errors and preserve edges. The stereo images from the Middlebury benchmark are used in the experiment. The experimental result show that the average RMSE of the improved SGM method is 12.64% lower than the raw SGM. The proposed method can effectively improve the accuracy of disparity map compared to the SGM algorithm.

Keywords: Semi-global matching · Radiometric variations ·
Histogram equalization · Binary singleton expansion · Weighted median filter

1 Introduction

Stereo correspondence has been investigated extensively and deeply in computer vision area. Stereo correspondence algorithm establishes the correspondence between the input stereo images and generates the resulting disparity. It has been widely used in autonomous driving, view synthesis, motion detection, etc. An excellent review of various stereo correspondence algorithms was provided by Scharstein [1]. They categorized the stereo correspondence algorithm according to the following fundamental stages: (1) cost computation stage (i.e., calculate corresponding points from stereo images), (2) support aggregation stage (i.e., aggregate initial costs within a support window), (3) disparity optimization stage (i.e., select disparity) and (4) disparity refinement stage (i.e., improve the accuracy of disparity map).

Stereo correspondence algorithm can be mainly divided into two categories based on the algorithm on how the disparity is been computed, namely local methods and global methods. In local stereo correspondence algorithm, the process of computing matching costs is aggregated over a window or region based on predefined size and winner-takes-all is applied to select the most suitable matching pixels. Local correspondence

© Springer Nature Singapore Pte Ltd. 2019
Y. Wang et al. (Eds.): IGTA 2019, CCIS 1043, pp. 382–391, 2019.
https://doi.org/10.1007/978-981-13-9917-6_37

algorithms are fast and simple. But, they are very sensitive to noises and disparity map needed further processing. Comparison with local correspondence methods, the global correspondence algorithms consider all pixels in the reference image to estimate the disparity values. In global algorithms, the energy function is minimized to obtain the disparity map. Most popular methods include graph cuts (GC) [2], belief propagation (BP) [3] and dynamic programming (DP) [4]. Although the quality of disparity maps obtained from global correspondence algorithms is much accurate than that from local correspondence algorithms, the lengthy computation time of global correspondence algorithms makes them unsuitable for real-time applications.

SGM, presented by Hirschmüller [5], shows more accurate and efficient and compared with local and global correspondence algorithms. It combines the efficiency of local algorithm with the accuracy of global algorithm. Although SGM algorithm provides a good trade-off between the time and accuracy, it achieves unsatisfactory result under varying radiometric variations. Figure 1 depicts the result for the 'Bowling' stereo images under radiometric variations (left image with exposure 1, illumination 3. Right image with exposure 2, illumination 3). Figure 1(c) the Ground truth. Figure 1(d) depicts the result computed from the SGM method.

To remedy this problem, in this paper an improved SGM method is presented to enhance the accuracy of disparity map under radiometric differences. In the proposed method, both histogram equalization and binary singleton expansion are adopted in the pre-processing to eliminate the discrepancy of illumination between the input stereo images. Another strategy is employed in disparity map refinement step, which use the WMF to reduce the erroneous matching of final result. The experimental result shows a significant improvement on the accuracy compared to raw SGM.

The rest of the paper is organized as follows: The previous job about SGM stereo correspondence is provided in Sect. 2. The proposed improved SGM method is detailed presented in Sect. 3, experimental result of this paper is presented in the Sect. 4. Finally, Sect. 5 is the conclusion of this paper.

(a)   (b)   (c)   (d)

Fig. 1. Stereo correspondence of 'Bowling' image under radiometric variations from Middlebury benchmark. (a) Left image with exposure 1 and illumination 3. (b) Right image with exposure 2 and illumination 3. (c) Ground truth. (d) Result computed from SGM.

2 Related Works

Most of the stereo correspondence algorithms are based on the consistency assumption: the matching points in the stereo images have similar intensity or color values. However, in real-world situation (indoor or outdoor), stereo images may be captured under radiometric variations such as illumination or exposure changes, causing the matching pixels cannot be same pixel values. SGM is an intensive area of research. In this part, we briefly introduce the SGM methods that presented in recent years to cope with the varying radiometric variation problems in this field.

The performance of existing matching cost functions on stereo images under radiometric variations was measured by Hirschmüller [6]. The light intensity, exposure and noise as variables in the experiment. CT achieved the best performance among the measured matching cost functions. In order to compensate for the differences in radiation between the stereo images, it was recommended to use the mutual information (MI) matching cost function [5]. However SGM method based on MI matching cost performs badly under severe varying illumination conditions, Loghman et al. [7] presented an improved SGM correspondence algorithm based on the census transform (CT). To enhance the quality of raw disparity map, a filter based on spatial Gaussian Weighted Averaging was implemented. A matching cost method based on color transformation [8] has been presented in which the color of a stereoscopic image is adaptively transformed such that the matching points have the same color. However, the algorithm does not consider the influence of the occlusion area.

Most of the parametric matching costs (such as SAD, SSD, NCC) are very sensitive to radiometric variations. In the work of [9], to overcome this problem, a new SGM method used sum of gradient magnitude differences is proposed. The method achieved well performance under the radiometric variations. The author in [10] presented an algorithm based on SGM and census transformation. Implement two sub-pixel interpolations to improve the sub-pixel level accuracy.

3 Proposed Method

In this paper, we define the left image as a reference image and the right image as the target image. In addition, the stereo images used in the experiment are all rectified by the eipolar constraint. The pipeline of the improved SGM method is showed in Fig. 2. It contains the following three steps: (1) HE and BSE are adopted in the pre-processing to eliminate the discrepancy of illumination between the stereo images. (2) A coarse disparity map obtained from the SGM method. (3) The disparities are validated by enforcing the LRC to filter out mismatching, and finally perform WMF to further improve the accuracy of result.

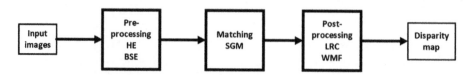

Fig. 2. Block diagram of the improved SGM method.

3.1   Pre-processing

The radiometric variation occurs due to global intensity change and local intensity change. The global intensity change is caused by camera gain and exposure, and the local intensity difference is caused by light intensity variation. In the pre-processing stage, both the histogram equalization (HE) and binary singleton expansion (BSE) are adopted to eliminate the radiometric variations.

3.1.1   Histogram Equalization

Histogram equalization (HE) [11], also called histogram flattening, is a widely useful technique for improving the image contrast due to its simplicity and comparatively better performance. In this paper, HE is used to reduce the large global intensity difference between the image pair and adjust luminance differences to be the same. The conversion formula is defined as:

$$D_B = D_{max} \int_0^{D_A} P_{D_A}(\mu)d\mu \tag{1}$$

Where D_B is the converted intensity value, D_A is the intensity value before the conversion, D_{max} is the maximum of the intensity. When the image is composed of discrete gray levels in the range of [0, 255], the formula is:

$$D_B = \frac{D_{max}}{A} \sum_{i=0}^{D_A} H_i \tag{2}$$

Where the A is the total number of the pixel, H_i is the number of pixels of the i gray scale. The result of the HE is showed in the Fig. 3(b).

3.1.2   Binary Singleton Expansion

BSE is adopted in order to reduce the local intensity differences by dividing the results of histogram equalized image with its column vector:

$$A = \max(I_{in}, [], 2) \tag{3}$$

$$\begin{aligned} I_{out} \\ = \text{bsxfun}(@ \text{rdivide}, I_{in}, A) \end{aligned} \tag{4}$$

where the A is a column vector containing the largest elements of every row of the input image I in obtained by histogram flattening, the I_{out} is the output image. The I_{out} obtained normalized values by element-wise dividing of I_{in} with I_{out} to perform SGM. The result obtained from BSE is showed in the Fig. 3(c).

The intensity histogram of the input stereo images under radiometric variations are showed in the Fig. 4. The resulting image after histogram equalization process is showed in Fig. 4(b) and (c) shows the resulting image after binary singleton expansion process.

Fig. 3. Results of pre-processing processing. (a) The radiometric variations input images. (b)The resulting image from HE. (c) The resulting image from BSE.

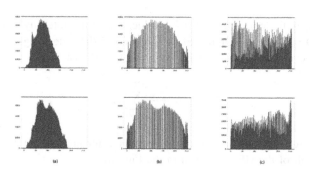

Fig. 4. (a) The histogram of the input stereo images. (b) The intensity histogram of the images processed by HE. (c) The intensity histogram of the images processed by BSE.

3.2 Semi-global Matching

SGM algorithm presented by Hirschmüller [5]. It has been introduced in order to compensate for the high computational load of global optimization methods and provide a robust optimization scheme. The SGM successfully combines the advantages of the other two algorithms.

The similarity criterion is computed, which in this case is the mutual information. The energy function in SGM consists three parts, as shown in Eq. (5): the first part named data term, which is the sum of all pixel matching costs. The second part adds a constant penalty P_1 for all pixels q in the neighborhood N_p of p. In order to cope with depth discontinuities regions, the last part provides a bigger constant P_2 ($P_2 > P_1$). D_p and D_q are the disparities of p and q, respectively.

$$E(D) = \sum_{p} C(p, D_p) + \sum_{q \in Np} P_1 T\big[\big|D_P - D_q\big| = 1\big] + \sum_{q \in N_p} p_2 T\big[\big|D_p - D_q\big| > 1\big]$$

$$(5)$$

This method minimizes the global energy in horizontal, vertical, and diagonal directions. The costs-path Lr (p, dp) of the pixel p (u, v) at disparity dp in direction r is calculated recursively as given by:

$$L_r(\boldsymbol{p}, d_p) = C(\boldsymbol{p}, d_p) + \min\big(L_r(\boldsymbol{p} - \boldsymbol{r}, d_p), L_r(\boldsymbol{p} - \boldsymbol{r}, d_p - 1)$$
$$+ P_1, L_r(\boldsymbol{p} - \boldsymbol{r}, d_p + 1) + P_1, min L_r(\boldsymbol{p} - \boldsymbol{r}, k) + P_2\big) \qquad (6)$$

Afterwards the costs S(p, dp) are summed up over all paths in all direction r (8 optimization directions are used in our method). The final disparity value is selected at the minimum cost.

$$S(\mathbf{p}, d_p) = \sum_{r} L_r(\boldsymbol{p}, d_p) \qquad (7)$$

3.3 Disparity Refinement

Disparity refinement stage is essential to obtain an accurate disparity map, which serves to find and correct those errors. There are many conventional refinement methods including: LRC, errors suppression, sub-pixel refinement, and filter strategies such as bilateral filter [12]. In this paper, we adopt the LRC and WMF to remove the outliers and improve the accuracy of the result.

3.3.1 Outliers Detection

LRC is employed to detect the outliers. This method was originally introduced in [13, 14]. This algorithm is based on the well-known uniqueness constraint, which assumes that in the right input image has a uniqueness matching match. This method checks if the disparity values in both directions are equal. In the occlusion regions, the two values do not match, because the image region in the left image is missing from the right image. Consequently, occlusion regions are should efficiently handled in the process of stereo correspondence. LRC needs to be employed two times using two different disparity maps as the reference. The result is obtained by interpolating the missing disparity for the least significant neighbors in the same image row using a piecewise constant function.

3.3.2 Weighted Median Filter

The weighted median filter proposed by Ma [15] can reduce noise and eliminate the high-frequently component of an image. It can be used in the post-processing stage to eliminate the outliers from the initial disparity map. In this paper, we introduce this filter as disparity refinement strategy after LRC check in our modified semi-global method due to its simplicity and nice properties. WMF is an operator, which replaces the pixel with weighted median of surrounding pixels in the current window. The weights w(p, q) between two pixels p and q are generated from the original image as shown in Eq. (8).

$$w(p, q) = \exp\left\{-|I(p) - I(q)|^2/2\sigma^2\right\} \tag{8}$$

WMF calculates the median of disparity values according to the color similarity and proximity functions.

4 Experimental Results

In this part, experiment is conducted to study the performance of the improved SGM algorithm. We mainly focus on the performance of the improved SGM method compared to initial SGM under radiometric variations. The performance of the comparison is evaluated using the rectified stereo image pair from the 2006 datasets of Middlebury benchmark. The test datasets consists of four pairs of stereo images (Fig. 5): "Baby" "Aloe", "Rocks", "Plastic". Each pair of images captured under different light conditions (the left image is taken with exposure 1 and illumination 3, the right image is taken with exposure 1 and illumination 2), which means they have different illumination color, lighting geometry, and gamma correlation. The root mean squared error (RMSE) is adopted to test the difference between the computed result dC(x, y) and ground truth dT(x, y), i.e.,

$$R = \left(\frac{1}{N}\sum_{(x,y)}|d_C(x, y) - d_T(x, y)|^2\right)^{\frac{1}{2}} \tag{9}$$

For all experiments, parameters were chosen empirically. All the experiments were running on CPU with core i3 2.53 GHz and 4 GB memories. The proposed method was implemented in python and Matlab and OpenCV.

The resulting map obtained from the improved SGM method is showed in Fig. 6. Figure 6(a) is the resulting maps of SGM for the stereo images in Fig. 5. Figure 6(b) is the resulting maps of the improved SGM. Figure 6(c) is Ground truth. Figure 6 demonstrates that the proposed method is more insensitive than SGM algorithm under different radiometric variations. The comparison of RMSE between SGM and the improved SGM in the images is showed in Table 1. The average RMSE of the SGM method is 56.44 and the proposed method is 43.8. That is to say, the improved SGM is 12.64% lower than the SGM. Consequently, we can find out that the improved SGM has lower RMSE than SGM in all images. The improved SGM performs better than SGM under radiometric variations. Although the performance of the improved SGM under radiometric variations is better than SGM method, it does not perform well in slanted and weak texture regions.

Fig. 5. Middlebury datasets under different illumination conditions used in the experiment the top image is taken with exposure 1 and illumination 3, the bottom image with exposure 1 and illumination 2. (a) Baby; (b) Aloe; (c) Rocks; (d) Plastic.

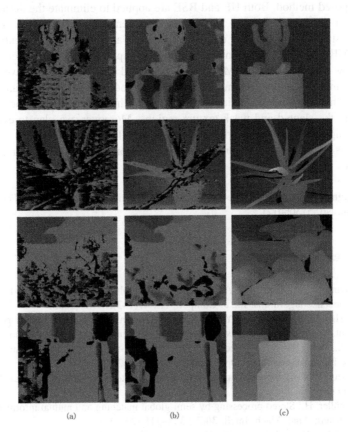

Fig. 6. Disparity map of test images. (a) SGM. (b) The proposed method. (c) The Ground truth.

Table 1. The RMSE of the proposed method and SGM algorithm in the different images.

Images	SGM	The proposed method
Baby	43.875	33.492
Aloe	57.705	41.257
Rocks	59.594	47.736
Plastic	64.588	52.721

5 Conclusion

A radiometric invariant improved SGM method is presented in this paper and evaluated under radiometric differences in indoors scene for the purpose of stereo correspondence. Compared to the SGM algorithm, there are two following additional strategies in the proposed method. Both HE and BSE are applied to eliminate the discrepancy of illumination difference globally and locally between the stereo images in the preprocessing stage. In the disparity refinement stage, in addition to the conventional LRC check, WMF is adopted to eliminate the outliers and preserve edges. The experimental results show that the average RMSE of the improved SGM is 12.64% lower than raw SGM. It demonstrates that the improved SGM method performs better than raw SGM under radiometric variation conditions. In the future, the improved SGM method can be modified in the slanted and weak texture regions. Moreover, we plan to evaluate the proposed algorithm on the Karlsruhe Institute of Technology (KITTI) dataset for autonomous driving, since this presents varying radiometric variations of real-life outdoor scenes.

Acknowledgments. This research is supported by the National Natural Science Foundation of China (Grant No. 51306012).

References

1. Scharstein, D., Szeliski, R.: A taxonomy and evaluation of dense two-frame stereo correspondence algorithms. Int. J. Comput. Vis. **47**(1–3), 7–42 (2002)
2. Wang, H.Q., Wu, M., Zhang, Y.B.: Effective stereo matching using reliable points based graph cut. In: Proceedings of Visual Communications and Image Processing, pp. 1–6 (2013)
3. Wang, X., Wang, H., Su, Y.: Accurate belief propagation with parametric and nonparametric measure for stereo matching. Optik **126**(5), 545–550 (2015)
4. Belhumeur, P.N.: A Bayesian approach to binocular stereopsis. Int. J. Comput. Vis. **19**(3), 237–260 (1996)
5. Hirschmüller, H.: Stereo processing by semi-global matching and mutual information. IEEE Trans. Pattern Anal. Mach. Intell. **30**(2), 328–341 (2008)
6. Hirschmüller, H., Scharstein, D.: Evaluation of stereo matching costs on images with radiometric differences. IEEE Trans. Pattern Anal. Mach. Intell. **31**(9), 1582–1599 (2009)
7. Loghman, M., Kim, J.: SGM-based dense disparity estimation using adaptive Census transform. In: International Conference on Connected Vehicles & Expo. IEEE (2014)

8. Jung, I.L., Chung, T.Y., Sim, J.Y., Kim, C.S.: Consistent stereo matching under varying radiometric conditions. IEEE Trans. Multi-media **15**, 56–69 (2013)

9. Hamzah, R.A., Ibrahim, H.: Improvement of stereo matching algorithm based on sum of gradient magnitude differences and semi-global method with refinement step. Electron. Lett. **54**(14), 876–878 (2018)

10. Pantilie, D., Nedevschi, S.: SORT-SGM: sub-pixel optimized real-time semi-global matching for intelligent vehicles. IEEE Trans. Veh. Technol. **61**(3), 1032–1042 (2012)

11. Gonzalez, R.C., Woods, R.E.: Digital Image Processing, 3rd. Prentice Hall, Upper Saddle River (2008)

12. Paris, S., Durand, F.: A fast approximation of the bilateral filter using a signal processing approach. Int. J. Comput. Vis. **81**(1), 24–52 (2009)

13. Cochran, S.D., Medioni, G.: 3-D surface description from binocular stereo. TPAMI **14**, 981–994 (1992)

14. Hirschmüller, H., Innocent, P.R., Garibaldi, J.: Real-time correlation based stereo vision with reduced border errors. Int. J. Comput. **47**(1–3), 229–246 (2002)

15. Ma, Z., He, K., Wei, Y., et al.: Constant time weighted median filtering for stereo matching and beyond. In: Proceedings of the 2013 IEEE International Conference on Computer Vision. IEEE (2013)

A Survey of Chinese Character Style Transfer

Yifei Ma[1,2], Yuntai Dong[1,2], Kang Li[1,2(✉)], Jian Ren[1],
Guohua Geng[1,2], and Mingquan Zhou[2,3]

[1] School of Information Science and Technology, Northwest University,
Xi'an 710127, Shaanxi, People's Republic of China
{201832034,dongyuntai,201631768}@stumail.nwu.edu.cn,
{likang,ghgeng}@nwu.edu.cn
[2] National-Local Joint Engineering Research Center of Cultural Heritage
Digitization, Northwest University, Xi'an 710127,
Shaanxi, People's Republic of China
[3] College of Information Science and Technology, Beijing Normal University,
Beijing 100875, People's Republic of China
mqzhou@bnu.edu.cn

Abstract. The transfer of Chinese character style is a method of transferring the original character style to other target characters written in different styles and generating the target characters with similar character styles as the original characters. This paper deeply analyzes the related research of character style transfer, summarizes the principle and main methods of character style transfer, and emphatically analyzes the latest progress of the in-depth learning method in the aspect of character style transfer. We finalize the report by the problems to be solved in this field and the future research direction.

Keywords: Chinese characters generated · Style transfer · Neural networks · Deep learning

1 Introduction

Meaning and form are the two fundamental elements in Chinese character writings. 'Meaning' is the basic element of language tool. 'Form' is unique and abstract, but it is transformed from eye to brain into concrete expression and represents the new "meaning", which has developed into a colorful art. Writing in the style of a specific font or calligrapher is called facsimile, which is a necessary part of learning calligraphy skills. The similarity of facsimile is also an important index to judge the calligrapher's calligraphy level.

Since the 1980s, with the enhancement of computer graphics and image processing capabilities, the application of computer methods to generate characters with specific writing styles has become the main way to reduce the technical requirements of copying and improve efficiency. The relevant method is called character style transfer, which can also be called stylized generation of calligraphy fonts. Related research is used to identify the writing style of specific calligraphers or generate calligraphers' style of writing, which is widely used in the fields of character-related font library generation, cultural relic restoration and the identification of true and false calligraphic works.

© Springer Nature Singapore Pte Ltd. 2019
Y. Wang et al. (Eds.): IGTA 2019, CCIS 1043, pp. 392–404, 2019.
https://doi.org/10.1007/978-981-13-9917-6_38

Based on computer graphics, the method of stylized generation of calligraphy fonts was born in the 1980s. The media laboratory of Massachusetts institute of technology, Zhejiang university and Jilin university started relevant research at the same time. It mainly includes three types of methods: simulation writing brush model, character splitting and synthesis, and character skeleton rendering. However, they all have problems such as low generation efficiency, poor result similarity, and easy loss of style feature information, which restrict the wide application of text style transfer.

In recent years, methods based on deep learning has been applied to the style transfer of characters. MIT, Zhejiang university and Peking University have achieved good results. This kind of method is mainly based on three kinds of network architectures: CNN, RNN and GAN. Although it has achieved good results to some extent, it is still limited by the problems of its own structure, and there is no good way to deal with complex Chinese character.

The rest of this survey is organized as follows. In Sect. 2, we introduce three main methods of stylized generation of calligraphy fonts based on computer graphics. Section 3 introduces the style transfer of characters method based on CNN. Section 3.2 introduces the style transfer of characters method based on RNN. Section 3.3 introduces the style transfer of characters method based on GAN. In summarizing the survey, we analyzed the results generated by various methods, which depended on the quality of the style transfer of characters and considered the future challenges in this field (Sect. 4).

2 Stylized Generation of Calligraphy Fonts Based on Computer Graphics

2.1 Simulation Writing Brush Model

In the 1980s, Strassmann [1] proposed a two-dimensional brush model to simulate the writing brush. The brush model consists of four units: Brush, Stroke (a trajectory of position and pressure), Dip and Paper. By selecting from brushes, dips, and papers, the stroke can take on a variety of expressive textures. At the same time, Pang et al. [2] proposed a computer-controlled pen plotter drawing system, by the using of brush and ink to achieve the simulation of brush calligraphy.

Lee [3] constructed a three-dimensional brush model. The model simulates the deformation of the writing brush in painting by calculating the elastic force. A mesh fiber paper was constructed to simulate the diffusion effect of ink on paper.

Wong [4] constructed an inverted cone-shaped brush model, which simulated the weight of the brush by drawing many different superimposed ellipses on the stroke path. However, the calculation of the brush model is too large to realize real-time rendering.

Zhang [5] proposed a triangular mesh writing brush model which simulates the stroke path through the Bezier curve. The model has a small amount of calculation and a strong real-time performance, which simulates the softness and elasticity of the writing brush. Figure 1 is a screenshot of Zhang's three-dimensional virtual calligraphy creation and application System.

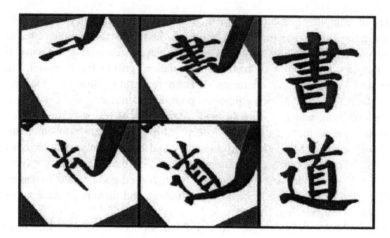

Fig. 1. The process of writing Chinese characters "shu" and "dao" in 3d virtual calligraphy creation.

It is inefficient to use writing brush model to generate calligraphy characters, which can only simulate the style of calligraphy fonts, but can't simulate the style features of higher levels.

2.2   Character Splitting and Synthesis

The method of character splitting and synthesis is to cut the existing calligraphy works, then transform and splice the cutting strokes, and finally synthesize the target characters.

Xu [6] proposed a six-layer model for characters splitting and synthesis, and the model structure is shown in Fig. 2.

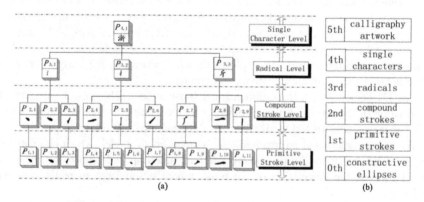

Fig. 2. Chinese calligraphy representation: (a) six-level representation hierarchy; (b) four levels in the representation for the Chinese character "zhe".

The model cuts the calligraphy into the most basic strokes by semi-automatic cutting method and the resulting strokes are organized into a small structured stroke database, which is then used by the constraint component to create text works in a new style.

Yu [7] constructed a calligraphy character synthesis system. In the synthesis step, Yu constructed a style evaluation model (SEM) to ensure the consistency of style. Figure 3 is the process of generating regular script "cheng" in Yu's calligraphy character synthesis system.

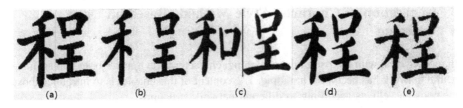

Fig. 3. (a) target calligraphy character (b) calligraphy character splitting (c) select radicals of Chinese characters(d) partial radical synthesis (e) results after adjustment with SEM

Zhang [8] divided the outline of the calligraphy character into small parts, expressed the outline as the characteristic curve according to the calculation of contour feature points, and then synthesized the overall outline of the new Chinese characters through the characteristic curve.

Although the character by synthesis can be used to synthesize character works in batches, the quality of synthesis is not high, and the style of synthesis is consistent, which can't simulate the style characteristics of a higher level. This method also has some difficulties in data preparation. Due to the irregularity of calligraphy, Chinese character cutting is mostly interactive, which is inefficient and consumes a lot of manpower.

2.3   Character Skeleton Rendering

Character skeleton rendering is to extract the skeleton of hand-written Chinese characters, add a specific style of rendering and stroke texture, and finally generate the target character. Zhang et al. [9] proposed a method to render handwriting into calligraphy characters. First, they established a library of calligraphy strokes. Then Special Nine Grid (SNG) is used to extract the strokes of handwriting. The corresponding Chinese calligraphy strokes were retrieved from the stroke database and the results were generated by using the rule-based stroke deformation algorithm. The deformation process is shown in Fig. 4.

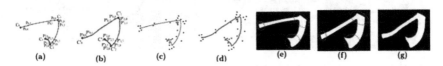

Fig. 4. (a) to (f) are the deformation and skeleton rendering process of hand-written Chinese characters

Velek [10] proposed an online Chinese character generation system, in which the calligraphy model combines online hand-written Chinese characters with calligraphy strokes to generate calligraphy characters. Most of the calligraphy characters generated by this method are synthesized with the handwriting of Chinese characters as the skeleton, which leads to low efficiency of characters generation and imperfect simulation of style.

3 Generation of Character Style Methods Based on Deep Learning

In recent years, with the rise of deep learning, character style transfer based on artificial neural network has become a hot topic. The content of this chapter is to introduce those methods and effects according to different network structures.

3.1 CNN Based Method

Manually identifying styles is quite difficult, which is relatively simple for CNN (convolution neural networks). CNN performs well in image classification, object recognition, neural style transfer, etc. In 2015, Gatys [11] first proposed a neural network-based style transfer algorithm. The algorithm uses a convolutional neural network to combine the content of the image with the style of another image to generate a new joint image. Since then, it has been tried to be applied to characters, but most of the research is based on character recognition. After that, Yu [12] tried to assign the style of the picture to the character and turn the character into an art form of any form. The experimental results are shown in Fig. 5. In fact, this experiment is not much different from Gatys, just changing the picture as the content for the text.

In 2017, Tian [13] proposed "Rewrite" based on CNN character style transfer. "Rewrite" employs a traditional top-down CNN structure and takes different sizes of convolution on different layers so that it captures different levels of detail. Experimental training data didn't do well on KaiTi. The experimental results are shown in Fig. 6. For some of the lighter fonts, only some blurred ink spots will appear. For some ink-over-fonts, only the outline can be captured, and the internal information can't be displayed. In general, the effect of this experiment is not satisfactory and there are certain defects.

Fig. 5. Yu's experimental result. The left is a style picture, and the three figures on the right are the generated character content.

邵 邵 宏 宏 歇 歇
捐 捐 肪 肪 敲 仙
没 没 档 档 丘 丘

Fig. 6. Rewrite's experimental result. Some of the font generation effects are OK, but the other can't recognize it at all.

From the current effect, CNN based methods are not suitable for character style transfer.

3.2 RNN Based Method

In the method of characters style transfer based on CNN and the other neural network, there is a lack of accurate description of specific font or hand-written style. In order to solve this problem, Lian et al. [14] proposed a style transfer method based on character stroke extraction and used RNN [15] (Recurrent Neural Network). In this paper, an automatic stroke extraction method is proposed. The character strokes are extracted and transferred in style. According to the composition of different characters, the strokes are spliced together to generate new characters. The main contribution of this paper is to establish the non-rigid localization registration for the font of each font, and exactly analyze the position of each part of each Chinese character. As shown in Fig. 7, these are the 32 basic strokes proposed in this paper. This method greatly reduces the demand for experimental data, and the training data is a way of decomposition and reassembly, significantly improving the effect of complex character style transfer. In general, the experimental effect of this method is better than the existing character style transfer method, as shown in Fig. 8. However, the data preparation process of this method is complex, which restricts its promotion and application.

Fig. 7. The strokes of Chinese characters are classified and summarized, and 32 basic strokes of Chinese characters are obtained

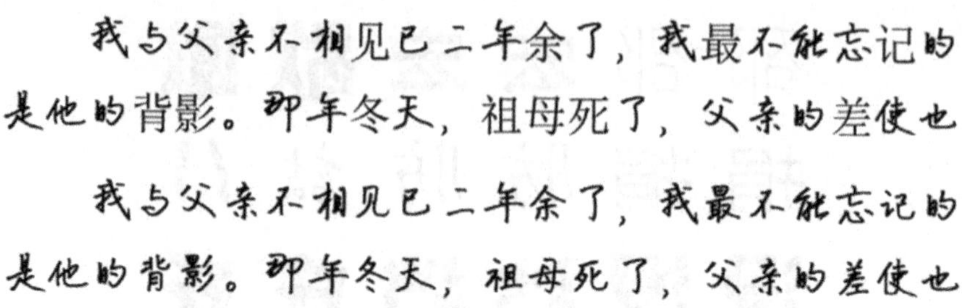

我与父亲不相见已二年余了，我最不能忘记的
是他的背影。那年冬天，祖母死了，父亲的差使也

我与父亲不相见已二年余了，我最不能忘记的
是他的背影。那年冬天，祖母死了，父亲的差使也

Fig. 8. Some experimental results of stylistic transfer method based on character stroke extraction are presented

3.3 GAN Based Method

With the rise of GAN [16] (Generative adversarial network), the development of style transfer has also diversified. The main application of GAN is image generation and data enhancement. Azadi et al. [17] proposed an end-to-end method with a new network architecture. This method can learn the style of font with a small number of English characters and generate 26 letters corresponding to the style. The experiment is not bad. But it is limited to normalized samples, and its generalization ability is weak.

Bhunia et al. [18] proposed a font transfer architecture based on Convolutional Recurrent Generative adversarial network. The images of English words with different widths can be processed equivalent to each other, and the consistency of the images can be maintained in the end. However, the model needs to be pre-trained for a different source font. The experimental results are shown in Fig. 9. Because the experimental data is all English letters, it is not convenient to promote it to other types of character.

Input (Arial)	Algerian	Arial Black	Bauhaus	Bookman	Forte	Magneto	Ravie	Times new Roman	Times Black
BLOCK	BLOCK BLOCK	**BLOCK** **BLOCK**	**BLOCK** **BLOCK**	BLOCK BLOCK	*BLOCK* *BLOCK*	*BLOCK* *BLOCK*	BLOCK BLOCK	BLOCK BLOCK	*BLOCK* *BLOCK*
CLAIM	CLAIM CLAIM	**CLAIM** **CLAIM**	**CLAIM** **CLAIM**	CLAIM CLAIM	*CLAIM* *CLAIM*	*CLAIM* *CLAIM*	CLAIM CLAIM	CLAIM CLAIM	*CLAIM* *CLAIM*
EXPECT	EXPECT EXPECT	**EXPECT** **EXPECT**	**EXPECT** **EXPECT**	EXPECT EXPECT	*EXPECT* *EXPECT*	*EXPECT* *EXPECT*	EXPECT EXPECT	EXPECT EXPECT	*EXPECT* *EXPECT*

Fig. 9. Ankan's experimental result. 1st row contains the ground truth images and this method results are shown in 2nd row.

Tian proposed a new method "zi2zi" [19] model based on the pix2pix [20] model. Referring to the zero-shot GNMT [21] paper, they bind the style embedding and the character embedding before passing the non-trained Gaussian noise through the decoder layer. When GAN mixes multiple styles, the model is likely to confuse different styles and ends up with characters that are not similar in each style. With the inspiration in the AC-GAN [22] model, the style of generated characters can be predicted. Add up the multi-level directory loss to identify the discriminator training and punish it, thereby retaining its own style. The experimental results are shown in Fig. 10. The experimental data not only contains Chinese fonts but also Korean fonts, and the experiment has good expandability. Most font styles can be well transformed, but when the font itself is too complex, the effect will be very bad. And it performs well on synthesis of thick typography style rather than hand-writing.

Fig. 10. "zi2zi" experimental result. The first three lines are Chinese fonts and the last two lines are Korean fonts.

After that, lots of different models based on GAN are proposed. Chang [23] et al. proposed an end-to-end model which can directly transfer typography style from a standard printed font to any other printed or hand-writing typography. Through corresponding the same convolution position and back-convolution adding, it improves performance on fonts transfer task since it can recover the details, such as subtle strokes, connections in characters. The experimental results are shown in Fig. 11. The experiment does get the relevant handwriting style, but when generating handwriting data, it will produce noise and data loss without orientation. In addition, Jie later proposed a new hierarchical adversarial network (HAN [24]). In the generator section, it also added the same data as the corresponding convolution and the back-convolution. The layered antagonistic discriminator is a multi-level structure. Through continuous iterative identification, the differences between data can be better identified to ensure more accurate data generation (Fig. 12).

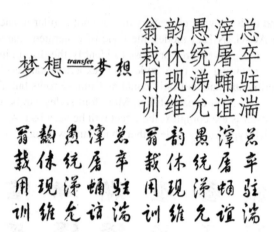

Fig. 11. Jie's results on handwriting fonts. The Upper right area is source fonts. The Lower left area is generated fonts. The Lower right area is the ground truth.

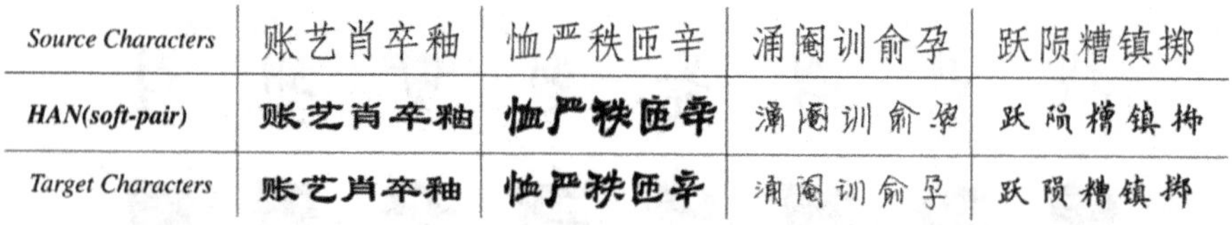

Source Characters	账艺肖卒釉	恤严秩匝辛	涌阉训俞孕	跃陨糟镇掷
HAN(soft-pair)	账艺肖卒釉	恤严秩匝辛	涌阉训俞孕	跃陨槽镇掷
Target Characters	账艺肖卒釉	恤严秩匝辛	涌阉训俞孕	跃陨糟镇掷

Fig. 12. The experimental results are in the second line. The others are the source characters and target characters.

The methods mentioned above are all based on many supporting data but not all of them have many pairs of data for us to use. Chang et al. [25] proposed a method named CycleGAN [26]. According to the idea of unsupervised data. The CycleGAN method greatly reduces the requirement for data itself and the degree of preprocessing. This method relies on ResNet [27] and DenseNet to generate information to improve the degree of acquiring information features. However, due to the limitations of CycleGAN itself, the generation effect does not meet our demand for high-precision imitation (Fig. 13).

Fig. 13. Bo's experimental results. (1) is matching corresponding data and (2) is irrelevant data.

Lyu et al. [28] simulated and generated the calligraphic works of ancient Chinese calligraphers with GAN. The standard data and input data are simultaneously sampled down and sampled up and the information finally passing through the network is presented. The generated simulated font, input font and standard font are superimposed on each other and put into the discriminator for training (Fig. 14).

Fig. 14. Mi Fu's experimental results. In fact, almost all characters can't recognize it.

After FontSL [29], Lian et al. proposed an end to end Chinese Font Generation System (DCFont [30]). They used the VGG16 network to extract text styles, and added the style vector, the content vector, and the category embedding as the next input. This generator structure is the same as the Jie's. Besides, they combined GAN and stroke category so that they proposed Structure-guided Chinese Font Generation via Deep Stacked Networks (SCFont). They differ from previous networks in that in deconvolution, the contents of each deconvolution layer include the corresponding the same position convolution, the overall content of the upper layer of the deconvolution layer, and the content of the upper layer of the deconvolution layer. In order to prevent generated characters from being ambiguous, they proposed to use twice GAN. The first generation result as input to the other GAN. In the other GAN, Resnet is specially added to increase the depth of the network and improve the ability to capture the features.

Based on the analysis of the above experimental results, through the continuous increase of the new network structure, experimental results have gradually improved and the expansion of the experiment has been better than before. Therefore, GAN is suitable for character style transfer.

4   Conclusions and Future Work

In general, the reason why methods are divided into two categories is that traditional methods were limited by the development of computer technology at that time. Although deep learning was proposed as early as the 1940s, due to the limitations of equipment technology, the research fell into a low ebb in the late 1960s. With the development of computer technology, hardware upgrade and data precipitation, the method based on deep learning has gradually returned to the forefront. It is also because the innovation of computer technology has changed the production efficiency that the deep learning mode is generally better than the traditional mode. For the sake of comparison, Fig. 15 summarizes the various methods and their advantages and disadvantages in detail.

Classes	Method	Experimental results	Features	Advantages & Disadvantages
computer graphics	simulation writing brush model		Generate style fonts by interacting with the system	character generation is slow, style features are easy to be lost, and data preparation is difficult
	character splitting and synthesis	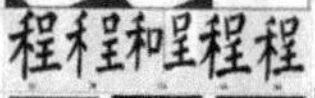		
	character skeleton rendering			
based on deep learning	CNN	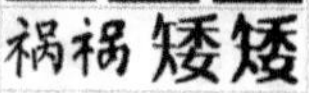	Models are trained continuously and the results are filtered artificially	Fast generation speed, easy expansion, unstable effect, easy to collapse
	GAN			
	RNN	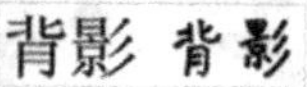		

Fig. 15. Computer graphics and deep learning in the transfer of Chinese character style comparison and summarize their advantages and disadvantages.

In general, with the improvement of deep learning network performance, the experimental effect is significantly improved. Specifically, the model based on GAN is obviously better than that based on CNN. However, the model based on RNN has outstanding effect because it disassembles and reassembles the strokes of characters, reduces the demand for data and improves the stylistic similarity of the details of characters, but it doesn't have the significance of universal promotion. Therefore, according to the current situation, GAN is the most suitable neural network for Chinese character style transformation.

Future work:

1. Small sample data. The essence of deep learning is to enable machines to continuously learn in the way of big data and acquire certain deep-level characteristics through the continuous deepening of the network, which are based on a large amount of data as the premise. When deep learning is relevant to life, there may not be enough basic data. At this time, we will face the problem of sample loss, so it is an urgent problem to improve the demand of the experimental model for the number of samples or increase the number of experimental samples.
2. Improve the performance of neural network. Each new network architecture is a new revolution of the deep learning system. However, when the network architecture is mature, the experimental results will be limited to the network itself. No matter how to adjust, the experimental results will only approach the threshold of the upper limit of the network architecture. Therefore, it is necessary to constantly improve the network and even create new structures to promote the continuous development of deep learning.

3. Combine with Chinese calligraphy culture. Chinese culture has a long history. From the original inscriptions on bones or tortoise shells to various modern fonts, Chinese calligraphy remains on cultural relics and historical sites. However, most of them have been damaged due to natural or human factors to a certain extent and the character is no longer complete. It is of great historical and cultural significance to restore the cultural relics by means of deep learning, and to display and restore calligraphers' works in a nearly real way. Furthermore, we can even have an in-depth study of the corresponding calligraphy styles of famous figures in different dynasties and complete the restoration of font calligraphy through existing technical means.

Acknowledgement. This work is supported by The National Key Research and Development Program of China (No. 2017YFB1402104).

References

1. Strassmann, S.: Hairy brushes. In: Conference on Computer Graphics & Interactive Techniques (1986)
2. 庞云阶, 尹丽娜. 计算机控制毛笔绘画系统 CCBPS. 计算机辅助设计与图形学学报 (1), 37–40 (1989)
3. Lee, J.: Simulating oriental black-ink painting. Comput. Graph. Appl. IEEE **19**(3), 74–81 (1999)
4. Wong, H.T.F., Ip, H.H.S.: Virtual brush: a model-based synthesis of Chinese calligraphy. Comput. Graph. **24**(1), 99–113 (2000)
5. 张振庭. 计算机书法创作模拟与渲染研究[D]. 浙江大学 (2011)
6. Xu, S., Lau, F.C.M., Cheung, W.K., et al.: Automatic generation of artistic Chinese calligraphy. Intell. Syst. IEEE **20**(3), 32–39 (2004)
7. 俞凯. 计算机书法若干关键技术研究. 浙江大学 (2010)
8. Zhang, J., Mao, G., Lin, H., Yu, J., Zhou, C.: Outline font generating from images of ancient chinese calligraphy. Trans. Edutainment **5**, 122–131 (2011). https://doi.org/10.1007/978-3-642-18452-9_10
9. Hunter, J., Lagoze, C., Giles, L., et al.: Proceedings of the 10th Annual Joint Conference on Digital Libraries
10. Velek, O., Liu, C.L., Nakagawa, M.: Generating realistic Kanji character images from on-line patterns (2001)
11. Gatys, L.A., Ecker, A.S., Bethge, M.: A neural algorithm of artistic style. Computer Science (2015)
12. Yuweiming70. Style_Migration_For_Artistic_Font_With_CNN (2017). https://github.com/yuweiming70/Style_Migration_For_Artistic_Font_With_CNN
13. Tian, Y.: ReWrite (2016). https://github.com/kaonashi-tyc/Rewrite/
14. Lian, Z., Zhao, B., Chen, X., Xiao, J.: EasyFont: a style learning-based system to easily build your large-scale handwriting fonts. ACM Trans. Graph. **38**, 1–18 (2018). https://doi.org/10.1145/3213767
15. Gregor, K., Danihelka, I., Graves, A., et al.: DRAW: a recurrent neural network for image generation. Computer Science 1462–1471 (2015)
16. Goodfellow, I.J., Pouget-Abadie, J., Mirza, M., et al.: Generative adversarial nets. In: International Conference on Neural Information Processing Systems. MIT Press (2014)

17. Azadi, S., Fisher, M., Kim, V., et al.: Multi-content GAN for few-shot font style transfer (2017)
18. Bhunia, A.K., Bhunia, A.K., Banerjee, P., et al.: Word level font-to-font image translation using convolutional recurrent generative adversarial networks (2018)
19. Tian, Y.: ReWrite (2017). https://github.com/kaonashi-tyc/zi2zi/
20. Isola, P., Zhu, J.Y., Zhou, T., et al.: Image-to-image translation with conditional adversarial networks (2016)
21. Johnson, M., Schuster, M., Le, Q.V., et al.: Google's multilingual neural machine translation system: enabling zero-shot translation (2016)
22. Odena, A., Olah, C., Shlens, J.: Conditional image synthesis with auxiliary classifier GANs (2016)
23. Chang, J., Gu, Y.: Chinese typography transfer (2017)
24. Chang, J., Gu, Y., Zhang, Y.: Chinese typeface transformation with hierarchical adversarial network (2017)
25. Chang, B., Zhang, Q., Pan, S., et al.: Generating handwritten Chinese characters using CycleGAN. In: 2018 IEEE Winter Conference on Applications of Computer Vision (WACV). IEEE (2018)
26. Zhu, J.Y., Park, T., Isola, P., et al.: Unpaired image-to-image translation using cycle-consistent adversarial networks (2017)
27. He, K., Zhang, X., Ren, S., et al.: Deep residual learning for image recognition (2015)
28. Lyu, P., Bai, X., Yao, C., et al.: Auto-encoder guided GAN for Chinese calligraphy synthesis. In: 2017 14th IAPR International Conference on Document Analysis and Recognition (ICDAR). IEEE Computer Society (2017)
29. Lian, Z., Zhao, B., Xiao, J.: Automatic generation of large-scale handwriting fonts via style learning. In: SIGGRAPH Asia Technical Briefs. ACM (2016)
30. Jiang, Y., Lian, Z., Tang, Y., et al.: DCFont: an end-to-end deep Chinese font generation system. In: SIGGRAPH Asia 2017 Technical Briefs. ACM (2017)

Deep Multi-resolution Feature Fusion Network Based 3D Object Recognition

Yang Xiao[1], Yanxin Ma[2(✉)], and Jun Zhang[1]

[1] College of Electronic Science, National University of Defense Technology,
Changsha, China
[2] College of Meteorology and Oceanography,
National University of Defense Technology, Changsha, China
mayanxin@nudt.edu.cn

Abstract. In recent years, deep learning has become a popular method for 3D object recognition with point clouds. In this work, we introduce a multi-resolution feature fusion convolution neural network using point cloud data for 3D object recognition. Experiments are conducted on ModelNet40 dataset. It achieves better accuracy with 86.9% for 3D object recognition on point cloud data through four different feature fusion. Experimental results have demonstrated the superior performance of the proposed multi-resolution feature fusion network.

Keywords: Point cloud · Deep learning · Multi-resolution · Object recognition

1 Introduction

With the development of computer vision, 3D object recognition has been applied in industry, transportation and robots. One of the fundamental challenges of 3D object recognition is to find the best way to represent more information in three-dimensional world, 3D information in particular. 3D object recognition has been considered as one of the most important components to interactions between humans and robots. As a result, 3D object recognition has become a critical research domain in computer vision and computer graphics. With developing of low-cost 3D sensors such as Microsoft Kinect, Google Tango, *etc.*, 3D data and 3D data analysis achieves a significant growth. Due to the numerous technology development such GPU and several large 3D datasets, it makes deep learning based 3D object recognition possible. Actually, Convolution Neural Networks (CNN) [1] have been increasingly applied in 3D object recognition systems.

Before the deep learning was applied to 3D computer vision, it has recently gained meaningfully state-of-the-art performance in tasks involving nature language proposing, voice recognition and image processing [2]. In recent years, deep learning has also been used for other challenging domains, for example, 3D data processing. Due to the fact that 3D data is not in a regular data format, most of researchers prefer to transform 3D data to 2D images, views or regular 3D voxel grids first and then apply the transformed data to deep networks [3, 4].

© Springer Nature Singapore Pte Ltd. 2019
Y. Wang et al. (Eds.): IGTA 2019, CCIS 1043, pp. 405–411, 2019.
https://doi.org/10.1007/978-981-13-9917-6_39

The method of feature learning for 3D object recognition can be roughly divided into three types, including Multi-view based methods [1, 2], volumetric representation based methods [5–7] and point cloud based methods [8, 9]. Multi-view based methods first project 3D shape to two-dimensional image space. Then deep learning is used to extract features of two-dimensional image. These methods can make full use of the superior performance of 2D network architecture, and also the existence of massive image data for pre-training. However, these methods would lose a part of spatial structure information which will bring negative influence for recognition performance. Besides, the multi-view methods only provide 2D contour representation of the 3D object. It does not include sufficient geometric information as a complete 3D representation because some details of that information are not encoded. 3D volumetric networks give a new direction. In detail, voxel convolution neural network, considers the 3D shape as the probability distribution in the 2D voxel grid, and thus expresses it as a 2D tensor or 3D tensor. The real breakthrough in this area was made by Wu et al. [5] in 2015. The convolution deep belief network is used for 3D object recognition and the 3D ModelNet dataset is built for training and testing. Subsequently, a number of 3D volumetric convolution neural networks have been proposed for 3D object recognition. Qi et al. [6] proposed a volumetric 3D CNN by subvolume supervision to reduce over fitting. Maturana and Scherer [7] designed a volumetric convolution neural network named VoxNet for real-time recognition of 3D object by. Qi et al. proposed PointNet [8] to directly process unstructured point cloud data by neural network. Although these works have made a great achievement, most of existing deep learning models have high computational cost and complex network architecture. In this paper, we focus on the invariance and completeness of 3D point cloud features which are extracted based on deep learning, and realize 3D object recognition by multi-resolution feature fusion.

Point cloud has simple and unified structure which avoids the combination irregularities and complexities of meshes. Therefore, point cloud is easier to be learned by neural networks. Recently, researchers pay more attention to this advantage and focus on using deep learning to process point cloud. PointNet has successfully achieved an end-to-end model to deal with irregular point cloud. We propose a multi-resolution feature fusion convolution neural network for 3D object recognition, it utilizes multi-resolution feature information to improve the performance of network.

The main contributions of this work are as follows:

(i)   A 3D CNN is proposed for 3D object recognition. It utilizes multi-resolution feature fusion information to get great improvement as compared to existing models including MVCNN [2], 3DShapeNets [5], Subvolume [6], VoxNet [7], PointNet [8] and PointNet++ [9].

(ii) Multi-resolution information is learned by changing the distance between points.

(iii) Comparative experiments have been conducted on the ModelNet dataset [5]. The experimental results show that proposed model provides a simple structure for 3D object recognition tasks with low computational cost and disorder point clouds processing.

This paper is structured as follows. Section 2 gives a literature review of 3D object recognition with CNN-based methods. Section 3 presents our model and introduces the implementation of multi-resolution feature fusion. Section 4 shows the experiment results of our model on ModelNet40 dataset. Finally, Sect. 5 concludes this paper.

2 Related Work

The core of 3D object recognition is to extract discernibility, simplicity and low dimension features of 3D shapes [10]. The classical approach is to design feature descriptors according to specific tasks and domain knowledge. The main purpose of these methods is to achieve 3D shape features with better discriminating ability, robustness, invariance and computability by extracting the spatial distribution of geometric attributes of 3D object space. On the contrary, deep learning automatically learns data characteristics, avoiding human intervention.

A number of convolution neural networks have been used to process 2D images and some achieve the state-of-the-art results. Recently, several attempts have been made to apply deep learning to 3D vision. Shi *et al.* [11] proposed a convolution neural network (namely, DeepPano) for 3D object recognition. It represented 3D object using panoramic images. Considering that although neural networks is robust to translation certainly, 2D projections will change when the object is rotated, which have significant influence on the features extracted by CNN. To overcome this negative effect, Shi *et al.* [11] firstly projected each 3D object into a panoramic image around the principal axis. Feature learning was performed on the panoramic images and the objects were classified using the learned features. The experimental results show that this method can preserve the shape information of 3D objects to a certain extent through transformation.

Voxel convolution neural network is a kind of neural network structure which considers 3D shape as a probability distribution in 3D voxel grid. The groundbreaking work in this area was initiated by Wu *et al.* [5] who designed a five-layer Convolution Deep Belief Network (namely, 3DShapeNets). The input of 3DShapeNets is binary voxelized 3D data, with 1 and 0 representing whether the voxel belong to the object or not. The training process of 3DShapeNets was conducted using pre-training and fine-tuning. Since then, Maturana and Scherer [7] designed a convolution neural network VoxNet for real-time 3D object recognition. Moreover, Sedaghat *et al.* [12] added an auxiliary task of object direction estimation task with the main recognition, by transforming estimation problem into classification problem. Consequently, the network can learn more favorable features and make a significant classification performance improvement. Qi *et al.* [8] proposed a deep learning network structure named PointNet which solves the problem that 3D CNN cannot directly process unstructured point cloud data. This network can directly deal with point cloud data and efficiently accomplish the classification and segmentation tasks. Moreover, Qi *et al.* [9] proposed PointNet++ to address that PointNet cannot extract local information of point clouds. Although a number of works have achieved state-of-the-art recognition performance on 3D data, most of these works transform 3D data to voxel or image which may lose original structural information of 3D data. In this paper, a deep network is proposed to learn multi-resolution feature information by changing the distance between points.

3 Model

The proposed model contains two parts, which are feature extraction part and feature fusion part. In the feature extraction part, convolution kernels are different according to different input to learn different features. In the fusion part, the extracted features are fused to achieve 3D object recognition.

3.1 Feature Extraction

Point cloud is a collection of massive points at the surface characteristics of the object. It can be used to keep a complete structural information when we deal with 3D object recognition and scene segmentation tasks. For most of 3D CNNs, the input of the models should be voxels, occupancy grids. Consequently, 3D data represented by mesh or point clouds must be converted to volumetric data before being recognized.

Specially, 3D point cloud data is expressed in the form of 3D coordinates, which contains a direct vector of spatial information. In the proposed network, point clouds are used as input. In detail, point cloud is directly put into the feature extraction block. As shown in Fig. 1, several convolution layers are used to learn powerful feature descriptor from the input points.

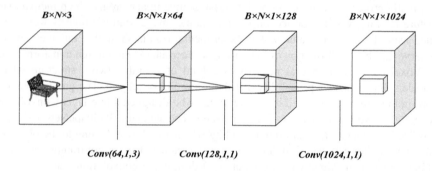

Fig. 1. Feature extraction block

3.2 Feature Fusion

To obtain different features of object, the input points were sampled to different resolutions as $N \times 3, N/2 \times 3, N/4 \times 3, N/8 \times 3$. The points with different resolutions were set into a same feature extraction block and four different features were obtained as $B \times N \times 1 \times 1024, B \times N/2 \times 1 \times 1024, B \times N/4 \times 1 \times 1024, B \times N/8 \times 1 \times 1024$. Then a max-pooling layer was used to get discerning features as $B \times 1 \times 1024$. After that, the four features learned from different resolutions input points were fused with a concat layer. Then, two fully connected layers with softmax were used to achieve 3D object recognition. The full structure of the proposed network is shown in Fig. 2.

Fig. 2. Multi-resolution convolution neural network

4 Experiments and Results

The proposed model is evaluated on ModelNet40 shape classification benchmark dataset [5] which is mostly used in 3D object recognition task. The ModelNet40 dataset contains 12,311 CAD models which consists of 9,843 CAD models for training and 2,468 for testing.

The proposed network achieves 3D object recognition using multi-resolution feature fusion. The experimental parameters of learning rate, decay rate and epoch are set to 0.001, 0.7, 400. Adam algorithm is used as optimizer function. The loss function and accuracy value changing curve could be seen in Fig. 3.

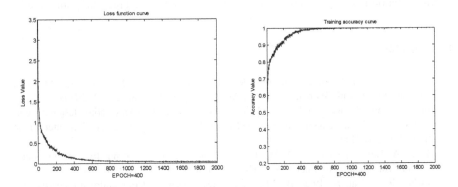

Fig. 3. Loss function and accuracy value curve

The comparing experimental results with state-of-the-art 3D object recognition methods are shown in Table 1. The results indicate that the proposed network achieves a comparable recognition accuracy.

It can be observed from Table 1 that the proposed model achieves a higher recognition accuracy than PointNet and other image and volume based recognition methods with an overall accuracy of 90.1%. Compared to PointNet++ (with an overall accuracy of 91.9%) which is built on a complex structure, the proposed network obtains a similar overall accuracy with lower computation cost. Simultaneously, it can be observed that the proposed model achieves an acceptable recognition efficiency.

Table 1. Classification results on ModelNet40

Method	Input	Accuracy average class (%)	Accuracy overall (%)
3DShapeNets [5]	Volume	77.3	84.7
VoxNet [7]	Volume	83.0	85.9
Subvolume [6]	Volume	86.0	89.2
MVCNN [2]	Image	90.1	–
PointNet [8]	Point	86.2	89.2
PointNet ++ [9]	Point	-	91.9
Ours	**Point**	**86.9**	**90.1**

5 Conclusion

In this paper, a multi-resolution feature fusion network is proposed for 3D object recognition and it directly used point cloud as input. The proposed network consists two blocks of feature extraction block and feature fusion block to learn more information from four different inputs. The experimental results show that the proposed multi-resolution network achieves comparable recognition accuracy on point cloud.

References

1. Ioannidou, A., Chatzilari, E., Nikolopoulos, S., Kompatsiaris, I.: Deep learning advances in computer vision with 3D data: a survey. ACM Comput. Surv. **50**(2), 20 (2017)
2. Su, H., Maji, S., Kalogerakis, E., Learned-Miller, E.: Multi-view convolutional neural networks for 3D shape recognition. In: IEEE International Conference on Computer Vision, pp. 945–953 (2015)
3. Brock, A., Lim, T., Ritchie, J.M., Weston, N.: Generative and discriminative voxel modeling with convolutional neural networks. arXiv preprint arXiv:1608.04236 (2016)
4. Socher, R., Huval, B., Bhat, B., Manning, C.D., Ng, A.Y.: Convolutional-recursive deep learning for 3D object classification. In: Neural Information Processing Systems, pp. 665–673 (2012)
5. Wu, Z., et al.: 3D ShapeNets: a deep representation for volumetric shapes. In: IEEE Conference on Computer Vision and Pattern Recognition, pp. 1912–1920 (2015)
6. Qi, C.R., Su, H., Nießner, M., Dai, A., Yan, M., Guibas, L.J.: Volumetric and multi-view CNNs for object classification on 3D data. In: IEEE Conference on Computer Vision and Pattern Recognition, pp. 5648–5656 (2016)
7. Maturana, D., Scherer, S.: VoxNet: a 3D convolutional neural network for real-time object recognition. In: IEEE/RSJ International Conference on Intelligent Robots and Systems, pp. 922–928 (2015)
8. Qi, C.R., Su, H., Mo, K., Guibas, L.J.: PointNet: deep learning on point sets for 3D classification and segmentation. arXiv preprint arXiv:1612.00593 (2016)
9. Qi, C.R., Yi, L., Su, H., Guibas, L.J.: PointNet ++: deep hierarchical feature learning on point sets in a metric space. arXiv preprint arXiv:1706.02413 (2017)

10. Sun, J., Ovsjanikov, M., Guibas, L.: A concise and provably informative multi-scale signature based on heat diffusion. Comput. Graph. Forum **128**, 1383–1392 (2009)
11. Shi, B., Bai, S., Zhou, Z., Bai, X.: Deeppano: deep panoramic representation for 3-D shape recognition. IEEE Signal Process. Lett. **22**(12), 2339–2343 (2015)
12. Sedaghat, N., Zolfaghari, M., Brox, T.: Orientation-boosted voxel nets for 3D object recognition. arXiv preprint arXiv:1604.03351 (2016)

Construction of Game-Based Teaching Environment for Animation Scene Scheduling Based on Virtual Reality

Xiaodong Wei and Yali Wu[✉]

School of Educational Technology, Northwest Normal University,
967 Anning East Road, Lanzhou 730070, People's Republic of China
a18909443699@163.com

Abstract. Audio-visual language is the language of film and television animation art. The scene scheduling in the audio-visual language of animation includes action design, the design of characters' moving routes in space, and the arrangement and design between the roles and the background. Traditional teaching methods are not enough to provide virtual scenes for learners to practice. Therefore, this paper develops an immersive gamification teaching environment for the practical teaching of scene scheduling content in audio-visual animation language, which includes three aspects: role scene scheduling, shot scene scheduling, role scheduling and shot scheduling. Given this teaching system we have carried on the teaching pilot experiment, the experimental results showed that the immersive teaching environment could improve students' learning effect, promote the construction of action program schemata, and promote the formation and maintenance of skills.

Keywords: Animation scene scheduling ·
Gamification teaching environment · Action program schema section

1 Introduction

The full application of virtual reality technology and augmented reality technology on mobile platforms has triggered the impact of VR/AR on educational concepts. How to use VR technology characteristics to drive educational features is an essential subject of educational technology research. VR/AR of the education thought to embody in it broke the traditional teaching mode, through the creation of teaching design. Teaching process and teaching implementation of VR/AR technology, complete the teaching type conversion, the transformation of teaching means, teaching method, teaching form transformation as well as the teaching space form transformation. Vividly demonstrates the nature of things, rule, and the inner link between elements [1–4]. Help the students to the current more profound and accurate understanding of the learning content to make them complete the multipath and personalised learning. In the technology and problems being under the function of the new consciousness and state, the close integration of understanding the world, perceiving the world and constructing knowledge can genuinely reflect the idea of technology serving education, and the

© Springer Nature Singapore Pte Ltd. 2019
Y. Wang et al. (Eds.): IGTA 2019, CCIS 1043, pp. 412–424, 2019.
https://doi.org/10.1007/978-981-13-9917-6_40

teaching effect will be higher than the original knowledge value effect, reaching the impact of $1 + 1 > 2$ [5]. With the continuous development of virtual reality technology, many language teaching attempts to use the method of immersion teaching; audio-visual language is no exception. Although audio-visual animation language is a theoretical course, it is closely related to practice and cannot separate from the test and summary of animation practice, as well as the application in practice. Scene scheduling in the audio-visual language of animation is to divide the scene space and determine the role positioning and positioning in the scene space. Scene scheduling of animation is both a technology and art. Technically speaking, scene scheduling requires not only profound theoretical knowledge but also rich practical experience. Scene scheduling technology can improve the quality of animation. From the perspective of art, scene scheduling is also an art, which can grasp the overall situation of animation and ensure the coherence of animation narration. However, the traditional teaching method only stays at the level of theoretical teaching, because it involves a lot of content, and the spatial structure includes, the learners generally feel that the teaching content is complicated and confusing.

In recent years, researches on virtual learning environment mainly include the following aspects: First, basic theoretical research on VR learning environment;

Second, research on teaching and learning methods based on VR learning environment; Third, the development and utilization of different types of VR learning environments; Fourth, the effect evaluation of VR learning environment; Fifth, studies on the fairness of multi-culture and gender in learning; Six is the student emotion and so on non-intelligence factor research. At present, VR learning environments that have widely used include desktop VR system, augmented VR system, immersive VR system and distributed VR system [6–8]. The development of a teaching environment for animation scene scheduling requires a VR system to provide a learning motivation framework for students so that students can apply the acquired knowledge into practice. In practical activities, teachers can guide students to conduct game animation scene scheduling, turn knowledge into ability, and form an action program schema for scene schedule. VR learning environment provides students with cognitive support and the ability to apply knowledge. Combined with the relevant theories of bloom and Gagne, it is not difficult to see that animation scene scheduling training belongs to procedural knowledge, and immersive VR system should be used to complete the construction of teaching environment.

2 Literature Review

2.1 Scene Scheduling in Animation Audio-Visual Language

Directions from the French Mise en - scene, it is the meaning of "put in place." The design used to describe the production of theatre or film is a visual artistic technique through spectroscopic and cinematographic design. It is also the director to put the ideological content of the script, the plot and character, environment and atmosphere, and rhythm, etc. Through their artistic conception, using scene scheduling method, a unique language to convey to the audience. It is introduced into the audio-visual language of animation to provide theoretical support for the narration of animation. The obvious challenge of scene scheduling is the concept of space, which is not a montage of scene editing or a combination of positive and negative shots, but an immersive long-lens picture. Scene scheduling is the key to animation creation. The low level of the camera application, weak sense of animation and unsmooth narration are common problems for learners to create animated short films. Wangcheng dress feather through the analysis of some of the animated short, probes into the directions can see as the opposite of montage of expression in the animated short film art creation. The application of pointed out that has the depth of the scene, to the scene scheduling provides a complete stereo space, make the picture out of the animated short film is often flat and alienable, let the audience easy to enter into the picture, and to generate a certain degree of emotional communication and role. This study provides certain theoretical guidance to matters only, not involve applying this knowledge to practice [9]. Chen by studying large scene scheduling case of excellent works put forward the scene scheduling learning method should be based on the deconstruction of excellent films, establish scene scheduling database. The study method of animation works, rhythm, visual effects, the art of narrative fluency can play a role in many respects, such as curing, but resources to inspire the students' thinking is not enough, knowledge to the ability of transformation degree is not high [10–13]. In general, for the scene scheduling method of teaching, the current study is less. on the one hand, the Chinese animation education and research, pure pursuit of technology and the picture. China to the United States for many years, the Japanese animation in the animation outsourcing drawing work, and cultivate a group of old animated drawing, when these animation people enter universities and training schools to teach animation courses and various software technologies, naturally pointed to the direction of technology and the picture [14, 15]. On the other hand, they deliberately pursued "Chinese characteristics," paid attention to the excavation and inheritance of traditional culture, and explored various forms of animation, such as ink animation, paper-cut animation, and puppet animation, etc., all of which made great achievements at that time and formed their unique artistic styles [16, 17]. Although there have been many textbooks on the audio-visual language of animation, most of them have adopted the theory of audio-visual language of film and television, supplemented by examples of animation works, and few of them have studied the natural regularity starting from the essential properties of animation. As for the scene scheduling of animation, it has a stronger sense of space than film and television works. The current teaching method is limited to academic teaching, and the teaching effect is not good. As a result, in the practical application, the students have a lower level of lens use. Given this situation, a new teaching environment developed in this paper, and the 3D scene of lens scheduling is simulated to promote teaching.

2.2 Immersive Virtual Reality Teaching Environment

Immersive virtual reality technology mainly includes immersive VR video and immersive virtual reality interactive system. Immersive video with two or more cameras from different angles at the same time multiple video shooting, to produce a fully 3D digital video, and using computer vision and computer graphics, for interactive video and TV viewers to provide a "virtual camera," make the watchers are free to choose the direction and perspectives. This teaching environment can switch perspectives freely, meet the needs of students to select and operate audio-visual objects from multiple perspectives and provide learners with a motivational framework. However, due to the weak interactivity, learners cannot fully participate in the practical learning of scene scheduling in the teaching environment, so this paper does not try.

The immersive virtual reality interactive system builds the immersive interactive environment by tracking the experiencer's location and cooperating with the computer-generated virtual scene, and interacts with the environment through the sensor device so that the user can obtain the immersive interactive experience [18]. Virtual reality technology widely used in medical, military, mechanical and another professional practice teaching has achieved good teaching results [19]. Studies have shown that tactile feedback and directional feedback can be used to simulate the target language environment in language learning, providing a platform for learners to interact with the target language environment and improving the learning effect. Therefore, by analysing the characteristics of scene scheduling in the audio-visual language of animation, this paper develops the teaching environment, selects appropriate interaction modes according to the different cognitive levels of students, and constructs a personalised and differentiated teaching environment to meet the learning needs of students with different cognitive levels.

3   Program Design

3.1   System Design

The immersive scene scheduling teaching environment is applied to the practical teaching of scene scheduling teaching content in the audio-visual language of animation. The system development firstly used 2d graphics software to carry out relevant graphic design, then used 3ds Max to conduct role modelling and scene modelling and endowed with maps and materials, and again used unity3D engine in combination with SteamVR plug-in and VRTK plug-in for system development, and finally used mobile HTC VIVE platform for interaction, as shown in Fig. 1(a), (b). This teaching environment includes three parts: role scene scheduling, scene scheduling, role scheduling, and scene scheduling:

(1) The design of the role scene scheduling part, respectively, carries out the action design of the role itself and the interaction between the character and the external environment. In the action design of the function itself, the composition of the position requires reference to the golden section or symmetrical proportion, trying to achieve harmonious and pleasing to the eye, expressive effect. The design of the interaction between characters and the external environment should not only maintain the perfect composition of the spatial relationship between characters and the setting but also reflect the style and express the theme. There are many scene scheduling methods for animated characters, which summarised in the system design: The characters make horizontal movement from the left or right side of the camera screen, which summarised as smooth scheduling. The characters move forward or back to the camera, which can be synthesised as ahead or

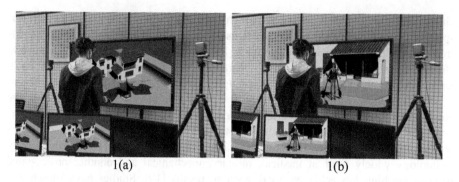

1(a)   1(b)

Fig. 1. Animation scene scheduling teaching environment

back scheduling. The characters move forward or back to the oblique Angle of the lens, which can summarise as oblique scheduling. The characters move in the opposite direction from the top or the bottom of the shot, which can summarise as up or down programming. The characters move up or down in the oblique direction in the shooting, which can summarise as slanting upward or downward. The characters move in a circular motion in front of the camera or around the position of the camera, which can summarise as circular scheduling. The role of free movement in front of the camera, summed up as amorphous scheduling.

(2) Camera scene scheduling refers to the use of camera position changes to the schedule, to make the audience feel like they are on the spot. Constantly from one place to another. Lens scene scheduling mainly, by means of field of view and shooting ways two lens scene scheduling is the lens movement way, namely the "push" and "pull", "rock", "shift" and "like", the scene scheduling can, in fact, two levels, a plane is the scheduling of a single lens, another level is the overall schedule for the entire animation.

(3) The combination of role scheduling and shot scheduling based on the logic of character behaviour determined by plot development, character and character relationship. There are usually three ways to combine these two kinds of scheduling: One is depth scheduling, that is, to make full use of various motion forms of the camera by the change of pole position in the multi-level space. For example, when shooting an animated character from close to far away, the perspective relationship should be used to enhance the sense of three-dimensional space. Second, repeated scheduling. In an animated cartoon, the repeated appearance of the same or similar role scheduling or lens scheduling will arouse the audience's association, understand its internal connection and enhance the appeal. Third, the contrast of scheduling, scheduling of the dynamic and static, fast and slow, and with the strength of sound. The light and shade of smooth shadow can make the atmosphere more intense.

3.2 Implementation Method

Scene Scheduling Teaching Environment was relying on mobile HTC VIVE platform for interaction, that is, through Steam VR plug-ins, VRTK plug-ins to achieve the interaction between the handle and UI interface. First, learners need to debug VR helmet and handle through Steam VR software to ensure its normal operation. When the learner enters the 360° virtual learning environment, it can see that there are three items to choose from in the virtual practice teaching environment, namely role scene schedule. Lens scene scheduling, the combination of scheduling and lens scheduling, learners learn by handle emission rays after selecting projects; the scene will automatically switch to the project. To meet the learning needs of students of different cognitive level, reflect the teaching environment of personalisation, each project set up a primary, intermediate, advanced, three different difficulty levels of learning scene for learners to choose. If learners can't get an accurate judgment about their cognitive level, don't know how to choose the difficulty level, UI interface design the help button, when learners use the handle after ray chose to help launch, Press the handle to open the knowledge question bank for the cognitive level test. At this time, learners begin to answer the questions, and the system will automatically mark the answers after the questions answered. At the same time, suggestions on the selection of difficulty levels will provide according to learners' answer scores. Learners use the handle to choose the difficulty level, the system automatically load study scene, set up in the scene and the learning environment related background music in order to express the theme better, make learners immerse in a variety of sensory stimulation, multi-angle many-side careful observation of the scene, using their theoretical knowledge to analysis need scene scheduling object. According to the circumstances of the animation of the development of route planning and scheduling, planning can be run in the system, after the completion of an operation after the teacher give corresponding learning evaluation and feedback.

3.3 Teaching Model

When virtual reality technology applies to education and teaching, its most core theoretical basis is constructivism learning theory. Constructivism advocates student-centred theory and requires students to change from passive recipients of knowledge to subjects of information processing and meaning construction. It also requires teachers to change from knowledge imparting and indoctrination to help students to construct the meaning of the promoter and guide. Relevant studies have shown that virtual reality technology provides similar resources for independent learning. By designing the teaching environment with immersive virtual reality technology, learners can choose their learning mode according to their cognitive level and test the learning effect through environmental feedback. At the same time, cognitive load theory holds that virtual reality environment design and learning script design should put students' limited cognitive resources into activities related to learning objectives. The animation scene scheduling teaching environment designed in this paper reduces the external cognitive load as much as possible, creates the sense of immersion as much as possible, takes the skill formation as the goal, helps learners to transform knowledge into skills, and improves students' ability to apply knowledge. Teaching activities divided into three stages: activity preparation, activity exploration, and evaluation and summary, including seven phases: preliminary development, problem presentation, problem analysis, problem-solving, achievement display, assessment and feedback, and later review. The teaching process is shown in Fig. 2.

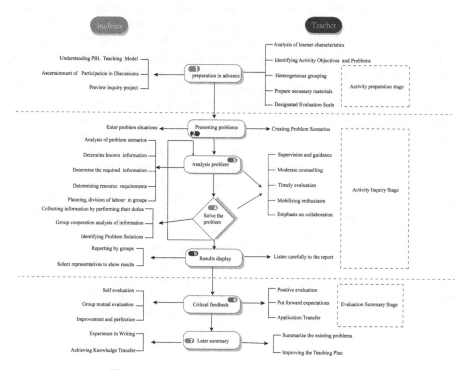

Fig. 2. Animation scene scheduling teaching model

(1) Activity preparation: Teachers need to analyse the characteristics of learners, divide students into groups, determine the objectives of practical teaching activities, prepare necessary materials and develop a learning evaluation scale. Students need to understand the PBL model, participate in a discussion of problems, and preview practical learning projects.

(2) Activity inquiry stage: Teachers create a problem situation for students. In the process of actual learning, students should be supervised and moderately tutored. Teachers also need to timely evaluate students' inquiry process to mobilise students' active participation and promote students' teamwork ability. Students need to actively enter into the problem situation, analyse the problem situation, and at the same time make a plan to solve the problem and divide the work into groups. In this stage, the team members shall perform their duties and cooperate to analyse the situation and determine the solution to the problem. When the activity completed, and the results are displayed, each group shall report the results to the selected representative, and the teacher shall listen to the report carefully.

(3) Evaluation and summary stage: Teachers should make positive evaluation and expectations for students, actively guide students to extend and transfer the knowledge they have learned, summarise the problems in practical teaching and improve the teaching plan. Students can conduct self-evaluation and group mutual evaluation, to enhance and enhance the solution to the problem, and carefully write the experience to achieve knowledge transfer.

4 Method

4.1 Participants

In this study, a total of 60 sophomore students majoring in digital media application technology were recruited to participate in the teaching experiment. None of them had previous experience in learning animation audio-visual language. Among them, 30 students form a class as the experimental group (group 1), and the other 30 as the control group (group 2). The same teacher teaches the two categories.

4.2 Procedure

The objective of this experiment is to learn the scene scheduling of a single lens, the scene scheduling of pushing, pulling, shaking, moving and following a single lens. The experimental group taught by the teaching system designed in this paper. Before class, each group equipped with HTC VIVE platform. The teacher demonstrated the application process of the practical teaching system to the students through multimedia video. The teaching mode is shown in Fig. 2 used for actual teaching. The control group used traditional multimedia teaching, and the teachers used the multimedia projector to display the animation scenes. The students in each group completed the design scheme according to the previous theoretical knowledge.

4.3 Measure Tools

The measurement tools in this study include pre-test and post-test. The purpose of the pre-test is to evaluate whether the two groups of students have the same cognitive level before participating in the experiment. The post-test includes two aspects: one is the evaluation of the teaching effectiveness of the students' immersion teaching system; The other is the evaluation of the influence of the teaching system on the construction of the students' action program schema. Therefore, the teaching effect assessment questionnaire was closely related to the teaching of the practice teaching content and teaching difficulty, shall be borne by two of the course teaching of teachers to discuss written questionnaire, including 10 questions (T1–T10), measurement of five dimensions (D1–D5), which is suitable for teaching target D1, D2 for thinking ability, D3 for comprehensive ability, D4 for knowledge migration, D5 for skill formation. The evaluation of the influence of the teaching system on the construction of students' action program schemata includes 15 questions (T1–T15) and three dimensions (d1–d3), among which D1 is cognition, D2 is connection and D3 is automation. Five-point

Likert scale used in all the questionnaires in this study and students in each group randomly selected for interviews.

5 Results

5.1 Data Analysis

Each data set of the two groups collected from different students. Therefore, they are unrelated and independent, so the independent sample t-test is suitable for analysing the results obtained from the questionnaire.

5.2 Evaluation of Teaching Effectiveness

Using independent sample t to evaluate the teaching effectiveness of the two teaching modes is different. Pre-test shows that there is no significant difference between group 1 and group 2 in the application of the research content. That is to say, the cognitive level of the two groups of students is the same. We calculated the average of the questionnaire results. One point is "completely consistent." Five points are "completely inconsistent." The back results show that the experimental group. The average value was higher than that of the control group, especially in D1 teaching objectives, D4 knowledge transfer, and D5 skills formation. The difference between the experimental group and the control group is obvious. The score of the experimental group is much higher than that of the control group. Independent sample t-test results showed that students in the experimental group were more likely to accomplish teaching objectives (D1, $F = 0.142$, $P = 0.000 < 0.001$), stimulate effective thinking such as analysis, synthesis, generalization and abstraction related to teaching content (D2, $F = 0.849$, $P = 0.000 < 0.001$), realize the connection and comprehensive application of knowledge (D3, $F = 2.202$, $P = 0.002 < 0.01$), transfer theoretical knowledge to practical environment to complete tasks (D4, $F = 1.146$, $P = 0.000 < 0.001$). < In summary, there is a significant difference in the teaching effect between the experimental group and the control group. The students who use this system for practical teaching have a higher level of mastery and application of knowledge than those who use traditional teaching mode, as shown in Table 1.

5.3 Assessment of the Impact of Teaching System on the Schema Construction of Students' Action Procedures

Similarly, independent sample t was used to evaluate the effect of the two teaching modes on the construction of students' action program schema. As can be seen from Table 2, the average score of the students in the experimental group was higher than that of the students in the control group. Especially in D2 connection stage and D3 automation stage. The average value of the experimental group was significantly higher than that of the control group. In the cognitive stage, the students in the experimental group had a slightly stronger ability to assess their task level (D1, $F = 0.510$, $P = 0.013 < 0.05$). In the contact stage, the ability of the two groups to turn cognition to

Table 1. Evaluation of teaching effectiveness

No.	Group	Mean	SD	F	Sig. (2-tailed)
D1	1	3.95	0.686	0.142	0.000
	2	2.25	0.639		
D2	1	4.00	0.649	0.849	0.000
	2	2.90	0.718		
D3	1	4.00	0.649	2.202	0.002
	2	3.25	0.786		
D4	1	4.00	0.725	1.146	0.000
	2	2.30	0.801		
D5	1	4.65	0.489	1.920	0.000
	2	2.85	0.745		

skills was significantly different, and the experimental group was significantly higher than the control group (D2, $F = 0.477$, $P = 0.000 < 0.001$). In the automation stage, the application of skills in the experimental group was more obvious in the schematic way of action procedures, a start. Motion signals can quickly and accurately complete tasks in a continuous manner according to the action procedure. Each action of skill has become a whole and maintained in time and space (D3, $F = 1.325$, $P = 0.000 < 0.001$). Generally speaking, there are significant differences between the experimental group and the control group in the contact stage and the automation stage. The immersion teaching system plays a positive role in promoting the construction of students' action program schema.

Table 2. Assessment of the impact of teaching system on the visual construction of students' action procedures

No.	Group	Mean	SD	F	Sig. (2-tailed)
D1	1	4.60	0.503	0.510	0.013
	2	4.15	0.587		
D2	1	4.65	0.489	0.477	0.000
	2	3.80	0.523		
D3	1	4.65	0.489	1.325	0.000
	2	3.45	0.510		

5.4 Interview Results

After the teaching experiment, we randomly selected some students from the experimental group and the control group for interviews. The results show that most of the students in the experimental group think that immersion scene scheduling teaching environment presents practical learning scenarios through a simulated virtual reality environment. In three-dimensional space, students can observe the experimental environment intuitively, to conduct a mirror. Head-and-face scheduling, knowledge transfer is easy to form, and learning objectives are relatively easy to achieve. At the same time, immersive practical teaching environment significantly stimulates students' learning motivation, which is conducive to the transfer of knowledge and the formation of skills. The students in the control group generally think that it is difficult to achieve the learning goal by using a multimedia projector to display the learning scene in this experiment. Because the scene scheduling of the lens is carried out in three-dimensional space, while the two-dimensional display platform requires each group of students to use their imagination to associate three-dimensional space with completing the practical learning task. The students in the whole learning process generally think that it is difficult and have no interest in learning. Interest in learning. The students in the control group hope that in the future practice teaching, they can transfer the theoretical knowledge of scene scheduling and transform the corresponding knowledge into skill learning mode in the simulated three-dimensional space corresponding to the learning situation.

6   Discussion

The animation audio-visual language teaching present situation is not very desirable, is difficult to obtain, maintain and stimulate students' attention and curiosity. Because "audio-visual animation language" is a course, in theory, most teachers use traditional teaching. Multimedia teaching mode and the directions of the teaching content applied in the three-dimensional space, the division of 3D scene space area, the determination of the role positioning and walked a two-dimensional learning environment for students to feel the teaching content is challenging. Traditional teaching makes the curriculum for inspiring the enthusiasm of students learning scene scheduling principle, and the students can't fully understand the related theory, Some students are not interested in the course. The teaching environment of animation scene scheduling based on immersive virtual reality technology allows learners to learn in the context by creating a three-dimensional virtual environment. At the same time, the simulation of virtual reality environment intuitively presents the practical learning situation, and students design the scene scheduling of shots in the three-dimensional space like immersive, which promotes the knowledge transfer and skills formation of students. This teaching system sets the background music of the theme according to the learning situation, which stimulates the visual and auditory senses of the learners, and improves the sense of immersion of the learners in the virtual environment.

Also, the teaching system is independently developed and designed according to the principle of animation scene scheduling, which reduces external influence, improves students' understanding of the principle of scene scheduling, and promotes the transformation of students' theoretical knowledge into skills. The development cost of this teaching system is low. Hardware environment is relatively easy to implement, and the operation is simple. Teachers have no use to spending a lot of time to decompose the learning tasks, and only need to explain the tasks through text, audio, image or video. The interactive part specially developed for guiding the learning, which will not make learners feel confused and boring. The task design of learning situation includes knowledge transfer and skill transformation. With minimal interference and a strong sense of reality, it urges students to enhance attention, improve learning effect, enhance learning motivation and promote skill formation.

7 Conclusion and Future Work

In this paper, an immersive virtual reality (VR) - based teaching environment for animation scene schedule developed for the practical teaching of the course "audio-visual animation language," and the influence of the immersive teaching environment on students' learning effects and skills formation discussed by using the situational teaching mode. The experimental results prove that this teaching environment can help students to transform knowledge into ability and promote the formation of students' professional skills. In the future work, we will continue to improve the teaching environment of animation scene scheduling and try to use new interactive technology to teach more teaching contents of audio-visual animation language, to realise the mutual benefit of teaching.

References

1. Wei, X., Guo, D., Weng, D.: A study of preschool instructional design based on augmented reality games. In: Wang, Y., Jiang, Z., Peng, Y. (eds.) IGTA 2018. CCIS, vol. 875, pp. 106–113. Springer, Singapore (2018). https://doi.org/10.1007/978-981-13-1702-6_11
2. Fonseca, D., Valls, F., Redondo, E., Villagrasa, S.: Informal interactions in 3D education. Comput. Hum. Behav. 55(PA), 504–518 (2016)
3. Villagrasa, S., Fonseca, D., Redondo, E., et al.: Teaching case of gamification and visual technologies for education. J. Cases Inf. Technol. (JCIT) 16(4), 38–57 (2014)
4. Li, X., Zhang, L.: Research on teaching design of mixed form in virtual reality/augmented reality. Audio-Visual Educ. Res. 20–25 (2017)
5. Li, X., Zhang, L.: Intelligent virtual reality/augmented reality research on the structure of teaching system. Audio-Visual Educ. Res. 97–104 (2018)
6. Gao, Y., Liu, D.: Virtual reality technology promotes the core elements of learning and its challenges. Audio-Visual Educ. Res. 77–85 (2016)
7. Zikas, P., et al.: Mixed reality serious games and gamification for smart education. In: European Conference on Games Based Learning. Academic Conferences International Limited (2016)
8. Liu, P., Peng, Z.: Gamification interaction design of online education. In: 2013 2nd International Symposium on Instrumentation and Measurement, Sensor Network and Automation (IMSNA). IEEE (2013)
9. Wang, C.: The Application of Scene Scheduling in Animation Short Film – Take the Opening Animation Short Film of Annecy International Animation Festival as an Example (2011)
10. Chen, L.: On the Application of Scene Scheduling in Animation – How to Improve Chinese Animation with Scene Scheduling (2009)
11. Wood, L., et al.: The role of gamification and game-based learning in authentic assessment within virtual environments. In: Research and Development in Higher Education: The Place of Learning and Teaching, pp. 514–523 (2013)

12. Lynch, T., Ghergulescu, I.: NEWTON virtual labs: introduction and teacher perspective. In: 2017 IEEE 17th International Conference on Advanced Learning Technologies (ICALT). IEEE (2017)
13. Freina, L., Ott, M.: A literature review on immersive virtual reality in education: state of the art and perspectives. In: The International Scientific Conference eLearning and Software for Education, vol. 1. "Carol I" National Defence University (2015)
14. Li, X.: The Application of Scene Scheduling in Animation (2018)
15. Vicent, L., et al.: Virtual learning scenarios for qualitative assessment in higher education 3D arts. J. Univers. Comput. Sci. 21, 1086–1105 (2015)
16. Chen, L.: On the scene in the animation scheduling. Sci. Technol. Inf. 244–245 (2010)
17. Charles, D., Charles, T., McNeill, M., et al.: Game-based feedback for educational multi-user virtual environments. Br. J. Educ. Technol. 42(4), 638–654 (2011)
18. Zhao, Y.: Research and Development of Immersive Virtual Interactive Platform (2018)
19. Hu, W.: Practical Research on Virtual Reality Technology (2018)

An Improved Dark Object Subtraction Method for Atmospheric Correction of Remote Sensing Images

Yu Wang[1,2(✉)], Xiaoyong Wang[1,2], Hongyan He[1,2], and Guoliang Tian[1,2]

[1] Beijing Institute of Space Mechanics and Electricity, Beijing 100094, China
93031@163.com
[2] Key Laboratory for Advanced Optical Remote Sensing Technology of Beijing, Beijing 100094, China

Abstract. Atmospheric correction is an important and essential procedure of high-quality remote sensing data for quantitative application and surface parameters retrieval, while aerosols and water vapor are larger temporal and spatial variation, which are the main factors restricting the accuracy of atmospheric correction. An Improved Dark Object Subtraction (IDOS) method is proposed in this paper. The new method retrieves the ancillary information on the aerosol optical depth (AOD) and total water vapor (TWV) from the multi-spectral information. The AOD and TWV obtained from the retrieval are used to optimize the DOS model. The experiment is carried out using data of Sentinel-2, which carries a Multispectral Instrument (MSI). The simulation results show that the visual effects, image clarity and image contrast of the remote sensing images are obviously improved; the atmospheric corrected reflectance curve is closer to measured typical objects reflectance curve in the terms of both spectral shape and reflectance value, indicating that the effect of atmosphere have been successfully removed by using the proposed algorithm. Compared with the traditional DOS technique, the IDOS method has greatly higher accuracy and practicality.

Keywords: Atmospheric correction · Dark Object Subtraction · Aerosol optical depth · Water vapor · Remote sensing images

1 Introduction

The atmosphere is a layer of dielectric composed of multiple gases and aerosols between the satellite remote sensor and the Earth's surface. When electromagnetic waves transmits from the surface of the Earth to the sensor, the atmosphere is a necessary passage. The effect of the atmosphere on electromagnetic waves can be roughly classified into two physical processes, absorption and scattering [1]. The absorption and scattering of the atmosphere can weaken the electromagnetic waves. Eliminating the influence of the atmosphere on the amount of electromagnetic waves by atmospheric correction and restoring its original appearance on the Earth's surface becomes an inevitable problem of quantitative remote sensing [2, 3].

© Springer Nature Singapore Pte Ltd. 2019
Y. Wang et al. (Eds.): IGTA 2019, CCIS 1043, pp. 425–435, 2019.
https://doi.org/10.1007/978-981-13-9917-6_41

Dark Object Subtraction (DOS) is a widely used and well-known simple image-based absolute atmospheric correction method. This approach assumes that there are at least a few pixels of dark objects throughout a satellite image scene, and they should have zero value, along with a horizontally homogeneous atmosphere [4, 5]. Thus, the minimum Digital Number (DN) value in the histogram considered as dark objects from the scene which is known as the atmospheric effects (mostly from haze), which accordingly is subtracted from all pixels. Atmospheric transmittance and path radiation are the key determinants of DOS atmospheric correction accuracy [6]. In four factors (atmospheric molecule, ozone content, aerosol and water vapor content) that affect atmospheric transmittance and path radiation, atmospheric molecules and ozone content are relatively stable with little difference in space, while aerosols and water vapor are larger temporal and spatial variation, which are the main factors restricting the accuracy of atmospheric correction. The variation makes it significantly harder to obtain the aerosol optical thickness and the water vapor optical thickness with high precision. However, the common practice is to ignore these two factors or make use of the weather station data, which seriously limits the atmospheric correction accuracy of the DOS.

Therefore, aiming to improve the estimates of surface reflectance through traditional image-based DOS method, this paper investigates to achieve the simultaneous acquisition of atmospheric radiation parameters based on the multi-spectral information. An Improved Dark Object Subtraction (IDOS) method that tends to correct the haze in terms of atmospheric scattering and path radiance for optical remote sensing image is presented. The new method retrieves the ancillary information on the aerosol optical depth (AOD) and total water vapor (TWV) from the multi-spectral information. AOD is retrieved using the Dense Dark Vegetation (DDV) algorithm. TWV retrieval over land is performed with the Atmospheric Pre-corrected Differential Absorption algorithm. Then, the AOD and TWV obtained from the retrieval are used to optimize the DOS model. This paper is organized as follows. Section 2 is a simple introduction to the DOS method. Section 3 is an improved DOS method. In Sect. 4, we provide some experimental results, discuss the proposed method and compare it with existing methods. Finally, we conclude in Sect. 5.

2   DOS Method

Remote sensing surface reflection inversion is based on the radiation transfer equation. Assuming surface uniformity, lambertian reflection, sky irradiance isotropic, and ignoring atmospheric refraction, polarization and proximity effects, surface radiance is expressed as:

$$L_0 = \rho \times \frac{(E_0 \cos(\theta_z)T_z + E_{down})}{\pi d^2} \tag{1}$$

The apparent radiance received by the satellite is a function of surface radiance, atmospheric transmission, atmospheric albedo, and upward atmospheric spectral radiance L_p due to atmospheric scattering.

$$L_{sat} = L_p + \frac{L_0 T_v}{1 - S\rho} \tag{2}$$

Where, L_0 is the spectral radiance at ground level ($W \cdot m^{-2} \cdot sr^{-1} \cdot \mu m^{-1}$),

L_{sat} is the spectral radiance at sensor level ($W \cdot m^{-2} \cdot sr^{-1} \cdot \mu m^{-1}$),

L_p is the spectral radiance received by the sensor from an area where there is only atmospheric contribution,

ρ is the spectral reflectance at ground level,

d is the Sun-Earth distance in astronomical units,

E_0 is the exoatmospheric spectral solar irradiance ($W \cdot m^{-2} \cdot sr^{-1} \cdot \mu m^{-1}$),

θ_z is the incidence angle between the solar vector and the normal vector of the terrain (accounting for its slope and aspect),

E_{down} is the down-welling spectral irradiance at the surface due to the scatted solar fluex in the atmosphere ($W \cdot m^{-2} \cdot sr^{-1} \cdot \mu m^{-1}$),

T_z is the atmospheric transmittance through the path Sun to Earth,

T_v is the atmospheric transmittance through the path Earth to Sun,

S is the spherical albedo of the atmosphere.

Since the value of S is small, it can usually be ignored. The surface reflectance is obtained by the Eq. (1) and the Eq. (2):

$$\rho = \frac{\pi(L_{sat} - L_p)d^2}{T_v[E_0 \cos(\theta_z)T_z + E_{down}]} \tag{3}$$

According to a study by Song et al. [7], assuming that the reflectance of a dark pixel is 0.01, then

$$L_p = L_{dark} - 0.01\{[E_0 \cos(\theta_z)T_z + E_{down}]T_v/(\pi d^2)\} \tag{4}$$

Where, L_{dark} is the dark pixel radiance in the image ($W \cdot m^{-2} \cdot sr^{-1} \cdot \mu m^{-1}$).

It can be seen from Eq. (3) that there are 4 variables. Based on research work such as Song and Clark [8, 9], According to different simplifying assumptions for T_z, T_v and E_{down}, different DOS atmospheric correction methods are obtained as shown in Table 1.

Table 1. Parameter settings for the four DOS approaches based on Eq. (3)

Methods	T_v	T_z	E_{down}
DOS1	1.0	$\cos\theta_z$	0.0
DOS2	$\exp(-\tau_r/\cos\theta_v)$	$\exp(-\tau_r/\cos\theta_v)$	$6SV$
DOS3	$\exp(-\tau_a/\cos\theta_v)$	$\exp(-\tau_a/\cos\theta_v)$	πL_p
DOS4	$6SV$	$6SV$	$6SV$

3 IDOS Method

3.1 Atmospheric Parameter Retrieval Based on Multi-spectral Information

Aerosol Optical Thickness Retrieval

Dense Dark Vegetation (DDV) is a commonly used aerosol optical thickness retrieval method, suitable for different remote sensors configured with short-wave infrared spectrum. The basic idea is to use the low reflectance of dense vegetation in red and blue bands and there is a certain linear relationship with the reflectance of the short-wave infrared band. The AOD information is extracted by distinguishing the contribution values of the surface and the atmosphere from the apparent reflectance observed by the satellite remote sensor.

Assuming that the surface is a Lambertian body and the atmospheric conditions are uniform, the apparent reflectivity of the top of the atmosphere received by the satellite remote sensor can be expressed as:

$$\rho_{TOA}(\theta_s, \theta_v, \phi) = \rho_0(\theta_s, \theta_v, \phi) + \frac{T(\theta_s)T(\theta_v)\rho_s(\theta_s, \theta_v, \phi)}{[1 - \rho_s(\theta_s, \theta_v, \phi)S]} \tag{5}$$

Where, ρ_{TOA} is the apparent reflectance,

ρ_0 is the path radiation equivalent reflectance,
ρ_s is the surface reflectance,
θ_s is the sun zenith,
θ_v is the zenith angle,
ϕ is the sun and the remote sensor relative azimuth,
$T(\theta_s)$ is the atmospheric transmittance of the sun-ground,
$T(\theta_v)$ is the atmospheric transmittance of ground-remote sensor.

The ρ_0, S and $T(\theta_s)T(\theta_v)$ three parameters are related to atmospheric optical properties from which the AOD can be retrieved [10]. When retrieving the AOD, the surface reflectance noise is removed by the decoupling of the ground gas. Calculate the correspondence between AOD and ρ_0, S, $T(\theta_s)T(\theta_v)$, using a radiation transfer model such as 6S. A look-up table is created to retrieve AOD.

Total Water Vapor Content Retrieval

It is relatively difficult to obtain the transmittance from the single water vapor absorption channel radiation value, and the water vapor content retrieval is based on the channel ratio method. In the given wavelength range, the effects of atmospheric scattering and surface reflection are removed, and the ratio of reflectance of different spectral channels is utilized to retrieve the water vapor content.

The radiance received at different wavelengths can be expressed as:

$$\rho * (\lambda) = \frac{L_{sensor}(\lambda)}{L_{sun}(\lambda)} = T(\lambda)\rho(\lambda) \tag{6}$$

Where, λ is the wavelength,
$L_{sensor}(\lambda)$ is the radiance received by the remote sensor,
$L_{sun}(\lambda)$ is the atmospheric top solar radiance,
$T(\lambda)$ is the atmospheric transmittance,
$\rho(\lambda)$ is the surface reflectance,
$L_{path}(\lambda)$ is the atmospheric path radiation.

If the surface reflectance is constant with wavelength, the path radiation can be considered as a small fraction of the direct reflected radiation of the sun [11]. Water vapor transmission rate of 0.945 μm channels $T_{obs}(0.945\,\mu m)$:

$$T_{obs}(0.945\,\mu m) = \frac{\rho(0.945\,\mu m)}{\rho(0.865\,\mu m)} \tag{7}$$

The water vapor transmission rate of the 0.945 μm channel is equal to the ratio of the surface reflectivity corresponding to the 0.945 μm channel to the surface reflectance of the adjacent atmospheric window channel.

3.2 Optimize the DOS Model for Atmospheric Correction

Since the AOD and TWV are the main parameters affecting the atmospheric transmittance, retrieving atmospheric parameters based on multi-spectral information can provide a more accurate transmission rate for the DOS atmospheric correction model. The atmospheric transmittance of the sun direction and the sensor observation direction can be expressed as:

$$T_z = \exp(-\tau/\cos\theta_z) = \exp[(-\tau_r - \tau_a - \tau_w)/\cos\theta_z] \tag{8}$$

$$T_z = \exp(-\tau/\cos\theta_v) = \exp[(-\tau_r - \tau_a - \tau_w)/\cos\theta_v] \tag{9}$$

Where, τ_r is the rayleigh scattering optical thickness,
τ_a is the AOD,
τ_w is the TWV optical thickness.

4 Experimental Results and Analysis

4.1 Data Introduction

The Sentinel-2A, launched on June 23, 2015, is used to observe the earth's land, forest cover change, coastline and deep-sea pollution between 84° north latitude and 56° south latitude. Multi-spectral setting can simultaneously detect distribute images such as clouds, aerosols, water vapor, ice and snow. The study area is located near Beijing (109°45′45″–109°46′10″, 21°32′45″–21°33′05″), imaging time is August 6, 2017. Bands for aerosol detection and water vapor detection are available in the Sentinel-2A band setup.

In order to verify the effectiveness of the IDOS atmospheric correction method, the DOS atmospheric correction method was selected for comparative experiments. The experimental flow is shown in Fig. 1.

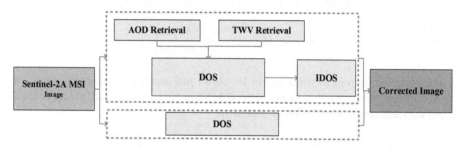

Fig. 1. Sentinel-2A IDOS atmospheric correction experiment procedure

4.2 Reflectance Image Before and After Correction

The experimental area covers urban areas and vegetation areas. The true color image before atmospheric correction is shown in Fig. 2(a). The true color image after DOS atmospheric correction is shown in Fig. 2(b), and the true color image after IDOS atmospheric correction is shown in Fig. 2(c).

Comparing the remote sensing images before and after correction, the image visual effects and pixel value contrasts change significantly, and the image details are enhanced. The original image is foggy and blurred above the urban area affected by the atmosphere, and the outline of the object is not obvious. The corrected image has better effect on subjective vision, the brightness is improved, the overall visibility of the image is enhanced, vegetation after atmospheric correction is more differentiated from bare land and surface buildings.

(a) Original Image   (b) DOS Atmospheric Correction Image

(c) IDOS Atmospheric Correction Image

Fig. 2. Comparison of different methods for atmospheric correction (Color figure online)

4.3 Evaluation of Clarity and Contrast Before and After Correction

The image clarity can be used to characterize the remote sensing image [12]. The larger the image clarity index value is, the clearer the remote sensing image is, indicating that the correction effect is better.

The formula for the definition evaluation function is as follows:

$$F = \frac{1}{M \times N} \sum_{x=1}^{M} \sum_{y=1}^{N} I_{xy}^2 \tag{10}$$

The Laplace neighborhood operator uses a four-neighbor operator, that is, the single-pixel Laplace algebra sum is:

$$I_{xy} = 4f(x,y) - f(x-1,y) - f(x+1,y) - f(x,y-1) - f(x,y+1) \tag{11}$$

The image contrast is used to represent the grayscale contrast of the contour, edge and texture of the remote sensing image. The larger the image contrast index value is, the clearer the image is. The smaller the value is, the more blurred the image is. When the two remote sensing images are compared, the image with unclear outline and weakened edges has a small contrast.

The formula for the contrast evaluation function is as follows:

$$C_{con} = \sum_{i=0}^{N-1}\sum_{j=0}^{N-1}\frac{[C(i) - C(i-1)]^2 + [C(j) - C(j-1)]^2 + [C(j) - C(j+1)]^2 + [C(i) - C(i+1)]^2}{4}$$

$$(12)$$

Where, $C(i,j)$ is the gray value of the pixel.

Image clarity and contrast were used to evaluate the blue, green, and red bands of pre-atmospheric correction image, the DOS atmospheric correction image, and the IDOS atmospheric correction image. The clarity evaluation is shown in Fig. 3, and the contrast evaluation is shown in Fig. 4. The results of the definition and definition of contrast are shown in Table 2.

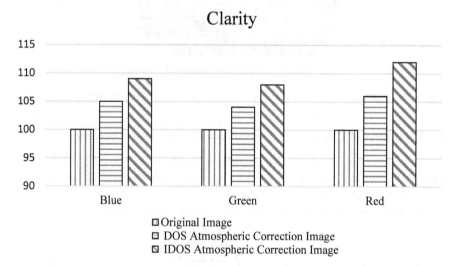

Fig. 3. Clarity evaluation of different correction method (Color figure online)

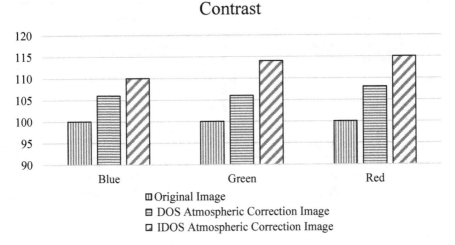

Fig. 4. Contrast evaluation of different correction method (Color figure online)

Table 2. Clarity and contrast evaluation of different correction method

		Blue	Green	Red
Improved clarity (%)	DOS	5.00	4.00	6.00
	IDOS	9.00	8.00	12.00
Improved contrast (%)	DOS	6.00	6.00	8.00
	IDOS	10.00	14.00	15.00

After using DOS atmospheric correction and IDOS atmospheric correction, the image clarity and contrast are obviously improved and the correction effect is different for different spectral band. Compared with the DOS atmospheric correction, IDOS has a more obvious effect on image enhancement, indicating that the method is more effective.

4.4 Spectral Characteristics Evaluation of Typical Ground Reflectivity

In order to evaluate the effect of atmospheric correction on the level of quantitative application. Four kinds of typical features such as water, vegetation, bare soil and architecture were selected for spectral curve comparison in the image before atmospheric correction, DOS atmospheric correction and IDOS atmospheric correction image. The results are shown in Fig. 5.

By comparing the spectral curves of typical objects before and after atmospheric correction, the typical spectral curve after IDOS atmospheric correction is closer to its standard spectral curve. Compared with DOS atmospheric correction, the spectral results obtained by this method are better, which is more conducive to quantitative remote sensing applications.

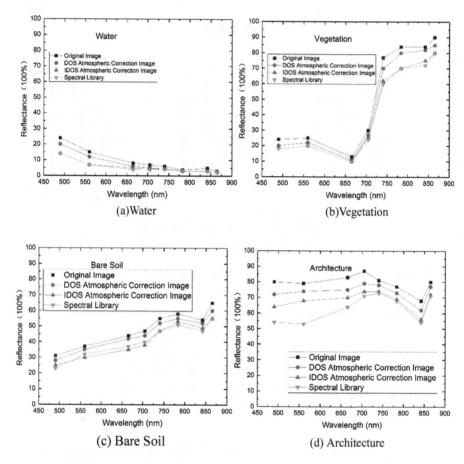

Fig. 5. Comparison between spectral curves of typical ground objects

5   Conclusion

This paper presents an improved dark object subtraction method for atmospheric correction of remote sensing images, using multi-spectral information to retrieve the atmospheric parameter. Verified by the experiment, compared with original one, evaluated from visual effects, clarity, contrast, and spectral characteristics, IDOS method in this paper can improve the quality of remote sensing image. In the future, we will combine the retrieved atmospheric parameters with radiation transfer models to achieve high accuracy atmospheric correction.

References

1. Vermote, E.F., Kotchenova, S.: Atmospheric correction for the monitoring of land surfaces. J. Geophys. Res.: Atmos. **113** (2008)
2. Mustak, Sk.: Correction of atmospheric haze in Resourcesat-1 Liss-4 MX Data for urban analysis: an improved dark object subtraction approach. Remote Sens. Spat. Inf. Sci. **XL**, 283–287 (2013)
3. Hadjimitsis, D.G., Papadavid, G., Agapiou, A., et al.: Atmospheric correction for satellite remotely sensed data intended for agricultural applications: impact on vegetation indices. Nat. Hazards Earth Syst. Sci. **10**, 89–95 (2010)
4. Levi, M., Rasmussen, C.: Considerations for atmospheric correction of surface reflectance for soil survey applications (2011)
5. Chang, J., Clay, D.E., Leigh, L., et al.: Evaluating modified atmospheric correction methods for landsat imagery: image-based and model-based calibration methods. Commun. Soil Sci. Plant Anal. **39**(9–10), 1532–1545 (2008)
6. Abdullah, H.M., Akiyama, T., Shibayama, M., et al.: Estimation and validation of biomass of a mountainous agroecosystem by means of sampling, spectral data and QuickBird satellite image. Int. J. Sustain. Dev. World Ecol. **18**(5), 384–392 (2011)
7. Song, C., Curtis, E., Woodcock, K.C.: Classification and change detection using landsat TM data. Remote Sens. Environ. **2** (2001)
8. Clark, B., Suomalainen, J., Pellikka, P.: A comparison of methods for the retrieval of surface reflectance factor from multitemporal SPOT HRV, HRVIR, and HRG multispectral satellite imagery. Can. J. Remote Sens. **36**(4), 397–411 (2010)
9. Chavez, P.S.: Image-based atmospheric correction—revisited and improved. Photogram. Eng. Remote Sens. **62**, 1025–1036 (1996)
10. Levy, R.C., Remer, L.A., Mattoo, S., et al.: Second-generation operational algorithm: retrieval of aerosol properties over land from inversion of moderate resolution imaging spectroradiometer spectral reflectance. J. Geophys. Res. Atmos. **112**(D13) (2007)
11. Bennartz, R., Fischer, J.: Retrieval of columnar water vapour over land from backscattered solar radiation using the medium resolution imaging spectrometer. Remote Sens. Environ. **78**(3), 274–283 (2001)
12. Eskicioglu, A.M., Fisher, P.S.: Image quality measures and their performance. IEEE Trans. Commun. **43**(12), 2959–2965 (1995)

The Influence of Mobile Augmented Reality-Based Sandbox Games on Chinese Characters Learning

Xiaodong Wei[1], Guodong Yang[1(✉)], and Dongdong Weng[2]

[1] School of Educational Technology, Northwest Normal University,
967 Anning East Road, Lanzhou 730070, People's Republic of China
ygd9565@163.com
[2] School of Optoelectronics, Beijing Institute of Technology,
No. 5, South Zhongguancun Street, Haidian Zone, Beijing 100081
People's Republic of China

Abstract. With the rapid development of augmented reality technology in the field of education, the availability of learning methods based on mobile AR technology has been verified. However, there is little research on the impact of mobile AR on Chinese character learning. This paper designed and developed a mobile AR Chinese characters sandbox game. Compared with the traditional Chinese characters learning applications, the game is more interesting and effective. The game combines 3D touch interaction, 2D interface interaction, image recognition-based AR interaction and so on. The game can intelligently recommend suitable learning content to learners. In the game, participants write Chinese characters by interacting with the real environment, while changing the virtual environment. The results of this study show that the game has a positive impact on learners' learning of Chinese characters. It can greatly improve learners' learning interest and motivation.

Keywords: Mobile learning · Argument reality ·
Human-computer interaction · Gamified learning · Chinese characters

1 Introduction

In recent years, mobile learning has developed rapidly all over the world. However, in order to meet the universality and sustainable development of mobile learning, continuous technological innovation and support are needed [1]. Mobile language learning has been in use since 2001 [2]. The popularity of smart phones further promotes the transmission of learning content and accelerates the development of mobile language learning [3]. Mobile learning allows language learners to set up learning tasks based on the current environment, weakening the boundary between formal learning and informal learning. Kukulska-Hulme, found that there was a strong link between game-based learning and mobile learning [4]. Gamified mobile learning methods promote students' learning outcomes through situational awareness and real environment, which is better than non-gamified mobile learning [5]. An interesting game can encourage

© Springer Nature Singapore Pte Ltd. 2019
Y. Wang et al. (Eds.): IGTA 2019, CCIS 1043, pp. 436–446, 2019.
https://doi.org/10.1007/978-981-13-9917-6_42

students to use again and again, and then repeat the language content of the study for many times [6].

Augmented reality (AR) technology has been gradually developed in various fields, and has also been emerging in the field of education in recent years. Researchers have found that AR has great development potential in education and can affect students' emotional and cognitive learning results [7]. Educators have found that games can attract players to immerse themselves in them, and gamified teaching methods can effectively improve students' learning performance. AR can further bridge the gap between games and education [8]. Hsu found through experimental research that AR language learning could achieve a high learning effect. At the same time, autonomous AR language learning could also form a higher flow experience, and to a certain extent, could reduce the sense of learning anxiety [9].

Vocabulary is the core of language learning and an important part of language development. Chinese character is a very ancient ideographic language, which is the carrier of Chinese civilization for thousands of years [10]. Therefore, Chinese characters are a necessary and important part of Chinese learning. In the process of teaching Chinese as a foreign language for many years, researchers have found many problems in the teaching of Chinese characters. Among them, compared with English writing, how the strokes of Chinese characters were combined and distributed, and how different Chinese characters were distinguished from each other was a difficulty in learning Chinese characters [11]. How to write Chinese characters in the correct order of strokes is a problem for many Chinese and foreigners alike [12].

However, the writing of Chinese characters has been neglected for a long time. Traditional Chinese characters writing exercises are usually repeated by students to reinforce their memory. But this method does not have the stroke order practice, writing is also very easy to make mistakes. Students could not get feedback in time, and repeated wrong writing strengthened their wrong memory of Chinese characters. The emergence of mobile Chinese characters learning has led to the emergence of strokes in Chinese characters learning, but error information cannot be fed back in time. There is no personalized intelligent push for the learning order of Chinese characters.

2 Literature Review

2.1 Mobile Learning (M-Learning)

So far, there is no definite definition of m-learning. Some researchers try to define m-learning with the equipment and technology required by m-learning, while others define it according to the learning characteristics of students [13]. Although there are different definitions of m-learning, a typical feature of m-learning is that students can keep moving [14]. In any case, the importance of m-learning can't be ignored. M-learning is common in all fields. It also provides and delivers learning content for formal and informal learning [3]. Some researchers have proposed that m-learning will be an important form of lifelong learning [15]. M-learning tool "Explorez", developed for first-year French university students, turned the campus into a virtual French-speaking world. The m-learning tool improved French by enabling students to interact with different objects on campus through task-based learning and AR. It also incorporated a variety of gamification elements to attract more users to take the initiative to learn [8]. Cavus, has designed a mobile English learning tool. Through experiments, it has been found that m-learning can help students improve their interests in learning English words and their learning performance, which has been well received by students [16].

2.2   Augment Reality (AR)

AR technology is the derivative of virtual reality technology. AR technology is to superimpose virtual objects in the real environment through computer vision technology, so as to enhance the experience of real things. AR technology has been widely used in many fields. For example, Chang, et al. applied AR to mobile navigation to guide tourists to learn the history and geography of tourist attractions [17]. Especially in the field of education has a great impact. Yip et al. used AR video to improve the quality of classroom teaching, which was more efficient than traditional teaching with handouts, and easier to understand complex problems [18]. Solak, applied AR technology to English classes to teach English words. The study found that AR technology had a positive impact on vocabulary learning in language classes and could effectively improve students' academic performance [19].

2.3   Gamified Learning (G-Learning)

Gamification is the use of game design elements in non-game environments [20], and gamification learning is the integration of game design principles into the learning process. Gamification can improve students' learning efficiency, but different from games, gamification learning needs to consider many obstructive factors [21]. Based on the mobile gamification learning system, Su applied the mobile gamification learning method to the learning process of scientific knowledge in primary schools, and found that gamification learning can not only improve students' learning motivation, but also have a positive impact on students' academic performance [22]. Gamification can be used not only for classroom learning, but also to improve users' participation and motivation in online learning. Nike ID, for example, allows users to design their own shoes. The health industry has launched a variety of g-learning apps [23].

3   System Development of the AR Educational Game

3.1   Preliminary Preparation and System Design

Designing a mobile AR system requires some preparatory work. AR can enhance real objects, so we need to prepare a real target object first. We specially designed a recognition card for the game (as shown in Fig. 1), to achieve the superposition with virtual objects. The card can identify different game objects and aims to learn different Chinese characters. In addition, we need to prepare a mobile device equipped with a camera to carry the system.

Fig. 1. AR sandbox game recognition card, used to achieve the superposition with virtual objects.

After the preparatory work is finished, we will begin to design and develop the mobile AR sandbox game to learn Chinese characters. To make the game more interesting and immersive, we designed a main story: animals live in a forest. One day, birds find a lot of different materials that can be used to make the forest more beautiful, but how to build it? The user is a small builder who helps animals complete the construction of the forest.

First, we need to design and make the game objects needed in the sandbox game. After making 3D models with 3D modeling tools, import them into the game engine. In addition, the design of game UI is also required, including the shape, color and style of UI. Then follow the design drawings for layout and construction. After the scene is made, it needs to be further processed in order to make it more realistic and beautiful. Add some particle effects in the 3d scene, and display the effects that cannot be seen in real life in the game with particle effects, making the game more delicate and interesting. At this point, the entire AR virtual environment is created.

The AR sandbox game is designed to help students write Chinese characters correctly. After students log in to the system, follow the system to guide the operation of the learning game. Then students can begin to learn the content of Chinese characters. The main learning content of the game is the writing of Chinese characters. Students identify the card through the mobile device's camera and swipe their fingers across the screen based on the virtual path. The writing process will be constantly tested and feedback. Every stroke of writing has a right or wrong judgment. If the stroke of the swipe is correct, a virtual animation demonstration will appear on the path, along with the corresponding animation and sound effects. While watching the cartoon, students can also observe the writing process of the strokes again. If the stroke is wrong, the virtual animation will not be displayed, and there will be an error message and sound effects.

The learning content of Chinese characters in the game is not programmed, but the intelligent recommendation is made by analyzing the learning situation of students.

According to the students' problems in writing, recommend the Chinese characters suitable for the students to learn next. For example, a student in the process of writing stroke " 丿 " always writing is not standard, system will recommend contains the stroke of Chinese characters. The specific system design process is shown in Fig. 2.

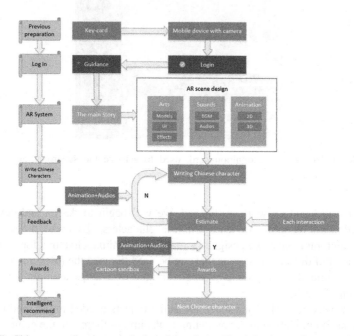

Fig. 2. AR Chinese sandbox game design flow chart. The left shows the overall structural process, and the right shows the diagram for each process.

After students successfully write Chinese characters, they will be given a complete sandbox. They can also watch the correct written animation over and over again.

3.2   Human-Computer Interaction

In the writing process of Chinese characters, there are various ways of interaction, such as AR interaction, two-dimensional interaction and three-dimensional interaction. Human-computer interaction is changing from single-channel interaction to multi-channel interaction, and people are also pursuing more natural interaction.

In the game, AR interaction is used to identify the card, and the real object is identified and processed by computer vision technology, thus the virtual object is superimposed on the card in the way of 3d registration. Students can observe the virtual sandbox from different angles and distances to give them an immersive experience (as shown in Fig. 3). To a certain extent, it can reduce students' learning anxiety and improve their learning interest.

Students can swipe and click on the user interface to select the materials they like (for making the sandbox) and the Chinese characters they want to learn (as shown in

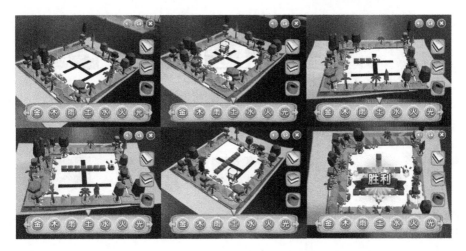

Fig. 3. Chinese characters sandbox from the perspective of AR. Overlay card and sandbox environment. The pictures show various situations during the writing process.

Fig. 3). Different virtual objects can be created by selecting different materials. Different Chinese characters can identify different sandbox scenes and learning contents, which will bring students a richer and more interesting experience.

After select the materials and Chinese characters, students need to click and swipe along the path of the Chinese characters in the virtual sandbox on the touch screen, and then the previously selected materials can be created on the path and superimposed with the virtual sandbox in real time. The feedback in the writing process of Chinese characters not only includes the animation of creating materials, but also the animation feedback and sound feedback after each writing is completed (as shown in Fig. 4). These feedback methods are more intense and timelier, so that students can better understand their writing and correct them. Prevent students from forming wrong reinforcement, which is difficult to correct in the end.

3.3   Intelligent Recommendation

Intelligent recommendation is to search the learning content suitable for users in the database and recommend it to users in the selected area of Chinese characters by analyzing users' operation and learning situation. At present, a lot of learning applications are designed in the background learning process, including learning contents and order. Students can't choose the contents of learning that are suitable for their current learning situation, which reduces the learning efficiency and autonomy of students.

The intelligent recommendation function in AR Chinese characters sandbox game can realize students' personalized learning, timely solve the problems in the learning process and carry out intensive training. In order to improve students' learning autonomy and initiative, they can get additional rewards by completing intelligent recommendation tasks.

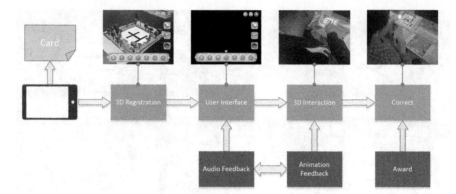

Fig. 4. Human-computer interaction flow chart. Interactive flow and feedback of AR sandbox games in use.

4 Method

4.1 Participants

There were 76 participants in this study, all of whom were sophomores majoring in digital media. Their mother tongue is Chinese, and they have a certain understanding of AR technology, with certain software evaluation ability. The students were divided into two groups, 38 of whom were assigned to the experimental group (Group 1) and the rest to the control group (Group 2). The two groups of students were taught by the same teacher, who works on virtual reality and Chinese characters. All students will be able to use the tablet and be familiar with a variety of interactive modes (Fig. 5).

Fig. 5. Pilot experiment process. The left picture is the AR environment, and the right picture is the traditional media environment.

4.2 Measuring Tools

The measurement methods used in this study were pre-test and post-test. Questionnaire survey was used to measure the differences of two different Chinese learning methods from four dimensions. The four dimensions are learning interest (D1), immersion (D2), interactivity (D3) and learning style (D4). The measurement method was independent sample t-test. Pre-test aims to measure whether the two groups of students are satisfied with the traditional Chinese characters learning methods. Post-test is to measure the satisfaction of two groups of students with AR Chinese characters learning method and Chinese characters learning method based on tablet computer through Likert five-point scale. The Cronbach's alpha value of the questionnaire was 0.916.

4.3 Procedure

The objective of this study is to compare the effect of AR Chinese characters learning method and tablet Chinese characters learning method. During the experiment, we first taught the students in the control group. Before the class, we prepared tablet computers for each student and selected a Chinese character learning app in the store. Before the class began, students' satisfaction with the traditional Chinese writing practice was measured to see if it was consistent with the experimental group. In class, the teacher asked the students to open the downloaded learning application of Chinese characters and learn the writing part of Chinese characters according to the learning mode of the APP. The writing part of Chinese characters was mainly evaluated. The method of writing Chinese characters is to give students a Chinese character and then ask them to describe it in red according to the system prompts, and they will be rewarded whether they are correct or not. After half an hour of learning, the students were asked to measure their satisfaction with this method of learning Chinese characters.

In the experimental group, the teacher prepared a tablet computer and a card for each student before class and pretested the students. In the course, since students have mastered AR technology, there is no need for instructions. Students open the AR Chinese characters sandbox system designed by us and learn the writing of Chinese characters through identifying the card and various interactive operations. Satisfaction was also measured after half an hour of learning.

5   Results

We got two sets of data during the experiment. The first set of data is a survey on the satisfaction of two groups of students with the traditional Chinese characters learning methods. As shown in Table 1, the satisfaction of the two groups of students is consistent. The data in Table 1 shows that the two groups of students are not satisfied with the traditional Chinese writing learning methods and there is no difference between them.

Table 1. The difference of group 1 and group 2

No.	Group	Mean	SD	F	p
D1	1	1.66	0.627	0.075	0.223
	2	1.84	0.679		
D2	1	1.92	0.712	0.843	0.432
	2	1.79	0.741		
D3	1	1.89	0.798	0.068	0.569
	2	2.00	0.805		
D4	1	1.74	0.795	4.396	0.748
	2	1.68	0.620		

As shown in Table 2, it can be seen from the average value of the two groups of data that the average value of the experimental group is higher than that of the control group as a whole. But compared with Table 1, the learning interest (D1, Mean1 = 4.29, Mean2 = 3.89), immersion (D2, Mean1 = 4.29, Mean2 = 3.84), interactivity (D3, Mean1 = 4.29, Mean2 = 3.76) and learning style (D4, Mean1 = 4.13, Mean2 = 3.68) of the experimental and control groups were significantly improved.

Table 2. Independent sample t test results of group 1 and group 2.

No.	Group	Mean	SD	F	p
D1	1	4.29	0.802	3.994	0.067
	2	3.89	1.034		
D2	1	4.29	0.694	10.006	0.038
	2	3.84	1.103		
D3	1	4.29	0.654	6.524	0.006
	2	3.76	0.943		
D4	1	4.13	0.777	1.652	0.021
	2	3.68	0.873		

Through the independent sample t test of the two groups of data, it is found that students are very interested in the two Chinese characters learning methods, and there is no significant difference (D1, F = 3.994, p = 0.067 > 0.05). However, Chinese characters learning games based on AR have better immersion (D2, F = 10.006, p = 0.038 < 0.05), interactivity (D3, F = 6.524, p = 0.006 < 0.01) and learning style (D4, F = 1.652, p = 0.021 < 0.05).

To sum up, students had good feedback on both learning styles, but the experimental group had better immersion, interaction and learning style than the control group.

6 Discussion

Mobile AR sandbox games use AR to superimpose virtual sandbox models on the card. Students can interact with virtual objects in the sandbox in real time. The game will give feedback in various ways, so as to master the correct writing method of Chinese characters in the process of playing the game, and obtain the corresponding rewards.

The students used AR to superimpose the card and virtual scenes in the game. AR firstly processes virtual scenes through computer vision technology and computer graphics, and then superimposes with real objects. Therefore, AR can integrate virtual objects with real objects in a very realistic way, giving people a strong sense of immersion [24, 25]. Students can freely control the Angle of observation and learning, and have more flexible operation. There are various sandbox scenes in the game, and students can choose different materials for secondary construction. The sandbox also contains animation of various small animals, which is very interesting. In addition, the interactive mode in the game is rich and the feedback is timely. While playing the game, students can timely find and correct mistakes. Finally, the whole process of the game is controlled by the students themselves, and the learning content can be selected according to their preferences and intelligent recommendations. To a certain extent, it can realize students' personalized learning of Chinese characters writing.

7 Conclusion

The paper designed and developed a Chinese characters learning game, which is presented in the form of AR sandbox. Students can choose sandbox scene and learning content in the game. The system combined various interactive modes properly and provided students with better interactive experience. In addition, the learning content of students is personalized recommendation through the intelligent recommendation system, so students can learn more suitable Chinese characters. In the future, we will improve the accuracy and judgment basis of intelligent recommendation, so that students can have more choices. Finally, we will also add other contents of Chinese characters, such as pronunciation, usage and so on.

Acknowledgement. This research was supported by the National Natural Science Foundation of China under Grant No. 31860285.

References

1. Traxler, J.: Learning in a mobile age. Int. J. Mob. Blended Learn. (IJMBL) **1**(1), 1–12 (2009)
2. Godwin-Jones, R.: Emerging technologies mobile apps for language learning. Lang. Learn. Technol. **15**(2), 2–11 (2011)
3. Chen, N.S., Hsieh, S.W.: Effects of short-term memory and content representation type on mobile language learning. Lang. Learn. Technol. **12**(3), 93–113 (2008)
4. Kukulska-Hulme, A., Shield, L.: An overview of mobile assisted language learning: from content delivery to supported collaboration and interaction. ReCALL **20**(3), 271–289 (2008)
5. Su, C.H., Cheng, C.H.: A mobile game-based insect learning system for improving the learning achievements. Procedia-Soc. Behav. Sci. **103**, 42–50 (2013)
6. Todd, R.W., Tepsuriwong, S.: Mobile mazes: investigating a mobile phone game for language learning. CALL-EJ Online **10**(1), 10–11 (2008)
7. Ibáñez, M.B., Di Serio, Á., Villarán, D., Kloos, C.D.: Experimenting with electromagnetism using augmented reality: impact on flow student experience and educational effectiveness. Comput. Educ. **71**, 1–13 (2014)
8. Perry, B.: Gamifying French Language Learning: a case study examining a quest-based, augmented reality mobile learning-tool. Procedia-Soc. Behav. Sci. **174**, 2308–2315 (2015)
9. Hsu, T.C.: Learning English with augmented reality: do learning styles matter? Comput. Educ. **106**, 137–149 (2017)
10. Ren, X.: Chinese character education and the inheritance of Chinese culture. Educ. Res. **39**(10), 98–103 (2008)
11. Li, Y.: Characteristics of Chinese characters and Chinese character teaching for foreign countries. World Chin. Teac. **28**(03), 356–367 (2014)

12. Tam, V., Yeung, K.W.: Learning to write Chinese characters with correct stroke sequences on mobile devices. In: 2010 2nd International Conference on Education Technology and Computer, vol. 4, p. V4-395. IEEE (2010)

13. John, T.: Defining discussing and evaluating mobile learning: the moving finger writes and having writ. Int. Rev. Res. Open Distance Learn. (IRRODL) **8**(2), 1–12 (2007)

14. Sharples, M., Taylor, J., Vavoula, G.: Towards a theory of mobile learning. In: Proceedings of mLearn, vol. 1, no. 1, pp. 1–9, October 2005

15. Holzinger, A., Nischelwitzer, A., Meisenberger, M.: Mobile phones as a challenge for m-learning: examples for mobile interactive learning objects (MILOs). In: Third IEEE International Conference on Pervasive Computing and Communications Workshops, pp. 307–311. IEEE, March 2005

16. Cavus, N., Ibrahim, D.: m-Learning: an experiment in using SMS to support learning new English language words. Br. J. Edu. Technol. **40**(1), 78–91 (2009)

17. Chang, Y.L., Hou, H.T., Pan, C.Y., Sung, Y.T., Chang, K.E.: Apply an augmented reality in a mobile guidance to increase sense of place for heritage places. J. Educ. Technol. Soc. **18**(2), 166–178 (2015)

18. Yip, J., Wong, S.H., Yick, K.L., Chan, K., Wong, K.H.: Improving quality of teaching and learning in classes by using augmented reality video. Comput. Educ. **128**, 88–101 (2019)

19. Solak, E., Cakir, R.: Exploring the effect of materials designed with augmented reality on language students' vocabulary learning. J. Educators Online **12**(2), 50–72 (2015)

20. Groh, F.: Gamification: state of the art definition and utilization. Inst. Media Inform. Ulm Univ. **39**, 31 (2012)

21. El-Masri, M., Tarhini, A., Hassouna, M., Elyas, T.: A design science approach to gamify education: from games to platforms. In: ECIS, May 2015

22. Su, C.H., Cheng, C.H.: A mobile gamification learning system for improving the learning motivation and achievements. J. Comput. Assist. Learn. **31**(3), 268–286 (2015)

23. Muntean, C.I.: Raising engagement in e-learning through gamification. In: Proceedings of 6th International Conference on Virtual Learning ICVL, vol. 1, October 2011

24. Wang, S., Tang, Z.: Research on teaching methods based on new mobile augmented reality technology. Chin. J. Educ. **S1–125**(3), 125–127 (2017)

25. Wei, X., Guo, D., Weng, D.: A study of preschool instructional design based on augmented reality games. In: Wang, Y., Jiang, Z., Peng, Y. (eds.) IGTA 2018. CCIS, vol. 875, pp. 106–113. Springer, Singapore (2018). https://doi.org/10.1007/978-981-13-1702-6_11

Impact of Teaching Aids Based on Virtual Role on Student's Design Thinking for Animation Course

Xiaodong Wei[1], Yang Liu[1(✉)], and Dongdong Weng[2]

[1] School of Educational Technology, Northwest Normal University,
967 Anning East Road, Lanzhou 730070, People's Republic of China
ly623326@163.com
[2] School of Optoelectronics, Beijing Institute of Technology,
No. 5, South Zhonguancun Street, Haidian Zone, Beijing 100081,
People's Republic of China

Abstract. This paper describes a teaching aid called ANIMA, which integrates the whole flow of animation design, and uses a virtual role and speech recognition technology to guide students to make animation. This paper examines the learning performance of two groups of participants: experimental group (ANIMA aids) and control group (traditional manufacturing tools). A quasi-experimental study was conducted on 44 college students. The learning performance of different production tools was evaluated, including learning effect and design thinking. The results showed that compared with the traditional animation tools, ANIMA can improve students' learning effect and cultivate their complete design thinking.

Keywords: Animation effect · Animation pedagogical agent ·
Speech recognition technology · Design thinking

1 Introduction

RE Mayer, a multimedia learning expert, believes that multimedia learning refers to learning through many kinds of media materials such as text, picture, video, animation and so on. Comparing the effects of different forms of media on learning is an important part of multimedia learning research [1]. In the process of multimedia learning, the principle of multimedia cognition holds that students learn better when they learn words and pictures than when they learn only words. Based on the multimedia cognitive principle, the animation effect explains the theory of multimedia cognitive principle more comprehensively. Animation effect refers to animation media compared with graphic and text media, animation media in learning effect is better.

The animation, which aims at education and has a relative unity, is also called an education animation [2]. At the same time, with the continuous development of mobile multimedia technology, educational animation has been widely welcomed by people

© Springer Nature Singapore Pte Ltd. 2019
Y. Wang et al. (Eds.): IGTA 2019, CCIS 1043, pp. 447–458, 2019.
https://doi.org/10.1007/978-981-13-9917-6_43

for its advantages such as fast spread speed, strong interaction, small file capacity, strong narrative and so on. And it has occupied the extremely important status in people's study life [3]. Therefore, the demand for educational animation is increasing rapidly in the market. However, faced the problem of scarce professionals and the long production cycle, the output of educational animation has been limited by a lot [4]. Therefore, how to reduce the threshold of animation production, shorten the animation production cycle, improve the output of animation are urgent problems to be solved.

Animation Pedagogical Agent (APA) refers to the character image presented on the computer screen. It can provide instruction and support to learners in the process of learning [5]. The introduction of APA in the process of animation production has a good effect on promoting learners' learning. In conclusion, in order to solve the above problems and improve the teaching effect, this paper designs a teaching aid called ANIMA, which has a huge database (Fig. 1). Users can quickly create their own animation through ANIMA. Improve animation production efficiency, shorten animation production cycle, and eventually increase animation production. At the same time, it also reduces the difficulty of making animations for users lacking artistic skills and reduces the threshold of animation production.

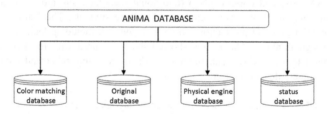

Fig. 1. ANIMA database

2   Literature Review

2.1   Animation Effect

In foreign countries, Shnotz et al. compared "the time phenomena caused by Earth rotation" under animation and graphic conditions, and found that learners' answers to jet lag under animation conditions were significantly better than those under graphic and textual conditions. Moreover, this effect is effective for learners with different levels of knowledge [6]. In China, Song studied the influence of subject background and presentation interaction on multimedia learning effect. She found that animation as a learning material for learning, can improve the learning effectiveness of arts and science students [7]. Through the research, Hu found that the learning effect of learning materials in the form of animation and commentary was more significant than that of text and pictures. The results of related eye movement behavior data are also in good agreement with the research conclusion [8]. Yan et al., taking 49 college students as subjects, divided into two groups to test. It is found that when learners use animation version of learning materials, learning time and error times are less [9]. All the above empirical studies confirm the real and effective existence of animation effect in the process of multimedia learning.

2.2 Animation Pedagogical Agent

In the multimedia learning environment, there is a lack of positive interaction between learners and learning resources, which leads to low learning efficiency. Multimedia learning experts introduce animation pedagogical agents into the multimedia learning process to make up for the problems existing between learners and learning resources. Animation Pedagogical Agent refers to the image of a person presented on a computer screen, which can provide instruction and support to learners in the process of learning. Empirical research shows that adding pedagogical agent in the process of multimedia learning can improve learners' performance in post-test. For example, Lusk and Atkinson found that the migration performance of the experimental group was better than that of the control group [10]. Through the research on the influence of animation pedagogical agent on multimedia learning, Li et al. found that adding animation pedagogical agent to multimedia learning cannot reduce learners' attention to learning content, and it can improve the effect of multimedia learning. This study supports the hypothesis of social agent theory. Adding the agent image that the learner likes will promote the learning, but adding the agent image which the learner does not like does not hinder the study [11]. However, APA are currently only used in knowledge learning, not in software learning.

At the same time, according to China's 2017 animation industry report, animation production is low, and animation available for education is scarcer [12]. How to improve the output of animation, shorten the animation production cycle, and reduce the threshold of animation production are the urgent problems to be solved at present.

3 System Design

ANIMA is designed according to the traditional animation process. Animation is divided into three stages: pre-production, mid-stage production and post-production, each stage contains a lot of concrete content, as shown in Fig. 2 [13]. The ANIMA aid is designed according to the three stages of animation, which is used to help users create educational animation.

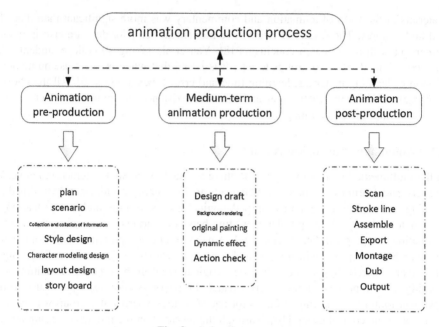

Fig. 2. Animation process

The aid includes the knowledge graph of the technology required for animation (Fig. 3), animation process guidance, and speech recognition caption technology. Knowledge graph classifies the key techniques of animation, including caption, symbol, motion, clip, frame and export. By completing the knowledge graph, users can master the key technology of animation. The process of using the teaching aid is as follows. The user needs to complete the knowledge graph firstly. Then enter the formal process of animation production, including content design, aesthetic design, technology guidance, subtitle synthesis and one-button export. In general, the aid has the following four main advantages:

1. In the preparation stage of animation production, the knowledge graph is inserted, and the animation pedagogical agent (APA) is used to explain it, which solve the anxiety of the first-time users. After the completion of knowledge graph, the user basically grasps the key technology of making animation.
2. When the animation is formally started, the teaching aid according to the content design, the corresponding technical prompt information appearing in the interface, convenient for the user to make the appropriate tool selection. This shortens the time consumed in the technology selection and reduces the error rates.
3. In subtitle synthesis, we used speech recognition technology. At the same time, the teaching aid can estimate the time needed for the picture to move according to the length of the caption.
4. The whole production process, including the three stages of animation production, train users to form complete design thinking, and improve the efficiency of animation output.

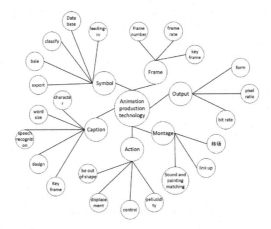

Fig. 3. Knowledge graph

Fig. 4. Knowledge graph training interface

Figure 4 shows the knowledge graph that the user needs to complete after opening the teaching aids. When the user completes the training of a technology, the graph in which the technology name is found will change from gray to color in the knowledge graph and be displayed in the prompt window of the interface. If the corresponding technical problem is encountered in the subsequent production process, users can also return to the knowledge graph for repeated practice.

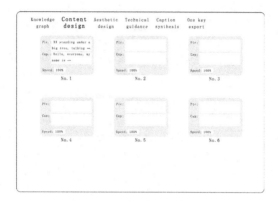

Fig. 5. Content design interface

Figure 5 shows that in the content analysis phase. According to the usage process, the user matches the screen content with the interpretation subtitle input, and selects the voice speed. Through these steps, users can estimate the length of the animation and the number of frames required for each screen. When the input is complete, the user needs to import the animation symbol or select the appropriate animation symbol in the database. The name of the symbol is changed to a unique recognizable name to match the content of the text message. For example: in the text message, "Baby picked up the water cup on the table." You need to name the corresponding components "Baby", "Table", "Water Cup". In addition, the content of the screen and caption can also be modified at any time.

In the aesthetic design stage, users can determine the overall style of animation and color matching. In the aspect of color matching, in order to facilitate the operation of users, a large number of color matching schemes are stored in the color matching database, and users can choose freely, so as to make the animated picture more harmonious and full of aesthetic feeling. And to those users that have higher aesthetic ability, they can undertake color collocation according to their be fond of, make the picture has distinctive artistic style thereby.

The technical guidance stage is the technical realization stage of animation production. In this stage, the user makes animation independently through this aids. During the production process, ANIMA will provide technical tips at the appropriate time according to the text information entered in the content analysis stage. Users can also add appropriate physical engines to the animation symbols in the physical engine database, so that the movement of symbols is more consistent with the movement of objects in the natural environment, and increase the sense of realism of animation. In addition to the physical engine database, the user can also add appropriate states to the animation symbols in the status database, for example, running, jumping, etc.

Subtitle synthesis is the final stage of animation production. Subtitle input is done during the content analysis phase. If the animation is finished and the subtitles do not match, you can also modify them at this stage. Users have two ways to modify, one is to continue to use speech recognition technology for subtitle matching, and the other is to manually input. According to the actual situation, users can choose a way of subtitle input. After the input is completed, the subtitle can be automatically matched according to the key frame. After the matching is completed, the animation is completed. Finally, the user can export the animation according to the prompts.

4 Research Method

4.1 Participants

Forty-four participants (22 women and 20 men, with an average age of 21 years) participated in the study. Participants from Northwestern Normal University's Institute of Education and Technology were divided into two groups, each with 22 people. The proportion of men and women in each group was the same. Each group uses different two-dimensional animation tools to create the specified animation. As far as professional background is concerned, 44 participants are third-year students majoring in digital publishing. In their previous studies, they have studied programming, graphics and image technology, 3D modeling technology, and so on. Through a survey of participants, none of them had access to two-dimensional animation software.

4.2 System Design

The quasi-experimental design is used in this study. Independent variables are two kinds of production modes: One group used AE, which is traditional two-dimensional animation software, and the other group used ANIMA. Dependent variables are production time, design thinking, and software ease of operation. The experiment was conducted in the multimedia classroom of the school, the experimental group (group 1) used the ANIMA to create the specified animation, and they also needed to complete the knowledge graph provided by the aid. Knowledge graph is explained by animation pedagogical agent (APA). The control group (group 2) used AE to create animation, considering that they had no contact with the production software, we prepared the AE operation guide for them in advance.

4.3 Measure Tools

4.3.1 Pre-test and Post-test of Animation Production
The purpose of the pre-test was to determine whether participants had the same cognitive level to ensure the validity of the sample. The pre-test consists of six subjects, all of which are related to the techniques used in the animation process. The post-test also included six multiple-choice questions (Q1–Q6), a total of 30 points. The topic is the knowledge involved in this experiment. The post-test is to evaluate students' understanding of two-dimensional animation production. A parallel test was conducted with 40 college students before the formal experiment. The reliability analysis coefficient is 0.815, which has internal consistency.

4.3.2 Interviews and Questionnaires
Interviews can be more intuitive to understand the user's feelings when using animation tools, through interviews to explore participants using different animation

software attitude, acceptance, as well as the advantages and disadvantages of the software. Throughout the interview, the interviewees used neutral language to minimize the impact on the interviewees' views. The questionnaire used the Richter scale method. We use the questionnaire to understand the participants' design thinking ability. The questionnaire includes 10 questions (T1–T10) and 5 dimensions (D1–D5). D1 is the ability to find problems, D2 is the ability to analyze problems, D3 is the ability to solve problems, D4 is the ability to expand, and D5 is the ability to innovate.

4.4   Teaching Scheme Design

This paper adopts the teaching method of "project-oriented and task-driven" to design the curriculum, turning the students into the leading role in the classroom, while the teacher acts as the guide. Teaching activities are divided into three stages: before class, in class and after class, each stage contains different sub-tasks. The teaching model is shown in Fig. 6.

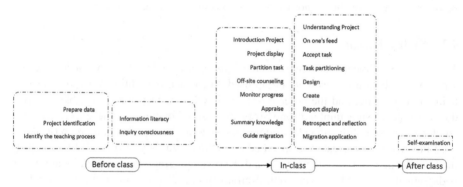

Fig. 6. Teaching model

In the first stage (before class), the teacher first sorts out and stores the prepared teaching resources, to show them to the students in class. Secondly, teachers should determine the teaching items and collect relevant materials. Finally, the teacher also needs to determine the teaching process to ensure the scientific and orderly course. At this stage, students should have corresponding inquiry awareness and information literacy. In the second stage (in class), the teacher first introduces the general situation of the project to the students and shows the multimedia materials related to the project to arouse the students' interest in learning. Secondly, teachers divide different subtasks according to the specific content of the project. Students clearly accept the task, and carry out independent design and creation. In the process of students' design and creation, teachers pay close attention to the students' dynamics at any time, provide timely guidance and monitor the students' progress. Thirdly, when students finish the creation, teachers should organize students to report and display. In the process of student report and display, teachers should evaluate and summarize students' achievements. Finally, the teacher guides the student to carry on the review reflection and the knowledge transfer, in order to enable the student to use in the future study life nimbly. In the third stage (after class), teachers reflect on teaching according to the specific class situation, and students reflect on learning according to their own learning situation.

4.5   Data Collection and Data Analysis

The collection data includes quantitative data and qualitative data. Quantitative data is the data of students' learning effect. This paper uses the independent sample T test to analyze the learning effect of the two groups of students. Univariate ANOVA was used to measure the difference in problem-solving ability between the two groups. The whole process was fully involved in all participants in this experiment, so the number of effective samples in the control group was 22, and the number of effective samples in the experimental group was 22. Qualitative data include interviews, video data and questionnaires. The overall reliability of the questionnaire is greater than 0.7, indicating that it is acceptable. During the experiment, participants turned on the recording device and were confirmed by the teacher.

5   Results

5.1   Learning Effect Analysis

Two groups of data were from the experimental group and the control group, respectively. The questionnaire used the five-point method of the Richter scale. The pre-test data showed that there was no significant difference between the experimental group and the control group. In the post-test results, we performed independent sample T test on the data of the two groups (Table 1). The results showed that there was significant difference between the two groups ($p = 0.002 < 0.01$). So the teaching effect of ANIMA teaching aid is obviously better than that of traditional two-dimensional animation software. At the same time, we recorded the duration of the experiment, and the results showed that the experimental time of the experimental group (120 min) was obviously shorter than that of the control group (200 min).

Table 1. T test of two sets of post-test results.

Group	Mean	SD	F	p
1	22.18	3.459	0.276	0.002
2	17.45	2.876		0.002

5.2   Evaluation of Design Thinking Ability

Independent sample T test was used to measure the difference of students' design thinking ability between the two teaching modes (Table 2). The results showed that the average value of the experimental group (group 1) was higher than that of the control group (group 2). Group 1 students are easier to analyze the problem according to the prescribed process (p = 0.000, p < 0.01), the speed of solving the problem is faster (p = 0.000, p < 0.01), and the ability of innovation is stronger (p = 0.000, p < 0.01). However, there was no significant difference between the problem-finding ability and the expansion ability between the two groups (p < 0.733, p > 0.05; p = 0.052, p > 0.05). To sum up, there were significant differences between group 1 and group 2, and the students in the experimental group showed a more complete ability of design thinking.

Table 2. Comparison of data from five dimensions of design thinking ability.

No.	Group	Mean	SD	F	p
D1	1	7.455	2.018	.920	0.733
	2	7.182	1.662		0.733
D2	1	7.272	1.679	4.125	0.000
	2	4.182	0.981		0.000
D3	1	7.273	1.490	2.442	0.000
	2	4.000	1.000		0.000
D4	1	7.182	1.167	5.353	0.045
	2	6.364	0.505		0.052
D5	1	7.727	1.191	.033	0.000
	2	3.636	1.120		0.000

5.3 Interview Analysis

The students in the experimental group thought that the ANIMA helped them to understand and strengthen the main process of animation production. It also cultivated students' systematic design thinking. At the same time the teaching aid operation process is simple, extremely easy to use, and through it user can quickly create their desired animation. However, ANIMA cannot complete some complex dynamic design, and the amount of database storage is limited. The students in the control group think that the traditional two-dimensional animation tool (AE) can fully realize their ideas, but the operation process is more complex and difficult. It takes a long time to complete the task and the output is low. At the same time, after this experiment, they cannot fully grasp the design process and design thinking. In the production process, the rework rate is higher.

6 Discussion

This paper discusses the impact of ANIMA teaching aids on students' design thinking and animation output. The results show that the ANIMA teaching aids can improve the teaching effect and the output of the animation. It also allows students to form complete design thinking. In future life, students can move it to other design activities. The ANIMA teaching aids can have such a good experimental effect, mainly because it combines the complete design process and further strengthens the design process when the students make the project. In the link of knowledge graph, the animation pedagogical agent (APA) is added, so that the learning effect of the multimedia is improved. This also makes a good preparation for the use of software. At the same time, all kinds of databases can save the students' time, reduce the difficulty of making animation, and enhance the enthusiasm of students. Through the "project-oriented, task-driven" teaching practice, students can expand the knowledge transfer to other learning tasks, and produce the same results. In the process of teaching, the teaching burden of teachers is also reduced, so that teachers have more energy to pay attention to students' thinking ability rather than software operation problems.

7 Conclusion

This paper describes a teaching aid called ANIMA, which guides students to make two-dimensional animation by integrating the complete design process and rich database. Through teaching experiments, we explore whether this teaching aid can improve the output of animation and cultivate students' design thinking ability. The results show that the ANIMA teaching aid can improve the production of animation, train students to form a complete design thinking ability, and enhance students' interest in animation production. The goal of this experiment is to study the teaching effect and influence of the ANIMA teaching aid, so many technical problems have not been effectively improved at this stage, such as the simple database, the limited number of resources and so on. In the future, we will further improve and expand the function of the ANIMA teaching aid. We will also explore the influence of this teaching aid on students' innovation ability through more experiments.

Acknowledgement. This research was supported by the National Natural Science Foundation of China under Grant No. 31860285.

References

1. Mayer, R.E.: The promise of multimedia learning: using the same instructional design methods across different media. Learn. Instr. **13**(2), 125–139 (2003)
2. Shuchao, C.: Educational animation research: ontology, form and function. Doctoral dissertation (2018)
3. Botong, C.: The advantages and feasibility of applying Flash animation to sports popularization education. Quotient (4) (2015)
4. Tiantian, T., Jingwen, Z.: Chinese animation industry market analysis report. Audiovisual (2), 73–76 (2011)
5. Ting, C.Y., Wong, C.O.: Supporting conceptual change in scientific inquiry learning via animated pedagogical agent. In: International Conference on Information Technology in Asia. IEEE (2011)
6. Schnotz, W., Rasch, T.: Enabling, facilitating, and inhibiting effects of animations in multimedia learning: why reduction of cognitive load can have negative results on learning. Educ. Technol. Res. Dev. **53**(3), 47–58 (2005)

7. Feifei, S.: An experimental study on the effects of subject background and presentation interaction on the effectiveness of animation multimedia learning. Doctoral dissertation, Liaoning normal University
8. Weixing, H.: An experimental study of multimedia learning in the context of animation. Doctoral discourses, Liaoning Normal University
9. Zhiming, Y.: Animation effects in skill acquisition. Mod. Educ. Technol. **20**(8), 32–36 (2010)
10. Atkinson, R.K.: Optimizing learning from examples using animated pedagogical agents. J. Educ. Psychol. **94**(2), 416–427 (2002)
11. Wenjing, L.: The influence of animation teaching agent on multimedia learning: the adjustment of learner's experience and preference. Psychol. Dev. Educ. (4), 453–462 (2016)
12. Anonymous. China animation industry report. I research consulting series research report (2017)
13. Jin, Y.: Animation production process. Zhejiang University Press (2006)
14. Yangfan, Z.: Reconstruction and practice of the teaching method based on project + task computer application. Electron. Prod. (4), 119–174 (2014)

Classification of Imagined Digits via Brain-Computer Interface Based on Electroencephalogram

Melvin Harsono[1,3], Lie-quan Liang[2], Xin-wei Zheng[2],
Forrest Fabian Jesse[3], Yi-gang Cen[1(✉)], and Wen Jin[4]

[1] Computer and Information Technology, Beijing Jiaotong University,
Beijing 100044, China
melvin_harsono@yahoo.com, ygcen@bjtu.edu.cn
[2] Information Science School, Guangdong University of Finance
and Economics, Guangzhou 510320, Guangdong, China
{lianglq, xinweizheng}@gdufe.edu.cn
[3] Xixuan Laboratory, 13th Floor, National University Technology Building,
Beijing 100044, China
jesse@jesse.org
[4] Jiangsu Jinhai Star Navigation Technology Co., Ltd.,
Zhenjiang 212000, Jiangsu, China
jw@jinhx.cn

Abstract. Brain-Computer Interface (BCI) aims to improve the detection and decoding of brain signals acquired by electroencephalogram (EEG). In the recent years, artificial intelligence development has stepped onto a new stage, which boosts the research of BCI. This paper focuses on implementation of BCI by recognition of imagined digits. The subject was asked to imagine a digit 0 or 1 without other stimulation. The experiment was conducted using a 14 electrode Electroencephalogram. The subject was asked to imagine a digit for 30 s and the signals were recorded for analysis. Based on the results of the classification and ERP analysis, the O1 and O2 electrode positions (10–20 system) were chosen. Four methods were proposed for the feature extraction by using Event Related Potential (ERP) analysis, Power Spectral Density Analysis (PSD), Independent Component Analysis (ICA) and Common Spatial Pattern (CSP). Finally, several classification methods were used to recognize the imagined digits based on the extracted features. Experimental results showed that the results obtained by Artificial Neural Network (ANN) after CSP performed the best. The classification accuracy achieves 66.88%.

Keywords: Brain Computer Interface (BCI) · Event-Related Potential (ERP) ·
Power Spectral Density (PSD) · Common Spatial Pattern (CSP) ·
Artificial Neural Network (ANN)

1 Introduction

A Brain-Computer Interface (BCI) system enables biological signals from the brain to be recognized by the computer. In some applications, the subject may be able to give commands to devices connected to the computer. A popular implementation of BCI is a

© Springer Nature Singapore Pte Ltd. 2019
Y. Wang et al. (Eds.): IGTA 2019, CCIS 1043, pp. 459–471, 2019.
https://doi.org/10.1007/978-981-13-9917-6_44

wheelchair controlled by a signal acquired from EEG. However, the implementation of BCI using EEG is not limited to the field of biomedical engineering for medical purposes. BCI is also popular for gaming and further application in virtual reality or augmented reality (VR, AR) [1] and even for improving the traditional education system by understanding the emotions. In [2], the author proposed the method which points out that human-computer interaction takes part in emotion building. This is important to show the relationship between emotion and learning.

In this paper, we propose a novel method for binary classification of imagined digits with the intention to enable more classification methods for the purposes of medical and other applications of BCI. It can also be used for supporting behavior learning as the measurement is done for cortex of human brain. Beard in [3] found that there is a significant effect of students can change the emotions of students' engagement in learning. By using the imagination recognition system, the emotion control system for learning in school can also be assisted.

For feature extraction from the EEG signal, Event Related Potential (ERP) and Common Spatial Pattern (CSP) are combined together. In addition to ERP, other EEG measurement methods such as Visual Evoked Potentials (VEP), Steady-State Visual Evoked Potentials (SSVEP), Event Related Desynchronization/Synchronization (ERD/ERS) can be used for the measurement. Due to the scenario of imagining the digit, unstimulated by the environment, we found that ERP analysis worked the best in this case. ERP enables the extraction of information from the EEG signals which are related to a certain motor event, cognitive, or specific sensory stimuli [4].

In this experiment, the ERP analysis was done for the whole group (of 10–20 system) electrodes used in the experiment. The ERP analysis was done by plotting the potential value on each epoch. One epoch is a 10 s span starting at 10 s and ending at 20 s within a 30 s recording. The ERP plot would then show the location of electrodes related to the events. Power Spectral Density (PSD) computation was then applied for removing bad electrodes and checking the amplitude of certain frequency ranges for the improvement of classification rate. PSD itself in this case is defined as the Discrete Time Fourier Transform (DTFT) of the covariance sequence [5].

After the ERP analysis and before the classification process, as a part of the classification method, Common Spatial Pattern (CSP) was applied. CSP is normally applied on multivariate signal processing such as the Electroencephalogram signal. It will find the spatial filters which maximize the variance of a class corresponding to the other classes. The author in [6] introduced the CSP method which is used to estimate the ERPs as they are naturally contaminated by biological and instrumental artifacts. CSP uses the multivariate spatio-temporal filtering to increase the signal-to-noise ratio. Besides enabling BCI to recognize a certain event (hand or leg movement for example), CSP can also be used for artifact cancelation in EEG implementation.

This study is also compared to the researches by Seto in [7]. The experiment done by Seto shows a similar recognition process as we proposed in this paper, by having the imagination of four directions. The signal processing and classification by Seto, however, used the band-pass filter, Fast Fourier Transform, Normalization, Principal Component Analysis (PCA), and three layers neural network. The identification rate using the 14 channels EEG is 46%.

2   Material and Experiment Setup

A. Electroencephalogram (EEG) Equipment

Emotiv EPOC+ is a commercial EEG, well known in practical EEG research. This EEG is a multi-channel portable system with a sequential sampling method. The system itself consists of 128 Hz sampling rate and 14 electrodes with 2 reference electrodes. The electrode position follows the 10–20 electrode positioning system in which they are: AF3, F7, F3, FC5, T7, P7, O1, O2, P8, T8, FC6, F4, F8, and AF4. Figure 1 shows the position of the electrodes corresponding to the naming in the 10–20 universal electrode positioning system [8].

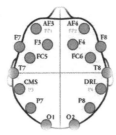

Fig. 1.   Emotiv EPOC+ Electrode positions (Color figure online)

Before wearing the EEG, each electrode should be given saline solution such that the impedance can be reduced. After wearing the EEG correctly, TestBench^{TM}, a software for the calibration of Emotiv EPOC+ is used. The electrode positioning in Fig. 1. should be all in green so that the EEG is ready for recording.

B. Experiment Setup

The experiment is meant to record the brain signal where subject was imagining binary digits (0 and 1). For the training dataset, there were 100 trials of experiments conducted for imagining 0 and 1 each. Within a single experiment, the subject was given 30 s of the whole single experiment time to imagine the digit 0 or 1. Before the experiment began, the subject was given a printed image of digit 0 or 1 such that there is a standard for the imagination process. After 30 s of recording, there were 20 s of resting time before the next recording round (Fig. 2). The recording for a single binary digit imagination recognition was 15 trials a day excluding the training time and low concentration in imagining trials.

Trial	Rest	Trial	Rest	...
30 sec	20 sec	30 sec	20 sec	...

1 Set

Fig. 2.   Experiment recording time setup

3 Data Preprocessing

The recordings of all trials in this experiment were put into folders. The data format of Emotiv EPOC+ recordings is European Data Format (EDF) file. In the beginning of data pre-processing, all of the EDF files were read all together and concatenated. Then, raw data was plotted to check which electrode should exist and could be selected for implementation. Obviously, the 14 essential electrodes as depicted from the Fig. 1, excluding the references node, are the electrodes which should be selected for the experiment. From the raw data plot as given in the Fig. 3, there were several electrodes which were not essential for the classification implementation.

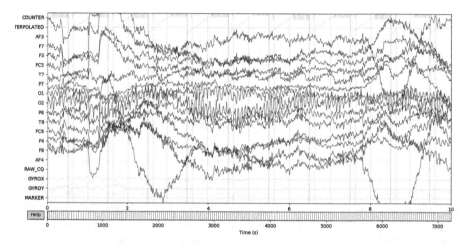

Fig. 3. Raw data plot

After that, a set of bad channels was pointed out such as Counter, Interpolated, Raw_Cq, Gyrox, Gyroy, Marker, Marker_hardware, Sync, Time_Stamp_s, Time_-Stamp_ms, CQ_AF3, CQ_F7, CQ_F3, CQ_FC5, CQ_T7, CQ_P7, CQ_O1, CQ_O2, CQ_P8, CQ_T8, CQ_FC6, CQ_F4, CQ_F8, CQ_AF4, CQ_CMS, and STI 014.

The essential 14 channels are marked in the black in the Fig. 3. plot while some other unessential channels such as Counter, Interpolated, Raw_Cq, Gyrox, Gyroy, and others are marked as grey (will not be used in the future). From Fig. 3, it can be seen that the signals were messy with noise interference. Therefore, the raw data consisted of the 14 channel raw EEG data which was then put into an Infinite-Impulse Response (IIR) band-pass filter within the range of 8–30 Hz [9]. The band-pass filter range was between 8–30 Hz because it followed the condition of the experiment scenario, including alpha and beta waves as given in Table 1. The transfer function of the IIR filter is shown in Eq. (1):

$$H(z) = \frac{\sum_{i=0}^{P} b_i z^{-i}}{1 + \sum_{j=1}^{Q} a_j z^{-j}} \qquad (1)$$

Where P is the feedforward filter order, b_i are the feedforward filter coefficients, Q is the feedback filter order, a_i are the feedback filter coefficients, and z is the symbol for applying the z-transformation.

Table 1. EEG frequency and state

Wave	Delta	Theta	Alpha	Beta	Gamma
Hz	1–3	4–7	8–13	13–30	30–
State	Deep sleep	Shallow sleep	Relax	Wakefulness	Excite

As shown in Table 1, delta wave ranging from 1–3 Hz will have high amplitude fluctuation whenever a person is in the condition of deep sleep [10]. Hence, for many other frequency ranges such as theta, alpha, beta, and gamma; each band will have high potential within the specific frequency range and states. In the experiment, the band pass filter will be done for the range of alpha and beta waves because these two bands happen when a person is in an awake condition. While delta and theta waves may have higher fluctuation when a person is sleeping. The band pass filter result of the raw data is given in Fig. 4. Noise on the 14 channels was suppressed, and the desired data could then be processed.

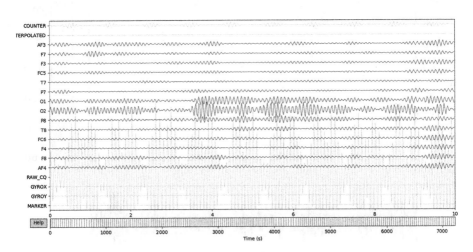

Fig. 4. The raw data plot of 14 channels after band pass filter

After band-pass filter, the raw data can be used for ERP analysis. Then, the ERP per channel was plotted to check whether a channel contained suitable data for classification or not.

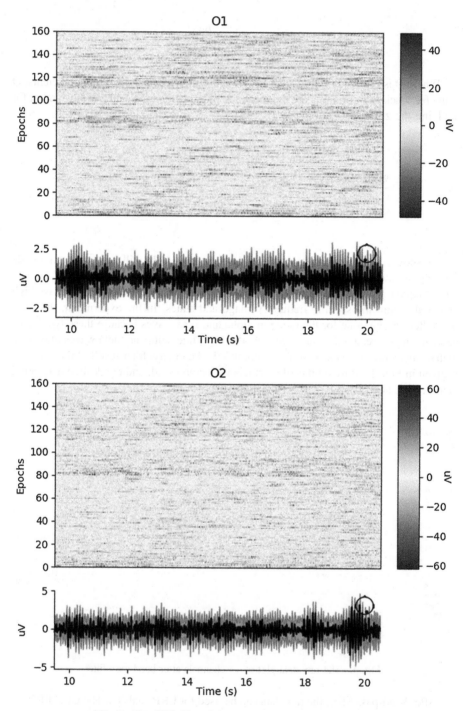

Fig. 5. The ERP Plot of O1 and O2 (Color figure online)

Figure 5 shows the ERP plot of O1 and O2 channels. The vertical axis shows quantity of epochs. The black waveform on the horizontal axis of the ERP plot shows the average electrical potential (of all epochs) for that electrode in the time domain. The small dots show synchronization in red, desynchronization in blue. Otherwise, the region will be mostly white, showing that there is less event related to the reaction from the subject. The more red and blue dots inside the graph, the higher the electrical potential fluctuation due to the event stimuli.

From the 14 electrode locations, 2 of them contain the most data correlated to the event, they are O1 and O2. To check the potential of noise on the chosen locations, Power Spectral Density (PSD) analysis was applied. A plot of PSD is shown in Fig. 6. It can be seen that there is a channel with high noise which should be considered as a bad channel, i.e. FC5. Based on the PSD analysis and after removal of FC5 from the PSD calculation, it can be seen that O1 and O2 showed the highest power in the range of 10 to 13 Hz. Then the data of O1 and O2 was filtered by a band-pass filter within the range of 10–13 Hz, as shown in Fig. 7. The filtered results of O1, O2 were both chosen for the classification.

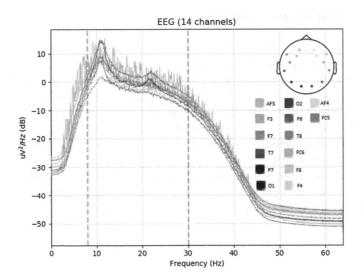

Fig. 6. PSD plot before re-filter

After choosing the electrode position and frequency for classification, the raw data was put into epochs. One epoch consists of one trial of imagining a digit. The time was limited within the range of 10–20 s per epoch before being concatenated. The events per epoch will be set as labels for classification. After epoching and labeling, the data was then processed by applying Fast Independent Component Analysis (Fast ICA) for a better classification result.

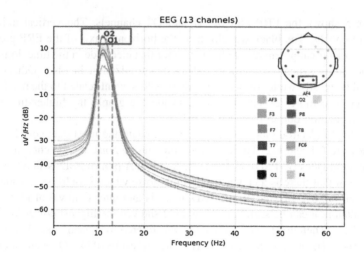

Fig. 7. PSD plot after frequency selection

4 Classification and Analysis

There were several methods used for classification in this experiment for comparison reasons. The main machine learning classification algorithms were Support Vector Machine (SVM), Artificial Neural Network – Multi Layer Perceptron (ANN-MLP), Logistic Regression, and Linear Discriminant Analysis (LDA). However, in order to increase the classification rate, Common Spatial Pattern (CSP) was applied in SVM, ANN-MLP, and LDA. A different method for Logistic Regression was applied by using the xDawn Covariance and Tangent Space algorithm. The whole classification method is given in Fig. 8.

All of the classification algorithms were evaluated using KFold validation with the parameter of 10. The result was determined by the confusion matrix, while the classification rate is determined by the accuracy with the formula:

$$Classification\ rate = \frac{tp + tn}{tp + fp + tn + fn} \tag{2}$$

Where *tp*, *tn*, *fp*, and *fn* are true positive, true negative, false positive, and false negative.

The classification rate (the accuracy to classify the given label) of LDA after CSP was 60% with the confusion matrix shown in Fig. 9. The elapsed time using the 10-Fold cross validation for the LDA method is 0.541 s.

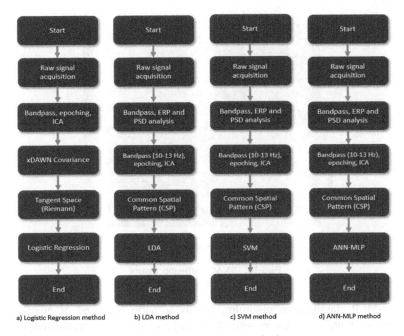

Fig. 8. Data processing methods

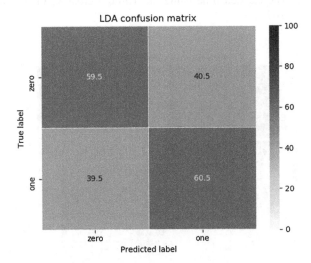

Fig. 9. LDA confusion matrix

For SVM classification, the configuration of SVM itself was RBF kernel with the C value 1. SVM is the general learning method based on statistical system and it is effective to process nonlinear and high dimensional pattern recognition [11]. The classification rate of SVM after CSP was 66.25% with the confusion matrix shown in Fig. 10. The elapsed time using the 10-Fold cross validation for the SVM method is 0.621 s.

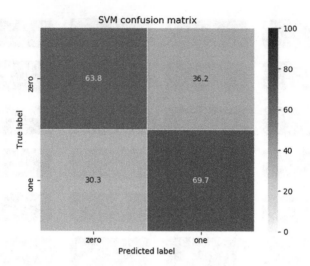

Fig. 10. SVM confusion matrix

ANN-MLP classification algorithm in this scenario consisted of quasi-Newton solver method with hidden layers with 14, 10, and 5 number of perceptron respectively. The classification rate of ANN-MLP after CSP was 66.88% with the confusion matrix given in Fig. 11. The elapsed time using the 10-Fold cross validation for the ANN-MLP method is 2.167 s.

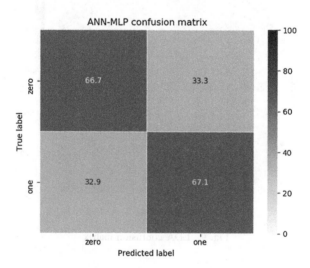

Fig. 11. ANN-MLP confusion matrix

The last classification algorithm used in this experiment was the Logistic Regression Algorithm. However, in order to optimize the result of Logistic Regression classification algorithm, instead of applying CSP before Logistic Regression, xDAWN Covariance was calculated and then the Riemann Tangent Space was projected. This method was applied on P300 BCI [12]. The classification rate of Logistic Regression with xDAWN Covariance and Riemann Tangent Space was 65.62% with the confusion matrix shown in Fig. 12. The elapsed time using the 10-Fold cross validation for Logistic Regression method is 1.949 s.

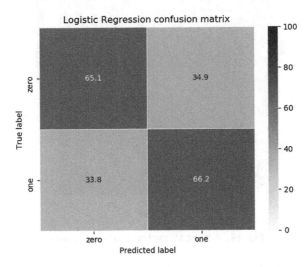

Fig. 12. Logistic Regression confusion matrix

After applying the all classification methods, the result of this experiment was compared with the data processing method of a similar imagination recognition experiment by Seto et al. in imagining direction. The data processing method proposed by Seto et al. did not select the electrode position with ERP and apply PSD analysis for feature selection and CSP for feature space enhancement. But as depicted in Fig. 13, the data was first band-pass filtered within the range of 8-30 Hz frequency including Alpha and Beta states, then the data from all electrodes would pass a band pass filter, be normalized, and processed by using Principal Component Analysis. After the pre-processing part, the data was classified by using a three-layer neural network and validated with 5-fold validation [13].

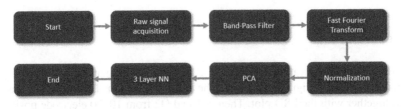

Fig. 13. Yuki Seto et al. data processing

By applying the same data processing method proposed by Seto et al. for our experiment scenario, the classification rate yields 52.5% with the confusion matrix shown in Fig. 14. The elapsed time using the 10-Fold cross validation is 3.406 s.

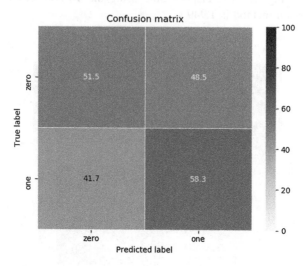

Fig. 14. Seto et al. method confusion matrix

The summary of the results classification rate for all data processing methods is listed in Table 2. It can be seen that the best classification method in this case is CSP +ANN MLP with the rate of 66.88%.

Table 2. Performance comparison of the four methods proposed in this paper and the method used in [12]

Type	Classification rate	Elapsed time (seconds)
CSP+LDA	60%	0.541
CSP+SVM	66.25%	0.621
CSP+ANN MLP	66.88%	2.167
xDAWN+TangentSpace+LogReg	65.62%	1.949
Y. Seto et al. method	52.5%	3.406

5   Conclusion

This paper has shown a novel method of classifying the human cognitive state when imagining the binary digit (0 or 1). For the feature selection, ERP analysis was conducted together with the PSD plot. Then, O1 and O2 from 10–20 electrode positioning system were chosen to give the best classification rate after they were filtered by a band-pass filter within the 10–13 Hz frequency range. The experimental results showed that the ANN-MLP after CSP process outperformed the other data processing methods. In a future experiment, the improvement of classification rate will be conducted by applying modern machine learning classification methods and more feature extraction methods such as Hjorth Parameter and Fractal Dimension, and Embedding Sequences Analysis. Furthermore, better cognitive state classification study will be applied using an EEG system with more electrodes. Additionally, the experiment using deep learning classification method with automatic feature extraction is being conducted.

Acknowledgement. This work was supported by the Science and Technology Program of Guangzhou (201804010271); National Natural Science Foundation of China (61872034, 61572067); Natural Science Foundation of Guizhou Province ([2019]1064); Special Innovative Projects in Key Platforms and Scientific Research Projects of Guangdong Universities in 2018.

References

1. Hsu, W.Y.: Brain-computer interface connected to telemedicine and telecommunication in virtual reality applications. J. Telematics Inform. **34**, 224–238 (2017)
2. Wei, Y., Sun, X.: A novel interaction system based on management of students' emotions. In: 11th Chinese Conference on Image and Graphics Technologies and Applications (IGTA), Springer, Singapore, vol. 634, pp. 77–84 (2016)
3. Beard, C.: Student achievement: the role of emotions in motivation to learn - emotional maps. Pedagogic Research Project Report, Sheffield Hallam University (2005)
4. Kropotov, J.D.: Functional Neuromarkers for Psychiatry Applications for Diagnosis and Treatment. Elsevier Inc., London (2016)
5. Stoica, P., Moses, R.: Spectral Analysis of Signals. Prentice Hall, Upper Saddle River (2005)
6. Congedo, M., et al.: Spatio-temporal common pattern: a companion method for ERP analysis in the time domain. HAL archieves-ouvertes (2016)
7. Seto, Y., Ako, S., Sakagami, K., et al.: Classification by EEG frequency distribution in imagination of directions. Procedia Comput. Sci. **35**, 1300–1306 (2014)
8. Emotiv EPOC Brain Computer Interface & scientific contextual EEG. https://emotiv.gitbook.io/epoc-user-manual/
9. Grout, I.: Digital Systems Design with FPGAs and CPLDs. Elsevier Ltd., Burlington (2008)
10. Bong, S.Z., Wan, K., Murugappan, M., et al.: Implementation of wavelet packet transform and non-linear analysis for emotion classification in stroke patient using brain signals. Biomed. Signal Process. Control **36**, 102–112 (2017)
11. He, J.-B., Zhang, H.-M., Liang, J., Jin, O., Li, X.: Paper currency denomination recognition based on GA and SVM. In: Tan, T., Ruan, Q., Wang, S., Ma, H., Di, K. (eds.) IGTA 2015. CCIS, vol. 525, pp. 366–374. Springer, Heidelberg (2015). https://doi.org/10.1007/978-3-662-47791-5_41
12. Rivet, B., Cecotti, H., Souloumiac, A., Maby, E., Mattout, J.: Theoretical analysis of xDAWN algorithm: application to an efficient sensor selection in a P300 BCI. In: 19th European Signal Processing Conference, pp. 1382–1386. IEEE, Barcelona (2011)
13. Seto, Y., Ako, S., Miura, H., et al.: Analysis of brain state in imaging directions by using EEG. In: The 35th Annual International Conference of the IEEE Engineering in Medicine and Biology Society, vol. 51, p. R-192. JSMBE, Osaka (2013)

Plant Identification Based on Multi-branch Convolutional Neural Network with Attention

Pengxi Li[1], Xiaoqing Gong[1], Xu Hu[2], Lianqi Shi[1], Xiaoting Xue[1], Jun Guo[1(✉)], Pengfei Xu[1(✉)], and Daguang Gan[3]

[1] School of Information Science and Technology, Northwest University,
Xi'an 710127, China
[2] School of Computer Science and Technology, Xidian University,
Xi'an 710071, China
[3] Wanfang Data, Beijing 100038, China

Abstract. The identification of plants has great significance in the study of plants, and it has applications in plant classification and medical research. With the development of computer vision, plants identification based on deep learning methods can effectively carry out. At present, most of the existing methods use the traditional features such as the shape and texture features for plant identification, and these methods are applicable to plants with large differences in their shapes. Therefore, we develop a multi-branch convolutional neural network with attention (MCNNA) to extract the effective features, and the first part of MCNNA is an attention block, which is used to reduce the influence of background, and the latter part is multi-branch convolutional neural network, which is used to extract the multi-view features through multi-channel. Experiments have shown that our proposed method has better performances for the classification of plants than the traditional methods. We tested our method on the dataset BJFU100 and obtained final accuracy of 97.89%, and we have the accuracy of 93.35% on our own image dataset.

Keywords: Plants identification · Multi-branch convolutional neural network · Attention block · Fusion block

1 Introduction

There are 350,000 species of plants on earth, and they widely distribute on the ground. Plants play an important role in soil and water conservation, maintaining ecological balance and agricultural production, and they also have ornamental value and medicinal value. In 1753, the Swedish botanist Linnaeus established a classification system for plants.

For plant identification, the artificial features, which includes image grayscale features, color features, texture features and gradient features, have been used in several existing methods [1]. For example, Qi et al. tried to extract the shape features and the edge characteristics of the leaves for plant identification [2]. Chen et al. proposed a classification method based on the shape and texture features of the leaf images, and using BP neural network to achieve the plant recognition with the accuracy of 92% [3].

© Springer Nature Singapore Pte Ltd. 2019
Y. Wang et al. (Eds.): IGTA 2019, CCIS 1043, pp. 472–481, 2019.
https://doi.org/10.1007/978-981-13-9917-6_45

Wei et al. selected ten effective parameters and utilized support vector machine (SVM) to recognize the plants with the accuracy of 95.8% [4]. However, the features used in these methods are traditional artificial features, which cannot express the nonlinear characteristics in complex images. With the wide applications of deep learning methods to image recognition, the performances of the image recognition have significantly improved. ResNet20 [5] has been used to identify the plants, and get better performances than the traditional methods. Therefore, the computer vision technologies can help us to recognize most kinds of plants quickly, and are beneficial to botanists on their ecological research of the plants. However, it is not easy to identify large number of plant species for the following challenges.

The natural factors including the light, weather and the complex background have adverse effects to plants recognition. In the existing public datasets of plants include Flavia [6], the images of plants or their leaves are collected under specific situation, and the background of the images is simple. Therefore, these plants can be identified by traditional methods with high accuracy. However, in most situations, the images of the plants have complex backgrounds and varied lighting, which results in great visual differences in plant images, and the difference information has adverse effects on the performances of the network model for plant recognition. In addition, the traditional methods cannot extract the deep features from the images with complex background. Therefore, how to extract the effective features of plants from the complex background is the key problem for the plant recognition methods.

At present, there are several feature extraction methods for object recognition [7]. However, these methods can only extract the shallow features, which cannot have an effective expression for the plant images with complex background, especially for the plants with similar appearance. The traditional methods only select the geometric features of the leaves for identifying the corresponding plants, and some other methods consider the texture features of the leaves for the same task. However, these traditional shape and texture features are difficult to identify the plants, which the leaves with the similar shape and texture features. Therefore, it is necessary to extract the deep features by deep network models to obtain a better expression of the leaves of different plants.

To solve the above problems, several deep learning methods have been used for plant identification. For example, fully convolutional networks model was proposed by Fan [8] to identify space plants, and Zhang [9] designed a deep learning model for plant recognition, this model contains 8 convolutional layers, and the final accuracy is 91.1%. Besides, Double Stream CNN was put forward for identifying the plants on the dataset Flavia [6]. Furthermore, other existing deep learning methods including ZFnet [10], VGG [11], GoogLeNet [12] and ResNet [13] may also be used to recognize the plants. However, these methods are not fine-grained identification for plants, and their performances still need to be improved due to lacking of attention mechanism on the key parts of the plants. In this paper, we propose a new method based on multi-branch convolutional neural network with attention for plant identification, and the proposed method consists of two parts: attention block and multi-branch convolutional neural network. The attention block is used to reduce the influence of background, and multi-branch convolutional neural network can extract the multi-view features through multi-channel.

2 Multi-branch Convolutional Neural Network with Attention

2.1 The Structure of MCNNA

The main structure of MCNNA is show in Fig. 1, and it consists of the following two parts: the attention block and multi-branch convolutional neural network. The attention block reduces the effects of background by focusing on the branches and leaves of plants. The multi-branch convolutional neural network contains three branches, which have different network structures and parameters. Finally, the feature maps are fused into a final feature vector for plant recognition.

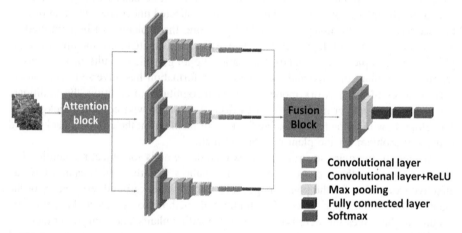

Fig. 1. The structure of MCNNA consisted of two parts: the attention block and MCNN.

2.2 The Attention Block

The attention block is the first part of MCNNA, and it consists of nine convolutional layers, two max pooling layers and one deconvolution layer, as shown in Fig. 2. The input images can have different sizes, for example, our input images have the size of 224 × 224.

In attention block, the size of the convolution kernel is 3 × 3 except for the convolutional layer in the lower side branch, as shown in Fig. 2. The upper side branch contains two convolutional layers and two max pooling layers for feature extraction, and the lower side branch consists of two layers, convolutional layer and deconvolution layer for feature selection. In the lower side branch, we use the convolution kernel with the size of 11 × 11 to reduce the dimension of the feature maps, and the receptive field of each pixel will become larger. After some iteration, the network will focus on the features on several key areas, which have significant difference from those of other plants. The deconvolution operation makes the reduced feature map enlarge as a new feature map, which has the same size as the feature map before dimension reduction.

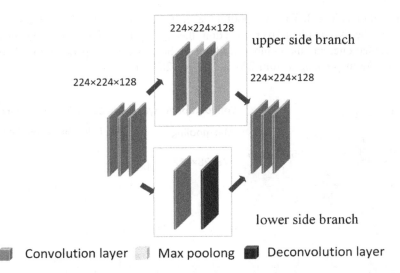

Fig. 2. The attention block

Finally, the fusion operation is to sum the values of each element in the feature maps from two branches.

The attention block enables the network to focus on plants and reduce the impact of background factors, as shown in Fig. 3. After attention block, the background is filtered while the branches and leavers of the plants are retained (Fig. 8).

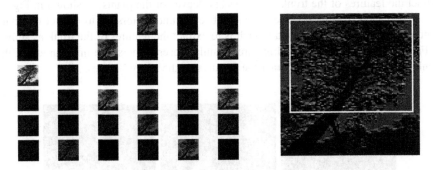

Fig. 3. The feature maps extracted by the attention block.

2.3 Multi-branch Convolutional Neural Network (MCNN)

This structure of MCNN is the latter part of MACNNA, and it contains three branches. The structure of each branch is similar, but their convolution kernels have different sizes, and some parameters of the max pooling layer are not the same. In each branch, there are 12 convolutional layers, 4 max pooling layers, and 2 fully connected layers, and the fully connected layer expands the feature map into a vector of 1×1000 dimensions finally, as shown in Fig. 4. The size of the convolution kernel in each convolution is 3 × 3. The max pooling layer has the size of 2 × 2 and the step size is 2. After the max pooling layer operation, the size of the feature map becomes half of the original one, and the number of filters doubles. After the operation of this branch, the feature map changes from 224 × 224 × 128 to 1 × 1000.

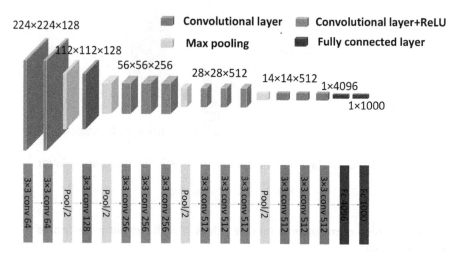

Fig. 4. One branch of MCNN and its parameter set

In MCNN, each branch has its own function, and the multiple branches are used to extract the features of the trunk, branches and leaves of the plants, as shown in Fig. 5. The first branch is to reduce the effects of background factors, as to extract the main features of the plant. The second branch is to extract the features of the trunk as shown in Fig. 5(b), and these extracted features mainly preserve the shape information of the trunk. The last branch is to extract the features of the plants' leaves.

Fig. 5. The feature maps extracted by multi-branch convolutional neural network.

At last, three branches will get three vectors with the size of 1 × 1000, which will be merged in the fusion block. Then we connect the three feature vectors into a 1 × 3000 vector. Finally, the vectors with the size of 1 × 100 can be obtained by the following convolution layers, and are used for plant recognition.

3 Experiments and Analysis

3.1 The Dataset BJFU100

In this paper, we test the comparison methods and our methods on the dataset BJFU100 created by Yun Sun et al. [5]. BJFU100 contains 100 plants, and each species of plant contains 100 images. Several images of the plants are shown in Fig. 6.

Fig. 6. The images of the plants in BJFU100. The dataset contains plants of high similarity, some of which show subtle differences in leaf shape.

3.2 Experimental Setup and the Parameters Our Network

The experiments run under the caffe framework, using cuda in version 8.0 and OpenCV in version 3.0. The hardware: Intel Xeon E5-2650 v4 processor, GeForce GTX 1080, and the memory is 64G.

The size of the input image is 224×224, and the value of batch size is set to 50. The initial learning rate is set to 0.0005, and the learning rate becomes half of the original per 3,000 iterations. The over-fitting reduces by using SGD's momentum method with a weight decay value of 0.0001 and a momentum value of 0.9.

3.3 The Analysis of the Experimental Results

In order to verify the effectiveness of the proposed method, we use a five-fold cross validation method to test the experimental methods on the dataset BJFU100 for five times, and we use Top-1 accuracy and testing accuracy as the parameters for evaluating the performances of different methods.

(1) Top-1 accuracy

We use Alexnet [16], VGG [11], ResNet26 [13], ResNet32 [13], DenseNet [14] and Double Stream CNN (DS-CNN) [15] as the comparison methods. The experimental results are shown in Table 1 and Fig. 7. On the Top-1 accuracy, we achieved the best result with the highest accuracy of 97.89% compared with the max accuracy of 95.56% obtained by other networks.

Table 1. The experimental data by cross-validation

Algorithm	1	2	3	4	5
Alexnet	0.8508	0.8485	0.8181	0.8596	0.8473
VGG	0.8927	0.9012	0.8824	0.9024	0.8856
Resnet26	0.9178	0.9245	0.9142	0.9123	0.9278
Resnet32	0.8457	0.9292	0.9472	0.9489	0.9556
Densenet	0.9209	0.9105	0.8989	0.9215	0.9117
DS-CNN	0.9269	0.9475	0.9433	0.9325	0.9321
MCNNA	0.9663	0.9654	0.9789	0.9621	0.9654

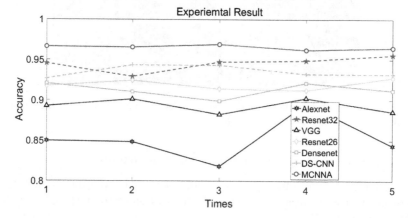

Fig. 7. The curves of the experimental results by different methods, our proposed method achieves the best result with the maximum accuracy of 97.89% and the results remain stable between 96%-98%.

(2) Testing Accuracy

The performance of the algorithm on the training data set does not really represent their performance. Therefore, we test all the methods on a new dataset collected by ourselves, as shown in Table 2. Our own image dataset have 3526 images of 32 kinds of plants, and these images are obtained by our mobile phone. Then our proposed method has the accuracy of 93.35%, which is higher than DS-CNN by 5.70%, which may be due to that we add the attention block at the beginning of the MCNN to reduce the impact of background factors.

Table 2. Testing experimental data

Algorithm	Testing accuracy
Alexnet	0.6587
VGG	0.6954
Resnet26	0.7889
Resnet32	0.8565
Densenet	0.8421
DS-CNN	0.8828
MCNNA	0.9335

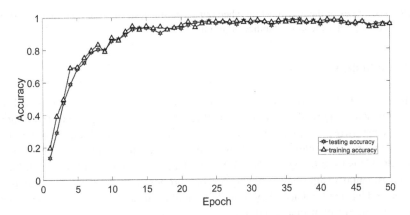

Fig. 8. Training accuracy and test accuracy in 50 iterative experiments

In the Fig. 9, we test our method on our own images of plants, with the increasing of the number of iterations, both the training accuracy and the test accuracy improve. After 15 training epochs, the training accuracy begins to fluctuate slightly between 90% and 95%, and gradually converges, while the test accuracy is stable at around 92%, showing a particularly small fluctuation. Based on the experimental results, we obtained the values of accuracy 0.80 and Recall 0.83, and the value of F1 is 0.81.

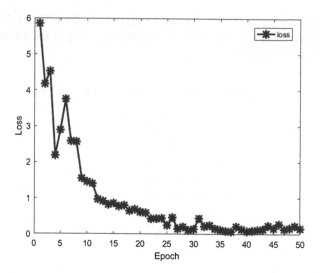

Fig. 9. The values of the loss function when our method is tested on our own images. After 25 epochs, the loss values tend to stabilize at around 0.77.

4 Conclusion

In order to identify the plants with higher accuracy, we develop a multi-branch convolutional neural network with attention (MCNNA) to extract the effective features. MCNNA has two parts including the attention block and multi-branch convolutional neural network. The attention block is used to reduce the influence of background, while MCNN is used to extract the multi-view features through multi-channel. Finally, the experimental results have shown that our proposed method has the best performances, and has the final accuracy of 97.89% on the dataset BJFU100 and the accuracy of 93.35% on our own image dataset.

Acknowledgement. This work was supported in part by the National Key Research and Development Program of China under Grant No. 2017YFB1400301.

References

1. Guan, W., Xue, X., An, Z.: Application progress and prospect of deep learning in video target tracking. Acta Automatica Sinica **42**(6), 834–847 (2016)
2. Qi, H., Shou, W., Jin, S.: Computer-aided plant identification model based on leaf features (2003)
3. Chen, W., Zhou, P.: Research on leaf shape and texture feature extraction of plants. J. Zhejiang Sci-Tech Univ. **30**(3), 394–398 (2013)
4. Wei, L., He, D.J., Qiao, Y.L.: Plant leaves classification based on image processing and SVM. J. Agric. Mech. Res. **35**(5), 12–15 (2013)
5. Sun, Y., et al.: Deep learning for plant identification in natural environment. Comput. Intell. Neurosci. **2017**, 6 (2017). Article no. 7361042

6. Wu, S.G., Bao, F.S., Xu, E.Y., et al.: A leaf recognition algorithm for plant classification using probabilistic neural network. In: 2007 IEEE International Symposium on Signal Processing and Information Technology, pp. 11–16. IEEE (2007)
7. Chaib, S., Gu, Y.F., Yao, H.X.: An informative feature selection method based on sparse PCA for VHR scene classification. IEEE Geosci. Remote Sens. Lett. **13**(2), 147–151 (2016)
8. Fan, S., Wang, X., Qi, Z.: Fast recognition of space plants image based on fully convolutional networks. J. Comput. Syst. **27**(11), 136–141 (2018)
9. Zhang, S., Huai, Y.J.: Leaf image recognition based on neural network deep learning. J. Beijing Forestry Univ. **38**(9), 108–115 (2016)
10. Zeiler, M.D., Fergus, R.: Visualizing and understanding convolutional networks. In: Fleet, D., Pajdla, T., Schiele, B., Tuytelaars, T. (eds.) ECCV 2014. LNCS, vol. 8689, pp. 818–833. Springer, Cham (2014). https://doi.org/10.1007/978-3-319-10590-1_53
11. Simonyan, K., Zisserman, A.: Very deep convolutional networks for large-scale image recognition. arXiv preprint arXiv:1409.1556 (2014)
12. Szegedy, C., Liu, W., Jia, Y., et al.: Going deeper with convolutions. In: Proceedings of the IEEE Conference on Computer Vision and Pattern Recognition, pp. 1–9 (2015)
13. He, K., Zhang, X., Ren, S., et al.: Deep residual learning for image recognition. In: Proceedings of the IEEE Conference on Computer Vision and Pattern
14. Huang, G., Liu, Z., Van Der Maaten, L., et al.: Densely connected convolutional networks. In: Proceedings of the IEEE Conference on Computer Vision and Pattern Recognition, pp. 4700–4708 (2017)
15. Liao, J., Cai, Y., Wang, Y., et al.: Plant disease identification technology based on convolutional neural network. Mod. Comput. (Prof. Ed.) (2018 19), 43–48, 53 (2018)
16. Krizhevsky, A., Sutskever, I., Hinton, G.E.: ImageNet classification with deep convolutional neural networks. In: Advances in Neural Information Processing Systems, pp. 1097–1105 (2012)

Verification Learning for Robust Visual Object Tracking

Linyu Fei, Rong Wang$^{(\boxtimes)}$, and Jianwei Ding

People's Public Security University of China, Beijing 102623, China
fei_linyu@163.com, dbdxwangrong@163.com

Abstract. Recent years have witnessed the rapid advances of Siamese Networks in visual tracking. Nevertheless, most Siamese-based trackers have poor generalization capability and merely focus on local region, leading to fail to handle hard cases such as out of view, occlusion and so on. In this paper, we employ verification learning method into Siamese-based trackers, by taking advantage of the accurate tracking performance of Siamese-based trackers and leveraging the fast speed of yolov3 network. Firstly, we adopt a Siamese-based tracker to locate the target and output tracking results. Then, a verifier is introduced to determine whether it is a failure and generate the validation result. Simultaneously, feedback mechanism will be stimulated, continuously adjusting and robustifying tracking results. The experiments are performed on VOT2018 benchmark, showing that our method achieves state-of-the-art performance.

Keywords: Visual tracking · Verification · Convolutional neural networks

1 Introduction

Recently, visual object tracking is extensively a hot topic in computer vision and has widely applied to video surveillance, automatic driving and so forth. More and more people have aroused great interest in visual tracking so far. While recent years have witnessed great improvements in visual tracking accuracy, the advancements in tracking robustness still remain challenging in case of many complicated factors.

Object tracking aims to locate a target and distinguish it from backgrounds in an image sequence, given only its initial frame. The existing visual tracking algorithms are often categorized as either correlation filter based methods or deep learning based methods. The early correlation filter based methods exploit circular matrix and operate in Fourier domain, ensuring accuracy and tracking speed at the same time. Latest correlation filter based methods apply deep features, further improving tracking accuracy. The higher accuracy of these trackers, however, comes at the cost of much slower speed [1, 2]. The deep learning based methods, especially Siamese-based methods, have proved to be superior in object tracking, where it achieves a trade-off between accuracy and speed.

Bertinetto et al. proposed SiamFC algorithm [3] which makes use of fully-convolutional network, allowing arbitrary input size. SiamRPN [4] further decomposes the tracking task into two parts: siamese network and region proposal network. Owing

© Springer Nature Singapore Pte Ltd. 2019
Y. Wang et al. (Eds.): IGTA 2019, CCIS 1043, pp. 482–491, 2019.
https://doi.org/10.1007/978-981-13-9917-6_46

to classification and regression, it can run at 160 fps while achieving leading performance.

As mentioned above, Siamese-based trackers foster significant advances in short-term tracking as the target keep in sight. The challenge, however, is that it is not quite robust in long-term tracking. What's worse, it frequently faces tracking failures under the circumstance of out-of-view and occlusion. To mitigate the above problem, we propose verification learning method that ensures its generalization capacity and adaptability when the tracking results are unreliable.

Instead of changing the tracking network directly, our method work from another perspective. Inspired by [5, 22, 23], we formulate tracking task as a verification problem. We introduce a verifying and correcting strategy to visual tracking, which enhances its adaptive ability and generalization. Our framework is constituted by two components: a tracker and a verifier. The tracker locates the target for real time. Tracking results are judged by an overlap score to verify the tracking performance. Once the tracking results are not confident, the correcting mechanism will be triggered and update location and size of the target. Then the corrected result will be feed back to the tracker again, forming a closed loop. With a feedback mechanism, the tracking process can be adapted to complex environment and maintain robust as in Fig. 1.

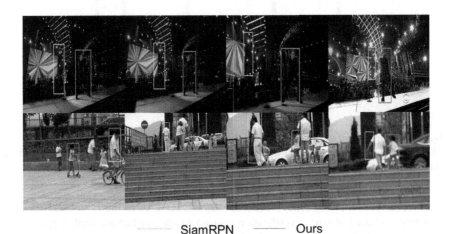

SiamRPN ———— Ours

Fig. 1. Comparisons of our method with SiamRPN.

Extensive experiments are performed on VOT2018 benchmark [6], where our method outperforms SiamRPN [4] in terms of robustness and achieves a higher EAO (expected average overlap) score [6], [14]. The proposed approach shows very promising results in comparison with state-of-the-arts.

The remainder of the article is structured as follows: the proposed method is described in detail in the second part. In the third part, we present the analysis and empirical results of our framework. Finally, we put forward a brief concluding section and discuss future research in the fourth part.

2   Method

2.1   Overview

In this part, our framework consists of two components: tracking and verifying, as shown in Fig. 2. Both of them collaborate with each other, which effectively and efficiently realize real-time and accurate tracking.

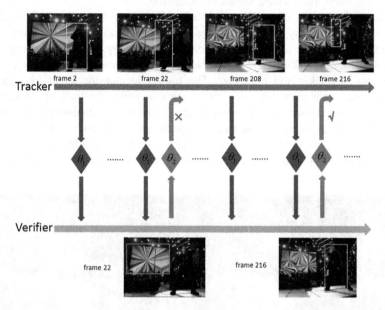

Fig. 2. The pipeline of our framework. The blue arrow (*top-down*) verifies the tracking results and the red arrow (*bottom-up*) is the correction part. The yellow rectangle represents the tracking result, while the green rectangle represents the verification result. (Color figure online)

For each frame in the video sequence, the tracker locates the target and mark it. After that, the tracker issues verification request to the verifier for further processing (whether to start the correction mechanism).

On the verifier side, it is made up of validation and correction. The validator compares tracking results with a threshold once receiving a request from the mentioned tracker. It runs per frame to realize high accuracy. The correction will be activative in case of a tracking failure. However, correction results may not be adopted, which depends on a comparison to a confidence score. Through continuous learning, our method keeps updating and improving tracking results.

2.2   Baseline

2.2.1   Siamese Region Proposal Network

We adopt Siamese Region Proposal Network (SiamRPN) as the base of our tracker. SiamRPN [4] can yield favorable performance with real-time speed against the competing trackers. Differ from traditional multi-scale testing and online finetuning, it leverages the power of region proposal network (RPN), thus leading to a compact boundary [7].

The structure of SiamRPN [4] is shown in Fig. 3. Features, especially appearance information, are extracted in a fully convolution network without padding. In Siamese network, we alter AlexNet [8] to adapt to inputs, from which we remove conv2 and conv4 layers. Template and detection frame (denoted as z, x, respectively) are operated in two analogous convolution network separately. Both of two processes share the same parameters. On the other hand, proposals can be generated in a region proposal network [7], which are then sent to classification and regression branches. By introducing anchor mechanism, we can obtain several proposals. Diverse scales and aspect ratios are taken into consideration, thereby leading to more robust performance.

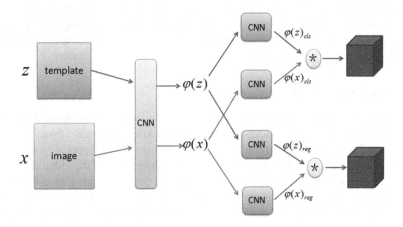

Fig. 3. The structure of SiamRPN.

Given that most detection tasks are based on category information, we formulate the tracking task as:

$$\min_{W} \frac{1}{n} \sum_{i=1}^{n} L(\zeta(\varphi(x_i; W); \varphi(z_i; W)), l_i) \tag{1}$$

where x denotes the detection frame and l_i represents the corresponding label. Similarly, z denotes the template sample. Function φ and ζ are carried out for feature extraction and region proposal selection. Besides, L aims to get the average loss of the subsequent function. n reflect the number of dataset, while value of parameter W needs to be acquired in advance as:

$$\min_{W} \frac{1}{n} \sum_{i=1}^{n} L(\phi(x_i; W), l_i) \tag{2}$$

note that ϕ is a predictor function. It is important to attain the parameter W that minimize the average loss L.

2.2.2 Yolov3 Network

To obtain fast and robust results, we exploit yolov3 network as our baseline [9]. The yolov3 network [9] is a full convolutional network, which uses a lot of residual skip connections. In this structure, a downsample layer with step size of 2 is used for downsampling, instead of max-pooling or average-pooling layer. At the same time, upsampling as well as route operations is an indispensable method. The author proposes a Feature Pyramid Network (FPN) which associates and assembles rich semantic information from various scales [10]. Detection at three different scales {32, 16, 8} has been respectively performed so that we can have a multi-scale feature map.

Deep features can be made full use of by upsampling, but shallow features are important as well, so there is a route layer to combine them. The feature map obtained by $16\times$ downsampling and the layer obtained by four downsampling are spliced together. It is good to do this concatenation. There is no doubt that learning deep and shallow features at the same time is more conducive to express feature.

2.3 Tracking by Verifying

SiamRPN [4] has been shown capable of tracking in short-term tracking. However, it provides suboptimal results under the long-term tracking challenge. Object is likely to move out of sight in the long-term tracking. Given the time to reappear is uncertain, it increases the difficulty of tracking. Since only the initial frame of the video is given, the tracker cannot recognize and track the re-emerged target, resulting in drift problem. Worsestill, it struggles in cases of similar appearance interference. The existing background is so complicated that foreground target often cannot be distinguished from it accurately. Consequently, it is not discriminative to hard negative samples, which greatly affects the effect and performance of our tracking.

Algorithm 1. Our Method.

Input: A video sequence with N frames, groundtruth of first frame.
Output: Tracking results of target on the video.
1: Initialization: tracker T, verifier V;
2: Run T and V until the end;

In order to alleviate the multi-scale problem, a feature pyramid network is introduced in yolov3 [9]. It integrates information of different layers, which is better for small target detection. In addition, it is a flexible way to detect and locate object with yolov3 network.

Motivated by tracking-by-detection [11–13], our verifier can also be treated as an extension of yolov3 detector [9]. We integrate a yolov3 detector [9] into the SiameseRPN tracker [4]. Target will be determined as lost if the score falls below θ_1. When track fails or tracking results are unreliable, the verifier will detect and find out the candidate proposal that is closest to the target. The proposal is considered as tracking result, sent back to correct the tracker subsequently.

Algorithm 2. Tracking Algorithm.

Input: The last tracking result R_{i-1}, the current frame i.

1: **While** $i = 2 ,..., N$ **do**
2:         track on the frame i;
3:         generate a temporary tracking result R_i;
4:         send a request to V;
5:         **if** received a message from V **then**
6:                 **if** tracking result is reliable **then**
7:                     update;
8:                 **else**
9:                     correct tracking result R_i;
10:                     retrack;
11:                 **end**
12:         **else**
13:                 maintain the current result R_i;
14:         **end**
15: **end**

Algorithm 3. Verifying Algorithm.

Input: The current tracking result R_i, the current frame i.

1: **While** $i = 2 ,..., N$ **do**
2:         **if** received a request from T **then**
3:                 verify the current result R_i;
4:                 **if** verification passed **then**
5:                     continue tracking;
6:                 **else**
7:                     activate correction;
8:                     **if** correction result is reliable **then**
9:                         correct R_i;
10:                   **end**
11:                 **end**
12:                 send verification results to T;
13:         **end**
14: **end**

Algorithm 1 summarizes our method. As shown in Fig. 2, a validation measure is carried out for every frame. We compare its verification score with a threshold θ_1. If the verification score is higher than θ_1, our verifier automatically determines that the tracking is successful. Then, it keeps the foregoing tracking result unchanged, and performs tracking of the next frame. At this time, the correction module continues to be on standby, in a dormant state. On the contrary, if the verification score is lower than θ_1, our verifier will view it as an unrealiable result. In this case, the tracker sends a message, with yolov3 [9] triggered for fast detection. To acquire a detection result, we introduce a formulation as:

$$\hat{p} = \arg\max_{p_i} V(x_i, p_i) \tag{3}$$

where p_i and x_i means candidate proposal and target respectively. While function V returns the verification score of former ones. $\hat{p}$ aims to get the proposal which maximizes the verification score. Then it feeds the detection score back to the tracker. It is worth noting that the detection result may not be a substitute for tracking result. That is to say, if the detection score is lower than the threshold θ_2, the tracking result will not be affected and maintains unchanged. In a contrasting manner, the correction result will be accepted and sent to the next frame. To an extent, the whole tracking process forms a feedback loop, from which tracking results can be constantly adjusted and updated. Figure 4 gives an example intuitively. The detail of the proposed algorithm is illustrated in Algorithms 2 and 3.

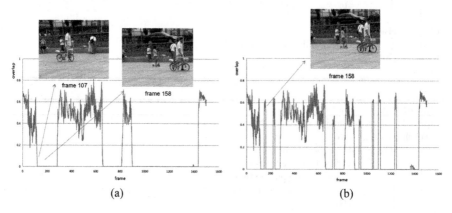

(a)   (b)

Fig. 4. The tracking results of *girl*. The tracking results of SiamRPN method and our method are shown separately in *(a)* and *(b)*. As is shown in *(a)*, the tracker in SiamRPN begins to drift from frame 107 and drifts completely at frame 158. With our method, the tracker resumes tracking at frame 158.

3   Experiment and Analysis

In this section, experiments are conducted to evaluate our framework on VOT2018 benchmark [6] with 60 videos. The performance of trackers is measured in terms of Accuracy (A), Robustness (R) and Expected Average Overlap (EAO).

3.1   Implementation Details

We use a modified AlexNet [8] as the base network of our tracker. Then we adjust parameters of yolov3 detector [9] in validation module. The thresholds θ_1 and θ_2 are set to 0.2 and 0.34, respectively.

Our tracker and verifier are implemented using python on a machine equipped with Intel E5-2650, 64 GB of RAM, and a NVIDIA GTX 2080Ti GPU accelerator. The experiments are carried out by Matlab R2016a with matconvnet toolbox.

3.2   Analysis on VOT 2018 Dataset

Here, we evaluate our approach on VOT2018 benchmark. The VOT2018 dataset contains 60 sequences, with each target marked by a bounding box. All videos are annotated with six properties: illumination changes, motion changes, size changes, occlusion, camera motion, and unassigned. There are three evaluation criteria for VOT2018 benchmark: robustness, accuracy and expected average overlap. The accuracy metric measures average overlap in the course of successful tracking. The robustness, also called failure rate, illustrates how many times the tracker loses the target (when the overlap rate is zero). While the expected average overlap (EAO) criterion evaluates the overall performance of a tracker, which averages the IoU without reset operation. All these do good to give insight into the behaviour of a tracker. We refer to [6] for further details.

We compare our tracker with baseline tracker SiamRPN [4] and 7 other state-of-the-art trackers including SRCT [18], SiamVGG [19], CCOT [2], CFCF [20], ECO [1], MCCT [21] and FSAN on VOT2018 benchmark [6]. Figure 1 indicates that our approach provides a more robust performance than the mentioned trackers. Compared with SiamRPN, the EAO score of our tracker has been improved a little. Table 1 lists the details. However, the above improvement of performance is at the expense of accuracy. As we can see in Fig. 5, it shows the Accuracy-Robustness plot, where the closer to the top, the higher accuracy a tracker has. Similarly, more closed to right means faster. Intuitively, Fig. 6 reports the results of ours against 8 other state-of-the-art trackers with regard to the EAO score.

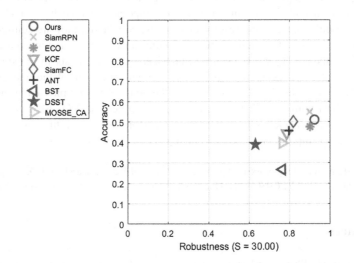

Fig. 5. Comparisons with 8 other trackers on VOT2018 dataset with A-R plot.

Table 1. Comparisons with other three trackers on VOT2018 Dataset.

	Ours	SiamRPN	LADCF	ECO
EAO	0.331	0.324	0.389	0.280
Accuracy	0.518	0.551	0.493	0.484

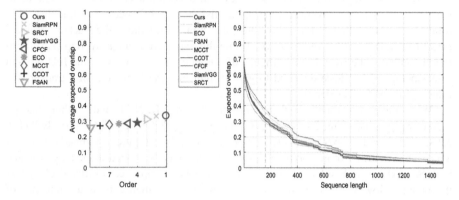

Fig. 6. The EAO score curve of our approach and 8 other trackers in the VOT2018 challenge.

4   Conclusions

In this paper, we propose a verification learning method for visual object tracking. The target is located and its tracking results are temporarily stored by a tracker. In the verifying module, the tracking results are determined whether they are confident or not by a threshold score. Depending on the circumstances, the correcting mechanism is triggered to update the target position and size. Since it adjusts the position of the target, the correcting mechanism guarantees the generalization of the tracker to some degree. Moreover, the tracking process can be adapted to complex environment and maintain robust with a feedback mechanism. Experiment on VOT2018 dataset proves that our approach achieves a state-of-the-art performance. In future, we will further explore how to improve accuracy of our tracker.

Acknowledgments. This work is supported by National Key Research and Development Plan under Grant No. 2016YFC0801005. This work is supported by Grant No. 2018JXYJ49.

References

1. Danelljan, M., Bhat, G., Khan, F.S., Felsberg, M.: ECO: efficient convolution operators for tracking (2016)
2. Danelljan, M., Robinson, A., Shahbaz Khan, F., Felsberg, M.: Beyond correlation filters: learning continuous convolution operators for visual tracking. In: Leibe, B., Matas, J., Sebe, N., Welling, M. (eds.) ECCV 2016. LNCS, vol. 9909, pp. 472–488. Springer, Cham (2016). https://doi.org/10.1007/978-3-319-46454-1_29

3. Bertinetto, L., Valmadre, J., Henriques, J.F., Vedaldi, A., Torr, P.H.S.: Fully-convolutional siamese networks for object tracking. In: Hua, G., Jégou, H. (eds.) ECCV 2016. LNCS, vol. 9914, pp. 850–865. Springer, Cham (2016). https://doi.org/10.1007/978-3-319-48881-3_56

4. Li, B., Yan, J., Wu, W., Zhu, Z., Hu, X.: High performance visual tracking with siamese region proposal network. In: Proceedings of the IEEE Conference on Computer Vision and Pattern Recognition, pp. 8971–8980 (2018)

5. Fan, H., Ling, H.: Parallel tracking and verifying: a framework for real-time and high accuracy visual tracking. In: 2017 IEEE International Conference on Computer Vision (ICCV), pp. 5487–5495 (2017)

6. Kristan, M., et al.: The sixth visual object tracking VOT2018 challenge results. In: Leal-Taixé, L., Roth, S. (eds.) ECCV 2018. LNCS, vol. 11129, pp. 3–53. Springer, Cham (2019). https://doi.org/10.1007/978-3-030-11009-3_1

7. Ren, S., He, K., Girshick, R., Sun, J.: Faster R-CNN: towards real-time object detection with region proposal networks. In: International Conference on Neural Information Processing Systems. IEEE Computer Society, Los Alamitos (2015)

8. Krizhevsky, A., Sutskever, I., Hinton, G.E.: ImageNet classification with deep convolutional neural networks. In: Proceedings of the Advances in Neural Information Processing Systems, pp. 1097–1105 (2012)

9. Redmon, J., Farhadi, A.: YOLOv3: an incremental improvement (2018)

10. Lin, T.Y., Dollár, P., Girshick, R., He, K., Hariharan, B., Belongie, S.: Feature pyramid networks for object detection (2016)

11. Avidan, S.: Support vector tracking. IEEE Trans. Pattern Anal. Mach. Intell. **26**, 0–1072 (2004)

12. Avidan, S.: Ensemble tracking. IEEE Trans. Pattern Anal. Mach. Intell. **29**, 261–271 (2007)

13. Ross, D.A., Lim, J., Lin, R.S., Yang, M.H.: Incremental learning for robust visual tracking. Int. J. Comput. Vis. **77**, 125–141 (2008)

14. Kristan, M., et al.: The visual object tracking VOT2016 challenge results. In: Hua, G., Jégou, H. (eds.) ECCV 2016. LNCS, vol. 9914, pp. 777–823. Springer, Cham (2016). https://doi.org/10.1007/978-3-319-48881-3_54

15. Henriques, J.F., Caseiro, R., Martins, P., Batista, J.: High-speed tracking with kernelized correlation filters. IEEE Trans. Pattern Anal. Mach. Intell. **37**, 583–596 (2015)

16. Bolme, D.S., Beveridge, J.R., Draper, B.A., Lui, Y.M.: Visual object tracking using adaptive correlation filters. In: The Twenty-Third IEEE Conference on Computer Vision and Pattern Recognition, pp. 13–18. IEEE (2010)

17. Danelljan, M., Hager, G., Khan, F.S., Felsberg, M.: Accurate scale estimation for robust visual tracking. In: Proceedings of the British Machine Vision Conference BMVC (2014)

18. Lee, H., Kim, D.: Salient region-based online object tracking. In: IEEE Winter Conference on Applications of Computer Vision (WACV), pp. 1170–1177. IEEE Computer Society, Los Alamitos (2018)

19. Li, Y., Zhang, X.: SiamVGG: visual tracking using deeper siamese networks (2019)

20. Gundogdu, E., Alatan, A.A.: Good features to correlate for visual tracking. IEEE Trans. Image Process. **27**, 2526–2540 (2018)

21. Wang, N., Zhou, W., Tian, Q., Hong, R., Wang, M., Li, H.: Multi-cue correlation filters for robust visual tracking. In: 2018 IEEE/CVF Conference on Computer Vision and Pattern Recognition, pp. 4844–4853. IEEE Computer Society, Los Alamitos (2018)

22. Zhou, J., Wang, R., Ding, J.: deep convolutional features for correlation filter based tracking with parallel network. In: Wang, Y., Jiang, Z., Peng, Y. (eds.) IGTA 2018. CCIS, vol. 875, pp. 461–470. Springer, Singapore (2018). https://doi.org/10.1007/978-981-13-1702-6_46

23. Jiang, S., Zhang, J., Zhang, Y., Qiu, F., Wang, D., Liu, X.: Long-term tracking algorithm with the combination of multi-feature fusion and YOLO. In: Wang, Y., Jiang, Z., Peng, Y. (eds.) IGTA 2018. CCIS, vol. 875, pp. 390–402. Springer, Singapore (2018). https://doi.org/10.1007/978-981-13-1702-6_39

Convolutional Randomized Binary Features for Keypoints Recognition

Jinming Zhang[✉], Zuren Feng, and Gang Li

State Key Laboratory for Manufacturing Systems Engineering,
Xi'an Jiaotong University, Xi'an 710049, China
zhang.jin.ming@stu.xjtu.edu.cn

Abstract. Randomized binary features have been used to recognize keypoints. However, the existing methods apply their sampling operations on raw or blurred images. The great success of convolutional neural networks has proved that convolution operator is a powerful feature extractor. So, we try to combine binary feature extractor with convolutional feature extractor to generate convolutional randomized binary features. In our method, we first generate multi-layer convolutional feature maps for an image and apply the pre-generated sampling operators to sample on theses convolutional feature maps. Finally, all the sampling values are binary encoded into bytes-like feature vector. The basic sampling operators of traditional binary features have only two points, which are not suitable for multi-layer images. While, the basic sampling operator we used to observe multi-layer convolutional feature maps is RID (Randomized Intensity Difference) operator. The strategy that applying RID to convolutional feature maps can improve binary feature quality. Our methods are compared with state-of-art methods on several image datasets. The experiment results show the excellent performance of our method.

Keywords: Random features · Binary features ·
Convolutional features

1 Introduction

Computer vision tasks including image classifying [17,18], registration [19], visual tracking [5,22], visual SLAM [6,11,12] and robot navigation [16] all depends on accurate matching of local features generated from different image views. There are several successful local invariant features including SURF [2], SIFT [10], ORB [15], BRIEF [3], and AKAZE [4]. However, hand-designed complicated sampling patterns are always carried to resist image distortions including zoom, rotation and view-point changes. The other way is to consider keypoints matching as a classification problem, in which each class corresponds to the set of a keypoint's all possible views. Classifiers such as RandomTrees [7,8,13], RandomFerns [8,14], restricted Boltzmann machine [20] are employed

© Springer Nature Singapore Pte Ltd. 2019
Y. Wang et al. (Eds.): IGTA 2019, CCIS 1043, pp. 492–504, 2019.
https://doi.org/10.1007/978-981-13-9917-6_47

to recognize keypoints. However, classifier-based methods focus on improving classifier but ignore the improvement of binary feature space quality. They use nonrandom-weighted aperture-fixed two-cells single-channel intensity test operators to construct feature space. The randomness of these traditional operators only reflects in position distribution within an size-fixed image patch. Furthermore, the sampling operations of all the above methods are carried out on the original image or the slightly blurred original image.

In this paper, we use RID sampling operator (a kind of more general randomized sampling operator) to sample on convolutional feature maps to construct binary feature space. The traditional randomized operators (they are called as RIT operator) used in ORB [15], RandomFerns [14], BRIEF [3] and RandomizedTrees [7] are not applicable to multi-layer feature maps. Instead, our RID sampling operators have two advantages. First, there are much more randomness in RID operators: sampling cells count, position distribution, aperture size, cells' weights and cells' sampling channels. Firstly, a specified number of RID operators are generated randomly, Then, they are divided into a specified number of groups; Finally, we apply binary encoding method on each group to build feature space. Due to the randomness, RID operators can observe multi-resolution information and bring much more sampling redundancy compared with those traditional RIT operators. Second, RID operators have more than two sampling cells within one operator, which can be used to process multi-channel image like multi-layer convolutional feature maps or multi-spectral images. The sampling cells of a RID operator can be placed in different channels to achieve multi-channel joint coding. RID operators do not need artificial design of sampling patterns compared with other constant multi-resolution patterns, for instance, FREAK [1] and BRISK [9]. Different kinds of convolutional RID features are embedded into RandomTrees and RandomFerns to test performance on image dataset. Our experimental results indicate that the combination between convolutional feature maps and RID operators can remarkably improve local binary feature quality and have competitive performance in the application of keypoints recognition.

2   Related Works

Randomized binary features have been used in patches and keypoints recognition. There are two characteristics in them: first is randomly sampling within image patches, second is sampling values binary encoding. Many methods, including ORB [15], BRIEF [3], AKAZE [4], extract a bits string from keypoint neighborhood as a descriptor then matched via Hamming distance. Randomized binary features have several advantages compared with gradient-based features: easily implementing, efficiently computing and competitively matching. The basic operators used in ORB, AKAZE and BRIEF are the same: the mean intensity test of two randomly pre-selected rectangular cells. However, the two rectangular cells are with fixed aperture, weight and channel. There are some non-randomized local binary features such as FREAK and BRISK which need hand-designed sampling patterns. The disadvantage of descriptor-like features is the need for rotation estimation. Their performances depend largely on accurate rotation estimations. Classification-based methods consider keypoints matching as classification and each class corresponds to the set of keypoint all possible views. These methods don't need rotation estimation. RandomizedTrees was proposed by Lepetit et al. [7] as classifier method. In their method, the tests at tree nodes are simple binary tests based on intensity difference of two points. Naive Bayesian classifier was also used as classification technique by Ozuysal et al. [14]. Naive Bayesian classifier uses hundreds of simple binary features, and they assumes the independence between arbitrary sets of features. The basic operators they employed are also two pre-selected blurred points. Two-stage randomizedtrees was also used for keypoints recognition by Shimizu and Fujiyoshi [13]. The viewpoints of image patches are classified in the first stage [21]; keypoint classification is done via the RTs in the second stage. The sampling operator in tree nodes are also binary tests similar to [7]. RBM classifier was also used by Yuan et al. [20] for keypoints recognition. The features set for training of RBM model is defined by a n-D binary vector based on intensity test of two pre-selected pixels. These classification-based methods differ from each other by the classifier they adopted but they all use the same basic sampling operator. RSLBP proposed by Wang et al. [18] is different from the original LBP operator or other LBP variants that adopt the difference between the neighboring pixels and the center pixel to describe the pixel. Point pairs are selected randomly from local neighborhood, then LBP encoding is made after sums of pixels neighboring are compared. The basic operator used by RSLBP is also pixel-pairs intensity tests, similar to [3,14].

Through the review of existing randomized binary features, we can find the common ground of these methods is that they all use single-channel aperture-fixed nonrandom-weighted point-pairs to build binary space. However, our researches indicate that those incompletely randomized operators are not conducive to the diversity and separability of binary features and can't give full play to binary features performance. Furthermore, the basic sampling operators of existing methods are applied on raw gray image patches instead of multi-layer feature maps as we do.

3   Our Methods

3.1   Convolutional Feature Maps Generation

We discuss how to generate convolutional feature maps from an original gray image in this subsection. First we need generate convolution kernels. The convolution kernel adopted in this paper is the random Gauss convolution kernel: each number in the convolution kernel obeys the standard normal distribution $N(0, 1)$. Since the size of keypoint neighborhood is chosen to be 31×31, the proper size of Gaussian convolution kernel is between 3×3 and 15×15. In practice, we find larger convolution kernels can improve the quality of the feature space better but require more computation. In the following experiments, we select three kernel sizes including 7×7, 9×9 and 11×11 to show the experiment results.

In order to explain why sampling on convolutional feature maps can improve feature space quality, we first convolute the same gray-scale image with different Gaussian convolution kernels, and then transform the pixel values of the convoluted floating-point feature map linearly, adjust them to between 0 and 255, and display them. The results are illustrated in Fig. 1. We can find from Fig. 1 that when the sum of the whole Gaussian convolution kernel is greater than zero, the feature map is consistent with the original image. The larger the sum, the more similar the feature map looks to the original image; the smaller the sum of convolution kernels but always greater than zero, the heavier the texture of the feature map becomes, and it seems that the original image is embossed. When the sum of the convolution kernels is less than zero, the brightness of the original image reverses and becomes like an undeveloped negative film. The more the sum of convolution kernel is less than 0, the more significant the brightness reversal effect is. A large number of sampling operators will take a lot of overlap when sampling in a size-fixed small area of a single channel image. The overlap of sampling operators will lead to a great correlation among feature components of the final descriptor vector. However, after the original single channel image is processed by different convolution kernels, convolution feature maps will show different appearances (see Fig. 1). when we randomly assign a large number of sampling operators to different feature map layers, we can reduce the overlapping area of sampling operators, and then reduce the correlation between different feature components (see Fig. 3). Therefore, for randomized binary features, random sampling on multi-layer feature maps is better than random sampling on original gray image.

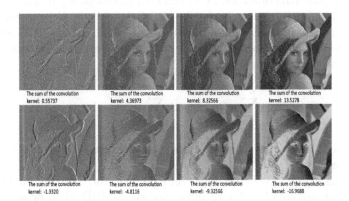

Fig. 1. This figure shows eight examples of convolutional feature maps obtained by randomly generated 9×9 Gauss convolution kernel. In the top row of feature maps, the sum of convolution kernel is greater than zero. In the second row, the sum of convolution kernel is less than zero.

3.2   Randomized Intensity Sampling Operators

We discuss how to design sampling operators in this subsection. The traditional sampling operators used in [7,14] and [20] are usually single-channel aperture-fixed nonrandom-weighted position-randomized operators. They have size-fixed smoothing aperture and can only be used on single-channel images. Their randomness reflects only on sampling positions. We denote the type of these traditional operators as RIT operator (Randomized Intensity Tests) according to [3,14] and [7]. One RIT test refers to sampling two smaller pixel areas randomly, defined as follows [14]:

$$\tau(p_1, p_2) = \tau(p_1 - p_2, 0) = \begin{cases} 1 & p_1 > p_2 \\ 0 & p_1 \le p_2 \end{cases} \tag{1}$$

RIT operators are also used in sampling patterns including ORB [15], FREAK [1], RSLBP [18] and BRISK [9].

Because each RIT operator has only two sampling points, it can cover only two layers of convolutional feature maps. Differently, in order to realize multi-channel joint sampling and coding, we use completely randomized RID operators (Randomized Intensity Difference) to sampling on multi-layer convolutional feature maps. RID operator is multi-channel multi-granular random-distributed random-weighted sampling operator, defined as follows:

$$fv = op(patch) = \sum_{i=1}^{n} w_i * mI(cell_i(x_i, y_i, w_i, h_i, c_i)) \tag{2}$$

Where $cell_i$ is a rectangular area at randomly pre-selected position. n is sampling cells count of one RID operator. every cell $cell_i$ has its position (x_i, y_i), aperture (w_i, h_i) and channel (c_i). w_i is the weight of the $cell_i$. $mI(\cdot)$ represents mean operation on sampling cell ranges from 0 to 255. To make sure RID operator to be gradient-like and theoretical mean of $op(patch)$ equals zero, all sampling cells weights meet the following conditions:

$$\sum_{i=1}^{n^+} w_i^+ = 1 \text{ and } \sum_{i=1}^{n^-} w_i^- = -1 \tag{3}$$

where w_i^- and w_i^+ represent the negative and positive weights within sampling operator, respectively. And $n^+ + n^- = n$.

Equations (2) and (3) define a general RID operator. The cell number of each RID operator can equal 2, 4, 6 or more. So, we use RID(n) to present RID cell number. For instance, RID(4) means $n = 4$ and RID(2) is just like the traditional RIT operator. We need pre-generate numbers of RID operators and put them into M groups to construct M-D feature space. All groups contain the same type and the same number of RID operators. RID aperture size is also pre-selected randomly within a specified range. Considering keypoint neighborhood is 31×31 patch, RID aperture range cannot be larger than 31×31. The aperture size of

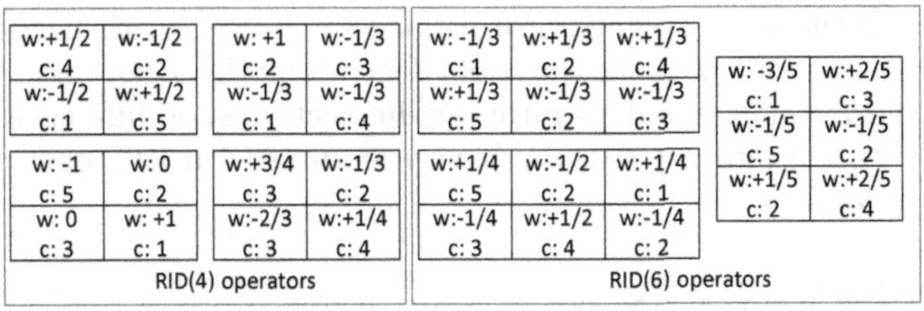

w:+1/2	w:-1/2	w: +1	w:-1/3
c: 4	c: 2	c: 2	c: 3
w:-1/2	w:+1/2	w:-1/3	w:-1/3
c: 1	c: 5	c: 1	c: 4
w: -1	w: 0	w:+3/4	w:-1/3
c: 5	c: 2	c: 3	c: 2
w: 0	w: +1	w:-2/3	w:+1/4
c: 3	c: 1	c: 3	c: 4

RID(4) operators

w: -1/3	w:+1/3	w:+1/3
c: 1	c: 2	c: 4
w:+1/3	w:-1/3	w:-1/3
c: 5	c: 2	c: 3
w:+1/4	w:-1/2	w:+1/4
c: 5	c: 2	c: 1
w:-1/4	w:+1/2	w:-1/4
c: 3	c: 4	c: 2

RID(6) operators

w: -3/5	w:+2/5
c: 1	c: 3
w:-1/5	w:-1/5
c: 5	c: 2
w:+1/5	w:+2/5
c: 2	c: 4

Fig. 2. Some examples of two kinds of RID operators that are applied on 5-layer convolutional feature maps. Sampling cells' weights (w) of each operator are randomly pre-selected according to Eq. (3). The number c at each cell represents the sampling channel of that cell. Each operator can arrange its sampling cells into different layers to implement multi-layer joint randomized binary coding. The randomized operators are pre-generated before applying them to images. And once generated, they keep the same for all keypoints.

both RID(4) and RID(6) operators are randomly selected in the range $[6 \times 6, 27 \times 27]$ in the following experiments. Cells' weights of RID operator are also generated randomly. Constrained by Eq. (3), There are four sampling cells in RID(4) operator and weights have many possible values (see Fig. 2). We can see RID(4) weights have much more randomness than RID(2) weights constrained by Eq. (3). Because RID(6) has more cells than RID(2) and RID(4), RID(6) weights also have many possible values (see Fig. 2) and consequently have much more randomness than RID(2) and RID(4). The advantage of multi-cells operators is that they can be extended to extract multi-layer convolutional maps. RID sampling cells are specified randomly into different channels, which implements multi-channel joint randomized binary coding.

3.3   Binary Feature Space Construction

This subsection discuss the building of binary feature space employing numbers of basic operators.

The M-D feature vector can be denoted as: $V = \{v_1, \cdots, v_m, \cdots, v_M\}$. Let $fv = op(patch)$ be a general sampler to a patch, where fv is sampled value and op is sampling operator. Each component v_m corresponds to a basic operator group, noted as $group_m = \{op_1, \cdots, op_s, \cdots, op_S\}$. Generally, building feature space is to design the mapping from $group_m$ to v_m, expressed as $v_m = h(group_m)$. We have many possible ways to design mapping $h(\cdot)$.

The mapping $h(\cdot)$ used in traditional binary features like BRIEF [3], RandomFerns [14], RandomTrees [7], RSLBP [18], ORB [15], FREAK [1] and BRISK [9] is applying many binary coding operations on $group_m$, as follows:

$$v_m = h(group_m) = \sum_{s=1}^{S}(2^{s-1} * \tau(op_s, T)), \quad op_s \in group_m \quad (4)$$

where $\tau(\cdot, \cdot)$ is the binary comparator defined by: if $v_1 < v_2$ then $\tau(v_1, v_2) = 0$; otherwise $\tau(v_1, v_2) = 1$. T is the threshold depends on the mean value of $group_m$. The threshold T equals zero if operators are intensity-test or difference operators. If we input Eq. (1) into Eq. (4), the binary features with RIT operator can be written as follows:

$$v_m = h(group_m) = \sum_{s=1}^{S}(2^{s-1} * \tau(p_i - p_j, 0)); \; here, \; op_s = p_i - p_j \quad (5)$$

The coding approach is to compare intensity-test with mean ($T = 0$), called "mean binary coding". In this paper, with the use of RID operator, the mapping h can also be the form of "cyclic binary coding", as follows:

$$v_m = h(group_m) = \sum_{s=1}^{S}(2^{s-1} * \tau(op_s, op_{(s+1)\%S})), \; op_s \in group_m \quad (6)$$

Since $\tau(\cdot, \cdot)$ equals either 1 or 0, the v_m value space is finite discrete integer set, as follows:

$$v_m \in F = \{0, 1, 2, \cdots, 2^S - 1\} \quad (7)$$

3.4   The Workflow of Our Methods

We show the workflow of our ConvRid feature methods in Algorithm 1.

4   Results

4.1   Variance and Correlation

High variance makes a feature more discriminative, because it can produce much more different responses to inputs. Another desirable property is to make the binary tests uncorrelated so that each test can contribute to the result. In order to analyze the correlation of binary tests in a feature vector, we compute the response to 100k keypoints for BRIEF and ConvRids. The results are illustrated in Fig. 3. The highest 40 eigenvalues are plotted after applying PCA on the data. We can see that BRIEF exhibit high initial eigenvalues, indicating correlation among the binary tests - essentially all the information is contained in the first 10 or 15 components. While, our ConvRids have low initial eigenvalues and spread all the information to more components, which indicates that there are less correlations among components of our ConvRid feature vectors and thus can make full use of all feature components.

4.2   Parameters Experiments

Sampling redundancy has crucial affects on feature quality. Given image patch size and operator aperture size, We have three parameters that affect sampling

---

Algorithm 1. The workflow of our convolutional RID feature extractor method

---

Input: The number of convolution kernels, K;
       The size of convolution kernels, $kernel\_size$;
       The number of groups for grouping all RID operators, M;
       The number of RID operators within each group, S;
       The number of sampling channels of RID operators, c;
       Image patch size surrounding a key point, $patch\_size$
       RID operator aperture size range, $aperture\_range$;
       The given gray image to detect keypoints and extract descriptors, $image$
Output: The descriptor vectors of all detected keypoints, $descriptors$;
1: Generating K convolution kernels randomly under the constraints of the parameters: $N(0,1)$ and $kernel\_size$;
2: Generating $M*S$ RID operators randomly in the parameter constraints;
3: Grouping $M*S$ operators randomly into M groups;
4: Randomly specifying $M*S$ operators into K convolutional feature maps. Each map has $M*S/K$ operators. Make sure K can divide $M*S$ exactly.
5: Detecting numbers of keypoints on the given image, $keypoints$;
6: Applying K convolution kernels on the given image $image$ to generate K-layers convolutional feature maps, $feat\_maps$;
7: **for** each $keypoint \in keypoints$ **do**
8:     extracting feature maps surrounding $keypoint$ from $feat\_maps$;
9:     applying RID operators to local feature maps to get grouped values.
10:     **for** each $group \in groups$ **do**
11:        applying binary coding on grouped values to get component value;
12:     **end for**
13:     all components are assembled into bytes vector as keypoint descriptor;
14: **end for**
15: bagging all keypoint descriptors into the descriptor set: $descriptors$.
16: **return** $descriptors$;

---

redundancy: component number M, group size S and conv-maps number K. To make the experiments, 300 keypoints are firstly detected on reference image and generate 1000 patches randomly, and evaluating RandomFerns method. The experiments are made under three cases: first case is that keeping the number of feature maps K fixed while increasing the number of RID operators on per feature map (see Fig. 4(a)); second case is that keeping the number of RID operators per feature map fixed while increasing the number of feature maps K (see Fig. 4(b)); third case is that keeping the total number of RID operators fixed while changing the number of feature maps and the number of RID operators on per map (see Fig. 5). In the two cases of Fig. 4, the total number of RID operators grows and so that the length of feature descriptor (component count M) become longer, which lead to the rise-up of recognition rate curves. In the experiment case of Fig. 5, although the number of RID operators on per feature map and the number of feature maps are changed, the total number of RID operators are kept unchanged and so that the length of feature descriptor are the same. We can find from Fig. 5 that when the number of sampling operators and the length

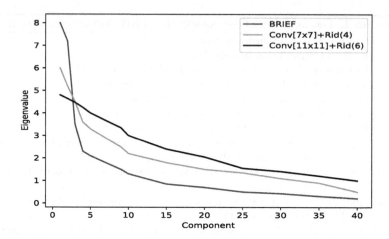

Fig. 3. Distribution of eigenvalues in the PCA decomposition over 100k keypoints of three feature vectors: BRIEF, and ConvRIDs.

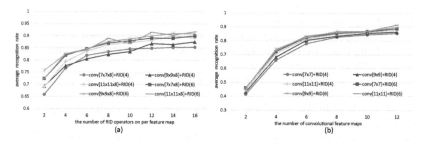

Fig. 4. (a) This figure shows the experiment result under the case that the number of feature maps K is fixed to be 8, the number of RID operators on per feature map increases from 2 to 16. Under these circumstances, the recognition rate curves of RandomFerns classifier rise up to saturation, because the descriptor become longer and more discriminative. (b) This figure shows the experiment result under the case that the number of RID operators on per feature map is fixed to be 6, the number of feature maps K increases from 2 to 12. Under these circumstances, the recognition rate curves of RandomFerns classifier rise up to saturation, this is also because the descriptor become longer and more discriminative.

of descriptors remain unchanged, the more convolution feature maps used, the better the recognition rate will be. This experimental phenomenon fully explains that it is better to construct randomized binary features on convolution feature maps than to construct them on original image.

4.3   Recognition Rate Tests on Images

We use RID(4) and RID(6) operators sampling on different kinds of convolutional feature maps to build binary features and combine them with Ran-

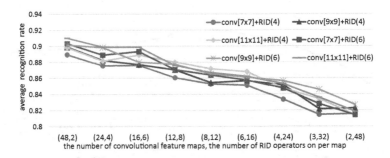

Fig. 5. This figure shows the experiment result under the case that the number of RID operators on per feature map increases, meanwhile the number of feature maps K decreases. Under these circumstances, descriptor length is unchanged. we see that the recognition rate curves of RandomFerns classifier are on the decline.

domTrees and RandomFerns [8] to evaluate recognition performance. Performance between our convolutional RID features and the non-convolutional RID features is compared. The non-convolutional RID features are denoted like this: "non-conv+RID(4)" and "non-conv+RID(6)", which means RID operators take operations on original image patches. While, our convolutional RID method is denoted as "conv[HxWxK]+RID(n)", where $n = 4$ or 6, H and W are height and width of convolution kernels, K is the number of convolution kernels. RID aperture is selected randomly in the range ($[6 \times 6]$, $[27 \times 27]$). For fairly comparison, we set $M = 40$ and $S = 8$ to stay feature space dimensions always same. The number of convolution kernels K is set to be 8, so the number of RID operators on per convolution feature map is $M * S/K = 40$. We make experiments on images from MSCOCO dataset. Each method is tested in two cases: first is keeping keypoints count equal 300 while increasing training samples count of each keypoint continuously. The corresponding experimental results are shown in (a) and (c) of Fig. 6. The second case is keeping training samples count of each keypoint equal 500 while increasing keypoints number detected from reference. The results are shown in (b) and (d) of Fig. 6.

The results in Fig. 6 indicate two points: the first is that recognition of ConvRID features is better than that of the non-convolutional RID features in both classifiers: RandomFerns and RandomTrees. This shows that sampling on multi-layer convolutional feature maps can improve feature quality effectively regardless of which classifier you use. The second is that performance of RID(6) operators is better than that of RID(4) operators. Those operators with more sampling cells have better recognition rate. The explanation for this is that there are more weights randomness in the operator with more sampling cells. And, more feature randomness brings out more feature diversity. The improvement of operators' diversity is beneficial to enhance feature distinctiveness.

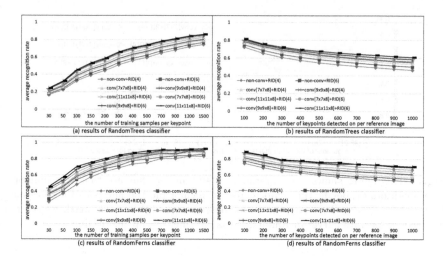

Fig. 6. Average recognition rate curves of RandomTrees and RandomFerns. (a) and (c): Keep the number of keypoints fixed to be 300 while continuously increase the number of training samples per keypoint. With the increasing of training samples, the recognition rate curves gradually increase. Different combinations of convolution kernels and RID operators have different performance. (b) and (d): Keep the number of training samples per keypoint fixed to be 500 while continuously increase the number of keypoints detected on each reference image. With the increasing of keypoints, the recognition rate curves gradually decrease. Different combinations of convolution kernels and RID operators have different performance.

4.4   Comparison with Existing State-of-Art Methods

Now we compare precision performance between ConvRID features and the existing methods in different situations, such as viewpoint changing, rotation, blurring, zooming, noises and light changing. The methods to be compared with ours include: SIFT, KAZE, SURF, BRIEF, ORB, AKAZE, RILBP, CSLBP, RandomTrees and RandomFerns. If a method own detector, we employ it; if not,

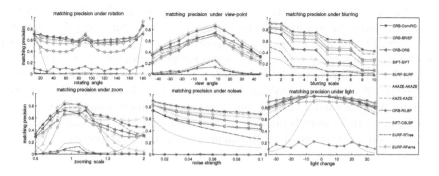

Fig. 7. matching precision results under image rotation and zooming

we adopt the detector in its original paper. These methods are implemented by OpenCV library. Our ConvRID feature method use the detector of ORB. So, our method is noted by ORB-ConvRID, which use 320 ($M = 40$, $S = 8$) RID(6) sampling operators and eight convolution kernels with size of 11×11.

The results are shown in Fig. 7. We can find that our ORB-ConvRID feature method has good enough performance in cases of zooming, rotation and viewangle change, while in blurring test, noises and light changes, ours performs best among all other methods.

5   Conclusions

In this paper, we carry out researches on convolutional randomized binary features for keypoints/patches recognition. We analyze several important parameters that have crucial affects on multi-resolution observation and sampling redundancy. We find from our experiments that our completely randomized convolutional binary features have excellent quality compared with those traditional incomplete features. Furthermore, the improvement of binary features by applying completely randomized intensity difference sampling operators on multi-layer convolutional feature maps is consistent no matter which classifier you employ. This kind of complete randomization cannot bring more computing burden and can be implemented easily with no need of comprehensive manual design. At present our ConvRID feature extractor can not be trained. In the follow-up studies, we will focus on trainable convolutional randomized binary feature method.

References

1. Alahi, A., Ortiz, R., Vandergheynst, P.: FREAK: fast retina keypoint. In: 2012 IEEE Conference on Computer Vision and Pattern Recognition, pp. 510–517 (2012). https://doi.org/10.1109/CVPR.2012.6247715
2. Bay, H., Ess, A., Tuytelaars, T., Van Gool, L.: Speeded-up robust features (SURF). Comput. Vis. Image Underst. **110**, 346–359 (2008). https://doi.org/10.1016/j.cviu.2007.09.014
3. Calonder, M., Lepetit, V., Ozuysal, M., Trzcinski, T., Strecha, C., Fua, P.: Brief: computing a local binary descriptor very fast. IEEE Trans. Pattern Anal. Mach. Intell. **34**(7), 1281–1298 (2012). https://doi.org/10.1109/TPAMI.2011.222
4. Alcantarilla, P.F.: Fast explicit diffusion for accelerated features in nonlinear scale spaces (2013). https://doi.org/10.5244/C.27.13
5. Gauglitz, S., Höllerer, T., Turk, M.: Evaluation of interest point detectors and feature descriptors for visual tracking. Int. J. Comput. Vis. **94**, 335–360 (2011). https://doi.org/10.1007/s11263-011-0431-5
6. Gil, A., Mozos, O., Ballesta, M., Reinoso, O.: A comparative evaluation of interest point detectors and local descriptors for visual slam. Mach. Vis. Appl. **21**, 905–920 (2010). https://doi.org/10.1007/s00138-009-0195-x
7. Lepetit, V., Fua, P.: Keypoint recognition using randomized trees. IEEE Trans. Pattern Anal. Mach. Intell. **28**(9), 1465–1479 (2006). https://doi.org/10.1109/TPAMI.2006.188

8. Lepetit, V., Fua, P.: Keypoint recognition using random forests and random ferns. In: Criminisi, A., Shotton, J. (eds.) Decision Forests for Computer Vision and Medical Image Analysis. ACVPR, pp. 111–124. Springer, London (2013). https://doi.org/10.1007/978-1-4471-4929-3_9

9. Leutenegger, S., Chli, M., Siegwart, R.Y.: Brisk: binary robust invariant scalable keypoints. In: 2011 International Conference on Computer Vision, pp. 2548–2555 (2011). https://doi.org/10.1109/ICCV.2011.6126542

10. Lowe, D.: Distinctive image features from scale-invariant keypoints. Int. J. Comput. Vision 60, 91–110 (2004). https://doi.org/10.1023/B:VISI.0000029664.99615.94

11. Mur-Artal, R., Montiel, J.M.M., Tardós, J.D.: ORB-SLAM: a versatile and accurate monocular SLAM system. IEEE Trans. Rob. 31(5), 1147–1163 (2015). https://doi.org/10.1109/TRO.2015.2463671

12. Mur-Artal, R., Tardós, J.D.: ORB-SLAM2: an open-source SLAM system for monocular, stereo, and RGB-D cameras. IEEE Trans. Rob. 33(5), 1255–1262 (2017). https://doi.org/10.1109/TRO.2017.2705103

13. Nishimura, T., Shimizu, S., Fujiyoshi, H.: Keypoint recognition with two-stage randomized trees. IEICE Trans. Inf. Syst. 97, 1766–1774 (2012). https://doi.org/10.1587/transinf.E95.D.1766

14. Ozuysal, M., Calonder, M., Lepetit, V., Fua, P.: Fast keypoint recognition using random ferns. IEEE Trans. Pattern Anal. Mach. Intell. 32(3), 448–461 (2010). https://doi.org/10.1109/TPAMI.2009.23

15. Rublee, E., Rabaud, V., Konolige, K., Bradski, G.: ORB: an efficient alternative to SIFT or SURF. In: 2011 International Conference on Computer Vision, pp. 2564–2571 (2011). https://doi.org/10.1109/ICCV.2011.6126544

16. Schmidt, A., Kraft, M., Fularz, M., Domagala, Z.: Comparative assessment of point feature detectors in the context of robot navigation. J. Autom. Mob. Robot. Intell. Syst. 7, 11–20 (2013)

17. Shen, F., Liu, J., Wu, P.: Double δ-LBP: a novel feature extraction method for facial expression recognition. In: Wang, Y., Jiang, Z., Peng, Y. (eds.) IGTA 2018. CCIS, vol. 875, pp. 370–379. Springer, Singapore (2018). https://doi.org/10.1007/978-981-13-1702-6_37

18. Wang, Q., Li, B., Chen, X., Luo, J., Hou, Y.: Random sampling local binary pattern encoding based on Gaussian distribution. IEEE Sig. Process. Lett. 24(9), 1358–1362 (2017). https://doi.org/10.1109/LSP.2017.2728122

19. Wang, Y., Ge, Z., Su, J., Wu, W.: SAR image registration using cluster analysis and anisotropic diffusion-based SIFT. In: Wang, Y., et al. (eds.) IGTA 2017. CCIS, vol. 757, pp. 1–11. Springer, Singapore (2018). https://doi.org/10.1007/978-981-10-7389-2_1

20. Yuan, M., Tang, H., Li, H.: Real-time keypoint recognition using restricted Boltzmann machine. IEEE Trans. Neural Netw. Learn. Syst. 25(11), 2119–2126 (2014). https://doi.org/10.1109/TNNLS.2014.2303478

21. Zhang, J., Wan, Y., Pan, Y.: A framework for multi-view feature selection via embedding space. In: Wang, Y., Jiang, Z., Peng, Y. (eds.) IGTA 2018. CCIS, vol. 875, pp. 57–69. Springer, Singapore (2018). https://doi.org/10.1007/978-981-13-1702-6_6

22. Zhang, X., Zhang, H., Wei, Q., Jiang, Z.: Pose estimation of space objects based on hybrid feature matching of contour points. In: Tan, T., et al. (eds.) IGTA 2016. CCIS, vol. 634, pp. 184–191. Springer, Singapore (2016). https://doi.org/10.1007/978-981-10-2260-9_21

A Novel Multi-image Encryption Algorithm Based on the RDFrMT and Cascaded Phase Retrieval

Haotian Yang, Tong Li, Sijiang Huang, Fei Qi, and Xuejing Kang[(⊠)]

Beijing University of Posts and Telecommunications, Beijing 100876, China
kangxuejing@bupt.edu.cn

Abstract. In this paper, a multi-image encryption method is presented by using the Random Discrete Fractional Mellin Transform (RDFrMT) and the cascaded phase retrieval algorithm (PRA). Firstly, we define the RDFrMT and discuss its properties including nonlinear, multi-parameter, and randomness. Then, based on the RDFrMT, a cascaded multiple-image encryption scheme is proposed. In our algorithm, an image generated by logistic map is transformed to the RDFrMT domain, and the resulting image is fed into the PRA. This nonlinear process makes our cryptosystem robust for potential attacks and ensures its security. Thereafter, the output is cut based on the Hamming distance and the keys are related to multiple input images, which makes our cryptosystem has distinct security level for different images. We repeat the above steps and get a cascaded encryption scheme. Numerical simulations demonstrate the security and feasibility of the proposed scheme.

Keywords: Multiple-image encryption · Phase retrieval ·
Random Discrete Fractional Mellin Transform

1 Introduction

With the rapid development of technology, the security of image information transmission plays an important role in modern society. Since image encryption is a direct way to protect image data, it has been getting the widespread concern in the academia in recent years. Plenty of encryption methods have been raised, generally, these methods can be classified into two category: encryption in the spatial domain, and encryption in the transform domain.

Spatial image encryption methods often perform confusion and diffusion strategy by using chaotic sequence [1], DNA coding [2], and CA coding [3], etc. In general, the spatial image encryption is high efficiency, and the encrypted image is ideal. But such methods are often not robust to noise channels, and can not resist data loss attacks. Moreover, they are not suitable for multi-image encryption. On other hand, image encryption in transform domain can solve these problems. Refregier and Javidi [4] introduced Fourier transform into image encryption for the first time. They proposed a double-random phase encoding

© Springer Nature Singapore Pte Ltd. 2019
Y. Wang et al. (Eds.): IGTA 2019, CCIS 1043, pp. 505–515, 2019.
https://doi.org/10.1007/978-981-13-9917-6_48

method, in which the cipher image is obtained by random-phase encoding in both the input and the Fourier planes. To further improve the security, Situ et al. [5] extended image encryption to Fresnel domain and proposed a lensless optical security system based on double random-phase encoding. Pei [10] introduced image encryption to fractional domain and defined random discrete fractional Fourier transform (RDFrFT) by randomizing both the eigenvectors and the eigenvalues. They enhance the security of multiple-parameter discrete fractional Fourier transform (MPDFrFT) and the random Fourier transform (DRFT). Based on their works, Kang et al. [6] proposed a multichannel random discrete fractional Fourier transform (MRFrFT) with random weighting coefficients and partial transform kernel functions. However, the above encryption methods in transform domain are all proposed for single image encryption. To further improve the efficiency of image encryption system, multi-image encryption has been applied in recent years. Li et al. [7] proposed a asymmetric multiple-image encryption scheme based on the cascaded fractional Fourier transform, and the asymmetric system can resist the attack of plaintext-ciphertext pairs. Liansheng et al. [8] proposed a multiple-image encryption scheme based on the phase retrieval process and phase mask multiplexing in the fractional Fourier transform domain, which have ideal encrypted image. Additionally, Hwang and Chang [9] proposed a new multi-image encryption technique based on a modified Gerchberg-Saxton algorithm (MGSA) and a phase modulation scheme in the Fresnel-transform (FrT) domain. However, due to the superposition of multiple encrypted information, each decrypted image is affected by crosstalk noise. The increase in the number of encrypted images leads to a significant degradation in the quality of the decrypted image, and the encryption capacity is limited. In addition, most encryption systems are linear, making the system vulnerable to potential attacks.

In this paper, we design a cascaded multi-image encryption system based on Random Discrete Fractional Mellin Transform (RDFrMT) and the phase retrieval algorithm (PRA). We firstly define the RDFrMT and discuss its properties. And then phase retrieval is used to obtain the phase key and generated it during the nonlinear encryption process. In this process, cascaded PRA make the decryption process of each images independent and can avoid the crosstalk noise. Thereafter, we maintain the matrix size by cutting images based on the Hamming distance and make our cascading system remain efficient when encrypting many images. In this process, the cutting method is associated with the previous encryption result, therefore our encryption system has a distinct security level for different encrypted images. Compared to parallel encryption systems, our systems can easily affect multiple images decryption by one key and can avoid various types of attacks based on plaintext and ciphertext pairs.

2   Preliminaries

In this section, we first review the RDFrFT proposed by Pei [10] and the phase retrieval algorithm [11,12], which are the basic of our encryption scheme.

2.1   Random Discrete Fractional Fourier Transform

The RDFrFT is defined as [10]

$$F_H^{\bar{a}} = \sum_{k=0}^{N-1} \lambda_k^{a_k} r_k r_k^T \tag{1}$$

where the eigenvalues $\lambda_k (k = 0 \cdots N - 1)$ is obtained by random vector $\bar{a}$, and $r_k (K = 0\ N - 1)$ is orthonormal eigenvector basis of a DFT commuting matrix H, which is obtained by:

$$K = F^2 = F^{-2} = \begin{bmatrix} 1 & 0 \\ 0 & J_{N-1} \end{bmatrix} \tag{2}$$

$$E = \frac{(D + KDK)}{2}, G = \frac{E + E^T}{2}, H = G + FGF^{-1} \tag{3}$$

where F is the Fourier transform matrix, J_{N-1} is the reversal matrix whose only nonzero entries are ones on the antidiagonal, D is a matrix generated randomly.

2.2   Phase Retrieval

Phase retrieval (PRA) [11,12] is the process of algorithmically finding solutions to the phase problem. The iterative process is shown in Fig. 1. Details about PRA can refer to [11,12].

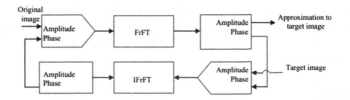

Fig. 1. Flowchart of phase retrieval algorithm in FrFT domain.

First of all, an arbitrary image is chosen as the input amplitude. And the initial phase is randomly generated with the distribution in $(0, 2\pi)$. Then after fractional Fourier transform, the complex function is obtained in the transform plane. The obtained phase is combined with the target image for inverse fractional Fourier transform. And the phase of the transformed result substitutes the phase of input and next loop starts. Loop ends until satisfying convergence criteria. Finally, the obtained phase is the desired phase distribution.

3   The Proposed RDFrMT

In this section, we firstly define the RDFrMT, and then discuss its properties.

3.1   Definition

Since the RDFrFT [10] is a linear transformation, encryption systems based on it is not safe enough. To enhance the security, we define the 2-D random discrete fractional Mellin transform (RDFrMT) as follows,

$$C = F_{M_1}^{\overline{a_1}} \cdot LPT_{c_x,c_y}(P) \cdot F_{M_2}^{\overline{a_2}} \tag{4}$$

where $LPT_{c_x,c_y}(\cdot)$ is the log-polar transform with the transform center at (c_x, c_y), $F_{M_1}^{\overline{a_1}}$ referring to the idea of fractional Mellin transformation (FrMT) in [11–14], P is the input image, and C is the output image.

The RDFrMT can be seen as two parts. The first part is the log-polar transform (LPT) which transform the image in Cartesian coordinate to log-polar coordinate and formulate as

$$\rho = \ln\sqrt{(x - c_x)^2 + (y - c_y)^2}, \theta = \arctan\frac{y - c_y}{x - c_x} \tag{5}$$

where c_x and c_y are the transform center in Cartesian coordinate.

After the log-polar transform, the results ρ and θ are always decimal and in a very small range. For example, if the range of x and y is $[1, 256]$, the range of ρ and θ is $[0, 5.5452]$. To solve this problem, we set an parameter k and get ρ', θ'

$$\rho' = [k \cdot \rho], \theta' = [k \cdot \theta] \tag{6}$$

where $[\cdot]$ is rounding operation. The algorithm for calculating k is described in detail in [15]. With this strategy, the size of the output image may be changed after the adjustment by k, to recover the image size, we propose a cutting strategy based on the Hamming distance in our encryption scheme by using the size of the original matrix and c_x, c_y (details see Sect. 4 Step 3).

The second part of our RDFrMT is the RDFrFT with orders a_1, a_2. If the size of the output of the LPT is $M_s \times N_s$, the $F_{M_1}^{\overline{a_1}}$ should be $M_s \times M_s$ and the $F_{M_2}^{\overline{a_2}}$ should be $N_s \times N_s$.

3.2   Properties

Similar to the FrMT [11–14] that is the FrFT in log-polar coordinates, our RDFrMT can be regarded as the RDFrFT in log-polar coordinates. So the basic characteristics of RDFrFT such as unitarity, identity, index additivity and commutativity are also inherited by our RDFrMT. Other unique properties of the proposed RDFrMT are discussed as follows.

(1) Non-linearity. Since LPT is non-linear, the RDFrMT is non-linear transform.
(2) FrMT matrix. If $a = [1, 1, \cdots]$, $F_H^{\overline{1}} = F$, where F is the DFT matrix, the RDFrMT degenerate to the FrMT.
(3) More free parameters. RDFrMT has more free parameters such as the N fractional orders $\overline{a}$ and $N \times N$ free values in the random matrix D, which enhances the randomness of the RDFrMT.
(4) Random magnitude and phase for the output. The eigenvectors and eigenvalues of the RDFrFT matrix $F_M^{\overline{a}}$ are random, which makes our RDFrMT more sensitive to the fractional orders than the FrMT.

4   The Proposed Image Encryption Scheme

In this section, we propose a cascade encryption system based on RDFrMT and PRA. The encryption flow chart is shown in Fig. 2. The concrete encryption steps are as follows.

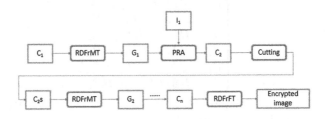

Fig. 2. The flowchart of encryption.

Step 1. Assume that the first plaintext image has the size of $M \times N$, we need to generate a random matrix C_1 with a smaller size $M_s \times N_s$. In our scheme, we use logistic map $x(n-1) = u \cdot x(n) \cdot (1 - x(n))$ to obtain a chaotic sequence X. To obtain better chaotic property, we set a length parameter p. Take out the $(p+1)_{th}$ value to the $(p + M_s \times N_s)_{th}$ value in sequence X to obtain the random matrix C_1. Then, transform C_1 to G_1 by RDFrMT with key $\bar{a}$, D_1, D_2 and center c_x and c_y. Note, the values of M_s and N_s is determined by M, N and LPT with parameters c_x, c_y.

Step 2. After obtaining the result image transformed by the RDFrMT, we fed it into the PRA as the original image. Because the original image and the phase key obtained by PRA are both indispensable in the decryption of PRA, the key of our cascaded PRA system can influence both front and back decryption images and solve the problem that a key only affects one image. In addition, due to the independence of each PRA process, the decryption of each images is independent, which can avoid the problem of crosstalk noise in multi-image encryption and make our cryptosystem more robust.

Step 3. Perform RDFrMT on C_2 whose size should be the same as the next plaintext image I_2. Note that the LPT in the RDFrMT may enlarge the size, if we perform RDFrMT directly on C_2, the result G_2 will be larger than the next plaintext image I_2. To continue using the PRA, we need to cut C_2 or expand I_2. Since the expansion will accumulate in the cascading system, which may affect our encryption efficiency, next we propose a cutting strategy and use the concept of Hamming distance [16].

– Compute the sum of each value in the previous level C_{i-1} when cutting $C_i(i = 2; \cdots)$.

- Convert each value (0–255) of encryption result of the previous level C_{i-1} to an 8-bit binary number B_i $(i = 1, 2, \cdots M \times N)$.
- Take out $B_i(j)$ and $B_i(j+2)$ $(j = 1, 2, 5, 6)$ in ascending order of i and put into $BP_{j(j+2)}$.
- Compute HMD between these four sequences to get six different values $d_i (i = 0, 1, \cdots 5)$.

$$\begin{cases} d_0 = HMD(BP_{13}, BP_{24}) \\ d_1 = HMD(BP_{13}, BP_{57}) \\ d_2 = HMD(BP_{13}, BP_{68}) \\ d_3 = HMD(BP_{24}, BP_{57}) \\ d_4 = HMD(BP_{24}, BP_{57}) \\ d_5 = HMD(BP_{57}, BP_{68}) \end{cases} \tag{7}$$

- Suppose we want to cut into $M_s \times N_s$ $(M_s < M, N_s < N)$. We can obtain the starting position (z_1, z_2) by follows.

$$k = mod(sum, 6)\, z_1 = round(mod(d_k, Ms)) \\ z_2 = round(mod(d_{mod(k+3, 6)}, Ns)) \tag{8}$$

- Take out the points form (z_1, z_2) to $(mod(z_1 + Ms, M), mod(z_2 + Ns, N))$ in C_i to obtain $C_i s$.

In our cutting strategy, we make the generation of the starting point related to C_{i-1} when cutting C_i. The advantage is that the association between the keys is established, so that the error of one key causes multiple encrypted images unable to be decrypted. And obviously, this effect will also accumulate. That is, the decryption affected by key C_1 is the most, key C_2 is the second, and so on. Conversely, for I_1, only C_1, C_2 and transform orders are required when decrypting. But for the last picture I_n, all C_i and transform orders are required. Thus in our system, different images have different security levels. When encrypting, we can select the plaintext input order according to your needs, so that the most important plaintext could have the highest security level.

Step 4. Repeat above three steps to encrypt the remaining images. After the last image being encrypted by PRA, we obtain C_n. Then transform C_n to C_{n+1} by RDFrMT because it does not involve the process restoring the original image from the cut image which affects our decryption. Therefore, we obtain the cascaded PRA encryption scheme which can generate the key in the encryption process, and have the ability to resist various types of attacks based on plaintext and ciphertext pairs.

In our scheme, fractional orders $\bar{a}$, random matrix D_1, D_2, the parameters used in logistic map u, x_0 and p, transformation center c_x and c_y serve as keys. Particularly, we need to generate C_1 as the same size as the first plaintext image. All other $C_i (i = 2; \cdots)$ are also secret keys.

The Decryption Scheme. The decryption process is the inverse process of encryption.

5   Simulation Result and Analysis

Numerical simulation is employed to test the feasibility and the security of our scheme. We choose three images to be plaintexts: Lena, Man and Cameraman with size 512×512. The fractional order a is set randomly by the function rand$(1, 512)$ in MATLAB and the random matrix D_1 and D_2 are generated by rand(512). Other parameters are set as $u = 4, x_0 = 0.7936, p = 17, (c_x, c_y) = (1, 1)$. The center position is set as $(c_x, c_y) = (1, 1)$. The encryption result and three decrypted images obtained with correct keys are shown in Fig. 3.

Fig. 3. Encrypted image and decrypted images.

5.1   Robustness to the Statistical Attack

Robustness to the statistical attack can be tested by analyzing the histograms. The results of our three plain images and encrypted images (both real part and imaginary part) are shown in Fig. 4. It is obvious that the histogram of the plaintext images is totally changed and presents a Gaussian distribution after encryption, which means attackers could not find any information regarding the distribution of intensity values.

Testing the pixel distribution by the correlation coefficient of the encrypted image is another way to analysis the robustness of the statistical attack. Correlation coefficient is computed by:

$$CC = \frac{\sum_{i=1}^{N}(x_i - \overline{x})(y_i - \overline{y})}{\sqrt{(\sum_{i=1}^{N}(x_i - \overline{x})^2)(\sum_{i=1}^{N}(y_i - \overline{y})^2)}} \tag{9}$$

where $\overline{x} = 1/N \sum_{i=1}^{N} x_i, \overline{y} = 1/N \sum_{i=1}^{N} y_i$.

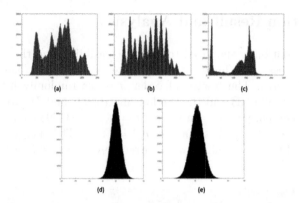

Fig. 4. Histogram of images.

Table 1. Comparison of correlation coefficient

	Lena	Man	Cameraman	Our real part	Our imaginary part	Li's [d]
Horizontal	0.9554	0.9904	0.9717	0.0096	0.0113	0.0167
Vertical	0.9223	0.9386	0.9858	0.0092	0.0098	0.0115
Diagonal	0.8727	0.9315	0.9599	0.0136	−0.0085	0.0174

In our experiment, we select 2000 pairs of adjacent pixels in horizontally, vertically and diagonally direction from each plain images and encrypted image. The results are listed in Table 1. It demonstrate that the correlation among pixels of plain images is broken after encryption compared with [7].

5.2   Robustness to the Noise

When the encrypted image is transmitted in channels, it may be disturbed by noise. An excellent encryption algorithm can decrypt the plaintext image with good quality from the disturbed dense image. We use the function randn in MATLAB to generate a standard Gaussian matrix as the simulation of channel noise. Figure 5(a) is the encrypted image added noise, Fig. 5(b)–(d) are the decrypted images. It is shown that the first two images are not affected, and the last image can be distinguished as well, which demonstrate our system provides robustness to the noise.

5.3   Robustness to the Data Loss

Data loss is another interference caused by channels. We occlude 25% of the encrypted image pixels in the upper left and lower right corner to test the robustness against data loss. Figure 6(a) and (e) are the encrypted image lost pixels. (b)–(d) are the decrypted images corresponding to (a). And (f)–(h) are the decrypted images corresponding to (e). It is shown that the first two images are

Fig. 5. Decrypted images compounding to noise.

not affected and the primary information of the last image can be recognized vaguely. Therefore, our system has robustness to the data loss.

Fig. 6. Decrypted images compounding to different data loss.

5.4 Sensitivity to the Keys

A secure encryption algorithm should have high sensitivity to the keys. That is, we can not decrypt images using wrong keys, even if the keys are changed little. We analyze the sensitivity to the fractional order a and the random matrix D.

From Fig. 7 ($a = a+0.001$) and Fig. 8 ($D(1,1) = D(1,1)+10^{-16}$), we can not get useful information from the decrypted images, which verify that our system is sensitive to the keys.

We also test the sensitivity to the key C_1, we set $x_0 = x_0+10^{-16}$ in Fig. 9(a)–(c), and set $u = u - 10^{15}$ in (d)–(f). The decrypted images are almost indistinguishable, which demonstrate the sensitivity to key and the characteristic that one key affects the decryption of multiple ciphertext images. Similar results can be obtained testing other C_i.

Fig. 7. Decrypted images with wrong fractional orders

Fig. 8. Decrypted images with wrong key.

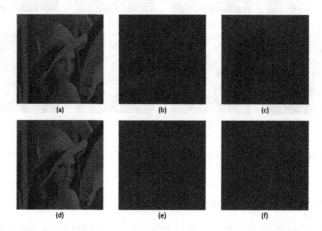

Fig. 9. Decrypted images with wrong logistic parameters

6   Conclusions

In this study, we proposed a cascaded multi-image encryption system. In this system, keys are generated in the encryption process to avoid plaintext attacks. And our cutting method makes up for the problem that the RDFrMT will change the size of the image and result in the decrease of encryption efficiency. Unlike other cascaded multi-image encryption system, our keys can affect the decryption of multiple pictures instead of one. Moreover, our system also can be used in image encryption of different security levels.

Acknowledgement. This work was supported in part by National Natural Science Foundation of China (61701036).

References

1. Tong, X., Cui, M.: Image encryption with compound chaotic sequence cipher shifting dynamically. Image Vis. Comput. **26**(6), 843–850 (2008)
2. Zhang, Q., Wang, Q., Wei, X.: A novel image encryption scheme based on DNA coding and multi-chaotic maps. Adv. Sci. Lett. **3**(4), 447–451 (2010)
3. Jeyaram, B.S., Radha, R., Raghavan, R.: New cellular automata-based image cryptosystem and a novel non-parametric pixel randomness test. Secur. Commun. Netw. **9**, 3365–3377 (2016)
4. Refregier, P., Javidi, B.: Optical image encryption using input plane and fourier plane random encoding. Opt. Lett. **20**(7), 767–769 (1995)
5. Situ, G., Zhang, J.: Double random-phase encoding in the Fresnel domain. Opt. Lett. **29**(14), 1584–1586 (2004)
6. Kang, X., Zhang, F., Tao, R.: Multichannel random discrete fractional Fourier transform. IEEE Sig. Process. Lett. **22**(9), 1340–1344 (2015)
7. Li, Y., Zhang, F., Li, Y., et al.: Asymmetric multiple-image encryption based on the cascaded fractional Fourier transform. Opt. Lasers Eng. **72**(Complete), 18–25 (2015)
8. Liansheng, S., Meiting, X., Ailing, T.: Multiple-image encryption based on phase mask multiplexing in fractional Fourier transform domain. Opt. Lett. **38**(11), 1996 (2013)
9. Hwang, H.E., Chang, H.T., Lie, W.N.: Multiple-image encryption and multiplexing using a modified Gerchberg-Saxton algorithm and phase modulation in Fresnel-transform domain. Opt. Lett. **34**(24), 3917–3919 (2009)
10. Pei, S.C., Hsue, W.L.: Random discrete fractional Fourier transform. IEEE Sig. Process. Lett. **16**(12), 1015–1018 (2009)
11. Shechtman, Y., Eldar, Y.C., Cohen, O., et al.: Phase retrieval with application to optical imaging. IEEE Sig. Process. Mag. **32**(3), 87–109 (2014)
12. Liu, X., Zhang, Y., et al.: Image encryption scheme based on fractional Mellin transform and phase; retrieval technique in fractional Fourier domain. Opt. Laser Technol. **47**(4), 341–346 (2013)
13. Zhou, N., Wang, Y., Gong, L., et al.: Novel color image encryption algorithm based on the reality preserving fractional Mellin transform. Opt. Laser Technol. **44**(7), 2270–2281 (2012)
14. Zhou, N., Wang, Y., Gong, L.: Novel optical image encryption scheme based on fractional Mellin transform. Opt. Commun. **284**(13), 3234–3242 (2011)
15. Lv, M., Zi, F., Li, Y.: Vision bionics and application on the design of imaging guidance head. In: MIPPR 2007: Automatic Target Recognition and Image Analysis; and Multispectral Image Acquisition. International Society for Optics and Photonics (2007)
16. Wei, X., Guo, L., Zhang, Q., et al.: A novel color image encryption algorithm based on DNA sequence operation and hyper-chaotic system. J. Syst. Softw. **85**(2), 290–299 (2012)

Analysis of Influence of the Spectral Channels of AWG on the Imaging Quality of Planar Interferometric Imaging System

Gongmin Yu$^{(\boxtimes)}$, Libing Jin, Feng Zhou, and Xiliang Tong

Beijing Institute of Space Mechanics and Electricity, Beijing 100094, China
yu_568651142@163.com

Abstract. The Planar Interferometric Imaging System samples the object visibility in the Fourier domain and then digitally reconstructs an image. Firstly, the principle of SPIDER imaging is studied, the principle of AWG is analyzed, and the influence of different bandwidth on the visibility of interference fringes is simulated. The results show that increasing the number of spectral channels of AWG can improve the visibility of interference fringes, effectively increase the spatial frequency coverage and improve the imaging quality.

Keywords: Visibility of fringe · Arrayed waveguide grating ·
Interferometric imaging · Photonic Integrated Circuit

1 Introduction

In 2012, the Segmented Planar Imaging Detector for EO Reconnaissance (SPIDER) [1–4] was developed by the researchers at the LM Advanced Technology Center and UC Davis. It is an interferometric imaging system based on Photonic Integrated Circuits (PIC) [5, 6]. Two-dimensional micro-lens arrays are used to obtain the optical information of the target, which is coupled to the optical waveguide. And then interference is implemented in the PIC. The high-resolution image is obtained by analyzing the amplitude and phase of the interference image and reconstructing the image, with a reduction of Size, Weight and Power (SWaP) by the factor of $10\times$–$100\times$ compared with the traditional imaging system. It has great potential in space optical remote sensing, Space Situation Awareness (SSA) [7] and other fields, and is one of the current research hot-spots. System structure and design principles for SPIDER are described in Refs. [8, 9]. The second generation PIC is developed, and the imaging capability of SPIDER is simulated and verified by experiments. Shanghai Institute of Technical Physics of the Chinese Academy of Sciences has analyzed the index of the SPIDER, optimized the micro-lens array, and expanded the application of the system [10, 11]. However, there is no research on the influence of arrayed waveguide grating on imaging and the selection of imaging spectrum in the PIC.

In this paper, the principle of SPIDER and Arrayed Waveguide Gratings (AWG) are studied. The relationship between the spectral channels of AWG and the visibility of interference fringes is analyzed. The influence of different spatial frequency coverage on image quality is simulated and analyzed. Finally, the principle of spectrum selection is given.

© Springer Nature Singapore Pte Ltd. 2019
Y. Wang et al. (Eds.): IGTA 2019, CCIS 1043, pp. 516–523, 2019.
https://doi.org/10.1007/978-981-13-9917-6_49

2   Basic Principle of SPIDER

SPIDER is a passive interferometric imaging technology based on PIC technology, as shown in Fig. 1. Standard lithography technology is used to integrate AWG, phase modulator, Multi Mode Interference (MMI) coupler and other components on a chip [12]. The micro-lens array collects the optical information from the target and couples it into the optical waveguide array. After subdividing the broad-band light into the corresponding narrow-band through the arrayed waveguide grating and adjusting the phase, the same wavelength light satisfies the interference condition, realizes the interference coupling in the MMI coupler, and finally detects the coupling output by Balanced Four-Quadrant Detection and obtains the target Light intensity distribution through the corresponding processing.

Planar Interferometric Imaging System is an incoherent optical imaging system, In order to obtain stable interference fringes on the image plane and facilitate the extraction of fringe visibility information and image reconstruction in the later stage, wavelength demultiplexing of broad-band light must be carried out to divide the broad-band into corresponding narrow-band. AWG is one of the key components of PIC, which can demultiplex the broad spectrum received by micro-lens into the corresponding narrow spectrum to meet the interference conditions.

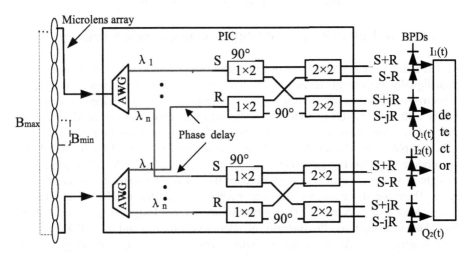

Fig. 1. The schematic diagram of the interference imaging system based PIC

As shown in the Fig. 2, AWG is mainly composed of input waveguide, star coupler, array waveguide and output waveguide. Two star couplers are symmetrically distributed on both sides of the arrayed waveguide grating. The optical signal is input from the input waveguide and diffracts in the star coupler. The phase of the diffracted light is the same, coupled into the array waveguide. The adjacent array waveguide has a length difference Δl. The phase difference produced by the same wavelength is the same $n\Delta l$, where n is waveguide refractive index. The same wavelength will be diffracted and focused on the same output waveguide, and different wavelengths will be output in different output waveguides. The light of two micro-lenses with the same baseline is input at two input terminals of the same AWG, which can reduce the Optical Path Difference (OPD).

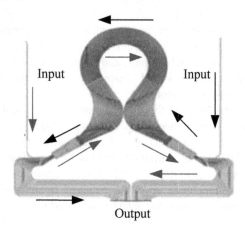

Fig. 2. The schematic diagram of the AWG

3   Effect of Bandwidth on Visibility of Interference Fringes

The SPIDER imager samples the object visibility function in the Fourier domain and then digitally reconstructs an image. The optical information of the target is coupled by a micro-lens, and then, the optical information from the target is divided into n narrow bands with the same bandwidth $\lambda_1 \sim \lambda_n$ through the AWG and the interference condition is satisfied by phase modulation. The interference is realized by 1×2 and 2×2 MMI couplers, and the interference fringe information is detected by Balanced Four Quadrature Detector. For optical interference with spectral width $\Delta\lambda$, Each wavelength of light produces its own set of interference fringes and Except for zero interference level, There are displacements between each other, and the overlap of interference fringes leads to the decrease of the contrast of interference fringes [13]. Figure 3 shows the relationship between the intensity of interference fringes and the OPD when two light beams λ, $\lambda + \Delta\lambda$ are equal in light intensity. Obviously, the fringe contrast decreases with the increase of optical path difference until it reaches zero.

The relationship between visibility of fringe and coherence length is expressed as Eqs. (1):

$$K = \left| \frac{\sin(\Delta k \frac{\Delta l}{2})}{\Delta k \frac{\Delta l}{2}} \right| \tag{1}$$

where K is visibility of fringe, $k = 2\pi/\lambda$ is wave number, Δl is OPD. The visibility of fringe decreases with the increase of optical path difference. The visibility of fringe is

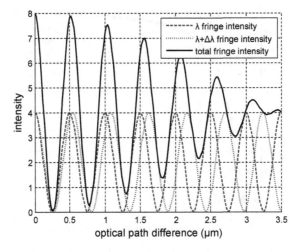

Fig. 3. Variation of intensity of superimposed fringes with OPD at different wavelengths

0.9, When the OPD equals to 1/4 coherent length ($\lambda^2/\Delta\lambda$). When the OPD is equal to one coherent length, the fringe visibility decreases to zero. Low visibility of fringe is bad for obtain the amplitude and phase information of the target, furthermore, it will reduce the signal-to-noise ratio of the system. As shown in the Fig. 4, visibility of fringe is generally required to be greater than 0.9.

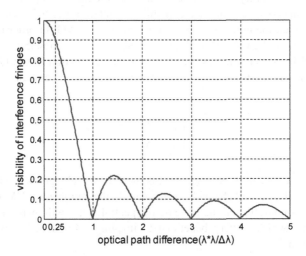

Fig. 4. The relationship between the visibility of fringes and the OPD

After the above analysis, the bandwidth and OPD of the two interfering beams affect the visibility of the interference fringes. The bandwidth of interferometric imaging system based on PIC is depends on the number of spectral channels of AWG.

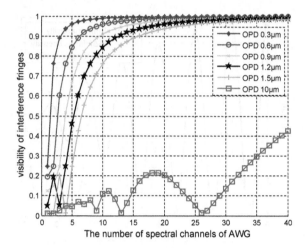

Fig. 5. The relationship between the number of spectral channels of AWG and the visibility of fringes

The relationship between the number of spectral channels of AWG and the visibility of fringes under different OPD is simulated and analyzed. The simulation conditions are set as follows: Imaging band 380 nm–760 nm, The fractional wave number of AWG is set to 1–40. As shown in Fig. 5, When OPD is small, The visibility of fringe increases with the number of spectral channels of AWG; At the same AWG fractional wavenumber, the visibility of fringe decreases with the increase of OPD; When OPD is much larger than coherence length, the visibility of interference fringes does not change monotonously with the number of spectral channels of AWG. In order to improve the visibility of fringes, the OPD should be reduced as much as possible.

The SPIDER imager samples the object visibility function in the Fourier domain and then digitally reconstructs an image. The spatial frequency domain (UV domain) is as follow:

$$\begin{cases} u = \Delta x/\lambda Z \\ v = \Delta y/\lambda Z \end{cases} \tag{2}$$

Where, Δx, Δy is length of baseline, λ is incident wavelength, Z is object distance. If the number of spectral channels is increased, the number of UV coverage will increase correspondingly, and the increase of spectral bands will increase the energy to the focal plane, which is very beneficial to imaging. Moreover it will increase the coherence length.

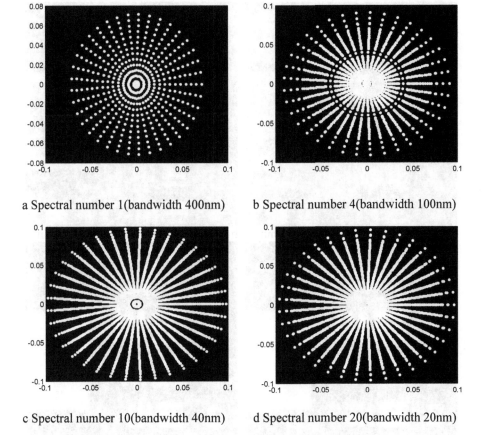

a Spectral number 1(bandwidth 400nm)   b Spectral number 4(bandwidth 100nm)

c Spectral number 10(bandwidth 40nm)   d Spectral number 20(bandwidth 20nm)

Fig. 6. UV coverage with different number of spectral channels of AWG

In SPIDER, AWG multiplexes a wide spectrum into several quasi-monochromatic channels. For an imaging system with 37 interferometer arms and 12 baselines for each interferometer arm, the number of UV sampling points is $12 \times 37 = 444$. As shown in Fig. 6, when the number of spectral channels is 4, 10 and 20, the UV coverage is shown in Fig. 6(b)–(d), in these three cases, the number of UV sampling points is 1776, 4440, 8880 respectively. Spatial frequency sampling multiplies with the increase of the number of spectral channels, and low frequency sampling is more intensive due to the radial arrangement of the interferometer arm.

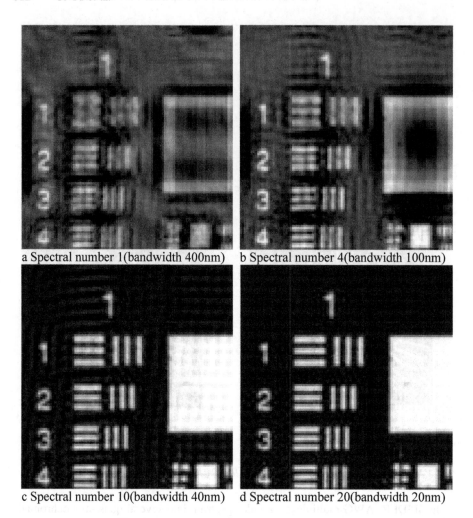

a Spectral number 1(bandwidth 400nm)   b Spectral number 4(bandwidth 100nm)

c Spectral number 10(bandwidth 40nm)   d Spectral number 20(bandwidth 20nm)

Fig. 7. Results of different UV coverage imaging

As shown in Fig. 7, the influence of different UV coverage on the imaging quality of Planar Interferometric Imaging System. With the increase of the number of spectral channels, the image quality is improved. It can be seen that increasing the number of spectrum channels of AWG can effectively improve the image quality of Planar Interferometric Imaging System. However, it can be seen from Fig. 7(c), (d), when the UV sampling points continue to increase, the improvement of imaging quality is not obvious.

Increasing the number of spectral channels of AWG can improve imaging quality, but it will multiply the number of output waveguides, Balanced Four-Quadrant Detection and other components, which will bring a burden to PIC integration. According to the analysis of Figs. 5 and 7, when the bandwidth is 10 nm–40 nm, the visibility of fringes can meet the requirements, and the imaging quality can be guaranteed.

4 Conclusion

AWG is one of the key components of interferometric imaging system based on PIC. The number of spectral channels of AWG affects the visibility of fringe and the quality of imaging. When the number of spectral channels of AWG is increased, the coherence length of the two beams and the visibility of the interference fringes are increased. The UV coverage is multiplied to improve the imaging quality; It is beneficial for design integrated optical devices separately in each spectral band, which is beneficial to the improvement of system performance. However The increase of the number of spectral channels of AWG will lead to the increase of waveguide output, thus increasing the burden of integration. According to the current development level of PIC, we can choose the number of spectral channels of AWG reasonably. Generally, the bandwidth of AWG is 10 nm–40 nm which can meet the requirement.

References

1. Duncan, A., Kendrick, R.: Segmented planar imaging detector for electro optic reconnaissance. US Patent No. 8913859 B1, United States, 16 December 2014
2. Kendrick, R., Duncan, A., Ogden, C., et al.: Flat panel space based space surveillance sensor. In: Advanced Maui Optical and Space Surveillance Technologies (AMOS) Conference, Maui, Hawaii (2013)
3. Scott, R., Su, T., Ogden, C., et al.: Demonstration of a photonic integrated circuit for multi-baseline interferometric imaging. In: 2014 IEEE Photonics Conference (IPC), San Diego, CA, USA, 12–16 October 2014
4. Badham, K., Duncan, A., Kendrick, R., et al.: Testbed experiment for SPIDER: a photonic integrated circuit-based interferometric imaging system. In: Advanced Maui Optical and Space Surveillance Technologies Conference (AMOS), Maui, Hawaii, USA (2017)
5. Shang, K., Payhak, S., Qin, C., et al.: Low-loss compact silicon nitride arrayed waveguide gratings for photonic integrated circuits. IEEE Photonics J. 9(5), 6601805 (2017)
6. Su, T.H., Liu, G.Y., Badham, K.E., et al.: Interferometric imaging using Si3N4 photonic integrated circuits for a SPIDER imager. Opt. Express 26(10), 12801–12812 (2018)
7. Su, T., Scott, R., Ogden, C., et al.: Experimental demonstration of interferometric imaging using photonic integrated circuits. Opt. Express 25(11), 12653–12665 (2017)
8. Chu, Q., Shen, Y., Yuan, M., et al.: Numerical simulation and optimal design of segmented planar imaging detector for electro-optical reconnaissance. Opt. Commun. 405, 288–296 (2017)
9. Duncan, A., Kendrick, R., Ogden, C., et al.: SPIDER next generation chip scale imaging sensor. In: Proceedings of the Advanced Maui Optical and Space Surveillance Technologies Conference, no. 1, p. 27, 15–18 September 2014, Maui, Hawaii, USA
10. Yu, Q., Wu, D., Chen, F.: Design of a wide-field target detection and tracking system using the segmented planar imaging detector for electro-optical reconnaissance. Chin. Opt. Lett. 16, 071101 (2018)
11. Yu, Q., Ge, B., Li, Y.: System design for a "checkerboard" imager. Appl. Opt. 57(35), 10218–10233 (2018)
12. Duncan, A., Kendrick, R.: Segmented planar imaging detector for electro-optic reconnaissance. U.S. Patent 8,913,859B1, 16 December 2014
13. Liang, Q.: Physical Optics. Publishing House of Electronics Industry (2012)

Remote Sensing Image Change Detection Algorithm Based on BM3D and PCANet

Yi Wan[1], Yongjin Liu[2], Qunnie Peng[2], Feiran Jie[2], and Delie Ming[1,2(✉)]

[1] National Key Laboratory of Science and Technology
on Multispectral Information Processing Technology,
Huazhong University of Science and Technology, Wuhan 430074, China
mingdelie@hust.edu.cn
[2] Science and Technology on Electro-optic Control Laboratory,
Luoyang 471009, China

Abstract. Image change detection is a process that analyzes images of the same scene taken at different times in order to identify changes that may have occurred between the multitemporal images. This letter proposes a remote sensing image change detection algorithm based on BM3D and PCANet. Firstly, the BM3D algorithm is utilized to remove the noise in the log-ratio image, then the gray level co-occurrence matrix (GLCM) and FCM algorithm are utilized to select the image patches which are used to train the PCANet model. Finally the pixels in the multitemporal images are classified by the trained PCANet model, the changed and unchanged pixels are combined to form the final change map. The experimental results obtained in this letter verify the effectiveness of the proposed algorithm.

Keywords: Remote sensing image · Change detection · BM3D · GLCM · PCANet

1 Introduction

With the development of science and technology, especially the rapid advancement of aerospace technology, humans can obtain various types of remote sensing images from high altitude through satellite. Among them, as an important application in remote sensing image analysis—change detection is widely used in the civil and military fields of the country [1]. Image change detection is a comparative analysis of multi-temporal images of the same location to obtain changes in the location and other attributes of the location. In the civil field, it is mainly used to monitor the development of urban land expansion, the geological environment changes in specific areas, especially the monitoring of natural disasters such as earthquakes, floods and forest fires [2]. For the military field, it is mainly used to monitor the deployment of military facilities, damage assessment after military strikes, etc. Therefore, the research of image change detection technology is significant to civil and military fields [3].

Since the multi-temporal remote sensing image is used for the change detection, it is inevitably affected by various noises due to multiple factors such as time and

© Springer Nature Singapore Pte Ltd. 2019
Y. Wang et al. (Eds.): IGTA 2019, CCIS 1043, pp. 524–531, 2019.
https://doi.org/10.1007/978-981-13-9917-6_50

weather. This makes the subsequent change detection analysis very difficult. The noise of the two images will be more serious, so it is an important part of this letter to suppress the correlation noise and improve the accuracy of the change detection. This letter applies the BM3D (Block-matching and 3D filtering) algorithm to the prepro-cessing stage of the change detection algorithm [4]. First, the logarithmic ratio of the two remote sensing images of different time phases is obtained to obtain the loga-rithmic ratio image, and then filtered by BM3D algorithm to obtain the final difference image. Then, the GLCM feature is extracted to form a feature vector [5], and then the FCM cluster is used to filter the changed pixels, the unchanged pixels and the unde-termined pixels to obtain a pre-classified change image [6]. Image block is taken centering on the changed pixel point and the unchanging pixel point, and is input as the training sample into the PCANet to train the model [7]. Finally, the undetermined pixel part is further divided into changed pixels and unchanged pixels through the trained PCANet model to obtain the final change detection map.

2 Methhodology

The framework of the proposed method in this paper is shown in Fig. 1.

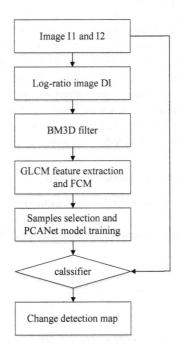

Fig. 1. Framework of the proposed method.

2.1   Block-Matching and 3D Filtering (BM3D)

The BM3D algorithm is mainly divided into two steps: firstly, we perform basic denoising through the original image matching to form a basic estimate. Then select an image reference block of size $N_1 \times N_1$ in the noisy image, and move to a plurality of reference blocks with a specific step size. Then search for the similar blocks in the area around each reference block and integrate them into a three-dimensional matrix. The similarity distance calculation method between the image block P_x and the image block P_y is as follows:

$$d(P_x, P_y) = \frac{\|P_x - P_y\|^2}{N_1 \times N_1} \tag{1}$$

Then, the formed three-dimensional matrix is three-dimensionally transformed, the noise is weakened by hard threshold processing on the transform domain coefficients, and then the estimation of all image blocks in the matrix is obtained through three-dimensional inverse transform. The resulting estimated block estimates are obtained by weighted averaging them to obtain a base estimate of the real image.

The second step is similar to the first step, but in block matching, the image is matched using the first step of the estimated image. Finding the similarity of similar blocks in the basic estimation graph by block matching forms two three-dimensional matrices: one is obtained by basic estimation, and the other is obtained by the coordinates of this matching in the original image with noise. Then, combined with Wiener filtering, the two three-dimensional matrices are three-dimensionally transformed, and the energy spectrum in the base estimation image is used as an energy spectrum to perform Wiener filtering on the three-dimensional matrix with noise. It is then inverse transformed to get an estimate of all image blocks and return them to their original position. Finally, the obtained estimated partial blocks are overlapped, and the final estimation of the real image is obtained by weighted averaging them.

2.2   Gray Level Co-occurrence Matrix (GLCM)

Gray level co-occurrence matrix (GLCM) is a method to describe image texture by studying the spatial correlation properties of image gray scale. The mathematical basis is the second-order moment combination conditional probability density function of the image:

$$P_{ij} = \frac{P_{ij}^{\delta\theta}}{\sum_{i=1}^{N_q} \sum_{j=1}^{N_q} P_{ij}^{\delta\theta}} \tag{2}$$

Where $P_{ij}^{\delta\theta}$ is the number of points where the gray values satisfying the conditions of δ and θ are i and j respectively. $\sum_{i=1}^{N_q} \sum_{j=1}^{N_q} P_{ij}^{\delta\theta}$ is the number of all points satisfying the conditions of δ and θ. P_{ij} is the probability that the number of points whose gradation values satisfy the δ and θ conditions are i and j respectively. δ is the step value of GLCM. θ is the generation direction of GLCM.

GLCM does not directly describe the texture features of the image. It needs to calculate a series of eigenvalues to characterize the texture. In this paper, four eigenvalues are selected, they are energy, contrast, inverse moment, and entropy. These four feature values are used to form a feature vector for the description of the image texture feature.

2.3 PCANet Model

PCANet is essentially a CNN network. In common CNN networks, the convolution templates of each layer in the network are randomly initialized. But PCANet uses the most basic PCA filter as the convolution layer filter, uses the binary hash coding process in the nonlinear layer, and uses the block extended histogram and the binary hash code in the resampling layer. The output of the sampling layer is the final feature extraction result of the entire PCANet network.

The first stage of PCANet: Around each pixel of the image, we take a patch of size $k_1 \times k_2$, and each patch is represented by a column vector, that is $x_{i,1}, x_{i,2}, \ldots,$ $x_{i,\tilde{m}\tilde{n}} \in \mathbb{R}^{k_1 k_2}$ where $x_{i,j}$ denotes the jth vectorized patch in image ϕ_i. Then We subtract patch mean from each patch and obtain $\bar{X}_i = [\bar{x}_{i,1}, \bar{x}_{i,2}, \ldots, \bar{x}_{i,mn}]$, where $\bar{x}_{i,j}$ is a mean-removed patch. Then we do the same works for the all image in the training set. Finally, we get the processed training sample matrix $X = [\bar{X}_1, \bar{X}_2, \ldots, \bar{X}_N] \in \mathbb{R}^{k_1 k_2 \times N\tilde{m}\tilde{n}}$. Assuming the number of filters in the layer i is L_i, the PCA algorithm is used to solve the standard orthogonal matrix V to minimize the reconstruction error.

$$\min_{V \in \mathbb{R}^{k_1 k_2 \times L_1}} \left\| X - VV^T X \right\|_F^2, \text{s.t.} V^T V = I_{L_1} \tag{3}$$

Where I_{L_1} is an identity matrix of size $L_1 \times L_1$. Then the corresponding PCA filters W_l^1 is

$$W_l^1 = mat_{k_1,k_2}\left(q_l\left(XX^T\right)\right) \in \mathbb{R}^{k_1 \times k_2}, l = 1, 2, \ldots, L_1 \tag{4}$$

Where $mat_{k_1,k_2}(v)$ denotes a function that maps the column vector v to a matrix of size $k_1 \times k_2$, $q_l(XX^T)$ denotes the l th main eigenvector of XX^T.

The second stage of PCANet: The mapping process of the second stage of PCANet is basically the same as that of the first stage. First, we calculate the mapped output of l th filter in the first stage $\phi_i^l = \phi_i * W_l^1$, i = 1, 2, ..., N, before we calculate the convolution operation, we must first perform the edge zeroing operation on the sample to ensure that the mapping result has the same size as the original image. Then we use the mapping output of the first stage as the input matrix of the second stage, $Y = [Y^1, Y^2, \ldots, Y^{L_1}] \in \mathbb{R}^{k_1 k_2 \times L_1 N \tilde{m} \tilde{n}}$, Then the PCA filters of the second stage are obtained as W_l^2.

$$W_l^2 = mat_{k_1,k_2}\left(q_l\left(YY^T\right)\right) \in \mathbb{R}^{k_1 \times k_2}, \ l = 1, 2, \ldots, L_2 \tag{5}$$

Since the first stage has L_1 filter kernels, L_1 output matrices are generated. For each input of the second stage, there are L_2 outputs, so the PCANet will generate $L_1 \times L_2$ Outputs: $O_i^l = \left\{\phi_i^l * W_l^2\right\}_{l=1}^{L_2}$.

The output stage of PCANet: we first binarize the filtered output of the second stage using a Heaviside step function whose value is one for positive input and zero otherwise. Then we calculate it as follows:

$$T_i^l = \sum_{l=1}^{L_2} 2^{l-1} H\left(\phi_i^l * W_l^2\right) \tag{6}$$

For each T_i^l, $l = 1, \ldots, L_1$, we partition it into B blocks of size $b_1 \times b_2$, then we calculate the histogram information h_k, $k = 1, \ldots, B$ for each block. We concatenate all the B histograms into one vector and denote as $Bhist\left(T_i^l\right) = [h_1, \ldots, h_B]$. Finally, the feature of the entire image can be expressed as

$$f_i = \left[Bhist\left(T_i^1\right), \ldots, Bhist\left(T_i^{L_1}\right)\right]^T \in \mathbb{R}^{(2^{L_2})L_1 B} \tag{7}$$

3   Experiment

In order to verify the feasibility and applicability of the proposed change detection algorithm, we select two data sets of remote sensing image. The first data set is the real image data of the Farmland D region of the Yellow River in 2008 and 2009, the second data set is the real image data of the Ottawa region in May 1997 and August 1997 (Figs. 2 and 3).

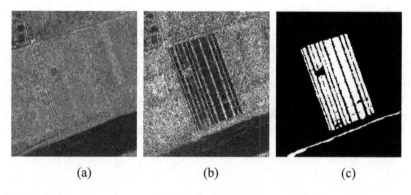

(a)   (b)   (c)

Fig. 2. Yellow River data set, (a) 2008.6, (b) 2009.6, (c) ground-truth change maps.

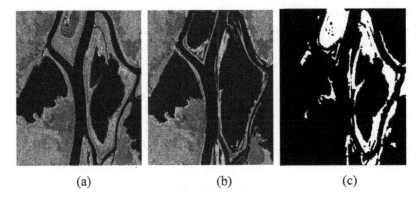

(a)   (b)   (c)

Fig. 3. Ottawa data set, (a) 1997.5, (b) 1997.8, (c) ground-truth change maps.

Follow the algorithm steps in this paper, we first get the log-ratio image by the log-ratio operator, and the BM3D algorithm is utilized to remove the noise in the log-ratio image, then GLCM feature vector and FCM algorithm are used to select pixels if interest that have high probability of being changed and unchanged. And the image patches centered at interested pixels are generated, they are used to train the PCANet model. Finally, the remaining pixels are separated into changed and unchanged classes using the trained PCANet model, the final change map is generated. In order to verify the applicability of the algorithm, we use other algorithms to do the comparative experiments. The methods are PCAKM [8], MRFFCM [9]. The results of experiment are shown in the Fig. 4.

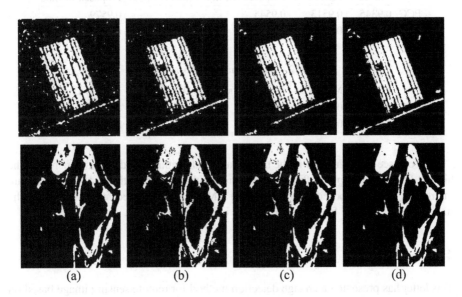

(a)   (b)   (c)   (d)

Fig. 4. The result of various change detection methods on the Yellow River data set and the Ottawa data set. (a) Results by PCAKM, (b) Results by MRFFCM, (c) Results by the proposed method without BM3D, (d) Results by the proposed method.

We use percentage correct classification (PCC) and Kappa coefficient (KC) as the performance evaluation of change detection. They are defined as follows

$$KC = \frac{PCC - PRE}{1 - PRE} \tag{8}$$

$$PCC = 1 - \frac{OE}{N} \tag{9}$$

$$PRE = \frac{(TP + FP) \cdot Nc + (FN + TN) \cdot Nu}{N^2} \tag{10}$$

$$TP = Nc - FN \tag{11}$$

$$TN = Nu - FP \tag{12}$$

$$OE = FN + FP \tag{13}$$

Where FN denotes the number of changed pixels are detected as unchanged, FP refers the number of unchanged pixels that are detected as changed, N refers the number of total pixels, Nc refers the number of changed pixels, Nu refers the number of unchanged pixels, TP refers the number of correctly changed pixels, TN refers the number of correctly unchanged pixels. The results are shown in Tables 1 and 2.

Table 1. Results on the Yellow River dataset.

	PCAKM	MRFFCM	Proposed method without BM3D	Proposed method
PCC	0.9345	0.9513	0.9545	0.9579
KC	0.7652	0.8238	0.8502	0.8675

Table 2. Results on the Ottawa dataset.

	PCAKM	MRFFCM	Proposed method without BM3D	Proposed method
PCC	0.9747	0.9779	0.9809	0.9830
KC	0.9035	0.9127	0.9303	0.9377

We can see from the data in the table that the algorithms used in this paper have the highest PCC and Kappa coefficients compared with other algorithms. And we compare the results of the proposed method without BM3D and proposed method, we find the importance of BM3D for image denoising in change detection.

4 Conclusion

This letter has presented a change detection method for remote sensing image based on BM3D and PCANet. The proposed method exploits the GLCM feature vector and FCM algorithm to select the image patches which are used to train the PCANet model.

And the proposed method is robust to the noise in image. And this will be the next works on how to reduce the running time of the algorithm.

References

1. Bruzzone, L., Bovolo, F.: A novel framework for the design of change-detection systems for very-high-resolution remote sensing images. Proc. IEEE **101**(3), 609–630 (2013)
2. Deng, J.S., Wang, K., Deng, Y.H., et al.: PCA-based land-use change detection and analysis using multitemporal and multisensor satellite data. Int. J. Remote Sens. **29**(16), 4823–4838 (2008)
3. Lv, P., Zhong, Y., Zhao, J., et al.: Change detection based on a multifeature probabilistic ensemble conditional random field model for high spatial resolution remote sensing imagery. IEEE Geosci. Remote Sens. Lett. **13**(12), 1965–1969 (2016)
4. Chierchia, G., El Gheche, M., Scarpa, G., et al.: Multitemporal SAR image despeckling based on block-matching and collaborative filtering. IEEE Trans. Geosci. Remote Sens. **55**(10), 5467–5480 (2017)
5. Haralick, R.M., Shanmugam, K.: Textural features for image classification. IEEE Trans. Syst. Man Cybern. **6**, 610–621 (1973)
6. Li, H., Celik, T., Longbotham, N., et al.: Gabor feature based unsupervised change detection of multitemporal SAR images based on two-level clustering. IEEE Geosci. Remote Sens. Lett. **12**(12), 2458–2462 (2015)
7. Chan, T., Jia, K., Gao, S., et al.: PCANet: a simple deep learning baseline for image classification? IEEE Trans. Image Process. **24**(12), 5017–5032 (2015)
8. Celik, T.: Unsupervised change detection in satellite images using principal component analysis and k-means clustering. IEEE Geosci. Remote Sens. Lett. **6**(4), 772–776 (2009)
9. Gong, M., Su, L., Jia, M., et al.: Fuzzy clustering with a modified MRF energy function for change detection in synthetic aperture radar images. IEEE Trans. Fuzzy Syst. **22**(1), 98–109 (2014)

Long-Tailed Contrastive Loss
for Video-Based Person Re-identification

Liqiang Bao$^{(\boxtimes)}$

School of Computer Science and Technology,
University of Chinese Academy of Sciences, Beijing 100049, China
`liqiang.bao@vipl.ict.ac.cn`

Abstract. Contrastive loss based deep metric learning has been generally used in video-based person re-identification, which learns a metric by preserving the distance between positive sample pairs close and negative sample pairs far on the embedding space. Yet contrastive loss still suffers not only from "hard" negative examples loosely defined by a hard margin, but also from severe sampling imbalance caused by equal sampling technique. To address these defeats, this paper presents a novel loss called Long-Tailed Contrastive Loss (LTCL). A Gaussian kernel function is used as the negative loss term, which takes into account the effect of long-range negative sample pairs. Meanwhile, a focusing factor is introduced for adaptive hard negative data mining and a rebalancing factor is used to compensate the sampling imbalance. Experiments conducted on two classic datasets demonstrate the effectiveness of the proposed method.

Keywords: Contrastive loss · Long-tailed contrastive loss ·
Hard margin · Sampling imbalance · Hard negative data mining

1 Introduction

To re-identify a person who has been previously captured by other non-overlapping cameras is commonly defined as the task of *person re-identification*. This task has been paid more and more attention for increasing concern of public safety and social service such as criminal tracking and missing people search. Important though it is, this task is quite challenging due to different environmental settings, view-port changes, illumination conditions, ineluctable occlusion and various appearances.

As the first application of person re-identification, image-based person re-identification has been extensively studied with methods falling into two categories. The first category contains approaches attempting to extract reliable feature representations [5,6,12,17,21], while the second category tries to learn a robust distance metric [1,8,22]. Recent DNN based methods combine these two processes into an end-to-end pipeline [4,25].

Massively studied as it is, image-based re-identification is recently considered of less potential than video-based re-identification. Being able to provide

© Springer Nature Singapore Pte Ltd. 2019
Y. Wang et al. (Eds.): IGTA 2019, CCIS 1043, pp. 532–540, 2019.
https://doi.org/10.1007/978-981-13-9917-6_51

rich samples and temporal information related to a person's motion, video-based re-identification is intuitively more close to the real world surveillance system. Existing classic methods for video-based re-identification include collecting interest-point descriptors over time [10] and analyzing biometric characteristics such as gait feature [2]. Karaman et al. [9] use a conditional random field (CRF) to model video so that similar images receive similar labels. Space-time features [11] are also learned to feed into a ranking function.

Recent state-of-the-art methods for video-based person re-identification have generally adopted deep metric learning that aims to learn an embedding representation of the data preserving the distance between similar data points close and dissimilar data far on the embedding space [16]. Due to lower computational cost than triplet loss, contrastive loss is particularly used in video-based re-identification. Specifically, Mclaughlin et al. [18] propose the first contrastive loss based DNN method (denote as CL) for video-based re-identification, which greatly improves the state-of-the-art. [23] propose to use contrastive loss together with attention vectors in both spatial and temporal dimensions between the extracted features. Chung et al. [3] design a two stream CNN architecture where each stream is a contrastive loss based Siamese network, thus spatial and temporal information can be learned separately.

Although yielding promising progress, contrastive loss still suffers from slow convergence and poor local optima [19]. This is mainly due to the lack of long-distance information of negative sample pairs. Contrastive loss uses the hinge loss function as its negative loss term, where a hard margin is applied to define "hard" examples, thus only the "hard" negative sample pairs whoes distances are within the margin have contribution to the loss, while the long-distance negative sample pairs are abruptly ignored. However, there is no absolute standard to judge whether a sample is hard or not in multi-identity case. For intractable classes whose intra-class distances are comparable to the margin, negative sample pairs with distances larger than the hard margin may also be hard enough.

Furthermore, contrastive loss generally applies equal sampling technique during training, which always inevitably leads to sampling imbalance. Sampling imbalance means the number of sampled pairs differs too much from the number of real sample pairs. Imagine we have m classes and each has n samples, then there are $\frac{1}{2}mn(n-1)$ possible positive sample pairs and $\frac{1}{2}m(m-1)n^2$ possible negative sample pairs in total. One concern rises that the imbalance between the positive pairs and negative pairs quickly becomes intractable when scaling up m or n. As a consequence, the training is inefficient as most pairs are negatives that contribute little intra-class information [14]. Though equal sampling is essential to avoid the class imbalance, it risks of slow convergence and poor local optima, because only limited negative classes are involved per each update during training [19].

In this paper, the negative loss term of contrastive loss is reformulated by a Gaussian kernel function, so that the loss is valid for negative sample pairs with even long distances (i.e., a globally effective loss function). The proposed loss has two hyperparameters, namely the focusing factor μ and the rebalancing factor γ.

Unlike the hard margin used in the hinge loss function, the focusing factor works like a soft margin, which is capable of performing hard negative data mining in a more adaptive and elegant way. And the rebalancing factor applies a relative weight to the negative loss term to regulate the sampling imbalance so that the weakened inter-class information is properly up-weighted.

2   Method

This section starts by discussing the contrastive loss, and then shows how modifications made in this paper to deal with the aforementioned problems.

2.1   Contrastive Loss

Contrastive loss was first proposed by LeCun [7] to learn a globally coherent nonlinear function that maps the input data evenly to the output manifold. Here, contrastive loss can be reformulated in the context of video-based re-identification.

Consider a pair of video sequences $(\mathbf{s}_i, \mathbf{s}_j)$, where each sequence consists of multiple consecutive frames of an unmatched person. A corresponding pair of feature vectors $\mathbf{v}_i = R(\mathbf{s}_i)$ and $\mathbf{v}_j = R(\mathbf{s}_j)$ are given as output after being processed using the feature extraction network. Objective function can be presented in two parts:

$$\mathcal{L}_P(i,j) = \frac{1}{2}\|\mathbf{v}_i - \mathbf{v}_j\|^2$$
$$\mathcal{L}_N(i,j) = \frac{1}{2}[\max(0, m - \|\mathbf{v}_i - \mathbf{v}_j\|)]^2$$

(1)

where $\|\mathbf{v}_i - \mathbf{v}_j\|$ is the Euclidean distance between the feature vectors, $m > 0$ is a margin. $\mathcal{L}_P$ refers to the loss function for positive pairs, in which sequences are from the same person, i.e., $i = j$, the loss function encourages the features $\mathbf{v}_i$ and $\mathbf{v}_j$ to be as close as possible in the Euclidean space, while $\mathcal{L}_N$, the loss function for negative pairs, encourages the features to be separated by a margin m.

2.2   Long-Tailed Contrastive Loss

In order to solve the problem that the loss of long-distance negative sample pairs is invalid in contrastive loss, A Gaussian kernel function is applied as the negative loss term, taking the place of the hinge loss function used in $\mathcal{L}_N$. With long-distance information used, a "maximum-margin" classification can be dynamically achieved in training.

Following the idea in [14] to apply OHEM with a special design in loss, a focusing factor μ is proposed to do the hard negative example mining job. In comparison with the "hard" margin, μ can be similarly considered a soft

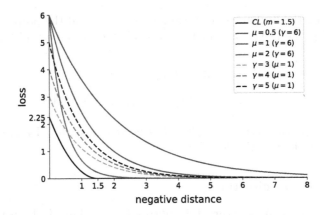

Fig. 1. Visualization of $\mathcal{L}_N$ for different μ and γ. For better understanding, the margin is manually set to 1.5 for CL. (better viewed in color)

margin, which regulates the relative balance of attention between the short-distance area and the long-distance area, meaning it adaptively defines the hard negative examples and further performs the hard negative data mining on them.

Sampling imbalance caused can be quite simply addressed by sampling more negative paris, yet a larger ratio rather than 1:1 brings in other unwanted problems, such as slow convergence. Thus a rebalancing factor γ is introduced to relatively compensate for the negative loss term instead of recruiting more negative sample pairs. Now the negative loss term can be written as:

$$\mathcal{L}_N = \gamma e^{-\mu \|\mathbf{v}_i - \mathbf{v}_j\|} \tag{2}$$

Visualization of $\mathcal{L}_N$ for several values of μ and γ is in Fig. 1. It can be observed that: (1) With the Gaussian kernel function applied, the loss of negative sample pairs is effective even when $\|\mathbf{v}_i - \mathbf{v}_j\|$ becomes very large. As $\|\mathbf{v}_i - \mathbf{v}_j\| \to \infty$, the loss of well-recognized sample pairs gradually vanished; (2) The focusing factor performs adaptive hard negative data mining by controlling the relative attention between short-distance area and long-distance area. For example, when $\mu = 2$, $\mathcal{L}_N$ mainly focuses on short-distance area, where the loss of negative pairs within the distance of 1.0 has a thumping majority. And as μ increases, the attention is extended to a longer range; (3) The rebalancing factor γ is only applied to the negative loss term $\mathcal{L}_N$, which directly compensate for the sampling imbalance. γ gives negative pairs an extra punishment while training, which makes us pay more attention to handle negative relationships. The larger γ is, the more compensation is made for the sampling imbalance.

Let $I(\cdot)$ denote a logic index function as follows:

$$I(i,j) = \begin{cases} 1 & i \text{ and } j \text{ belong to the same person} \\ 0 & \text{otherwise} \end{cases} \tag{3}$$

Combining the unchanged positive loss term $\mathcal{L}_P$ and the proposed negative loss term $\mathcal{L}_N$, the newly proposed contrastive loss can be completely reformulated as:

$$\mathcal{L}(R, i, j) = \frac{1}{2} I(i, j) \|\mathbf{v}_i - \mathbf{v}_j\|^2$$
$$+ \frac{1}{2}(1 - I(i, j))\gamma e^{-\mu\|\mathbf{v}_i - \mathbf{v}_j\|}. \tag{4}$$

This loss is named the *Long-Tailed Contrastive Loss* (LTCL), after the long-tailed curve of the negative loss term.

2.3   Network Architecture

In terms of network architecture, the network proposed in CL [18] is used, where each frame and its optical flow are first processed by a CNN to produce a feature vector representing the person's appearance and motion at a single time-step. Then the features are iteratively further processed by a RNN layer, and the outputs from all time-steps are summarized with temporal pooling. The use of RNN and temporal pooling is deemed to exploit temporal information within the sequence. A Siamese network that takes a pair of samples is used to accomplish the comparison between features with LTCL as the objective function. Simultaneously, softmax loss is also used for better performance.

3   Experiments

The proposed method for video-based re-identification is evaluated on two datasets: iLIDS-VID and PRID2011. Based on the assumption that the real person re-identification system should have the trajectory for each identity, the iLIDS-VID dataset contains 600 trajectories for 300 identities, where each person is represented by two video sequences captured by non-overlapping cameras. Due to heavy occlusion and various lighting conditions, iLIDS-VID is very challenging for re-identification task. The dataset PRID-2011 includes 385 and 749 trajectories coming from two non-overlapping cameras. Among them, only 200 people appear in both cameras. Problem of this dataset is that some trajectories are not well-synchronized, which mean the person might "jump" between consecutive frames. Following the protocol used in [18, 20], only the first 200 persons who appear in both cameras are considered.

In order to have a fair comparison, the experimental settings in CL [18] is strictly followed. More details can be found in [18].

3.1   Hyperparameters

In this experiment, How CMC curves varies with regard to the selection of different hyperparameters is investigated. Since there are two hyperparameters in

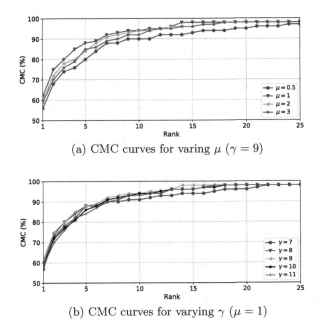

(a) CMC curves for varing μ ($\gamma = 9$)

(b) CMC curves for varying γ ($\mu = 1$)

Fig. 2. CMC curves for varying μ and γ on iLIDS-VIS dataset (better viewed in color).

the proposed loss function, verifying every combination would be ineffective and meaningless. Instead, the best performance is obtained by iteratively searching for the optimal state for each hyperparameter, and for simplicity, only integers are considered (except for $\mu = 0.5$). The tests performed on the iLIDS-VID dataset show that when $\mu = 1$ and $\gamma = 9$, the proposed approach gives the best performance, see Fig. 2.

Notice that when $\mu = 1$, LTCL shows the largest gain on CMC performance, meaning that the adaptive definition of hard negative examples is properly achieved at $\mu = 1$. A lower focusing factor, for example, $\mu = 0.5$, gives a worse performance, this is because the loss is gradually extended to a longer range, thus the hard negative examples are relatively down-weighted. As μ increases, the performance also shows a slow decline, which verifies the effectiveness of long-distance information. In a nutshell, it proves that the focusing factor successfully acts as a soft margin that adaptively performs the hard negative data mining.

Figure 2(b) illustrates that, as the rebalancing factor γ gets larger, the overall performance shows a tendency to rise first and then decrease slightly, indicating that the compensation for sample imbalance is reasonable. It is also noteworthy that when the maximum compensation performance is achieved, any sustained

Table 1. Comparison with related methods on iLIDS-VID and PRID-2011 datasets.

Dataset	iLIDS-VID				PRID-2011			
CMC rank	1	5	10	20	1	5	10	20
VR [20]	35	57	68	78	42	65	78	89
AFDA [13]	38	63	73	82	43	73	85	92
STA [15]	44	72	84	92	64	87	90	92
RFA [24]	49	77	85	92	64	86	93	98
CL [18]	58	84	91	96	70	90	95	97
LTCL	**62**	**88**	**94**	**98**	**76**	**94**	**99**	**99**

rise only brings a slight decline. This may be due to the very large sampling imbalance caused by the sampling technique, small permutation in rebalancing factor does not have a great impact.

3.2   Comparison with the State-of-the-Art

The performance of the proposed is compared against state-of-the-art approaches from the literature. The CMC results on two datasets are presented in Table 1. Comparing with the CL method, it can be confidently concluded that, with long-distance information and two hyperparameters used, the proposed method outperforms all mentioned methods by a great margin and reaches the start-of-the-art. LTCL achieves a remarkable overall improvement in matching rate on both PRID2011 dataset and even challenging iLIDS-VID dataset. And even for rank-1, it exceeds the CL method by 4% on iLIDS-VID and 6%. It can further observed that LTCL displays more robust generalization ability since on both datasets, LTCL shows a rapid increasement over CMC accuracies.

3.3   Evaluation Without Softmax Loss

Contrastive loss is one the most widely used loss for metric learning, but only a few have reported strong experimental performance using this loss alone, many have combined with classification loss to reach better performances. This may be due to the strict convergence condition while classification helps to alleviate this problem by enforcing a more discriminative model. Here the real power of CL and LTCL without using classification loss is investigated.

The CMC results of CL and LTCL without classification loss are showed in Table 2. It can observed that LTCL greatly outperforms CL on both datasets with absolute superiority, which indicates that the proposed LTCL is a more promising choice to learn expressive representations for metric learning tasks such as video-based re-identification.

Table 2. Comparison of CL and LTCL without classification loss on iLIDS-VID and PRID2011.

Dataset	iLIDS-VID				PRID-2011			
CMC rank	1	5	10	20	1	5	10	20
CL [18]	11	27	44	67	21	51	73	85
LTCL	21	50	70	83	42	72	82	90

4   Conclusion

The long-tailed contrastive loss is proposed in this paper for video-based person re-identification. To overcome the defeats of the conventional contrastive loss, the Gaussian kernel function is applied to take into account the long-distance negative information. Meanwhile, two hyperparameters are introduced to address the problems of hard negative data mining and sampling imbalance respectively. Results are evaluated on two standard datasets, which shows that the proposed LTCL outperforms the state-of-the-art methods from the literature. Moreover, experiments strongly support the superiority of the LTCL for metric learning.

References

1. Bar-Hillel, A., Hertz, T., Shental, N., Weinshall, D.: Learning a mahalanobis metric from equivalence constraints. J. Mach. Learn. Res. **6**(6), 937–965 (2005)
2. Boulgouris, N.V., Hatzinakos, D., Plataniotis, K.N.: Gait recognition: a challenging signal processing technology for biometric identification. IEEE Sig. Process. Mag. **22**(6), 78–90 (2005)
3. Chung, D., Tahboub, K., Delp, E.J.: A two stream Siamese convolutional neural network for person re-identification. In: Proceedings of the IEEE Conference on Computer Vision and Pattern Recognition, pp. 1983–1991 (2017)
4. Ding, S., Lin, L., Wang, G., Chao, H.: Deep feature learning with relative distance comparison for person re-identification. Pattern Recognit. **48**(10), 2993–3003 (2015)
5. Dong, S.C., Cristani, M., Stoppa, M., Bazzani, L., Murino, V.: Custom pictorial structures for re-identification, pp. 68.1–68.11 (2011)
6. Farenzena, M., Bazzani, L., Perina, A., Murino, V., Cristani, M.: Person re-identification by symmetry-driven accumulation of local features. In: Computer Vision and Pattern Recognition, pp. 2360–2367 (2010)
7. Hadsell, R., Chopra, S., Lecun, Y.: Dimensionality reduction by learning an invariant mapping. In: IEEE Computer Society Conference on Computer Vision and Pattern Recognition, pp. 1735–1742 (2006)
8. Hirzer, M., Roth, P.M., Kstinger, M., Bischof, H.: Relaxed pairwise learned metric for person re-identification. In: European Conference on Computer Vision, pp. 780–793 (2012)
9. Karaman, S., Bagdanov, A.D.: Identity inference: generalizing person re-identification scenarios. In: Fusiello, A., Murino, V., Cucchiara, R. (eds.) ECCV 2012. LNCS, vol. 7583, pp. 443–452. Springer, Heidelberg (2012). https://doi.org/10.1007/978-3-642-33863-2_44

10. Karanam, S., Li, Y., Radke, R.J.: Person re-identification with discriminatively trained viewpoint invariant dictionaries. In: IEEE International Conference on Computer Vision, pp. 4516–4524 (2015)
11. Klaser, A., Marszałek, M., Schmid, C.: A spatio-temporal descriptor based on 3D-gradients. In: 19th British Machine Vision Conference BMVC 2008, p. 275-1. British Machine Vision Association (2008)
12. Kviatkovsky, I., Adam, A., Rivlin, E.: Color invariants for person reidentification. IEEE Trans. Pattern Anal. Mach. Intell. 35(7), 1622–34 (2013)
13. Li, Y., Wu, Z., Karanam, S., Radke, R.J.: Multi-shot human re-identification using adaptive fisher discriminant analysis. In: British Machine Vision Conference, pp. 73.1–73.12 (2015)
14. Lin, T.Y., Goyal, P., Girshick, R., He, K., Dollr, P.: Focal loss for dense object detection (2017)
15. Liu, K., Ma, B., Zhang, W., Huang, R.: A spatio-temporal appearance representation for video-based pedestrian re-identification. In: IEEE International Conference on Computer Vision, pp. 3810–3818 (2015)
16. Lowe, D.G.: Similarity metric learning for a variable-kernel classifier. Neural Comput. 7(1), 72–85 (1995)
17. Ma, B., Su, Y., Jurie, F.: Local descriptors encoded by fisher vectors for person re-identification. In: Fusiello, A., Murino, V., Cucchiara, R. (eds.) ECCV 2012. LNCS, vol. 7583, pp. 413–422. Springer, Heidelberg (2012). https://doi.org/10.1007/978-3-642-33863-2_41
18. Mclaughlin, N., Rincon, J.M.D., Miller, P.: Recurrent convolutional network for video-based person re-identification. In: IEEE Conference on Computer Vision and Pattern Recognition, pp. 1325–1334 (2016)
19. Sohn, K.: Improved deep metric learning with multi-class n-pair loss objective. In: Advances in Neural Information Processing Systems, pp. 1857–1865 (2016)
20. Wang, T., Gong, S., Zhu, X., Wang, S.: Person re-identification by video ranking. In: European Conference on Computer Vision, pp. 688–703 (2014)
21. Wang, X., Doretto, G., Sebastian, T., Rittscher, J.: Shape and appearance context modeling. In: IEEE International Conference on Computer Vision, pp. 1–8 (2007)
22. Weinberger, K.Q., Saul, L.K.: Distance metric learning for large margin nearest neighbor classification. J. Mach. Learn. Res. 10(1), 207–244 (2009)
23. Xu, S., Cheng, Y., Gu, K., Yang, Y., Chang, S., Zhou, P.: Jointly attentive spatial-temporal pooling networks for video-based person re-identification (2017)
24. Yan, Y., Ni, B., Song, Z., Ma, C., Yan, Y., Yang, X.: Person re-identification via recurrent feature aggregation. In: European Conference on Computer Vision, pp. 701–716 (2016)
25. Yi, D., Lei, Z., Li, S.Z.: Deep metric learning for practical person re-identification, pp. 34–39. Computer Science (2014)

A Novel Image Super-Resolution Method Based on Cross Classification Trees and Cascaded Network

Yuan Lv, Ziqi Wang, Peiqi Duan, and Xuejing Kang$^{(\boxtimes)}$

Beijing University of Posts and Telecommunications, Beijing, China
{lvyuan,kangxuejing}@bupt.edu.cn

Abstract. In this paper, we propose an efficient and high-quality super-resolution method by combining Cross Classification Trees (CCTs)-based sample classification rule and Deep Forest mapping relationship. Firstly, we use a number of mapping kernels to divide sample space into overlapping subspaces and use decision trees to realize the classification function. In this process, the CCTs are used to classify samples, which can remarkably improve the coverage rate of the sample subspaces and increase the classification accuracy. Then, for each leaf node of CCTs, a Cascade Network (CN) is learned, which simultaneously uses priori and posteriori information to map low-resolution (LR) image patches to high-resolution (HR) image patches for each subspace. This is an ensemble approach in a data-dependent way with a larger sample and fewer hyper-parameters. Extensive experiment results demonstrate that the proposed method achieves better performance and costs less time.

Keywords: Image super-resolution · Decision trees ·
Cross Classification Tree · Random forest · Machine learning

1 Introduction

Single image super-resolution (SR) is a common fundamental problem in the field of image application, which is widely used in various fields and has a significant practical value. Single image SR method aims to reconstruct a high resolution (HR) image from low-resolution (LR) input that is generated from the HR image by a down-sampling process and a blurring process. This is well known as an ill-posed inverse problem [1] because the information will be lost in the nonlinear degradation process. Therefore, the solution of HR images estimated from an LR image may not be unique.

Multifarious SR methods have been proposed to improve the quality of natural images, such as sharp edges and rich texture. Among various SR methods, classic models can be mainly classified as interpolation-based [2, 3], reconstruction-based [4, 5] and learning-based methods [6–18]. Currently, state-of-the-art SR reconstruction methods with high quality are mostly implemented by external-example learning-based algorithms [8–17]. These methods obtain a set of optimized mapping models by endlessly training to estimate HR patches from their corresponding LR patches. ANR [12] method and its extended version A+ [11] divide training image patches into

© Springer Nature Singapore Pte Ltd. 2019
Y. Wang et al. (Eds.): IGTA 2019, CCIS 1043, pp. 541–552, 2019.
https://doi.org/10.1007/978-981-13-9917-6_52

clusters, and jointly learn HR/LR patch pair dictionary by least-squares. But it is difficult to reconstruct high-frequency information with a limited improvement of visual effect. As for k-means clustering and linear regression, they give preset weights which are trained by posterior probability to the nearest LR patches to reconstruct the HR image. However, it is time-consuming for the input image patches to find the closest clusters. Decision trees and random forest have also been used in image super-resolution (SR) methods to classify the natural image patch space into countable multivariate subspaces that are mutually exclusive to obtain a highly-fitting mapping. Nevertheless, it is time-consuming to train a high precision decision tree, because it is always necessary to have accurate data of manually labelled training set.

In this paper, we propose a novel super-resolution method by combing two methods together: a sample-classification decision tree based on Cross Classification Trees (CCTs) classification rule, and a mapping learning model based on Cascade Networks (CNs), which can obtain a more rational division of sample subspaces and guarantee reconstruction quality and speed at patch classification stage and linear regression stage. In the patch classification stage, we use the CCTs, a non-binary classification model, to divide sample space into overlapping subspaces to increase the coverage rate of the sample subspace and improve classification accuracy. And in the linear regression stage, we use the CNs to improve the quality of the reconstruction stage layer-by-layer. Our CNs is a set of hierarchical nets that can make full use of priori information to model their correspondences for each class. Also, the priori information can be learned by extracting the statistic relationship between LR and HR patches. Extensive experiment results demonstrate that the proposed method achieves less time-spending, as it is 43.1 s less than SCSR method and 1.31 s less than ANR method. Moreover, our method can increase the sample utilization rate and enhance the optimal regression results' coverage rate of the sample subspaces.

The rest of the paper is organized as follows. Section 2 introduces the relative work of classification and regression of natural image patch pairs. Section 3 introduces our super-resolution method based on the CCTs and the CNs regression model, and Sect. 4 describes the experiment of the proposed framework and presents the results of our method. Section 5 draws a conclusion.

2   Related Work

As a hotspot of SR, some researchers attempt to classify LR patches by applying Random Tree, Decision Trees or Deep Forest method, and to learn the mapping between LR and HR patches by sparse representation [8, 11, 12, 18–20] or multivariate regression [13, 15]. Broadly speaking, their testing processes aim to solve the following optimization problems:

$$\min_i \sum\nolimits_{i=1}^{k} \|S_i - f(l_i)\|_2^2 \tag{1}$$

$$\min_{c, M_c} \sum\nolimits_{c=1}^{k} \sum\nolimits_{l_i \in c} \|h_i - M_c l_i\|_2^2. \tag{2}$$

where l_i and h_i denotes LR and HR patch vectors collected from the training set, S_i represents the class that l_i belongs to, c is the class label or dictionary atom and M_c means the desired mapping of c. These methods tend to solve the following two core problems: the classification rule of external LR-HR patch pairs and the solving method of M_c. Appropriate sample classification rule and mapping solving method can ensure the optimization of the solutions of the Eqs. (2) and (3). In the testing process, LR patches find the corresponding c and generate desired HR patches through the corresponding mapping M_c. Next, we will introduce the related works of these two core problems.

Sample classification is the precondition of mapping-learning. Ordinarily, to obtain a set of highly-fitting mapping, sample space is classified into sets of multivariate subspaces that are mutually exclusive. The decision tree is a classic classification model of machine learning methods which is widely used in academic and commercial applications. The architecture of decision trees is optimized by training data and it also enjoys a lightweight forecast as a single path on the tree to divide sample space into countable clusters. However, to train a high precision decision tree, it is always necessary to have accurate data of manually labelled training set.

Besides, the mutual exclusive classification is not reasonable for the SR problem because numerous patches may not just belong to any of these subsets.

Zhou [9] uses Deep Forest methods as the classification basis. By using a non-differentiable model that does not use the BP algorithm and imitating the characteristics of layer-by-layer processing, in-model feature transformation and sufficient model complexity, the performance of representation learning is improved. However, though the accuracy of classification is improved, the high complexity still costs a large amount of time, and the unknowable and unexplainable problems also exist. Adaptive Tree method [10] improves classification accuracy by adding both decision trees for in-model feature transformation and pruning. However, in the process of training, a large number of samples are still left unused. Random forest-based methods [8] utilize Cascaded Decision Trees to form forests to classify samples. However, a binary classification-based method will inevitably lead to marginal error and sample waste. The CCTs classification approach we provide is an effective method to be applied in much more areas of data processing field.

3   The Proposed Super-Resolution Method

In this section, we propose an efficient and high-quality SR method that uses Cross Tree-based sample classification rule and obtains Cascade Network mapping relationship between LR and HR dimensional spaces. Figure 1 shows the flow chart of the proposed method. In the training process, we classify samples by using the CCTs based sample classification rule. Then, decision trees are learned for each non-leaf node and CNs are learned for each class (leaf node) which can obtain a highly-fitting mapping. In addition, a decision scheme is used to ensure the validity and reliability of node branching in real time. In the testing process, overlapping LR patches are matched with different leaf nodes by the Decision Tree and the mapping process is completed by the corresponding Deep Forest. Next, we will introduce our SR method in detail.

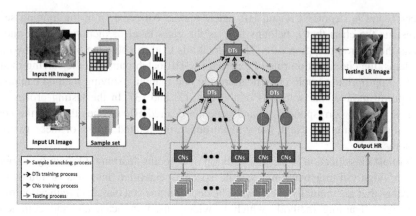

Fig. 1. The flow chart of our proposed method

3.1 Sample Classification Decision Tree Based on Cross Classification Tree

Inspired by [10], for one LR image, our method directly uses a neighbourhood patch of size $n \times n$ to amplify each pixel. Specifically, assuming that the up-sampling factor is s, we collect overlapping LR patch $l \in \mathbb{R}^{n \times n}$ from the training LR images, initialize them with bilinear or bicubic process, and find the corresponding HR patch $h \in \mathbb{R}^{1 \times 1}$ from HR images in the training process.

Different from the methods introduced above, which extract features of LR patch to classify LR-HR patch pairs, the proposed SR method uses Cross Classification Tree, which is the LR-to-HR mapping kernel of each sample, as the classification basis to classify the sample space into overlapping sample subspaces. Our method enhances the accuracy of classification by blurring the boundary of classification. Consider a vectorized single sample $p_k : \{l_k, h_k\}$, there exists a mapping relationship $h_k = m_k l_k$ and we define the matrix $m_k \in \mathbb{R}^{1 \times n^2}$ as the Sample Individual Mapping-Kernel (SIMK) of the sample p_k, which is calculated as $m_k = h_k l_k^{-1}$, where l_k^{-1} denotes the pseudo-inverse of l_k. According to this, the optimization Eq. (2) can be further expressed as:

$$\min_{c, M_c} \sum_{c=1}^{k} \sum_{m_i \in c} \|(m_i - M_c)l_i\|_2^2 \tag{3}$$

This equation clearly shows that for LR-HR patch-pairs in one class c, the aggregation degree of set $\{m_i \in c\}$ directly affects the optimization result. We randomly extract 10,000 sample-groups from the training set to calculate the difference of regression errors. In a sample space, we define the radiation energy of the mapping kernels E_n as

$$E_n = \log \frac{1}{d} \sum_{k=1} |h_k - ml_k| \tag{4}$$

The radiation range V as

$$V = \{h_i, l_i | E_i < \log \varepsilon\} \tag{5}$$

And the fraction of coverage v as

$$v = \frac{1}{d} \sum_{i=1} D_i, \quad \text{where} \quad D_i = \begin{cases} 1, E_i < \log \varepsilon \\ 0, E_i \geq \log \varepsilon \end{cases} \tag{6}$$

where E_i is the single-sample energy, ε is the error threshold and d is the sample number. Within the permitted range, a large sample space has small radiation energy, while the radiation range and the coverage rate is high. Also, the radiation energy is getting higher as it gets closer to the centre of radiation, and the radiation range also satisfy the acceptable regression error. We aim to reach the balance between the radiation energy and the radiation range. In binomial classification system or multinomial classification system, we divide the sample space into two or more mutually exclusive sample subspaces and obtain the mapping kernels of each LR-HR patch pair in its subspace by training each sample subspace. The mapping core is at the mapping centre. Since $V \subseteq P$, which means the radiation range is contained in the sample subspace, it could be easily seen that the radiation ranges of different mapping kernels do not intersect, and also it is easy to cause over-fitting problems. By blurring the boundaries of the sample subspace, we expand each sample subspace so that adjacent sample subspaces are included with each other, therefore the radiation ranges intersect (or tangent) to achieve the largest coverage of the sample space as a whole. Figure 2 shows the process of classification.

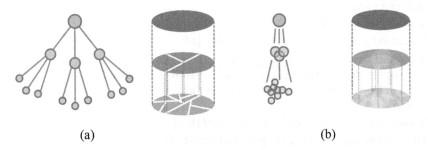

(a)   (b)

Fig. 2. (a) Traditional classification method and its coverage of sample subspaces, which are mutually exclusive, (b) CCTs classification method and its coverage of sample subspaces, which are overlapped.

The Decision Tree is an efficient structure and we utilize it to perform Cross Tree-based sample classification. The purpose of each branching process is to gradually approach the idealized optimal result of the Eq. (3). Specifically, we randomly collect LR-HR patch-pairs of the same scale as training sets multiple times from the sample set, and train q mapping kernels $\{m_i\}$ from the collected training sets.

After the sample sets $\{p_k^l\}(k = 1,\ldots,d)$ are processed by mapping kernels m_k, the error matrix $E \in \mathbb{R}^{q \times d}$ and data matrix $S \in \mathbb{R}^{q \times d}$ will be obtained. $E(q,d)$ and $S \in \mathbb{R}^{q \times d}$ satisfy the following constraint:

$$\text{If } E(i,k) = |m_k l_i - h_i| < \varepsilon, S(i,k) = 1, \text{ otherwise } S(i,k) = 0 \tag{7}$$

By calculating the equation, the sample space can be divided into r overlapping subspaces. Assume the number of classification subsets is t, then the number of possible combinations of the subspaces is $\binom{t}{r}$. We select the combination with the largest sample coverage rate as a classified subspace by the current non-leaf node. The algorithm mentioned above is listed in Algorithm 1.

Algorithm 1. The proposed node-branching process

Input: training set of the father node $\{fj\}$, validation set $\{vs\}$.

Initialization: vector the LR and HR patches to l and h, and standardize $\{fj\}$ to $\{fj|fj\epsilon\{l,h\}\}$.

1. randomly collect 100 groups of samples$\{fs\}$;

2. calculate m for each group sample as $\{m\}$;

3. **for** each LR/HR patch pairs of fj:

    Calculate the regression error$\{E_{i,j}|E_{i,j}\epsilon E\}$ of each m of $\{m\}$.

   end

4. statistical the coverage rate of each combination of m and chose the best combination $\{M\}$;

5. divide $\{fs\}$ into four child nodes $\{cs\}_1, \{cs\}_2, \{cs\}_3, \{cs\}_4$, by combination $\{M\}$ and error square E;

6. record the labels $\{z|z\epsilon\{1,2,3,4\}\}$;

7. learning a decision tree between $\{l\}$ and $\{z\}$;

8. **for** each validation sample $vs_k \in \{vs\}$

    put $l \in vs_k$ into the decision tree and determine the label z';

    Put $l \in vs_k$ into M, generate cgh_k and fgh_k;

   end

9. calculate the E_c between $\{cgh\}$ and $\{h|h\epsilon\{vs\}\}$.

10. calculate the E_f between $\{fgh\}$ and $\{h|h\epsilon\{vs\}\}$.

11. determine whether to divide the father node by comparing E_c and E_f.

3.2   Mapping Learning for LR Patch Based on Cascaded Network

Traditional learning-based algorithms require a large number of sample data and hyperparameters. Not only the training process is complicated, but high-performance equipment is also required. These limited the performance of the traditional algorithms. With the Deep Forest model, Zhou [9] enhanced the learning ability by introducing posterior in each layer and improved the accuracy of classification. Unlike Zhou's Deep Forest methods that only solve classification problem [9], we apply deep forest in mapping learning and uses Cascaded Network to achieve mapping learning. For training sets $p_k : \{l_k, h_k\}$, there exists $m \sim h_k l_k^{-1} (k = 1, \ldots, d)$, thus the optimization equation can be further expressed as:

$$\min_i \sum_{i=1}^{k} \|h_i - ml_i\|_2^2 \tag{8}$$

We collect the same number of samples from the sample set multiple times as the training set. The mapping kernels $m_c (c = 1, \ldots, x)$ is learned by BP algorithm. The sample sets $l_k \in \mathbb{R}^{1 \times n^2} (k = 1, \ldots, d)$ are passed to the mapping kernel m_c, thus we can obtain the error matrix $E \in \mathbb{R}^{x \times d}$, and furthermore, obtain the average error coefficient $\varepsilon_k (k = 1, \ldots, x)$, which represents the performance of regression of the mapping kernel. We then select w best networks with the smallest ε_k from c mapping kernels and link the mapping result to the end of the sample set to get the next training set $p_k^2 : \{l_k^2, h_k\}$, where $l_k^2 \in \mathbb{R}^{1 \times (n^2 + w)}$. We further calculate the mapping kernel m_c^2 by BP algorithm. The end-to-end optimization equation can also be further expressed as:

$$\min_i \sum_{i=1}^{k} \left\| h_i - m_c^2 \left(l_i + \sum_{c=1}^{w} m_c^1 l_i \right) \right\|_2^2 \tag{9}$$

As the above method shows, we can train the Cascaded Network to any depth. This Cascaded Network uses the prediction of one layer as the priori of the input of the next layer to improve the performance of each layer. Meanwhile, it limits the error from accumulating when iterating. This improves the depth and complexity of the network and ensures the optimization of the SR method.

4 Experiment

In this section, we first discuss the optimal settings of the parameter sets of the Cross Tree, the Cascaded Network and the Decision Tree size. Then, to demonstrate the superiority of our SR quality, the proposed method is compared with several state-of-the-art methods in terms of objective and visual quality assessments. In our experiments, we use 88 images as the training set. To further improve the diversity of training images, we generate 704 images from these 88 images through the mirror and rotation transformation. In the training and testing process, LR input images are created by downsizing HR images with Bicubic interpolation and Gaussian blur. In order to balance the reconstruction quality and speed, we collect LR patches with size 5×5 from the training set. To objectively evaluate the SR quality, PSNR, SSIM [14] and runtime are applied for objective quality assessments. The experiments are implemented on a computer with Intel-i7, 3.2 GHz CPU and 16G memory under Windows 10 system, and the simulation environment is MATLAB R2017b.

4.1   The Network Parameter Set of Cascaded Network and Decision Tree

Our method uses the BP algorithm to train our Cascaded Network. Proper network parameter set can optimize network performance and runtime. For Cascaded Network, the input and output vector sizes are 25×1 and 1×1 respectively. And the input and output vector sizes of the first layer are 25×1 and 4×1 respectively. The rest are 29×1 and 4×1 respectively. We choose the average value of the outputs as the final mapping result of each patch. We use a four-layers network model to achieve high accuracy regression mapping, which includes three hidden layers. We set the numbers of nodes in each layer of mapping network to $\{25, 16, 9, 4, 1\}$, which can achieve desired classification accuracy as well as fast speed. In the process of training the Cascaded Network, we randomly collect 100 groups of samples from the sample set to train 100 mapping kernels, and each group contains 600,000 samples. By testing their performances, we select 4 best networks. As Fig. 3 shows, with the number of the cascades increases, the regression optimizes as the depth of the network equals 3.

Similarly, the scale of Decision Trees also affects the reconstruction quality and speed of SR. To expand the sample space, each sample in the sample space is labelled with the subspace it belongs to. We randomly collect 100 groups of samples from the expanded sample set to train the Decision Tree, and each group contains 1,000,000 samples. By testing the impact of the smallest sample in a leaf node on the performance of the Decision Tree, the value *minleaf* is set to prune the Decision Tree and generate optimized Decision Tree. And we select the best Decision Tree by classification accuracy test.

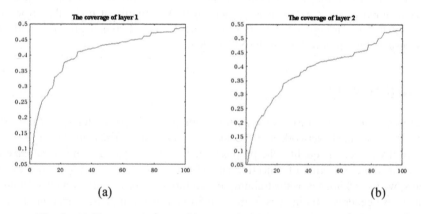

Fig. 3. (a) The coverage rate of layer 1, (b) The coverage rate of layer 2

4.2   The Determination of the Decision Tree Size

To ensure the validity of node branching, we design a validity check to control the expansion of the Cross Tree. Generally, when the classification accuracy is reliable, the more classes there are, the better fitting degree of the m-NN obtained for each class will be.

By BP algorithm, we use a three-layers network model to achieve mapping, which includes two hidden layers. The numbers of nodes in each layer of the mapping net are set as {25, 15, 16, 9, 4, 1} to obtain 100 mapping kernels. From the sample set, we randomly collect 100 groups of samples, which contains 600,000 samples each, and pass them into each mapping kernel. We then label each sample with a mapping result that is less than 0.5. When the number of networks reaches 97, the sample space could be covered completely.

To obtain a larger fraction of sample coverage and a faster speed of classification, we select and divide the 4 best networks. There will be 3,921,225 different kinds of combinations. The average fraction of coverage of a single network is 36.7%. By selection, the combination with the highest coverage rate could be 78.6%. The labelled sample is used as the sample set of the subspace in the next layer. A single sample could be classified into multiple classes. When the average mapping capacity of the child node is lower than the parent node, the parent node is set as a leaf node to stop the growth of the branch.

4.3   The Quantitative Evaluation of Single Image SR

In our method, we calculate the PSNR and runtime for both visual and objective quality evaluation. Table 1. shows the results of PSNR and runtime of our method compared with other algorithms. The proposed method yields the fastest reconstruction speed with acceptable reconstruction quality. This is obvious that our method shortens the runtime, and the lightweight Cascade Network can also greatly reduce the reconstruction time. Extensive experiment results show that the proposed CCTs method achieves on less time-spending, as it is 43.1 s less than SCSR [8] method and 1.31 s less than ANR [12] method. Figure 4 shows the result of the reconstructed images (Fig. 5).

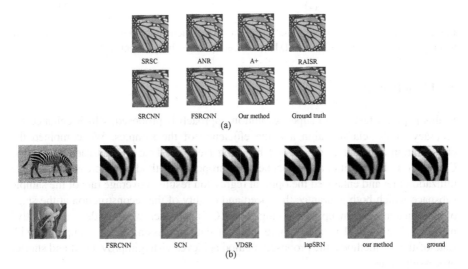

Fig. 4. (a) The comparison of the reconstruction of butterfly_GT by different methods, (b) The comparison of the reconstruction by different methods

Table 1. The results of PSNR (dB), SSIM and runtime(s) on the Set5

Set5 images	Bicubic			SCSR			ANR			A+			SRCNN			Our methods		
	PSNR	SSIM	Time	PSNR	SSIM	Time	PSNR	SSIM	Time	PSNR	SSIM	Time	PSNR	SSIM	Time	PSNR	SSIM	Time
baby_GT	36.5	0.93	–	37.6	0.94	110	38.1	0.92	2.86	38.2	0.93	38.1	38.1	0.95	4.77	32.27	0.93	2.24
bird_GT	36.0	0.96	–	38.5	0.97	31	39.2	0.97	1.61	40.1	0.97	40.1	40.1	0.98	1.72	34.11	0.95	0.75
butterfly_GT	26.8	0.88	–	29.7	0.93	25	29.7	0.92	0.66	31.0	0.92	31.5	31.5	0.94	1.52	27.97	0.93	0.90
head_GT	34.5	0.79	–	35.2	0.82	28	35.4	0.81	**1.01**	35.6	0.81	35.5	35.5	0.83	1.96	29.99	0.77	0.98
woman _GT	31.5	0.93	–	33.6	0.95	27	33.9	0.92	1.02	34.6	0.93	34.7	34.7	0.96	1.61	31.34	0.94	0.75
Average	33.05	0.90	–	34.90	0.92	44.2	35.29	0.91	1.43	35.89	0.91	35.98	35.98	0.93	2.32	31.14	0.91	1.12

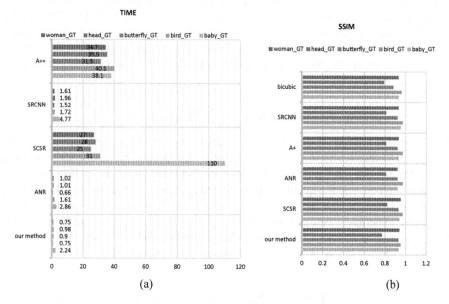

Fig. 5. (a) The comparison of time spent on reconstructing different pictures by different methods. (b) The comparison of SSIM of different pictures by different methods.

5   Conclusion

In this paper, a fast image super-resolution approach is proposed, which enhance the accuracy of the classification and the efficiency of the samples. We combined the classification and regression process by using Decision Tree and Cascaded Network. Compared to the traditional approaches, our proposed method can increase the sample utilization rate and enhanced the optimal regression results' coverage rate of the sample subspace which both guarantee the speed and quality of the reconstruction at the stage of classification and mapping-learning. The CCTs approach we provide is an effective method to be applied in much more areas of data processing field. Comparing with state-of-the-art methods, the proposed method achieves visual improvement and shorter processing time.

Acknowledgment. This work was supported in part by the National Natural Science Foundation of China (61701036).

References

1. Kim, K.I., Kwon, Y.: Single-image super-resolution using sparse regression and natural image prior. IEEE Trans. Pattern Anal. Mach. Intell. **32**(6), 1127–1133 (2010)
2. Hou, H.S., Andrews, H.C.: Cubic splines for image interpolation and digital ltering. IEEE Trans. Image Process. **26**, 508–517 (1978)
3. Zhang, X., Wu, X.: Image interpolation by adaptive 2-D autoregressive modeling and soft-decision estimation. IEEE Trans. Image Process. **17**, 887–896 (2008)
4. Zhang, X., Jiang, J., Li, J., Peng, S.: Manifold learning-based sample selection method for facial image super-resolution. Opt. Eng. **4**(51), 7003 (2012)
5. Zhang, X., Jiang, J., Peng, S.: Commutability of blur and affine warping in super-resolution with application to joint estimation of triple-coupled variables. IEEE Trans. Image Process. **21**(4), 1796–1808 (2012)
6. Buades, A., Coll, B., Morel, J.M.: A review of image denoising algorithms, with a new one. SIAM Journal on Multiscale Modeling and Simulation **4**(2), 490–530 (2005)
7. Takeda, H., Farsiu, S., Milanfar, P.: Kernel regression for image processing and reconstruction. IEEE Trans. Image Processing **16**(2), 349–366 (2007)
8. Yang, J., Wright, J., Huang, T.S., Ma, Y.: Image super-resolution via sparse representation. IEEE Trans. Image Process. **19**(11), 2861–2873 (2010)
9. Chang, H., Yeung, D.Y., Xiong, Y.: Super-resolution through neighbor embedding. In: Proceedings of the 2004 IEEE Computer Society Conference on Computer Vision and Pattern Recognition, CVPR 2004, Washington, DC, USA, USA (2004)
10. Li, B., Chang, H., Shan, S., Chen, X.: Locality reserving constraints for super-resolution with neighbor embedding. In: 2009 16th IEEE International Conference on Image Processing (ICIP), Cairo, Egypt (2009)
11. Timofte, R., Smet, V.D., Gool, L.V.: Adjusted anchored neighborhood regression for fast super-resolution. In: Asian Conference on Computer Vision (2014)
12. Timofte, R., Smet, V.D., Gool, L.V.: Anchored neighborhood regression for fast examplebased super-resolution. In: 2013 IEEE International Conference on Computer Vision, Sydney, NSW, Australia, 1–8 December 2013
13. Choi, J.S., Kim, M.: Super-interpolation with edge-orientation-based mapping kernels for low complex 2x upscaling. IEEE Trans. Image Process. **25**(1), 469–482 (2016)
14. Zhao, Y., Wang, R., Jia, W., Yang, J., Wang, W., Gao, W.: Local patch classification based framework for single image super-resolution, arXiv:1703.04088 (2017)
15. Romano, Y., Isidoro, J., Milanfar, P.: Rapid and accurate image super resolution, arXiv: 1606.01299, June 2016
16. Dong, C., Loy, C.C., Tang, X.: Accelerating the super-resolution convolutional neural network, arXiv:1608.00367, August 2016
17. Dong, C., Loy, C.C., He, K., Tang, X.: Learning a deep convolutional network for image super-resolution. In: Fleet, D., Pajdla, T., Schiele, B., Tuytelaars, T. (eds.) ECCV 2014. LNCS, vol. 8692, pp. 184–199. Springer, Cham (2014). https://doi.org/10.1007/978-3-319-10593-2_13
18. Tanno, R., Arulkumaran, K., Alexander, D.C., Criminisi, A., Nori, A.: Adaptive neural trees, arXiv:1807.06699v1 (2018)

19. Huang, J.: Learning hierarchical decision trees for single-image super-resolution. IEEE Trans. Circuits Syst. Video Technol. **27**(5), 937–950 (2017)
20. Huang, J., Siu, W., Liu, T.: Fast image interpolation via random forests. IEEE Trans. Image Process. **24**(10), 3232–3245 (2015)
21. Liu, Z., Siu, W.: Cascaded ramdom forests for fast image super-resolution. In: IEEE International Conference on Image Processing (2018)
22. Zhou, Z., Feng, J.: Deep forest: towards an alternative to deep neural networks. In: Proceedings of the Twenty-Sixth International Joint Conference on Artificial Intelligence (2017)
23. Wang, R., Han, C., Li, M., Guo, T.: Single image super-resolution reconstruction based on edge-preserving with external and internal gradient prior knowledge. In: Chen, C.-S., Lu, J., Ma, K.-K. (eds.) ACCV 2016. LNCS, vol. 10116, pp. 191–205. Springer, Cham (2017). https://doi.org/10.1007/978-3-319-54407-6_13

Diagnostic Classification of Pulmonary Nodules Using a Multi-scale and Multi-input DenseNet

Mengsong Wang, Hansheng Li, Yifan Wu, Qirong Bu[✉],
and Jun Feng

Department of Information Science and Technology, Northwest University,
Xi'an 710127, China
boqirong@nwu.edu.cn

Abstract. Pulmonary nodule is the early symptoms of lung cancer. Diagnosis classification of pulmonary nodule from CT is a challenging task. Recently, Convolution Neural Networks (CNNs) have been proposed to address this task. However, the inexplicability of deep networks make it is difficult for Radiologists to accept. In this paper we present a Multi-scale and Multi-input DenseNet (MsMi-DenseNet). First, MsMi-DensNet mixes multiple window widths and levels together to gain more information from the CT images. Second, MsMi-DenseNet combines the features of two scales of nodule images. Third, in order to improve the interpretability of deep networks, the manual features of nodule are added to the network to be trained. We tested MsMi-DenseNet on the LIDC-IDRI dataset, the sensitivity, specificity, accuracy of the network and the area of ROC curve are 96.65%, 92.93%, 94.17% and 0.9820 respectively. Comparing with the existing methods, MsMi-DenseNet has made significant improvements in the diagnosis of pulmonary nodules.

Keywords: Pulmonary nodules diagnosis · Computed Tomography ·
Manual feature · Computer Aided Diagnosis

1 Introduction

Lung cancer is the most common cause of cancer death in worldwide. In 2015, 1.69 million people dead due to lung cancer. In 2018, about 234,030 new cases are diagnosed as lung or bronchial cancer, and the number of deaths reached 154,050 [1]. Therefore, how to improve the diagnose accuracy of lung cancer is very important. Diagnosing lung cancer in early stage is the key to improve the survival rate of the patients. Pulmonary nodules are the early symptoms of lung cancer, which can be effectively detected by low-dose Computed Tomography (CT) and it has been proved that can reduce the mortality rate of pulmonary cancer [2]. But there are subtle differences between benign and malignant pulmonary nodules, lung cancer diagnosis is an arduous task even for expert doctors. Besides, the result of CT diagnosis relies heavily on subjective experience of clinicians, and results are not very reliable. Based on the above reasons, computer aided diagnosis (CAD) can provide a non-invasive solution and objective prediction for assisting radiologists with pulmonary nodules diagnosis.

© Springer Nature Singapore Pte Ltd. 2019
Y. Wang et al. (Eds.): IGTA 2019, CCIS 1043, pp. 553–564, 2019.
https://doi.org/10.1007/978-981-13-9917-6_53

There are two types of CAD for nodule classification: Classification model based on manual extraction features [3–5] and deep neural network based on automatic feature extraction [6–11]. The first method usually extracts the low-level features from pulmonary nodules, such as size, position, shape, texture and so on. Then selecting classifiers to determine benign or malignancy of the pulmonary nodules. Li et al. predicted the two properties of "texture" and "subtlety" through five texture features of pulmonary nodules [12]. Zionvev et al. extracted 64 low-level features from the shape, size, grayscale and texture, then use the support vector machine and decision tree to predict the semantic attributes such as "subtlety", "margin" and "malignancy" [13]. However, since it is not easy to extract and select useful subsets of pulmonary nodule features, more researchers have focused their study on the second method, the method which is based on deep neural network and can learn the diagnostic features of lung CT images automatically. In literature [14], Dey et al. proposed multi-scale input, and fuse the features from every Dense Block to do classification, resulting in 90.40% accuracy and 90.47% sensitivity, and the area of AUC is 0.9548. Although the deep learning model has achieved good results in the field of classification, it is just a "black box", we don't know what features are used,which is difficult to be accepted by radiologists and clinicians.

Therefore, we simulate the doctor's diagnostic process to train the classification model in this paper. First, inspired from the doctor's observation CT images process, we translate our data into the three-channel data which different channel has different window widths and window levels. This enriches the information of the nodule because different sizes of pulmonary have more information and can provide help to the classification of the nodules. We use multi-window widths and multi-window levels data at two scales as the input of the deep network. This can fuse the training features of the two input sizes and can make the classification diagnosis of benign and malignant pulmonary nodules more accurately. To further improve the performance, manual features (semantic, texture, size and morphological features) of pulmonary nodules were added to the deep network.

Our contributions are outlined as follows:

- We propose a multi-scales multi-inputs DenseNet (MsMi-DenseNet) algorithm in this paper.
- The proposed MsMi-DenseNet utilizes multiple window widths and window levels, which enriches nodule information. Manual features are also exploited to improve the performance of the task.
- Extensive experiments are implemented on LIDC-IDRI dataset, which shows that the proposed MsMi-DenseNet achieves the best performance in terms of segmentation, attributes and malignancy prediction compared with previous the state-of-the-art methods. The sensitivity, accuracy and specificity of the method in our paper are 96.65%, 94.17%, 92.93%, and the ROC curve area is 0.9823.

2   Pulmonary Nodules Diagnosis with MsMi-DenseNet

In the paper, we proposed a new deep network framework: MsMi-DenseNet. As showed in Fig. 1, the framework has multi-inputs and single-output. The four inputs are the two scales pulmonary nodule images and the corresponding 68-dimensional manual features. The MsMi-DenseNet network framework combines the features of the pulmonary nodules and the environmental information of the tissues and organs around them, which is more conducive to the benign and malignant classification of pulmonary nodules. The manual features are added to the MsMi-DenseNet network for training, combining traditional features and deep can enrich classification feature set, which was also conducive to the application of CAD in clinical medicine accepted by doctors.

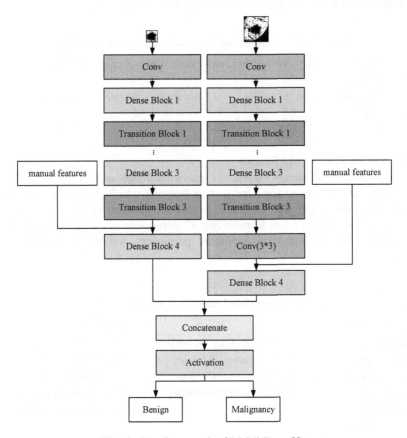

Fig. 1. The framework of MsMi-DenseNet

2.1   Extracting the Manual Features of Pulmonary Nodule

Due to the lack of medical image data, deep networks cannot extract valid features, so adding some manual features will help provide classification performance.

The CT image of the lung is a grayscale DICOM image with a 512 * 512 resolution. The difference in grayscale reflects the difference in the absorption of X-rays by organs. In the process of benign and malignant diagnosis of pulmonary nodules, doctors mainly judge the morphological features, texture features and size features of pulmonary nodules, as well as some of the most commonly used semantic features, such as lobulation, spiculation, calcification, cavity and roundness, etc.

(1) Extraction of semantic features
   The dataset used in this paper contains nine semantic features for each nodule, namely "subtlety", "internal structure", "calcification", "sphericity", "margin", "lobulation", "spiculation", "texture" and "malignancy", the grade of this features is shown in Table 1. In this paper, the first eight features are added to the manual feature set for the training of the classification model.

Table 1. The semantic attribute grade of pulmonary nodules

Attribute	subtlety	internal structure	calcification	sphericity	–
Grade	5	4	6	5	–
Attribute	margin	lobulation	spiculation	texture	malignancy
Grade	5	5	5	5	5

(2) Extraction of low-level features
   The image of pulmonary nodule is a grayscale image, and its low-level features mainly include shape, size, and texture features, which play a vital role in the diagnosis of benign and malignant pulmonary nodules. In this paper, 15 morphological features, 5 size features and 40 texture features were extracted to form a 60-dimensional low-level feature of pulmonary nodules. It is illustrated in Table 2.

Table 2. The low-level features of pulmonary nodules

Morphological features		Size features
X_1: plumpness	X_6: Circular Error Probable	X_{16}: area
X_2: eccentricity	X_7: the number of convex	X_{17}: Perimeter
X_3: Rectangularity	X_8: the number of concave	X_{18}: EquivDiameter
X_4: compactness	X_9–X_{15}: invariant moments	X_{19}: MajorAxisLength
X_5: circularity		X_{20}: MinorAxisLength
Texture features 1 110		
X_{21}–X_{28}	The features calculated from gray level co-occurrence matrix (the mean and variance of energy, entropy, moment of inertia correlation at 0°, 45°, 90°, 135°)	
X_{29}–X_{60}	32-dimensional Gabor texture features 101	

The specific steps we extracted the morphological features and size characteristics of the pulmonary nodule are as follows:

Step1: Extracting the coordinates of pulmonary nodules.
Step2: According to the coordinates, binarizing the CT image.
Step3: Calculating the fullness, eccentricity, and squareness of pulmonary nodules.
Step4: The convex and concave points on the edge of pulmonary nodules are calculated according to the contour coordinates.

In LIDC-IDRI dataset, the nodule boundaries on each CT slice were independently drawn by four radiologists and stored in xml files. In order to make the nodule boundaries more authoritative, radiologists only consider the nodules labeled with three or four radiologists. The combined rule of three or four different figures of a nodule on each slice is to extract all image pixels within the drawing boundary and select at least three intersections drawn by the radiologist as the nodule area in the slice. The algorithm of extracting the intersection region on a single 2D image slice is outlined as follows.

Step 1: Read all the pixels on the boundary of the nodule in a single image slice.
Step 2: Fill the inner pixels inside each of the radiologists' painting boundaries.
Step 3: Calculate the times (t_n) of each pixel being contained by all the boundaries.
Step 4: Label the inner pixels with $t_n \geq 3$.
Step 5: Combine the labeled pixels as the final region data in one 2D slice of the candidate nodule.

The CT image of the lung covers the physiological organization and structural information of the pulmonary nodules. Therefore, in addition to extracting the morphological features and size features of pulmonary nodules, we also extracted some texture features of pulmonary nodules. For the extraction of texture features, we mainly used the Haralick feature of 8-dimensional in gray scale co-occurrence matrix and the texture feature of 32-dimensional Gabor filter.

2.2 Multi-scales and Multi-inputs DenseNet

Nowadays, because the deep network is still only a "black box", most doctors still have difficulty accepting the results obtained by the deep network. The doctors can understand the meaning of traditional manual features. Therefore, we improve the DenseNet [15] and proposes a MsMi-DenseNet for the diagnosis of benign and malignant pulmonary nodules. Combining depth features with traditional features improves performance and makes it easier for doctors to understand.

Firstly, we modified the format of input data for DenseNet network. The original lung CT image is the DICOM image, a lossless format that contains a wealth of lesion information. The depth of each pixel may be 8 bits, 16 bits, 32 bits etc. But the pixel on ordinary JPEG and BMP images is only 8 bits. The input of the DenseNet is mostly JPEG and BMP format images. If the DICOM images are converted to JPEG or other formats, information loss is inevitably during the conversion process. In order to avoid the loss of information affecting the benign and malignant classification of pulmonary nodules, we made the original data into Python 16bit npy data storage format and

Table 3. The structure and parameters of MsMi-DenseNet

Layers	Output size (50 * 50)		Output size (100 * 100)		MsMi-DenseNet
	Feature map	Channels	Feature map	Channels	
Convolution	25 * 25	64	50 * 50	64	7 * 7 conv, stride 2
Pooling	13 * 13	64	25 * 25	64	3 * 3 max pool, stride 2
Dense Block (1)	13 * 13	256	25 * 25	256	$\begin{bmatrix} 1*1 & conv \\ 3*3 & conv \end{bmatrix} * 6$
Transition Layer (1)	13 * 13	128	25 * 25	128	1 * 1 conv
	6 * 6	128	12 * 12	128	2 * 2 average pool, stride 2
Dense Block (2)	6 * 6	512	12 * 12	512	$\begin{bmatrix} 1*1 & conv \\ 3*3 & conv \end{bmatrix} * 12$
Transition Layer (2)	6 * 6	256	12 * 12	256	1 * 1 conv
	3 * 3	256	6 * 6	256	2 * 2 average pool, stride 2
Dense Block (3)	3 * 3	1024	6 * 6	1024	$\begin{bmatrix} 1*1 & conv \\ 3*3 & conv \end{bmatrix} * 24$
Transition Layer (3)	3 * 3	512	6 * 6	512	1 * 1 conv
	1 * 1	512	3 * 3	512	2 * 2 average pool, stride 2
Concatenate Layer (1)	1 * 1	512	1 * 1	512	3 * 3 conv
		580	1 * 1	580	68-dimensional manual features
Dense Block (4)	1 * 1	1092	1 * 1	1092	$\begin{bmatrix} 1*1 & conv \\ 3*3 & conv \end{bmatrix} * 16$
Concatenate Layer (2)	2184				
Classification Layer	1 * 1 * 2184				7 * 7 global average pool
					2D, softmax

modified the interface code of the network data reading. Furthermore, during data processing period, learning from the doctor's reading CT habits, we adjust the window width of the three commonly used lung CT, and then superimposed three single-channel data to enrich the information of the nodules, then the size of the input data is m * n * 3.

Secondly, we modify the DenseNet framework to the multi-input and single-output because different pulmonary nodules have a lot of differences in size. The environmental information around the pulmonary nodules is significant for its benign and malignant classification, in order to preserve the environmental information, according to the size distribution of the pulmonary nodules in the dataset, we take two scales centered on the center of the nodule. The two size are 50 * 50 and 100 * 100. The 50 * 50 size nodule image can contain the largest nodule in the dataset, and the 100 * 100 size nodule image contains the surrounding environment information of all nodules in the dataset. We extract the corresponding 68-dimensional manual features (semantic, shape, size and texture features) for the data of two scales. Finally, added two 68-dimensional manual features to the pulmonary nodule areas as input data to the network for training.

Table 3 shows the network framework and the parameters of each layer. During the network training process, the 68-dimensional manual features can be seen as a 68 channels 1 * 1 feature map. As can be seen from Table 3, the output size of feature map of nodules with the size of 50 * 50 after the third Transition Layer is 1 * 1, we add a concatenate layer after transition layer, change the original 512 channels feature map to 580 channels feature map. The feature map size is 100 * 100 after the process of the transition layer, the output feature map is 3 * 3, and the feature vector size of manual features is 1 * 1. We add a convolution layer which has 3 * 3 convolution kernel, transfer the feature map from 3 * 3 to 1 * 1, it is more convenient to concatenate with the manual feature which has the same size. We add a concatenate layer in front of the global average pool at the end of the network. This layer concatenates two sizes of data to get more features and improve the result of the classification.

The loss function of the MsMi-DenseNet we proposed in this paper is categorical cross entropy function shows in formula 1. Categorical cross entropy is mainly used to evaluate the difference between the probability distribution and the real distribution obtained by the current model. n represents the total number of samples, y_i represents the actual label of the ith sample, and y_i^* represents the sample label of the network prediction.

$$C = -\frac{1}{n}\sum_i y_i \ln y_i^* + (1 - y_i) \ln(1 - y_i^*) \tag{1}$$

3   The Result of Experiments and Analysis

3.1   LIDC-IDRI Pulmonary Nodule Image Dataset

LIDC-IDRI dataset is the world's largest public medical image dataset, including CT scan images of 1012 patients, each set of CT includes one or more pulmonary nodules. The dataset is annotated by four radiologists and stored in xml files which marks the medical signs of the corresponding CT images and the outline information of the nodules. According to the CT images and xml files, we can check pulmonary nodules and extract the DICOM section of the pulmonary nodule, the outline of the nodule, and the sign information. As it shows in Fig. 2, (a) is the original image of pulmonary nodule, (b) is the result of the combination of the outlines by four doctors.

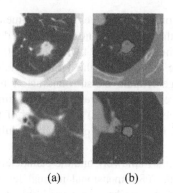

(a)   (b)

Fig. 2. The original image and boundary of pulmonary nodule

The basis for labeling benign and malignant pulmonary nodules is the malignancy marked by the radiologist in Table 1. In the xml file, radiologists classified the malignancy measurement into five levels: 1, 2, 3, 4, and 5. Different researches use different rules to classify the nodules according to the level, in general there are three types. The first method is to mark the malignant grades 1, 2, 3 as benign pulmonary nodules, and the malignant grades 4, 5 as malignant pulmonary nodules. The second method is to mark the malignant degree of 1, 2 as a benign pulmonary nodule, and the malignant grades 3, 4, 5 as malignant pulmonary nodules. The third treatment is to label the malignant degree of 1, 2 as a benign pulmonary nodule, the malignant grade of 4, 5 as a malignant pulmonary nodule. The processing method selected in this article is the first one.

3.2   Multiple Window Widths and Window Levels CT Images

In LIDC-IDRI database, the DICOM images are gray single-channel images. We use three commonly used lung window widths (WW) window levels (WL). As it shows in Fig. 3, (a) is an example of a CT image of the lungs with a window width of 1600 and a window level of −600. And (b) is a CT image with a window width of 190, window level of 80. (c) is the image with 3500 of window width and 750 of window level. And then we combine these three images into one image with three channels, this image has more details of nodule. (d) is the visualization of CT image with three-channel of lung.

At the end of this section, the central coordinates of the nodule are obtained according to the outline coordinates of the nodule. Two different scale nodule areas were taken as the dataset centered on the center of the nodule, which were 50 * 50 and 100 * 100. A total of 4,974 lung CT sections are extracted, of which 2,395 were benign nodule sections and 2,579 were malignant nodule sections. The ratio of training set, verification set, and test set in the experiment is 6:2:2.

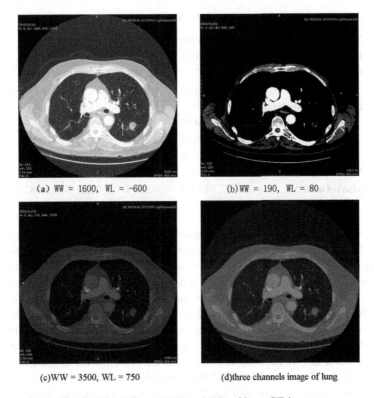

(a) WW = 1600, WL = -600   (b) WW = 190, WL = 80

(c) WW = 3500, WL = 750   (d) three channels image of lung

Fig. 3. The different WW and WL of lung CT images

3.3 The Parameters of the Experiment

We use Keras as our training model to classify the benign and malignant pulmonary nodules, and Tensorflow as the backend of Keras. Keras is available for Python 2.7–3.6 versions. And it has the following advantages: high modularity, minimal simplicity and scalability.

In order to reduce the impact caused by the lack of medical image data, the pre-training model used in this paper is the model obtained from of DenseNet121 training on the ImageNet dataset. We set the batch size as 4, and train 100 times. And the growth rate of DenseNet k = 32, the compression θ of transition layer is 0.5. We set the learning rate as 0.001, the dropout as 0.1. And we use stochastic gradient descent (SGD) as our optimizer. In order to check our method, we use 5 fold cross validation.

3.4 Experiment Result and Analysis

We use 5 fold cross validation on LIDC-IDRI dataset to test our MsMi-DenseNet. In order to evaluate our model, we compare it with several methods which have good performance recently, the comparison results are shown in Table 4. Among them, Han, Dhara et al. use traditional machine learning methods to diagnose the benign and malignant pulmonary nodules, Shen, Dey R, Xie Y et al. use depth network to do this.

Table 4. Comparing the performance of MsMi-DenseNet with state-of-the-art methods

Method		Sensitivity	Specificity	Accuracy	AUC
Han et al. [16]		89.35%	86.02%	–	0.9405
Dhara et al. [17]		89.73%	86.36%	–	0.9505
Shen et al. [18]		77.00%	93.00%	87.14%	0.9300
Dey et al. [14]	Basic CNN	87.50%	81.20%	84.35%	0.9064
	Multi-Output	88.99%	82.69%	85.84%	0.9205
	DenseNet	88.50%	88.33%	88.42%	0.9451
	MoDenseNet	90.47%	90.33%	90.40%	0.9548
Xie et al. [19]		91.43%	94.09%	93.40%	0.9778
MsMi-DenseNet		**96.65%**	**92.83%**	**94.17%**	**0.9820**

Han et al. [16] extracted Haralick features, Gabor features and LBP (local binary patterns) features and used SVM classifiers for classification. The sensitivity and specificity were 89.5% and 86.02% respectively. Dhara et al. [17] based on shape, edge and texture features to achieve benign and malignant classification. However, the feature set extracted by hand is not perfect enough to determine whether the difference between different types of pulmonary nodules can be accurately described. Shen et al. [18] proposed a network Mc-CNN (Multi-crop CNN) for the classification of benign and malignant pulmonary nodules, which is a multi-scale input network. Dey et al. [13] proposed a multi-output network based on the DenseNet, achieving an accuracy of 90.4%. Xie et al. [19] produced three different nodule image inputs, used ResNet-50 to train the classification model, and finally merged the three output features, but the fusion method is to map the output characteristics of the three networks to two. On the neuron, the final fusion is performed, making it difficult to determine if there is a loss of features.

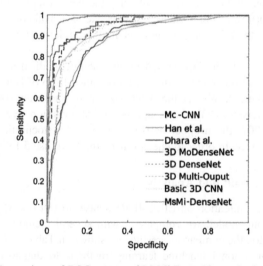

Fig. 4. Comparison of ROC curves of MsMi-DenseNet and other methods

Although the classification accuracy of these deep networks has been improved, the effect in the classification of pulmonary nodules has not reached the effect on the ImageNet dataset. In addition, the deep network is still a "black box", which doesn't consider the traditional low-level features, many radiologists can't accept this diagnosis method. Therefore, our proposed MsMi-DenseNet network which combine with manual features. We can see the performance of it in Table 4, our method achieved 96.65% sensitivity and 94.17% accuracy, which is much higher than other algorithms. However, the specificity of our proposed method is 92.93%, which is lower than 94.09% of XIE Y et al. Sensitivity indicates the proportion of malignant pulmonary nodules diagnosed correctly, and the specificity indicates the proportion of benign pulmonary nodules diagnosed correctly. Both of them have important clinical diagnostic significance, and the cost of malignant pulmonary nodules being diagnosed as benign pulmonary nodules is greater than the cost of benign pulmonary nodules being diagnosed as malignant pulmonary nodules. Therefore, our method is more practical.

As shown in Fig. 4, the ROC curve of our method is better than other algorithm's curves. It can be seen that the proposed method achieves the highest AUC value of 0.9820.

4   Conclusion

In this paper, according to the deficiencies of the current diagnostic methods for benign and malignant pulmonary nodules proposed by researchers and the situation that radiologists do not approve of the deep network method, we use the experience and habits of doctors for reference to improve DenseNet network, which has the best classification effect at present. Our contribution is that (1) in order to prevent the loss of important information, this paper retains the int16 type data of the DICOM image, and adjusted the three window widths and window levels to make the pulmonary nodule data into three-channel data. (2) Considering the multi-scale information of pulmonary nodules, the input format of the DenseNet network was modified to change DenseNet to a network structure with multiple inputs and single outputs. (3) Drawing lessons from traditional CAD methods and extracted 68 dimensional features of the pulmonary nodules and trained in MsMi-DenseNet network. (4) Finally, in this article, the MsMi-DenseNet network was evaluated on the LIDC-IDRI dataset, which was compared with other researchers' algorithms. It is concluded that our algorithm has better performance, sensitivity of 96.65%, specificity of 92.83, accuracy of 94.17%, and the area of AUC reached 0.9820.

The result shows that the MsMi-DenseNet network model is reliable for the diagnosis of benign and malignant pulmonary nodules, and the predicted results can be used as the "third eye" for clinical diagnosis.

Acknowledgments. This work is supported by the National Natural Science Foundation of China under Grant No. 61701404; Major Program of National Natural Science Foundation of China under Grant No. 81727802.

References

1. Siegel, R.L., Miller, K.D., Jemal, A.: Cancer statistics 2018. CA Cancer J. Clin. (2018). https://doi.org/10.3322/caac.21442
2. National Lung Screening Trial Research Team et al.: Reduced lung-cancer mortality with low-dose computed tomographic screening. N. Engl. J. Med. **365**, 395–409 (2011)
3. Krishnamurthy, S., Narasimhan, G., Rengasamy, U.: Three-dimensional lung nodule segmentation and shape variance analysis to detect lung cancer with reduced false positives. Proc. Inst. Mech. Eng. Part H: J. Eng. Med. **230**(1), 58–70 (2016)
4. Liu, Y., et al.: Radiological image traits predictive of cancer status in pulmonary nodules. Clin. Cancer Res. **23**, 1442–1449 (2016). https://doi.org/10.1158/1078-0432.CCR-15-3102
5. Shewaye, T.N., Mekonnen, A.A.: Benign-malignant lung nodule classification with geometric and appearance histogram features. arXiv preprint arXiv:1605.08350 (2016)
6. Shen, W., Zhou, M., Yang, F., Yang, C., Tian, J.: Multi-scale convolutional neural networks for lung nodule classification. In: Ourselin, S., Alexander, D.C., Westin, C.-F., Cardoso, M. Jorge (eds.) IPMI 2015. LNCS, vol. 9123, pp. 588–599. Springer, Cham (2015). https://doi.org/10.1007/978-3-319-19992-4_46
7. Nibali, A., He, Z., Wollersheim, D.: Pulmonary nodule classification with deep residual networks. Int. J. Comput. Assist. Radiol. Surg. 1–10 (2017)
8. Liu, K., Kang, G.: Multiview convolutional neural networks for lung nodule classification. Int. J. Imaging Syst. Technol. **27**(1), 12–22 (2017)
9. Hussein, S., Cao, K., Song, Q., Bagci, U.: Risk stratification of lung nodules using 3D CNN-based multi-task learning. In: Niethammer, M., et al. (eds.) IPMI 2017. LNCS, vol. 10265, pp. 249–260. Springer, Cham (2017). https://doi.org/10.1007/978-3-319-59050-9_20
10. Zhu, W., Liu, C., Fan, W., Xie, X.: DeepLung: 3D deep convolutional nets for automated pulmonary nodule detection and classification. arXiv preprint arXiv:1709.05538 (2017)
11. Wu, Y., Shi, W., Cui, L., Wang, H., Bu, Q., Feng, J.: Automatic mass detection from mammograms with region-based convolutional neural network. In: Wang, Y., Jiang, Z., Peng, Y. (eds.) IGTA 2018. CCIS, vol. 875, pp. 442–450. Springer, Singapore (2018). https://doi.org/10.1007/978-981-13-1702-6_44
12. Li, G., Kim, H., Tan, J.K., et al.: Semantic characteristics prediction of pulmonary nodule using artificial neural networks. In: Conference Proceedings IEEE Engineering in Medicine and Biology Society 2013, pp. 5465–5468 (2013)
13. Zinovev, D., Raicu, D., Furst, J., et al.: Predicting radiological panel opinions using a panel of machine learning classifiers. Algorithms **2**(4), 1473–1502 (2009)
14. Dey, R., Lu, Z., Yi, H.: Diagnostic classification of lung nodules using 3D neural networks (2018)
15. Huang, G., Liu, Z., van der Maaten, L., et al.: Densely connected convolutional networks (2017)
16. Han, F., Wang, H., Zhang, G., et al.: Texture feature analysis for computer-aided diagnosis on pulmonary nodules. J. Digit. Imaging **28**(1), 99–115 (2014)
17. Dhara, A.K., Mukhopadhyay, S., Dutta, A., et al.: A combination of shape and texture features for classification of pulmonary nodules in lung CT images. J. Digit. Imaging **29**(4), 466–475 (2016)
18. Shen, W., Zhou, M., Yang, F., et al.: Multi-crop convolutional neural networks for lung nodule malignancy suspiciousness classification. Pattern Recogn. **61**(61), 663–673 (2017)
19. Xie, Y., Xia, Y., Zhang, J., Feng, D.D., Fulham, M., Cai, W.: Transferable multi-model ensemble for benign-malignant lung nodule classification on chest CT. In: Descoteaux, M., Maier-Hein, L., Franz, A., Jannin, P., Collins, D.L., Duchesne, S. (eds.) MICCAI 2017. LNCS, vol. 10435, pp. 656–664. Springer, Cham (2017). https://doi.org/10.1007/978-3-319-66179-7_75

SAR Ship Detection Under Complex Background Based on Attention Mechanism

Chen Chen[✉], Changhua Hu, Chuan He,
Hong Pei, Zhenan Pang, and Tong Zhao

Rocket Force University of Engineering, 204 Unit, Xi'an 710025, China
chenchen_9407@163.com, hch_reu@sina.net,
hechuan8512@163.com, ph2010hph@sina.com,
pznfatfight@163.com, 601080018@qq.com

Abstract. SAR ship detection based on deep learning has wide application, however there exist the following three problems for SAR ship detection. Firstly, the ships in the port are seriously disturbed by the onshore buildings. The existing detection methods cannot effectively distinguish the target from the background. Secondly, the algorithm cannot accurately locate the closely arranged ship targets. Finally, the ships in SAR images have a variety of scales, and the existing algorithms have poor positioning effect on ship targets of different scales. To solve the above problems, this paper proposes an object detection network which combines attention mechanism to enhance the network's ability to accurately locate targets in complex background. To deal with the diversity of ship target scales, we propose a loss function that incorporates Generalized Intersection over Union (GIoU) loss to reduce the sensitivity of the algorithm to scale. The proposed algorithm achieves good results for ship target detection in complex backgrounds based on the extended SAR Ship Detection Dataset (SSDD), while maintaining a fast detection speed.

Keywords: SAR · Ship detection · Deep learning · Attention mechanism

1 Introduction

With the development of maritime trade, ships play an increasingly important role in the process of marine development and transportation. Monitoring and controlling ships can effectively improve the efficiency of marine transportation and reduce maritime traffic accidents. Synthetic Aperture Radar (SAR) is widely used in marine ship detection because of its advantages of all-day, strong anti-jamming ability and strong penetration [1]. In recent years, the rapid development of TerraSAR-X, RADARSAT-2 and Sentinel-1 has promoted the research of ship target detection in SAR images [2].

With the powerful feature extraction ability of convolutional neural network, deep learning has achieved great success in object detection tasks. Object detection methods based on deep learning are mainly divided into two categories: two-stage detection algorithms such as Faster R-CNN [3] and single-stage detection algorithms such as SSD [4], RFBnet [5]. Two-stage detection algorithm has high positioning accuracy, and in contrast, single-stage detection algorithm has absolute advantage in terms of

© Springer Nature Singapore Pte Ltd. 2019
Y. Wang et al. (Eds.): IGTA 2019, CCIS 1043, pp. 565–578, 2019.
https://doi.org/10.1007/978-981-13-9917-6_54

speed. Both algorithms are widely used in automatic driving, intelligent security, remote sensing detection and other fields. In SAR image object detection task, compared with the traditional Constant False Alarm Rate (CFAR) algorithm, the ship detection algorithm based on deep learning does not require complex modeling process, thus it has attracted more attention and research from scholars. Li et al. applied the improved Faster R-CNN detection algorithm to ship detection in SAR images [6]. Kang et al. combined the traditional CAFR algorithm with Faster R-CNN [7]. Jiao et al. proposed a Fast R-CNN SAR image ship detection method with dense connections [8]. However, there are still some problems for ship detection in SAR images based on deep learning. Firstly, the background of the ship adjacent to the port is complex, and is seriously disturbed by the wharf and shore buildings. The algorithms above cannot effectively distinguish the target from the background and effectively segment the closely arranged ship targets. Secondly, the SAR ship target has the diversity of scale, and for the small-scale ship target, these algorithms cannot effectively detect and locate. Finally, the ship detection algorithm based on deep learning mostly adopts the two-stage detection framework based on Faster R-CNN, which pays more attention on the detection accuracy and ignores the detection speed, thus failing to detect the target in real time.

Visual attention model has been widely applied in object detection, object recognition, object tracking and other fields [9]. The core idea of attention mechanism is to make the model learn to focus on the key information and ignore the irrelevant information. Target detection method based on visual attention mechanism usually obtains saliency feature map through attention model, and then calibrates the target in the image by analyzing saliency map. In the task of ship detection, Song et al. combined the sparse saliency of the target through the attention model with the Local Binary Pattern (LBP), and proposed an automatic ship detection algorithm applied to optical satellite image. The algorithm has good robustness to the interference of cloud and light [10]. With the development of deep learning in the field of computer vision, it is becoming more and more important to build a neural network with attention mechanism. On the one hand, the neural network can learn the attention mechanism independently. On the other hand, the attention mechanism can contribute to us understanding the neural network in turn [11]. In terms of the combination of visual attention mechanism and neural network, Wang et al. proposed a residual network combining attention model, which achieved good results in image classification [12]. Zheng et al. proposed a component learning method of convolutional neural network based on multi-attention model, which enabled the network to obtain better fine-grained features of images [13].

When building SAR ship detection model based on convolution neural network, we need to fully consider the difference between optical image and SAR image, and design convolution neural network model pertinently. In this paper, we propose a single-stage object detection algorithm which combines attention mechanism to solve the existing problems of ship detection in SAR images. The contribution of this paper is threefold. Firstly, in view of the complex background and the difficulty of distinguishing the target from the background in SAR images, we integrate the attention mechanism into the feature pyramid to obtain salient feature maps of different depths, and fuse these features of different depths, which improves the accuracy of the network to detect and locate ship targets in complex background and closely arranged. Secondly, GIoU Loss [14] is introduced into the loss function to reduce the sensitivity of the network to scale. Finally, we apply the single-stage detection algorithm to the task of ship detection in SAR image, and realize the real-time detection of ship target in SAR image.

The rest of the paper is organized as follows. Section 2 illustrates our proposed method and network structure. Section 3 presents the experiments and the results. The paper is concluded in Sect. 4.

2 Method

This paper proposes a ship detection method based on attention mechanism in SAR image. The main flow of the algorithm is as follows. Firstly, feature extraction network is constructed by residual module to obtain multi-level target mapping features. Secondly, the saliency of mapping features is enhanced by attention mechanism to obtain saliency feature maps; then the features expressed in different depths are fused by feature fusion method; on the fused feature maps, the position and confidence scores of targets are predicted. Finally, the predicted values are filtered by non-maximum suppression NMS, and the final detection results are obtained.

2.1 Construction of Feature Extraction Network

To deal with the characteristics of ship target in SAR image, we use Inception-ResNet. [15] as the basic unit to construct feature network and acquire image feature pyramid. The network structure in the algorithm is shown in the Fig. 1. The residual part of the residual module is replaced by Inception module in the network. By the extension of Inception module, the transmission ability of the network to the upper information is enhanced. The introduced shortcut method solves the phenomenon of gradient disappearance and makes the network deeper. We superimpose two convolutions of 3 * 3 size in Inception branch, so that we can get the same size of Receptive Fields (RF) as

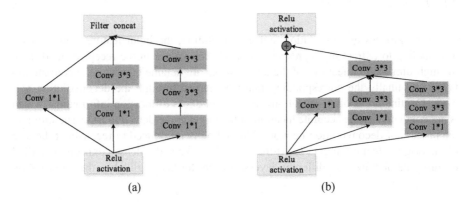

(a)   (b)

Fig. 1. The Inception-ResNet module. (a) The original Inception module. (b) Inception model combined with ResNet.

5 * 5 [16]. The larger Receptive Fields can get a wider range of information, which is conducive to distinguishing ship targets from complex background. The Inception module is introduced to form a multi-branch convolution structure. The convolution cores of different sizes in each branch increase the diversity of feature information obtained. In the network, 1 * 1 convolution channel is adopted to reduce the dimension, which reduces the number of parameters of each inception model. At the same time, linear convolution is used for dimension stitching to match the dimension of input and output.

2.2 Object Detection Network with Attention Mechanism

The innovation of this paper is to integrate the attention mechanism into the detection network and obtain salient features of ship targets through the attention mechanism, so as to obtain more accurate location information.

The attention model in this paper is mainly composed of two branches: convolution branch and mask branch. Among them, the network structure of the mask branch is an hourglass-like symmetrical structure, including two stages of convolution and deconvolution, as shown in the Fig. 2.

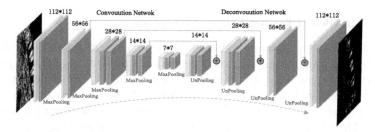

Fig. 2. Convolution and deconvolution network. Pink represents the pooling layer, blue represents the feature layer acquired through learning, and numbers represent the size of the feature map. Through this process, the mask map of the target can be learned. (Color figure online)

In the process of convolution and deconvolution, the input feature map is firstly Maxpooling to extract the representative activation values in the receptive field; then the high-dimensional features of the target image are obtained through the convolution layer; and finally the corresponding mask is learned through the deconvolution network. Continuous pooling operations results in the loss of location information, which is not conducive to the accurate location of the target in the detection task. Therefore, in the process of deconvolution network, Unpooling is introduced to reconstruct the size of the original feature map [17]. At the same time, we add a dense connection method to fuse the features of different layers, which further highlights the information characteristics of the mask map. Mask maps act on convolutional feature maps by Eq. (1). In this way, elements in mask maps are similar to the weight of feature maps, which enhances regions of interest and suppresses non-target regions.

$$A_{i,n} = M_{i,n} * C_{i,n}. \tag{1}$$

where A is the output of attention model, M is the output of mask branch, C is the output of convolution branch, i is the location of points in space, n is the number of convolution channels.

The network structure of the attention model is shown in Fig. 3. The saliency features are obtained by multiplying the corresponding elements between the mask map and the feature map. In order to avoid the difference between different levels of feature maps caused by attention model, Sigmoid is used as activation function to normalize the pixel values in mask maps into [0, 1]. However, in the process of constructing the network, multiple attention models are stacked and multiplied, which makes the element values in the feature map smaller and smaller. This will destroy the original characteristics of the network. When the network layer becomes deeper, it is easier to fall into local optimum. Therefore, the idea of identical mapping in Resnet [18] is introduced into the attention model. In the convolution branch, an identical mapping branch is added to the original output. On the one hand, the idea of shortcut solves the gradient problem in the network, which can make the network deeper; on the other hand, through addition operation, the salient features of model output are more obvious, and the discrimination of target features is enhanced. The corresponding network can be described as:

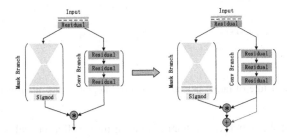

Fig. 3. The Attention module. The left side of the graph is the mask branch. The hourglass structure represents the process of convolution and deconvolution. The green part represents 1 * 1 convolution and is used to adjust the dimension. (Color figure online)

$$A_{i,n} = M_{i,n} * C_{i,n} + C_{i,n} = \left(1 + M_{i,n}\right) * C_{i,n}. \tag{2}$$

Most of the algorithms use the fusion of shallow location information and deep semantic information to solve the problem of missing target location information in the process of network downsampling [19, 20]. However, ships in SAR images are seriously disturbed by background, and it is difficult to obtain effective location features in shallow network. If effective location information cannot be obtained in shallow network, feature fusion of different depths will also be meaningless. Therefore, a new feature fusion method is proposed in this paper. Firstly, the attention model is fused into the detection network to enhance the saliency of the location information of the target in the shallow features through the attention mechanism. Then, the saliency features of different depths are fused using the structure mode of Feature Pyramid Networks (FPN), which not only retains more semantic information, but also ensures the accuracy of location information. The overall structure of the network is shown in Fig. 4. Firstly, the dimension of the input image is adjusted by 7 * 7 convolution layer, and then downsampling is done by Maxpooling layer. The feature extraction network consists of four stages. Each stage uses Inception-ResNet as the basic unit to construct the feature pyramid, which can enhance the ability to acquire upper information. In each stage, salient feature maps of different depths are obtained by concatenating several attention models in series, and the features of different depths are fused to highlight the advantages of location.

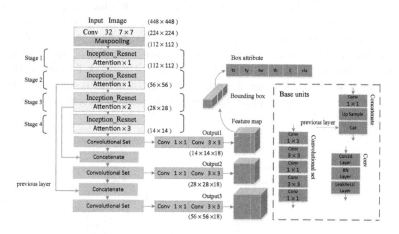

Fig. 4. Structure of target detection network integrating attention mechanism

The output of the network is a feature map of three different scales. The algorithm divides the tensor of the feature map into several grids according to the scale. Each grid includes the location attributes of the bounding box and the confidence score of the object. The network output is filtered by confidence threshold and Non-Maximum Suppression (NMS), and the final prediction results are obtained.

2.3   Loss Function

In detection tasks, Mean Squared Error (MSE) Loss is used as a loss function in most detection algorithms to evaluate the effect of bounding box regression. For SAR ship target, the size of ship target varies greatly with different resolution, while MSE Loss is sensitive to scale. Using MSE Loss as loss function will affect the positioning effect of ship target. Therefore, we introduce generalized IoU (GIoU) [15] into loss function to reduce the sensitivity of loss function to scale. The definition of GIoU as follow

$$GIoU = IoU - \frac{|C \backslash (A \cup B)|}{|C|}, \quad IoU = \frac{|A \cap B|}{|A \cup B|}. \tag{3}$$

Where C is the smallest enclosed shape that completely contains A and B. $|C \backslash (A \cup B)|$ is the area in C that does not cover $A \cup B$. GIoU losses can also be defined as $L_{GIoU} = 1 - GIoU$. In our scheme, the following method is used to calculate L_{GIoU}. Firstly, the coordinates of the predicted bounding box and the real bounding box are obtained by the location information x, y, w, h of the network prediction.

$$\begin{aligned} x_1 &= w/2 - x, x_2 = w/2 + x \\ y_1 &= h/2 - y, y_2 = h/2 + y \end{aligned}. \tag{4}$$

In Eq. (4), x_1, y_1, x_2, y_2 are the coordinate of the predicted bounding box, and the coordinate $x_1^*, y_1^*, x_2^*, y_2^*$ of the corresponding real bounding box can also be calculated according to the label. We can calculate the intersection area S_I of these two boxes.

$$S_I = \begin{cases} \left(x_2^I - x_1^I\right) * \left(y_2^I - y_1^I\right) & x_2^I > x_1^I, y_2^I > y_1^I \\ 0 & otherwise \end{cases}. \tag{5}$$

Where $x_1^I = \max\left(x_1, x_1^*\right), x_2^I = \min\left(x_2, x_2^*\right), y_1^I = \max\left(y_1, x_1^*\right), y_2^I = \min\left(x_2, x_2^*\right)$. At the same time, the coordinates of the boundary points of the minimal closed graph B_C can be determined and the corresponding area S_C can be formulated as:

$$S_C = \left(x_2^C - x_1^C\right) * \left(y_2^C - y_1^C\right). \tag{7}$$

Where $x_1^C = \min\left(x_1, x_1^*\right), x_2^C = \max\left(x_2, x_2^*\right), y_1^C = \min\left(y_1, y_1^*\right), y_2^C = \max\left(y_2, y_2^*\right)$ Through the above steps, $GIoU$ and L_{GIoU} can be calculated as:

$$\begin{aligned} GIoU &= IoU - \frac{S_C - U}{S_C} \\ L_{GIoU} &= 1 - GIoU \end{aligned}. \tag{8}$$

Ship detection belongs to single object detection. The loss function of network consists of two parts: location loss and confidence score loss. The loss function of fusion $GIoU$ can be expressed as:

$$\begin{aligned} Loss &= Loss_{coord} + Loss_{conf} \\ &= \alpha \sum_{i=0}^{S^2} \sum_{j=0}^{B} l_{ij}^{obj} L_{GIoU} + \sum_{i=0}^{S^2} \sum_{j=0}^{B} l_{ij}^{obj} f\left(C_i, C_i^*\right) \\ &+ \beta \sum_{i=0}^{S^2} \sum_{j=0}^{B} l_{ij}^{noobj} f\left(C_i, C_i^*\right) \end{aligned} \tag{9}$$

In Eq. (9), α is the balance factor of location loss. S and B represent the number of grid partitions and the number of boundaries contained in each grid on the characteristic graph of network prediction. β is the penalty factor, which reduces the impact of bounding box without targets on the loss function. C and C^* are confidence score and corresponding label of the prediction. Because the output of the algorithm is normalized by the Sigmoid, the cross-entropy loss function as shown in Eq. (10) can get better convergence effect.

$$f(x,x^*) = -\frac{1}{N}\sum_{i=1}^{N}\left[x_i^* \log(x_i) + (1 - x_i)\log\left(1 - x_i^*\right)\right]. \tag{10}$$

3 Experiments

In this section, we describe the experiments carried out in this paper, including network training and analysis of the experimental results.

3.1 Training

Experimental Platform and Dataset Introduction. All the experiments are implemented on a workstation with the Intel(R) Xeon Silver 4114@2.20 Hz × 20 CPU, NVIDIA GTX TITAN-XP GPU, 128G memory and Pytorch framework. In order to evaluate the detection performance of the model, the open SAR ship object data set SSDD [12] is utilized for the experiments. The data set includes ship objects of different resolutions (1 m to 15 m) and sizes under different backgrounds (coastal, offshore). The scenes diversity of samples ensures that the trained model has stronger generalization ability. In addition, because the ship target is small in low resolution image, it is difficult to judge, so only ship targets with more than three pixels are labeled. Therefore, the data set contains 1160 images with multi-scale ship targets in different scenes. In order to make the trained model more robust, we extend the data set. The specific implementation is that the 12 TerraSAR-X images containing ship targets are cut into small slices and tagged according to the format of PASCAL VOC. Finally, the number of images in the data set is expanded to 1706. The details of extended SSDD are shown in Table 1. We divide the data into training set, verification set and test set according to the ratio of 7:1:2.

Table 1. The details of SSDD.

Sensors	Polarization	Resolution	Position	Number
RadarSat-2	HH, VV	1 m–15 m	inshore	1706
TerraSAR-X	HV, VH		offshore	
Sentinel-1				

Hyper-parameters Selection. In this paper, the hyper-parameters are selected through many experiments. On the basis of using pre-training weights, the feature extraction network is fine-tuned. The initial learning rate of the feature extraction network is set to 0.001, the initial learning rate of the detection layer is set to 0.01, the attenuation coefficient is 0.1, and the total number of training rounds is 210. The optimization algorithm uses SGD, momentum parameter is 0.9, and the attenuation coefficient is 0.00004, batch size is set to 6 * 3 (GPU parallel operation), the balance factor is 0.5, and the penalty factor is 0.1. The variation of loss function during training is shown in the figure. After 20000 steps of iteration, the network converges completely, and the total loss value is 0. 04483. The loss curve is shown in Fig. 5(a). At the same time, the training time is recorded. As shown in Fig. 5(b), the training time of single sample is about 42 s.

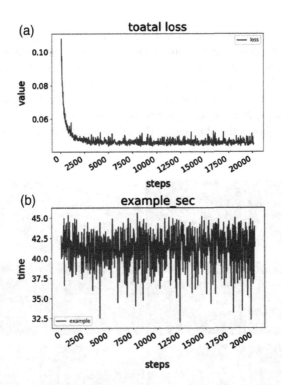

Fig. 5. The curves of loss and training time of single sample

3.2   Object Detection Experiments

Evaluation Metrics. In order to evaluate the detection effect of the model quantitatively, the performance of the detector is described by the following criteria.

$$precision = \frac{N_{tp}}{N_{tp}+N_{fp}}. \tag{13}$$

$$recall = \frac{N_{tp}}{N_{tp}+N_{fn}}. \tag{14}$$

Where N_{tp} is the correctly detected ship target, N_{fp} is the incorrectly detected target and N_{fn} is the missing ship target. We use F1 score to represent the comprehensive performance of the algorithm. We define the predicted bounding box is correct when it has IoU greater 0.5 with a single ground-truth.

$$F1 = \frac{2 \times precision \times recall}{precision + recall}. \tag{15}$$

Experimental Results. In order to test the validity of the network model, the ship detection results under different environment conditions in the extended SSDD data set are analyzed, as shown in the Fig. 6. In the first line, we show the detection results of ship targets closely arranged, which is a difficult problem in ship target detection in SAR image. It can be seen that the algorithm in this paper can effectively distinguish closely spaced ships, and also can effectively segment ship targets close to the coast. The second line shows the ship target detection under the ambiguous background.

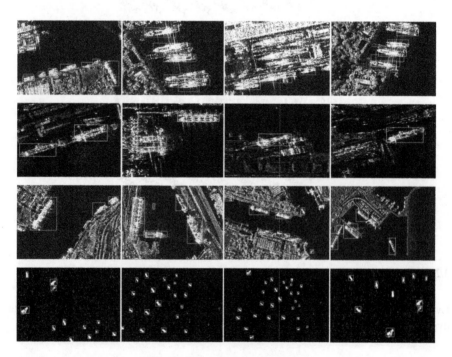

Fig. 6. The experimental results

This kind of ship target is characterized by unclear outline and unclear boundary between the target and the background. We can find that the algorithm can effectively distinguish the target from the background. The third line shows the results of ship detection in different sizes and directions in the same image. It can be found that the algorithm can accurately locate the target. The fourth line shows the detection results of small targets with sparse distribution. It can be seen that the algorithm has a better detection effect for small targets and a lower missed detection rate.

Contrast Experiments. In this paper, through further experiments, the method is compared quantitatively with several mainstream single-stage target detection algorithms based on deep learning in precision, recall, F1 score and detection speed. The quantitative comparison results are shown in the Table 2.

Table 2. The detection performance of the proposed method and other methods

Method	Backbone	Precision	Recall	F1%	Time
SSD	Vgg16	82.1%	70.2%	75.6%	24 ms
	Darknet-53	85.7%	72.5%	78.5%	29 ms
RFBNet	Vgg16	84.9%	72.7%	78.3%	**20 ms**
	Darknet-53	86.1%	73.6%	79.3%	22 ms
Proposed method	Attention-Resnet	**86.5%**	**74.7%**	80.1%	24 ms

It can be seen from the table that the proposed method achieves the highest precision and recall on the extended SSDD compared with the SSD [4] and RFBNet [5] of different backbone networks. Although it is not as fast as RFBNet, single image detection time of 24 ms can sufficiently achieve real-time detection [21]. It is noted that experiments on different platforms may have some impact on the detection time. In order to intuitively compare the detection results of different algorithms, we show the detection results in Fig. 7. Most of the samples have the same detection results under the three algorithms. In order to show the difference of the detection results more clearly, we select more complex samples for display. It can be seen that the three algorithms can effectively detect ship targets, but in terms of positioning accuracy, the method proposed in this paper has the best effect. At the same time, due to the introduction of attention mechanism, the network can learn more fine features. Compared with the other two algorithms, this algorithm can effectively distinguish closely arranged ships.

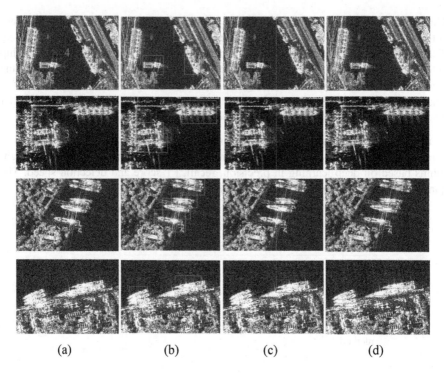

Fig. 7. The comparison results of our proposed method and other methods on SSDD. (a) the ground truth, (b) the result of SSD, (c) the result of RFBnet, (d) the result of proposed network.

4   Conclusions

In this paper, a single-stage object detection algorithm based on attention mechanism is proposed, and the effectiveness of the algorithm is verified on the open data set SSDD. In this paper, we use the modified residual model as the basic unit of feature extraction network, which enhances the network's ability to acquire upper target information. At the same time, the attention mechanism is integrated into the neural network, which improves the ability to detect and locate the target, and makes the algorithm can effectively distinguish the closely arranged ships. In view of the multi-scale characteristics of ship targets in SAR images, GIoU Loss is introduced into the loss function, which reduces the sensitivity of the network to scale. Another advantage of our proposed algorithm is that it is fast. The detection time of a single image on SSDD is only 24 ms, which can realize real-time ship detection. It should be noted that the algorithm cannot accurately locate ship targets with rotational characteristics, which is a problem we need to solve in the future. The continuous development of SAR will enable us to obtain more high-quality data, which will strongly promote the research of deep learning algorithm in SAR image processing field.

Acknowledgments. This research was supported by the National Natural Science Foundation of China under grant No. 61773389, 61833016, 61573365.

References

1. Yang, X., Sun, H., Fu, K.: Automatic ship detection in remote sensing images from google earth of complex scenes based on multiscale rotation dense feature pyramid networks. Remote Sens. **10**(1), 132 (2018)
2. Leng, X., Ji, K., Zhou, S.: An adaptive ship detection scheme for spaceborne SAR imagery. Sensors **16**(9), 1345 (2016)
3. Ren, S., He, K., Girshick, R.B.: Faster R-CNN: towards real-time object detection with region proposal networks. In: Neural Information Processing Systems, pp. 91–99. ACM, Montreal (2015)
4. Liu, W., et al.: SSD: single shot multibox detector. In: Leibe, B., Matas, J., Sebe, N., Welling, M. (eds.) ECCV 2016. LNCS, vol. 9905, pp. 21–37. Springer, Cham (2016). https://doi.org/10.1007/978-3-319-46448-0_2
5. Liu, S., Huang, D., Wang, Y.: Receptive field block net for accurate and fast object detection. In: Ferrari, V., Hebert, M., Sminchisescu, C., Weiss, Y. (eds.) ECCV 2018. LNCS, vol. 11215, pp. 404–419. Springer, Cham (2018). https://doi.org/10.1007/978-3-030-01252-6_24
6. Li, J., Qu, C., Shao, J.: Ship detection in SAR images based on an improved faster R-CNN. In: SAR in Big Data Era: Models, Methods & Applications. IEEE Press, Beijing (2017)
7. Kang, M., Leng, X., Lin, Z.: A modified faster R-CNN based on CAFR algorithm for SAR ship detection. In: International Workshop on Remote Sensing with Intelligent Processing. IEEE Press, ShangHai (2017)
8. Jiao, J., Zhang, Y., Sun, H.: A densely connected end-to-end neural network for multiscale and multiscene SAR ship detection. IEEE Access **6**(99), 20881–20892 (2018)
9. Li, W., Wang, P., Qiao, H.: A survey of visual attention based methods for object tracking. Acta Automatica Sinica **40**(4), 561–576 (2014)
10. Song, Z., Sui, H., Wang, Y.: Automatic ship detection for optical satellite images based on visual attention model and LBP. In: IEEE Workshop on Electronics, Computer & Applications. IEEE Press, Ottawa (2014)
11. Zhang, Q., Nian Wu, Y., Zhu, S.-C.: Interpretable convolutional neural networks. In: Proceedings of the IEEE Conference on Computer Vision and Pattern Recognition, pp. 8827–8836. IEEE Press, Salt Lake City (2018)
12. Wang, F., Jiang, M., Qian, C.: Residual attention network for image classification. In: Proceedings of the IEEE Conference on Computer Vision and Pattern Recognition, pp. 3156–3164. IEEE Press, Hawaii (2017)
13. Zheng, H., Fu, J., Tao, M.: Learning multi-attention convolutional neural network for fine-grained image recognition. In: IEEE International Conference on Computer Vision. IEEE Press, Hawaii (2017)
14. Rezatofighi, H., Tsoi, N., Gwak, J.: Generalized intersection over union: a metric and a loss for bounding box regression. arXiv preprint arXiv:1902.09630 (2019)
15. Szegedy, C., Ioffe, S., Vanhoucke, V.: Inception-v4, inception-ResNet and the impact of residual connections on learning. In: Thirty-First AAAI Conference on Artificial Intelligence, San Francisco (2017)
16. Szegedy, C., Vanhoucke, V., Ioffe, S.: Rethinking the inception architecture for computer vision. In: Computer Vision & Pattern Recognition. IEEE Press, Las Levas (2016)

17. Noh, H., Hong, S., Han, B.: Learning deconvolution network for semantic segmentation. In: IEEE International Conference on Computer Vision. IEEE Press, Liverpool (2015)
18. He, K., Zhang, X., Ren, S.: Deep residual learning for image recognition. In: Proceedings of the IEEE Conference on Computer Vision and Pattern Recognition, pp. 770–778. IEEE Press, Las Levas (2016)
19. Lin, T.-Y., Dollár, P., Girshick, R.: Feature pyramid networks for object detection. In: Proceedings of the IEEE Conference on Computer Vision and Pattern Recognition, pp. 2117–2125. IEEE Press, Hawaii (2017)
20. Luo, Z., Zhang, H., Zhang, Z., Yang, Y., Li, J.: Object detection based on multiscale merged feature map. In: Wang, Y., Jiang, Z., Peng, Y. (eds.) IGTA 2018. CCIS, vol. 875, pp. 80–87. Springer, Singapore (2018). https://doi.org/10.1007/978-981-13-1702-6_8
21. Wang, R., Zou, J., Che, M., Xiong, C.: Robust and real-time visual tracking based on single-layer convolutional features and accurate scale estimation. In: Wang, Y., Jiang, Z., Peng, Y. (eds.) IGTA 2018. CCIS, vol. 875, pp. 471–482. Springer, Singapore (2018). https://doi.org/10.1007/978-981-13-1702-6_47

A Beam Adjustment Algorithm Based on Star-Sensor Geometric Imaging Link Model with Distance Constraint

Guoliang Tian[✉], Qiaolin Huang, Hongyan He, Yu Wang,
and Zhongqiu Xia

Beijing Institute of Space Mechanics and Electricity, Beijing 100094, China
tglmingbai@163.com

Abstract. The geometric link model of integrated remote sensing imaging of star sensor and camera is proposed in order to improve the geometric positioning accuracy of remote sensing satellite image, reduce the error between satellite coordinate system and other coordinate systems, and increase the installation stability between star sensor and satellite platform. Based on the model, the beam adjustment algorithm of the star-sensing camera integrated remote sensing imaging geometric link model with additional distance constraints is proposed. The simulation results, using the initial adjustment parameters of ZY-3, show that the beam adjustment algorithm can effectively eliminate the systematic error component in the geometric positioning error and improve the geometric positioning accuracy of the remote sensing satellite image.

Keywords: Remote sensing satellite · Geometric link model · Beam adjustment algorithm · Star sensor · Geometric positioning accuracy

1 Introduction

As the increasing of high-resolution optical remote sensing satellites successfully launched and in orbit, as well as the development of remote sensing hardware equipment and the improvement of production capacity, China has the ability of acquiring high-resolution optical remote sensing images with wide range, high-resolution, and fast speed [1]. However, the acquisition of remote sensing images does not mean that it can be applied in related fields, because a large number of remote sensing images are of low resolution, and a few images with application value are also limited due to geometric positioning errors. With the improvement of remote sensing image resolution and radiation quality, remote sensing images can acquire images of ground targets clearly, but the ability to analyze their locations is weak under the premise of identifying targets. Therefore, research on geometric positioning accuracy is extremely important, which measures geometric positioning accuracy of satellite-to-ground remote sensing [2].

In the study of geometric positioning accuracy, many studies use different parameters to construct models [3], and analyze the difficulties of satellite photogrammetry without ground control points [4]. Based on error propagation, Bettemir

© Springer Nature Singapore Pte Ltd. 2019
Y. Wang et al. (Eds.): IGTA 2019, CCIS 1043, pp. 579–590, 2019.
https://doi.org/10.1007/978-981-13-9917-6_55

estimates the positioning accuracy of push-broom imaging using the star sensor accuracy, GPS accuracy, imaging time accuracy, and the assumed value of the orientation element accuracy of the camera; Yu et al. analyzed the effects of random errors such as the internal and external orientation elements [5]; Wang et al. made quantitative analysis used a star-sensitive camera full-link error simulation and evaluation mathematical model [6]. Common to these research is that most of the parameters in satellite photogrammetry are discussed, and only the random errors of each parameter are considered, and the indicators affecting the positioning accuracy in the overall design of high-resolution optical remote sensing satellites are less involved [7]. In the actual design, these indicators not only have random errors, but also systematic errors [8]. For example, Yuan Xiuxiao and others have verified the existence of the attitude angle constant error and conducted the attitude angle error correction, and check the systematic error [9, 10].

In the field of space remote sensing, due to the large-scale and large-field remote sensing system, in the traditional beam adjustment process, using the actual geographical coordinates of the control points to solve the system's scale factor can not meet the current satellite remote sensing terrain fluctuations. At the same time, the existing geometric imaging model can not fully reflect the actual situation of remote sensing imaging. Therefore, based on the beam adjustment, the distance between multiple pairs of control points is introduced as the constraint to solve the scale factor. The geometric link imaging model integrated by the star-sensitive camera is used to solve the three-dimensional coordinates of the target, and then a distance based on distance is proposed. The beam adjustment algorithm of the constrained star-sensitive camera integrated geometric link imaging model is used to complete the geometric ground processing of remote sensing images and improve the geometric positioning accuracy of remote sensing images.

2   Principle Analysis

2.1   Star-Sensitive Camera Integrated Geometric Link Model

In the process of high-resolution optical remote sensing satellite imaging, many factors can affect the geometric positioning accuracy of the image. To improve geometric positioning accuracy, we must first analyze its influencing factors and construct a complete geometric imaging link model, which involves observation targets (topographic relief, earth curvature), atmospheric refraction, remote sensors (optical systems, detectors), satellite platforms (orbits, attitudes), ground processing, accuracy evaluation, etc. We should also consider the stability of the remote sensor caused by the large-caliber, long-focus optical system and orbital attitude, among which the indicators affecting the positioning accuracy are the main research in the stereo positioning of high-resolution optical remote sensing satellites [12] (Fig. 1).

For high-resolution space cameras, the geometric model should consider distortion under large field of view conditions, and the geometric model introduced into the distortion is

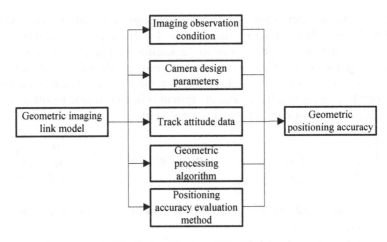

Fig. 1. Imaging condition diagram

$$\begin{bmatrix} X \\ Y \\ Z \end{bmatrix}_{WGS84} = \begin{bmatrix} X_{GPS} \\ Y_{GPS} \\ Z_{GPS} \end{bmatrix}_{WGS84} + R_{J2000}^{WGS84} R_{Orbit}^{J2000} R_{Satellite}^{Orbit} \left(\begin{bmatrix} E_x \\ E_y \\ E_z \end{bmatrix} + \begin{bmatrix} e_x \\ e_y \\ e_z \end{bmatrix} + m R_{Camera}^{Satellite} \begin{bmatrix} 0 \\ y - y_0 - D \\ -f \end{bmatrix} \right).$$

(1)

$\begin{bmatrix} E_x & E_y & E_z \end{bmatrix}^T$ is Offset for the GPS phase center in the satellite coordinate system, $\begin{bmatrix} e_x & e_y & e_z \end{bmatrix}^T$ is the offset between the origin of the camera and the satellite coordinate system.

However, the measurement accuracy of star sensor refers to the accuracy of the measured inertial attitude, and the inertia attitude has a conversion relationship with the ground posture:

$$R_{Satellite}^{Orbit} = R_{Orbit}^{J2000^{-1}} \cdot R_{Star}^{J2000} \cdot R_{Satellite}^{Star}.$$

(2)

It can be seen that the orbital error and the star sensor installation error are introduced during the conversion. In the geometric link design of high-resolution optical remote sensing satellites, the accuracy of inertial attitude measurement of star sensors is an important indicator and should be introduced in modeling. Therefore, the geometric model of the inertial attitude measurement accuracy of the star sensor is:

$$\begin{bmatrix} X \\ Y \\ Z \end{bmatrix}_{WGS84} = \begin{bmatrix} X_{GPS} \\ Y_{GPS} \\ Z_{GPS} \end{bmatrix}_{WGS84} + R_{J2000}^{WGS84} R_{Star}^{J2000} R_{Satellite}^{Star} \left(\begin{bmatrix} E_x \\ E_y \\ E_z \end{bmatrix} + \begin{bmatrix} e_x \\ e_y \\ e_z \end{bmatrix} + m R_{Camera}^{Satellite} \begin{bmatrix} 0 \\ y - y_0 - D \\ -f \end{bmatrix} \right).$$

(3)

The above model means that the star sensor is installed on the satellite star and converted to the camera coordinate system via the satellite coordinate system, which is not only the measurement error of the correlation angle between the coordinate systems, but also the additional error caused by the deformation of the satellite structure. An effective way to remove errors due to the satellite coordinate system is to use an integrated installation of the camera and the star sensor. If the offset of the GPS phase center in the satellite coordinate system is 0, then the offset of the camera coordinate system origin from the satellite coordinate system is 0, a geometric model is available for high-resolution optical remote sensing satellite imaging.

$$
\begin{bmatrix} X \\ Y \\ Z \end{bmatrix}_{WGS84} = \begin{bmatrix} X_{GPS} \\ Y_{GPS} \\ Z_{GPS} \end{bmatrix}_{WGS84} + mR_{J2000}^{WGS84} R_{Star}^{J2000} R_{Camera}^{Star} \begin{bmatrix} 0 \\ y - y_0 - D \\ -f \end{bmatrix}. \quad (4)
$$

R_{Camera}^{Star} is the transformation matrix of the camera coordinate system to the star sensor coordinate system.

In this paper, the orthogonal transformation matrix of the geocentric rectangular coordinate system to the satellite trajectory plane coordinate system is used to transform the spatial rectangular coordinates into plane coordinates and elevation coordinates.

$$
\begin{bmatrix} X \\ Y \\ Z \end{bmatrix}_{Terrain} = R_{WGS84}^{Terrain} \begin{bmatrix} X_{GPS} \\ Y_{GPS} \\ Z_{GPS} \end{bmatrix}_{WGS84} + mR_{WGS84}^{Terrain} R_{J2000}^{WGS84} R_{Star}^{J2000} R_{Camera}^{Star} \begin{bmatrix} 0 \\ y - y_0 - D \\ -f \end{bmatrix}.
$$

$$(5)$$

Specially, if $R_{WGS84}^{Terrain} = R_{J2000}^{WGS84} = I$:

$$
\begin{bmatrix} X \\ Y \\ Z \end{bmatrix}_{Terrain} = \begin{bmatrix} X_{GPS} \\ Y_{GPS} \\ Z_{GPS} \end{bmatrix}_{Terrain} + mR_{Star}^{Terrain} R_{Camera}^{Star} \begin{bmatrix} 0 \\ y - y_0 - D \\ -f \end{bmatrix}. \quad (6)
$$

$$
R_{Star}^{Terrain} R_{Camera}^{Star} = \begin{bmatrix} \cos\varphi & 0 & -\sin\varphi \\ 0 & 1 & 0 \\ \sin\varphi & 0 & \cos\varphi \end{bmatrix} \begin{bmatrix} 1 & 0 & 0 \\ 0 & \cos\omega & -\sin\omega \\ 0 & \sin\omega & \cos\omega \end{bmatrix} \begin{bmatrix} \cos\kappa & -\sin\kappa & 0 \\ \sin\kappa & \cos\kappa & 0 \\ 0 & 0 & 1 \end{bmatrix}. \quad (7)
$$

φ, ω, κ are the data provided by the star sensor and the gyro.

$R_{rotate} = R_{Star}^{Terrain} R_{Camera}^{Star}$, then the star-sensitive camera integrated geometric link imaging model is:

$$
\begin{bmatrix} X \\ Y \\ Z \end{bmatrix}_{Terrain} = \begin{bmatrix} X_{GPS} \\ Y_{GPS} \\ Z_{GPS} \end{bmatrix}_{Terrain} + mR_{rotote} \begin{bmatrix} 0 \\ y - y_0 - D \\ -f \end{bmatrix}. \quad (8)
$$

The optical remote sensing satellite under the integrated installation of the star-sensitive camera can effectively eliminate the angular measurement error between the coordinate systems introduced by the satellite coordinate system, and improve the stability of remote sensing imaging and reduce the remote sensing caused by the deformation of the satellite structure. Measuring the uncertainty and constructing a geometric imaging link model reflecting this installation method can accurately reflect the geometric imaging process and reduce the geometric positioning error.

2.2 Beam Adjustment Algorithm Based on Distance Constraint for Star Sensor Camera Integrated Geometric Link Imaging Model

In the high-resolution optical remote sensing satellite two-line array push-broom imaging process, geometric imaging is an error equation based on the collinear equation.

$$
\begin{cases}
x - x_0 + \Delta x = -f \dfrac{a_1(X - X_s) + b_1(Y - Y_s) + c_1(Z - Z_s)}{a_3(X - X_s) + b_3(Y - Y_s) + c_3(Z - Z_s)} \\
y - y_0 + \Delta y = -f \dfrac{a_2(X - X_s) + b_2(Y - Y_s) + c_2(Z - Z_s)}{a_3(X - X_s) + b_3(Y - Y_s) + c_3(Z - Z_s)}
\end{cases}
\tag{9}
$$

x_0, y_0 are the main points, f is the main distance, XS, YS, ZS are the line elements, X, Y, Z are the coordinates of the target point in the object space coordinate system, Δx, Δy are the image plane coordinate system Error. a_1, a_2, a_3, b_1, b_2, b_3, c_1, c_2, and c_3 are direction cosines, which are determined by the roll angle ω, the pitch angle φ, and the yaw angle κ. The calculation is as below:

$$
\begin{cases}
a_1 = \cos \varphi \cos \kappa - \sin \varphi \sin \omega \sin \kappa \\
a_2 = -\cos \varphi \sin \kappa - \sin \varphi \sin \omega \cos \kappa \\
a_3 = -\sin \varphi \cos \omega \\
b_1 = \cos \omega \sin \kappa \\
b_2 = \cos \omega \cos \kappa \\
b_3 = -\sin \omega \\
c_1 = \sin \varphi \cos \kappa + \cos \varphi \sin \omega \sin \kappa \\
c_2 = -\sin \varphi \sin \kappa + \cos \varphi \sin \omega \cos \kappa \\
c_3 = \cos \varphi \cos \omega
\end{cases}
\tag{10}
$$

The rotation matrix element is expressed as a function of the outer orientation element, and the formula (9) is developed according to the Taylor formula, and the term is obtained once to obtain the error equation of the imaging geometric model:

$$
\begin{cases}
e_x = \frac{\partial x}{\partial x_0} \Delta x_0 + \frac{\partial x}{\partial f} \Delta f + \frac{\partial x}{\partial X_s} \Delta X_s + \frac{\partial x}{\partial Y_s} \Delta Y_s + \frac{\partial x}{\partial Z_s} \Delta Z_s + \frac{\partial x}{\partial \omega} \Delta \omega + \\
\frac{\partial x}{\partial \phi} \Delta \varphi + \frac{\partial x}{\partial \kappa} \Delta \kappa + \frac{\partial x}{\partial X} \Delta X + \frac{\partial x}{\partial Y} \Delta Y + \frac{\partial x}{\partial Z} \Delta Z - (x - x^0) - \Delta x \\
e_y = \frac{\partial y}{\partial y_0} \Delta y_0 + \frac{\partial y}{\partial f} \Delta f + \frac{\partial y}{\partial X_s} \Delta X_s + \frac{\partial y}{\partial Y_s} \Delta Y_s + \frac{\partial y}{\partial Z_s} \Delta Z_s + \frac{\partial y}{\partial \omega} \Delta \omega + \\
\frac{\partial y}{\partial \phi} \Delta \varphi + \frac{\partial y}{\partial \kappa} \Delta \kappa + \frac{\partial y}{\partial X} \Delta X + \frac{\partial y}{\partial Y} \Delta Y + \frac{\partial y}{\partial Z} \Delta Z - (y - y^0) - \Delta y
\end{cases}
\tag{11}
$$

e_x and e_y are image point coordinate residuals, x and y are the image point coordinates corresponding to the known control points, and x_0 and y_0 are the image point coordinates calculated by substituting the approximate values of the pending parameters into the collinear equation. When the ground point coordinate errors ΔX, ΔY, ΔZ are introduced, corresponding weights are introduced to the ground point coordinates to reflect the precision characteristics of the control points. The image point observation weights are equal and $P = I$. The matrix form is:

$$E = AF - L, \ P = L. \tag{12}$$

$$F = [\Delta x_0, \Delta y_0, \Delta f, \Delta X_s, \Delta Y_s, \Delta Z_s, \Delta \omega, \Delta \varphi, \Delta \kappa, \Delta X, \Delta Y, \Delta Z, -\Delta x, -\Delta y]^T$$

For every pixel:

$$E_i = [e_x, e_y]^T. \tag{13}$$

$$A_i = \left[\begin{matrix} \frac{\partial x}{\partial x_0}, \frac{\partial x}{\partial y_0}, \frac{\partial x}{\partial f}, \frac{\partial x}{\partial X_s}, \frac{\partial x}{\partial Y_s}, \frac{\partial x}{\partial Z_s}, \frac{\partial x}{\partial \omega}, \frac{\partial x}{\partial \varphi}, \frac{\partial x}{\partial \kappa}, \frac{\partial x}{\partial X}, \frac{\partial x}{\partial Y}, \frac{\partial x}{\partial Z}, 1, 0 \\ \frac{\partial y}{\partial x_0}, \frac{\partial y}{\partial y_0}, \frac{\partial y}{\partial f}, \frac{\partial y}{\partial X_s}, \frac{\partial y}{\partial Y_s}, \frac{\partial y}{\partial Z_s}, \frac{\partial y}{\partial \omega}, \frac{\partial y}{\partial \varphi}, \frac{\partial y}{\partial \kappa}, \frac{\partial y}{\partial X}, \frac{\partial y}{\partial Y}, \frac{\partial y}{\partial Z}, 0, 1 \end{matrix} \right]. \tag{14}$$

$$L_i = [l_x, l_y]^T = [x - x^0, y - y^0]^T. \tag{15}$$

When using linearized error equations to calculate the corrections, there are 14 unknowns. At least 14 equations need to be listed. Each pair of square and object points can list 2 equations, so if there are 7 known The control points of the ground coordinates can solve each correction number. According to the principle of least squares indirect adjustment, the equations can be listed.

$$A^T P A F^* = A^T P L. \tag{16}$$

P is the weight matrix of the observation value, which reflects the measurement accuracy of the observation value. The observation value of all the image point coordinates is generally considered to be an equal precision measurement, then P is the unit matrix, thus obtaining the solution of the normal equation.

$$F^* = (A^T A)^{-1} A^T L. \tag{17}$$

Each of the correction numbers Δx_0, Δy_0, Δf, ΔX_S, ΔY_S, ΔZ_S, $\Delta \omega$, $\Delta \varphi$, $\Delta \kappa$, ΔX, ΔY, ΔZ, Δx, Δy can be obtained. The sum of the initial values of x0, y0, f, XS, YS, ZS, ω, φ, κ and the corresponding corrections after each iteration is the initial value of the next iteration, and a new correction is obtained until the correction is made. The numbers Δx_0, Δy_0, Δf, ΔX_S, ΔY_S, ΔZ_S, $\Delta \omega$, $\Delta \varphi$, and $\Delta \kappa$ are less than a certain limit [13].

Based on the traditional beam adjustment, the star sensor camera integrated imaging geometric link model is introduced. In the calculation of the scale factor, the additional distance constraint is added to obtain the beam of the star-sensitive camera integrated imaging geometric link model based on distance constraint. Adjustment algorithm, the flow chart is as follows (Fig. 2):

As shown in the above figure, it can effectively improve the sensitivity of the beam adjustment algorithm to the elevation data, as the star-sensing camera integrated

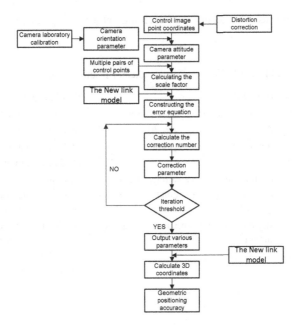

Fig. 2. Algorithm flowchart

geometric imaging link model is brought into the adjustment process based on the traditional beam adjustment, and when calculating the scale factor, the traditional three-dimensional coordinates of the actual control point are replaced by the distance between the actual three-dimensional point pairs.

3   Simulation Verification

In the high-resolution optical remote sensing satellite geometric link, the influencing factors of geometric positioning accuracy include systematic error and random error, and the random error is mainly related to the geometric stability of the high-resolution optical remote sensing satellite. Firstly, the design parameters of the remote sensing satellite of the ZY-3 are used to simulate the remote sensing satellite imaging by the high-resolution optical remote sensing satellite geometric link imaging model with of systematic error and random error. Secondly, the beam adjustment algorithm based on the distance-constrained star-sensitive camera integrated imaging geometric link model is used to simulate the remote sensing satellite imaging at the same conditions. The distribution of geometric positioning errors in the two simulation results is analyzed to verify the correction effect of the new adjustment algorithm on geometric positioning error.

Set the satellite orbit height to 506 km, the camera's main distance is 1700 mm, the line array length is 16384 pixels, the pixel size is 10 μm, the front and rear view cameras and the front view camera are at an angle of 22°, and the ground sampling terrain is mountainous. The accuracy of each indicator in the geometric link is listed in Table 1.

Table 1. Accuracy of each indicator in the geometric link

Source of error	System item	Random item
Main point	Measurement error: $\varepsilon_{y0} = 2$ μm	Stability accuracy: $\sigma_{y0} = 2$ μm
Main distance	Measurement error: $\varepsilon_f = 20$ μm	Stability accuracy: $\sigma_f = 2$ μm
Distortion	Measurement error: $\varepsilon_D = 2$ μm	Stability accuracy: $\sigma_D = 2$ μm
Orbit	–	Orbital accuracy: $\sigma_P = 0.05$ m
Attitude	Satellite attitude measurement and determination of systematic errors: $\varepsilon_\varphi = \varepsilon_\omega = \varepsilon_\kappa = 5''$	Satellite attitude measurement and determination accuracy: $\sigma_\varphi = \sigma_\omega = \sigma_\kappa = 0.8''$
	Angle error between star-sensing and camera: $\varepsilon_\theta = 1''$	Angle stability between star sensor and camera: $\sigma_\theta = 0.5''$
Time synchronization	–	Time synchronization accuracy: $\sigma_t = 20$ μs

A two-line camera is positioned based on the same name on a stereo image. Remote sensing imaging direct positioning simulation, the simulation steps are as follows:

(1) Set both systematic and random errors to exist.
(2) Select 11 identical positions at equal intervals on each array of front and rear view cameras, and calculate the positioning error at the selected position.
(3) Repeating the operation 10 times is equivalent to selecting 10 × 11 points on each satellite image.
(4) Calculate the positioning accuracy by using the positioning accuracy evaluation method based on the round error probability.
(5) Set the system error to 0 and repeat steps (2)–(4).

Table 2. Simulated imaging X, Y coordinate positioning error in presence of systematic errors

	Y1	Y2	Y3	Y 4	Y5	Y6	Y7	Y8	Y9	Y10	Y11
y/pixels	−8192	−6554	−4915	−3277	−1638	0	1638	3277	4915	6554	8192
Ex/m	20.65	21.66	22.72	23.85	25.02	26.26	27.58	28.94	30.42	32	33.67
Ey/m	−107.2	−112.0	−117.1	−122.7	−128.7	−135.3	−142.4	−150.2	−158.7	−168.0	−178.3

The X coordinate positioning error and the Y coordinate positioning error in the presence of systematic errors are listed in Table 2, respectively.

The error distribution is shown in Fig. 3.

When the systematic error exists, the positioning error is large, the direction of the positioning error vector is systematic, and the positioning errors at different positions on the same array are similar, indicating that the imaging axes at the different positions

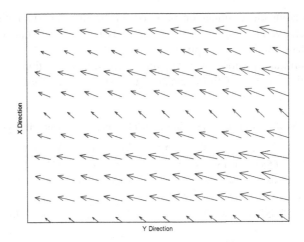

Fig. 3. Distribution of positioning error in the presence of systematic errors

on the same array have the same orbit and attitude parameters, which match the actual situation.

In addition, the simulation results are calculated as: $\hat{u}_X = 26.62$, $\hat{u}_Y = -138.28$, $\hat{\sigma}_X = 5.12$, $\hat{\sigma}_Y = 51.11$, $\hat{\rho} = -0.0389$, and then according to the positioning accuracy evaluation model based on the circular probability error, it is calculated that when R = 205.62 m, P = 0.9, that is, the positioning accuracy based on the 90% probability

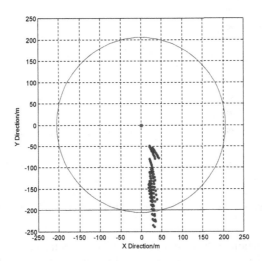

Fig. 4. Positioning accuracy with systematic errors (CE 90)

of the circle error is 205.62 m. The positioning accuracy based on the circular probability error is shown in Fig. 4 [11].

The beam adjustment simulation is based on the imaging simulation. The mean value of the iterative threshold distance constraint is 1 m, and the standard deviation of the image surface residual is 0.5 pixel.

The X coordinate positioning error, the Y coordinate positioning error, and the elevation positioning error with systematic errors are listed in Table 3.

Table 3. X, Y, Z coordinate positioning error of beam adjustment with systematic error

	Y1	Y2	Y3	Y 4	Y5	Y6	Y7	Y8	Y9	Y10	Y11
y/pixels	−8192	−6554	−4915	−3277	−1638	0	1638	3277	4915	6554	8192
Ex/m	7.39	7.68	7.94	8.2	8.54	8.84	9.21	9.58	10	10.36	10.83
Ey/m	4.846	5.01	5.155	5.332	5.53	5.743	5.952	6.202	6.501	6.807	7.087
Ez/m	2.58	2.651	2.738	2.844	2.922	3.043	3.16	3.268	3.401	3.571	3.745

In addition, the simulation results are calculated as: $\hat{u}_X = 0.90$, $\hat{\sigma}_X = 4.17$, $\hat{\mu}_Y = 5.83$, $\hat{\sigma}_Y = 39.16$, $\hat{\mu}_Z = 3.08$, $\hat{\sigma}_z = 19.66$. Firstly, testing the sample for normality and independence came to the conclusion, $\hat{\rho} = -0.099$. Then, according to the positioning accuracy evaluation model based on the circular probability error, it is calculated that when R = 63.89 m, P = 0.9, that is the positioning accuracy is 63.89 m based on the 90% probability of the circle error. A schematic diagram of positioning accuracy based on circular probability error is shown in Fig. 5.

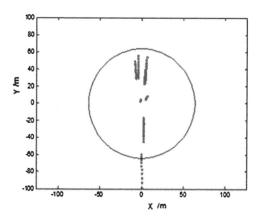

Fig. 5. Positioning accuracy with systematic errors (CE 90)

Firstly, the direction of the positioning error vector obtained from Tables 2 and 3 is more random, and the positioning errors at different positions on the same array are similar, indicating that the imaging moments at the different positions on the same array have the same orbit and attitude. This is consistent with the actual situation.

Secondly, it can be seen from the analysis of Figs. 4 and 5 that the error is distributed around the center of the circle, indicating that the system error component is small and the random error component is large; and in the case of some coarse errors, the geometric ground processing results are still steadily converged, which verifies the algorithm's stability.

Compared with the simulation results of the geometrical positioning accuracy of the push-pull imaging of the bilinear camera, the plane positioning error is greatly reduced, and the plane positioning accuracy is reduced from 205.62 m to 63.89 m (CE90), but the mean value of the plane positioning error is 0.90 m and 5.83 m., indicating that the systematic error has not been completely eliminated.

Finally, the target to be measured is a discrete point obtained by the mountain terrain. We obtained that elevation accuracy is 19.66 m (1σ) by processing the simulated remote sensing image. It is verified that the beam adjustment algorithm based on the distance constraint-based star-sensitive camera integrated geometric imaging link model is feasible under the condition of mountain topography observation.

4 Summary

The beam adjustment algorithm based on the distance constraint-based star-sensitive camera integrated geometric imaging link model is simulated by selecting ZY-3 design parameters. The simulation results show that the algorithm can not correct the positioning error caused by random error. But it can effectively eliminate the systematic error component in the positioning error, and greatly improve the geometric positioning accuracy of remote sensing satellite imaging. It is of great significance to enhance the geometric positioning capability of remote sensing satellites.

References

1. Huang, Q., Jiang, W.: A study of the new direction of space-borne hi-resolution optical remote sensor. Spacecr. Recovery Remote Sens. **28**(4), 48–50 (2007). (in Chinese)
2. Xia, Z., Huang, Q., He, H., et al.: Analysis of geolocation accuracy of high resolution optical remote sensing satellite geometric chain. Spacecr. Recovery Remote Sens. **37**(3), 111–119 (2016). (in Chinese)
3. Xia, Z., Huang, Q., He, H., et al.: Study on geometric performance assessment method of high resolution optical remote sensing satellite imagery. In: Eighth International Symposium on Advanced Optical Manufacturing & Testing Technology, Suzhou, vol. 9682, p. 96820N (2016)
4. Ruan, N., Zhuang, X., Li, T., et al.: End to end simulation and analysis of space optical remote sensing system. Spacecr. Recovery Remote Sens. **34**(6), 36–43 (2013). (in Chinese)
5. Yu, J.: Accurate Geometric Positioning of High Resolution Satellite Remote Sensing Imagery. Wuhan University, Wuhan (2009). (in Chinese)
6. Wang, R., Wang, J., Hu, X.: Preliminary location accuracy assessments of 3rd satellite of TH-1. Acta Geodaetica et Cartographica Sinica **45**(10), 1135–1139 (2016). (in Chinese)
7. Sheng, Q., Xiao, H.: Satellite Remote Sensing and Photogrammetry. Science Publishing House, Beijing (2015). (in Chinese)
8. Wang, J., Wang, R., Hu, X.: Discussion on evaluation of satellite imagery location accuracy. Spacecr. Recovery Remote Sens. **38**(1), 1–5 (2017). (in Chinese)

9. Tao, J.I.N., Zhen, L.I., Ting, L.I., et al.: System design and analysis for improving geometric accuracy of high-resolution optical remote sensing satellite image. J. Astronaut. **34**(8), 1160–1165 (2013). (in Chinese)

10. Zhou, N., He, H.: Research of geometric exterior calibration of space-borne linear array sensor. Spacecr. Recovery Remote Sens. **36**(5), 111–118 (2016). (in Chinese)

11. Tian, G., Huang, Q., He, H., et al.: Analysis on geometric positioning accuracy evaluation of remote sensing satellite image. Spacecr. Recovery Remote Sens. **38**(10), 111–119 (2017). (in Chinese)

12. Tian, G., Huang, Q., He, H., et al.: Analysis of the influence of undulate terrain on the geometric accuracy of remote sensing images. IMCCC 2018 (2018)

13. Zhang, G.: Line Push-broom Remote Sensing Satellite Geometry to Deal with High Precision. Science Publishing House, Beijing (2016). (in Chinese)

Dynamic Load Balancing Algorithm Based on Per-pixel Rendering Cost Estimation for Parallel Ray Tracing on PC Clusters

Chaozhi Yang, Chunyi Chen[(✉)], Xiaojuan Hu, and Huamin Yang

School of Computer Science and Technology, Changchun University of Science and Technology, Changchun 130022, China
chenchunyi@hotmail.com

Abstract. Load balancing determines the performance of the sort-first rendering clusters. A dynamic load balancing algorithm based on per-pixel rendering cost is proposed. Firstly, a 3D scene is rendered by ray tracing. At the same time, the number of intersection points between rays and scene objects in a pixel is obtained. Then, a rendering-cost map is created according to these numbers in a frame. Based on the render history, the rendering-cost map in a previous frame is used to estimate the real distribution of the ray tracing rendering cost in a future frame. Finally, a load assignment strategy is proposed to make rendering cost more uniform among rendering nodes. The experimental results show that the proposed algorithm can render continuously the next frame by subdividing future frames in advance. It is better than the compared algorithm in terms of load balancing and frame rate.

Keywords: Ray tracing · PC-clusters · Load balancing · Parallel rendering · Sort-first

1 Introduction

Due to recent technological advancements, the virtual reality (VR), 3D and interactive games are achieving rapid development. Photorealism and rendering speed are two key issues in these applications. Although the computing power of existing single computer has been greatly improved compared with the past, it is still difficult to meet the computing needs of current applications. Cluster-based parallel graphics rendering system is one of the high-performance solutions [1]. Those rendering applications, such as 3D scenes, are very suitable for parallel processing in cluster computing environment.

There are three major categories of methods for parallel rendering systems, namely sort-first architecture, sort-middle architecture and sort-last architecture [2]. The combination of sort-first parallel rendering architecture and personal computer (PC) clusters is an efficient way to speed up the ray tracing algorithm. Besides, good load balancing is crucial in order to fully exploit the available computational power of sort-first clusters [3].

To solve the load balancing problem in the cluster, we propose a dynamic load balancing algorithm based on per-pixel rendering cost estimation (abbreviated as PRCE

© Springer Nature Singapore Pte Ltd. 2019
Y. Wang et al. (Eds.): IGTA 2019, CCIS 1043, pp. 591–601, 2019.
https://doi.org/10.1007/978-981-13-9917-6_56

algorithm). The PRCE algorithm can solve the load balancing problem in single-frame screen partition of sort-first clusters. It adopts load estimation based on the spatial-temporal coherence [4] of parallel ray tracing. Take the pixel's rendering cost of the last frame as the load estimation of the future frame. The pixel's rendering cost is relative with the number of intersection points between ray and geometric object. Using the PRCE algorithm, the scenes could render efficiently under the complex illumination.

The rest of this paper are organized as follows: Sect. 2 presents some related works about the load balancing and cluster architecture. In Sect. 3, we clarify the proposed algorithm in detail. In Sect. 4, we conducted the experiments and analysis the results. Finally, we conclude this paper in Sect. 5.

2 Related Work

2.1 Load Balancing

For the problem of rendering load balancing between multiple nodes, many researchers have given solutions and discussions. Such as Abraham et al. [5] proposed a load balancing algorithm based on the render history. The algorithm uses the rendering time of the previous frame to estimate the workload of the next frame, which is simple and easy to implement. Chang et al. [6] proposed a method that based on the 2-pass rendering character of deferred shading to predict the rendering load distribution among the screen space. It achieved per-pixel load distribution as a gray image in real-time by utilizing fragment shader and alpha blending in GPU. Serina et al. [7] presented a reservoir technology, which reduces the communication overhead among rendering nodes and improves the efficiency of the cluster. Ji et al. [8] presents a dynamic load balancing strategy based on screen partition of dual division and 3D space division. They realized the load balancing of physical simulation load in the parallel system. Wang et al. [9] solves the load balancing problem by the feedback data of rendering nodes. Rincón-Nigro et al. [10] estimated the overhead of processing each task by performing a reduced traversal of the rays over bounding volume hierarchies (BVH). It can enhance common balancing strategies and reduce rendering times. Cosenza et al. [11] proposed a method based on deferred shading and image sampling to compute a cost map. It can be used for adaptive task partitioning and enhanced dynamic load balancing. Lin et al. [12] proposed an adaptive task division method based on prediction binary tree (PBT), which significantly improved the performance of the sort-first parallel rendering system. Li et al. [13] proposed a dynamic feedback strategy. It could reduce the rendering time by introducing load ratio and adding exponential filter.

Most of above methods are achieved based on rendering history, which treats the rendering time of the previous frame as the estimation cost of the next frame. After the image of the previous frame is rendered, the division of the next frame begins. We have to wait for the end of the division before we render the next frame. It could generate a vacuum of rendering and reduce the efficiency of cluster. The PRCE algorithm solved this problem, which can render continuously the future frame and distribute evenly the rendering cost.

2.2   Cluster Architecture

This paper adopted the sort-first parallel rendering cluster to render the dynamic complex scenes. The cluster used in this paper includes a control node, four rendering nodes and a Gigabit Ethernet switch. The control node is mainly responsible for load division and allocation, synchronization of the global clock, and display of the final result. Each rendering node is a complete computer with the independent operating system. The data of test scenes, which included the model data, the scene layout and the configuration, is stored on the hard disks of the corresponding rendering node. Each rendering node is equipped with a graphics processing unit (GPU) for powerful graphics interactive ability, and is installed GPU development tools to realize the real-time rendering of 3D photorealistic scenes (Fig. 1).

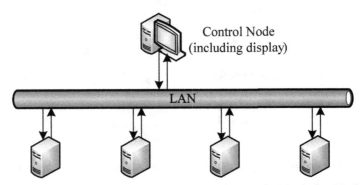

Fig. 1. The sort-first parallel rendering cluster.

3   Dynamic Load Balancing Algorithm Based on Per-pixel Rendering Cost Estimation

Focusing on the load balancing problem in sort-first rendering clusters, we proposed the PRCE algorithm. It adopts the load prediction based on the render history. The screen space of a future frame is subdivided based on a rendering-cost map of the previous frame. The proposed algorithm has two important processes. One is calculating the rendering-cost map of each frame. Another is that the control node divides the screen space according to a cost assignment strategy.

3.1   Create the Map of Rendering Cost

In ray tracing, the intersection detection of the rays and scene objects is the most time-consuming [11]. Direct and indirect illumination rays could intersect objects of different materials, such as diffuse surfaces, specular reflected surfaces, specular transparent surfaces, and more [14]. When they intersected, a shadow test ray will be launched. And it has intersection detection, too. All of the above intersection detections are accelerated using the bounding volume hierarchy (BVH). If these rays don't intersect with the BVH, their computation cost can be ignored. If intersected, they require a lot of time and space. The more intersections, the greater the amount of calculation [15]. Besides, the number of intersections is easily obtained in ray tracing process. Therefore, we take the number of intersections as the rendering cost estimation of a pixel. The rendering-cost map is made up of these numbers of all pixel and it is used to estimate the real distribution of the ray tracing rendering cost in a future frame (Fig. 2).

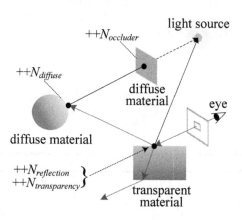

Fig. 2. The statistical process of intersection points in a pixel based on ray tracing.

In the PRCE algorithm, we divide the intersection points into diffuse-points, reflection-points, transparency-points and occluder-points. The process of counting the number of these points in a pixel is described as follows. When the direct illumination ray intersects the diffuse material surface, the number of diffuse-points plus one. A new indirect illumination ray (reflection or transparency) will be launched when a direct or indirect illumination ray intersects a surface with the reflected or transparent. And the number of corresponding intersection points is added by one. When the shadow test ray intersects an object, the number of occluder-points is added by one. Finally, the program ends if the termination condition is satisfied. According to the number of intersection points, the rendering cost formula is described.

$$C_{rendering} = \left(N_{diffuse} + N_{reflection} + N_{transparency}\right) \times c + N_{occluder} \quad (c \in N^*). \quad (1)$$

Where, $C_{rendering}$ denotes the rendering cost estimation of the pixel in screen. $N_{diffuse}$, $N_{reflection}$, $N_{transparency}$ and $N_{occluder}$ denote the number of diffuse-points, reflection-points, transparency-points and occluder-points in this pixel, respectively. The c is an experiential parameter. Because the occluder-point from the shadow test ray needn't to calculate the value of the pixel color, we multiply the other intersections by a positive integer parameter to make the pixel's rendering cost estimation more accurate.

3.2   Divide the Screen Space

As Fig. 3 shows, the proposed algorithm could subdivide the screen space of the future frame in advance. The division process of the next frame has been completed before the end of the last frame's rendering. And it is demonstrated in the experimental chapter. Due to the nature of this method, the rendering-cost maps of the first frame and second frame cannot be obtained in advance. So, these two frames are divided by static load balancing.

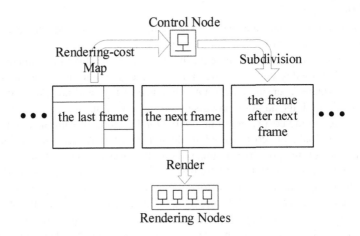

Fig. 3.   The schematic diagram of subdividing the frame after next frame in advance.

In load balancing, one of the most important processes is to equally distribute tasks. We split the screen according to a cost assignment strategy in this paper, which ensures that the rendering cost of each screen-tile is basically the same. In the implementation, a special linear list (queue) is used. First, we put the entire image in the queue. Then, the image is dequeued and subdivided into two tiles. The split-axis is found on the longest edge of the divided image. Next, these new tiles are queued in order. When the number of tiles is same as the number of rendering nodes, the division of this frame is finished. There are 2^x rendering nodes and the x is a positive integer. Finally, we record its location and index at the original image and the data is sent to rendering nodes.

If the longest edge of the original image is along the X-axis, the process that control node splits this image into two tiles is described as follows. The resolution of this image is *width* × *height*.

Step 1. Calculate the sum of rendering cost in rendering-cost map. The rendering cost of all pixel are stored in the cache *Cost[width, height]*. The cache *Cost* is traversed column by column and its value is added column by column. These sums are placed in the array *Sum[width]*.

Step 2. Determine the location of the split-axis. The array of *Sum* is naturally an ascending sequence. Then we use the method of binary search to find the first value that is equal to or greater than *half_sum* (a half of the rendering cost total) in *Sum*. We record the location (*axis*) of this value in *Sum* and the *axis* is the split-axis.

Step 3. According to the optimization principle, the image is divided:

IF $|Sum[axis]\text{-}half\_sum| \geq |Sum[axis\text{-}1]\text{-}half\_sum|$ **THEN**

The rendering cost in *axis* belongs to the right. Take this column and right pixels as the right tile. The remaining pixels are the left tile.

ELSE

Take this column and left pixels as the left tile. The remaining pixels are the right tile.

END IF

Step 4. Record the starting and ending of the two tiles in the screen coordinate system. This process of subdivision is end.

For the above cost assignment strategy, there are three additional explanations. First, the pattern that divides an image along the longest edge could make the shape of tiles similar to a square. It ensures a certain coherence of rays and has good acceleration with BVH. Second, the addition process of the cache *Cost* in step 1 is shown in Fig. 4. The sum of rendering cost is stored in *Sum[width-1]*. Third, the optimization principle in step 3 could make the cost of the left tile and right tile more balanced. Figure 5 is an example about this principle. In this picture, the rendering cost of the gray and the white are most balanced. But the tile must be a rectangle. So, the *axis* belongs to either the left tile or the right tile. S_1 is the total rendering cost above *h* in *axis*. S_2 is the rest in *axis*. If *axis* is a part of the left tile, S_2 is the extra cost in the left. If not, S_1 is the extra cost in the right. When S_2 is greater than or equal to S_1, the extra cost caused by putting *axis* in the right is less than left. So, it is more suitable that puts *axis* in the right tile in this example.

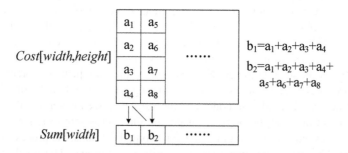

Fig. 4. The addition process of the rendering cost in cache *Cost*.

4   Results and Analysis

The cluster used in the experiment consists of four rendering computers, a control computer and a Gigabit Ethernet switch. The configuration of rendering nodes is same as control node. Them include an Intel(R) Xeon(R) CPU E3-1225 v3 @3.20 GHz together with 8 GB RAM. The GPUs of rendering nodes are uniformly equipped with a

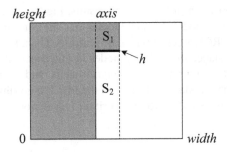

Fig. 5. The optimization principle in division.

4 GB NVIDIA Quadro K2000 graphics card. The GPU development tools are the NVIDIA OptiX SDK 4.1.1 and NVIDIA CUDA SDK 7.5. The switch is HUAWEI S5700-24TP-SI-AC. The test scenes are dynamic. And the images shown later are generated at a resolution of 1024(width) × 768(height). The value of the experiential parameter c in formula (1) is 3. Rendering nodes use BVH to accelerate during ray tracing. And the maximum depth of recursion is 15. In order to reflect the effectiveness of the PRCE algorithm, the load balancing algorithm in reference [12] is taken as the compared algorithm. And for short, it is abbreviated as PBT algorithm.

4.1 The Analysis About Load Balancing

Figure 6 shows the test scene. Some walls and floor are made of reflective material. The irregular green cube in the middle is transparent. And the material of other objects is diffuse. This scene contains 770k surfaces and has a large number of intersection detections. There are many reflection rays and transparency rays in the interior of the irregular green cube. Much of the rendering cost is concentrated in this area. So, this scene can be used for load balancing testing.

Fig. 6. The test scene rendered by ray tracing (Color figure online)

Figure 7 is a comparison of the division results. Figures 8 and 9 are the rendering time of the four rendering nodes. It can be found that, the consuming time of each node in same frame by the PRCE algorithm is more uniform. Then, the Standard Deviation is used to evaluate the balance of rendering nodes in this paper. When it is equal to 0, it means that the load of the four rendering nodes is same, and the most balanced state is reached. In Fig. 10, the Standard Deviation of the PRCE algorithm is generally smaller than the PBT algorithm. So, the PRCE algorithm is superior to the PBT algorithm in load balancing.

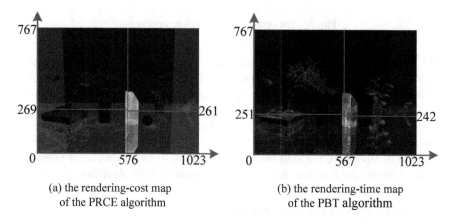

(a) the rendering-cost map
of the PRCE algorithm

(b) the rendering-time map
of the PBT algorithm

Fig. 7. The different subdivision result of the test scene.

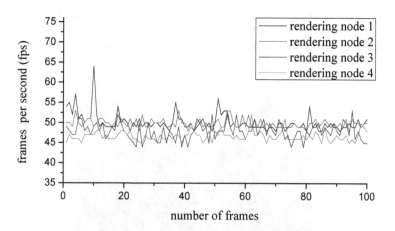

Fig. 8. The rendering time of each rendering node by the PRCE algorithm.

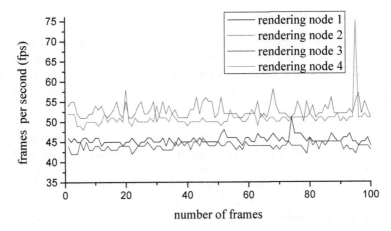

Fig. 9. The rendering time of each rendering node by the PBT algorithm.

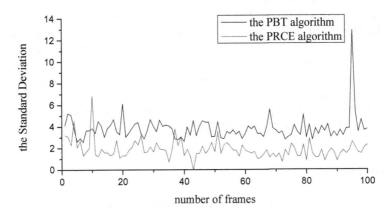

Fig. 10. The comparison of load balancing through the Standard Deviation.

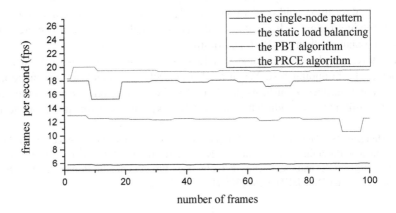

Fig. 11. The comparison of frame rate with different algorithms.

4.2   The Analysis About Efficiency

Figure 11 shows the comparison of frame rate in the same scene. In addition to the single-node pattern, the rest algorithms used four rendering nodes. The performance of cluster based on these load balancing algorithms is better than the single-node pattern. In terms of the frame rate, the PRCE algorithm is significantly better than other algorithms.

In PRCE algorithm, T_{divi} is the time of dividing screen space. T_{recv_max} is the maximal time of receiving result in control node. T_{rend_max} is the maximal time of rendering a tile in rendering nodes. In the ray-tracing engine of OptiX, the RGB values of a pixel RGB uses 4 bytes for storage, and the rendering cost of a pixel uses 1byte. In theory, an average rendering node in each frame sends 1 MB ($1024 \times 768 \times 5B/4$) data. The average transmission time of these data in the switch used in the experiment is 8 ms. Because the load distribution is generally unbalanced, T_{recv_max} is greater than 8 ms. The data volume of a rendering-cost map and all RGB value is same in every frame. So, T_{divi} in each frame is similar, about 10 ms. The screen-tile index data volume is very little. So, this transmission time can be ignored. And the rendering nodes sends the result of the last frame while rendering the next frame by using multithreading. Then, T_{recv_max} plus T_{divi} is about 23 ms at the test scenes. However, T_{rend_max} is about 54 ms. It can be found that the sum of the dividing time and transmission time is significantly less than the rendering time. So, the division process of the next frame has been completed before the end of the last frame's rendering. Compared with the PBT algorithm, the PRCE algorithm that divides future frame in advance sacrifices little temporal coherence in ray tracing, but it could render continuously the next frame and optimize the entire process.

5   Conclusion

This paper proposes a dynamic load balancing algorithm based on per-pixel rendering cost estimation for sort-first clusters. We gain easily the rendering-cost map based on ray tracing. The rendering-cost map in the last frame could be taken as the estimation of real distribution of the ray tracing rendering cost in the frame after next frame. The PRCE algorithm could render continuously the next frame and reduce the waiting time of dividing progress. It sacrifices little temporal coherence, but it is more efficient and more balanced than the PBT algorithm.

In future, we plan to add some new factors to refine the formula (1), such as the number of the bounding box. When a ray intersects the model of same material but with different number of surfaces, the bounding box is different. It makes the time of calculation different. So, adding this factor will make the cost estimation more accurate.

Acknowledgments. This work was supported by Jilin Provincial Science & Technology Development Program of China (No. 20170101005JC, No. 20180519012JH, No. 20190302113GX) and the Science & Technology Program of Jilin Provincial Department of Education of China (No. JJKH20181136KJ).

References

1. Mueller, C.: The sort-first rendering architecture for high-performance graphics. In: Proceedings of the 1995 Symposium on Interactive 3D Graphics, pp. 75–85. ACM (1995)
2. Molnar, S., Cox, M., Ellsworth, D., Fuchs, H.: A sorting classification of parallel rendering. IEEE Comput. Graph. Appl. **14**, 23–32 (1994)
3. Yaseen, A., Ji, H., Li, Y.: A load-balancing workload distribution scheme for three-body interaction computation on graphics processing units (GPU). J. Parallel Distrib. Comput. **87**, 91–101 (2016)
4. Cosenza, B., Cordasco, G., Chiara, R.D., Erra, U., Scarano, V.: On estimating the effectiveness of temporal and spatial coherence in parallel ray tracing. In: 6th Eurographics Italian Chapter Conference, pp. 97–104 (2008)
5. Abraham, F., Filho, W.C., Cerqueira, R., Campos, J.L.: A load-balancing strategy for sort-first distributed rendering. In: 17th Brazilian Symposium on Computer Graphics and Image Processing, pp. 292–299. IEEE (2004)
6. Chang, H., Lei, X., Dai S.: A dynamic load balancing algorithm for sort-first rendering clusters. In: 2009 2nd IEEE International Conference on Computer Science and Information Technology, pp. 515–519. IEEE (2009)
7. Serina, F.J., Madamba, J.A.R.: Reservoir: an alternative load balancing technique for parallel ray tracing. In: 2011 Fifth Asia Modelling Symposium, pp. 193–197. IEEE (2011)
8. Ji, Z., He, B.: A dynamic load balancing method for parallel rendering and physical simulation system based sort-first architecture. In: Proceedings of 2011 International Conference on Computer Science and Network Technology, vol. 3, pp. 1792–1796. IEEE (2011)
9. Wang, W., Zhao, Z.X., Xu, Q., Liu, T.: Design and implementation of adaptive dynamic load balancing distributed parallel rendering system based on sort-first. Adv. Mater. Res. **798**, 693–698 (2013)
10. Rincón-Nigro, M., Deng Z.G.: Cost-based workload balancing for ray tracing on multi-GPU systems. In: ACM SIGGRAPH 2013 Posters, pp. 41–42. ACM (2013)
11. Cosenza, B., Dachsbacher, C., Erra, U.: GPU cost estimation for load balancing in parallel ray tracing. In: International Conference on Computer Graphics Theory and Applications, pp. 139–151 (2018)
12. Lin, Z., Zhao, L., Yuan, Q., Lu, D., Li, Y.: Immersive virtual tour using multi-projection with remote cluster rendering. In: 3rd International Conference on Multimedia Technology, pp. 570–580 (2013)
13. Li, Q., Wu, W., Gao, L., Wang, L., Huang, J.: A dynamic load balancing strategy based on feedback for cluster rendering system. In: Lu, Y., Wu, X., Zhang, X. (eds.) ISCTCS 2014. CCIS, vol. 520, pp. 41–47. Springer, Heidelberg (2015). https://doi.org/10.1007/978-3-662-47401-3_6
14. Luo, D., Zhang, J.: Real-time soft shadow by A-Buffer. In: Wang, Y., Jiang, Z., Peng, Y. (eds.) IGTA 2018. CCIS, vol. 875, pp. 168–179. Springer, Singapore (2018). https://doi.org/10.1007/978-981-13-1702-6_17
15. Gao, X., Wang, X., Yang, B., Liu, Y.: Design of a computer-aided-design system for museum exhibition based on virtual reality. In: Wang, Y., et al. (eds.) IGTA 2017. CCIS, vol. 757, pp. 157–167. Springer, Singapore (2018). https://doi.org/10.1007/978-981-10-7389-2_16

Research on Warehouse Object Detection Algorithm Based on Fused DenseNet and SSD

Liangjie Chen[1], Fei Wang[2], Li Wang[1], and Lin Wang[1(✉)]

[1] College of Data Science and Information Engineering,
Guizhou Minzu University, Guiyang 550025, China
wanglin@gzmu.edu.cn
[2] College of Humanities and Sciences of Guizhou Minzu University,
Guiyang 550025, China

Abstract. Aiming at the problem that the object detection accuracy of SSD algorithm in warehouse environment is not too high, a warehouse object detection algorithm based on improved SSD that fusion of DenseNet and SSD is proposed (Dense-SSD). Firstly, a large number of images containing cargos, trays and forklifts in real warehouse environment are collected through the camera, and the collected images are labeled to building the warehouse object dataset. Further the based network of the improved algorithm based on SSD pipeline is adapted with DenseNet, the Dense-SSD is trained from scratch on the PASCAL VOC and self-built warehouse object dataset, respectively. Finally, the trained models are tested on the above two datasets respectively. Experimental results show that the proposed method can reach 77.62% mAP on the PASCAL VOC, which is higher than SSD by 5.15 points. And the Dense-SSD can reach 93.85% mAP on the self-built warehouse object dataset while the model size is only 62.9 MB, which is higher than SSD by 1.43 points. Meanwhile, the model size is reduced by 31.8 MB than SSD.

Keywords: Warehouse object detection · DenseNet · SSD

1 Introduction

Object detection is one of the popular research topics in the computer vision, which combines advanced technologies in the fields of image processing, pattern recognition, artificial intelligence and automatic control. And it has a wide range of applications in intelligent transportation, video surveillance, medical diagnostics and industrial detection, etc. The main task of object detection is to locate the position of the object of interest in the image and indicate the name of the category to which it belongs.

The object detection algorithm based on convolutional neural network (CNN) can be divided into two series: based on two stages and based on single stage. The algorithms based on two stages mainly including R-CNN [1], SPPnet [2], Fast R-CNN [3], Faster R-CNN [4] and R-FCN [5].

The R-CNN algorithm first uses selective search (SS) [6] to extract the regions of the image that may contain objects, then these regions of interest (RoI) are scaled to a uniform size, and fed into CNN for feature extraction, finally, the extracted feature

© Springer Nature Singapore Pte Ltd. 2019
Y. Wang et al. (Eds.): IGTA 2019, CCIS 1043, pp. 602–611, 2019.
https://doi.org/10.1007/978-981-13-9917-6_57

vectors are classified by SVM classifier. The SPPnet algorithm mainly avoids the repetitive calculation of convolution features, thus realizing the speed faster than R-CNN algorithm. Its main advantage is that extracted regardless of the image size, one feature map is calculated only once in the whole image, and then the feature is concentrated in any region (sub-image) to generate a fixed length representation for the training detector. The Fast R-CNN algorithm mainly adopts the idea that shared convolution calculation of region proposal, and adds a RoI pooling layer between the last convolution layer and the first fully connected layer, so that a fixed length feature is extracted for each RoI, which improves the speed and accuracy of object detection. The Faster R-CNN algorithm uses the region proposal network (RPN) instead of the SS extract region proposal, which can simultaneously share the full image convolution feature with the detection network, achieving End-to-End object detection. The R-FCN algorithm improves object detection speed and accuracy by removing the fully connected layer and using the position-sensitive score graphs for final detection.

The object detection algorithm only based on single stage mainly including YOLO (You Only Look Once) [7], SSD (Single Shot MultiBox Detector) [8] and their variants. This type algorithms mainly remove the stage of region proposal and directly predict object categories and specific locations by adopting a single feedforward convolutional neural network. YOLO realizes conversion of the object detection into a regression problem, which improves the detection speed of the object. However, the detection accuracy of object is not too high due to YOLO algorithm cancels the candidate region extraction mechanism of R-CNN, only a relatively small mesh is used for regression. SSD combines predictions from multiple feature maps of different resolutions to handle objects of various scales naturally. Which integrates the regression idea of the YOLO algorithm and the anchor mechanism of the Faster R-CNN algorithm, adopting multi-scale regional features for regression, a higher detection speed is obtained, while still maintaining high detection accuracy. Deconvolutional Single Shot Detector (DSSD) [9] combines a state-of-the-art classifier (Residual-101 [10]) with the SSD, and then the deconvolution layers are used to augment SSD + Residual-101 to introduce additional large-scale contexts and improve accuracy in object detection, especially for small objects. ESSD [11] improves the detection accuracy of small objects by extending better semantic information to the shallow part of the SSD. The feature pyramid detection method for SSD is difficult to fuse the features from different scales, and FSSD [12] introduces a novel and lightweight feature fusion module into the SSD. Which enables features from different layers with different scales are concatenated together, followed by the generation of new feature pyramids by some down-sampling blocks, that are finally fed to a multi-box detector to predict the final detection results.

At present, the warehouse object detection based on CNN become a new research hotspot in the field of computer vision gradually. However, most object detection methods are based on natural scenes or indoor scenes in the current. Such as two public object detection datasets commonly used ImageNet and Pascal VOC (Pascal Visual Object Classes) are collected images from natural scenes. There are few public datasets based on industrial detection scenarios [13], and there are more fewer open datasets for object detection based on the warehouse environment, almost no. Therefore, it is of great importance to create a large-scale and highly quality warehouse object dataset, if adopting CNN to achieve object detection based on warehouse environment.

In this paper, a large number of images in real warehouse environment first are collected and labeled to create the warehouse object dataset by cooperating with companies. Further we train the Dense-SSD from scratch on the PASCAL VOC and self-built warehouse object dataset respectively. Finally, the trained models are tested on the above two datasets respectively, and the trained model on the self-built warehouse object dataset is used to detect cargos, trays and forklifts in the warehouse environment by optimizing the model parameters.

2 Warehouse Object Detection Algorithm Based on Fused DenseNet and SSD

2.1 The Warehouse Object Detection Overall Framework Based on Fused DenseNet and SSD

The warehouse object detection framework based on fused DenseNet [14] and SSD (Dense-SSD) is an object detection algorithm based on CNN and is similar to the SSD multi-scale proposal-free detection framework. Its network structure mainly consists of the backbone sub-network and the prediction sub-network, where the core part is the backbone sub-network that is mainly used to extract image features. The backbone sub-network is a variant of the deeply supervised DenseNet structure, which is composed of a stem block, four dense blocks, two transition layers and two transition w/o pooling layers. The prediction sub-network is mainly used to prediction over multi-scale response maps, which fuses multi-scale prediction responses with an elaborated dense structure. The network structure of Dense-SSD as shown in Table 1.

Table 1. The network architectures of Dense-SSD (each "Pooling" shown in the table corresponds the Max Pooling)

Layers		Kernel	Stride
Stem	Convolution	3×3	2
	Convolution	3×3	1
	Convolution	3×3	1
	Convolution	3×3	1
	Pooling	2×2	2
Dense Block (1)	$\begin{bmatrix} 1 \times 1\ conv \\ 3 \times 3\ conv \end{bmatrix} \times 6$		1
Transition Layer (1)	Convolution	3×3	1
	Pooling	2×2	2
Dense Block (2)	$\begin{bmatrix} 1 \times 1\ conv \\ 3 \times 3\ conv \end{bmatrix} \times 6$		1

(continued)

Table 1. (*continued*)

Layers		Kernel	Stride
Transition Layer (2)	Convolution	1×1	1
	Pooling	2×2	2
Dense Block (3)	$\begin{bmatrix} 1 \times 1\ conv \\ 3 \times 3\ conv \end{bmatrix} \times 10$		1
Transition w/o Pooling Layer (1)	Convolution	1×1	1
Dense Block (4)	$\begin{bmatrix} 1 \times 1\ conv \\ 3 \times 3\ conv \end{bmatrix} \times 12$		1
Transition w/o Pooling Layer (2)	Convolution	1×1	1
Prediction Layers	Dense		

2.2 The Design Ideas of Dense-SSD

In order to achieve good performance, most of the advanced object detection frameworks fine-tuning networks pre-trained on ImageNet. Its advantages are that there are many state-of-the-art deep models publicly available, and it is very convenient to reuse them for object detection, while requiring less instance-level annotated training data.

However, there are also serious limitations when adopting fine-tuning networks from pre-trained models for object detection. Model fine-tuning limits the structural design space of the object detection network, learning bias is caused by differences in both the loss functions and the classification distributions between classification and detection tasks, there may be huge domain differences from the fields of pre-trained models to the fields of object detection, such as, it is very difficult to transfer RGB images to depth images and medical images.

Compared with other object detection scenarios, the warehouse environment is relatively special, and those public object detection datasets usually not include the warehouse object categories. In order to effectively avoid the difficulty of huge differences from pre-trained model fields to the object detection fields, and in view of the superior performance of implicit deep supervision for object detection proposed dense connections in DenseNet, we fused DenseNet and SSD in this paper. Adopting dense hierarchical connections in DenseNet, each layer of the network has direct access to the gradients from the loss function and the original input signal. Further, the dense connections have a regularizing effect, which reduces overfitting on tasks with smaller training set sizes to a certain extent. As mentioned above and inspired by [15], the pre-trained on ImageNet classification dataset is no longer required by the proposed fusion algorithm Dense-SSD, but the network is trained from scratch on the detection dataset. The design ideas of Dense-SSD detection framework are as follows:

(1) The pre-trained model on ImageNet is no longer required. The backbone network DenseNet instead of adopting the pre-trained model on ImageNet, the detection network is trained from scratch directly on the object dataset.

(2) Deep supervision learning. Its core idea is to provide integrated objective function as direct supervision to the earlier hidden layers, rather than only at the output layer. And it is attached to the hidden layer can effectively mitigate the gradient disappearance problem. The SSD detection framework contains both classification loss and localization loss, adding complex side output layers is an explicit solution to introduce objective functions for the detection task at each hidden layer. Here we empower deep supervision with a dense layer-wise connection as introduced in DenseNet, a dense hierarchical connection (dense blocks) of DenseNet is used. Hence, the earlier layer in the DenseNet can be supervised directly by the objective function with the skip connections.

(3) Each component of the feature extraction network. To reduce the information loss of original input images, we follow the idea that converting a large convolution kernel into a stack consisting of multiple small convolution kernels. The primeval design in DenseNet (7×7 conv-layer, stride = 2 followed by a 3×3 max pooling, stride = 2) is changed to a stack of four 3×3 convolution layers followed by a 2×2 max pooling layer, and this structure is defined as stem block. The transition layer between two adjacent dense blocks consists of a 1×1 convolution layer followed by a 2×2 max pooling layer. The transition w/o pooling layer eliminates this restriction of the number of dense blocks in Dense-SSD architecture, so that increase the number of dense blocks without reducing the final feature map resolution.

(4) Multi-scale dense prediction structure. Similar with multi-scale prediction structure of SSD, Dense-SSD also applies six scales of feature maps to predict the detected objects. The six scales are 38×38, 19×19, 10×10, 5×5, 3×3, 1×1 respectively. Dense structures are not only adopted in the backbone sub-network, but also in the front-end multi-scale prediction layers. In the prediction structure of SSD, each later scale is converted directly from the adjacent previous scale, while in the dense prediction structure of Dense-SSD, a 1×1 convolution layer followed by a 3×3 convolution layer are used between two contiguous scales of feature maps to integrate each scale to obtain multi-scale information. Figure 1 illustrates the comparison of the front-end prediction layer structure between the SSD and Dense-SSD detection frameworks. For simplicity, restricting that each scale outputs the same number of channels for the prediction feature maps.

(5) Learning half and reusing half. In Dense-SSD, in each scale (except 38×38), half of the feature maps are learned from the previous scale with a series of conv-layers, while the remaining half feature maps are directly down-sampled from the contiguous high-resolution feature maps. The down-sampling block consists of a 2×2, stride = 2 max pooling layer followed by a 1×1, stride = 1 convolution layer. Figure 2 illustrates schematic diagram of the down-sampling block. The pooling layer aims to match resolution to current size during concatenation. The conv-layer is used to reduce the number of channels to 50%. For each scale of Dense-SSD, only half of new feature maps are learned and reuse the remaining half of the previous ones.

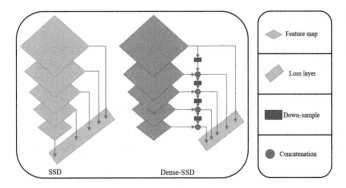

Fig. 1. SSD prediction layer with multi-scale structure and Dense-SSD prediction layer with multi-scale dense structure

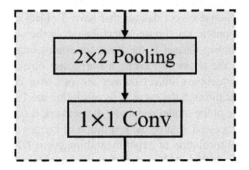

Fig. 2. Schematic diagram of the down-sampling block

2.3 Training Settings

Most of our training strategies follow SSD. Firstly, we have to match a set of default boxes to object ground truth boxes. For each ground truth box, we match it with the best overlapped default box and any default boxes whose Jaccard overlap is larger than a threshold with 0.5. Among the non-matched default boxes, we select certain boxes as negative samples based on the confidence loss so that the ratio with the matched ones is 3:1. Secondly, we adopt the L2 normalization technique to scale the feature norm to 20 on all outputs, since each scale of Dense-SSD feature maps is concatenated from multiple resolutions. Finally, the horizontal flip technique is used to augmented data, while we have our own learning rate scheduling and mini-batch size settings. Details will be given in the experimental section.

3   Experiments

The hardware and software configurations adopted for experiments in this paper are shown in Table 2, and the Caffe framework in deep learning is used.

Table 2. Experimental configuration

Operating system	CPU	Memory	GPU	CUDA
Ubuntu 16.04	Intel i7-7700K	16 GB	NVIDIA TITAN X	CUDA8.0

3.1   Experimental Datasets

In order to verify the effectiveness of the proposed Dense-SSD algorithm, we conduct experiments on the widely used PASCAL VOC dataset that have 20 object categories and the self-built warehouse object dataset that have 3 object categories respectively. At present, there is no public warehouse object dataset in the warehouse environment, while the warehouse object dataset is the basis for completing the warehouse object detection tasks. Given the above, we create a warehouse object dataset in this paper. those images in the warehouse object dataset are our own collected from the real warehouse environment through the camera, its resolution are 1920 × 1080. In order to reduce the training time of the model and make the network is converged more quickly, those images are preprocessed, that is, the resolution of images are reduced by 3 times. Consequently, the final resolution of experimental images is 640 × 360. In this paper, there are 10450 images in the self-built warehouse object dataset, which contain three object categories of cargos, trays and forklifts, where 7893 images containing cargos and trays, and 2557 images containing forklifts.

Before training the model, we first randomly divide the self-built warehouse object dataset into the training validation set and the test set with 4:1, and then randomly divide the training validation set into the training set and the validation set according to the ratio of 4:1. Of these, there are 6688 images included in training sets, 2090 images included in test sets, and 1672 images included in verification sets.

3.2   PASCAL VOC

We trained Dense-SSD on the union of PASCAL VOC2007 trainval and 2012 trainval, and the model is tested on the PASCAL VOC2007 test. We compare against SSD, two methods use 300 × 300 input. We set the number of trainings to 80000, the initial learning rate is set to 0.1, and then divided by 10 after every 20000 iterations, the training finished when reaching 80000 iterations. Meanwhile, the SGD with a momentum of 0.9, a weight decay of 0.0005 and the batch size of 5 is used to train the model from scratch on the dataset. The detection results on PASCAL VOC2007 test are shown in Table 3.

Table 3. PASCAL VOC2007 test detection results

Methods	Number of test images	Size of the model	mAP
SSD	4952	101	72.47
Dense-SSD	4952	**70.6**	**77.62**

According to Table 3, the mean Average Precision (mAP) of Dense-SSD proposed in this paper on PASCAL VOC2007 is improved from SSD's 72.47% to 77.62%, which is higher than SSD by 5.15 points. Meanwhile, the model size is reduced by 30.4 MB than SSD.

3.3 The Self-built Warehouse Object Dataset

On the self-built warehouse object dataset, our model training settings are the same as in Sect. 3.2. In the case of same training set and test set, we compared Dense-SSD with Faster R-CNN and SSD, and the detection results compared as shown in Table 4.

Table 4. Comparison of detection results with different methods

Methods	Number of test images	Size of the model	mAP
Faster R-CNN	2090	235.8	93.74
SSD	2090	94.7	92.42
Dense-SSD	2090	**62.9**	**93.85**

According to Table 4, the Dense-SSD proposed in this paper can reach 93.85% mAP on the self-built warehouse object dataset, and the model size is only 62.9 MB. Which is higher than Faster R-CNN and SSD by 0.11 and 1.43 points respectively. Moreover, the model size is reduced by 172.9 MB and 31.8 MB respectively. Consequently, compared with most CNN-based detection solutions require a huge memory space to store the massive parameters, Dense-SSD shows great potential for applications on mobile low-end devices.

Detection effect diagrams of the test image of some warehouse objects are given, as shown in Fig. 3.

As can be observed from Fig. 3, whether it is light conditions, shooting angle, the changes of object color or scale, or more complex warehouse environment (such as: object partial occlusion), Dense-SSD can obtain a more satisfactory detection effect based on warehouse objects.

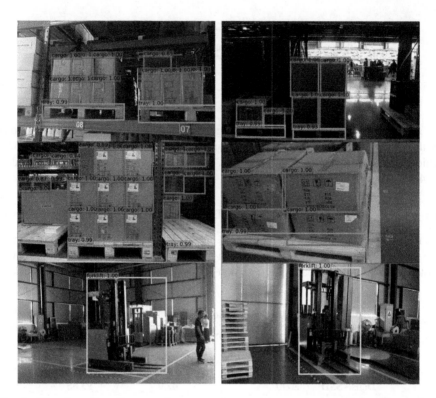

Fig. 3. Detection effect diagrams of some warehouse object test images (Color figure online)

4 Conclusion

The application scenario based on warehouse environment, an object detection algorithm based on improved SSD that fused DenseNet and SSD (Dense-SSD) is used to detect the warehouse object in this paper. Mainly the Dense-SSD object detector is trained from scratch on the PASCAL VOC and the self-built warehouse object dataset respectively. And the trained model based on the warehouse object dataset is applied to the fields of warehouse object detection by optimizing the model parameters. The detection accuracy of the Dense-SSD is higher than both Faster R-CNN and SSD, the model size, however, is smaller than both Faster R-CNN and SSD. Moreover, it has good robustness to the change of object color, scale and illumination condition, and obtains the satisfactory detection effect of warehouse object. However, for some occluded, small-scale warehouse objects, the proposed warehouse object detection algorithm still has a miss detection phenomenon. Our future work will focus on this situation, and improve the detection accuracy and efficiency of warehouse objects while further improving the warehouse object dataset.

Acknowledgments. The work in this paper is supported in part by the Innovation Group Major Research Project of Guizhou Provincial Department of Education (QIAN JIAO HE KY ZI [2018] 018), in part by the Research Foundation Project of Guizhou Minzu University (2017YB065), in part by the Foundation Research Project of College of Humanities & Sciences of Guizhou Minzu University (18rwjs016). We would like to thank the previous researchers for their outstanding achievements. Thanks for Professor Wang's instruction and help.

References

1. Girshick, R., Donahue, J., Darrell, T., et al.: Rich feature hierarchies for accurate object detection and semantic segmentation. In: IEEE Conference on Computer Vision and Pattern Recognition, pp. 580–587 (2014)
2. He, K., Zhang, X., Ren, S., et al.: Spatial pyramid pooling in deep convolutional networks for visual recognition. IEEE Trans. Pattern Anal. Mach. Intell. **37**(9), 1904–1916 (2014)
3. Girshick, R.: Fast R-CNN. In: IEEE International Conference on Computer Vision, pp. 1440–1448 (2015)
4. Ren, S., He, K., Girshick, R., et al.: Faster R-CNN: towards real-time object detection with region proposal networks. Advances in Neural Information Processing Systems, pp. 91–99 (2015)
5. Dai, J., Li, Y., He, K., et al.: R-FCN: object detection via region-based fully convolutional networks. Advances in Neural Information Processing Systems, pp. 379–387 (2016)
6. Uijlings, J.R.R., van de Sande, K.E.A., Gevers, T., et al.: Selective search for object recognition. Int. J. Comput. Vis. **104**(2), 154–171 (2013)
7. Redmon, J., Divvala, S., Girshick, R., et al.: You only look once: unified, real-time object detection. In: IEEE Conference on Computer Vision and Pattern Recognition, pp. 779–788 (2015)
8. Liu, W., et al.: SSD: Single Shot MultiBox Detector. In: Leibe, B., Matas, J., Sebe, N., Welling, M. (eds.) ECCV 2016. LNCS, vol. 9905, pp. 21–37. Springer, Cham (2016). https://doi.org/10.1007/978-3-319-46448-0_2
9. Fu, C.Y., Liu, W., Ranga, A., et al.: DSSD: deconvolutional single shot detector. arXiv Preprint arXiv:1701.06659, pp. 1–11 (2017)
10. He, K., Zhang, X., Ren, S., et al.: Deep residual learning for image recognition. In: IEEE Conference on Computer Vision and Pattern Recognition, pp. 770–778 (2015)
11. Zheng, L., Fu, C., Zhao, Y.: Extend the shallow part of single shot multibox detector via convolutional neural network. arXiv Preprint arXiv:1801.05918, pp. 1–7 (2018)
12. Li, Z., Zhou, F.: FSSD: feature fusion single shot multibox detector. arXiv Preprint arXiv: 1712.00960, pp. 1–10 (2018)
13. Li, T., Huang, B., Liu, J., et al.: Application of convolution neural network object detection algorithm in logistics warehouse. Comput. Eng. **44**(6), 176–181 (2018)
14. Huang, G., Liu, Z., van der Maaten, L., et al.: Densely connected convolutional networks. In: IEEE Conference on Computer Vision and Pattern Recognition, pp. 2261–2269 (2017)
15. Shen, Z., Liu, Z., Li, J., et al.: DSOD: learning deeply supervised object detectors from scratch. In: IEEE International Conference on Computer Vision, pp. 1919–1927 (2017)

Study on 3D Modeling of Complex Coal Mine Interface

Qian-lin Dong[1], Yang-ming Jiang[2], Zhi-chao Hao[3], Wei-dong Li[1],
Ke Wang[1], Xing-dong Wang[1], and Qing-yuan Li[4(✉)]

[1] College of Information Science and Engineering,
Henan University of Technology, Zhengzhou 450001, China
dql2008@126.com
[2] Institute of Remote Sensing and Digital Earth of CAS, Beijing 100094, China
[3] College of Geosciences' and Surveying Engineering,
China University of Mining and Technology, Beijing 100083, China
[4] Key Laboratory of Chinese Academy of Surveying and Mapping,
Beijing 100830, China
liqy@casm.ac.cn

Abstract. Coal seam floor, fault are important geological interfaces to be focused in the process of coal exploration and mining. This paper analyzes in detail the characteristics of complex coal seam floor and fault and proposes corresponding effective 3D reconstruction method for them respectively. For complex coal seam floor surface, this paper proposes blocking partition 3D reconstruction method in which complex coal seam floor surface is decomposed by boundary lines into modeling blocks with single internal structure. These modeling blocks are reconstructed in 3D form separately. Meanwhile, this paper puts forward a new method which adopts multi-source, multi- category geological data to collaboratively reconstruct 3D fault model in the exploration area. It makes full use of the advantages of each type of fault data and makes up disadvantages. The methods mentioned above have good effect of 3D geological modeling in Sanlutian exploration area of Muli area, Qinghai province. So these methods will have wide application prospect.

Keywords: Block-divided 3D modeling · Coal seam floor 3D reconstruction · Multi-source multi-category data · Fault reconstruction

1 Introduction

Geological interfaces such as unconformity, stratigraphic interface, coal seam roof/floor and fault plane are important signs in coalfield geology research which are the basis for morphological modeling of coalfield research areas. They are also very important for studying coal resource structural & sedimentary evolution, coal gas resources generation & migration coalbed methane. In the process of coal exploration and exploitation, coal seam floor contour map is an important map for preparation of exploration design, layout exploration project, reserve calculation and submission of geological report. It also plays an important role in all stages of mine design, construction and production. During coal mining, faults will affect both reserves and coal recovery and also will

© Springer Nature Singapore Pte Ltd. 2019
Y. Wang et al. (Eds.): IGTA 2019, CCIS 1043, pp. 612–624, 2019.
https://doi.org/10.1007/978-981-13-9917-6_58

increase support difficulty and cost, as well as induce coal and gas outburst accidents. Therefore, it is very important to determine faults before coal exploration and production. However, current coal seam floor contour maps and exploration line profiles submitted after coalfield geological exploration are basically two-dimensional. In the background of 3D computer simulation for all stage of mine design, well construction and production management, it is urgent to upgrade the expression of coalfield geological exploration results from 2D to 3D to provide an intuitive and three-dimensional mining environment for the design, construction and production departments.

As front technology, 3D geological modeling is very beneficial to coal geological structure study [1]. Reconstruction methods of coal seam, fault plane and stratum unconformity are always the basis of 3D modeling research [2]. Since closed surface model can generate volume model by mesh filling or meshing, 3D geological interface construction is also the key and foundation for constructing real 3D geological body model. Yu used surface spline function interpolation to reconstruct coal floor surface for the first time [3]. Yfantis used the fractal method to simulate the geological interface [4], Mallet proposed discrete smooth interpolation [5], Fisher et al. [6], Zheng et al. [7] used NURBS to simulate geological surface and entities, a 3D geological modeling method based on multi-source data integration is realized by Wu and Xu [8], Wu et al. [9] used a single plane or multiple planes to simulate fault surface and provided mathematical description of fault spatial geometry. Due to sparse sampling data, unreasonable spatial distribution and non-uniform data model [10], geological data provided by engineers also has the characteristics such as multi-source, multi-scale, multi-temporal, etc., geological bodies studied have typical grey information characteristics [11], these all have determined complexity and uncertainty of 3D geological modeling. At present, most data used in 3D mine geology modeling are single which is either limited to drilling data or to surface survey data, In general, these data have not been effectively and comprehensively utilized and mutual constraint relationships between them are not fully reflected. Plan view (including topographic geological map, coal seam floor contour map) and section view are commonly used basic geological data. They are all dimensionally-reduced expressions for 3D geological body. There are a lot of errors due to various reasons when drawing. However, these errors can be easily found and tested by corresponding 3D geological model.

Because of the importance of coal seam floor and fault in coal mining exploration and mining process and the complexity of 3D geological modeling, this paper analyzes in detail the characteristics of complex coal seam floor and fault data and proposes 3D reconstruction methods both for complex coal seam floor and fault. Based on comprehensive integration of multi-source and multi-class geological data, this paper transforms geological data of different sources and types (including original MapGIS, CAD, and text files) using 3D geological modeling software -GD3A and the authors extended its functional modules through VC++ and OpenGL programming to construct reliable 3D geological model for Sanlutian exploration area in Muli, Qinghai Province of China. The 3D geological model constructed fully reveals underground geological characteristics of study area and provides important reference for future coal resources mining in the area.

2 Complex Coal Seam Floors Partitioned Blocking Reconstruction

2.1 Basic Principle of Partitioned Blocking 3D Reconstruction

Faults cut original coal seams seriously due to extremely complicated regional geological structure evolution during long geological history. Original complete coal seams are often cut into many small coal seam blocks by faults. The top/floor surfaces of these numerous sub-block coal seams, which were divided by fault line, coal seam boundary line, etc., can be fitted by different interpolation algorithms. This partitioned block fitting process conforms to the idea of local interpolation in mathematics, which not only improves the computational efficiency of the algorithm, but also ensures reasonable accuracy. It obviously lays the foundation for the establishment of accurate 3D geological models.

The 3D block geological modeling method decompose complex large-area 3D geological modeling areas into small-area modeling geological blocks or units with relatively simple internal structures by the geological boundaries such as faults, coal seam boundaries and rock mass boundaries [12]. Then 3D geological modeling is carried out for these relatively simple small-area geological units. Finally all units are integrated to form the three-dimensional geological model of the whole region. The block-based 3D geological modeling method decomposing complex global problems into several simple local problems and solve them locally, which conforms to the general habit of scientific research. The block-based 3D geological modeling method has two principles. Firstly, the extent of the partition must be a closed area surrounded by fractures, coal seam boundaries or rock mass boundaries. Secondly, the selection of geological boundaries should be based on the actual geological conditions of the study area. If there are many smaller closed geological boundaries in the small area, they can be neglected and modeled separately. This method has the advantages of simplifying the process of 3D geological modeling effectively, modifying and perfecting the model easily, and integrating the model easily.

The core principle the block 3D geological modeling is the global decomposition, block modeling, gradual improvement and comprehensive integration. It support to modify the unreasonable parts of the model on block-by-block or object by object based on the block modeling individually with the continuous updating of survey data and the deepening of geological understanding. Finally, the constructed block or 3D geological object models are unified in the same three-dimensional space coordinate system, where the three-dimensional spatial topological relationship between the geological objects can be edited and modified, to form the whole 3D geological model for the research area. The geological model established by the block 3D modeling method only need to update the data within the block range when the survey data changes, which can improve the speed of data update. The blocks out of the frustum range can be eliminated in the visualization progress of 3D geological model data, which reduce the number of triangles drawn, and improve the display speed of the three-dimensional geological model data.

2.2   Single Block Coal Seam Floor Reconstruction Method

2.2.1   Intersection Between Fault Line, Boundary Line and Floor Elevation Line

In China, Coal seam floor contour map is always drawled by MapGIS/AutoCAD software. When geological engineering technicians draw the map, they only label elevation value beside the contour line, while seam floor contour map is still 2-dimensional graphic. It does not reflect ups and downs of coal seam floor surface from real 3-dimensional angle. So we need to endow these 2-dimensional floor contour lines with elevation value to transfer into 3-dimensional contour lines. Then Delaunay triangulation is carried out based on constrained condition of seam floor contour lines to make it real 3-dimensional coal seam floor map.

Similarly, both fault line and boundary line in the floor contour map are two-dimensional lines. Compared with floor contour lines, they even do not have elevation attribute values. Therefore, we need to obtain three-dimensional both fault lines and floor contour lines. To achieve this aim, this paper carries out line intersecting operation between each fault line and its adjacent floor contour line. In the same way, the line intersecting operation is done between each coal seam boundary line and its adjacent floor contour line. As results, a series of new intersection points are generated both in fault line and coal seam boundary line, then we endow them with elevation value in association with corresponding contour line. So we obtain a series of intersection points with real 3-dimensional coordinate. Finally, 3-dimensional fault line and coal seam boundary line are obtained through linear interpolation. Here the key algorithm is 2-dimensional line intersection algorithm. It is basic problem of CAD, Computer Graphics, GIS, etc. Line section can be expressed by mathematical formula below [13]:

$$\begin{cases} x = x_m + s * (x_n - x_m) \\ y = y_m + t * (y_n - y_m) \end{cases} \qquad (0 \le s \le 1, 0 \le t \le 1) \qquad (1)$$

Where $(x_m, y_m), (x_n, y_n)$ are two endpoints of a line section, s, t are the two parameters to be solved. Given two lines MN and KL in which the start point and end point are $(x_m, y_m), (x_n, y_n), (x_k, y_k), (x_l, y_l)$ separately. Two variables can be calculated separately based on the line formula (1) above.

$$s = \frac{(x_n - x_m)(y_m - y_k) - (y_n - y_m)(x_m - x_k)}{(x_n - x_m)(y_l - y_k) - (y_n - y_m)(x_l - x_k)} \qquad (2)$$

$$t = \frac{(x_l - x_k)(y_m - y_k) - (y_l - y_k)(x_m - x_k)}{(x_n - x_m)(y_l - y_k) - (y_n - y_m)(x_l - x_k)} \qquad (3)$$

If the value of s, t are between [0, 1], then there is a intersection point of Line MN and Line KL. We substitute s into parametric equation of Line MN or substitute t into parametric equation of Line KL, then we can obtain the coordinate of intersection point. If the value of s, t are out of [0, 1], there is no intersection point between Line MN and Line KL.

In this case, it is relatively simple to find the intersection point directly when two lines intersect, but in fact, this often happens: because of imprecise operation, the contours and fault lines that should intersect do not intersect, but the end of contours is close enough to fault line, which is often used in the process of GIS graphics editing. Then the phenomenon of "undershot" appears [14]. At this time, we can set a tolerance or threshold and stipulate that as long as the distance between the two lines is within tolerance range, the default is that the two lines intersect, and continue to extend the end of the contour to intersect with the fault line to obtain the intersection point.

2.2.2   The Transformation of Constrained Delaunay from 2D to 3D

Triangle is the simplex in plane domain, triangulation network is particularly suitable for fitting complex topography surface, geological interface, etc. In other words, triangulation network mainly represents surface in the 3D solid geometric modeling system. The circumcircle of each triangle in Delaunay Triangulation does not contain any other point inside it. 2D Delaunay triangulation has strict mathematical definition and complete theoretical basis, meanwhile, it has good capability of representing boundaries and constrained adaptability, so it is widely used in three dimensional geological modeling fields. Complex geological bodies often contain a lot of faults, the relationship among these faults is also very complex, these faults can be seen as constrained condition of triangulation for geological interfaces cut by faults. Currently the most popular constrained Delaunay triangulation algorithm was proposed by Chew in 1989 [15]. The basic idea is that constrained lines are divided into smaller sub-lines and then triangulation is carried out.

3-dimensional scattered point set on the non-overlapping single-value surface is generally transferred through projection transformation into 2-dimensional plane points and then Delaunay triangulation is carried out to fulfill the construction of 3D TIN surface. For multi-Z value geological surface such as overturned folds, they are usually divided into two single-value surfaces and are reconstructed separately [16]. In this paper, constrained Delaunay triangulation is carried out based on constrained condition such as fault lines, coal seam boundary lines, contour lines, etc. to reconstruct coal seam floor surface and ground surface.

2.3   Example for Complex Coal Seam Floor Reconstruction

Coal seam floor contour map contains elevation level of coal seam in stratum, geological structure and their mutual relationship, etc. It is foundation of coal mining design, improvement, extension, etc. It is also basis of coal reserve calculation, dynamic change management and mining engineering production design. Meanwhile, it is a good and effective way to reconstruct 3-dimensional coal seam using floor contour map with its abundant geological information. The geological data collected by the Research for 3D modeling of coal seam floor in the Sanlutian exploration area include contour maps of Shang4 coal seams, Shang 5 coal seams and Xia1 coal seam floor (the position relationship of three coal seams from top to bottom) and 43 borehole data in the exploration area. Based on coal seam floor contour map, this model uses the method of partition block to reconstruct 3D coal seam floor. At the same time, the modeling results are verified and calibrated with the existing borehole histogram. The overall technical route adopted for the three-dimensional reconstruction of complex coal mine floor is shown in Fig. 1 below.

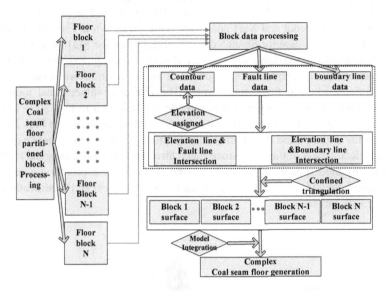

Fig. 1. Complex coal seam bottom surface reconstruction technology route map

Specifically, Xia1 coal seam processing process is taken as example: Original data format of Xia1 coal seam contour map is MapGIS data format. We intersect fault line and coal seam boundary line with contour line which has been given elevation value to get real three-dimensional fault line and coal seam boundary line in practice. Due to staggered cutting of faults, complete primary coal seams are cut into sheet coal seams. In order to facilitate the three-dimensional modeling, it is necessary to separate three-dimensional modeling for each sheet coal seam. With the corresponding contours, fault lines and coal seam boundary lines as restrictive conditions, Delaunay triangulation is applied to each flake or block coal seam. Finally, Delaunay triangulation map of complex floor surface of the whole Xia1 coal is obtained, as shown in Fig. 2(a) below (the Y axis points northward).

Once fault line or coal seam boundary line are updated, or engineers and technicians adopt more suitable interpolation algorithm, we only need to modify the block of coal seam floor associated with corresponding fault line or coal seam boundary line. It is obvious that other blocks of coal seam floor surface do not need to be changed. This is very helpful to modify and improve the model. When the number of triangles in the triangular network of coal seam floor is huge, we only need to display triangular network of corresponding block in coal seam floor in the visual cone when displaying graphics, which will greatly improve the displaying speed of 3D geological model. Obviously, the method of portioned block 3D geological modeling will show very complex coal seam floor surface to the geological and mining staff intuitively and clearly in three-dimensional way, which undoubtedly provides an important scientific basis for mine design, reconstruction, expansion and extension.

According to the same principle, Shang4 and Shang 5 coal seam floor are reconstructed by portioned block 3D geological modeling method. The overlapping map of Shang4 coal, Shang5 coal and Xia1 coal seam floor are shown in Fig. 2(b) below (red for Shang4 coal seam, blue for Shang5 coal seam and black for Xia1 coal seam). Based on two-dimensional topographic and geological map of mining area, the corresponding three-dimensional topographic map is obtained by using transformation technology from two-dimensional to three-dimensional. The fine three-dimensional topographic map of exploration area after illumination rendering is shown in Fig. 2(c). The overlapping map of ground surface and three coal seam floor is shown in Fig. 2(d). Figure 2(e) is the underground distribution map of drilling holes in the whole exploration area. The effectiveness of the above-mentioned three-dimensional geological model can be verified by the exposure of the underground strata in the exploration area through each drilling hole and reasonable suggestions for improvement and modification could be more easily put forward.

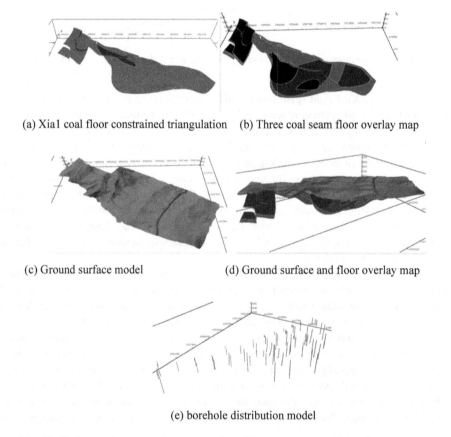

(a) Xia1 coal floor constrained triangulation   (b) Three coal seam floor overlay map

(c) Ground surface model   (d) Ground surface and floor overlay map

(e) borehole distribution model

Fig. 2. Coal seam bottom and ground surface 3D reconstruction (Color figure online)

3 Fault Reconstruction Based on Multi-source and Multi-category Geological Data

In the field of coalfield geological exploration, cross section, coal seam floor contour map of and topographic geological map are three basic maps with great importance. Cross sections reflect underground stratum distribution (stratum framework structure) and structural characteristics of faults and folds along the line. Cross sections are two-dimensional maps drawn by connecting various geological boundaries according to metallogenic law, during the preparation process, the geologists comprehensively analyzed the survey data, prospecting and mining engineering data. It is an exploration result with expert knowledge, and is more credible than other geological prospecting data. Therefore, it can be used as an important data source for three-dimensional geological modeling and visualization. Obviously, the more intensive exploration line layout in the exploration profiles, the more complete the exposure of underground faults will be. The contour map of coal seam floor is the projection map of the intersection line of the floor surface of coal seam and each elevation plane on the plane. Coal seam floor contour map can better express fault distribution in the coal seam on the horizontal plane, meanwhile, according to the elevation information of the floor contour, it can also reflect the extension of the fault in the vertical direction to a certain extent. Topographic geological maps are comprehensive maps reflecting regional topographic features, outcrop distribution of strata and geological structural characteristics of faults and folds. Compared with the data of deep underground geological faults obtained by other means, the data obtained by geological mapping have the characteristics of high accuracy, data-rich, great continuity, easy obtaining, low cost and permissible modifiability. All in all, it could better denote the outcrop of faults in the field, that is, the distribution of faults in the horizontal direction of the surface, but it lacks the relevant information to describe how the faults extend in the deep underground. Therefore, fault data in topographic and geological maps can be used as a strong constraint on the ground, and the reconstructed faults from exploration profiles and contour maps of coal seam floor can be reasonably extended to the ground.

Based on the analysis of cross sections, coal seam floor contour map and geological topography map, this paper proposes a collaborative reconstruction method for faults by means of combining those multi-source & multi-category geological data above in exploration area. we firstly adopt Minimum Span Length Algorithms to construct original triangulation based on constraints like fault trail line in cross sections and intersecting line between fault & coal seam, then we secondly adopt thin plate spline function to complete and fine fault model constructed above based on ground constraints like fault outcrop line in the topographic geological map. In the end, complete and fine fault model is constructed in the exploration area which would undoubtedly provide geological and mining engineers with a new method and approach to analyze fault structures.

3.1 Fault Reconstruction Based on Coal Seam Floor Contour Map

Taking the normal faults shown in the contour map of the coal seam floor in the exploration area as an example, we elaborate the construction process in detail (the construction principle of the reverse faults based on the floor surface in this modeling is the same as that of the normal faults). Based on the division of the original floor surface by fault boundary and coal seam boundary line, the real three-dimensional floor surface is generated by using the limited Delaney triangulation technology from two-dimensional to three-dimensional transformation. See the discussion in the preceding section, and it will not be repeated here. At this time, we can clearly see that the extension of normal faults separates the original coal seam into two separate small seams (as shown in the F7 fault) or that the original coal seam is only partially separated and does not become two separate small seams (as shown in the F24 fault). Faults cut coal seams and intersect with the roof and floor of the coal seam is called the intersection of coal seams. The fault coal intersection line reflects the coal seam cut by the fault and its shape. The range between the top and bottom fault coal intersection line is the action range of the fault in the coal seam. The relative relationship between the intersection lines of coal faults at the corresponding layers of the two faults reflects the nature of the faults, and the distance between them reflects the displacement of the faults. Figure 3(a) reflects the intersection line of the coal seam floor under the cutting of normal faults F7 and F24. We use the intersection line of upper and lower faulted coal (that is, the intersection line between fault plane and coal floor) as the constraint line to restrict triangulation to generate partial normal fault model in exploration area. Taking F7 normal fault as an example, F7 fault cuts the lower 1 coal, the upper 5 coal and the upper 4 coal, and produces two intersecting lines with each coal seam floor, totally 6 intersecting lines. The F7 fault triangulation network is reconstructed by limited triangulation using the six intersecting lines of coal faults as constraints. The F7 fault model is generated by illumination rendering as shown in Fig. 3(b) and (c) is part of the fault construction based on the floor contour map in the exploration area.

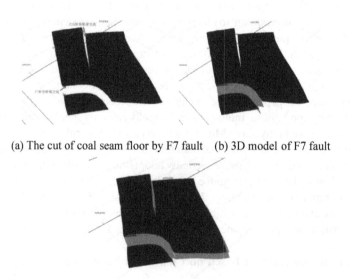

(a) The cut of coal seam floor by F7 fault   (b) 3D model of F7 fault

(c) 3D model of normal fault

Fig. 3. Faults reconstructed by coal seam floor map in exploration area

3.2 Faults Reconstruction Based on Cross Sections

Three-dimensional geological modeling technology based on cross sections is one of the hotspots in geological modeling. However, few domestic literatures have introduced the details of how to transform two-dimensional plane profile to real three-dimensional exploration profile. Exploration profiles usually exist in one plane, that is, the so-called flat section. At present, most of the geological profiles used in coal exploration and production in China belong to horizontal profiles, and usually have a variety of data formats, such as CAD, MapGIS, ArcGIS formats, etc. In the process of three-dimensional geological modeling, how to make full use of these flat profile data and avoid the waste of manpower and material resources in reconstructing profiles, we need to study how to transform these data from two-dimensional to three-dimensional. At the same time, because the drilling holes on the exploration line are not always arranged in a straight line during the transformation of the section coordinates of exploration line, that is, the so-called bending exploration line. In the three-dimensional geological modeling platform, we should also provide the function of converting the horizontal profile data of the corresponding bending exploration line to the real bending profile data.

3.2.1 Real 3D Cross Section Generation

It is an important method to reconstruct 3-dimensional fault surface using cross sections generated by coal geological exploration. Firstly, conventional 2-dimensional cross sections should be converted into real 3-dimensional ones. In other words, we need to generate real 3-dimensional cross sections. Here the key point is how 2-dimensional points in cross sections are converted into 3D space coordinate system.

The transformation principle and implementation method of 2-dimensional cross section converted to real 3-dimensional ones is: (1) Firstly, we divide 2-dimensional cross section into several small parts based on the start point, the end point of cross section line and borehole orifice point in the prospect line; (2) Secondly, we establish 3-dimensional cross section framework based on 2-dimensional prospect polyline; (3) Finally, we transform feature points in 2-dimensional cross section into 3-dimensional space coordinate system step by step. Meanwhile, we add turning control points for the long lines which step across turning points of cross section.

There are 13 cross sections in Sanlutian exploration area and the format of the original map is MAPGIS data format. Firstly, we transform them to DXF format and then import them into D3A platform to transform them into DS format. To make it convenient for establishing three-dimensional model, the cross sections in DS format should be pre-processed, and we divide the lines of cross sections into many sub-layers, such as fault line layer, stratum interface line layer, drill line layer, ground surface line layer, elevation line layer and so on. Then, we assign the same code number for fault lines on 13 cross sections of the same fault. The code numbers are like F1, F2, F26, F27, F28, and so on. The original 2D cross section of prospecting line 1 drawled in MapGIS software is shown in Fig. 4(a), meanwhile the corresponding 3D real cross section transformed by programming is shown in Fig. 4(b). Figure 4(c) is the overall effect map of real 3D cross sections in exploration areas.

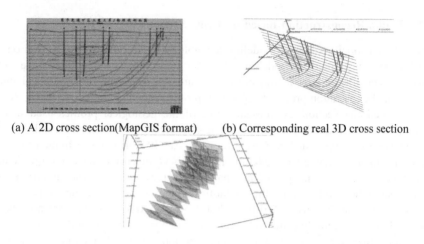

(a) A 2D cross section(MapGIS format)   (b) Corresponding real 3D cross section

(c) Overall real 3D cross sections

Fig. 4. Transformation from 2D cross sections to real 3D cross sections

3.2.2   Fault Reconstruction Based on Real Folded Profile

There are thirteen cross sections in Sanlutian exploration areas, Qinghai province, China. Original map format is MapGIS file format. Firstly, original cross section is converted into DXF format, and then imported into D3A software platform and converted into DS format. In order to facilitate three-dimensional reconstruction of faults, it is necessary to pre-process DS-format cross section. The lines on cross sections are divided into the following layers: fault line map, exploration line map, stratum line map, borehole line map and ground line map. Then, the same fault lines on 13 cross sections are given the same coding number, such as F1, F2, F26, F27, F28 etc.

Based on fault line coding number above, we adopt minimum span length distance algorithm to carry out constrained triangulation with the same code of fault line as constrained boundary. Minimum span length distance algorithm is also called minimum diagonal line algorithm which is the most common local optimized algorithm. Finally, we generate 3-dimensional reverse fault surface of all coding number. It is a simple example of coding number for fault lines in adjacent cross sections as shown in Fig. 5(a). The triangulation mesh of each reverse fault is constructed based on fault lines with the same coding number is shown in Fig. 5(b). The final 3-dimensional graph of reverse fault is shown in Fig. 5(c) which has no illumination rendering effect. The illumination rendering effect graph of all fault surfaces including both normal faults and reverse faults is shown in Fig. 5(d). The ground surface and fault overlay graph is shown in Fig. 5(e). Figure 5(f) shows us that how the faults in exploration area cut Xia1 coal seam. The re-constructed result of faults clearly shows us how the faults extend to the depths of underground and how the faults cut the main coal seam and make the coal seam move. Obviously, it provides important reference to mining engineering technician about how they could design and arrange laneway. Due to the inefficiency of original data, the reconstructed fault surface is only part of real fault, we should further consider how to extend these faults both to ground surface and to the depth of underground deep in the earth.

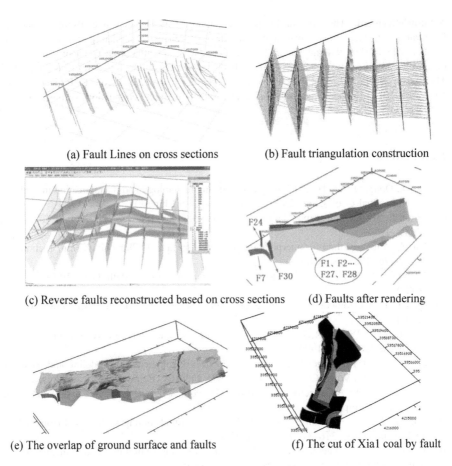

(a) Fault Lines on cross sections   (b) Fault triangulation construction

(c) Reverse faults reconstructed based on cross sections   (d) Faults after rendering

(e) The overlap of ground surface and faults   (f) The cut of Xia1 coal by fault

Fig. 5. Faults 3D reconstruction

4 Conclusion

The key to constructing 3D geological model is the reconstruction of 3D geological interface. The complexity of geological interface itself determines its reconstruction difficulty. Obviously it is necessary to carry out in-depth research on its construction theory and method. In this paper, construction theories and methods of two main geological interfaces of complex coal seam floor and fault plane are elaborated in detail. It is proved by examples that partitioned block 3D geological modeling method has obvious advantages for reconstructing complex coal seam floor surface and give us very good effective for geological body simulation. Meanwhile, collaborative reconstruction method for faults by combining multi-source & multi-category geological data is beneficial to constructing fine 3D fault model.

Acknowledgement. The work in this paper is supported by Henan University of Technology Doctoral Fund "Geological Form and Attribute comprehensive modeling research" (Project number 2018BS075), National Nature Science Foundation of China project "Theory and method of anisotropic property field inner geology body based on volume function" (Project number 41272367), Henan Provincial Science and Technology Research Project (Project number 192102210101), Henan University of Technology Research Foundation (Project number 2016XTCX05).

References

1. Li, Q., Dong, Q., Jia, H.: 3D geological modeling technology and its application in coalfield structure. Coal Geol. China **26**(8), 39–44 (2014). (in Chinese)
2. Ming, J.: 3D geological modeling research. Geogr. Geog. Inf. Sci. **27**(4), 14–20 (2011). (in Chinese)
3. Yu, Z.: A new method for interpolating geological surface. J. China Univ. Min. Technol. **16**(4), 69–76 (1987). (in Chinese)
4. Yfantis, E.A.: Simulation of geological surfaces using fractals. Math. Geol. **20**(6), 667–672 (1988)
5. Mallet, J.L.: Geomodeling. Applied Geostatics Series. Oxford University Press, Oxford (2002)
6. Fisher, T.R., Wales, R.Q.: 3D solid modeling of sandstone reservoirs using NURBS. Geobyte **5**(1), 39–41 (1990)
7. Zheng, D., Li, M.: Water Conservancy and Power Geological 3D Modeling and Analysis, vol. 168. China Water Conservancy and Power Industry, Beijing (2005). (in Chinese)
8. Wu, Q., Xu, H.: An effective method for 3D geological modeling with multi-source data integration. Comput. Geosci. **34**(3), 35–43 (2008)
9. Wu, Q., Xu, H.: 3D fault modeling technique in virtual mining system. J. Liaoning Eng. Tech. Univ. **24**(3), 316–319 (2005). (in Chinese)
10. Wu, Q., Xu, H.: 3D geological modeling method and application in digital mine. China Sci. (Earth Ed.) **43**(12), 1996–2006 (2013). (in Chinese)
11. Mao, S.: Gray geographical information system-the theory and technology of correct geological spatial data dynamically[J]. Acta Scicentiarum Naturalum Universitis Pekinesis **38**(4), 556–562 (2002). (In Chinese)
12. Xue, L., Li, W., Zhang, W., et al.: A method of block-divided 3D geologic modeling in regional scale. J. Jilin Univ. (Earth Sci. Ed.) **44**(6), 2051–2058 (2014). (in Chinese)
13. Li, C.: Research on intersection of two-dimensional curves and related algorithms. Hehai University (2004). (in Chinese)
14. General Administration of Quality Supervision, Inspection and Quarantine of the People's Republic of China, National Standardization Management Committee of China. GB/T 23707–2009/ISO 19107:2003. Geographic Information Spatial Model. China Standards Publishing House, Beijing (2009). (in Chinese)
15. Yang, Q.: Constraint Triangle Meshing Technology, pp. 5–7. Electronic Industry Press (2005). (in Chinese)
16. Wang, Z., Pan, M.: Delaunay triangulation algorithm of 3D folded cross-section[J]. Comput. Eng. Appl. **44**(1), 94–96 (2008). (in Chinese)

Enhanced Subtraction Image Guided Convolutional Neural Network for Coronary Artery Segmentation

Jingfan Fan[1], Chenbin Du[2], Shuang Song[2], Weijian Cong[1(✉)], Aimin Hao[1], and Jian Yang[1]

[1] School of Computer Science and Engineering,
Beihang University, Beijing 100191, China
forceyes@126.com

[2] Beijing Engineering Research Center of Mixed Reality
and Advanced Display, School of Optics and Photonics,
Beijing Institute of Technology, Beijing 100081, China

Abstract. Digital subtraction angiography (DSA) is a fluoroscopic technique used to clearly visualize blood vessels. However, accurate segmentation of coronary arteries cannot be directly obtained from DSA images because of motion artifacts. In this paper, a fully convolutional network is designed to segment the coronary arteries from DSA images instead of angiographic images. First, an ORPCA method with intra-frame and inter-frame constraints is introduced to enhance the vessel structure in DSA. Then, an enhanced DSA image-guided segmentation network, which is a fully convolutional network composed of an encoder path and a decoder path, is proposed to extract the coronary arteries to learn the vascular features from the enhanced vascular structures. The experimental results demonstrate that the proposed method is more effective and accurate in coronary artery segmentation, compared with state-of-the-art methods.

Keywords: Coronary artery · Subtraction angiography · Segmentation · Convolutional neural network

1 Introduction

Coronary artery disease (CAD) is a serious threat to human health. X-ray angiography (XRA) is the gold standard for the diagnosis of CAD because of its fast imaging speed, high spatial resolution, and its powerful ability to visualize the vascular structure of the coronary artery [1]. The accurate segmentation of the vascular structure from XRA images gives important guidance for doctors' diagnosis and treatment [2]. However, it is a highly challenging task because of the complex non-vascular information, overlapping structures, and uneven illumination. Recent studies have proposed numerous methods of vascular segmentation [2, 3]. Methods based on deep learning techniques have become popular because of their advantages, such as fast speed and high accuracy.

© Springer Nature Singapore Pte Ltd. 2019
Y. Wang et al. (Eds.): IGTA 2019, CCIS 1043, pp. 625–632, 2019.
https://doi.org/10.1007/978-981-13-9917-6_59

Learning-based vascular segmentation methods generally obtain hidden information from input image-related features without prior knowledge and then train the classification model to achieve vascular segmentation. Hassouna et al. [4] modeled the blood vessels and background as Rayleigh and normal distribution, and estimated the parameters of distribution using the expectation maximization algorithm. Goceri et al. [5] used k-means clustering to classify the vessels. Lupascu et al. [6] trained an AdaBoost classifier ground-truth images to distinguish vessel and nonvessel pixels and then used it to classify new coming images. Orlando et al. [7, 8] employed a fully connected conditional random field (CRF) model to segment thin and elongated structures in blood vessels. Fu et al. [9] and Luo et al. [10] combined a multi-scale and multi-level convolutional neural network with CRF into an integrated deep network named DeepVessel to solve the segmentation problem of retinal vessel. However, this type of segmentation methods has a specific application assumption and cannot automatically and robustly segment the coronary artery from angiographic images.

Digital subtraction angiography (DSA) and vascular enhancement techniques can highlight the vascular structures in the images but still with enhanced noise and motion artifacts. In this paper, we propose a fully convolutional network, which take enhanced DSA images as input [11] to classify the vessels from enhanced vascular structures to improve the precision of segmentation results, as shown in Fig. 1.

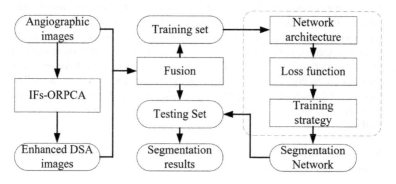

Fig. 1. The framework of the proposed method.

2 Methodology

2.1 Vascular Enhancement

Angiographic images include very complex background structure and pseudo-vessel structure, all of which increase the challenge of coronary artery segmentation. In previous works, we proposed an intra-frame and inter-frame constraint online and robust PCA (Ifs-ORPCA) [11] to enhance vessel-to-background contrast in the angiographic image sequence. First, in order to remove motion artefacts, a morphological filter operator is utilized to recover the motion of respiratory and patient. Second, an inter-frame constraint-based ORPCA is applied to extract the initial vessel layer. Consequently, the motion artefacts in initial vessel layer are removed by inter-frame constraint. Finally, an intra-frame constraint-based ORPCA algorithm is pro-posed to refine the topological structure of the extracted vessel. The Ifs-ORPCA method is effective to remove non-vascular structures, motion artefacts, and other non-uniform illumination-caused noise. Figure 2(b) shows the enhanced DSA image by the proposed method, which obviously highlights the vascular structures and will help segment the coronary arteries. To verify its segmentation effect, we compare the deep segmentation networks with three inputs, including the original angiographic image, the enhanced DSA image by the proposed Ifs-ORPCA, and the enhanced angiographic image. The enhanced angiographic image is fused by the original angiographic image I and the enhanced DSA image S, satisfying $F = I + \rho S, \rho > 0$.

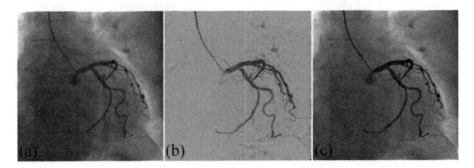

Fig. 2. The enhanced angiographic images. (a) The original angiographic image. (b) The enhanced DSA image. (c) The enhanced angiographic image.

2.2   Deep Convolutional Network

To considerate the global semantic information, a segmentation model based on fully convolutional neural network (FCN) [13] is proposed for end-to-end segmentation of the coronary arteries. This network consists of two parts: the encoder path and the decoder path. The encoder-decoder architecture is shown in Fig. 3. In the encoder path shown in the left side, the input image first passes through two 3×3 convolutional layers, which have 64 feature channels, zero padding (stride of 1), and ReLU [14] activation function. Then, we connect a max pooling layer with 2×2 stride to down-sample the features. The same operation is repeated four times to obtain the lowest resolution level, and during each down-sampling, we double the numbers of each feature channel. A dropout layer [15] layer is added to the last two levels to reduce overfitting. In the right side of Fig. 2, the decoder path, which is symmetric to the encoder path, four de-convolutional layers increases the resolution level until the feature resolution is the same to image's size. In each de-convolutional layer, two convolutional layers are performed also with ReLU activation, and the number of feature channel is halved. To recover the lost sharpness of the feature maps in up-sampling de-convolutional layer, we import a skip concatenation to merge the feature maps from the encoder path with the up-sampled feature maps. Finally, the segmen-tation map is calculated by a fully convolutional layer with 1×1 stride and sigmoid activation. The parameters of the network can be trained by using the training data with ground-truth labels of the coronary arteries.

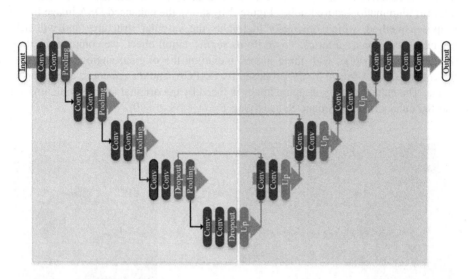

Fig. 3. Architecture of the proposed segmentation network.

3 Experimental Results

This study includes 170 angiographic images, and all the images are manually labeled by radiologists from the collaborating hospital. Add up to, 150 angiographic images are taken as the training set and the other 20 angiographic images are chosen as the testing set. The deep learning network is implemented via Keras using a computer with a single GPU (i.e., NVIDIA GTX 1080 8 GB), and the learning parameters are set in Table 1.

Table 1. Parameters in the deep learning model.

Parameters	Value
Image size	512×512
Number of epochs	30
Batch size	1
Optimizer	Adam
Learning rate	1e−4
Decade	0.9

To evaluate the segmentation performance of our method, we introduce various evaluation metrics. For the segmentation result, true positive (TP) denotes the number of predicted vascular pixels inside the ground-truth vascular segmentation; false positive (FP) denotes the number of predicted vascular pixels outside the ground-truth vascular segmentation; true negative (TN) denotes the number of predicted background pixels outside the ground-truth vascular segmentation; and false negative (FN) denotes the number of predicted background pixels inside the ground-truth vascular segmentation. The accuracy (Acc), sensitivity (Sen), specificity (Spe), precision (Pre), and F1-score are defined as:

$$\begin{cases} acc = \frac{TP+TN}{TP+TN+FP+FN} \\ sen = \frac{TP}{TP+FN} \\ spe = \frac{TN}{TN+FP} \\ pre = \frac{TP}{TP+FP} \\ F1 = \frac{2 \cdot pre \cdot sen}{pre+sen} \end{cases} \qquad (1)$$

The above five indicators range in [0, 1], and the larger the value, the better the segmentation results.

The proposed deep learning model accepts three different images, including the original angiographic image, the enhanced DSA image, and the enhanced angiographic image. Figure 4 shows the segmentation results take different inputs of the left coronary artery (LCA) and the right coronary artery (RCA). Figure 4(a4) and (b4) demonstrate the segmentation results obtained by inputting the original angiographic image to network, where segmentation noise exists in the background region and where the vascular boundary and connection relationship are unclear in the complex vessel regions. Figure 4(a5) and (b5) illustrate the segmentation results achieved by inputting the enhanced DSA image. In these results, the details of the vessels are clearly segmented, whereas some breaks and unsmooth connections occur in the vascular regions. Figure 4(a6) and (b6) illustrate the segmentation results achieved by inputting the enhanced angiographic image combined with the original angiographic image and the enhanced DSA image. The deficiency between these two images can be effectively balanced, the background noise is reduced, and the connection relationship of the blood vessels is well represented.

The quantitative segmentation results are reported in Table 2. This results demonstrate that the enhanced DSA images or angiographic images significantly improve the performance of the segmentation network. In terms of Sen, enhanced angiographic image obtain the best performance, and in other terms, the enhanced DSA image perform better.

To quantitatively evaluate the accuracy of the segmentation results, we compare the proposed method with CRF [8] and LevelSet [12]. For fair comparison, all the training and testing sets are consistent with those of the proposed method. The first column of Fig. 5 shows three angiographic images in contrast filling phase from the test set; the second to fifth columns represent the ground-truth segmentation and segmentation results obtained by CRF, LevelSet, and the proposed method, respectively. The segmentation results of CRF contain a large amount of noise in the background region and disconnections in the blood vessel regions. In addition, compared with the ground-truth, the radius of the blood vessel becomes smaller. The segmentation results of

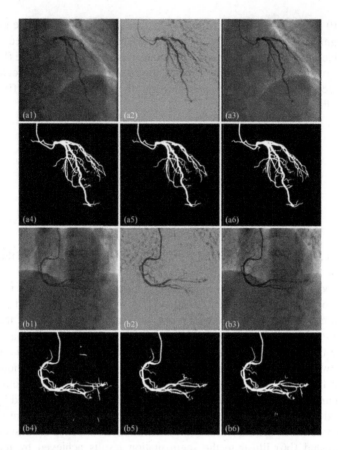

Fig. 4. Illustration of the segmentation results achieved by the same network with different inputs. (a1) Original image. (a2) Enhanced DSA image. (a3) Enhanced angiographic image. (a4)–(a6) Segmentation results of (a1)–(a3). (b1)–(b6) The images from RCA, corresponding to (a1)–(a6) from LCA.

Table 2. The average segmentation performance, in terms of Pre, Sen, Spe, Acc and F1-score, obtained by different input type including original image, enhanced DSA image and enhanced angiographic image for the 20 testing images.

Input	Acc	Sen	Spe	Pre	F1
Original image	0.9820	0.8595	0.9879	0.7667	0.8070
Enhanced DSA image	**0.9836**	0.8773	**0.9890**	**0.7847**	**0.8259**
Enhanced angiographic image	0.9815	**0.8975**	0.9856	0.7436	0.8106

LevelSet perform good segmentation of large blood vessels, but obvious burrs can be found in small blood vessels, meanwhile, the LevelSet method need to choose seed points manually. By contrast, our method is fully automatic and the segmentation results obtained by our method are most similar to the results of manual annotation in the test set data, especially for the small vascular region.

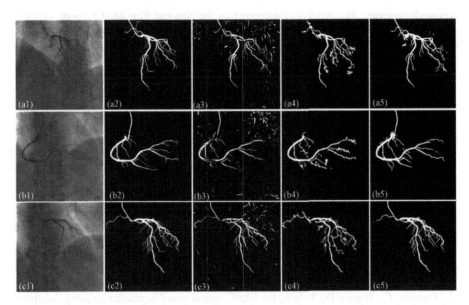

Fig. 5. Illustration of the segmentation results achieved by ground-truth, CRF, LevelSet, and the proposed method; the three rows indicate three sets of results.

The quantitative segmentation results are reported in Table 3. The proposed method achieves the best results in coronary artery segmentation in terms of all five evaluation criteria. This results demonstrate that the enhanced DSA images or angiographic images significantly improve the performance of the segmentation network.

Table 3. The average segmentation performance, in terms of Pre, Sen, Spe, Acc and F1-score, obtained by CRF, LevelSet, and the proposed method for the 20 testing images.

Methods	Acc	Sen	Spe	Pre	F1
CRF	0.9691	0.6932	0.9830	0.6416	0.6576
LevelSet	0.9756	0.7628	0.9855	0.7143	0.7350
Proposed	**0.9815**	**0.8975**	**0.9856**	**0.7436**	**0.8106**

4   Conclusion

In this paper, we proposed a FCN model to achieve end-to-end segmentation of coronary arteries based on the enhanced DSA images. Compared with the segmentation network based on the original angiographic images, the proposed method improves segmentation by enhancing the vascular structure in low-contrast angiograms, especially for removing catheters and artifacts. Experimental results demonstrate that the proposed enhanced subtraction image guided convolutional neural network is effective to achieve good results.

Acknowledgement. This work was supported by the National Key R&D Program of China (2017YFC0107900), the China Postdoctoral Science Foundation (2015M580962), and the National Science Foundation Program of China (61672099, 61501030).

References

1. Yang, J., Wang, Y., Tang, S.: Multiresolution elastic registration of x-ray angiography images using thin-plate spline. IEEE Trans. Nucl. Sci. **54**, 152–166 (2007)
2. Moccia, S., De Momi, E., Hadji, S.: Blood vessel segmentation algorithms—review of methods, datasets and evaluation metrics. Comput. Methods Programs Biomed. **158**, 71–91 (2018)
3. Fraz, M., Remagnino, P., Hoppe, A.: Blood vessel segmentation methodologies in retinal images–a survey. Comput. Methods Programs Biomed. **108**, 407–433 (2012)
4. Hassouna, M., Farag, A., Hushek, S.: Cerebrovascular segmentation from TOF using stochastic models. Med. Image Anal. **10**, 2–18 (2006)
5. Goceri, E., Shah, Z., Gurcan, M.: Vessel segmentation from abdominal magnetic resonance images: adaptive and reconstructive approach. Int. J. Numer. Methods Biomed. Eng. **33**, e2811 (2017)
6. Lupascu, C., Tegolo, D., Trucco, E.: FABC: retinal vessel segmentation using AdaBoost. IEEE Trans. Inf. Technol. Biomed. **14**, 1267–1274 (2010)
7. Orlando, J., Blaschko, M.: Learning fully-connected CRFs for blood vessel segmentation in retinal images. In: International Conference on Medical Image Computing and Computer-Assisted Intervention, pp. 634–641 (2014)
8. Orlando, J., Prokofyeva, E., Blaschko, M.: A discriminatively trained fully connected conditional random field model for blood vessel segmentation in fundus images. IEEE Trans. Biomed. Eng. **64**, 16–27 (2017)
9. Fu, H., Xu, Y., Lin, S.: Deepvessel: retinal vessel segmentation via deep learning and conditional random field. In: International Conference on Medical Image Computing and Computer-Assisted Intervention, pp. 132–139 (2016)
10. Luo, Y., Yang, L., Wang, L.: Efficient CNN-CRF network for retinal image segmentation. In: International Conference on Cognitive Systems and Signal Processing, pp. 157–165 (2016)
11. Du, C., Song, S., Ai, D.: Inter/intra-constraints optimization for fast vessel enhancement in x-ray angiographic image sequence. In: IEEE International Conference on Bioinformatics and Biomedicine, pp. 859–863 (2018)
12. Läthén, G., Jonasson, J., Borga, M.: Blood vessel segmentation using multi-scale quadrature filtering. Pattern Recogn. Lett. **31**, 762–767 (2010)
13. Fan, J., Yang, J., Wang, Y.: Multichannel fully convolutional network for coronary artery segmentation in x-ray angiograms. IEEE Access **6**, 44635–44643 (2018)
14. Krizhevsky, A., Sutskever, I., Hinton, G.: ImageNet classification with deep convolutional neural networks. In: Advances in Neural Information Processing Systems, pp. 1097–1105 (2012)
15. Srivastava, N., Hinton, G., Krizhevsky, A.: Dropout: a simple way to prevent neural networks from overfitting. J. Mach. Learn. Res. **15**, 1929–1958 (2014)

Visual Tracking Based on Multi-cue Proposals and Long Short-Term Features Learning

Jiaming Wei[1], Huimin Ma[1(✉)], Ruiqi Lu[1], and Xiong Luo[2]

[1] Department of Electronic Engineering,
Tsinghua University, Beijing 100084, China
{wjml6,lrql7}@mails.tsinghua.edu.cn,
mhmpub@tsinghua.edu.cn
[2] School of Computer and Communication Engineering & Institute of
Artificial Intelligence, University of Science and Technology Beijing,
Beijing 100083, China
xluo@ustb.edu.cn

Abstract. Tracking-by-detection frameworks have made significant progress in recent years. However, proposal and classification of this framework could still be severely affected by occlusion and motion. In this paper, we propose a tracking algorithm MPLST to improve the accuracy and robustness of proposal and classification under challenges. First, we provide a multi-cue proposal method, which combines Gaussian sampling utilizing previous target state, and motion and appearance selective search making use of the motion and appearance features of the target respectively. Second, we provide a long short-term features learning approach for target classification and network updating. The long-term features are robust to occlusion, and the short-term features can keep up with the fast motion of the target. Experiments on the OTB100 [1] and VOT2015 [2] datasets demonstrate that our MPLST can effectively deal with occlusion and motion, and achieve competitive performance against state-of-the-art trackers.

Keywords: Visual tracking · Region proposal · Long short-term features

1 Introduction

Tracking-by-detection mainly contains two stages: proposals and classification. This framework has made significant progress in improving accuracy for regular tracking. However, it sometimes fails under the challenges like occlusion and motion, which would strongly influence both two stages of detection. Tracking algorithms require cautious updating under occlusion but need to be fast updated for following the fast motion of the target. As a result, tracking algorithms suffer from the challenges of dynamic occlusion and motion. Specifically, in the proposal stage, Gaussian sampling [3] relies too much on the previous target state and fails under camera motion and target deformation. Region proposal networks [7] and selective search [6] only utilize the appearance features of objects and usually leave out the small and occluded target. In the classification stage, the most important process is to learn the target features and

© Springer Nature Singapore Pte Ltd. 2019
Y. Wang et al. (Eds.): IGTA 2019, CCIS 1043, pp. 633–644, 2019.
https://doi.org/10.1007/978-981-13-9917-6_60

online update a target classifier. However, robust classifiers [3–5] usually cautiously update the network and fail to follow the fast changes of the target. In contrast, other classifiers [10–13] which continuously keep up with the target are sensitive to occlusion and could fall into tracking drift easily.

In this paper, we propose a tracking algorithm MPLST based on multi-cue proposals and long short-term features learning. We balance fast learning and robust tracking, in order to solve dynamic occlusion and motion. Main contributions of our work are summarized as the following three folds:

(1) **Multi-cue proposals:** We provide a multi-cue proposal method to extract more accurate proposals by utilizing cues of previous target state, motion and appearance features. The Gaussian sampling is robust to occlusion. The motion-appearance selective search can generate high-quality proposals under motion and deformation.

(2) **Long short-term features learning:** We propose a feature learning and target classification method. Long-term features are robust to occlusion, while short-term features can keep up with fast motion of the target. The optimal representation of the target is obtained by combining long-term and short-term target features.

(3) **Accuracy and robustness balancing:** We evaluate our MPLST on two tracking benchmarks, the OTB100 [1] and VOT2015 [2] datasets. The experiments demonstrate that MPLST can deal with occlusion and motion, and achieve competitive performance on both accuracy and robustness against state-of-the-art trackers.

2 Related Work

2.1 Challenges Handling

Challenges of tracking include occlusion, scale change, deformation, illuminate variation and so on [1]. Occlusion is the dominant challenge followed by scale change and fast motion [2]. To handle fast motion, [22] utilizes the image template of the previous target and a regression network; [12–14, 30] use discriminative correlation filters to model the target. Those approaches can adapt to current target features quickly but suffer from wrong training samples caused by occlusion. As a contrast, [3–5, 23, 31] initialize and update the deep neural networks [24] using hundreds of training samples to resist the influence of occlusion. However, those approaches usually fail under fast motion because of the slow learning rate of the network.

2.2 Region Proposals

Proposals generation is the first stage of tracking-by-detection framework. [3–5] utilize Gaussian sampling to randomly extract proposals around the previous target by the Gaussian distribution. Gaussian sampling only relies on the previous location and size of the target and achieves robust performance under heavy occlusion. However, it cannot deal with fast motion and deformation due to the lack of target motion features. [25] utilizes selective search [6] to make use of appearance features of the target. [26] generates flexible and tight proposals using deep features of the target extracted by region proposal network [7] and takes advantages of appearance contrasts between the target and background. However, those methods usually extract proposals on salient objects and ignore small and occluded target, leading to tracking drift as a result.

2.3 Classification and Updating

Classification and model updating also suffer from dynamic occlusion and motion. Classifiers used in state-of-the-art trackers can be roughly categorized into two types: convolutional neural network (CNN) based models [3–5, 23] and discriminative correlation filters (DCF) based models [10–13, 16]. CNN based models take advantages of stable deep semantic features of the target to achieve better performance under heavy occlusion, but suffer from fast motion because a large number of samples and learning iterations are needed to online update the model. On the other hand, DCF based models only need several samples to update the classifier and can follow the fast change of the target. However, those methods usually fail when update models with wrong samples under heavy occlusion. Classifiers for tracking have to deal with dynamic occlusion and motion at the same time to achieve better performance.

3 Overview of Tracking Framework

Our MPLST is a tracking-by-detection framework with four parts as shown in Fig. 1. The fundamental purpose of MPLST is making better proposals and classification to handle the challenge of dynamic occlusion and motion in one tracking framework.

The first part of MPLST is feature extraction. The inputs are the current frame and the previous target states. We compute the optical flow map and extract motion and appearance features of the whole image using convolutional layers. The motion and appearance features are further concatenated as the feature maps. We utilize a network with only three layers because the targets are usually small and a shallow network will increase location precision. The networks are the convolutional layers of the VGG-M [14] network pre-trained on the ImageNet [8] dataset.

Second, 256 candidates are extracted by the multi-cue proposal approach combining Gaussian sampling and motion-appearance selective search. The Gaussian sampling generates 128 candidates by randomly sampling around the previous target state, which is robust to occlusion. The motion-appearance selective search extract 64 samples on the optical flow map and the current image respectively by standard selective search, which is more flexible for motion and deformation. We limit the search region around the target and choose candidates through previous target state. ROI pooling is further performed to obtain features of the candidates with a size of $3 \times 3 \times 1024$.

Third, the target-background classification is performed by combining long-term and short-term features of the target. The long-term features extracted by fully connected layers trained using samples collected over a long time period (100 frames). In contrast, the other path responses to the short-term features of the target which are learned using samples collected in a short time (10 frames). Those two paths also have different network architectures. We delete one fully connected layer for faster learning of the short-term features. The optimal representation of the target is obtained by training the classifier combining the long-term and short-term features. The reason for using two complementary features is that the long-term features are robust to occlusion and the short-term features can keep up with fast motion of the target.

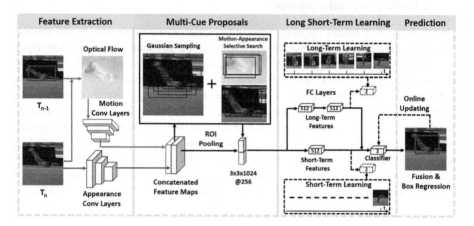

Fig. 1. Overview of our MPLST tracking frameworks which has four parts. The motion and appearance feature maps are extracted by the convolutional neural networks. The multi-cue proposal which combines Gaussian Sampling and motion-appearance selective search generates accurate proposals under occlusion and motion. The multi-path fully connected layers classify proposals utilizing the long-term and short-term features. Several high score proposals will be fused and a box regression is performed to refine the target state.

Finally, the boxes with the highest scores will be fused into one prediction box in the fourth part. We perform a linear bounding box regression to refine the target box. The regression model is trained by 1000 target samples collected in the first frame. Positive and negative samples are collected in each frame for online updating.

4   Multi-cue Proposals

The multi-cue proposal method combines three algorithms to generate better candidates. The Gaussian sampling makes use of the previous state of the target. Motion selective search utilizes optical flow map as motion features for sampling. Appearance selective search generates candidates using appearance contrasts between objects. Those three methods are complementary for handling multiple challenges.

4.1   Optical Flow Map

The states of proposals mainly depend on the motion of the target. The target motion usually contains two parts, the camera motion and the object motion. The camera motion influences the absolute locations of objects and the search region of tracking algorithms. The object motion influences the relative positions of objects and the posture of the target. Hence, we first calculate the optical flow between two frames to obtain the motion features of the target. The Horn-Schunck method [9] is performed to calculate dense optical flow around the target. The visual optical flow map is further generated by a pseudo-color transformation approach [29]. We make use of the optical flow map in two ways. First, the average optical flow outside the previous target state is regarded as the camera motion. The search region of our tracking algorithm is relocated according to the camera motion. Second, the optical flow around the previous target is regarded as the object motion and utilized for motion selective search.

4.2 Gaussian Sampling

Gaussian sampling is widely used in state-of-the-art tracking algorithms [3–5]. We choose Gaussian sampling as the basic proposal method of our tracking framework. In each frame, 128 samples are generated by translation and scale dimension of the target state in the previous frame. The translation is subject to Gaussian distribution whose mean is previous target state and the covariance is $0.09r^2$, where r is the mean of the height and width of the target. The scale s_t is also subject to Gaussian distribution whose mean is the initial target scale and the covariance is 0.25. The scale of candidates is calculated by multiply 1.05^{s_t} to previous target scale. The camera motion has been excluded before the Gaussian sampling. Because the Gaussian sampling mainly utilizes the previous target state, it is a highly effective proposal method for small target or target whose motion is not too large.

4.3 Motion-Appearance Selective Search

In order to utilize the motion and appearance features of the target, we draw 64 samples with motion selective search and 64 samples with appearance selective search. We choose motion and appearance features because those features are complementary features. A target that remains stationary will not be influenced by motion blur and has clear appearance contrast with backgrounds. On the other hand, a target with large motion will be salient on the optical flow map. We first determine the search region because performing selective search on the whole image is a waste of computation and could extract too many background objects. A region that is two times larger than the previous target is regarded as the search region. Next, selective search [6] is performed on the optical flow map and the current image respectively. We generate 256 samples in total with the Gaussian sampling and the motion-appearance selective search. The results of the proposals are demonstrated in Fig. 1.

5 Long Short-Term Features Learning

The features of the target usually continuously change during tracking. The long-term features can resist interference and increase tracking robustness. The short-term features represent the recent states of the target and increase tracking accuracy. In order to balance the accuracy and robustness, we propose a long short-term features learning method to make use of long-term and short-term features at the same time.

5.1 Motion and Appearance Features

The convolutional features of the current frame represent the appearance features of the target. Although they are widely used in tracking algorithms, the appearance features are not enough to deal with fast motion and scale change. Hence, we extract the motion features of the target on the optical flow map using pre-trained convolutional networks. The motion features and the appearance features are further concatenated as the target features and used to classify the target and the backgrounds. The features of candidates with a size of $3 \times 3 \times 1024$ are generated after ROI pooling on the concatenated feature maps.

5.2 Long-Term Features

The fully connected layers are used to further extract the feature vectors of the candidates and perform target/background classification. The single path of fully connected layers [3] is duplicated into two paths for learning long-term and short-term features respectively. The long-term features are robust to occlusion because the true target samples are much more than noisy occluded samples. The long-term path has two fully-connected layers with a size of $3 \times 3 \times 1024 \times 512$ and $1 \times 1 \times 512 \times 512$. This path extracts the long-term high-level features of the target using relatively deeper FC layers, in order to improve updating robustness under occlusion. The target samples for online updating are collected in a long time as shown in Fig. 1. We choose target samples in recent 100 frames, about 4 s, which are long enough during tracking. Finally, the long-term feature vector with 512 channels is generated.

5.3 Short-Term Features

The short-term path has shallower fully connected layers than the long-term path for quickly online updating. This path is used to learn fast feature change of the target under big motion and deformation. Hence, the short-term features focus on what the target exactly looks like recently. We force the network branch to learn the short-term features in two ways. First, the second fully-connected layers are deleted to learn the low-level target features. A shallow network is also easy to online update. Second, only target samples extracted in recent 10 frames are used to train the short-term path, in order to exclude the influence of the long-term target samples. The short-term feature vector also has 512 channels as the long-term vector.

5.4 Classification and Online Updating

The long-term and short-term features are concatenated into one feature vector with 1024 channels for target/background classification. The classifier is a fully connected layer with a size of $1 \times 1 \times 1024 \times 2$. The classifier generates a target score $P^+(x_i)$ and a background score $P^-(x_i)$ for each candidate x_i. The target scores are used to evaluate the similarity between candidates and previous target features. The optimal target state x^* is predicted by Eq. 1.

$$x^* = \text{argmax}_{x_i} P^+(x_i). \tag{1}$$

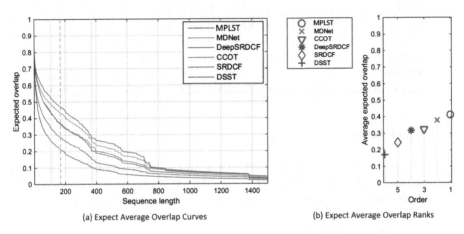

(a) Expect Average Overlap Curves   (b) Expect Average Overlap Ranks

Fig. 2. Expect average overlap curves and ratios ranks from right to left.

The classifier and the long short-term paths are updated using a three-step method. First, positive and negative training samples are collected during tracking. We collect 50 positive samples and 200 negative samples in each frame. The positive samples have > 0.7 IoU overlap ratios with the predicted target. The negative samples have < 0.5 IoU overlap ratios. Second, the long-term path and the short-term path are trained using positive samples collected in recent 100 frames and 10 frames. The negative samples in recent 20 frames are used. The loss function is softmax loss as Eq. 2 with K = 2. Where f_j denotes the score of category j, f_{y_i} denotes the score of the ground-truth category. Stochastic gradient descent (SGD) is used for loss backpropagation.

$$L = -f_{y_i} + log \sum_{j=1}^{K} e^{f_j}. \tag{2}$$

Third, the target/background classifier is trained to make use of long-term and short-term features at the same time. The positive and the negative samples in recent 20 frames are used. The purpose of our network architecture is to obtain the optimal representation of the target using long short-term features. The loss function is also softmax loss as Eq. 2. The classifier and the long short-term paths are initialized in the first frame with 500 positive samples and 5000 negative samples.

Table 1. Accuracy and Robustness evaluation of our MPLST and state-of-the-art trackers on VOT2015 [2] dataset under challenges including camera motion, illumination change, motion change, occlusion and size change. Left of slash is accuracy and right of slash is robustness. Top performance is highlighted in bold.

	empty	camera	illume	motion	occlu	size	mean
DSST	61.1/37	55.8/69	67.3/7	49.1/61	38.4/28	52.2/33	54.0/39.2
SRDCF	58.0/16	53.6/43	69.2/8	48.6/36	42.1/22	47.2/21	53.1/24.3
CCOT	57.0/11	53.5/24	66.0/2	46.4/20	44.5/14	49.1/13	52.8/14.0
DeepSRDCF	62.8/9	56.4/25	66.5/0	49.7/23	45.2/26	53.1/8	55.6/15.2
MDNet	65.0/6	61.0/20	68.0/1	56.0/15	54.3/14	56.0/11	60.0/11.4
MPLST (Ours)	**65.0/4**	**61.9/17**	**70.6/0**	**56.6/13**	**56.3/13**	**58.1/9**	**61.4/9.3**

6   Experiments

Our challenges handling network (MPLST) is evaluated on two large-scale visual tracking benchmarks: the VOT2015 [2] and OTB100 [1] datasets. We compare our tracking algorithm with other state-of-art trackers under multiple challenges.

6.1   Evaluation on VOT2015

VOT2015 [2] is a commonly used dataset which contains 60 sequences with full annotation. The 60 videos provide different challenges, including camera motion, illumination change, motion change, occlusion and size change. Three main metrics including accuracy, robustness and expect average overlap (EAO) are utilized to evaluate the performance of trackers. We compare our tracker MPLST with state-of-art trackers including MDNet [3], DeepSRDCF [13], CCOT [12], SRDCF [11] and DSST [10]. Our tracker is pre-trained using sequences in OTB100 [1] datasets excluding sequences in VOT2015 [2].

Table 1 illustrates the accuracy (left) and robustness (right) evaluation of trackers under challenges. Our MPLST achieves better performance on most challenges, especially on occlusion and size change. We improve the accuracy by 2.0% on occlusion, 2.1% on size change and 1.4% in the average. And the robustness is also improved under most challenges, especially on camera motion and size change. Figure 2 plots the expect average overlap (EAO) curves and the ranks of trackers. EAO evaluates the expected accuracy of the results on long-term tracking. Our MPLST has better feature learning ability for long-term tracking as shown in Fig. 2.

6.2   Evaluation on OTB100

OTB100 [1] is consist of 100 fully annotated videos with different attributes including fast motion, occlusion, deformation, etc. The one-pass evaluation (OPE) is performed on our MPLST comparing with 14 state-of-art trackers including MDNet [3], CCOT [12], DeepSRDCF [13], HDT [15], SRDCFdecon [16], CF2 [17], CNN-SVM [18], SRDCF [11], staple [19], MEEM [20], SAMF [21], LCT [27], KCF [28] and DSST [10]. The main metrics for performance evaluation are precision and success plots. The precision plot measures the accuracy of the target location. The success plot evaluates the bounding box overlap ratio. Our tracker is pre-trained on VOT2015 [2], excluding sequences in OTB100 [1].

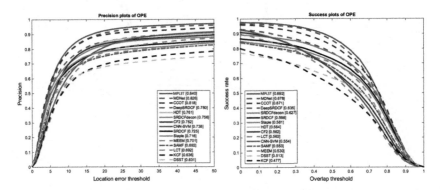

Fig. 3. Precision and success plots of OPE on OTB100 [1], comparing our tracker MPLST with state-of-the-art trackers.

Figure 3 illustrates the precision and success plots of OPE on the OTB100 [1] dataset. Our MPLST outperforms state-of-the-art trackers on both location accuracy and bounding box overlap. We make progress of 1.4% on precision and 1.4% on success. We further evaluate trackers under different attributes and plot the precision curves as shown in Fig. 4. Our MPLST performs better on most attributes, especially scale variation, out-plane rotation, and fast motion. The experiment results demonstrate that our MPLST can handle multiple dynamic challenges in one framework.

6.3 Experimental Analysis

The experiments mainly evaluate the accuracy and robustness of trackers under challenges. We summarize the results of experiments in three folds:

First, our MPLST achieves competitive performance against state-of-art trackers on both accuracy and robustness on the OTB100 [1] and VOT2015 [2] datasets. MPLST improves both proposal and classification stage of a tracking-by-detection framework. The multi-cue proposal method is utilized to generate more accurate candidates. The long short-term learning method learns features of the target in different time periods.

Second, our MPLST achieves better performance on multiple challenges, especially deformation, fast motion, and occlusion. The experiments results achieve the fundamental purpose of our tracking frameworks. Complementary approaches are effective to deal with dynamic occlusion and motion at the same time.

Third, some future work needs to be done to further improve our tracking performance. MPLST cannot deal with the extremely small target and similar background. The features of the small target will be lost after convolution and pooling in deep layers. Also, our tracker cannot distinguish the target and similar background because their features are almost the same (Fig. 5).

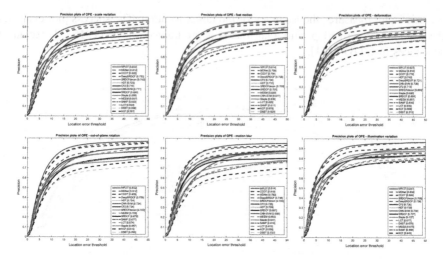

Fig. 4. Precision plots of OPE under different attributes on OTB100 [1]. The attributes include scale variation, fast motion, deformation, out-plane-rotation, motion blur, and illumination variation.

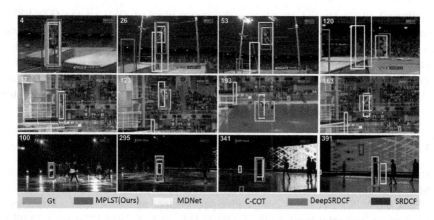

Fig. 5. Qualitative results of our MPLST comparing with other state-of-the-art trackers.

7   Conclusions

The proposed MPLST tracking framework handles the challenge of dynamic occlusion and motion simultaneously by multi-cue proposals and long short-term features learning. The multi-cue proposal method which combines Gaussian sampling and motion-appearance selective search improves the robustness of proposal under occlusion and the accuracy of proposals under fast motion. The long short-term features learning approach constructs the optimal representation of the target by combining long-term and short-term target features. Our MPLST resists occlusion using the long-term features and keeps up with fast motion of the target using short-term features. Our tracking algorithm improves both tracking accuracy and robustness under challenges including occlusion, motion, deformation, and scale variation and achieves competitive performance against state-of-the-art trackers. In the future work, the feature pyramid networks could be utilized to learn low-level features and handle small targets. The training frequency should be adaptively adjusted to improve real-time performance.

Acknowledgment. This work was supported by the National Key R&D Plan (No. 2016YFB0100901), the National Natural Science Foundation of China (No. 61773231).

References

1. Wu, Y., Lim, J., Yang, M.H.: Object tracking benchmark. IEEE Trans. Pattern Anal. Mach. Intell. **37**(9), 1834–1848 (2015)
2. Kristan, M., et al.: The visual object tracking VOT2015 challenge results. In: Proceedings of the IEEE International Conference on Computer Vision Workshops, pp. 1–23 (2015)
3. Nam, H., Han, B.: Learning multi-domain convolutional neural networks for visual tracking. In: Proceedings of the IEEE Conference on Computer Vision and Pattern Recognition, pp. 4293–4302 (2016)
4. Han, B., Sim, J., Adam, H.: BranchOut: regularization for online ensemble tracking with convolutional neural networks. In: Proceedings of the IEEE Conference on Computer Vision and Pattern Recognition, pp. 3356–3365 (2017)
5. Nam, H., Baek, M., Han, B.: Modeling and propagating CNNs in a tree structure for visual tracking. arXiv preprint arXiv:1608.07242 (2016)
6. Uijlings, J.R., Van De Sande, K.E., Gevers, T., Smeulders, A.W.: Selective search for object recognition. Int. J. Comput. Vis. **104**(2), 154–171 (2013)
7. Ren, S., He, K., Girshick, R., Sun, J.: Faster R-CNN: towards real-time object detection with region proposal networks. IEEE Trans. Pattern Anal. Mach. Intell. **39**(6), 1137–1149 (2017)
8. Krizhevsky, A., Sutskever, I., Hinton, G.E.: ImageNet classification with deep convolutional neural networks. In: Advances in Neural Information Processing Systems, pp. 1097–1105 (2012)
9. Horn, B.K., Schunck, B.G.: Determining optical flow. Artif. Intell. **17**(1–3), 185–203 (1981)
10. Danelljan, M., Häger, G., Khan, F., Felsberg, M.: Accurate scale estimation for robust visual tracking. In: British Machine Vision Conference, Nottingham, 1–5 September 2014. BMVA Press (2014)
11. Danelljan, M., Hager, G., Shahbaz Khan, F., Felsberg, M.: Learning spatially regularized correlation filters for visual tracking. In: Proceedings of the IEEE International Conference on Computer Vision, pp. 4310–4318 (2015)
12. Danelljan, M., Robinson, A., Shahbaz Khan, F., Felsberg, M.: Beyond correlation filters: learning continuous convolution operators for visual tracking. In: Leibe, B., Matas, J., Sebe, N., Welling, M. (eds.) ECCV 2016. LNCS, vol. 9909, pp. 472–488. Springer, Cham (2016). https://doi.org/10.1007/978-3-319-46454-1_29
13. Danelljan, M., Hager, G., Shahbaz Khan, F., Felsberg, M.: Convolutional features for correlation filter based visual tracking. In: Proceedings of the IEEE International Conference on Computer Vision Workshops, pp. 58–66 (2015)
14. Chatfield, K., Simonyan, K., Vedaldi, A., Zisserman, A.: Return of the devil in the details: delving deep into convolutional nets. arXiv preprint arXiv:1405.3531 (2014)
15. Qi, Y., et al.: Hedged deep tracking. In: Proceedings of the IEEE Conference on Computer Vision and Pattern Recognition, pp. 4303–4311 (2016)

16. Danelljan, M., Hager, G., Shahbaz Khan, F., Felsberg, M.: Adaptive decontamination of the training set: a unified formulation for discriminative visual tracking. In: Proceedings of the IEEE Conference on Computer Vision and Pattern Recognition, pp. 1430–1438 (2016)

17. Ma, C., Huang, J.B., Yang, X., Yang, M.H.: Hierarchical convolutional features for visual tracking. In: Proceedings of the IEEE International Conference on Computer Vision, pp. 3074–3082 (2015)

18. Niu, X.X., Suen, C.Y.: A novel hybrid CNN–SVM classifier for recognizing handwritten digits. Pattern Recogn. **45**(4), 1318–1325 (2012)

19. Bertinetto, L., Valmadre, J., Golodetz, S., Miksik, O., Torr, P.H.: Staple: complementary learners for real-time tracking. In: Proceedings of the IEEE Conference on Computer Vision and Pattern Recognition, pp. 1401–1409 (2016)

20. Zhang, J., Ma, S., Sclaroff, S.: MEEM: robust tracking via multiple experts using entropy minimization. In: Fleet, D., Pajdla, T., Schiele, B., Tuytelaars, T. (eds.) ECCV 2014. LNCS, vol. 8694, pp. 188–203. Springer, Cham (2014). https://doi.org/10.1007/978-3-319-10599-4_13

21. Li, Y., Zhu, J.: A scale adaptive kernel correlation filter tracker with feature integration. In: Agapito, L., Bronstein, M.M., Rother, C. (eds.) ECCV 2014. LNCS, vol. 8926, pp. 254–265. Springer, Cham (2015). https://doi.org/10.1007/978-3-319-16181-5_18

22. Held, D., Thrun, S., Savarese, S.: Learning to track at 100 FPS with deep regression networks. In: Leibe, B., Matas, J., Sebe, N., Welling, M. (eds.) ECCV 2016. LNCS, vol. 9905, pp. 749–765. Springer, Cham (2016). https://doi.org/10.1007/978-3-319-46448-0_45

23. Fan, H., Ling, H.: SANet: structure-aware network for visual tracking. In: Proceedings of the IEEE Conference on Computer Vision and Pattern Recognition Workshops, pp. 42–49 (2017)

24. LeCun, Y., et al.: Backpropagation applied to handwritten zip code recognition. Neural Comput. **1**(4), 541–551 (1989)

25. Keuper, M., Tang, S., Zhongjie, Y., Andres, B., Brox, T., Schiele, B.: A multi-cut formulation for joint segmentation and tracking of multiple objects. arXiv preprint arXiv:1607.06317 (2016)

26. Ren, J., et al.: Robust tracking using region proposal networks. arXiv preprint arXiv:1705.10447 (2017)

27. Ma, C., Yang, X., Zhang, C., Yang, M.H.: Long-term correlation tracking. In: Proceedings of the IEEE Conference on Computer Vision and Pattern Recognition, pp. 5388–5396 (2015)

28. Henriques, J.F., Caseiro, R., Martins, P., Batista, J.: High-speed tracking with kernelized correlation filters. IEEE Trans. Pattern Anal. Mach. Intell. **37**(3), 583–596 (2015)

29. Jain, S.D., Xiong, B., Grauman, K.: FusionSeg: learning to combine motion and appearance for fully automatic segmentation of generic objects in videos. In: 2017 IEEE Conference on Computer Vision and Pattern Recognition, pp. 2117–2126. IEEE (2017)

30. Zhou, J., Wang, R., Ding, J.: Deep convolutional features for correlation filter based tracking with parallel network. In: Wang, Y., Jiang, Z., Peng, Y. (eds.) IGTA 2018. CCIS, vol. 875, pp. 461–470. Springer, Singapore (2018). https://doi.org/10.1007/978-981-13-1702-6_46

31. Wang, R., Zou, J., Che, M., Xiong, C.: Robust and real-time visual tracking based on single-layer convolutional features and accurate scale estimation. In: Wang, Y., Jiang, Z., Peng, Y. (eds.) IGTA 2018. CCIS, vol. 875, pp. 471–482. Springer, Singapore (2018). https://doi.org/10.1007/978-981-13-1702-6_47

MMRPet: Modular Mixed Reality Pet System Based on Passive Props

Yaqiong Xue[1], Dongdong Weng[1,2(✉)], Haiyan Jiang[1], and Qing Gao[3]

[1] Beijing Engineering Research Center of Mixed Reality and Advanced Display,
School of Optics and Photonics, Beijing Institute of Technology, Beijing, China
crgj@bit.edu.cn
[2] AICFVE of Beijing Film Academy, 4, Xitucheng Road,
Haidian, Beijing, China
[3] Zhejiang University of Media and Communications,
Hangzhou, Zhejiang, China

Abstract. We present MMRPet, a modular mixed reality pet system based on passive props. In addition to superimposing virtual pets onto pet entities to take advantages of physical interactions provided by pet entities and personalized appearance and rich expressional capabilities provided by virtual pets, the key idea behind MMRPet is the modular design of pet entities. The user can reconfigure limited modules to construct pet entities of various forms and structures. These modular pet entities can provide flexible haptic feedback and support the system to render virtual pets of personalized form and structure. By integrating tracking information from the head and hands of the user, as well as each module of pet entities, MMRPet can infer rich interaction intents and support rich human-pet interactions when the user touches, moves, rotates or gazes each module. We explore the design space for the construction of modular pet entities and the design space of the human-pet interaction enabled by MMRPet. Furthermore, a series of prototypes demonstrate the advantages of using modular entities in a mixed reality pet system.

Keywords: Virtual reality · Mixed reality · Pet ·
Modular Mixed Reality Embodiment · Passive haptics ·
Modular design · Tangible user interfaces · Tangible interaction

1 Introduction

Human-pet interaction can benefit a lot to human's mental health and social skills [1–3]. However, there are many obstacles in keeping pets, such as hygiene, allergies, bites, and the frequent infeasibility of caring for a pet. Retaining benefits of interacting with pets while addressing its restrictions has already inspired considerable research in artificial pets. From the screen-based 2D pets Nintendogs, Tamagotchi to virtual reality-based 3D pets, the appearance of virtual pets is increasingly diverse and expressive, but its untouchable intrinsic features restrict the realism of the interaction. In contrast, pet robots can provide rich physical interactions (such as touch) by integrating various sensors and actuators on their physical entities [4, 5]. The rich physical interactions significantly increase the social presence that physical robots can provide

Y. Wang et al. (Eds.): IGTA 2019, CCIS 1043, pp. 645–658, 2019.
https://doi.org/10.1007/978-981-13-9917-6_61

[6]. However, the visual information of physical robots is difficult to alter as it is fixed to the physical nature of the robots in the real world. Only a few have a fully actuated head that supports dynamic facial expressions to express emotions [7, 23].

In order to overcome limitations of a purely virtual or physical embodiment while taking advantage of both, some researchers propose the mixed reality agent [32] that superimposes the virtual embodiment onto the physical one [25]. In these systems, the physical embodiments provide physical presence and allow the system to support physical interactions, whilst the virtual embodiments provide personalized appearance and rich expressional capabilities.

Unfortunately, because of the fixed form and structure of physical embodiments, the user is required to possess a large number of physical embodiments of different forms and structures to support the system to render the virtual embodiment of personalized form and structure. This makes approaches based on mixed reality embodiment very inefficient, especially in the field of artificial pet where different pets may have different forms or structures (such as serpentine, bipedal, tetrapod, etc.).

In this paper, we propose the Modular Mixed Reality Embodiment (MMRE). In addition to superimposing the virtual embodiment onto the physical one to combine the advantages of both embodiments, the key idea behind MMRE is the modular design of physical embodiment. The user can reconfigure limited modules to construct physical embodiments of various forms and structures. These modular physical embodiments can provide flexible haptic feedback and support the system to render the virtual embodiments of personalized form and structure.

We present MMRPet, a pet system based on MMRE. It contains a module set from which users can select different combinations of modules and connect them to each other to construct pet entities of different forms and structures. In order to determine how to superimpose a virtual pet on a pet entity to achieve registration of visual and haptic information, we fix a marker containing rich texture features on the surface of each module and utilize a vision-based method to track each module separately. In addition, we track the position and orientation of the user's head and hands. Combining the above three types of tracking data, the system can support rich human-pet interaction when the user connects, touches, moves, rotates or gazes each module.

Our contributions are:

- We present Modular Mixed Reality Embodiment (MMRE) and a pet system based on MMRE.
- We explore new possibilities can be brought to human-pet interaction by the modular design of pet entities.
- We explore the design space for the construction of modular pet entities.

2   Related Work

2.1   Haptics in VR

In order to incorporate sense of touch in the virtual environment, many researchers have developed a variety of active haptic devices to create virtual forces in three-dimensional space, including grounded devices [9, 10], hand-held devices [11, 12], and wearable devices [13, 14]. Most of these devices can only provide kinesthetic feedback (shape, weight, hardness, etc.) [9–14], or tactile feedback (texture, roughness, temperature, etc.) [12]. Moreover, user is required to maintain contact with the device throughout the entire interaction process to feel the haptic feedback generated by the device, even when the device does not create any haptic feedback, which can impair the user's perception accuracy and immersion in virtual environment.

In contrast to active haptic devices, passive haptic systems focus on using existing objects to provide all haptic sensations simultaneously. The user does not need to wear or continuously hold the device, but rather encounters it when interacting with a virtual object. That is when the user touches or manipulates an object in the virtual world, he simultaneously also touches or manipulates a physical object at the same location. Previous work has shown that passive haptics can significantly increase the sense of presence in virtual environments [19]. It can also improve performance in manipulation task [27] and the closer the alignment, the better the performance [28]. Passive haptics has been widely used for scientific visualization [26], military training [30], entertainment and education [29] and other fields. However, there is a trade-off between the complexity of the system and the accuracy of haptic feedback due to the fixed shape of the passive props. The user is required to have plenty of passive props that are approximately 1:1 to their virtual counterparts [20], or has to use a generic passive prop to provide haptic feedback that is not sufficiently accurate for all virtual objects [26].

By introducing modular design in passive haptics, a variety of passive props can be assembled using one or a few common modules, and provide haptic feedback that better balances accuracy and versatility. TurkDeck [17] used "human actuators" to reposition and assemble a series of common modules into passive props when and where the user can actually reach them. Zhao et al. explored robotic assembly of passive props and used magnetic attraction forces to connect adjacent blocks [18]. Although these systems made passive haptics more flexible by utilizing modular design, in these systems the user can only interact with the modular props by moving or rotating them, as if the modular props were still rigid bodies. Very few have been concerned with the new possibilities can be brought to human-prop interaction by the modular design of passive props.

2.2 Embodiment of Agents

The visual information of virtual character, including the type of character that the agent represents (humanoid, zoomorphic, etc.) and virtual facial expression, can be generated and controlled by computers easily. Thus, virtual character can support various types of character, and express the variation of mental state through dynamic facial expressions, actions and other virtual content. However, due to the lack of physical embodiment, the physical presence which virtual character can bring is limited [31].

Physical robots can provide physical interactions (allows for touch, etc.) by integrating various sensors and actuators. NeCoRo [22] and Huggable [4] can detect whether they are picked up, tilted or rotated by the user through their built-in inertial measurement unit. AIBO [21] and NeCoRo [22] both are embedded with touch sensors that can detect whether they are touched on a certain position. Paro [15] uses an airbag-like tactile sensor wrapped around the entire robot to measure position and force when user touch the robot. Haptic Creature [16] uses an array of 60 pressure sensors to identify (through touch) the user's current emotional state. Huggable [4] uses pressure sensors to measure the position and force of user's touch and the electric field sensing to detect light touch that would never be detected by the pressure sensors. In addition, thermistors are used to detect prolonged contact such as being hugged in someone's arms and potentiometers is used to sense the user-driven actions to Huggable. The rich physical interactions significantly increase the social presence that physical robots can provide [6]. However, the visual information of physical robot is difficult to alter as it is fixed to the physical nature of the robot in the real world. Only few have a fully actuated head that supports dynamic facial expressions to express emotions, but the richness and realism of facial expression are hardly comparable to those of virtual characters [7, 23].

In order to overcome limitations of both types of embodiment (e.g. physical robots and virtual agents) and benefit from their advantages, some researchers proposed Mixed Reality Agent [32] that equips a physical robot with a virtual character through mixed reality visualization. Shoji et al. overlaid a humanoid agent onto a robot, thus created a mixed reality humanoid character that the user can touch and interact with [24]. Shimizu et al. proposed MR RUI that combines computer graphics models in the virtual world and robotic user interface in the physical world [25]. In these systems, the physical embodiments provide physical presence and allow the system to support physical interactions, whilst the virtual embodiments provide personalized appearance and rich expressional capabilities that are complex and expensive to implement with purely hardware-based solutions.

3 Modular Mixed Reality Embodiment

In mixed reality embodiment systems [24, 25], the physical embodiment is the skeleton of the agent and provides haptic information with fixed form and structure, whilst the virtual embodiment can be considered as virtual skin that envelops the physical embodiment and provides variable visual information. It is feasible and easy to modify and control the appearance and facial expression of the virtual embodiment. However, changing the form or structure of the virtual embodiment dramatically can lead to inconsistencies between visual information and haptic information. This huge mismatch between visual and haptic sensations can be easily perceived by the user and makes him think what he touches is not what he sees. For example, when a serpentine virtual character is superimposed on a bipedal robot, it is difficult for the user to believe that the visual information and haptic information are coupled with each other.

Thus, in order to support the system to render the virtual embodiment of personalized form and structure, the user is required to possess a large number of physical embodiments of different forms and structures. This makes approaches based on mixed reality embodiment very inefficient, especially in the field of artificial pet where different pets may have different forms or structures (such as serpent, biped, quadruped, etc.).

Thus, we propose the Modular Mixed Reality Embodiment (MMRE). In addition to superimposing the virtual embodiment onto the physical one to combine the advantages of both embodiments, the key idea behind MMRE is the modular design of physical embodiment. The user can reconfigure limited modules to construct physical embodiments of various forms and structures. These modular physical embodiments can provide flexible haptic feedback and support the system to render the virtual embodiments of personalized form and structure.

4 System Design

4.1 The Idea of MMRPet

MMRPet is a modular mixed reality pet system based on passive props. By superimposing virtual pets onto pet entities (Fig. 1a), the system can support both physical interactions provided by pet entities and personalized appearance and rich expressional capabilities provided by virtual pets. At the same time, the modular pet entities used in the system can provide flexible haptic feedback and support the system to render the virtual pets of personalized form and structure.

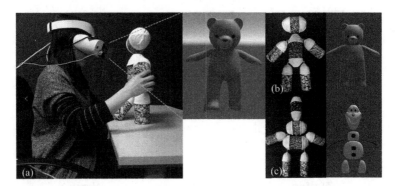

Fig. 1. (a) The user interacting with Teddy Bear in MMRPet. (b–c) Modular pet entities can provide flexible haptic feedback and support the system to render virtual pets of personalized form and structure.

MMRPet is composed of a module set and a tracking system. The module set contains a series of modules with different shapes. The user can select different combinations of modules and connect them to each other to construct pet entities of different forms and structures. The tracking system contains three functions as follows: (1) Track the 6DOF pose of each module to determine the way a virtual pet superimposed on a pet entity and achieve registration of visual and haptic information. (2) Track the position and orientation of the HMD worn by the user to determine the pose of the user's head. (3) Track the pose and motion of users' hands and visualize them in the virtual environment.

By integrating tracking information from the head and hands of the user, as well as each module of pet entities, MMRPet can infer rich interaction intents and support human-pet interaction when the user touches, moves, rotates or gazes each module.

In order to illustrate diverse choices in the construction of modular pet entities and rich human-pet interaction enabled by MMRPet, we will introduce the design space of both in the following section.

4.2   The Design Space for Construction of Modular Pet Entities

We introduce below the three-dimensional design space for construction of modular pet entities that clarify the choices in designing these reconfigurable modules (Fig. 2).

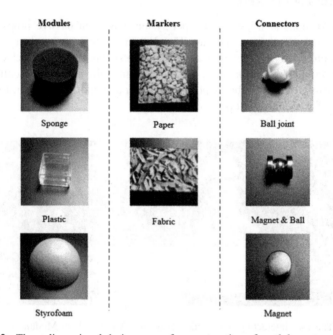

Fig. 2. Three-dimensional design space for construction of modular pet entities.

4.2.1   Modules

Modules provide haptic experience with specific physical properties, such as shape, size, stiffness, etc. In order to create a module set that contains as few modules as possible while provides rich and accurate haptic feedback, the shape of modules should be abstract enough, such as spheres, capsules, cuboids and other simple geometric objects, which can maximize the versatility of the system. The size of modules should be neither too small that affect tracking stability, nor too large that unsuitable for handheld interaction. A variety of materials with different tactile sensations, such as cardboard, plastic sheet, sponge and ABS, can be used to make modules, which can provide haptic feedback with different tactile features for different pets. Since no sensors are need to be integrated into the modules, these materials can be used to make modules by rapid prototyping technologies, such as die cutting and 3D printing, in minutes or hours' time.

4.2.2 Markers

Each module needs to be tracked separately to determine how to visualize the pet in the virtual environment, including the overall position and orientation of the pet and the posture of pet determined by the relative pose of each module, and enable interaction between user and system.

Markers are the one used for module-tracking. They are fixed on the surface of each module and tracked by a camera. They contain rich texture features which are distinct to each other. Since markers cover the surface of modules, they also play a role in providing haptic experience with specific physical properties, such as texture.

4.2.3 Connectors

A variety of connectors can be used to connect all modules as a whole. They may also support movement between modules within a certain degrees of freedom, such as ball and socket joints support 3-DOF rotational movement, universal joints support 2-DOF rotational movement, hinges support 1-DOF rotational movement, springs support translational movement and magnets support no movement.

4.3 The Design Space for Human-Pet Interaction

4.3.1 Consistency Between Virtual and Physical Motion

In order to ensure the registration of visual information and haptic information, the consistency between physical motion and the virtual motion needs to be maintained throughout the entire interaction process. That is, the user-driven motion on the pet entity will drive the virtual pet to act the same motion.

Intuitively, we can superimpose the body components of virtual pet onto each physical module. The user-driven motion on each physical module will drive the virtual body components superimposed on that physical module to act the same motion, thus achieve the consistency between virtual and physical motion. This method is suitable for pets that have body components separate from each another, such as Olaf (Fig. 1c).

However, for pets that have a continuous body, such as a Teddy Bear (Fig. 1b), detaching the body components would lead to adverse visual effects. For this kind of pet, virtual pets could be superimposed on the main module as a whole, and the tracking data of remaining modules could be used to control the motion of corresponding virtual body components using inverse kinematics method. For example, in Teddy Bear, the main module is the body module, and the remaining modules are the head module and limb modules.

4.3.2 Detecting Interaction Intent

Three types of tracking data can be obtained in MMRPet: (1) the pose of user's head; (2) the pose and motion of user's hands and (3) the pose of each module. In the following sections, we will describe how to use these three types of tracking data to detect the interaction intent of users. The MMRPet framework was implemented in Unity, whose terminology we use to describe our system.

Pose Interaction Intent: It detects whether the user drives the pet entity to a particular posture.

Gaze Interaction Intent: We simulate the emission of a ray from the center of the screen of the HMD, and consider the target hit by the ray within a certain distance as a rough estimation of the gaze of the user. If the gaze of the user turns from the surrounding environment to the pet, a Gaze Interaction Intent can be detected.

Touch Interaction Intent: We set an array of triggers on the virtual pet. A trigger detection that detects whether the virtual hands of the user penetrate these triggers runs in each frame of Unity. If a virtual penetration occurs, a Touch Interaction Intent can be detected.

Tilt Interaction Intent: We calculate the exponentially weighted average of the pose data of the main module, and use this value to determine whether the pet is tilted. Due to the adoption of the average pose of the pet for a period of time, it is ensured that even if the pet is in a transient upright state during the process of being tilted back and forth, it will not disengage from the Tilt Interaction Intent.

Proximity Interaction Intent: It detects whether the user is close enough to the pet by monitoring the horizontal distance between the main module in the pet entity and the user's head.

Lift Interaction Intent: It detects whether the user holds the pet up by monitoring the vertical distance between the main module in the pet entity and the user's head.

5 System Implementation

5.1 Tracking System

The entire system adopts a unified inside-out tracking strategy and is portable (Fig. 3a). The system uses Microsoft Mixed Reality HMD to track the position and orientation of the user's head. The HMD supports 6DOF spatial positioning by its built-in cameras and sensors, without the need for external sensors placed throughout a room.

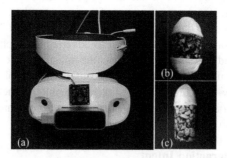

Fig. 3. (a) The HMD with a camera and a Leap Motion fixed on the front side of it. (b–c) Modules with markers fixed on them.

In order to achieve natural interaction where the user's hands are free, without requiring the user to wear data gloves or optical tracking marker, we use a Leap Motion controller to obtain, process and visualize hand information of the user, and fix it on the front side of the HMD.

The tracking of each module mainly depends on markers (Fig. 3b–c) fixed on the surface of each module and a camera fixed on the front side of the HMD. Each marker contains rich texture features and has its own id. The camera used in our system is customized. It is a 150° wide-angle USB camera and has performed pre-distortion processing on the hardware circuitry to enhance module tracking accuracy. The camera captures 30 frames per second at a resolution of 1920 * 1080. All virtual scenes were implemented in Unity and relative poses between each module and the head of the user can be obtained by using Vuforia.

Since Vuforia utilizes a feature-based tracking strategy, the tracking is fairly robust to partial occlusion as long as the remaining marker after occlusion has sufficient contrast-based feature.

5.2 Module Set

We have created two versions of module set, which contains seven modules shown in Fig. 4a. Each module uses a capsule-shaped which is the approximation of limbs and bodies of most pets. The modules come in three sizes with a scale ratio 2:3 in height (B modules versus A modules) or diameter (C modules versus A modules) aspect, based on the Fibonacci ratio that describes scaling in growing systems like mammalian skeletons [8]. Markers are arranged on the side surface of the cylindrical part of the capsule. In order to improve the tracking stability by adding texture features, we made some modifications to all C modules, replacing the bottom hemisphere with a plane arranged with an extra marker.

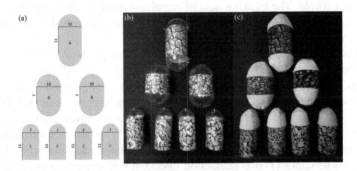

Fig. 4. (a) The specifications of the module set (unit: cm) (b) The first version of module set (plastic modules attached by markers made by paper). (c) The second version of module set (soft sponge modules wrapped by markers made by Short Plush).

We made one version from plastic and attached markers made by paper (Fig. 4b). To offer the user an even better tactile experience, we also created a second version where the sponge module was wrapped by markers made by short plush cloth (Fig. 4c). The sponge modules are neither too stiff that the user feels uncomfortable, nor too soft that may cause significant deformation when grasped, which weaken tracking accuracy. The short plush cloth markers was made by digital-printing markers on the short plush cloth. And it made tactile experience of the modules close to real pets.

Each module is connected to each other by a "Magnet & Ball" connector (Fig. 5), which is easy to assemble and disassemble and supports 3DOF rotational movement between modules. The placement of connectors is suitable for bipeds and quadrupeds that are the most common type for pets.

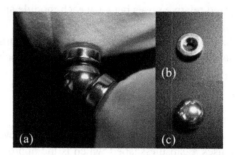

Fig. 5. (a) "Magnet & Ball" connector where (b) two perforation magnets are fixed on two modules and (c) a ferromagnetic ball is sandwiched between two perforation magnets.

5.3   Proof-of-Concept Prototypes

5.3.1   Teddy Bear

The physical entity of Teddy Bear is constructed by one A module, one B module and four C modules (Fig. 1b). The virtual model is superimposed on the body module (A module) as a whole. The tracking data of remaining modules (head module and limb modules) is used to control the motion of the corresponding virtual body components using inverse kinematics method.

The Teddy Bear is designed as an anthropomorphic pet bear. When the user touches the top of its head gently (Touch Interaction Intent), it will show a smile and emit love hearts to the user (Fig. 6a). When the user tilts its body (Tilt Interaction Intent), it will become dizzy (Fig. 6b). When the user holds it up over his head (Lift Interaction Intent), it will burst into cheer (Fig. 6c). When the user moves his head close to it (Proximity Interaction Intent), it will be shy (Fig. 6d). When the user raises its one arm (pose Interaction Intent), it will naughtily stick out its tongue and blink (Fig. 6e). When the user pulls its hands (Touch Interaction Intent), it will response a sweet kiss. When the gaze of the user turns from the surrounding environment to it (Gaze Interaction Intent), it will show a happy smile (Fig. 6f).

5.3.2   Olaf

The physical entity of Olaf is constructed by one A module, two B modules and four C modules (Fig. 1c). Each body components of virtual pet are superimposed onto the corresponding physical module. The user-driven motion on each physical module will drive the virtual body components superimposed on that physical module to act the same motion, thus achieve the consistency between virtual and physical motion.

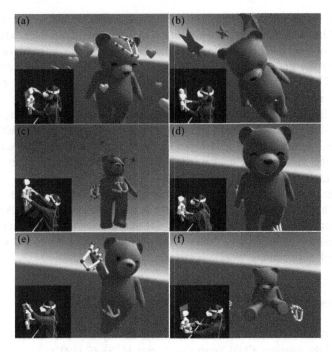

Fig. 6. The user interacts with Teddy Bear: (a) Touch interaction. (b) Tilt interaction. (c) Lift interaction. (d) Proximity interaction. (e) Pose interaction. (f) Gaze interaction.

6 Conclusion and Future Work

In this paper, we present MMRPet, a modular mixed reality pet system based on passive props. The user can reconfigure limited modules to construct pet entities of various forms and structures. These modular pet entities can provide flexible haptic feedback and support the system to render virtual pets of personalized form and structure. By integrating tracking information from the head and hands of the user, as well as each module of pet entities, MMRPet can infer rich interaction intents and support rich human-pet interactions when the user touches, moves, rotates or gazes each module. Since the sensor is not integrated into the physical modules and only markers are needed to track the position and orientation of each module, it is essentially feasible that a variety of materials can be used to make modules.

Leveraging the rich customization capabilities, a large number of novel applications can be enabled by MMRPet. One promising domain is VR storytelling. The user can customize both appearance and form of pets or other agents. By controlling the modules of physical entities, the user can tell their stories in their own hands.

In the future, we would like to replace the current hand-tracking method (Leap Motion) with a vision-based method. Leap Motion uses a binocular camera to capture the reflected light field formed by the infrared radiation reflected by objects in the work area and detect the poles (the tip of a finger or an object) and large-sized reflection surfaces of specific shapes (palm) in the reflected light field. When the hand is operating in the air, the reflected light field is generated mainly by the hand, so the detection of hands' feature is relatively stable. In MR system, however, when the hand touches an object, the object and the hand both reflect the infrared radiation and contribute to the generation of the reflected light field, which may cause tracking instability. Using a vision-based hand-tracking method, the system can also be streamlined, eliminating the need for an extra hand-tracking device.

We would also like to replace the current connection mechanism (Magnet & Ball) between modules with some plug-and-play motors to support more proactive interactions of pets. Meanwhile, the data fusion between the data from angle sensors in the motor and the vision-based tracking data of each module can support better pose tracking of each module.

MMRPet is a modular mixed reality pet system based on passive props. It may lose accuracy of haptic feedback within a certain extent while pursuing the versatility of the module. Integrating haptic retargeting [33, 34] that utilizes visual dominance to minimize user-perceived differences between the modular passive props and virtual shape is also a goal of our future work.

References

1. Mallon, G.P.: Utilization of animals as therapeutic adjuncts with children and youth: a review of the literature. Child Youth Care Forum **21**, 53–67 (1992)
2. Kruger, K., Serpell, J., Fine, A.: Animal-assisted interventions in mental health: definitions and theoretical foundations. In: Handbook on Animal-Assisted Therapy: Theoretical Foundations and Guidelines for Practice, 2nd edn, pp. 21–38 (2006)
3. Wilson, C.C., Turner, D.C.: Companion Animals in Human Health London. Sage, Upper Saddle River (1998)
4. Stiehl, W.D., Breazeal, C., Han, K.H., et al.: The huggable: a therapeutic robotic companion for relational, affective touch. In: IEEE International Workshop on Robot and Human Interactive Communication, pp. 408–415. IEEE, New York (2006)
5. Yohanan, S., Maclean, K.E.: A tool to study affective touch: goals & design of the haptic creature. In: 27th International Conference Extended Abstracts on Human Factors in Computing Systems, pp. 4153–4158. ACM, New York (2009)
6. Lee, K.M., Jung, Y., Kim, J., Kim, S.R.: Are physically embodied social agents better than disembodied social agents?: the effects of physical embodiment, tactile interaction, and people's loneliness in human–robot interaction. Int. J. Hum.-Comput. Stud. **64**, 962–973 (2006)
7. Goris, K., Saldien, J., Vanderniepen, I., Lefeber, D.: The huggable robot probo, a multi-disciplinary research platform. In: Gottscheber, A., Enderle, S., Obdrzalek, D. (eds.) EUROBOT 2008. CCIS, vol. 33, pp. 29–41. Springer, Heidelberg (2009). https://doi.org/10.1007/978-3-642-03558-6_4
8. Raffle, H.S., Parkes, A.J., Ishii, H.: Topobo: a constructive assembly system with kinetic memory. In: SIGCHI Conference on Human Factors in Computing Systems, pp. 647–654. ACM, New York (2004)
9. Sato, M.: Development of string-based force display: SPIDAR. In: 8th International Conference on Virtual Systems and Multimedia (2002)

10. Massie, H.: The PHANToM haptic interface: a device for probing virtual objects. In: Proceedings of the ASME Winter Annual Meeting, Symposium on Haptic Interfaces for Virtual Environment and Teleoperator Systems, vol. 55, pp. 295–300 (1994)

11. Achibet, M., Marchal, M., Argelaguet, F., Lecuyer, A.: The virtual mitten: a novel interaction paradigm for visuo-haptic manipulation of objects using grip force. In: Symposium on 3D User Interfaces, pp. 59–66. IEEE, New York (2014)

12. Benko, H., Holz, C., Sinclair, M., Ofek, E.: NormalTouch and TextureTouch: high-fidelity 3D haptic shape rendering on handheld virtual reality controllers. In: Symposium on User Interface Software and Technology, pp. 717–728. ACM, New York (2016)

13. Gu, X., Zhang, Y., Sun, W., Bian, Y., Zhou, D., Kristensson, P.O.: Dexmo: An Inexpensive and Lightweight Mechanical Exoskeleton for Motion Capture and Force Feedback in VR. In: Conference on Human Factors in Computing Systems, pp. 1991–1995. ACM, New York (2016)

14. Schorr, S.B., Okamura, A.M.: Fingertip tactile devices for virtual object manipulation and exploration. In: Conference on Human Factors in Computing Systems, pp. 3115–3119. ACM, New York (2017)

15. Shibata, T.: An overview of human interactive robots for psychological enrichment. Proc. IEEE **92**, 1749–1758 (2004)

16. Chang, J., MacLean, K., Yohanan, S.: Gesture recognition in the haptic creature. In: Kappers, A.M.L., van Erp, J.B.F., Bergmann Tiest, W.M., van der Helm, F.C.T. (eds.) EuroHaptics 2010. LNCS, vol. 6191, pp. 385–391. Springer, Heidelberg (2010). https://doi.org/10.1007/978-3-642-14064-8_56

17. Cheng, L.P., Roumen, T., Rantzsch, H., Sven K., Schmidt, P., Kovacs, R.: TurkDeck: physical virtual reality based on people. In: Symposium on User Interface Software and Technology, pp. 417–426. ACM, New York (2015)

18. Zhao, Y., Kim, L.H., Wang, Y., Le Goc, M., Follmer, S.: Robotic assembly of haptic proxy objects for tangible interaction and virtual reality. In: The Interactive Surfaces and Spaces, pp. 82–91. ACM, New York (2017)

19. Hoffman, H.G.: Physically touching virtual objects using tactile augmentation enhances the realism of virtual environments. In: IEEE 1998 Virtual Reality Annual International Symposium, pp. 59–63. IEEE, New York (1998)

20. Hettiarachchi, A., Wigdor, D.: Annexing reality: enabling opportunistic use of everyday objects as tangible proxies in augmented reality. In: Conference on Human Factors in Computing Systems, pp. 1957–1967. ACM, New York (2016)

21. Kanamori, M., Suzuki, M., Oshiro, H., Tanaka, M., Inoguchi, T., Takasugi, H.: Pilot study on improvement of quality of life among elderly using a pet-type robot. In: IEEE International Symposium on Computational Intelligence in Robotics and Automation, pp. 107–112. IEEE, New York (2003)

22. Libin, A.V., Libin, E.V.: Person-robot interactions from the robopsychologists' point of view: the robotic psychology and robotherapy approach. Proc. IEEE **92**, 1789–1803 (2004)

23. Breemen, A.V., Yan, X., Meerbeek, B.: iCat: an animated user-interface robot with personality. In: 4th International Joint Conference on Autonomous Agents and Multiagent Systems, pp. 143–144. ACM, New York (2005)

24. Shoji, M., Miura, K., Konno, A.: U-Tsu-Shi-O-Mi: the virtual humanoid you can reach. In: SIGGRAPH 2006 Emerging Technologies, p. 34. ACM, New York (2006)

25. Shimizu, N., Sugimoto, M., Sekiguchi, D., Hasegawa, S., Inami, M.: Mixed reality robotic user interface: virtual kinematics to enhance robot motion. In: International Conference on Advances in Computer Entertainment Technology, pp. 166–169. ACM, New York (2008)

26. Hinckley, K., Pausch, R., Goble, J.C., Kassell, N.F.: Passive real-world interface props for neurosurgical visualization. In: Conference on Human Factors in Computing Systems, pp. 452–458. ACM, New York (1994)
27. Lok, B., Naik, S., Whitton, M., Brooks, F.P.: Effects of handling real objects and avatar fidelity on cognitive task performance in virtual environments. In: IEEE Virtual Reality, January 2003, pp. 125–132 (2003)
28. Kwon, E., Kim, G.J., Lee, S.: Effects of sizes and shapes of props in tangible augmented reality. In: IEEE International Symposium on Mixed and Augmented Reality, pp. 201–202. IEEE, New York (2009)
29. Shapira, L., Amores, J., Benavides, X.: TactileVR: integrating physical toys into learn and play virtual reality experiences. In: IEEE International Symposium on Mixed and Augmented Reality, pp. 100–106. IEEE, New York (2016)
30. Wurpts, M.: Poster: updating an obsolete trainer using passive haptics and pressure sensors. In: IEEE Symposium on 3D User Interfaces, pp. 155–156. IEEE, New York (2009)
31. Chesney, T., Lawson, S.: The illusion of love: does a virtual pet provide the same companionship as a real one? Interact. Stud. **8**, 337–342 (2007)
32. Holz, T., Campbell, A.G., O'Hare, G.M.P., Stafford, J.W., Martin, A., Dragone, M.: MiRA —mixed reality agents. Int. J. Hum. Comput. Stud. **69**, 251–268 (2011)
33. Kim, Y., Park, H., Bang, S., Lee, S.H.: Retargeting human-object interaction to virtual avatars. IEEE Trans. Visual Comput. Graph. **22**, 2405–2412 (2016)
34. Zhao, Y., Follmer, S.: A functional optimization based approach for continuous 3D retargeted touch of arbitrary, complex boundaries in haptic virtual reality. In: CHI Conference on Human Factors in Computing Systems, p. 544. ACM, New York (2018)

ReFall: Real-Time Fall Detection of Continuous Depth Maps with RFD-Net

Yujia Zheng[1], Siyi Liu[1], Zairong Wang[2], and Yunbo Rao[1(✉)]

[1] School of Information and Software Engineering,
University of Electronic Science and Technology of China,
Chengdu 610054, China
raoyb@uestc.edu.cn
[2] Neijiang Normal University, Neijiang 641100, China

Abstract. With the growth in the elderly population, fall detection methods for the elderly are of great significance. In this paper, we propose a deep learning-based method for real-time fall detection continuous depth maps with Residual Fall Detection Network (RFD-Net). Our method incorporates feature extraction with fall detection. In feature extraction part, seven important features that accurately represent the body posture are extracted from the depth maps to reduce the computation load. In the fall detection part, a novel RFD-Net is proposed to recognize body posture for fall detection. Meanwhile, two other networks are developed to compare with RFD-Net. The experimental results show that the extracted features are good representative of the body posture, and our method delivers performance with a fall detection accuracy of 98.51%, which is higher than other related methods.

Keywords: Fall detection · Depth maps · RFD-Net · Posture recognition

1 Introduction

Fall detection has active importance in the health of the elderly, and its immediate discovery can make rescue timelier. In this paper, we propose a fall detection method that utilizes the 3D motion sensor to acquire the frame of the human body, extracts seven important features from the human body frame, and then we propose a novel network structure to process the features and automatically determine if a fall has occurred.

Our method consists of two sequential stages: feature extraction and fall detection. In the first stage, a body frame is built from depth maps that are acquired using a 3D motion sensor. Acquiring depth maps with sensors provide a strong and comprehensive data to be obtained in real-time and in fast frame rates (30 FPS). Afterwards, seven important features are extracted from the human body frame and these include *body centroid height, left hip angle, right hip angle, left knee angle, right knee angle, left feet height, right feet height*. Experiments show that the seven features not only meet the real-time requirement but also recognize the body's posture with high accuracy and robustness.

In the fall detection stage, features obtained from the feature extraction stage are inputs to deep learning models. These models use the features as the posture of the

© Springer Nature Singapore Pte Ltd. 2019
Y. Wang et al. (Eds.): IGTA 2019, CCIS 1043, pp. 659–673, 2019.
https://doi.org/10.1007/978-981-13-9917-6_62

human. Moreover, our method presents a novel fall detection mechanism to distinguish the precise condition of the posture, for example, whether the user is lying down on the ground (which means dangerous) or on the bed or sofa (which means normal condition). To study the performance of other kinds of networks, we improved RNN to compare with RFD-Net, which named *RNN for Fall Detection* (RNN4FD) and *Attention-based RNN combine Fully Connected Network* (ARNN-FCN).

The main contributions of this paper are as follows:

- Compared with traditional methods, few features are extracted from the human body frame to reduce the computation load enormously and achieved real-time demand. Meanwhile, our method using few features can detect more precise information on the fall condition.
- A novel RFD-Net is proposed for fall detection, which uses Exponential Linear Unit (ELU) to replace the traditional Relu and Res-Net to promote the detect effect.
- In order to show our method well, RNN for fall detection and attention-based RNN combine fully connected network are developed to compare with the RFD-Net.

2 Related Work

From the view of the device, the traditional fall detection methods can be divided into three categories: the wearable device-based category, the RGB sensor-based category, and environmental signals sensor-based category.

Wearable device mainly includes devices with pressure, acceleration, or inclination sensors, and is easy to manufacture and relatively simple to generalize. Quadros et al. [1] proposed a fall detection method based on wrist-worn device. The method applied the combination of different sensors and uses the machine learning and rule-based way for detection. Kau et al. [2] proposed a method that uses smart phone to detect fall event. The proposed method is based on accelerometer and electronic compass in the cellphone to get the angle information for inputs. However, the major weaknesses of these method are that, its devices are inconvenient for the elderly to regularly wear and its accuracy is not high enough. To ease its use, the physical sizes of these wearable devices are shrinking, but this limits their battery capacities, leading to the frequent need to charge them. For the elderly with gradually declining memory, this is a difficult task to often remember.

RGB sensor-based methods are convenient to apply in daily life, and the rapid development in computing creates diverse new methods for specific tasks in the fall detection method, such as human body recognition, body joints tracking and noise processing. Doulamis et al. [3] proposed an RGB sensor-based method using deep learning network. In this work, RGB-camera is used to acquire the visual information as the input of network to distinguish the human body. Soni et al. [4] applied background detection and contour extraction to detect falls. Mixture of Gaussian method is used for moving object detection, which based on the video information obtained by RGB sensor. However, these methods lead to privacy disclosure and are with highly environmental sensitivity. Almost all RGB sensor-based methods need to receive the original video information on the human activity in the private house, which for most countries and places, is illegal. Meanwhile, the RGB sensor-based methods need to extract features from these original RGB data, which can be easily influenced by environmental factors. For example, the illumination variation may decrease the accuracy of detection, and the occlusion as well as image noise also influence the method.

Environmental signals sensor-based method is easy to use and accurate on the basis of privacy protection, but the process of making and installing is cumbersome and expensive. Cheffena et al. [5] developed a fall detection method based on audio analysis. The method uses a circular array of microphones to receive audio signals and avoid direct contact with the human body. Popescu et al. [6] developed a fall detection method based on ground vibration and audio analysis. The method monitors the ground vibration amplitude signal through the acceleration sensors, and uses microphones to obtain the audio signal when the fall occurs, then calculate the precise time and position of the fall event. However, the installation processes of these methods are complex and the production cost is relatively high, which i obstructs large-scale manufacturing. And these methods do not have a strong anti-false alarm mechanism, which makes them less robust.

Taking advantage of depth maps, 3D sensors are widely used to tackle the problems of traditional fall detection methods mentioned above. Abobakr et al. [7] applied the Microsoft Kinect to extract the depth information of pixels in the body area, then use support vector machine to detect the fall event by characterizing the fall event as abrupt posture changes, different from the typical lying posture. However, using this body pixel information, attains a high detection accuracy, but also have a huge impact on computation load, which is not suitable for real-time application. Solbach et al. [8] used the stereo camera to get the depth map. In this work, the human posture is recognized with the stereo data captured by stereo camera and CNN is used as the classifier. The stereo camera uses the color image information obtained from connected cameras to calculate the depth maps and this is able to change the detection range. However, this work has some shortcomings: because the installation of the method is also very complex and the detection effect highly relates to the location of the device, it is difficult for this method to be daily applied in realistic environments. Additionally, unlike Kinect, stereo camera has no in-built infrared ray for detection, so ambient brightness has a great impact on its performance. It is not practical or necessary to externally install a fall detector.

To achieve the goal of developing a robust fall detection method with high accuracy, deep learning approaches, like CNN and *Long Shor Term Memory* (LSTM) are applied to extract the features from original data and make the final decision on whether a fall has occurred. Marcos et al. [9] used CNN to decide if a sequence of frames contains a person falling. In this work, the network transferred from VGG-16 extracts the generic features information of the input optical flow, which is then conveniently compared with selected features. Lu et al. [10] had built a method based on 3D CNN combined with LSTM. In this work, 3D CNN is used to get spatial information that cannot be obtained by 2D CNN, and LSTM is applied to deal with the time relationship between the frames. The method gets an average classification accuracy of 92.01 ± 0.35 on dataset UCF11. However, the problem of these works is that highly complex network structures with a large number of parameters and does not meet the speed requirement of real-time detection. The accuracy of the detection cannot be achieved by a simple stack of layers. He et al. [11] proposed deep residual learning optimization of deep network training. Though generic features are more convenient and flexible, too much data can lead to heavy computation load.

In recent years, ResNet achieves state-of-art performance in many computer vision related tasks. It is a very deep network but has a strong ability to avoid overfitting and provide suitable solution to the notorious vanishing gradient problem. In our work, we applied the residual learning framework to wrap convolutional layer(s) by residual block to ease the optimization of the deep generative architecture. To the best of found knowledge, this is also the first work in terms of adopting ResNet to model the fall detection.

3   Real-Time Fall Detection Method

In this session, we will focus on our model of fall detection method. Section 3.1 clarifies how we get the features for the model and the effectiveness of features, Sect. 3.2 demonstrates the structure of RFD-Net, Sect. 3.3 illustrates the mechanism of detecting fall event based on the posture information, and Sect. 3.4 discusses two other networks to compare with RFD-Net. Figure 1 illustrates the workflow of our method.

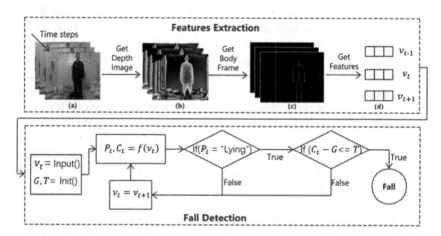

Fig. 1. The workflow of fall detection method (features extraction and fall detection). G represents ground level; T represents preset height; v_t, P_t and C_t represent features, posture and centroid height at t moment respectively.

3.1   Feature Extraction

The commonly used motion sensors in the field of computer vision, can extract depth maps from images and calculate the human frame at very high speed (30 FPS), as Fig. 2 shows. These methods have high accuracy and speed, but are not suitable for the fall detection, because the human frame features are complex with 750 coordinates per second, which cannot achieve the demanding of the real-time fall detection. In our work, we propose a practical feature extraction method based on the human frame results to reduce the computational load, which can also guarantee a high accuracy on fall detection.

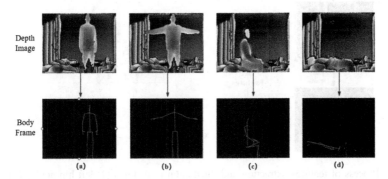

Fig. 2. Depth maps of four different human pose obtained by Kinect and corresponding body frame (a): standing. (b): open arms. (c): sitting. (d): lying down.

As shown in Fig. 2, the gray value in the depth map represents the distance between the object and sensor. And in the case of insufficient lighting conditions, the depth map can still provide the information we need. Using this depth information, we can extract the 3D coordinates of the users' body joints.

As the sensor works at a frame rate of 30 Hz, we can get 750 coordinates per second. Because we intend to design a high speed real-time detection method that does not depend on high-performance hardware facilities in the home environment, a key step in our work is to extract some important features (*body centroid height, left hip angle, right hip angle, left knee angle, right knee angle, left feet height, right feet height*) from a large amount of data, for the fall detection.

By analyzing the angles of the human body joints, we find that the "hips angle" and "knees angle" changed a lot between the two states (lying down or not). For fall detection, another significant feature is the "height" of the human body centroid. When the elderly is injured after a fall, an important observation made is that they cannot instantly stand up, which means that, the height of their body centroids stays low for a period of time. Besides, in order to get the precise position where the human is lying down, we put the "height" of the two feet into our features. Our method achieves this by first initializing for a while, the height of the floor, and then, when the human is not lying down, the method saves for ten seconds, his/her two-foot coordinate data as the heights. Then, it assigns the minimum height of these two feet as the new floor height. This approach proves useful because during data collection, it was observed that, before initializing the fall detection method, the human will commonly not stand on their feet for a long time, especially after reading the instruction which were presented to them a screen. Finally, we extract seven important features: four body joints angles combined with the height of body centroid for posture recognition, and two heights of the feet for floor level recognition. Process of features extraction is shown in Fig. 3.

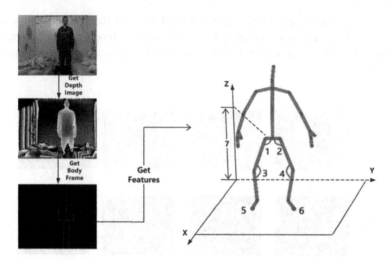

Fig. 3. Process of features extraction and illustration of features (1: left hip angle, 2: right hip angle, 3: left knee angle, 4: right knee angle, 5: left feet height, 6: right feet height, 7: body centroid height)

3.2   The Proposed RFD-Net for Posture Recognition

The basic idea of ResNet is to stack multiple convolutional layers together as a block and then employ a skip connection scheme that passes the previous layers' feature information to its posterior layer. The skip connection allows fitting the residual mapping rather than fitting the original identity mapping, which can maintain the input information and thus enlarge the propagated gradients. However, because of the highly complicated architectures of the typical ResNet (ResNet 34, 50, 101), they are not suitable for real-time applications, which are high speed and performs robustly. In our work, we propose a novel based on ResNet network architecture to meet the requirement of fall detection. Figure 4 shows our improved network architecture of RFD-Net.

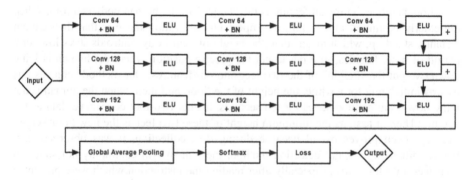

Fig. 4. Improved network architecture of RFD-Net

First, we built the convolutional block. The typical basic block is composed by the CNN layer, Batch Normalization (BN) layer, and the ReLU activation layers. ReLU is a widely used activation function, which filters all negative values and turns them into zero. The function of ReLU is $f(x) = \max(0, x)$. It has been proven that ReLU can better reduce the likelihood of varnishing gradient problem and is more efficient than tanh/sigmoid. However, it also ignores the negative part of the input and can trigger "dying ReLU" problem, which forces the function to eliminate the negative bias and thus make some units never to activate. This characteristic also forces ReLU to zero out all negative values. To improve the speed and accuracy of the model, we use ELU instead of ReLU. The activation functions of ELU is

$$f(x) = \begin{cases} a(e^x - 1), & x < 0 \\ x, & x \geq 0 \end{cases} \tag{1}$$

Compared with ReLU, ELU can accelerate training and improve classification accuracy. It has the following characteristics:

- It can better alleviate the varnishing gradient problem.
- Compared with ReLU, ELU has a negative value, which can push the average output value closer to zero, and this can reduce the migration effect to make gradient closer to the natural gradient.
- Elu is an exponential function when the value is negative, which means it is qualitative but not quantitative.

In our work, we improved ELU method, the proposed convolutional block is built as follows,

$$\begin{aligned} y &= W \otimes x + b \\ s &= BN(y) \\ h &= ELU(s) \end{aligned} \tag{2}$$

Here, $\otimes$ is the convolution operator. Because it is a time series classification task, we excluded the pooling layers in the basic convolution block to prevent overfitting and speed it up. We also applied the BN layer to make the model more general and faster. After the construction of the convolution blocks, we can use them to build each residual block, which is:

$$\begin{aligned} h_1 &= RB_{64}(x) \\ h_2 &= RB_{128}(h_1) \\ h_3 &= RB_{192}(h_2) \\ y &= h_3 + x \\ h &= ELU(y) \end{aligned} \tag{3}$$

We defined RB_i as the convolutional block with the number of filters i, and we set the $i = \{64, 128, 192\}$. To build the final ResNet-based architecture, we stacked the three residual blocks together, and followed by a global pooling layer. Compared with deeper ResNet, such as ResNet-34 and ResNet-50, the relatively simple structure of

RFD-Net proves that our experiment is a real-time application, as well, it achieves high performance in detecting human falls. To meet the demand of classification, we set a SoftMax layer as the last layer.

3.3   Fall Detection Mechanism

Based on the posture obtained from the network model, our proposed fall detection mechanism can be applied to distinguish whether the human victim is in the dangerous situation that needs emergency medical help. The proposed mechanism uses the height of human body centroid with the ground level to exclude the misjudgment that the human may be lying on the sofa or bed. By considering duration as a factor, our mechanism makes the method more robust. The proposed mechanism can be concluded as Algorithm 1.

Algorithm 1. Mechanism of Fall Detection

Input: The posture, P; The threshold, T; The height of centroid, C; The Height of ground, G; Features, F;
Output: The fall detection signal, F.

```
1: F = FeatureExtraction();
2: P = PostureRecognition(F);
3: G = F(0);
```
Distinguish the effective posture of "lying".
```
4: T = 3, count = 0;
5: if (P = "Lying") then
6:   if (C-G<=30cm) then
7:     count = count + 1;
8:   end if
9: end if
```
If the user is lying on the ground for more than 3 seconds (count >= 30FPS*3s = 90), we define that as "Fall down".
```
10: if count >= 90
11:    F = 1;
12: end if
13: return F;
```

3.4   Developed Network to Compare with RFD-Net

a. RNN4FD

RNN-based networks are popular in dealing with the time series classification because of the ability to fully exploit the dependencies between the series of data and the memory of the previous instance. Because the posture recognition is a time series classification task, we proposed RNN4FD to evaluate the performance of this kind of networks.

LSTM is a special kind of RNN, which can study the long-term pertinent information and has the ability to forget the irrelevant information. The special design of LSTM cell solves the varnishing gradient problem to some extent, which is always be found in the original RNN model. As a result, LSTM is more suitable for time series classification than original RNN. Graves et al. [12] used the follows to calculate the LSTM cell:

$$
\begin{aligned}
g^u &= \sigma(W^u h_{t-1} + I^u x_t) \\
g^f &= \sigma(W^f h_{t-1} + I^f x_t) \\
g^o &= \sigma(W^o h_{t-1} + I^o x_t) \\
g^c &= \sigma(W^c h_{t-1} + I^c x_t) \\
m_t &= g^f \odot m_{t-1} + g^u \odot g^c \\
h_t &= \tanh(g^o \odot m_t)
\end{aligned}
\tag{4}
$$

To full apply LSTM to the fall detection method, which needs high speed and stable performance, we did not make it deeper but put a Gaussian Dropout (GD) into the networks. GD is a combination of dropout and Gaussian noise. The GD layer multiplies Gaussian noise data centered on the value of one with the standard deviation of $\sqrt[2]{p(1=p)}$ into the input data, in which the p represents the rate in the common dropout. Adding Gaussian noise is a natural process for real input values. It only works while the network is training. Besides, the ELU does not set the data to zero as the ReLU would have done, so the GD combined with ELU produces better results than dropout combined with ReLU in our method, which is a kind of interaction. Finally, we build our LSTM-based architecture, which is shown in Fig. 5(a).

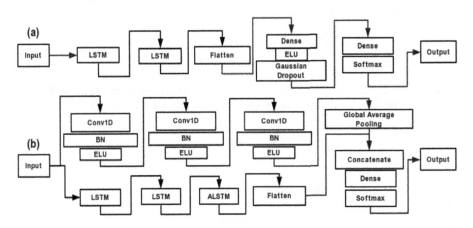

Fig. 5. Network architectures for compare methods (a: RNN4FD, b: ARNN-FCN)

b. ARNN-FCN

Intuitively, if the information in the data is fully utilized, the effect of the model will generally be improved. To exploit the spatial construction information of our data, we applied FCN to the RNN-based network.

Inspired by Zhao et al. [14], we applied the Attention model [13] to RNN, which was named as ARNN. The proposed method combines FCN and the temporal convolution to performance on the time series classification. To meet the requirement of real-time fall detection, we adjusted the architecture for the common networks and attained better performance as a result.

The FCN part consists of three temporal convolutional blocks, as shown in Fig. 5 (b). And each of them comprises a temporal convolutional layer and the combination of BN and ELU. The output dimensions of each convolutional layer are 32, 64, and 32, respectively. The kernel size is 2. At last, we applied a global average pooling layer after the final temporal convolutional block.

The ARNN part mainly reuses the architecture we built in the RNN4FD Network. To make the detection more accurate, we import the attention model into the traditional LSTM network. The attention model is usually applied for text tasks. In these kinds of tasks, the attention model will focus on the surrounding words of the target word to save computing resources, increase processing speed, and improve accuracy. The key idea of attention model comes from humans. When we perceive the scene in front of us, we will not pay attention to everything, but only look at what we want to see. Attention model will also only focus on several important things, which makes it efficient. In the application of LSTM, the attention model preserves the intermediate output of the input sequence using the LSTM encoder and then trains a model selectively learn these inputs before it associates the output sequence with them to get the results. In LSTM encoder, the frame features $(v_1, v_2 \ldots, v_t)$ are encoded into $(h_1, h_2 \ldots, h_t)$, then we use alignment model to get important scores of each h_i:

$$a(s_{i-1}, h_i) = v_a^T \tanh(W_a s_{i-1} + U_a h_i)$$
$$e_i = a(s_{i-1}, h_i) \tag{5}$$

where: $W_a \in \mathbb{R}^{n \times n}$, $U_a \in \mathbb{R}^{n \times 2n}$, $v_a \in \mathbb{R}^n$ are the weight matrices and s_{i-1} are the state of LSTM. The important scores are then normalized to get the context vector c_t:

$$c_t = \sum_{i=1}^{t} a_i h_i \tag{6}$$

The weight a_{ij} of h_j is represented as below:

$$a_i = \frac{\exp(e_i)}{\sum_{k=1}^{t} \exp(e_k)} \tag{7}$$

Then concatenate context vector c_t with FCN final output to combine the feature information extracted by the two sub-models.

4   Experiments and Results

To simulate common home hardware conditions, all experiments are deployed on an Intel i5-6200U processor, 8G RAM and GPU GTX 920M(2G). We also build a stable and generalizable dataset. The user's experience is the most key points we should consider, which divided the user's needs into the following points:

- The method can be used in most home environments, and maintain a robust performance regardless of any variations in location.
- The method can detect almost every fall event that threatens the health of users, and has a low probability of false alarm.
- The method can be real-time, and maintain stable operation for a long time.

Based on analysis, we set up three simulation scenarios according to the common usage environment. We invited users aged from 20–49 as our human test subject. To reduce the influence of individual differences in the experimental results, these test subjects had variant body structures and types. For all the simulations, 49 tests were done in the living room, 51 in the bathroom, and 101 in the bedroom. The detailed process of our simulation environment is in Table 1 as follows.

Table 1. Detailed process of our simulation environment.

Environment	Room's area	Sensor's location	Testers' behavior	Instruction
Living room	36 m²	SL_1	TB1	Most of the daily activities of users take place
Bathroom	5 m²	SL_2	TB1	Elderly people are very easy to slip in the bathroom and get badly hurt
Bedroom	15 m²	SL_3	TB2	Chaos layout in the bedroom makes detection challenging, and people sleeping on the bed is easy to be mistaken for a fall

Here, SL_1 = 45 cm above the ground, on the TV stand across the sofa. SL_2 = 1.3 m above the ground, on the shelf close to the wall; SL_3 = 50 cm above the ground, on the TV stand across the bed; TB1 = Standing, walking, sitting, squatting and falling down; TB2 = Simulate fall event in different directions and lie in bed randomly to simulate sleep.

4.1   Feature Extraction

To prove the validity of the features, we applied T-distributed Stochastic Neighbor Embedding (t-SNE) [15] with a squared Euclidean kernel to reduce the dimensionality of item embedding vectors to two. The Joint Probability Distribution q_{ij} is given by

$$q_{ij} = \frac{\left(1 + \|y_i - y_j\|^2\right)^{-1}}{\sum_{k \neq l}\left(1 + \|y_k - y_l\|^2\right)^{-1}} \tag{8}$$

Here, we use the Kullback–Leibler divergence to estimate the similarity between different distributions. Mathematically, the gradient d is given as follows.

$$d = 4\sum\left(p_{ij} - q_{ij}\right)\left(y_i - y_j\right)\left(1 + \|y_i - y_j\|^2\right)^{-1} \tag{9}$$

We colored each frame feature point according to the body posture (lying down or not lying down) in this frame. Figure 6 presents the 2D embedding produced by t-SNE. The clustering boundaries are clear, which means that the features we extracted are good representations of the body posture. Table 2 presents the data sample of the feature.

Table 2. Data sample of the features (1: left hip angle, 2: right hip angle, 3: left knee angle, 4: right knee angle, 5: left feet height, 6: right feet height, 7: body centroid height, T: Lying, F: Not Lying) (m)

1	2	3	4	5	6	7	Label
75.3235	127.9524	139.8139	97.7934	0.0327	0.1087	0.3629	T
75.0253	127.8068	145.4735	97.3098	0.0311	0.1043	0.3562	T
75.9478	127.1783	145.7521	97.5275	0.0395	0.0989	0.3722	T
123.2492	131.3814	117.0836	125.3936	0.1164	0.1362	1.3073	F
123.0412	130.9366	117.6974	125.4878	0.1215	0.1214	1.3131	F
121.3228	131.8005	118.0703	124.5992	0.1105	0.1373	1.3382	F

Fig. 6. t-SNE embedding for frame features, orange dots represent fall and blue dots represent not fall (Color figure online)

4.2   Compare with RFD-Net

To compare the performance of RFD-Net with the other two networks, we first carried out an experiment to establish the accuracy of posture recognition. In this experiment, we made some structural adjustments to the other two networks in order to increase the number of comparison models. Because the FPS of the sensor is 30 Hz, we set it as the standard for the real-time. Experimental results are shown in Table 3.

Table 3. Results of the accuracy of posture recognition. (LI: Living room, BA: Bathroom, BE: Bedroom, M: Method, R: reach the real-time demand ($\geq$ 30 Hz)) (%)

Method	LI lying	BA lying	BE lying	R
M1(RNN4FD)	93.88	88.12	84.31	Yes
M2(M1 + 1-Dense)	95.92	93.09	84.31	Yes
M3(M2 + 2-Dense)	93.88	91.09	92.16	Yes
M4(ARNN-FCN)	97.96	95.05	98.04	No
M5(M4 + 1-Dense)	97.96	96.03	96.07	No
M6(M4 + 2-Dense)	95.92	99.01	98.04	No
RFD-Net	97.96	96.03	96.07	Yes

From Table 3, we can find that the ARNN-FCN based networks (M4, M5, M6) and RFD-Net attain better accuracy than the RNN4FD (M1, M2, M3). The accuracy of the RFD-Net in the three environments is 97.96%, 96.03%, and 96.07%, respectively. The accuracy of ARNN-FCN is 97.96%, 95.05, and 98.04%. However, all the three ARNN-FCN-based networks do not attain the real-time requirement. In addition, we can see that as the number of hidden layers increases, the accuracy generally increases. Nevertheless, we cannot add too many layers because speed is very essential in order to achieve the real-time requirement.

We also test the accuracy of fall event detection. Identical to the posture recognition experiment, we also tested this accuracy in the three different environments as mentioned above. Table 4 shows results of the accuracy of fall detection.

Table 4. Results of the accuracy of fall detection. (LI: Living room, BA: Bathroom, BE: Bedroom, M: Method) (%)

Method	LI fall	BA fall	BE fall
M1(RNN4FD)	93.07	93.88	94.12
M2(M1 + 1-Dense)	94.06	95.92	94.12
M3(M2 + 2-Dense)	95.05	93.88	92.16
M4(ARNN-FCN)	98.02	97.95	98.04
M5(M4 + 1-Dense)	97.03	97.95	98.04
M6(M4 + 2-Dense)	98.02	100	96.08
RFD-Net	98.02	100	**98.04**

In Table 4, the RFD-Net model achieves the highest accuracy of 98.02%, 100%, and 98.04%, respectively. The ARNN-FCN-based models show lower accuracy than the RFD-Net model in the real-time fall detection experiments, which may because the cooperation between the net structure of ARNN-FCN based model and our fall detection mechanism is not as well as that with the RFD-Net. Based on the results of the two experiments, we finally choose the RFD-Net as the networks of our posture recognition model.

To evaluate the performance of our method its accuracy rates are compared with similar methods of fall detection. The comparison is presented in Table 5. The table shows that, for detecting falls of humans, our method has 98.51% accuracy, 99.02% precision, 98.06 recall, and 98.54% F1 score. Apparently, our method has the highest average accuracy, precision and F1 score among the other concerned methods.

Table 5. Results comparison among the concerned methods (Ac: accuracy, Pr: precision, Re: recall, F1: F1 score) (%)

Method	Ac	Pr	Re	F1
Solbach et al. [8]	90.55	88.99	93.27	91.08
Marcos et al. [9]	96.52	98.04	95.24	96.62
Abobakr et al. [7]	98.01	97.14	*99.03*	98.08
Our method	*98.51*	*99.02*	98.06	*98.54*

5 Conclusion

This work developed a real-time fall detection method for family use. We used the 3D motion sensor to obtain the depth map of the users and extracted the 3D coordinates of body joints. To make the method sufficient and economical, we extracted seven different features for the posture recognition model. After that, we proposed a novel network architecture as our model, and two other networks for comparison. In order to better test the performance of these network architectures, three different day-to-day environments were simulated in an experiment. The results show that the RFD-Net fits better with our fall detection mechanism than the two other networks, and obtains a superior performance compared with other related methods.

References

1. Quadros, T., Lazzaretti, A.E., Schneider, F.K.: A movement decomposition and machine learning-based fall detection system using wrist wearable device. IEEE Sens. J. **18**(12), 5082–5089 (2018)
2. Kau, L.J., Chen, C.S.: A smart phone-based pocket falls accident detection, positioning, and rescue method. IEEE J. Biomed. Health Inform. **19**(1), 44–56 (2015)
3. Doulamis, A., Doulamis, N.: Adaptive deep learning for a vision-based fall detection. In: The 11th Pervasive Technologies Related to Assistive Environments Conference, Corfu, Greece, 26–29 June 2018, pp. 558–565 (2018)
4. Soni, P.K., Choudhary, A.: Automated fall detection using computer vision. In: Tiwary, U.S. (ed.) IHCI 2018. LNCS, vol. 11278, pp. 220–229. Springer, Cham (2018). https://doi.org/10.1007/978-3-030-04021-5_20

5. Cheffena, M.: Fall detection using smartphone audio features. IEEE J. Biomed. Health Inform. **20**(4), 1073–1080 (2016)
6. Popescu, M., Mahnot, A.: Acoustic fall detection using one-class classifiers. In: 2009 Annual International Conference of the IEEE Engineering in Medicine and Biology Society, Minneapolis/St. Paul, Minnesota, 2–6 September 2009, pp. 3505–3508 (2009)
7. Abobakr, A., Hossny, M., Nahavandi, S.: A skeleton-free fall detection method from depth maps using random decision forest. IEEE Methods J. **12**(3), 2994–3005 (2018)
8. Solbach, M.D., Tsotsos, J.K.: Vision-based fallen person detection for the elderly. In: IEEE International Conference on Computer Vision Workshops, Venice, Italy, 22–29 October 2017, pp. 1433–1442 (2017)
9. Núñez-Marcos, A., Azkune, G., Arganda-Carreras, I.: Vision-based fall detection with convolutional neural networks. Wirel. Commun. Mob. Comput. **2017**, 1–16 (2017)
10. Lu, N., Wu, Y., Feng, L., Song, J.: Deep learning for fall detection: three-dimensional CNN combined with LSTM on video Kinematic data. IEEE J. Biomed. Health Inform. **23**(1), 314–323 (2019)
11. He, K.M., Zhang, X.Y., Re, S.Q., Sun, J.: Deep residual learning for image recognition. In: IEEE Conference on Computer Vision and Pattern Recognition, Las Vegas, NV, USA, 27–30 June 2016, pp. 770–778 (2016)
12. Graves, A.: Supervised Sequence Labelling with Recurrent Neural Networks. Studies in Computational Intelligence, vol. 385, pp. 345–352. Springer, Heidelberg (2012). https://doi.org/10.1007/978-3-642-24797-2
13. Bahdanau, D., Cho, K., Bengio, Y.: Neural machine translation by jointly learning to align and translate. In: International Conference of Learning Representations, San Diego, USA, 7–9 May 2015, pp. 1–15 (2015)
14. Zhao, B., Lu, H., Chen, S., Liu, J., Wu, D.: Convolutional neural networks for time series classification. J. Methods Eng. Electron. **28**(1), 162–169 (2017)
15. Maaten, L.J., Hinton, G.E.: Visualizing high-dimensional data using t-SNE. J. Mach. Learn. Res. **9**, 2579–2605 (2008)

Parametric Display Surface Geometric Calibration Method Based on Parameter Estimation

Xiang Li[1(✉)], Shanshan Chen[2], Xiaoying Sun[1], Feng Chen[2], and Dongdong Weng[2,3]

[1] College of Communication Engineering, Jilin University, 5372 Nanhu Street, Changchun, Jilin, China
lx_is_flying@qq.com, sunxy@jlu.edu.cn
[2] School of Optics and Photonics,
Beijing Engineering Research Center for Mixed
Reality and Novel Display Technology, Beijing Institute of Technology,
No. 5 Zhongguancun South Street, Beijing, China
shanchen0923@gmail.com, {chenfeng, crgj}@bit.edu.cn
[3] AICFVE of Beijing Film Academy, 4, Xitucheng Rd, Haidian, Beijing, China

Abstract. With the rapid development of computer vision, image processing and projection display technology, multi-projector display has been widely applied in information visualization, industrial design, military simulation, exhibition and so on. But current curved-surface calibration methods still have unsolved issues in practical applications. Here, we proposed a geometric calibration method based on parameter estimation. Camera parameters and surface parameters estimated from the curved surface constraints were used to realize the geometry calibration. Our results demonstrated the validation of this method in calibration accuracy and simplification of calibration process.

Keywords: Multi-projector calibration system · Geometric calibration · Parametric display surface · Parameter estimation

1 Introduction

The rapid development of computing power and storage induces larger scale of scientific computing, while the development of computer display system is relatively lagging. Thus, an urgent problem that needs to be solved is how to display massive amounts of data quickly and accurately. Nowadays, the new multi-projector calibration system can provide a feasible technical way to solve the above problems. Among them, as the curved surface projection has the characteristics of high resolution, high immersion, and low cost, it has been widely used in scientific research, virtual simulation, exhibition and display, creative industry, and other fields [1].

Raskar [2], Baar [3], Wang [4, 5], Sajadi [6–8], Sun [9], Harville [10] and others have done a lot of research on surface projection splicing. In 2004, Raskar proposed a method of projection stitching, which used quadric equations for surface projection stitching [2]. The specification of this method was in taking the quadric formula as the

© Springer Nature Singapore Pte Ltd. 2019
Y. Wang et al. (Eds.): IGTA 2019, CCIS 1043, pp. 674–685, 2019.
https://doi.org/10.1007/978-981-13-9917-6_63

unknown quantity and through the corresponding relationship between the projector image space Ω_P^i and the camera image space Ω_C to estimate the equation of the surface. However, as too many parameters needed to be estimated in this method, the projection stitching error was larger, for example, in some cases, the error was even larger than 5 pixels. In 2006, Wang Xiuhui et al. used a single camera to project the splicing of the cylindrical projection surface [4, 5]. They proposed a method to determine the effective projection region of the arc projection curtain, but the projection splicing method was related to the observer perspective. In 2009, Sajadi et al. of the University of California, Irvine, proposed a nonlinear optimization algorithm for surface projection stitching [6], in which the internal and external parameters of the projector and the parameters of the projection surface were unknown. Geometric calibration was carried out by using a single uncalibrated camera and the constraints of the surface boundary to estimate the unknown parameters. In 2011, Sajadi et al. extended the method to the hemispherical projection screen [7] and the CAVE-like projection screen [8]. However, the author assumed that the camera was the ideal and only the focal length f was unknown. In addition, the influence of factors such as camera lens distortion on the projection stitching result was not considered. Therefore, large errors occurred in the method, limiting the wide application of the method.

In order to solve the problems such as complex system structure, large splicing error, weak stability, and practicability, we first proposed a free-form surface projection splicing method based on parameter estimation. In this method, by using the surface which was formed by a straight line perpendicular to the ground moving along an arbitrary curve as its constraint condition, the parameters in the projector and the rotation translation matrix were estimated and the surface parameters were restored, then the surface projection splicing was carried out. We then tested our method by using the evaluation method of projection splicing geometric calibration error to verify the feasibility and accuracy of the proposed method.

2 Analysis of Parametric Surface Projection System

2.1 Spatial Definition

The main purpose of multi-projector geometric calibration is to combine images projected by multiple projectors into a unified large picture. In order to achieve the purpose above, we establish the corresponding relationship between the projection image space and the midpoint in the display image space by using the camera-based multi-projector splicing system.

The camera image space is defined as Ω_C, the projection surface space is Ω_P, and the image space of each projector is Ω_P^i (i as the projector number), and the display image space is Ω_D. The 2D coordinates of the Ω_C, Ω_P^i, Ω_D are marked as (x_c, y_c), (x_{pi}, y_{pi}), (x_d, y_d) in turn. Mark the correspondence Ω_C and the point Ω_P^i as $C(x_c, y_c) \rightarrow P_i(x_{pi}, y_{pi})$, abbreviated to M_{Ci}. Mark $P_i(x_{pi}, y_{pi}) \rightarrow C(x_c, y_c)$ as M_{Ci}^{-1}; mark the correspondence between Ω_D and Ω_C as $(x_d, y_d) \rightarrow C(x_c, y_c)$, abbreviated as M_D; $C(x_c, y_c) \rightarrow D(x_d, y_d)$ abbreviated as M_D^{-1}. M does not represent a homograph matrix, M^{-1} does not represent an inverse matrix of M, but only represents the correspondence between points. The relationship of Ω_C, Ω_P^i, Ω_D is shown in Fig. 1:

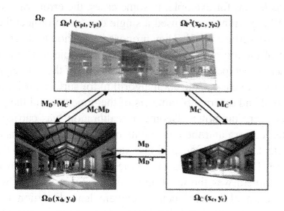

Fig. 1. Relationship between image space, projection space, and camera space.

2.2   Basic Method of Parametric Display Surface

There are two different ways to realize parametric surface projection splicing. The first is the fixed viewing angle surface projection splicing effect (as shown in Fig. 2); the other is the non-fixed viewing angle surface projection splicing method, or the wallpaper surface projection splicing method (as shown in Fig. 3).

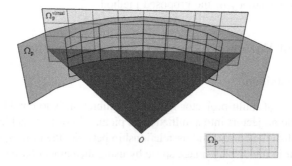

Fig. 2. Schematic diagram of fixed perspective surface projection.

As shown in Fig. 2, the surface projection splicing effect with a fixed angle of view is equivalent to a virtual projection plane $\Omega_P^{Virtual}$ after the projection surface space Ω_P, showing that the image in image space Ω_D is projected onto the virtual plane $\Omega_P^{Virtual}$ in full accordance with the Euclidean transform. That is, from the O point, all the lines in Ω_D are still straight lines after passing through geometric calibration.

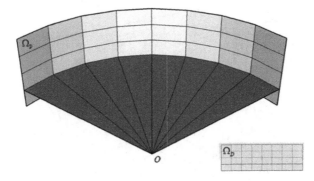

Fig. 3. Schematic diagram of non-fixed viewing angle surface projection.

For surface projection splicing and plane projection splicing, their purpose is to find the corresponding relationship between the display image space and the projector image space is $D(x_d, y_d) \rightarrow P_i\left(x'_{pi}, y'_{pi}\right)$, which can be obtained through the corresponding relationship M_{Ci} between the camera image space and the projector image space. $C(x_c, y_c) \rightarrow P_i(x_{pi}, y_{pi})$ and the correspondence between the display image space and the camera image space $M_D: D(x_d, y_d) \rightarrow C(x_c, y_c)$ are obtained. Because the Bezier surface can fit the continuous surface well, in general, the Bezier surface fitting method is used to calculate the projection splicing M_{Ci} of the surface. Generally, the M_D of the planar projection splicing and the fixed viewing angle surface projection splicing is linear, so it can be directly represented by the homograph matrix H_D. In order to solve the problem that the M_D of unfixed angle surface projection splicing is nonlinear, the following surface projection splicing method is proposed in this paper.

3 Geometric Calibration Method Based on Parameter Estimation

We use free surface projection splicing method based on parameter estimation to estimate the external parameters and surface parameters of the camera by using the curved surface formed by a straight line moving along a straight line perpendicular to the ground as a constraint. Figure 4 shows the variables used in the method and their relationships.

Based on the method proposed in [13], the parameter estimation surface projection splicing method uses a calibration camera to reduce camera lens distortion and estimate the camera focal length error and simplify the parameter estimation method. As shown in Fig. 4, in this method, the coordinates of the image space are displayed as three-dimensional coordinates, and the two-dimensional coordinates projected to the Z = 0 plane by Ω_D are (x, y). The 3D coordinates corresponding to the point is marked (X (x, y), Y (x, y), Z (x, y). The 2D coordinates of the camera image space Ω_C and the projection surface space Ω_P midpoint is sequentially labeled as (x_c, y_c), (x_p, y_p), and the sitting mark of the image map is expected to be (x_d, y_d). Where (x_c, y_c) is in pixels,

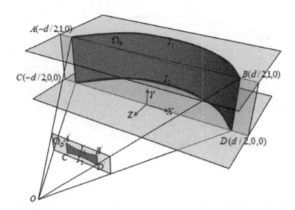

Fig. 4. Curve parameter estimation projection stitching method parameter relationship diagram

and (x_d, y_d) uses normalized coordinates. The above parameters meet the following constraints:

(1) Because the projection surface is a curved surface formed by a straight line moving perpendicular to the ground along an arbitrary curve, the upper and lower endpoints A and C of the starting segment and the two endpoints B and D of the terminating segment must be coplanar and set to Z = 0 plane. On this plane, the aspect ratio of the projected region is d. The coordinates of A, B, C and D are $A(-d/2, 1, 0)$, $B(d/2, 1, 0)$, $C(-d/2, 0, 0)$, $D(d/2, 0, 0)$;

(2) The curves at the top and bottom are located on the planes of Y = 1 and Y = 0, respectively, so Y(x, 0) = 0 and Y(x, 1) = 1;

(3) Since the bottom and top curves are the same, there are X(x, 0) = X(x, 1), Z(x, 0) = Z(x, 1);

(4) X, Z are only related to x, Y is only related to y, that is to say $X = X(x, y) = X(x) = x$, $Z = Z(x, y) = F_z(x)$, $Y = Y(x, y) = Y(y) = y$.

The splicing method of parameter estimation surface projection is to calibrate the camera, and then restore the surface parameters according to the above constraints. The specific methods are as follows:

(1) **Calibration of the camera and correction of distortion:**

By locating the camera positioned at point O, the internal reference K_c and the lens distortion parameter $[k_1, k_2, k_3, p_1, p_2]$ are obtained, and then the camera image is corrected for distortion [12].

(2) **Calculation of effective projection area:**

As shown in Fig. 5, according to the process shown, the effective projection region Ω_{P_in} can be obtained, and the curve fitting algorithm can be used to fit the edge of Ω_{P_in}. As shown in Fig. 6, the fitted upper and lower edge curves are denoted as l_1' and l_2', respectively. The coordinates of the four corners in the camera image space Ω_C are calculated and recorded as A', B', C', D', respectively.

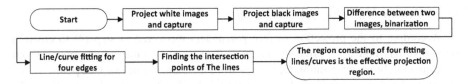

Fig. 5. Flow chart of the method for determining the effective projection area with a border.

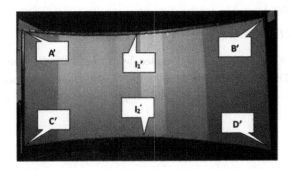

Fig. 6. Fit results of effective projection area and edge curve.

(3) **Calculate the external parameters of the camera:**

According to the pinhole camera model, can get

$$Z_c \begin{bmatrix} x_c \\ y_c \\ 1 \end{bmatrix} = K_p [R_p|T_p] \begin{bmatrix} X(x,y) \\ Y(x,y) \\ Z(x,y) \\ 1 \end{bmatrix} \tag{1}$$

Among them, K_c is a known quantity, and the projected aspect ratio d can be measured. The camera external parameters R_c and T_c can be obtained by taking the three-dimensional coordinates of the four corner points in Ω_P and the four corner coordinates in the corresponding Ω_C into Eq. (1).

(4) **Restore the parameters of the display surface:**

According to the process of step (3), after calculating R_c and T_c, the coordinates of the points on the plane Y = 0 and Y = 1 in Ω_D can be obtained by taking the points in I'_1 and I'_2 in Ω_C respectively. Then, according to the constraint condition (2), the curves I_1 and I_2 on the Y = 0 and Y = 1 plane should be the same. However, due to the existence of the calculation error, I_1 and I_2 are not completely identical. For this purpose, the average values of the corresponding points X (x, y) and Z (x, y) coordinates on I_1 and I_2 are taken as their common coordinate values. Curves I_1 and I_2 are then obtained by fitting these points using a polynomial curve fitting method. According to the constraint condition (4), we can know $X = x$, $Y = y$, $Z = F_Z(x)$, where Z can be obtained from the fitted curve.

(5) **Calculate M_D^{-1}: $C(x_c, y_c) \rightarrow D(x_d, y_d)$:**

According to the projection surface parameters recovered in step (4) to create a surface virtual model, the projected image is then taken as a map of the model. From the camera light center position O, the ray from the camera image space point (x_c, y_c) intersects the above surface model at a point (X, Y, Z). Then, according to (X, Y, Z), image map coordinates (x_d, y_d) are obtained, and the above operations are sequentially performed on all points of the display image space, and then M_D^{-1}: $C(x_c, y_c) \rightarrow D(x_d, y_d)$ is obtained.

(6) **Calculate M_{Ci}^{-1}: $P_i(x_{pi}, y_{pi}) \rightarrow C(x_c, y_c)$:**

M_{Ci}^{-1}: $P_i(x_{pi}, y_{pi}) \rightarrow C(x_c, y_c)$ is obtained by fitting the projection stitching using Bezier surface. Then, according to M_D^{-1} and M_{Ci}^{-1}, the relationship between the coordinate (x_d, y_d) of any point in Ω_D and the image coordinates of any projector can be obtained:

$$(x_d, y_d) = M_D^{-1}\left(M_{Ci}^{-1}\left(x_{pi}, y_{pi}\right)\right) \tag{2}$$

4 Experiment of Parameter Estimation Method

4.1 Experimental Environment

The experimental platform is shown in Fig. 7. The experimental platform includes: Sanyo 1050 LCD projector × 3 (nominal brightness 4500 lm, resolution 1024 × 768), Canon 5000D camera (image resolution 2352 × 1568 pixels); computer, Canon 5000D camera. Multi-screen distributor.

Fig. 7. Surface projection stitching experimental platform.

In the experiment, the projection screen is a 5.0 m chord length and 2.2 m high arc projection screen (shown in Fig. 8(a)), and a curved surface formed by a straight line perpendicular to the ground moving along an arbitrary curve (as shown in Fig. 8(b)).

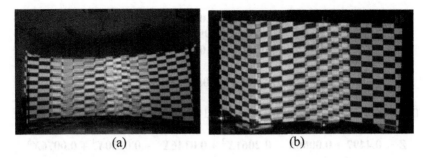

Fig. 8. Projection surface used in the experiment (a) Cylindrical projection surface (b) A curved projection surface formed by a straight line moving perpendicular to the ground along an arbitrary curve.

4.2 Experiment

The experimental steps are as follows: Calibrate the camera and perform distortion correction; obtain an effective projection area; calculate camera aspect and projection surface aspect ratio d; Restore projection surface parameters; Find the correspondence between the camera image space and the display image space M_D^{-1}: $C(x_c, y_c) \rightarrow D(x_d, y_d)$; The corresponding relationship M_{Ci}^{-1}: $P_i(x_{pi}, y_{pi}) \rightarrow C(x_c, y_c)$ between projector image space and camera image space is obtained by using Bezier surface fitting. The results of the experiment were subsequently analyzed using the method of [14].

In experiment 1, the surface parameter estimation projection splicing method is carried out according to the cylindrical projection surface shown in Fig. 8(a). In experiment 2, the surface parameter estimation projection splicing method is carried out according to the surface formed by a straight line perpendicular to the ground moving along an arbitrary curve shown in Fig. 8(b).

For the cylindrical projection surface in Experiment 1, the position of the LED of the projection edge used is taken as the expected projection position, and the internal expected projection position is obtained by bilinear difference between the edge points, thereby calculating RE_{mn}^i. In Experiment 2, the projection surface was unable to obtain the edge marker points and the position of the key points, so the expected projection position could not be obtained, so RE_{mn}^i was not calculated in this experiment.

In Experiment 1, the calibrated camera internal parameters and distortion parameters are:

$$K_c = \begin{bmatrix} 2398.468 & 0 & 1208.382 \\ 0 & 2394.730 & 772.251 \\ 0 & 0 & 1 \end{bmatrix}$$

$$[k_{c1}, k_{c2}, k_{c3}, p_{c1}, p_{c2}] = [-0.081743 \quad 0.133827 \quad 0.000197 \quad 0.000103 \quad -0.0253682]$$

The ratio of width to height of Z = 0 plane measured is $d = 2.732$, by which the external parameters R and T of the camera are calculated as follows:

$$R_c = \begin{bmatrix} 0.988 & -0.031 & -0.150 \\ 0.044 & 0.995 & 0.084 \\ 0.147 & -0.089 & 0.985 \end{bmatrix}$$

$$T_c = \begin{bmatrix} 0.573 & 0.068 & 2.423 \end{bmatrix}^T$$

The fitted curve $I_1 = I_2$ of the Y = 1 and Y = 0 planes is:

$$Z = 0.4497 + 0.0066X - 0.2061X^2 + 0.0146X^3 - 0.0230X^4 + 0.0076X^5$$

The virtual camera perspective projection matrix is set according to the internal parameters of the actual camera, as shown in Fig. 9, the projection surface model reconstructed at the camera angle of view.

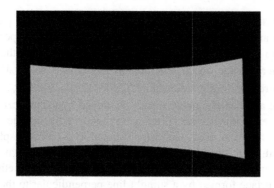

Fig. 9. Projection surface model reconstructed from the camera's perspective.

As shown in Fig. 10, the figure is the result of projection splicing in experiment 1, the magnification of superposition area, the distribution map of reprojection error $\left(RE_{mn}^1\right)$ of projector 1, and the distribution map of reprojection error $\left(RE_{mn}^2\right)$ of projector 2. The reprojection error $\left(RE_{mn}^3\right)$ distribution of projector 3, the result of text display, and the result of picture rendering.

In Experiment 1, the average reprojection errors of the three projectors are $ARE^1 = 1.01$, $ARE^2 = 1.54$, $ARE^3 = 0.74$, and the average superimposed area error AOE = 1.03.

Figure 11 shows the results of mesh stitching, overlay area magnification, text display and image rendering in experiment 2. In experiment 2, the average superposition area error is 0.96. From the experimental results, this method can achieve the pixel-level projection splicing effect, and can meet the needs of surface projection splicing.

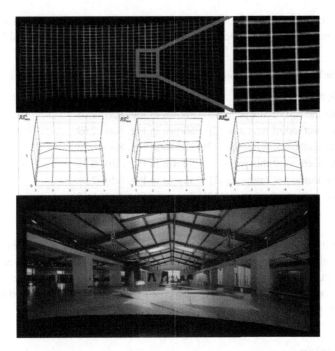

Fig. 10. Results of surface projection splicing experiment 1 (sequential grid mosaic: superimposed area enlargement, RE_{mn}^1 distribution map, RE_{mn}^2 distribution map, RE_{mn}^3 distribution map and image rendering result).

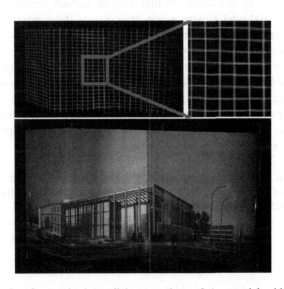

Fig. 11. Results of surface projection splicing experiment 2 (sequential grid mosaic: superimposed area enlargement and image rendering result).

In order to make a comparison, the method proposed in reference [13] is used to carry out experiments. The conclusion of the experiment is shown in Table 1:

Table 1. Experimental conclusion of surface projection on parametric surface

Method	Projection surface	AOE (average error)
The method of this paper	Shown in Fig. 8(a)	1.03
The method of reference [2]	Shown in Fig. 8(a)	2.69
The method of reference [13]	Shown in Fig. 8(a)	1.72
The method of this paper	Shown in Fig. 8(b)	0.96
The method of reference [2]	Shown in Fig. 8(b)	2.98
The method of reference [13]	Shown in Fig. 8(b)	1.69

Our results show that the parametric surface projection splicing method based on parameter estimation proposed in this paper can achieve the pixel-level projection splicing effect. Compared with the quadric equation method [2] and the uncalibrated camera method [13], the error of the superposition region is obviously reduced, which can meet the needs of parametric surface projection splicing.

5   Conclusion

Projection splicing display technology has been widely used in exhibition display, product release, virtual simulation, and so on. In order to solve the problems existing in surface projection splicing, we proposed a projection splicing method based on parameter estimation. In this study, we first used the surface formed by a straight line perpendicular to the ground moving along any curve as the constraint condition, then estimated the parameters of the projector and the rotation translation matrix and recovered the surface parameters, to carry out the projection splicing of the surface. The parametric surface projection splicing method had the characteristics of fast, stable, and accurate, thus could quickly complete the automatic surface projection splicing in the case of unattended. Moreover, we carried out experimental verification, error analysis, and data comparison of the proposed method. Our results showed that the parametric surface projection splicing method achieved the pixel-level projection splicing effect and met the needs of surface projection splicing.

Acknowledgments. This work was supported by the National Key Research and Development Program of China (No. 2016YFB1001401) and the National Natural Science Foundation of China (No. U1605254) and the 111 Project (B18005).

References

1. Disz, T., Papka, M.E., Stevens, R.: UbiWorld: an environment integrating virtual reality, supercomputing, and design. In: 1997 Proceedings Sixth Heterogeneous Computing Workshop (HCW 1997), pp. 46–57. IEEE (1997)
2. Raskar, R., Baar, J., Willwacher, T., et al.: Quadric transfer for immersive curved screen displays. Comput. Graph. Forum **23**(3), 451–460 (2004)
3. Baar, J., Willwacher, T., Rao, S., et al.: Seamless multi-projector display on curved screens. In: 2003 Proceedings of the Workshop on Virtual Environments, pp. 281–286. ACM (2003)
4. Wang, X.: Research on picture correction and 3D interaction technology for multi-projection display wall. Zhejiang University (2007)
5. Wang, X.: Picture correction technology for multi-projection display wall. J. Softw. **18**(11), 2955–2964 (2007)
6. Sajadi, B., Majumder, A.: Markerless view-independent registration of multiple distorted projectors on extruded surfaces using an uncalibrated camera. IEEE Trans. Vis. Comput. Graph. **15**(6), 1307–1316 (2009)
7. Sajadi, B., Majumder, A.: Automatic registration of multi-projector domes using a single uncalibrated camera. Comput. Graph. Forum **30**(3), 1161–1170 (2011)
8. Sajadi, B., Majumder, A.: Autocalibration of multi-projector CAVE-like immersive environments. IEEE Trans. Vis. Comput. Graph. **18**(3), 381–393 (2012)
9. Sun, W., Sobel, I., Culbertson, B., et al.: Calibrating multi-projector cylindrically curved displays for wallpaper projection. In: Proceedings of the 5th ACM/IEEE International Workshop on Projector camera systems, p. 1. ACM (2008)
10. Harville, M., Culbertson, B., Sobel, I., et al.: Practical methods for geometric and photometric correction of tiled projector. In: 2006 Conference on Computer Vision and Pattern Recognition Workshop, CVPRW 2006, p. 5. IEEE (2006)
11. Raskar, R., Baar, J.V., Willwacher, T., Rao, S.: Quadric transfer function for immersive curved screen displays. In: Eurographics (2004)
12. Hartley, R., Zisserman, A.: Multiple View Geometry in Computer Vision. Cambridge University Press, Cambridge (2000)
13. Raskar, R., Brown, M.S., Yang, R., et al.: Multi-projector displays using camera-based registration. In: Proceedings of Visualization 1999, pp. 161–522. IEEE (1999)
14. Xiang, L., Xie, J., Liu, Y.: Multi-projector geometric calibration error analysis. J. Comput.-Aided Des. Comput. Graph. 106–113 (2015)

An Optimization Method for Large Format Multi-projector Displays

Xiang Li[1(✉)], Shanshan Chen[2], Dong Li[2], Xiaoying Sun[1],
and Dongdong Weng[2,3]

[1] College of Communication Engineering, Jilin University, 5372 Nanhu Street,
Changchun, Jilin, China
lx_is_flying@qq.com, sunxy@jlu.edu.cn

[2] School of Optics and Photonics, Beijing Engineering Research Center for
Mixed Reality and Novel Display Technology, Beijing Institute of Technology,
No. 5 Zhongguancun South Street, Beijing, China
shanchen0923@gmail.com, {lidong, crgj}@bit.edu.cn

[3] AICFVE of Beijing Film Academy, 4, Xitucheng Rd, Haidian, Beijing, China

Abstract. Large-format arbitrary surface projection technology has been widely used in exhibitions, product launches, and virtual simulations in recent years. To solve the key point matching problem caused by the application of traditional structured light scanning method in large format arbitrary surface technology, we presented an optimization method including objective function derivation and constraint establishment. The objective function was used to minimize the distance between display image space and key points in projector's image space, while the constraint was used to ensure the production of expected shapes for control points and meshes of the Bezier surface. Our results showed significant reduce of registration error of the key points.

Keywords: Multi-projector calibration system · Large-format projection · Arbitrary display surface · Optimization method

1 Introduction

The large-format arbitrary display surface projection has large display size, irregular spatial shape change, and strong visual impact [1, 2], therefore, fits well for outdoor large-scale events, exhibitions, new product releases, and so on. In recent years, the cultural performance market has been rapid development, and there is more and more cross-border integration with tourism, animation, large-scale exhibitions, and so on. In the new media cultural performance, the audience are not satisfied with the superb performance of the live actors, but have higher requirements for environment setting of the stage and enjoyment of audio-visual than before. With the continuous improvement of the audience's requirements, the comprehensive use of large-format arbitrary display surface projection stitching technology has become an urgent need for modern cultural performances. However, most of the research related to projection method of the arbitrary display surface are focused on the smaller projection surface, the large-format

© Springer Nature Singapore Pte Ltd. 2019
Y. Wang et al. (Eds.): IGTA 2019, CCIS 1043, pp. 686–698, 2019.
https://doi.org/10.1007/978-981-13-9917-6_64

arbitrary display surface multi-projector calibration system is mostly manually adjusted.

In the arbitrary display surface, a projection plane cannot be represented by a parameter, a three-dimensional model, or a point correspondence. Raskar [3, 5, 11], Surati [6], Brown [7], Lee [8], Gross [9], and Zollmann [10] have done a lot of research related to the arbitrary display surface projection splicing method.

In 1999, Raskar et al. proposed an arbitrary display surface projection splicing method using multi-camera to reconstruct the three-dimensional model of projection surface and the position of projector [3]. In this method, the position of the observer was calculated by the head tracking device. However, considering that many parameters such as camera, projector, and projection surface parameters needed to be estimated, the projection splicing error was large. Thus, many researchers had focused on method improvement [4]. Raskar [5] and Surati [6] proposed a method for projection switching on any surface based on two-channel rendering technology. In 2001, Raskar et al. proposed a projection splicing method called Shader Lamps [11] in which, a probe-type 3D scanner was used to create a virtual 3D model. However, the feasible prerequisite was that it needed to use probe 3D scanner to build virtual 3D model, which could not be directly applied in large-format arbitrary display surface multi-projector calibration system.

In 2009, Yuan proposed a splicing method for projection on complex surfaces [12]. In his method, the relationship between camera image space and projector image space was established by using coded structured light scanning. However, because of the complexity of arbitrary display surface, it was inevitable that many key points were not be aligned. Therefore, in order to get better results, it is necessary to optimize the projection splicing results of the above methods.

Coolux [13] in Germany and arKaos in Belgium are two representative systems in commercial software domain [14]. Both are based on the manual tuning method to produce large-format arbitrary display surface multi-projector calibration system.

To solve the remaining problem of current large-format arbitrary display surface projection splicing, here we first proposed a large-format free representation of the projection splicing optimization method. This method can quickly optimize the results of automatic or manual splicing, thus effectively reduce the error of arbitrary display surface projection splicing and easily align the key points in arbitrary display surface. Then we demonstrate the feasibility and accuracy of the method through experiments and practical application cases.

2 Large-Format Arbitrary Display Surface Projection Stitching Optimization Method

2.1 Spatial Definition and Basic Method of Large-Format Arbitrary Display Surface

The main purpose of geometric correction is to combine images projected by multiple projectors into a single unified picture. In order to achieve the purpose above, we use camera-based multi-projector splicing system. This method is to establish the corresponding relationship between the projected image space and the points in the display image space by using the camera.

The camera image space is defined as Ω_C, the projection surface space is Ω_P, and the image space of each projector is Ω_P^i (i as the projector number), and the display image space is Ω_D. The 2D coordinates of the Ω_C, Ω_P^i, Ω_D are marked as (x_c, y_c), (x_{pi}, y_{pi}), (x_d, y_d) in turn. Mark the correspondence Ω_C and the point Ω_P^i as $C(x_c, y_c) \rightarrow P_i(x_{pi}, y_{pi})$, abbreviated to M_{Ci}. Mark $P_i(x_{pi}, y_{pi}) \rightarrow C(x_c, y_c)$ as M_{Ci}^{-1}; mark the correspondence between Ω_D and Ω_C as $(x_d, y_d) \rightarrow C(x_c, y_c)$, abbreviated as M_D; $C(x_c, y_c) \rightarrow D(x_d, y_d)$ abbreviated as M_D^{-1}. M does not represent a homograph matrix, M^{-1} does not represent an inverse matrix of M, but only represents the correspondence between points. The relationship of Ω_C, Ω_P^i, Ω_D is shown in Fig. 1:

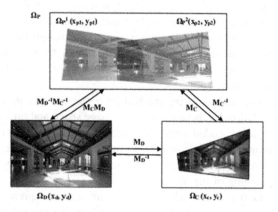

Fig. 1. Relationship between image space, projection space, and camera space.

In the arbitrary display surface projection splicing, the coding structured light scanning method is usually used to establish the corresponding relationship between the camera image space Ω_C and the projector image space Ω_P^i, M_{Ci}: $C(x_c, y_c) \rightarrow P_i(x_{pi}, y_{pi})$. Moreover, an image of the corresponding projector angle of view is obtained according to the correspondence between the display image space Ω_D and the camera image space Ω_C, M_D: $D(x_d, y_d) \rightarrow C(x_c, y_c)$, and is aligned with the projection surface after being projected by the projector [15].

The complex surface shape and the serious influence of ambient light are the characteristics of large-format arbitrary display surface projection. Therefore, when the traditional structured light scanning method is applied to large-format arbitrary display surface projection splicing, there will be many defect points (that is, points with no corresponding relationship), and will affect the effect of projection splicing. Therefore, in order to address the above problems, it is necessary to optimize the results of the projection splicing in the above method. At present, the existing fine adjustment method is to divide the whole display image space into mesh Ω_D, and then manually move the intersection of the mesh to align the key points. However, the drawback of this method is that if the mesh is too sparse, it is difficult to align each key point. If the mesh is too dense, there are many points that need to be adjusted. In order to solve the above problems, the best way is to correct the projection stitching error by using the most optimization method, and then select some of the corresponding points between the display image space Ω_D and the projector image space Ω_P^i. According to these corresponding points and the constraints of the projected surface, the key points of the projected surface are accurately aligned. The specific steps of this method are: manually marking the position of the key point Ω_D, then marking the corresponding key point in Ω_P^i, and automatically fitting the correspondence between Ω_D and Ω_P^i according to the key points corresponding to the input using the Bezier surface. However, the disadvantage of this method is that the adjustment time of this method is long, the requirement of personnel ability is high, and the result of adjustment completely depends on the experience and feeling of the adjustment personnel, so it is difficult to guarantee the quality. Therefore, in this paper, a large-format arbitrary display surface projection splicing optimization method is proposed.

In the projection splicing result optimization method, including the derivation of the objective function and the establishment of constraint conditions. In this method, the objective function is used to minimize the distance between the key points and the constraints used to ensure that the control points and meshes of the Bezier surface are the expected shapes.

2.2 Derivation of Objective Function

The coordinate of point Ω_D is $X_d = (x_d, y_d)$ and the coordinate of control point is $C_d = (c_d, c_d)$. The coordinate of point Ω_P^i after the Bezier surface transformation is $X_p = (x_p, y_p)$. According to Bezier surface Eq. (1), the relationship between X_p and X_d can be obtained as Eq. (2):

$$(x', y') = \mathrm{NB}(x,y) = \sum_{i=0}^{M} \sum_{j=0}^{N} P_{ij} B_i^M(x) B_j^N(y) \tag{1}$$

$$X_p = \mathrm{NB}(X_d, C_d) = \sum_{i=0}^{M} \sum_{j=0}^{N} P_{ij} B_i^M(x_d) B_j^N(y_d) \tag{2}$$

Among them, the number of control points is $M \times N$.

Let the expected projection position in Ω_P^i corresponding to point X_d in Ω_D be $X_{p0} = (x_{p0}, y_{p0})$, and the single group error distance can be obtained as follows:

$$\left\| X_p - X_{p0} \right\|_2^2 \tag{3}$$

The purpose of the arbitrary display surface projection splicing result optimization method is to find the coordinates of the control points and minimize the error distance of the selected m groups of corresponding key pairs, which is mathematically described as follows:

$$min \sum_{i=1}^{m} \left\| X_p^i - X_{p0}^i \right\|_2^2 \tag{4}$$

For ease of calculation, let $\bar{x}$ be the position of all control points:

$$f(\bar{x}) = \frac{1}{2} \sum_{i=1}^{m} \left\| X_p^i - X_{p0}^i \right\|_2^2 \tag{5}$$

Then the question is:

$$\begin{cases} \min f(\bar{x}) \\ \bar{x} = \left[p_x^{11}, p_y^{11}, p_x^{12}, p_y^{12}, \ldots, p_x^{MN}, p_y^{MN} \right] \end{cases} \tag{6}$$

At this point, the objective function $f(\bar{x})$ is obtained.

In order to quickly find the $\bar{x}$ of $f(\bar{x})$ with constrained minimization, it is necessary to solve the gradient of $f(\bar{x})$. Note as:

$$\|F(x)\|_2^2 = \sum_{i=1}^{m} \left\| X_p^i - X_{p0}^i \right\|_2^2 \tag{7}$$

Among them:

$$F(x) = \begin{bmatrix} x_p^1 - x_{p0}^1 \\ y_p^1 - y_{p0}^1 \\ x_p^2 - x_{p0}^2 \\ y_p^2 - y_{p0}^2 \\ \vdots \\ x_p^m - x_{p0}^m \\ y_p^m - y_{p0}^m \end{bmatrix} \tag{8}$$

To get the minimum value of $f(\bar{x})$, calculate the gradient and get:

$$\nabla f(\bar{x}) = \frac{\partial}{\partial \bar{x}} \left(\frac{1}{2} F(x)^T F(x) \right) \tag{9}$$

According to the relevant knowledge of matrix derivation, can get:

$$\nabla f(\bar{x}) = \frac{\partial}{\partial \bar{x}} \left(\frac{1}{2} F(x)^T F(x)\right) = J(x)^T F(x) \tag{10}$$

Among them:

$$J(x) = F'(x) = [\nabla F_1(x), \nabla F_2(x), \ldots, \nabla F_{2m}(x) \tag{11}$$

Deriving the items in $J(x)$, can get:

$$\frac{\partial F_1(x)}{\partial x} = \frac{\partial}{\partial \bar{x}} \left(x_p^1 - x_{p0}^1\right) = \frac{\partial}{\partial \bar{x}} \left(\sum_{s=0}^{M} \sum_{t=0}^{N} P_{st} B_s^M(x_d) B_t^N(y_d) - x_{p0}^1\right) \tag{12}$$

According to formula (8), can get:

$$\frac{\partial F_1(x)}{\partial x} = \left[B_1^M(y_d^1) B_1^N(x_d^1), 0, B_1^M(y_d^1) B_2^N(x_d^1), 0, \ldots, B_M^M(y_d^1) B_N^N(x_d^1), 0\right] \tag{13}$$

For any item $\frac{\partial F_i(x)}{\partial p_{x/y}^{st}}$, there will be:

$$\begin{cases} B_s^M\left(y_d^{\frac{i+1}{2}}\right) B_t^N\left(x_d^{\frac{i+1}{2}}\right) \ldots i = odd, \quad Derivation \ of \ p_y^{st} \ is \ 0 \\ B_s^M\left(y_d^{\frac{i}{2}}\right) B_t^N\left(x_d^{\frac{i}{2}}\right) \ldots \ldots i = even, \quad Derivation \ of \ p_y^{st} \ is \ 0 \end{cases} \tag{14}$$

For $\nabla F_i(x)$, there will be:

$$\nabla F_i(x) = C \cdot P \tag{15}$$

Where x is the column vector of $2MN \times 1$ and:

$$C = diag\left(i\%2, (i+1)\%2, i\%2, (i+1)\%2, \ldots, i\%2, (i+1)\%2\right)^{2MN \times 2MN} \tag{16}$$

$$P = \begin{bmatrix} B_1^M(y_d^k) B_1^N(x_d^k) \\ B_1^M(y_d^k) B_1^N(x_d^k) \\ \ldots \\ \ldots \\ B_s^M(y_d^k) B_t^N(x_d^k) \\ B_s^M(y_d^k) B_t^N(x_d^k) \\ \ldots \\ \ldots \\ B_M^M(y_d^k) B_M^N(x_d^k) \\ B_M^M(y_d^k) B_M^N(x_d^k) \end{bmatrix} \tag{17}$$

Among them, $k = floor\left(\frac{i-1}{2}\right) + 1$, $i = 1, 2, \ldots, 2m$, and $F(x)$ have 2m items.

According to the formula (11) and the formula (15), the gradient $\nabla f(\bar{x})$ of $f(\bar{x})$ can be obtained according to the formula (10).

2.3   Establishment of Constraints

It is necessary to constrain the position of the control point in order to make the position of the control point obtained by minimizing conform to the requirements of projection stitching. The constraint used is that the quadrilateral consisting of control points needs to satisfy that the diagonals cannot intersect. For example, in Fig. 2(a) (b), it is the position of the control point that meets the constraints. In Fig. 2(c) (d), it is the position of the control point that does not meet the constraints.

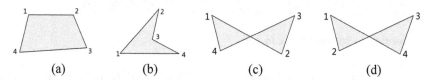

Fig. 2. (a) (b) the position of the control point that meets the constraint; (c) (d) the position of the control point that does not meet the constraint

If the coordinate of the upper left control point is $x_{s,t}$, which represents the point in the s row and t column of all control points, then the coordinates of the other three control points are $x_{s,t+1}, x_{s+1,t+1}, x_{s+1,t}$ in turn. If expressed by the variable $\bar{x}$ in the optimization objective function, then $x_{s,t}$ and x can be expressed as formula (18):

$$x_{s,t} = \begin{bmatrix} x(i(s,t)-1) \\ x(i(s,t)) \end{bmatrix} = \begin{bmatrix} p_x^{s,t} \\ p_y^{s,t} \end{bmatrix} \tag{18}$$

Where $x(w)$ represents the w item in $\bar{x}$ and:

$$i(s,t) = 2 \times ((s-1)N+t) \tag{19}$$

The four sides of the quadrilateral are described by vectors as $\vec{L}_{12}, \vec{L}_{23}, \vec{L}_{34}$ and $\vec{L}_{14}$, respectively. The fact that $\vec{L}_{12}$ and $\vec{L}_{34}$ do not intersect can be expressed as points 3 and 4 on the same side of vector $\vec{L}_{12}$, using Eq. (20) to describe:

$$\left(\vec{L}_{14} \times \vec{L}_{12}\right) \cdot \left(\vec{L}_{13} \times \vec{L}_{12}\right) > 0 \tag{20}$$

According to the same principle, can get

$$\left(\vec{L}_{14} \times \vec{L}_{12}\right) \cdot \left(\vec{L}_{14} \times \vec{L}_{13}\right) > 0 \tag{21}$$

Since there are $\left(\bar{L}_{14} \times \bar{L}_{12}\right)$ in both Eqs. (20) and (21), the constraint on edge disjoint can be simplified as:

$$\left(\bar{L}_{13} \times \bar{L}_{12}\right) \cdot \left(\bar{L}_{14} \times \bar{L}_{13}\right) > 0 \tag{22}$$

Substituting $\bar{L}_{12} = x_{s,t+1} - x_{s,t}$, $\bar{L}_{13} = x_{s+1,t+1} - x_{s,t}$, and $\bar{L}_{14} = x_{s+1,t} - x_{s,t}$ into Eq. (22), can get:

$$\left(\bar{L}_{13} \times \bar{L}_{12}\right) \cdot \left(\bar{L}_{14} \times \bar{L}_{13}\right) = \left(\begin{bmatrix} p_x^{s+1,t+1} - p_x^{s,t} \\ p_y^{s+1,t+1} - p_y^{s,t} \end{bmatrix} \times \begin{bmatrix} p_x^{s,t+1} - p_x^{s,t} \\ p_y^{s,t+1} - p_y^{s,t} \end{bmatrix}\right)$$
$$\cdot \left(\begin{bmatrix} p_x^{s+1,t} - p_x^{s,t} \\ p_y^{s+1,t} - p_y^{s,t} \end{bmatrix} \times \begin{bmatrix} p_x^{s+1,t+1} - p_x^{s,t} \\ p_y^{s+1,t+1} - p_y^{s,t} \end{bmatrix}\right) \tag{23}$$

The control points are a total of M × N, and the total constraint equations obtained by traversing the control points of $s = 1, 2, \ldots, M - 1$, $t = 1, 2, \ldots, N - 1$, are:

$$C(\bar{x}) = - \begin{bmatrix} \left(\bar{L}_{(1,1) \to (2,2)} \times \bar{L}_{(1,1) \to (1,2)}\right) \cdot \left(\bar{L}_{(1,1) \to (2,1)} \times \bar{L}_{(1,1) \to (2,2)}\right) \\ \left(\bar{L}_{(1,2) \to (2,3)} \times \bar{L}_{(1,2) \to (1,3)}\right) \cdot \left(\bar{L}_{(1,2) \to (2,2)} \times \bar{L}_{(1,2) \to (2,3)}\right) \\ \cdots \\ \left(\bar{L}_{(s,t) \to (s+1,t+1)} \times \bar{L}_{(s,t) \to (s,t+1)}\right) \cdot \left(\bar{L}_{(s,t) \to (s+1,t)} \times \bar{L}_{(s,t) \to (s+1,t+1)}\right) \\ \cdots \\ \left(\bar{L}_{(m-1,n-1) \to (m,n)} \times \bar{L}_{(m-1,n-1) \to (m-1,n)}\right) \cdot \left(\bar{L}_{(m-1,n-1) \to (m,n-1)} \times \bar{L}_{(m-1,n-1) \to (m,n)}\right) \end{bmatrix} < 0 \tag{24}$$

So far, the objective function $f(\bar{x})$, the gradient $\nabla f(\bar{x})$ of the objective function and the constraint condition $C(\bar{x}) < 0$ are obtained, and the optimal solution of the control point position $\bar{x}$ can be obtained through the constrained minimum function fmincon in the Matlab optimization tool.

In this interface, we first select the position of the key point in Ω_D (the position of the blue point in the figure), and then select the expected projection position of the point in the projector image space Ω_P^i (the position of the red point in the figure). Then, after pointing out all the key pairs that need to be optimized in turn, we use the above method to optimize. Figure 3(b) shows the results of unconstrained optimization, Fig. 3(c) shows the results of constrained optimization, and Fig. 3(d) and (e) show the meshes and images in Ω_P^i after constrained optimization.

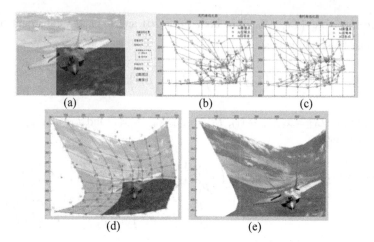

Fig. 3. (a) User interface; (b) Unconstrained optimization results; (c) Constrained optimization results; (d) Grid map with constrained optimization; (e) Image with constrained optimization (Color figure online)

3   Experiment and Application

3.1   Experiment

In order to verify the large-format arbitrary display surface projection splicing optimization method, the projection splicing experiment is carried out on the model shown in Fig. 4. The model has a length of 3 m and a height of 0.55 m. The projection surface is composed of 11 discontinuous folds, and the intersection line formed by each discontinuous surface of the building model and the intersection point of each intersection line are key points of the projection surface. Figure 4 shows the key position and number on the surface of the model, where the red dot is a possible key obtained using the corner detection method, and the green dot is the key position determined manually on this basis.

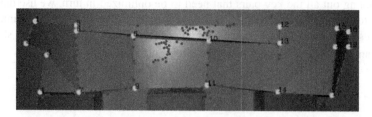

Fig. 4. Projection surface used in the experiment and the key point number and position of the projection surface (Color figure online)

The experimental platform includes two BenQ W1070 DLP projectors (nominal brightness 2000 lumens, focal length 16.88–21.88 mm, experimental resolution 1024 × 768) and a Canon 5000D camera (acquisition image resolution 2352 × 1568).

The specific steps of optimization method experiment with projection splicing results are as follows: Projection splicing using the splicing method of large-format free-form surface projection in [15]; The image material of non-fixed angle projection is made, and the situation that the key points Ω_D deviate from the expected projection position in the display image space are simulated. Manually selected pairs of key points Ω_D and Ω_p^i corresponding to the middle; The method of the most optimization is used to estimate the position of the control points of the Bezier surface. Re-rendering the image based on the Bezier surface control point position; The multi-projection error evaluation method in [16] was used to calculate the key point registration error KME_{mn}^i and the average superposition area error AOE before and after optimization.

In Fig. 5(a) (b), the position of the Bezier surface control point after the constraint optimization is performed for the left and right projectors respectively. Figure 5(c) is the result of the key point deviating from the expected projection position in the middle (where the green point represents the expected projection position of the key point, and the red point represents the actual projection position of the key point). Figure 5(d) is the result of the projection after optimization.

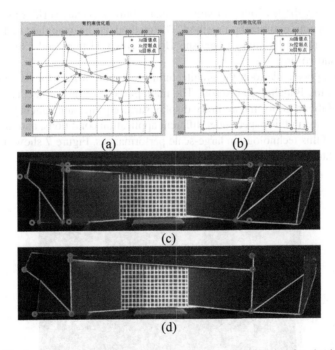

Fig. 5. (a) (b) shows the position of the Bezier surface control point for the left and right projectors with constrained optimization. (c) Projection stitching results of key points deviating from the expected position. (d) Optimized projection stitching results. (Color figure online)

Figure 6(a) (b) is the key point registration error of the two projectors before and after optimization. Figure 6(c) (d) is the key registration error of the optimized left and right projectors, where the key points are marked as shown in Fig. 6(b). From these images, we can see that after using the projection splicing result optimization method, the registration error of the selected key points is significantly reduced, while the registration error of the largest key points is reduced from 40 to less than 4. As for other unselected key points, the registration error is slightly increased, but both are below 3. Before calibration, the average stack region error AOE = 0.85, calibrates the average stack region error AOE = 1.37. After optimization, the average stack region error AOE also increases, but it can fully meet the requirements of projection splicing effect.

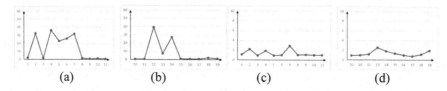

| (a) | (b) | (c) | (d) |

Fig. 6. (a) (b). Key point registration error; (c) (d). Of left and right projectors before optimization Key point registration error of left and right projectors after optimization

3.2 Application

In order to verify the feasibility of large-format arbitrary display surface projection, we proposed a splicing optimization method. The method has been applied to the Badaling Ski Resort Summer Evening, Changsha Huayi Town Theater and Church Building Projection and so on.

The laboratory undertook the architectural projection project for the summer evening party at the Badaling Ski Resort. The main purpose of this project is to verify the feasibility of the large-format arbitrary display surface projection splicing optimization method proposed in this paper under different application conditions, and to explore the application of this technology in large-scale performances. Figure 7 shows the effect of projection stitching and party scene.

Fig. 7. Field effect of the Badaling Ski Resort Summer Evening Party.

In 2018, the large-format arbitrary display surface projection optimization method proposed in this paper was also used in the architectural projection project of Huayi Town Theater in Changsha. In this project, the engineer used only 5 h to complete the on-site projection splicing work. Figure 8 shows a photo of the project site.

(a)   (b)

Fig. 8. (a) scene effect of projection of Changsha Huayi Town Theater (b) scene effect of Church projection of Changsha Huayi Town

4 Conclusion

In this paper, we proposed a large-format arbitrary display surface projection splicing optimization method. By carrying out experiments, we showed that this method was capable of quickly optimizing the traditional structured light scanning method with many defects and wrong key points. We then tested the feasibility and stability of the proposed method in practical application including stage performances and large outdoor activities.

Acknowledgments. This work was supported by the National Key Research and Development Program of China (No. 2017YFB1002805) and the National Natural Science Foundation of China (No. U1605254) and the 111 Project (B18005).

References

1. Chon, S., Lee, H., Yoon, J.: 3D architectural projection, Light Wall. Leonardo **44**(2), 172–173 (2011)
2. Head, A.: Exploring the issues of digital outdoor architectural projections (2012)
3. Raskar, R., Brown, M.S., Yang, R., et al.: Multi-projector displays using camera-based registration. In: Proceedings of Visualization 1999, pp. 161–522. IEEE (1999)
4. Low, K.L., Ilie, A., Welch, G., et al.: Combining head-mounted and projector-based displays for surgical training. In: 2003 IEEE Proceedings of Virtual Reality, pp. 110–117. IEEE (2003)
5. Raskar, R., Welch, G., Fuchs, H.: Seamless projection overlaps using image warping and intensity blending. In: Fourth International Conference on Virtual Systems and Multimedia, Gifu, Japan (1998)

6. Surati, R.J.: Scalable self-calibrating display technology for seamless large-scale displays. Massachusetts Institute of Technology (1999)
7. Brown, M.S., Seales, W.B.: A practical and flexible tiled display system. In: 2002 Proceedings of 10th Pacific Conference on Computer Graphics and Applications, pp. 194–203. IEEE (2002)
8. Lee, J.C., Dietz, P.H., Maynes-Aminzade, D., et al.: Automatic projector calibration with embedded light sensors. In: 2004 Proceedings of the 17th Annual ACM Symposium on User Interface Software and Technology, pp. 123–126. ACM (2004)
9. Gross, M., Würmlin, S., Naef, M., et al.: Blue-c: a spatially immersive display and 3D video portal for telepresence. ACM Trans. Graph. (TOG) 22(3), 819–827 (2003)
10. Zollmann, S., Langlotz, T., Bimber, O.: Passive-active geometric calibration for view-dependent projections onto arbitrary surfaces. J. Virtual Reality Broadcast. 4(6) (2007)
11. Raskar, R., Welch, G., Low, K.L., et al.: Shader lamps: animating real objects with image-based illumination. In: Gortler, S.J., Myszkowski, K. (eds.) Rendering Techniques 2001, pp. 89–102. Springer, Vienna (2001). https://doi.org/10.1007/978-3-7091-6242-2_9
12. Yuan, Q.: Research on Digital Interactive Exhibition Technology and System. Zhejiang University (2009)
13. arKaos Pro. http://www.arkaospro.com/arkaos-pro
14. Coolux Media System. http://www.coolux.de/
15. Xiang, L., Liu, Y.: Study on large-format arbitrary-surface multi-projector display for 3D architectural models. Opt. Tech. 40(2), 151–155 (2014)
16. Xiang, L., Xie, J., Liu, Y.: Multi-projector geometric calibration error analysis. J. Comput.-Aided Des. Comput. Graph. 106–113 (2015)

Study on Electromagnetic Visualization Experiment System Based on Augmented Reality

Xiaoxu Liu[1(✉)], Cong Wang[2], Jun Huang[1], Yue Liu[1,3],
and Yongtian Wang[1,3]

[1] Beijing Engineering Research Center of Mixed Reality and Advanced Display,
School of Optics and Photonics, Beijing Institute of Technology,
Beijing 100081, China
{2120160540,huangjun,liuyue,wyt}@bit.edu.cn

[2] China Electronics Standardization Institute, Beijing 100007, China
wangcong@cesi.cn

[3] AICFVE of Beijing Film Academy, 4, Xitucheng Rd, Haidian,
Beijing 100088, China

Abstract. When learning physics, electromagnetism is one of the most difficult concepts for students to understand. This paper proposes a real time visualization method for 3D magnetic field based on the augmented reality (AR) technology, which can not only visualize magnetic flux lines in real time, but also simulate the approximate sparse distribution of magnetic flux lines in space. An application utilizing the proposed approach is also presented, which permits students to freely and interactively move the magnets in 3D space and observe the magnetic flux lines in real time. An experiment is conducted to evaluate the application and its result shows that the application utilizing the proposed method can visualize the invisible physical phenomenon of 3D magnetic field, which has significant supplemental learning effects for students.

Keywords: Augmented reality · Real time visualization · Magnetic flux lines

1 Introduction

In the field of education, augmented reality technology is a new means of cross-border integration. Students can explore independently in the most natural way in the context of the fusion of virtual and reality. This kind of technology that can present knowledge entities and facilitate people's firsthand experience makes knowledge more and more contextual.

Electromagnetism is abstract and cognitively demanding, thus it is one of the most difficult subjects for students to master [1]. The main obstacle for students to learn is that they have difficulties in understanding or imagining abstract electromagnetic phenomena [2]. Unlike other physical concepts, when dealing with electromagnetism, students have no real-life references [3]. Such concerns were addressed in the MIT Technology Enabled Active Learning (TEAL)/Studio Project where students developed much better intuition about, and conceptual models of, physical phenomena

© Springer Nature Singapore Pte Ltd. 2019
Y. Wang et al. (Eds.): IGTA 2019, CCIS 1043, pp. 699–712, 2019.
https://doi.org/10.1007/978-981-13-9917-6_65

through the use of visualization in an electricity and magnetism course using web-based technologies [4, 5]. Consequently, developing effective pedagogical strategies and using emergent technologies for helping students in this endeavor will be a step ahead to validate TEAL Project findings when using AR technology. The visual features of augmented reality technology have been successfully applied to improve the spatial cognitive ability of science and engineering. Therefore, it will have a superb application prospect for helping students understand the abstract electromagnetic concept [6, 7].

In response to the aforementioned issue, the aim of this paper is to propose a real time visualization method for 3D magnetic field based on the augmented reality technology, with which students will have real-life reference when studying electromagnetism. In fact, some related methods have been proposed. For example, A Buchau et al. used the finite element method to calculate the 3D magnetic field, showing three examples of using the augmented reality to display the static magnetic field [8]. F Mannus et al. introduced an interactive magnetic field simulation system in the augmented reality scene [9]. Shinya Matsutomo et al. proposed a new real-time visualization system for magnetic fields, using augmented reality to synthesize the magnetic source and its generated magnetic field into a visual image [10]. However, most of these methods only focus on the drawing process of the magnetic flux lines in space, ignoring the sparse distribution of the calculated magnetic flux lines affected by the field strength [11, 12]. Therefore, we propose a real-time magnetic line visualization method that can simultaneously simulate the spatial distribution of magnetic lines.

In the proposed method, we first determine the number of magnetic flux lines and the approximate sparse distribution in the high field region, then obtain the magnetic flux intensity by the derived analytical expression of the 3D magnetic field, finally use the particle tracking method to simulate the calculated spatial trajectory of the magnetic flux line. One application that conveys the advantages of the proposed method is also presented. Meanwhile, in order to evaluate the performance of the proposed method, we recruited some students to participate in the user study in order to examine its impact on students' cognitive performance and investigate students' attitudes toward it.

The rest of this paper is organized as follows. The proposed approach is discussed in Sect. 2, Sect. 3 introduces the AR application utilizing the proposed approach. The methodology of the experiment and its results are shown in Sect. 4. Section 5 concludes this paper.

2 Algorithm

In order to realize real-time visualization of magnetic lines, we first derive the analytical formula of the spatial magnetic field, calculate the spatial distribution of the magnetic flux lines, and then track the spatial shape of the magnetic flux lines.

2.1   Computation of Magnetic Field

The basic law of electromagnetic field is Maxwell's equations, and its solving process is complicated. In order to simplify the calculation of permanent magnetic field, different researchers proposed a series of mathematical models which is equivalent to magnetic field. In this paper, we adopt the equivalent current model which consists of the Ampere molecular circulation hypothesis [13] and Biot-Savar's law [14] to calculate the 3D magnetic field of permanent magnets.

The magnetic field vector is represented by the magnetic flux density $\boldsymbol{B}$. According to Biot-Savart's law, the magnetic flux density $\boldsymbol{B}$ generated at a spatial point P of a complete current loop is:

$$\boldsymbol{B} = \frac{\mu_0}{4\pi} \oint_l \frac{Idl \times (\boldsymbol{r} - \boldsymbol{r'})}{|\boldsymbol{r} - \boldsymbol{r'}|^3} \tag{1}$$

where $\boldsymbol{r}$ is the arrow diameter of origin point, $\boldsymbol{r'}$ is the arrow diameter of field point $P(x, y, z)$, μ_0 is the vacuum permeability.

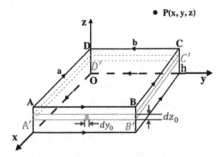

Fig. 1. Rectangular magnet model using molecular current

Let the size of rectangular permanent magnet be $a \times b \times h$, as shown in Fig. 1. It can be known from the Ampere molecular circulation hypothesis that the magnetic field at any point in the outer space of the magnet is excited by the closed current loop $ABCDA$ which is on the permanent magnet side surface. Here, the coordinate of the field point P is (x, y, z), and the current loop $A'B'C'D'A'$ with thickness dz_0 is selected, then the magnetic field generated at P is $d\boldsymbol{B}$ [15]. Thus, the total magnetic field $\boldsymbol{B}$ generated by all of the current loops at point P is:

$$\boldsymbol{B} = B_x\boldsymbol{i} + B_y\boldsymbol{j} + B_z\boldsymbol{k} = \int_0^h dB_x\boldsymbol{i} + dB_y\boldsymbol{j} + dB_z\boldsymbol{k} \tag{2}$$

Combined with the previously mentioned Biot-Savart's law, the final analytical expression can be derived as:

$$B_x = \frac{K}{2}[-\Gamma(a-x,b-y,z) - \Gamma(a-x,y,z) + \Gamma(x,b-y,z) + \Gamma(x,y,z)]. \quad (3)$$

$$B_y = \frac{K}{2}[-\Gamma(b-y,a-x,z) - \Gamma(b-y,x,z) + \Gamma(y,a-x,z) + \Gamma(y,x,z)] \quad (4)$$

$$B_z = K\left[\begin{array}{c} -\Psi(b-y,a-x,z) - \Psi(y,a-x,z) - \Psi(a-x,b-y,z) \\ -\Psi(x,b-y,z) - \Psi(b-y,x,z) - \Psi(y,x,z) - \Psi(a-x,y,z) \\ -\Psi(x,y,z) \end{array}\right] \quad (5)$$

2.2 Drawing of the Magnetic Flux Lines in 3-D Space

Asanuma et al. [16] corresponded the magnetic line to the streamline in the fluid flow region, for which many experimental visualization methods have been proposed. The virtual particle tracking method [17] used in the 3D magnetic flux lines algorithm proposed by Yamashita et al. [18] is a general method for calculating three-dimensional magnetic flux lines.

Virtual particle tracking is a very important method used in the visualization and analysis of flow field data. The idea of virtual particle tracking is to release a certain amount of massless particles at a specified location in the flow field and then track the trajectories of those particles in the domain. In a stable flow field, the generated trajectory is called a streamline, and in a flow field that changes in real time, the generated trajectory is called a path [19].

(1) A single particle is initially placed on the starting point P_0 of each magnetic flux line, which is calculated through the method described before.

(2) Determination of the path is carried out by a predictor–corrector method, as illustrated in Fig. 2a. Beginning at point P_0, the magnetic flux density $\boldsymbol{B}$ can be calculated and used to predict the particle location P_0' at a specified distance.

(3) At point P_0' a new magnetic flux density $\boldsymbol{B}'$ can be obtained and averaged with $\boldsymbol{B}$ to create a corrected magnetic flux density $\boldsymbol{B}''$. This corrected magnetic flux density is used to find a new location P_0'', which is used as the point of origin for movement in the next tracking step.

This technique is applied in succession (as demonstrated in the Fig. 2b) until the magnetic flux line flows out of the analysis domain or returns to the starting point P_0.

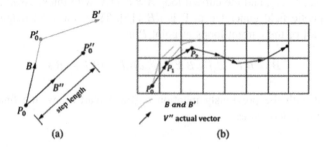

Fig. 2. Virtual particle tracking method (a) Path is determined. (b) Particle tracking.

2.3   Definition of Number and Starting Point of Magnetic Flux Lines

Although we have solved the calculation of the magnetic field and magnetic flux line's shape, we still have no solution on how to define the position of the starting point of each magnetic flux line. In general, in order to understand the magnetic field phenomenon easier, researchers expect that the number of magnetic flux lines is denser in the region where the field strength is higher and is sparse in the region where the field strength is lower. In order to achieve this goal, we place all the starting points in a common plane, that is, the N pole of the magnet. By dividing the plane area according to the magnitude of the field strength, the starting point of all the magnetic flux lines is determined, thereby generating the magnetic line. The specific process is as follows:

(1) Define the N pole of a rectangular permanent magnet as plane S, from which the flux lines will emerge. Define the value of total number of flux lines Num.
(2) Divide plane S into n sub-planes equally, the magnetic flux densities B_j of each vertex can be calculated separately (Fig. 3a). Define the average flux value $\bar{\phi}_i$ for each sub-plane i, then

$$\bar{\phi}_i = \frac{\sum_{j=1}^{4} B_j}{4} \cdot S_i \qquad (6)$$

where S_i is the area of sub-plane i.
(3) Compute the number of flux lines N_i (Fig. 3b) assigned to each sub-plane i according to the average flux value $\bar{\phi}_i$

$$N_i = \frac{\bar{\phi}_i}{\sum_{k=1}^{n} \bar{\phi}_k} \cdot Num \qquad (7)$$

(4) Randomly assign the starting point (x, y) within the range of each sub-plane i according to the value of N_i.

With the aforementioned method we can get the nearly optimal position of each magnetic flux line's starting point.

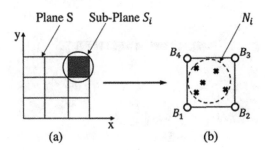

(a)   (b)

Fig. 3. Definition of number and starting point of magnetic flux lines (a) Plane S with its subplanes. (b) Definition of the number of magnetic flux lines.

3 Application

We have implemented the visualization method of the magnetic flux lines by adopting the method into Unity 3D, which is a 3D engine that can construct augmented reality applications with the support of Vuforia AR SDK. A web camera is used to capture the real-time video, from which Vuforia AR SDK can easily identify pictures and objects, and recreate environmental content of electromagnetic field in the real world [20]. The common way to use Vuforia for AR applications is to define a target picture. Vuforia identifies the target by detecting the matching of natural feature points in the picture. In addition, in order to study the usability of the proposed method, we designed an experimental application. The experimental scenes in the application are designed according to the Hall effect experiment, which is a classical experiment in electromagnetism.

The application consists of three parts (see Fig. 4). Figure 4(a) (b) is scene 1, the main task for students in scene 1 is to observe the distribution of the magnetic flux lines of a single magnet and learn the spatial magnetic field; Fig. 4(c) (d) is scene 2, the main task for students in scene 2 is to observe the interaction of the two magnets. The spatial variation of the magnetic flux lines will help students understand how to manipulate the

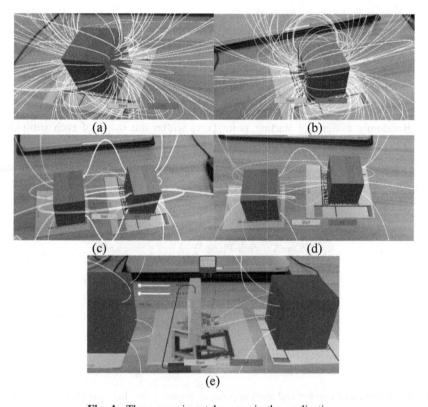

Fig. 4. Three experimental scenes in the application.

magnets to change the spatial magnetic field in the Hall effect experimental in scene 3; Fig. 4(e) is scene 3, in which students can manipulate the magnet or the conductor through the marker on the desktop, and the current can be changed by the slider. The column on the upper left records the magnitude of the current magnetic field and current passing through the conductor, and displays the current value of Hall voltage. In addition, the electrons in the conductor will also exhibit different ways of movement as the Lorentz force is changed.

With the help of the proposed application, learners can easily observe the electromagnetic phenomenon in the way the magnetic flux lines are visualized in real-time, and also learn the microscopic invisible principle of Hall effect experimental.

4 Experiment

The experiment involved 22 students from different middle schools in Beijing. The grades of these students range from the second year of junior high school to the first year of high school. We have investigated the user experience of AR applications for students. Some students indicated that they had experienced AR applications, where $M = 0.2$, $SD = 0.4$ (0 = never experienced, 1 = occasionally experienced, 2 = often experience).

4.1 Research Rationale and Experiment Preparation

This study mainly focuses on the effect of supplemental learning of the proposed AR-based learning application in an electromagnetic course. We investigated the current situation of the electromagnetic course's learning of middle school students before developing this AR application. Through the interviews with teachers and students, we learnt that because the learning content of the electromagnetic courses is rather boring, students are not very motivated to learn the content of this chapter, and they do not fully understand the contents of this chapter. Therefore, it's necessary to provide students an augmented reality application to stimulate students' interest and promote outcomes in learning electromagnetic courses. For such reasons, the experiment did not include a control group. The pre-test scores will represent the student's learning outcomes when using the textbook, and the post-test scores will represent the student's learning outcomes after using the augmented reality-based learning application. Any applications used in learning activities using the augmented reality application including software and activity forms, did not provide the exact knowledge points included in the test, which means that the student's test answer will be that the result they observe and explore by themselves during the learning process. Thus we suggests that the difference between the pretest and posttest scores will represent the learning effect of the application. The questionnaire after the experiment is mainly to investigate the students' attitude towards the augmented reality-based learning application. The experiment consists of five parts as shown in Table 1.

Table 1. Experiment design

Experiment parts	Operation methods
Pre-test	Each student is required to complete a paper and pencil test independently
Learning activities based on augmented reality application	Without teacher's guidance, each student is required to use the augmented reality application to learn according to the requirements of the activity form
Post-test	Each student is required to independently complete the same test used for the pre-test
Questionnaire survey	Each student is required to independently complete a paper and pencil questionnaire
Interview	Each student is interviewed about their feelings during the AR-based learning process

4.2   Measurement Instruments

(1) Pre-post test

The test is designed based on the high school physics syllabus. It mainly examines students' comprehension and retention of several key knowledge points about the characteristics of magnetic fields and Hall effect. The paper and pencil test includes multiple choice and calculation questions associated to the learning content and has a full mark of 30 points.

Prior to the experiment, all the students were required to complete the pre-test. After that, each student used the AR application presented in this section to complete the learning activity. After learning, a post-test was performed using the same quiz. The questions are briefly summarized as:

- Are the magnetic flux lines of intersection cross or not?
- Are the distribution of magnetic flux lines uniform?
- Are the magnetic flux lines a closed curve or a non-closed curve?
- What does the tangential direction of the magnetic flux lines represent?
- What is the relationship between the Hall voltage and the current flowing through the conductor?
- What is the relationship between the Hall voltage and the magnetic field that passes through the conductor?

(2) Instruction and activity form

In this study, an activity form was designed based on the content of the application to help them understand the learning process. According to the survey, all students were exposed to Augmented Reality teaching for the first time. And in the absence of teacher guidance, students are placed in self-exploration scenarios. Thus the activity table is designed to show them how to use hardware devices to interact with the computer and observe correctly.

(3) Post-questionnaire

The questionnaire uses the Likert scale, and the students score the questions based on their experience. The score ranges from "1 (very disagree)" to "5 (very agree)". The "Learning Attitudes" section consists of five questions that are modifications to the questions extracted from the questionnaire presented by Hwang et al. [21]. The "Satisfaction with Application" section covers four different directions. These problems were originally revised by Chu et al. [22], and in this experiment some minor changes were made based on the experimental content. The "cognitive effectiveness" part consists of three questions and the "cognitive accessibility" part consists of five questions, which are extracted from the problems revised by Chu et al. [22] and modified in this experiment.

Each student is given the copies of the questionnaire survey after they finished the post-test, and all of which were considered to be valid.

(4) Interview protocol

Finally, each student will have an oral interview survey which is designed to further explore the learning experience of students by using the application. In the interview, we asked the students the following questions.

- Do you think that this AR application will help the study of electromagnetism?
- In what ways can the application help you?
- Do you want to use such AR applications to learn electromagnetism in the future?
- Why do you want to use such AR applications?
- What applications do you usually use when studying electromagnetics in class?
- Do you think that the AR application is better than these applications?
- In what ways do you think that the AR application is better than those applications?
- Can you provide some suggestions for improving our visualization application?

4.3 Data Analysis and Findings

(1) Overall cognitive performance

The experiment produced 22 * 2 test samples (22 for pre-test and 22 for post-test), all of which were considered valid. The full score of test is 45 points. We performed a paired t-test on the pre-test and post-test scores [23]. The test variables were post-test scores minus the pre-test scores, indicating the difference in scores before and after each student's using the experimental system. The results are shown in Table 2.

Table 2. Paired t-test for pre-test and post-test score variables.

	Paired differences				t	Sig (2-tailed)
	Mean	Std. deviation	95% Confidence interval of the difference			
			Lower	Upper		
post-test score - pre-test score	11.6	1.855	9.974	13.226	-10.472	0.00023

Table 2 shows that the p-value (two-tailed) of the mean is close to zero ($t = -10.472$, p-value = 0.000), which suggests that students' scores after using the magnetic visualization application are significantly higher than those attained before the learning activity. As a result, we conclude that with other unobserved variables controlled, the magnetic visualization application has a statistically significant improvement on the score of the adopted cognitive quiz test, and students' averages scores increased by 11.6 points.

(2) Attitudes toward the application through questionnaire analysis

When analyzing the questionnaire analysis, we calculated the score of each part by averaging all of the corresponding items within each part. The descriptive statistics obtained are shown in Table 3.

Table 3. Descriptive statistics for the four questionnaire parts.

Variable	Max	Min	Mean	Std. deviation
Learning attitude	5	2	4.32	0.384
Satisfaction	5	3	4.1	0.308
Cognitive validity	5	3	4.4	0.298
Cognitive accessibility	5	2	4.4	0.349

It can be observed from Table 3 that the cognitive validity of using the application and the cognitive accessibility about the application have the highest mean value, which suggested that students think that the application is intuitive and interesting, and it can help their study. Therefore, students accepted our application well. In other words, the data can reflect the usability of the application and play a supporting role in student learning. In contrast, the "Satisfaction" constructs have the lowest mean value, which suggests that some features of this application still need improvement, such as the design of the UI interface, optimization of performance, etc.

(3) Students' experience exploration through interviews

When interviewing students after the end of the experiment, eight questions based on the interview questionnaire were asked to them and they were encouraged to discuss their views on the application [24].

The interview content was recorded through the recording equipment, and then was organized into text content. The content analysis method is adopted to analyze the data collected from interviews. Firstly the theme in the text content is sorted out, and then code the content according to the theme. When analyzing the results, link the text content with the numbers by the frequency of the topic, and then it can be qualitatively represented through the digital way, which can make it more intuitive and easy to understand [25] (see Table 4).

Table 4. The student's comments.

	Comments	Responses
Do you think that this AR application will help the study of electromagnetism?	It will help the study of electromagnetism	5
In what ways can the application help you?	It allows people to visually observe the sparse distribution of magnetic flux lines	4
	Obviously observe the process of magnetic flux lines changes when two magnetics interact with each other	3
	Learn the behavior of the magnetic field in space	4
	Increase the interesting of learning	2
Do you want to use such AR applications to learn electromagnetism in the future?	Yes, I want	5
Why do you want to use such AR applications?	The application offers the opportunity for experiment	3
	3D applications are more impressive than 2D	3
What applications do you usually use when study electromagnetics in class?	Watch the video	4
	Draw on the blackboard	3
Do you think the AR application is better than these applications?	Yes	5
In what ways do you think that the AR application is better than those applications?	More immersive	3
	It can be operated according to your own comprehension	4
Can you provide some suggestions for improving our visualization application?	Enhance interactivity	2
	Add more elements	2

It can be seen clearly from the interview that the students think that the magnetic field visualization will help their study of electromagnetism and they want to use such AR applications to learn electromagnetism in the future. Most of the students stated that the application allows them to visually observe the sparse distribution of magnetic flux lines and obviously observe the process of magnetic flux lines changes when two magnetics interact with each other. Compared with other applications used when studying electromagnetics in school, students said that this application is more immersive and it allows them to operate according to their own comprehension, which can increase the interests of learning. Finally, some students said they expect more elements to be added to the interactive scene, such as the interaction between magnets and iron block, etc.

5 Discussions and Conclusions

5.1 Discussions

Based on the above experimental results, we can get some conclusions as the following.

First, magnetic field visualization application based on augmented reality can significantly improve students' academic performance. The experiment verifies the supplementary learning effect of the application. The pre-test scores represent the learning effect of the students when using the textbooks, and the post-test scores represent the learning effects of the students using the augmented reality application. The experimental result shows that the post-test score is significantly higher than the pre-test score, which indicates that the augmented reality application has a positive impact on the improvement of academic performance.

Second, from the test results of students' attitudes towards learning, we can see that students have a positive attitude towards the learning activity. In the four parts of the questionnaire, the rating of "satisfaction" is relatively low, while still within the positive category, which indicates that some functions of the application need to be improved, such as UI interface design, performance optimization and so on. At the same time, the data of this questionnaire also reflects that this application can be accepted by students, they are willing to use our application to learn.

Third, students stated that this application is more immersive than the applications they usually used in school, and it allows them to operate according to their own comprehension, which can increase the interests of learning. We also found that students view the diversification of elements of the application as unsatisfactory. The main reason is that more elements require higher calculations, and we will add these elements after we optimize the visualization in the future.

5.2 Conclusions

We propose a real-time visualization method of magnetic field, which not only realizes the visualization of magnetic lines, but also simulates the approximate sparse distribution of magnetic flux lines in space. We also present an application utilizing this method, with which students can operate the magnet arbitrarily in an augmented reality environment to observe real-time change of the magnetic flux lines. This enables a student to easily interact with the magnetic field and observe its behavior.

In order to evaluate the value of the application, we invited some students to participate in the experiment. The result shows that the AR-based magnetic field visualization application is beneficial in improving middle school students' cognitive test performance on electromagnetic content. Additionally, students generally hold a positive attitude toward the AR application and enjoyed the exploration experience. Based on the findings, we wish to further employ this application as a remedial learning application in middle school course that require students to memorize abstract electromagnetic concepts.

Acknowledgements. This work was supported by the National Key Research and Development Program of China (No. 2018YFB1005002) and the National Natural Science Foundation of China (No. 61727808) and the 111 Project (B18005).

References

1. Ibáñez, M.B., Di Serio, Á., Villarán, D., et al.: Experimenting with electromagnetism using augmented reality: impact on flow student experience and educational effectiveness. Comput. Educ. **71**, 1–13 (2014)
2. Matsutomo, S., Mitsufuji, K., Hiasa, Y., et al.: Real time simulation method of magnetic field for visualization system with augmented reality technology. IEEE Trans. Magn. **49**(5), 1665–1668 (2013)
3. Maloney, D.P., O'Kuma, T.L., Hieggelke, C.J., Van Heuvelen, A.: Surveying students' conceptual knowledge of electricity and magnetism. Am. J. Phys. **69**(7 Suppl. 1), S12–S23 (2001)
4. Belcher, J.W., Bessette, R.M.: MIT educators share success. ACM SIGGRAPH Comput. Graph. **35**(1), 18–21 (2001)
5. Dori, Y.J., Hult, E., Belcher, B.J.W.: How much have they retained? Making unseen concepts seen in a freshman electromagnetism course at MIT. J. Sci. Educ. Technol. **16**(4), 299–323 (2007)
6. Dünser, A., Steinbügl, K., Kaufmann, H., et al.: Virtual and augmented reality as spatial ability training applications. In: Proceedings of the 6th ACM SIGCHI New Zealand Chapter's International Conference on Computer-Human Interaction Design Centered HCI – CHINZ 2006, Christchurch, New Zealand, 06–07 July 2006, pp. 125–132. ACM Press (2006)
7. Martín-Gutiérrez, J., Saorín, J.L., Contero, M., et al.: Design and validation of an augmented book for spatial abilities development in engineering students. Comput. Graph. **34**(1), 77–91 (2010)
8. Buchau, A., Rucker, W.M., Wössner, U., Becker, M.: Augmented reality in teaching of electrodynamics. COMPEL - Int. J. Comput. Math. Electr. Electron. Eng. **28**(4), 948–963 (2009)
9. Mannus, F., Rübel, J., Wagner, C., et al.: Augmenting magnetic field lines for school experiments. In: IEEE International Symposium on Mixed & Augmented Reality. IEEE Computer Society (2011)
10. Matsutomo, S., Miyauchi, T., Noguchi, S., et al.: Real-time visualization system of magnetic field utilizing augmented reality technology for education. IEEE Trans. Magn. **48**(2), 531–534 (2012)
11. Cingoski, V., Kuribayashi, T., Kaneda, K., et al.: Improved interactive visualization of magnetic flux lines in 3-D space using edge finite elements. IEEE Trans. Magn. **32**(3), 1477–1480 (1996)
12. Noguchi, S., Yoshigai, T., Yamashita, H.: Analytical computation and visualization of magnetic flux lines in 3-D space from hexahedral edge finite element results. IEEE Trans. Magn. **41**(5), 1820–1823 (2005)
13. Engel-Herbert, R., Hesjedal, T.: Calculation of the magnetic stray field of a uniaxial magnetic domain. J. Appl. Phys. **97**(7), 1579 (2005)
14. Stratton, J.A.: Electromagnetic Theory. McGraw-Hill, New York (1941)
15. Janet, F., Coulomb, J.L., Chillet, C., et al.: Simplified magnetic moment method applied to current transformer modeling. IEEE Trans. Magn. **40**(2), 818–821 (2004)

16. Asanuma, K.: Flow Visualization Handbook. Asakura, Tokyo (1977)
17. Shiroyama, S.: Flow visualization by imaginary particle tracing method. In: The 4th Symposium of Numerical Methods in Flow Dynamics, p. 483 (1990)
18. Yamashita, H., Harada, K., Nakamae, E., et al.: Stereographic display on three dimensional magnetic fields of electromagnetic machines. IEEE Trans. Power Apparatus Syst. **PAS-100** (11), 4692–4697 (2007)
19. Zhang, J., Yuan, X.: A survey of parallel particle tracing algorithms in flow visualization. J. Vis. **21**(5), 351–368 (2018)
20. Sun, H.L., Zhang, Z.L., Liu, X.X., et al.: Employing different viewpoints for remote guidance in a collaborative augmented environment. In: ChineseCHI 2018 (2018)
21. Hwang, G.J., Chang, H.F.: A formative assessment-based mobile learning approach to improving the learning attitudes and achievements of students. Comput. Educ. **56**(4), 1023–1031 (2011)
22. Chu, H.C., Hwang, G.J., Tsai, C.C., et al.: A two-tier test approach to developing location-aware mobile learning systems for natural science courses. Comput. Educ. **55**(4), 1618–1627 (2010)
23. Wei, X., Weng, D., Liu, Y., et al.: Teaching based on augmented reality for a technical creative design course. Comput. Educ. **81**, 221–234 (2015)
24. Akçayır, M., Akçayır, G., Pektaş, H.M., Ocak, M.A.: Augmented reality in science laboratories: the effects of augmented reality on university students' laboratory skills and attitudes toward science laboratories. Comput. Hum. Behav. **57**, 334–342 (2016)
25. Dündar, H., Akçayır, M.: Implementing tablet PCs in schools: students' attitudes and opinions. Comput. Hum. Behav. **32**, 40–46 (2014)

Research on Battle Damage Analysis Methods Based on Collaborative Simulation for Armored Equipment

Jun-qing Huang$^{(\boxtimes)}$, Wei Zhang, Wei Liu, and Tuan Wang

Training Center, Army Armored Military Academy, Beijing, China
tigerhjq@126.com, weizhang@126.com, weiliu@126.com,
tuanwang@126.com

Abstract. The method of collaborative simulation is used here to guide the research of battle damage simulation of armored equipment involving complex technologies in multiple fields. Based on basic functional components of specified armored equipment, an solid model of armored equipment is established by constructing a platform with the high-resolution solid model of equipment. The numerical model of ammunition power field is established based on the non-linear finite element dynamic analysis program. Basic data for equipment damage analysis are obtained through numerical analysis. The spatial intersection relationship of missile-and-target is established by analyzing the interaction between missiles and targets, where the targets are realized with the solid model of armored equipment. The situation of damage about the armored equipment is determined according to characteristics of the damaging elements of ammunitions and criteria to the damaged equipment components. As verified in practice, this method is feasible and operatable, and can be used as a guideline for damage analysis for armored equipment.

Keywords: Armored equipment · Battle damage · Collaborative simulation

1 Introduction

With the development of simulation technology, it has evolved gradually from simulations of single discipline and non-collaboration to those of multi-discipline and cross-domain collaboration for complex projects. As for a simulated environment as complex as involving battle damages to armored equipment, many fields and disciplines, including mechanics and kinetics, are necessary to further improve and refine the simulation model of battle damages to armored equipment. This kind of complex technical problems involves many fields so that it is impossible to solve them with a single simulation tool only.

Nowadays, CAD software with 3D solid modeling technology as its core and CAE software with finite element technology as its core are becoming more and more mature, and have been widely used in designing and analyzing mechanical products. Though, while providing effective analysis tools for kinds of simulation, professional software in various disciplines also has different emphasis. CAD software focuses on designing 3D entities but is relatively weak in analysis abilities, while CAE software

© Springer Nature Singapore Pte Ltd. 2019
Y. Wang et al. (Eds.): IGTA 2019, CCIS 1043, pp. 713–723, 2019.
https://doi.org/10.1007/978-981-13-9917-6_66

provides strong engineering analysis abilities but is weak in modeling abilities. These characteristics affect the full play of software functions somehow. It is enabled by the progresses of collaborative simulation that different software can be introduced into a simulated environment of battle damages of armored equipment so that the influence of many factors can be analyzed in a much more complex battlefield environment more deeply and concretely, thus the battle damage situation of those equipment can be acknowledged more comprehensively and trustworthy.

The basic idea of collaborative simulation based research of battle damages to equipment is that: in damage analysis for armored equipment in a simulated system-of-systems combat environment, the solid model of equipment should be constructed before the establishment of the material model of protection armors of the equipment. Then, the damaging effect to the armored equipment can be analyzed with finite element methods according to different attacking conditions to obtain a mapping table between the attacking conditions and the damaged components of the equipment. This ensures a more reasonable result of damaged components and degree of damages of the equipment corresponding to specific damaging event parameters in such a system-of-systems combat simulation of armored equipment so as to provide component-level damage data for damaging effects in this system-of-systems combat simulation for armored equipment, and then improve the accuracy of simulation. The collaborative simulation framework is shown in Fig. 1.

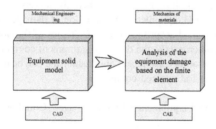

Fig. 1. The collaborative simulation framework of damages to armored equipment

2 Solid Model of Armored Equipment

Equipment battle damage analysis needs to establish equipment description model. With the development of computer simulation technology and through the combination of equipment battle damage analysis technology and computer application technology, a high-resolution solid model for equipment description has been produced. That is, based on the 3D solid model of equipment component level, the functional relationship between the components and the systems of the equipment has been established, and the geometry, structure and functional information of the equipment has been described completely, so as to provide a foundation for high precision assessments to equipment battle damages. To construct a solid model of equipment that can meet the needs of equipment battle damage analysis, the basic functional components of the armored equipment should be determined first, and then the solid model of the equipment can be constructed with solid modeling tools.

2.1 Determining Basic Components of Armored Equipment

The basic function of armored equipment refers to the indispensable function of armored equipment to complete the current task. Using system sketch or function block diagram, the subsystems, assemblies and components are analyzed one by one from top to bottom to determine the components that are essential to basic functions. For example, according to its operational tasks, the basic functions of a tracked infantry vehicle can be divided into four groups: firepower, maneuverability, protection and communication capabilities. According to the division principle of basic functional components, the basic functional components of the tracked infantry vehicle are analyzed from the two aspects of scope and granularity comprehensively and determined as listed in Table 1.

Table 1. The basic functional components of an armored object

Systems	Basic functional components	Systems	Basic functional components
lubrication system	Oil radiator	Caterpillar system	Inducer
	Oil line		Loading wheel
	...		...
...	...	...	...

2.2 Constructing Solid Model of Equipment

Based on the identified basic functional components of armored equipment, a solid equipment model can be established by constructing a platform with high-resolution solid models of the equipment. The main platforms for building high-resolution equipment solid models include WORKBENCH, SOLIWORKS, LS-DYNA, etc. They integrate CAD and CAE technologies, have abundant model interfaces, and have strong material and structure analysis functions. They can provide high-resolution model data for equipment battle damage analysis. Figure 2 is a collaborative environment based on ANSYS Workbench. Figure 3 is a 3D solid model of the internal and external components of a type of tank based on the actual size and basic functional components (some of the components have been simplified reasonably) using WORKBENCH platform.

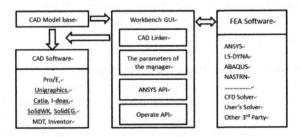

Fig. 2. A collaborative environment based on ANSYS workbench

Fig. 3. The 3D solid model of a type of tank

3   Equipment Damage Analysis Based on Finite Element Method

Equipment damage analysis based on finite element method mainly adopts the non-linear dynamic analysis program based on the finite element method to establish the numerical model of the ammunition power field and obtain the basic data for equipment damage analysis through numerical analysis. Taking the equipment solid model as the target, through the interaction analysis of missile and target, the space relationship of the missile-target rendezvous is established. The situation of damage about the equipment is determined according to characteristics of the damaging elements of ammunitions and criteria to the damaged equipment components so as to provide basic data for damage effect analysis to armored equipment in system-of-systems combat simulation environment.

3.1   Numerical Simulation Analysis of Power Field of Ammunition Warheads

The numerical simulation analysis of power field of ammunition warheads is based on the analysis of impact effect and penetration effect of ammunition to establish the numerical simulation model of ammunition warheads. The simulation results of ammunition power field (mass, position, shape, velocity, kinetic energy, momentum, etc. of the fragments and jet-flows) are obtained by dynamic analysis based on finite element method and provide necessary basic data for equipment damage analysis.

3.1.1   Power Field of Ammunition Warheads

The power field of ammunition warheads refers to the collection of all elements formed by ammunition warheads inside or near the target that can damage the target. Such an element is called "damaging element". Every damaging element is a material carrier with damaging ability and can generate damaging effect. It is also the smallest component of ammunition power field.

3.1.2   Numerical Simulation Based on Finite Element

With the rapid development of computer hardware technology and the emergence of large-scale fluid coding, numerical simulation based on finite element method (FEM) is becoming an effective means to study high-speed collision, explosion and other problems. At present, the finite element software tools that can analyze the impact dynamics of non-linear structures mainly include ANSYS/DYNA, ESIA and AUTO-DYN. Among these software, AUTODYN is capable not only to display and analyze the impact dynamics of non-linear structures by finite element method, but also to obtain fragments data generated by high-speed impact and explosion. And it has rich model interfaces and a good man-machine interface. Therefore, AUTODYN can be used as an effective finite element analysis tool for armored equipment damage research.

3.1.3   Numerical Simulation Analysis of Power Field of Ammunition Warheads

By establishing a numerical analysis model that can reflects the structure and material properties of ammunition, which means a solid model describing the structure characteristics of ammunition warhead and a material model reflecting the material properties, and combining with the specified boundary conditions, the numerical simulation data of ammunition power field can be obtained through the numerical analysis based on the finite element analysis tool of AUTODYN.

(1) Numerical analysis model

To obtain numerical simulation results of the power field of ammunition warheads, it is necessary to establish scientific and reasonable numerical analysis models for ammunition warheads, which include the definition of unit types, structural dimensions, material parameters, contact types, and etc.

1. Solid models

To intuitively represent the formation process of the power field and the state of a damaging element in the process of numerical simulation analysis to an ammunition power field, it is necessary to establish a solid model for the ammunition warheads, which includes the composition and structure of the ammunition warheads, the definition of the unit types and the gridding of the model. According to the tactical performance requirements and the structural characteristics of the ammunition, the solid model of ammunition warheads is established with ANSYS/WORKBENCH modeling tools. Figure 4 is the solid model of a certain type of ammunition warheads.

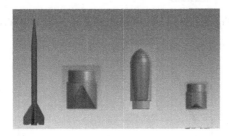

Fig. 4. Solid model of a typical ammunition warhead

2. Material models

Material model is a kind of model that describes the properties and states of materials. It reflects the states and properties of the materials. It is mainly described by the constitutive equation and the state equation.

The constitutive equation reflects the biased response of materials, which is related to strain, strain rate, internal energy and grain size. In finite element dynamic analysis, the constitutive relationship of a kind of material is mainly reflected by the strength model which can describe the nonlinear elastic-plastic response of the object. At present, the strength models used in dynamic analysis programs mainly include Johnson-Cook model, Steinberg Guinan model and so on. A state equation of a kind of materials is an expression that relates its pressure, density and thermodynamic parameters to reflect the volume characteristics of the material. The state equations available in dynamic analysis of ammunition damaging effect include mainly the Linear and the JWL state Equation.

(2)   Numerical simulation of power field of ammunition warhead

According to the solid model and the material model of an ammunition warhead, combined with the specified boundary conditions, and through the non-linear dynamic analysis based on finite element method, the continuum medium is discretized into finite elements to solve the problem. The numerical simulation results of ammunition power field obtained include the formation process of ammunition power field and the characteristics of damaging elements, i.e. velocity, energy and pressure. The analysis process of AUTODYN, a non-linear dynamic analysis program based on finite element method, is shown in Fig. 5. Figure 6 illustrates the fragmentation of a certain type of armor-piercing projectile after penetrating the target plate through finite element dynamic analysis.

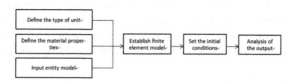

Fig. 5. Flowchart of analyzing with AUTODYN

Fig. 6. Fragmentation of a certain type of armor-piercing projectile after penetrating the target plate

3.2   Calculating Damaged Components of Equipment

3.2.1   Vulnerability Analysis of Armored Equipment

Analysis to vulnerability of an armored equipment focus mainly the characteristics of geometry, structure and function of the armored equipment as the target of different damaging elements of ammunitions. Usually, anti-armor ammunition such as armor-penetrating or armor-piercing projectiles are the main kinds of ammunition that can damage or destroy armored equipment. They mainly rely on the large amount of fragments produced by the projectile or jet-flow after it breaks through the armor of the armored equipment to apply damaging or destroying effect to internal components of the equipment. The capability of the protective armor of an armored equipment against penetration by the jet-flow of armor-penetrating or armor-piercing projectiles is relevant with its material, structure, thickness and inclination.

3.2.2   Missile-Target Spatial Intersection Relationship Analysis

The missile-target spatial intersection relationship is established by using a visual simulation platform. Add data about the damaging elements of ammunition (such as space coordinates, azimuth angles, etc.) and the solid model of equipment into the visual simulation platform and invoke its intersection behavior analysis module. After simulation and analysis, the visible process of how the damaging routines of the damaging elements are formed out and then how they intersect with components of the equipment as well as the statistical data of the intersected components can be obtained. This kind of platform includes mainly VEGA, CRY, VIRTOOLS and so on. Figure 7 shows the process of the formation of damaging routines based on VIRTOOLS and the solution of intersection with components of armored equipment.

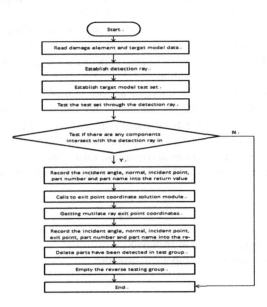

Fig. 7. Flowchart of formation of damaging routines and solution of intersection with targets

Because the ammunition power field and the intersection between damaging elements and targets are simulated on two different simulation platforms and there is no collaborative simulation interface for data interaction between them, but the two platforms have implemented interfaces to relevant programming language (such as C, C++, DELPHI languages, etc.) programs and capability of file operations, thus make it possible for them to achieve collaborative simulation in an indirect way by sharing data files through those programming languages.

Figure 8 is the simulated result of the intersection of the fragments of an armor-piercing projectile and the internal components of a vehicle after the projectile breaks through the protective armor of the vehicle in a coordinated simulation of ammunition power field and intersection of damaging elements and targets.

Fig. 8. Intersection of fragments and internal components of a vehicle

3.2.3 Damage Determination of Components of Armored Equipment

The situation of damage about an armored equipment can be determined through missile-target spatial intersection relationship analysis according to the power of ammunition and the vulnerability of the armored equipment. It is necessary to specify a set of criteria of damage accordingly to determine the damages to armored equipment by damaging elements of ammunition.

The theory of "equivalent thickness of armor" is used to evaluate the protective capability of components of different structures and materials against damages due to impact effect caused by fragments or remaining jet-flows. "Equivalent thickness of armor" is the equivalent thickness of armor steel, which is converted from components of different materials and structures according to their material density and geometric parameters. "Equivalent armor thickness" can be converted with the following formula:

$$h_d = \frac{r}{7.85} \times h.$$

Where, r - Density of original materials
h - Geometric thickness of component structure

Usually, the kinetic energy or specific kinetic energy of the fragment is used to measure its damaging capability. The specific kinetic energy of a piece of mass fragment can be calculated with the following formula:

$$e = m^{1/3}v^2/k$$

Where, m - Mass of the fragment (kg)
v - Velocity of the fragment (m/s)
k - Shape factor of the fragment

When the specific kinetic energy of the fragment and the equivalent armor thickness of the target component are known, the damage degree of the mass fragment to the component can be determined. For homogeneous armor steel, the average specific kinetic energy of fragment consumed per millimeter thickness is 470 J/cm². Given the equivalent thickness h of a component, the specific kinetic energy of fragment consumed by the component can be determined as 470 X h. By comparing the specific kinetic energy of a fragment with the specific kinetic energy of the fragment consumed by a components, whether the component would be damaged is easy to determine:

$$e_s = e_p - e_b$$

Where, e_s- Remaining specific kinetic energy
e_p - Specific kinetic energy of the fragment
e_b - specific kinetic energy of the fragment consumed by the component

The judging flowchart is as follows:
If $e_s > 0$, the component will be damaged, go to the next component ahead of the damaging routine after calculating its residual penetration energy. If $e_s = 0$, the component will be damaged, go to the next fragment damaging routine.
If $e_s < 0$, the component will not be damaged, go to the next fragment damaging routine.
For analysis of damaged components, it is necessary to determine the damage to every component in the direction of every fragment damaging routine one by one.

3.2.4 Database of Damaged Equipment Components
The database of damaged equipment components is constructed through equipment damage simulation analysis based on finite element method. The database consists of several ammunition damage efficiency data tables and an index table, as shown in Fig. 9. It is used mainly for the purpose of providing basic data support for system-of-systems combat simulations for armored equipment.

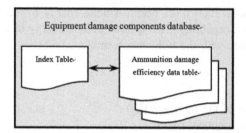

Fig. 9. Database of damaged equipment components

The ammunition damage efficiency data tables are divided into tables according to the type of the ammunitions and the equipment. The combination of ammunitions and equipment in each table does not overlap with other tables. For the convenience of inquiry, the ammunition damage efficiency data tables are named uniformly as "ammunition damage efficiency data table of ×× (ammunition) to ×× (equipment)". These tables all use component-level descriptive structures.

The index table is used to quickly locate the ammunition damage efficiency data table that needs to be queried. Its data structure includes three fields: "Ammunition name", "Equipment name" and "Table name". Among them, "Ammunition name" and "Equipment name" are indexed items, and "Table name" is a pointer item. When querying the table, it is necessary to match the keywords in the "Ammunition name" and "Equipment name" rows with the names of ammunition and target produced in the combat simulation. If the keywords are the same, the matching will be successful. Then the record can be retrieved. According to the pointer item "Table name" in the record, the corresponding ammunition damage efficiency data table can be located.

4 Summary

In course of an equipment combat simulation, locate the corresponding data table in the database of damaged equipment components online as soon as an event of ammunition damaging equipment happens. Query the damage data for the attacked equipment online quickly according to the terminal trajectory information given by the simulation, so as to improve the accuracy and reliability of battle damage simulation in simulated system-of-systems combat involving armored equipment.

References

1. Held, M.: Warhed hit distribution on main battle tanks in the Gulf war. J. Battlefield Technol. **13**(1), 31–38 (2000)
2. LSTC. AUTODYN Keyword User's Manual. Ver. 970. Livemore Software Technology, USA (2003)
3. Chou, P.C., Carleone, J.: The stability of shaped charge jet. J. Appl. Phys. **48**(10), 4187–4195 (1977)

4. Hm, W.: Predicting the penetration and perforation of targets struck by projectiles at normal incidence. Mech. Struct. Mach. **30**(4), 543–577 (2002)
5. Ben-Dor, G., Dubinsky, A., Elperin, T.: Shape optimization of penetrators nose. Theoret. Appl. Fract. Mech. **35**(3), 261–270 (2001)

Author Index

Printed in the United States
By Bookmasters